WINNING IN CHRIST
Seeing Through The Book Of Revelation

Robert Blair

Fairway Press
Lima, Ohio

WINNING IN CHRIST

FIRST EDITION
Copyright © 2023
by Robert Blair

All rights reserved. No portion of this book may be reproduced or utilized in any form or by any means, electronic or mechanical including photocopying, without permission in writing from the author. Inquiries should be addressed to: nwb1937@yahoo.com

All scripture quotations, unless otherwise indicated, are taken from the Holy Bible, New International Version®, NIV®. Copyright ©1973, 1978, 1984, 2011 by Biblica, Inc.™ Used by permission of Zondervan. All rights reserved worldwide. www.zondervan.com The "NIV" and "New International Version" are trademarks registered in the United States Patent and Trademark Office by Biblica, Inc.™

Scripture quotations marked (GNB or TEV) are from the Good News Bible, in Today's English Version. Copyright © American Bible Society 1966, 1971, 1976. Used by permission.

Library of Congress Control Number: 2023913596

e-book:
ISBN-13: 978-0-7880-4107-5
ISBN-10: 0-7880-4107-X

ISBN-13: 978-0-7880-4106-8
ISBN-10: 0-7880-4106-1   PRINTED IN USA

Contents

Preface 5
Introduction 9
Chapter 1 24
Chapter 2 41
Chapter 3 54
Chapter 4 67
Chapter 5 80
Chapter 6 95
Chapter 7 111
Chapter 8 125
Chapter 9 141
Chapter 10 161
Chapter 11 180
Chapter 12, Part 1 212
Chapter 12, Part 2 239
Bibliography — Books 267
Index 271
Acknowledgements 285
About Robert And Norma Blair 287

Preface

In the latter part of the first century AD, Christians in eastern areas of the Roman Empire underwent brutal persecution. The Holy Spirit designed *Revelation* to give strong hope to those beleaguered believers.[1] Because government authorities meted out much of the harassment, this divinely inspired letter of encouragement required coded language. Using covert terms and illustrations, this document reminds God's people how to endure and overcome in Christ.

The original recipients' life-situations remarkably resembled the circumstances many Christians currently face. Comprehending *Revelation* benefits all believers. *Revelation's* message enhances confidence in God's working, but the Spirit's "secret language" baffles most readers. Regrettably, few interpreters biblically identify *Revelation's* numerous, but necessary signs. Instead most commentaries add to the bewilderment about the book. Readers come away perplexed and further confounded.

To report a fire or to help folks find building exits does not require licensed safety experts. Neither does understanding *Revelation's* message require credentialed scholars. I consider myself an amateur "fire fighter," who sincerely desires that innocent people receive proper warning so they can safely find the exits God provides. Believers also need to know that once they get through "those doors," an unimaginably secure future awaits them.

Finding a consistent *Revelation* interpreter is difficult. Of the numerous commentaries I have read, none provided a uniform rendering of its symbols. Had I discovered a reliable one that overcame the major interpretive obstacles, I would not have begun this project.

Most interpreters share the same glaring problem. They tend to accept some *Revelation* words and phrases symbolically; others they take literally. Yet they rarely present logical reasons for their choices.

In *Revelation* 7, for instance, a group of 144,000 appears identified as servants of God with his seal on their foreheads. That company is comprised of 12,000 from each of Israel's Twelve tribes. The same large assemblage reappears in Chapter 14 mightily singing praises. *Revelation* 14: 4 identifies all 144,000 as men who had not defiled themselves

---

1. Some think that a person named John in the second century AD penned *Revelation*. Strong evidence supports the view that, about 90 AD, John, one of the Twelve, wrote the book. The structure and the incredibly complex use of sources, words, phrases, and incidents from most of the *Old Testament* books blended with Jesus' teachings, and so on, convince me of *Revelation's* superhuman origin. Even using sophisticated word processing methods, composition of such a book seems to exceed human abilities. *Revelation's* authorship is beyond the scope of this work, but see article on *"Revelation, Book of"* by L.L Morris in *The New Bible Dictionary*, J. D. Douglas, Organizing Editor, Intervarsity Press, London, 1965, pp 1093-1095.

with women. The Watchtower Society, which guides and oversees Jehovah's Witnesses, interprets the number 144,000 as literal. But the expression "male virgins" is figurative, they contend.

Most non-Jehovah's Witness interpreters regard the number 144,000 in chapters seven and fourteen as symbolic. In *Revelation* 20:6, however, many commentators join the Watchtower Society in regarding the number 1,000 concerning the earthly reign of Christ as literal. In fact, the NIV translators use this heading for verses 1-6: *The Thousand Years.*

Why should readers accept one set of numbers literally and regard others as symbolic? In other words, why are so many analysts consistently inconsistent? God does not promote confusion.

Is this interpretation biblical?

Basing conclusions on sound biblical and historical data is vital. In view of that, did I fluctuate in my explanations and interpretations? I aimed to harmonize them as much as possible. I welcome your comments on my results.

Did I plumb the full depths of *Revelation's* mysteries? That remains impossible until the Lord concludes history. Did I thoroughly cover the book's mysteries? Attaining that is unthinkable. No multi-volume tome on *Revelation* could accomplish that goal—even if the work filled the United States Library of Congress.

A natural sense of direction guides some people, but not me. In my hiking days, I wasted hours crawling over sharp-edged boulders, scrambling through thickets, and trudging back from dead ends. Divine illumination did not suddenly overwhelm me.

A basic knowledge of Greek and Hebrew helps. The greatest insights I gained, however, came as a result of a daily routine. Decades ago, I started reading through the *Bible* every year. My interest in *Revelation* increased over time. As it did, I began noticing links between *Old Testament* occurrences and *Revelation*. Numerous symbols seem based on Jesus' parables and his teachings. One should also not overlook instructions found in the Epistles. The best *Revelation* guidance comes through dedicated daily reading of God's Word so that one becomes acquainted with the entire *Bible*.[2]

Should readers expect a consistently unfolding plot—a straight route through *Revelation*? The path does not lead as the crow flies. Some novels and biographies progress that way, but not *the Apocalypse*. Its

---

2. Some assume that standard Lectionaries adequately cover all of the Bible's content if one follows them three consecutive years. Lectionaries tend to avoid certain vital subjects and important teachings. For example, they barely "touch" the so-called Pastoral Epistles and skip huge sections of the *New Testament's* only historical book, the *Acts of the Apostles*. It's no wonder that churches suffer vexing divisions.

plot would give a homing pigeon headaches. Yet serious readers can negotiate its daunting backwaters and dark alleyways.

"The path of the righteous is like the morning sun, shining ever brighter till the full light of day," says *Proverbs*.[3] *Revelation's* first-time readers sometimes expect to immediately find light. Instead, darkness frequently envelopes them. The trek through *Revelation* often twists and retraces mysterious, shadowy trails. On occasion, "nightfall" prevails.

To ascend a mountain, one usually has to reverse directions and patiently endure switchbacks. At times the ascent seems slight. Climbers often doubt their progress. On parts of the trail, a hiker might see neither the starting point nor the goal. *Revelation* leads one to similar "zigzags" and "blind spots." Most readers get lost and frustrated. Others become scared and quit.

Is there a path through the maze? I wobbled feebly through my early tours into *Revelation's* jumbles. Various students in Bible classes I taught kept insisting that we explore it. For mostly that reason, I first ventured into *Revelation's* "wilderness." Later my curiosity pressed me to search and survey. Still, understanding the book seemed hopeless. But tips here and there coupled with further research aided me to find a path. I cannot identify every rock and tree along the way. I am not sure the Lord intended that we should. One can, though, get through this uncannily designed labyrinth.[4]

Years ago some friends took me backpacking in the Sierra Nevada Mountains of California. On my first trip, we camped at the top of a pass more than 10,000 feet in elevation. One of those friends and I took an extended hike the next day. After a few hours, we came to the edge of King's Canyon National Park. We paused and gazed down slopes that extended thousands of feet. Stunned by sights, echoes, and colors, I tried to imbed the view in my memory. Unforgettable as that hiking experience was, *Revelation's* effects on me far exceed that stunning vista.

- **Explore.** Trek amidst covert passages, tangled symbols, and cryptic math.
- **Be awed.** Complex, signs amaze. Musical interludes mesmerize you.
- **Persevere.** The "hike" leads to refreshing waters and healing greenness.
- **Find hope.** The Holy Spirit rewards with boldness and reinforced faith. He changed my life perspective. I invite you

---

3. Proverbs 4:18 NIV

4. Charles Erdman's brief commentary gave me my first hints.

to travel with him. The Lord invites you to benefit from the victories he's already won for you.

I pray that maximum numbers of readers may benefit from this book with no traces of greed in its production, promotion, or sales.

Introduction

What Kind Of Writing Is *Revelation*?
Because I wanted this treatise to reflect the *Revelation's* real theme—*triumph*, I chose the title: *Winning in Christ*. Conquest dominates most relationships. "Who is in charge here?" we ask. "Who holds the real power behind the throne?" we query.

Though some insist that children should play non-competitive sports, the kids probably realize at some level that sports, where no winner is acclaimed are part of the pretense that surrounds childhood. Santa, the elf on the shelf, and the Easter bunny comprise only a portion of an American youngster's make-believe cast of characters. In truth, those who push non-competitive sports enjoy winning, too. To institute their practice of non-winning, they probably triumphed in a community or school board meeting. All the time, though, kids know that big boys and girls, and adults play to win—big time.

You have probably won many victories, or wish you had—in sports, board games, finances, puzzles, and so on. We treasure scrapbooks, trophies, plaques and the like that "prove" our success. The few victory mementoes I've earned rust, collect dust, or fade in storage boxes. In the meantime, I become increasingly fragile, inside and out.

Revelation tells of permanent victory for those who lay aside today's successes in order to gratefully serve our merciful Creator. They experience new birth and inherit life that doesn't fade or perish. *Revelation* promises this in secret language meant for believers.

Those unfamiliar with God's word find a different message. Shadowy, malicious powers wreak injury and death. Dark, malevolent forces bring violent world destruction. Many people think *Revelation* presents repeatedly disastrous scenes. Does *Revelation* largely depict calamity? English translations of the book usually begin: "The revelation of Jesus Christ." Would it amaze you to learn that *The Book of Revelation's* first word in its original (Greek) is *Apocalypse*? The book begins: "Apocalypse [of] Jesus Christ."[5]

Apocalyptic
The Greek word "apocalypse" did not originally denote fiery ruin as most today use the term. *New Testament* writers regularly used "apocalypse" to mean "reveal" or "appear." When Joseph and Mary brought

---

5. ἀποκάλυψις ἰησοῦ χριστοῦ The Westcott & Hort text fully capitalizes all three words, but with no breathing or accent marks. Nestles caps only the first letter in each, but includes the breathing and accent marks.

the child Jesus to dedicate him at the Temple, Simeon took Jesus into his arms and praised God saying: "Sovereign Lord, as you have promised . . . my eyes have seen your salvation . . . a light for <u>revelation</u> to the Gentiles . . ." (Revelation here translates *apocalypse*).[6] No one regards that tender, touching moment in the Temple with Simeon as menacing.

Paul used the word *apocalypse* in both letters to the Thessalonians. A passage in his second letter reads: "Don't let anyone deceive you in any way, for that day will not come until the rebellion occurs and the man of lawlessness is revealed, the man doomed to destruction."[7] A*pocalypse* intimates neither good nor bad; only that something not previously known or seen becomes visible. A fact, person, or information once concealed is identified. The *Book of Revelation* discloses (reveals) Jesus, and God's plans to defeat all forms of evil through Christ. As Jesus won, faithful believers can, too! That people connect *apocalypse* with calamity impresses me as both odd and sad.

The Holy Spirit didn't design the book to terrify believers. The Lord meant to encourage the first century faithful and us. God never forsakes those who love him. Does *Revelation* predict catastrophe? Yes, but only for those who give up, disown, or reject Christ. Following, trusting, and obeying Jesus ensure security and victory. *The Apocalypse* reveals Christ as capable and powerful—superior to first century Caesars. Christ remains infinitely more potent than twenty-first-century presidents, prime ministers, dictators, tech wizards, gurus, and rocket scientists.

In some ways, *Revelation* resembles other books classed as apocalyptic literature. This type of writing emphasizes God's sovereignty, his preeminent rule of the world. Powerful forces oppose God. At times he intervenes in world events using dreadful methods to counteract evil. In this fixed future, Apocalyptic literature features visions, angels, and vivid symbolism. Human effort, good or bad, can't alter God's will.[8]

To summarize; in John's *Apocalypse,* individuals can change their future by obeying God. In addition; regardless of its usage in other literature, apocalypse in *Revelation* refers to a revealing of something not previously known. Finally, *The Apocalypse of Jesus Christ* discloses both good and bad news. Jesus saves those who believe in him. He judges and punishes those who reject him and do evil.

---

6. Luke 2:29-32 NIV

7. 2 Thessalonians 2:3 NIV

8. For a fuller explanation, consult the *Cambridge Bible Commentary*, "Revelation of John," by T.F. Glasson

Comedy Or Tragedy?
You likely recognize the elements of a good story? First-rate books, plays, and movies contain unresolved tension. In case you've forgotten what that is, the following serves as an example:
1. Boy loves girl.
2. The girl is indecisive in her love for the boy.
3. Will he succeed in convincing her to love him?
4. If she becomes attracted to the boy, her parents will hate him.

Elements two, three, and four provide tension. Will the girl ever love the boy? If she loves the boy, will her parents accept him? Filmmakers, dramatists, and novelists rehash these simple themes.

Other considerations come into play.

- In comedies, the girl and the boy "live happily ever after."
- In tragedies they never get together; such as in *"Romeo and Juliet."*
- Adding an evil third person or force that threatens the lives and relationships of the characters adds further tension.
- Finding too soon how the story ends leads to boredom.

Is *Revelation* a comedy with a happy ending? Or is it a tragedy? *Revelation's* mystery maintains continuing **conflict.** Following our simple analogy:
- God is the "boy."
- The people of God represent the "girl."
- The evil third person is the devil aided by his nefarious allies.
- Satan (the devil, dragon) tries to interrupt the love relationship between God (the boy) and his people (the girl).

Revelation's theme speaks to all ages and cultures. As each person learns, life's unfolding brings ongoing tension. Every generation hopes to see good prevail. Right wins occasional victories. Yet decency's triumphs rarely endure. The devil and his cronies seem to constantly win. Frustration dogs the godly.

Revelation's Riddles
The enigma of *Revelation's* beastly characters, bloodshed, and violence combined with dark symbolism befuddles most readers. Most folks

consider *The Apocalypse* a tragedy. Is that classification correct? As we noted, the Holy Spirit prepared *Revelation* as a first century survival manual. He sent the letter to Christians living in an area known as Asia Minor (now Western Turkey). The book included warnings and teachings for seven regional churches. Jesus assigned John, his last surviving Apostle, as the delivery agent.

Revelation tells a simple message. The "boy-girl" love between God and his people stood in peril. The devil attacked and seduced the girl (the church) in two ways. First, societal influences strongly tempted God's folks. Lust, greed, and pride lured them (**Conflict** in **Chaos**).

Second, the devil endangered her (the church) through violent harassment. As his agent, Satan used a government to threaten, persecute, and kill some of God's people. In addition, as you know, the devil also uses envious and careless church folks as his allies.

The Survival Manual For Folks In Chaos

To guide and preserve his servants, the Lord gave *Revelation* as a "wilderness" manual. As they journeyed, God's people encountered internal and external hazards. This short, Holy Spirit handbook warned the church of involvement in greed, illicit sex, and pride. From without, a fearsome menace developed. Rome increasingly demanded emperor-worship.

The good news: in the same way God took care of Israel in the wilderness, Christ's living presence (the Holy Spirit)[9] accompanies his church.[10] Moreover, Christ, the Word made flesh, became a perfect role model. If believers trust and utilize God's ample equipping, he enables them to prevail over various tests and threats. The Lord assures: his love, word, and power always win. God's people can triumph, too.

Winning requires two types of action:

- First, believers must strive to attain Christ's purity and resist Satan's seductions;
- Second, they need to trust the Almighty's presence in his Spirit and persist faithfully to his word through persecution.

In the midst of our testing journey, each generation tends to miss this vital point: in Christ, God already won our victory. How do we know that?

---

9. Acts 16:6-10 illustrates some of the difficulty in defining the Godhead.

10. 1 Corinthians 10 informs us that Christ actually accompanied Israel in the wilderness. With the cloud of God's Spirit over them and walls of sea water on each side, the Lord immersed the whole nation. The Rock (petra) that accompanied them was Christ (verses 1-5).

1. When he visited this planet, God's Son Jesus resisted every temptation known to human beings.
2. Jesus perfected love and trust in God.
3. Though evil forces crucified him, Jesus came back from the dead.[11]
4. By his sacrificial blood and his resurrection power, God's Messiah (Christ) Jesus made our victory possible.
5. *Revelation* 5:13, 14 tell us: Christ, the lamb, now stands at the center of God's throne.[12] No earthly force ever equals Jesus' power and permanence.
6. He, the lamb, will return to reward those who remain faithful during persecution.
7. He will punish those who succumb to evil (**Comfort**).
8. Jesus the lamb deserves eternal honor and praise.

To protect his loyal followers, the Lord used symbols they understood but authorities would think nonsense.

We presently face the following questions:

- Where did *Revelation's* symbols originate?
- Are the "keys" to the signs available to us?
- Can we decipher them and properly apply their messages?

Current societal and political trends challenge the faith of Christians. In this country, believers face obstacles our parents and grandparents could not imagine. Wise people prepare themselves. Getting ready requires:

- Knowing what *Revelation* says about God's plans, trusting him, loving him, glorifying him, and faithfully following Jesus' model of obedience;
- Resisting increasingly lurid temptations;
- Learning how to deal with hostile governments.

Previous Attempts To Break *Revelation's* Codes

Adam Clarke first published his commentary about 1817. Some once considered Clarke's a superlative work. Many preachers would have considered their library incomplete without his multi-volume commentary. Adam Clarke apparently knew Hebrew, Greek, Latin, and

---

11. God's prophets predicted that his plan included a suffering servant and betrayal, cf. Acts 2:14-36

12. Jesus' close relationship with the Father is sometimes described as being at God's right hand. See Acts 2:33; 5:31 for example.

Arabic and frequently referred to writings in those languages. He comfortably quoted classical Greek and Latin authors. Clarke also knew ancient Anglo-Saxon. How many contemporary academics can equal Clarke's linguistic and educational qualifications?

Adam Clarke made extensive notes on every book of the *Bible*. When he got to *Revelation* in his commentary, however, he quit. The scholar lamented: "I do not understand the book (*Revelation*)." he evidently did not expect his readers to believe him. A few lines later, he said, "I repeat, I do not understand this book." Clarke cited a few academics but wrote little of his own commentary on *Revelation*.

The formidable mysteries in *Revelation* leave many serious readers scratching their heads. F. F. Bruce attained the respect of many twentieth-century scholars. Consult Bruce's *Revelation* notes in the *New International Commentary*.[13] You will find only succinct comments on *The Apocalypse*. John Calvin penned about as many words on religion as anyone in history. The famous reformer hardly "touched" *Revelation*.

Archbishop Edward White Benson died before he finished his *Revelation* commentary. In his "Introduction," however, Benson related this: "In answer once to the question, 'What is the form the book presents to you?' the reply of an intelligent, devout reader was, 'It is chaos'."[14]

William Barclay concisely assessed the views of Luther, Zwingli, et al:

- "One despairing commentator said that there are as many riddles in the *Revelation* as there are words."
- "Another that the study of the *Revelation* either finds or leaves a man mad."
- Luther disparaged it: "Christ is neither taught nor acknowledged; and the inspiration of the Holy Spirit is not perceptible in it."
- Ulrich Zwingli regarded *Revelation* with hostility.[15]

The Twenty-First-Century Challenge

In the twenty-first century, understanding *The Apocalypse* carries an added challenge. Recall the old expression, "It's hard to see the trees

---

13. F.F. Bruce, General Editor, *New International Bible Commentary*, Zondervan, Grand Rapids, 1979.

14. *THE APOCALYPSE, AN INTRODUCTORY STUDY OF THE REVELATION OF ST. JOHN THE DIVINE*, Edward White Benson, Margaret Benson, MacMillan and Co. Limited, London 1900. A Nabu Public Domain Reprint, p 2.

15. *The Revelation of John*, William Barclay, Vol. I, The Westminster Press, Philadelphia, 1976, p 1.

because of the forest"? Folks presently see neither *Revelation's* "trees" nor its "forest." Why? Graffito covers nearly every tree.

When Norma (my wife) and I dated, we visited the Oregon Caves. As we descended some stairs into the grotto, we saw multiple inscriptions on the walls. Someday those writings might be called petroglyphs. At that time, they seemed ugly graffito. Previous visitors etched names or statements on nearly every square inch of visible wall. Before we left, it shames me to say that on one of the few open spaces, I scrawled something akin to "Bob loves Norma."

In like manner, Bible teachers leave bizarre marks all over *Revelation* They began scratching in the second century. Preachers still scribble unfounded interpretations and wild ideas. In order to decipher *Revelation,* one must often unscramble, erase, and undo etchings "carved" by past and present "experts."

Recently while channel surfing, I happened on a prominent, "scholarly" radio speaker. "This should be interesting," I thought, when he mentioned his subject that day: *Revelation.* The preacher spoke with little of Adam Clarke's modesty. His presentation consisted mostly of speculation involving what would happen to the Jews left on earth after the so-called "Rapture." He opined that every *Revelation* detail symbolizes something.

Revelation's Importance Today

Rejection of Jesus' values and ethics troubles us. Repeated horrific sights and war rumbles sadden us. Child abuse, greed, drunkenness, drug addiction, and government intervention into families rip present society apart. Extremism frightens and dismays nearly everyone. **Chaos** dominates the world.

The Lord designed *Revelation's* message for times like ours. The book's significance infinitely exceeds the importance of any event covered on the nightly news, emailed, or posted on social media. *Revelation* advises us how to understand and react to the appalling reports we hear. God's word helps us keep bad and good news in context.

Are you looking for life perspective? *Revelation* aids in understanding God's plans for the world and us. By unlocking *Revelation's* mysteries, we find coping assistance. Anxiety and bitterness ebb. We can become what the Lord wants us to be.

At this very moment, coaches plan strategies for games their teams will soon play. Their tactics include anticipating tricks their opponents will use so they can prepare their defenses. *Revelation* alerts us to our mortal enemies' maneuvers. With proper understanding in the Lord, we can defend ourselves and conquer in him.

There's more. Coaches often use the strategy of surprise, i.e. catch their opponents off guard. *Revelation* readies us for situations that leave most folks ill-equipped. The book also includes: How to pull surprises on offense. As we utilize the Spirit's advice, counsel, and warnings, the Lord supplies us with resources that amaze the opposition and us. We win by trusting and using God's unlimited powers.

Code-Breaking Essentials

Extensive imagery accomplished *Revelation's* success. The fact that the book contains more than one type of sign adds to its mystery. Sometimes the Spirit used codes within codes. Familiarity with the different types enables us to grasp most of the content. A few passages are literal. But they are not where most folks expect them.

Where do we find solutions for this intriguing puzzle? Keep in mind the severe persecution that required *Revelation's* creative writing. Harassment began under the Roman emperor Nero (54-68 AD).[16] During the reign of Domitian (81-96 AD), cruel mistreatment grew intensely in certain parts of western Turkey (Asia Minor).

When the Lord commissioned the Apostle John[17] to write seven churches in the area, each church had its own conditions and needs. In the individual letters to churches, John used symbols unique and familiar to each area.[18] He intimately knew the recipients and their cities. We shall decode a sampling and give instances of their local flavor.

Revelation contains more signs and symbols than an advanced algebra test. Ciphers vary and they come from numerous sources. Though no "answer" pages can be found in the "back of the book," keys to *The Apocalypse* lie throughout the *Bible*. Jesus' parables contain answers as do the Epistles. Persistent *Bible* reading helps us discover clues, which enable us to crack most of *The Apocalypse* codes.

The Love Story

Ventures through *Revelation* evoke many emotions. Its symbols mystify, intrigue, and often repulse. As we've noted, scholarly reactions to the book vary. Some say they can decipher every detail. Others approach *Revelation* reluctantly.

In a TV commercial about the book series called *Left Behind*, a spokesperson referred to *"apocalypse"* as cosmic disaster. As we previously noted, *apocalypse* does not mean cataclysm. The term denotes

---

16. Christians had already been affected by Roman attitudes toward Jews. Luke noted in Acts 18:2 that Aquila a Jew from Pontus (near the Black Sea) and his wife Priscilla had been forced to leave Rome by the Emperor Claudius (ruled 41-54), who "ordered all the Jews to leave…"

17. In my opinion, the apostle John authored *Revelation* after his banishment to the Island of Patmos by Emperor Domitian. Not everyone accepts this view.

18. E.M Blaicklock's *Cities of the New Testament* presents fascinating background information on each city.

making something known; an unveiling, as when a curtain first opens. *Revelation* discloses a many-faceted Jesus:

- A Lamb, once dead but now gloriously alive;
- The ruler of the kings of the earth;
- A conqueror;
- And a judge who will return to pronounce condemnation on unbelievers.

The *Old Testament* prophets predicted a Messiah's[19] presence among us. Worshipers of God waited centuries for him to appear. The *New Testament* Gospels, especially *Matthew*, show how Jesus of Nazareth fulfilled those messianic predictions. He was and is God's anointed. The Word, our Creator, became flesh and lived among human beings on this planet.[20] His enemies brutally beat Jesus and crucified him. Friends entombed his lifeless body, but he rose from the dead and ascended to the Father.

The *Apocalypse* or *Revelation*[21] reveals how Jesus, though not visible to human eyes, remains active and present in our world until all see him. Jesus is not now visible. Yet he pledged to his disciples that he would remain with them. In his great commission, Jesus assured the apostles: *"And surely I am with you always, to the very end of the age."*[22] *Revelation* foretells the moment Jesus will become visible and then judge every person who has lived.

We compared *Revelation* to a love story with God as the boy and the people of God as the girl. As happens in many stories, the boy loves the girl; she does not love him. Does that comparison to a boy-girl relationship trouble you? Through Jeremiah, the Lord asked the people of Israel: *"What is my beloved doing in my temple as she, with many others, works out her evil schemes?"*[23] Picture a wayward wife coming home after a night of partying. Her husband meets her at the front door. "You've been out being unfaithful all night. Why did you come home?" he asks.

We are God's beloved. In spite of the Lord's love for us, we often grieve him. What saddens God? We displease God when we refuse to honor him or rely on him. Unbelief, immorality, fear, greed, grum-

---

19. In Hebrew, Messiah means an anointed one. Christ is the Greek equivalent of the term.

20. John 1:1-14.

21. We shall be referring to the book using both terms: *Revelation* and *Apocalypse*.

22. Matthew 28:20 NIV.

23. Jeremiah 11:15 NIV.

bling, gossip, hate, selfishness, and pride—all upset God. The *OT* repeatedly tells how these actions and attitudes offend him. Israel's lack of trust led to forty years of wilderness wandering and thousands of deaths.[24]

Honoring God often puts us at odds with our families, culture, and governments. Christians worldwide currently confront serious faith challenges. Secular societies and authorities exert increasing pressure on American Christians to turn from God and his word (**Conflict**). Compare society's early twenty-first-century values with those emphasized in *Romans* 1:18-32, *1 Corinthians* 6:9-20, and *Galatians* 5:13-26.

How does this faith-conflict relate to *Revelation*? Begin with this reality: The Bible teaches us to respect civil powers.[25] Yet our faithful service to God disturbs some in government. Authorities often misconstrue dependence on God with disloyalty to their control. Though belief and obedience to Christ should make us better citizens, government agents do not always see it that way. Many government representatives jealously guard their power and the attention they crave.

In the first century, some Roman authorities insisted that citizens worship only the Emperor.[26] Would you renounce Christ if the government ordered you to do that? Would you stop going to church if agents of the state tell you that you must quit or else go to jail? Many contemporaries stop worshiping for lesser reasons than the above.

We earlier noted that during the latter decades of the first century, God's people in western Turkey suffered harassment from Roman officials. For his folks facing persecution the Lord encouraged patient endurance. At the same time, some Christians became arrogant, greedy, and depraved. *Revelation* gravely warned those involved in illicit behavior and self-indulgence. The Lord punishes all evildoers. The present distress, upheaval, and turmoil does not signify a hopeless situation, said the Lord. He remains in control—always.

Not One Code, But Many

As you can imagine, the letter (*Revelation*) bearing the Spirit's assurance, warnings, and counsel brought potential hazard to its recipients. Thus the Lord devised specially coded communication. We must unravel several types of strange symbols. That fact makes the task of interpret-

---

24. 1 Corinthians 10:1-13.

25. Romans 13, Titus 3:1, 2.

26. For a fuller discussion of how Christianity became an "illicit" religion, consult H.E Dana, *"The New Testament World,* Third Edition, Broadman Press, Nashville, pp. 164-177.

ing *Revelation* difficult for modern readers. What made multi-codes necessary? Why do folks now suffer such snags in grasping them?

Suppose authorities found copies in the hands of Christians, a letter that urged them to put God before the Emperor. Possessing that correspondence could be considered treasonous. People faithful to the Lord might die. If to government officials, however, the memo appeared to be only nonsensical stories, the so-called evidence might seem absurd and laughable and disloyalty difficult to prove.

Through John's pen, the Holy Spirit skillfully wove writings from previous books together as part of his secret code. By stages we shall figure out *Revelation's* signs. We also face the fact that *Revelation* often seems like drivel to new readers. One of my California students used to say, "Bob, I think John was smoking something." At the time, she lacked appreciation for the book's ingenious arrangement.

Revelation "borrows" and utilizes hundreds of words and phrases from numerous OT and NT authors as well as quotations from those who knew Jesus. Yet *Revelation* is no verbal jumble. The "author-editor" systematically arranged the phrases, terms, and expressions so that they tell their own story.

That's not all. The letter tells a vital message, communicating its meaning to those who need to understand it. At the same time, the composition obfuscates understanding for those who oppose the Lord. John did not devise the phrasing and coding. As a man "in Spirit," God's Spirit guided him.

Before we outline our view of *Revelation,* we shall briefly review the four recognized major interpretations of the book. We also want to ask a logical question concerning accepting any one of this quartet of opinions. Imagine that you suffer an ailment and you consult a physician. He/she examines you and says to you, "You have such and such a disease." The doctor informs you that medical specialists usually treat this malady using one of four approaches.

"Which of the four do you recommend?" you ask. "Actually," says the doctor, "none of them works perfectly. None will cure you. But at least you will have tried something." Would you waste money or time on any of the four dubious treatments?

In the same way, you probably think; "If none of these interpretive methods works, why tell me about them?" By itself, no view adequately interprets the book. Still, each approach contains basic information necessary to comprehending *Revelation* as a whole. With that in mind, let's review the four.

The four major views of interpreting Revelation:
1. Past — (Some use the term "preterist," which refers to someone chiefly interested in the past). *Revelation* was written to Christians during the late first century AD. Preterists think the book applied to that time, but to no subsequent age. The author intended to help the original recipients deal with their unique situation. Those days exist no longer. No one now lives under the same circumstances so *Revelation* lacks present significance other than as part of history.

For a preterist, reading the letter resembles reading last week's sport's page. Or like advice given to hostages during a bank robbery. Once they are released or time passes, that counsel no longer remains meaningful. No one today fathoms it anyhow. Why bother?

A Roman naturalist and author named Pliny, called "the elder" and his nephew, Pliny "the younger," wrote in the mid to late first century. Literary students, natural history buffs, and those interested in ancient Roman life are familiar with the Plinys. Preterists would say that *Revelation* is of no more value than reading the works of either Pliny. *The Apocalypse* provides little value for present day.

Was *Revelation* written to first-century Christians? Absolutely. Trying to remove it from its historical context makes no more sense than attempting to move a skyscraper from its foundations. We can't remove this letter from its original setting.

Geographical locations change names. Yet, earth's human inhabitants keep making the same mistakes. Genes and chromosomes pass from parents to children. Experience does not. All individuals must learn life's lessons for themselves. Human behavior never changes over the millennia. The *Old Testament* tells the tragic truth of repeated human error. As he tested Adam and Eve, God tests every one of their descendants.

Revelation's message remains vital. Fad diets come and go; truly healthful diets remain the same. The Lord's cryptic message enabled first-century Christians to find meaning in a changing, hostile world. While hate, war, and spite consumed unbelievers, believers overcame anxious fear. Confidence in God's rule and his ultimate righteous judgment gave them purpose and endurance. To find maturity, wholeness, and the "peace that passes understanding," believers still need the Lord's assuring message. Sadly, prevalent misinterpretations result in the majority of believers not benefiting from *Revelation's* divine encouragement.

2. Future
Because *Revelation* speaks of things to come as well as the past and present, many see merit in the futurist view. Futurists think the book provides info for the last generations. It looks toward history's end. Over the centuries, many have accepted and agreed with this view—

that *The Apocalypse* deals primarily with the end time events. The book clearly speaks of the last days and the Last Day (the Judgment). One big obstacle undermines the futurist theory. No one knows when that Last Day will occur.

Significant numbers in every generation presume they live in the end times. Folks routinely assume: "Times can't get worse than they are today." The same mistaken opinion dominates era after era. Some people thought that at the end of the first century. Many presently draw that conclusion. History will end abruptly, but no one knows the day or the hour. No reliable indicators or signs exist. Neither does any human being know whether we are close. Numerous fourth century AD folks thought that they faced the end times. So did people who lived just prior to 1,000 AD and those in the 1500s. In the late 1700s, many thought that horrible events of the French Revolution portended the end.

Just before 2,000 AD, some popular preachers promoted the idea that world events signified the end. Many present preachers say the same thing. The *Left Behind* book series[27] marketed that idea. Book sales made its authors rich and famous. They left their readers behind and bewildered. Any person who claims to know the precise end time is, in the words of Shakespeare, "one full of sound and fury signifying nothing."

If the Lord designed *Revelation* for only the end time, and we are not in the end, of what value is it? This compares to a football team using a two-minute-drill in the middle of the game. The book speaks of finality—the Judgment. Several scenes depict it. Yet *Revelation* also deals with various meaningful events between the creation and the end.

To summarize, futurists face the following problem; no one knows when the Lord will bring the Last Day. Every generation thinks that it lives in the worst of times and therefore assumes the end must be near. For nearly 2,000 years, people have miscalculated. The futurist view creaks as weakly as the past view.

3. Continuous-Historical

Advocates of this view think that *The Apocalypse* predicts the significant events of history. Start with the noteworthy happenings predicted in *Revelation* Chapter Four (some say Chapter One; others Chapter Six), and go through Chapter 22. Correctly connect all the dots, and one can predict the history of God's dealings with humankind. Martin Luther apparently favored the Continuous–Historical theory. If this theory enables one to accurately foresee, however, by now there should be some general agreement on how to tie *Revelation*'s predic-

---

27. *Left Behind* is a series consisting of sixteen Christian novels written by Tim LaHaye and Jerry Jenkins published between 1995 and 2007.

tions to historical events. On that subject, few religious analysts accord with the views of other Continuous-Historical predictors.

Want an example of the problem with the theory's weakness? In the 1800s, a Catholic scholar named Walmsley of Wells College wrote a work called *The General History of the Christian Church*. He used the pseudo name of Signior Pastorini. Walmsley (Pastorini) predicted the end of all Protestant churches in 1825.[28] In the 20th century, Central and South American Protestant churches probably grew faster than all other religious groups. Current "continuous-historical advocates" will likely suffer similar posthumous embarrassment. They seem not to grasp *Revelation's* style and format.

4. Symbolic

The symbolic theory considers everything allegory or metaphor. Symbolists present a strong case. No other book's content compares with *Revelation's* rich similes and striking symbols. Yet the symbolic view also suffers feebly. Symbolists rarely agree with one another on how to connect *The Apocalypse's* "figurative dots." 'Though most have difficulty ascertaining them, *Revelation* contains both logical structure and a definite narrative that we shall later explore. The symbolic approach makes it virtually impossible to make any sense of the narrative. Those who do connect the "dots" rarely agree with anyone else's interpretation. Everyone "connects dots" in his or her own way. The continuous-historical view errs in taking all of *Revelation's* stories literally. Believers in the symbolic view fail to understand that even though the book does not always present its scenes in chronological historical sequence, *Revelation's* overall narrative progresses from creation to consummation.

Further Analysis Of The Four Theories

As is evident, not one of those views fully expounds all the factors in the book. Why try to use any of the four major views of interpretation when none of them works?

We are left with four inadequate remedies.

- Each has some merit.
- Each also contains major flaws.
- Combining them seems impossible.

We shall present a view that uses the strengths of each interpretive view, but avoids each one's weaknesses. We also intend to resolve a question many scholars ask about *Revelation's* structure. In his brief commentary on *Revelation*, Charles Erdman intimated what he called

---

28. Cf. Adam Clarke, Volume VI, p. 962.

telescoping but to my knowledge, he never fully developed that concept. Various writers suggested other approaches, but never finished their theories. Though *Revelation* contains vexingly complex symbols, a consistent story line advances. Readers must "climb" and endure many "switchbacks" before their journey concludes. The zigzags throw most folks dizzily off-balance. When we look for the proper clues in the right places, we improve our chances of grasping this Holy Spirit crafted book.

Revelation hides it message in symbolism. Where do we search for the keys? Few modern believers know the *Old Testament* as first century Christians did. In addition, not many Christians learn Jesus' and the Apostles' doctrine[29] as did many faith pioneers.

Is learning the *Bible* including *Revelation* worth our effort? Suppose grandma dies and leaves you her large jewelry collection. Some of your inheritance is exceedingly valuable; most is trinkets. To foil thieves, grandma purposely mixed the cheap with the precious. Identifying the costly requires sorting, comparing, and matching. Ascertaining grandma's exquisite stuff is well worth the effort involved.

You do not have to be a scholar to discover *Revelation's* treasure. Breaking *Revelation's* code isn't something only intellectuals can accomplish. By carefully noting similarities and parallels between *Revelation* and other parts of God's word, most anyone capable of reading can comprehend the book's vital message.

Incentive is the key to most success, not necessarily brainpower. Motivation to learn about God and his word spurred me to keep investigating. The rest of the *Bible* provides keys to most of *The Apocalypse* codes. In coming chapters, we shall reveal keys and clues I've uncovered mostly through reading the Bible cover to cover every year. Reading through several different translations also benefited me.[30]

---

29. See Acts 2:42

30. Over the years, I have read through the King James Version, The American Standard Version, The Revised Standard Version, The New American Standard Bible, James Moffatt's *A New Translation,* Today's English Version, and The Living Bible. I have also done lengthy readings in the J.B. Philips Translation, The Holy Scriptures from the Masoretic Text, and the Septuagint.

Chapter 1

Why Is *Revelation* So Difficult To Understand?
Revelation poses the ultimate riddle. Popular puzzle books and some text books supply answers in "the back." If an "official" *Apocalypse* answer-book ever existed, eyes haven't beheld it for centuries. From start to finish, *Revelation's* verses baffle steadfastly.

Some folks fancy that *Revelation* teems with Last Days data. The book brims with precise end-time prophecies, they say. Interpreters try to pinpoint the when, where, and how of supposed significant events. Generations come and go taking virtually all such *Apocalypse*-speculators with them.

We like clear-cut answers. We detest "maybes" and hype. "Give us facts," we demand. Yet whether we read *Revelation's* pages twice or twenty-five times, perplexity prevails. Multiple readings leave some students more confused. What qualities keep *The Apocalypse* so impenetrable?

The Lord made *Revelation's* message difficult for good reasons. Even as it comforted and aided believers, the Holy Spirit purposely designed the letter to confound hostile authorities. He intended for the book's complex symbolic structure to befuddle Christ's opponents.

Questions That Need Answers
What circumstances produced this intriguing script? The unique, new Christian fellowship unsettled and upset influential segments of society in Asia Minor (present western Turkey). Most citizens there viewed the Emperor as god. Christians followed Jesus' example of showing respect to "Caesar," yet steadfastly refused, as Jesus did, to "have any other gods before them." They could not venerate Rome's Emperor. He stood as an idol to which Christians could not and would not bow. Because of this failure to conform, God's church faced harsh antagonism. Persecution, harassment, and torture constantly beset believers.

The practice of exalting Rome's leaders began with Octavian about 31 BC. The Roman senate showered him with numerous titles including *Augustus*, meaning revered. Veneration progressed. Although enforcement of the law varied from place to place, Rome's government considered Christianity illegal. Authorities in the eastern parts of the Roman Empire strongly enforced the ban.

Second, in many communities, long-established trade guilds created and maintained strong, tightly-knit social bonds. Guild members thought Christian brotherhood, which God's churches practiced, threatened their cozy fraternal networks.

According to local legend, Diana (or Artemis), a fertility goddess, fell from the sky near the city of Ephesus (chief city in Asia Minor). Cult followers built a huge shrine to the eminent female deity. That temple functioned also as a bank, museum, art gallery, and elite meeting place. Guild associates manufactured souvenir shrines (silver models) of Diana. Local shops sold those mementos to tourists and devotees.

Craftsmen in those ancient guilds fretted about their industry's future. Christ's people did not purchase the souvenir idols the workers crafted. In addition Christians rarely frequented butcher shops and the profitable pagan temple eating places.

The temple dedicated to Artemis (Diana) of the Ephesians likely drew greater percentages of tourists than the Chinese Theater and film studios bring to Hollywood or the Empire State Building and Statue of Liberty entice to New York City. Decades prior to *Revelation*, guild members began rioting against missionary-teacher Paul in the city's massive semicircular amphitheater.[31] Acts 19 describes the swiftly formed, intense animosity toward Christ's people.

Ephesus workers and citizens foresaw shrinking tourism and relic sales if people worshiped God in Christ as Paul and his fellow missionaries taught.[32] Residents of nearby sister cities: Smyrna, Pergamum, Thyatira, and so on, shared similar concerns. For these and other reasons, the government, guild members, and citizens resented Christians. Hate toward the new movement increased. Intimidation of believers widened. Disciples in the Philadelphia church received maltreatment. A prominent church leader was slain in Smyrna. As persecution escalated, God's people needed encouragement.

Opposition to Christians came from another quarter. As the *Book of Acts* records, various Jewish leaders fomented hostility toward Christians. In the same manner that the Jewish hierarchy envied and harshly resented Jesus, some Jewish synagogue leaders throughout the Roman Empire reacted belligerently toward believers in Christ. The subject of resurrection particularly enraged the Sadducean sect of the Jews.[33]

Consider another significant aspect. The world constantly lures and tempts. The *Old Testament* records Israel's frequent surrender to sexual cravings promoted by devotees of pagan fertility gods. In the first century AD, similar enticements seduced believers in Asia Minor. Greek and Roman cities openly displayed sensual, erotic public art

---

31. Some estimate the amphitheater's seat capacity as 25,000.

32. See Acts 19:21-41.

33. The Pharisees believed in the resurrection; the more elite, wealthy Sadducees did not. See Matthew 22:23-33; Acts 4: 1-22; 23:1-11; 1 Corinthians 15.

and statuary. As the prophet Balaam and later Queen Jezebel led many Israelites astray, Artemis (Diana) and hosts of other fertility idols drew numbers of first century believers off course. Unbelief, lust, and greed lured them from obeying God's word.[34] The above factors generated the need for *Revelation*.

The Apocalypse fulfilled its intended goals. The Spirit's primary objectives: reinforce belief and create stronger commitment to Christ. The book bolstered believers' faith and warned those who wavered because of pagan temptations or fear of persecution. At the same time, the letter's unfamiliar symbols befuddled readers opposed to Christ.

Irony currently surrounds *The Apocalypse* confidence in Christ as *Revelation's* main message, but the menacing images and secret symbols the book employs frighten many readers. Clever minds routinely try to crack *The Apocalypse* code yet its secrets remain intact and mostly misinterpreted. As a result, few who need spiritual support find *Revelation's* encouragement. Believers who wander from God's truth never perceive the letter's stern warnings. Too few discover *Revelation's* long-buried treasures: profound hope and victory.

War Messages

God's people once understood *Revelation's* ciphers. Now, the book's encryption bamboozles even well-read scholars. Wrongly interpreted signs send sincere readers in manifold directions. Difficulty stems mainly from the tendency to overlook or neglect sources of *Revelation's* symbolism. Also, many readers fail to understand that they are attempting to crack "wartime-style" secret messaging.[35]

Revelation supplied vital information for people contending with a raging war. Consider this unique fact about the never ending battle which keeps Christians engaged. In most conflicts, combatants aim to inflict suffering on the opposition. They try to debilitate or annihilate their foes. *Revelation's* "battle plan" differs in this regard.

In his attempts to destroy the seemingly helpless, defenseless people of God, the great dragon-serpent continues evolving, changing his appearance and methods. Satan's strategies include callous, inhumane

---

34. See Numbers 22-25; Matthew 15: 16-20; 1 Corinthians 5, 6, & 10:1-12; Revelation 2:12-29; 9:20, 21; 21:6-8.

35. Many historians say that a Chinese military man called Sun Tzu (sixth- century BC) devised the first espionage system. Various factions utilized intelligence operations and perplexing codes during the French Revolution. Napoleon also used them. Russian Czars sent secret messages in vain efforts to suppress rebellions. In WWI, Mata Hari conducted her infamous spy activities. The French caught up with Mata Hari and executed her in 1917. Was Ms. Hari careless with her ciphers? Many know of the Navajo language "code" employed by the United States military in World War II. For centuries, North American Navajo Indians spoke it. The Germans never solved the Navajo "riddle."

disregard for human life. His multitudes of troops constantly attempt to humiliate and exterminate their presumably "weaker" opponents. The devil's mission: debase and obliterate all who obey God. Absolutely devoid of ethics, Satan's forces fight brutally, spitefully, heartlessly.

By contrast, the "lesser force" (believers in Christ) never resorts to unscrupulous methods. Unlike their evil foe, they stay a decent, benevolent course. This "smaller" army intends no harm to the malicious force striving to eradicate it. God's people resist retribution and reprisal. Though Christians arm themselves using the defensive equipment Paul recommended in *Ephesians* 6, they leave all vengeance to God.[36]

Secret Communications Needed

To succeed in their survival strategy of enduring and encouraging one another, God's church needed protected communications. From the onset of the "war," coded messages were essential. Without the benefit of secret symbols, God's "smaller" army would suffer staggering numbers of casualties.

Survival was not the "lesser" forces lone goal. Jesus commissioned all his followers to tell his Good News. Proclaiming the Lord's decisive, upbeat message of hope remains essential. Every army deals with morale. Godly "soldiers" need reassurance and inspiration. Troops must stay upbeat.

Written and oral communications to hearten, cheer, and inform require total concealment. Because enemy agents might intercept messages, memos must be sent and received in a secure, covert language. Legal circumstances required a code so cryptic and puzzling it would seem nonsensical if the enemy wanted to present the letter as evidence in court.

The Lord provided what his force needed. The small survival manual brilliantly succeeded. The handbook gave them coping strategies and effectively warned the troops against giving up or siding with the enemy. The instruction cheered the targeted audience. What made the clandestine "booklet" effective? The primary reason: God's Spirit and word continually confound human intellect.[37]

As an example, consider how *Revelation's* design probably perplexed Roman government officials trying to decipher the book. They likely experienced "aha" moments while reading the letter's opening lines:

> *The revelation from Jesus Christ, which God gave him to show his servants what must soon take place. he made it known by sending*

---

36. See also Romans 12:1-21.

37. See 1 Corinthians 2.

> his angel to his servant John, who testifies to everything he saw—that is, the word of God and the testimony of Jesus Christ. Blessed is the one who reads aloud the words of this prophecy, and blessed are those who hear it and take to heart what is written in it, because the time is near.38

This paragraph appears to divulge and disclose Jesus, the name associated with the new religion the Romans knew as Christianity. Yet when a Roman reader came to the section we know as verse 12 of Chapter 1, however, he/she must have thought *Revelation's* writer suffered hallucinations.

> I turned around to see the voice that was speaking to me. And when I turned I saw seven golden lampstands, and among the lampstands was someone like a son of man, dressed in a robe reaching down to his feet and with a golden sash around his chest. The hair on his head was white like wool, as white as snow, and his eyes were like blazing fire. His feet were like bronze glowing in a furnace, and his voice was like the sound of rushing waters. In his right hand he held seven stars, and coming out of his mouth was a sharp, double-edged sword. His face was like the sun shining in all its brilliance.

Could the average church-goer identify the sources for the various symbols found in 1:12-16? For this one paragraph, Nestle's Greek text lists more than twenty *Old Testament* references from *Ezekiel*, *Daniel*, and *Judges*, as well as Jesus' transfiguration scene in *Matthew* 17: 2.[39] In the prior section, 1: 4-8, Nestle identified about thirty references from ten different OT books. The *Revelation* writer evidently utilized both the Hebrew text and the Greek translation known as the Septuagint, which many first century Jews and Christians used.

In addition *Revelation's* author sourced the gospels of *Luke* and *John*, and mentioned the priesthood of believers as had the Apostle Peter in one of his epistles.[40] These facts confirm that we cannot overestimate the extents and complexities of the symbols *The Apocalypse* uses. Imagine a prosecutor, ancient or modern, trying to convincingly explain this jumble of evidence in a court of law. *Revelation* employed more than one code. These numerous types of symbols compound the book's mystery. This multi-cipher tactic greatly factored in *Revelation's* success.

---

38. Revelation 1:1-3 NIV.

39. *NOVUM TESTAMENTUM GRAECE ET LATINE*, Eb. Nestle, Stuttgart, 1909.

40. 1 Peter 2:5, 9.

A major focus of this study centers on the variety of codes and how Jesus' people benefited from them. Why are these codes so important? The war between good and evil persists. The battle continually rages. Fatality rates soar. Satan and his forces constantly resist our loving Creator. Many believers fall to temptation; others weary and stumble in the fight. Comprehending *Revelation's* hope-filled message can inspire twenty-first century believers as it aided first century disciples.

The Battlefield

The conflict enmeshes every being in the Cosmos. Even extra-terrestrial beings become entangled.[41] As the strife persists into the twenty-first century, forces of darkness keep inflicting heavy losses on the forces of light. Yet those who stay faithful to God will witness and enjoy his victory.

The original form of *The Apocalypse* letter remains intact. When properly understood, the book still encourages, strengthens, and protects present innocent troops. Two obstacles confront us. First, we must avoid the tendency to neglect the admittedly difficult work of obtaining *Revelation's* valuable messages. Second, we must also be wary of those who mishandle the word.[42] Well-meaning "experts" often misapply the signs the Holy Spirit provided.

The effects of misinformation resemble the spread of rumors after serious incidents. Many people believe and act on the first reports. Once authorities identify the facts, they face the challenges of correcting all the hubbub, buzz, and speculation originally circulated.

A few years ago, television and radio reporters told the story of devastation related to an Oklahoma disaster. For the second time in two weeks, tornadoes struck an area south of Oklahoma City. Officials notified residents of the impending storms. They warned folks several minutes in advance. For some reason, however, misinformation reigned for a while. Many residents thought authorities wanted them to escape the storms by driving away from them. Cars crowded highways and Interstates. Vehicles sat stalled, bumper to bumper, when the tornadoes struck. Catastrophe resulted.

Undoing effects of initial false reports remains a communication nightmare. Erroneous *Revelation* interpretations create similar effects. Conjecturers brashly assert wild theories. Advocates boldly preach flawed explanations. The effects include ridicule of God's Word, huge financial losses for folks who panic from false prophecies, and tragic disruption of Jesus' Great Commission.

---

41. See 2 Peter 2: 4-12.

42. Matthew 22: 29; 2 Timothy 2:15; 2 Peter 3:16.

Many "experts" contend that we waste valuable time trying to solve *Revelation's* riddles. Some "seasoned veterans" refuse to venture into the book. For these and other reasons, *The Apocalypse's* codes remain largely unbroken.

We must not forget that God's Spirit produced *Revelation* as a survival guide. He wrote the letter to prepare and sustain Jesus' followers for fiery ordeals. In the first century AD, intense trials persisted. The emperor's agents meant to stamp out the faithful. They aimed to exterminate those who believed in Jesus' resurrection. Despite their vehement efforts, *Revelation's* message inspired the church to endure furious first- and second-century tribulations.

Today a new era of persecution tests God's faithful. Increasing world-wide opposition to Christianity makes *Revelation's* message imperative. The challenges require dependence on God and our faithful perseverance. *Revelation* brings needed hope, information, and encouragement. Heeding its message leads to immortality—joyous eternity. But can we unseal this mystery—break *Revelation's* many codes? I think so.

Who Is Winning This War And How Will It End?

During my decades of awareness, many have expressed fear of earth's imminent obliteration. Those anxious ones included religious "experts" prophesying quick perdition. Wretched end-time assessments aren't unique to my short sojourn. Libraries and digital "warehouses" provide ample proof of prominent prior "experts" opining their generation's rapid advance toward the Abyss. The regularity of gloomy predictions probably prompted this Ecclesiastes advice: "Do not say, 'Why were the old days better than these?'"[43]

Countless believers think that *Revelation* tells the official what, when, why, and where of a catastrophic end. No wonder, that to many Christians and non-Christians, the word *apocalypse* means fearsome disaster.[44] This misrepresentation explains why to untold folks, current events seem a hopeless, confused joke. They plead for Divine intervention, often questioning why God fails at times to "uphold the righteous."

---

43. Ecclesiastes 7:10a NIV.

44. Those readers not convinced of this truth should note the Apostle Peter's use of the term *apocalypse* in 1 Peter 1. In verses 5 & 6, Peter wrote of the "salvation that is ready to be revealed in the last time. In this you rejoice." In verse 7, he spoke of the "praise, glory and honor when Jesus Christ is **revealed**." In both instances, the Greek text uses forms of the word *apocalypse*. In contemporary English speech, the term *apocalypse* is exceedingly and regularly misused.

Two prominent *New Testament* words[45] help us understand the nearly perpetual dilemmas Christians face in a world seemingly dominated by evil. No *Revelation* study can be complete without considering this pair of terms. About 15 times in his Gospel, Matthew used one of these expressions or its derivatives. I refer to the word *pleroma* (πλήρωμα) "to fulfill." John's Gospel uses the term about ten times. Though appearing less often in *Revelation*, the word occurs in significant contexts. *Pleroma* slightly impacts the English language,[46] but conveys an extremely important concept. Jesus declared to the Apostles: "This is what I told you while I was still with you: Everything must be **fulfilled** that is written about me in the Law of Moses, the Prophets and the Psalms."[47] Jesus fully accomplished God's messianic plan outlined in the *OT*. He then defined elements of the Divine strategy that involve subsequent generations, individuals, and societies:

> *This is what is written: The Messiah will suffer and rise from the dead on the third day, and repentance for the forgiveness of sins will be preached in his name to all nations, beginning at Jerusalem. You are witnesses of these things.*[48]

Jesus foresaw future disciples preaching his name to countries, cultures, and populations not yet then in existence and possibly yet to come.[49] That God expects all era's disciples to participate in completing his plan appears evident in the Great Commission.[50] In the *Revelation* letter to the Sardis church, the Lord warned: "I have not found your deeds *complete in* the eyes of my God. Remember what you have received and heard: obey it and repent".[51]

---

45. They also appear in the *Septuagint*.

46. Exceptions include plerosis, a medical term; pleromorph, geology; botany, Pleroma violet; and plerergate, a worker ant with a swollen abdomen.

47. Luke 24:44 NIV, **bold** emphasis mine. Jews then and now divide the same 39 books contained in most Protestant Bible Old Testaments into three categories as noted here. What he referred to as the **Psalms** most Jewish Bibles label as the **Writings**.

48. Ibid, verses 46-48 NIV.

49. He bluntly prophesied that future in Matthew 24, Mark 13, and Luke 21.

50. "Go and make disciples of all nations, baptizing them in the name of the Father and of the Son and of the Holy Spirit, and teaching them to obey everything I have commanded you. And surely I am with you always, to the very end of the age" Matthew 28:19, 20 NIV.

51. 3:2, 3a NIV.

Gerhard Delling's research of pleroma led him to define its meaning: "To fill up completely a specific measure."[52] A form of pleroma appears in The Septuagint, as God ratified a covenant with Abraham, promising him that his descendants would one day inherit the land where at the time he only sojourned. Genesis 15: 15 and 16 relate the Lord saying to the Patriarch:

> "You, however, will go to your ancestors in peace and be buried at a good old age. In the fourth generation your descendants will come back here, for the sin of the Amorites has not yet **reached its full measure.**"[53]

As *Daniel* 10:3 reads in an English translation of the *Septuagint*: "I ate no pleasant bread, and no flesh or wine entered into my mouth, neither did I anoint myself with oil, until three whole weeks were *accomplished* (πληρώσεως)." A similar form of *pleroma* with the prefix *ana*[54] appears in *Daniel* 12:13 where the Lord advised Daniel: "But go thou and rest; for there are yet days and seasons to the *fulfillment* of the end."[55]

This evidence leads me to conclude that God allotted a specific time for human history and also specific numbers related to certain events as *Revelation* 6: 11 appears to state: "until the number of their fellow servants and brothers who were to be killed as they had been was *completed* (πληρωθῶσιν)." On those subjects, no human being knows or receives any specific information. That's why Jesus counselled preparedness and watchfulness. "No one knows the day or the hour." God's plan remains beyond human comprehension. Further speculation on these matters amounts to idle idolatry.

In the *Daniel* 12:13 *Septuagint* passage above, a form of our second important term, *telos* (τέλος)[56] also appears. *Telos* occurs frequently in

---

52. See *The Theological Dictionary of the New Testament*, Vol. VI, pp. 283-311 for Delling's full treatise.

53. **Bold** emphasis mine, ἀναπεπλήρωνται –Perfect m/p verb ind. 3rd pers. pl. of ἀναπληρόω. Jesus similarly warned his contemporaries in Matthew 23:32 (πληρώσατε).

54. The prefix "ana" also preceded the term in Genesis 15:16.

55. THE SEPTUAGINT WITH APOCRYPHA: GREEK AND ENGLISH, Sir Lancelot C.L. Brenton, Hendrickson Publishers, Seventeenth Printing, February 2015. Originally published by Samuel Bagster & Sons, London, 1851.

56. This is the noun form of the word. Greek nouns usually add suffixes depending on their case and gender in the sentence. At least four different verb forms relate to telos. Verbs add prefixes and suffixes depending on their tense, mood, and voice in addition to whether they are singular or plural. In the case of *telos*, the stem *tel* is usually recognizable.

the *Apocalypse*.[57] NT writers frequently used it. English versions translate *telos* as fulfill, fill, accomplish, complete, perfection, finish, and end. Keep in mind a goal or task to be carried out. In the previously mentioned *1 Peter* passage, Peter told of the living hope, which benefits believers. Regarding the grand finale of being in Christ, he wrote: "You are receiving the end result (telos- τέλος) of your faith, the salvation of your souls."[58]

All humans must conform to God's grand strategy and goals. These include, as John wrote:

> *The one who says, "I have come to know him," and does not keep his commandments, is a liar, and the truth is not in him; but whoever keeps his word, in him the love of God **has truly been perfected**. By this we know that we are in Him: the one who says he abides in him ought himself to walk in the same manner as he walked.[59]*

Those who resist the Lord and his commands move toward a tragic conclusion.[60] As we saw, the *Daniel* passage reads: "there are yet days and seasons to the fulfillment of the end." At that moment, God will consummate his plan "It is done. I am the Alpha and Omega, the Beginning and the **End**."[61] "In the beginning God created the heavens and the earth." he also will finish-end (telos) the heavens and the earth. Peter warned of the finality's suddenness:

> *But the day of the Lord will come like a thief. The heavens will disappear with a roar; the elements will be destroyed by fire, and the earth and everything in it will be laid bare. Since everything will be destroyed in this way, what kind of people ought you to be? You ought to live holy and godly lives as you look forward to the day of God and speed its coming. That day will bring about the destruction of the heavens by fire, and the elements will melt in the heat. But in keeping with his promise we are looking forward to a new heaven and a new earth, where righteousness dwells. So then, dear friends, since you are looking forward to this, make every effort to be found spotless, blameless and at peace with him.[62]*

---

57. For example Revelation 10: 7; 11:7;15:1, 8; 17:17; 20:3, 7.

58. 1 Peter 1:9 NIV.

59. 1 John 2:4-6 NASB teteleiotai τετελείωται (**bold** emphasis mine).

60. Jesus warned his own countrymen; as noted earlier in Matthew 23:32, NASB, "Fill up, then, the measure *of the guilt* of your fathers."

61. Revelation 21:6 NIV.

62. 2 Peter 3: 10-14 NIV.

As the following Scriptures emphasize, the writer of *Hebrews* counseled God's people to believe, obey, and honor the Lord, submitting to his plans and principles, and enduring all opposition:

> *For every house is built by someone, but the builder of all things is God. Now Moses was faithful in all his house as a servant, for a testimony of those things which were to be spoken later; but Christ was faithful as a Son over his house—whose house we are, if we hold fast our confidence and the boast of our hope firm until the end . . .*
>
> *For we have become partakers of Christ, if we hold fast the beginning of our assurance firm until the end, while it is said, "TODAY IF YOU HEAR HIS VOICE, DO NOT HARDEN YOUR HEARTS, AS WHEN THEY PROVOKED ME."*[63]

Hebrews refers to the moment God's overall plan comes together in fulfillment-totality:

> *"And all these, having gained approval through their faith, did not receive what was promised, because God had provided something better for us, so that apart from us they would not be made perfect."*[64]

The Lord's Teaching Methods

The presence of Jewish synagogues, each with its scrolls of the Torah, Prophets and Writings (what Christians now call the *Old Testament*) assured that most Jewish young men and some women would know *Old Testament* history and laws. As C.L. Feinberg wrote: "In the first century AD, synagogues existed wherever Jews lived."[65]

The Assyrians' conquering of Israel's Northern kingdom in 722/721 BC and the Babylonian takeover of the Southern kingdom in 587/586 BC began the diaspora or dispersion of the Jewish people over the globe. Though many Jews returned after the Babylonian Captivity, the majority never returned to the homeland. In fact, James, half-brother of Jesus, addressed his epistle "to the twelve tribes who are dispersed abroad."[66] Jews expecting God's Messiah later constituted great fertile missionary soil for Jesus the Messiah's, Good News.

---

63. Hebrews 3:4-6 & 14, 15 NASB. The NIV and NRSV lack emphasis on **telos-end** in their renderings of these Scriptures.

64. Hebrews 11: 39, 40 NASB (τελειωθῶσιν) underline emphasis mine.

65. "Synagogue" C.L. Feinberg, *The New Bible Dictionary*, J.D. Douglas, org. ed., Inter-Varsity Press, London, 1962.

66. James 1:1 NASB.

Intense persecution arose after Stephen's death causing early disciples to leave Jerusalem and its environs. *Acts* 11 reported: "Now those who had been scattered by the persecution that broke out when Stephen was killed traveled as far as Phoenicia, Cyprus, and Antioch, spreading the word only among Jews."[67] For years, as *Acts* informs us, Paul's *modus operandi* included going first to synagogues when arriving in new cities. The Greek word *synagogue* compounds "syn" *with* or *together* and "ago" a verb meaning *to lead*. **Synagogue** primarily means *gather, gather together, or call together*. The word eventually described the building where, once their Temple became inaccessible, Jews gathered to pray, worship, meet, and learn.

In the first century, boys ages 7-15 regularly attended synagogue schools learning the Torah, its laws and history, The prophets, and the writings (including the praise, prayers and music of the *Psalms* as well as the wisdom from *Job, Proverbs, Ecclesiastes*, and so on). The prevalence of Greek education and wisdom after Alexander the Great's time affected Jewish and popular Christian thought more widely and profoundly than most people realize. Proof of its effects: the translation of the *Old Testament* into Greek, known as the *Septuagint* or *LXX*.[68] Legends tell that about 250-100 BC, 72 Jewish scholars in Alexandria, Egypt translated the work in 72 days. Many *New Testament* authors quoted from the *LXX*.

The ancient Jewish writings known as the Mishnah and the Talmud relate numerous fascinating instances of Rabbinic teaching methods carried out in synagogues and other places of instruction. Whether the Apostles and their disciples learned the majority of their *Old Testament* knowledge in synagogue lessons or whether Jesus "schooled" them or refreshed them, they seemed to know the Jewish Bible well. On the Day of Pentecost and later occasions, Peter and the other Apostles quoted lengthy passages and referred often to *OT* incidents and people.[69]

Effective teaching requires certain amounts of **rote** or **repetition, remembering, testing, discipline, attentiveness (hearing** and **listening)**, and producing fruit from one's learning. In *Revelation's* various scenes, the above factors come into play. Loud (mega) audio and dy-

---

67. Acts 11:19 NIV Interestingly, the word translated *scattered* is a form of Greek diaspora and the word translated persecution is *thlipsis* aka *tribulation*.

68. The very fact that a Jewish worship place is called synagogue, a word of Greek origin, is convincing. How strongly Greek philosophy and thought have affected modern Jewish and Christian conceptions of body, soul, and spirit deserves careful consideration and study.

69. Most reference Bibles indicate the multiple times Peter and others quoted not just the OT, but referred to Jesus' teaching as well. Many of OT quotations come from the Septuagint Version.

namic visual scenes enhance the learning process. Note the following sobering, instructive examples:

> ***Rote*** — *"Blessed is the one who reads aloud the words of this prophecy, and blessed are those who hear it and take to heart what is written in it . . . "(1:3 NIV).*[70]

> *"I warn everyone who hears the words of the prophecy of this scroll: If anyone adds anything to them, God will add to that person the plagues described in this scroll. And if anyone takes words away from this scroll of prophecy, God will take away from that person any share in the tree of life and in the Holy City, which are described in this scroll" (22:18, 19 NIV).*

> ***Remembering***[71] – *"Consider (earlier NIV versions translated "remember") how far you have fallen! Repent and do the things you did at first. If you do not repent, I will come to you and remove your lampstand from its place (2:5 NIV).*

> *"Remember, therefore, what you have received and heard; hold it fast, and repent. But if you do not wake up, I will come like a thief, and you will not know at what time I will come to you" (3:3 NIV).*

> **Testing** *or* **Trying** – *"I know your deeds, your hard work and your perseverance. I know that you cannot tolerate wicked people, that you have **tested** those who claim to be apostles but are not, and have found them false" (2:2 NIV).*

> *"Do not be afraid of what you are about to suffer. I tell you, the devil will put some of you in prison to **test** you, and you will suffer persecution for ten days. Be faithful, even to the point of death, and I will give you life as your victor's crown" (2:10 NIV).*

> *"Since you have kept my command to endure patiently, I will also keep you from the hour of **trial** that is going to come on the whole*

---

70. Because the NIV undergoes continual revision, there may be some variation in translation according to the date of publication.

71. *Remember* translates forms of mimnāskomai (μιμνήσκομαι) to remember, keep in mind, be concerned about. Contrary to popular ideas, God remembers un-repented of sins; see Revelation 9:20, 21; 16:16-21; & 18:4-8.

*world to **test** the inhabitants of the earth" (3:10 NIV).*[72]

Discipline or Teach – In *Revelation*, often used in a negative sense.

*"Nevertheless, I have a few things against you: There are some among you who hold to the **teaching** of Balaam, who **taught** Balak to entice the Israelites to sin so that they ate food sacrificed to idols and committed sexual immorality" (2:14 NIV).*

*"Nevertheless, I have this against you: You tolerate that woman Jezebel, who calls herself a prophet. By her **teaching** she misleads my servants into sexual immorality and the eating of food sacrificed to idols. I have given her time to repent of her immorality, but she is unwilling. So I will cast her on a bed of suffering, and I will make those who commit adultery with her suffer intensely, unless they repent of her ways." (2:20-22 NIV).*[73]

Attentiveness (hearing and **listening)** Calls to hear and listen occurred in each of the Letters to the Seven Churches and repeatedly throughout *Rev:* [74]*"He who has an ear, let him hear what the Spirit says to the churches."*

Jesus constantly emphasized kingdom **productivity in his parables.** The Lord expects his servants **to produce fruit from their learning.** *Revelation's* narrative focuses on deeds and reward of labor and the harvest.

Choosing The Right Scouts And Guides

Imagine the *Book of Revelation* as a forest filled not just with incredible curiosities, but more importantly, extraordinary life-enhancing sights. Unusual phenomena seem to symbolize upcoming events. Various forest guides advertise their expertise. All objects predict or signify something meaningful, say the "experts." As you tour, you clearly see

---

72. These instances translate peirasmós (πειρασμός), which often refers to a period of fiery testing; closely related to dokimadzo (δοκιμάζω) meaning to approve, test, demonstrate, or prove.

73. Didásko (διδάσκω) teach.

74. Akoúo (ἀκούω) hear, give heed to, understand, and so on **Bold** emphasis mine in all the above.

strange terrain. The visuals and sounds differ from anything you ever experienced.

Many "professional" escorts allege that the extraordinary phenomena symbolize a complex sequence of events that results horribly for some folks. Explanations of the "territory" seem inconsistent. Interpretations appear contradictory and outlandish. After you walk in the woods a while, you feel bewildered and disorientated. You want out.

Many *Revelation* guides predict a sudden and calamitous end of the world on a day they audaciously announce. The designated date arrives and passes. The guides rationalize their inaccuracies by claiming they did not correctly "tweak" some data. They blame "unexpected" events for their previous lack of fine-tuning. After they make a few "adjustments," the guides make new predictions.

If you think I overstate this point, consult the predictions made by 19th century "guides" like William Miller. Beginning in about 1831, Miller predicted the date of Christ's second coming as 1843. Later he revised it to 1844. Time keeps proving the bogus nature of human interpretations and prophecies. Hal Lindsey, among others made the same gaffe in the twentieth century.[75] As the twenty-first century arrived, he kept predicting and apparently some still believed his false forecasts.

You decide to consult more scholarly guides and confer with those whose backgrounds include university and seminary tutelage. Most inform you that four main interpretive routes lead into *Revelation's* "forest." When you ask which path they advise, they tell you something appalling. All express personal preferences, but they also acknowledge that none of the four routes gets you completely through the forest. All the major interpretive views available to scholars contain flaws, they admit. "You could get lost out there." Would you hire one of those "guides"? If all of the known trails into that dense forest lead to dead ends, why set out on any of them?

Adam Clarke explored *Revelation's* mystery, but quit. He explained his reasons for not trying to interpret the book:

> *My readers will therefore excuse me from any exposure of my ignorance or folly by attempting to do what many, with much more wisdom and learning, have attempted, and what every man to the present day has failed in, who has preceded me in expositions of this book. I have no other mountain to heap on those already piled up; and if I had, I have not strength to lift it; those who have courage may again make the trial; already we have had a sufficiency of vain efforts.*

---

75. You can see samples of Lindsey's erroneous predictions in his 1970s work: *The Late Great Planet Earth*.

Ter sunt conati imponere Pelio Ossam Scilicet, Atque Ossæ Frondosum Involvere Olympum Ter Pater Extructos Disjecit Fulmine Montes. Virg., G i. 281.

With mountains piled on mountains thrice they strove To scale the steepy battlement of Jove; And thrice his lightning and red thunder play'd, And their demolished works in ruin laid. Dryden76

Despite Clarke's dire warnings, surely the Lord would not have preserved the book if it has no value for our time.

In this work, I plan to introduce and provide keys for interpreting *Revelation* unhampered by weaknesses inherent in other views. As I researched for this book, it became clear that a few sages had already proposed parts of the view. Even these researchers, however, neglected important ciphers. The Lord willing, we shall detail the errors as we "travel."

To comment on every chapter and verse requires more than one volume. In this book, I plan to cover some building blocks necessary to understanding *Revelation*. A few seem elementary. But so are blocking and tackling to the game of football. We shall accomplish this only if God wills, of course.

Seven common words that begin with the letter "C" (**Seven Cs**) will assist us throughout this study. God is **Creator** of heaven and earth. Jesus **Christ,** (the Lamb slain) is God's faithful witness. When the people God creates refuse to love, honor, and obey Him, **Chaos** (bedlam, disorder, and lawlessness) result. Because of **Chaos** and confusion in their midst, godly people feel **Conflicted.** Will justice ever be restored? Will right ever prevail? Has God forgotten his people? In *Revelation,* God answered those questions for first century believers. Three other **Cs** will cover subjects we discussed in the Introduction. More importantly, they recap the Holy Spirit's purpose in *Revelation.*

First — Comfort
The Holy Spirit reminded Christians, who were undergoing suffering that all seemingly invincible, wicked, worldly powers must answer to the King of kings and Lord of lords. Furthermore, the Almighty intimately knows his churches. Those who continue to trust the **Creator** and his faithful true witness (Jesus **Christ,** the Lamb slain) through the present tribulation will find **Comfort.** They will attain permanent residence in the New Jerusalem (Jesus' glorified church), which God will reveal from heaven.

---

76. *Clarke's Commentary,* Adam Clarke, Abingdon Press, New York, Vol. VI, p 966.

Second – Caution And Convict

Those who succumbed to "Jezebel's" temptations gave in to greed and to fearsome earthly powers. The Holy Spirit convicted (found them guilty of wrongdoing). They must repent and turn to God. We shall see how he brings about conditions that should motivate all people to end their pride, change their ways, and honor Him. Many refuse to listen to their loving, all-wise **Creator**.

Third – Confound

The Lord coded the communications intended to comfort and convict believers by using signs and symbols designed to confuse the Lamb's enemies. Early Christians understood the Spirit's veiled, oblique language because they knew the *Old Testament*, Jesus' messages, and the Apostle's teaching.[77] Unless readers now consult all the Scriptures, they will remain confused.

We are involved in a titanic struggle—a battle for lives and souls. God will win. We shall win with Him—if we trust him and persevere in **Christ,** living by his example. Are you ready to explore the Word? The themes of most chapters in *Revelation* can be defined using one or more of the **Seven Cs:**

1. Creator
2. Christ
3. Chaos
4. Conflict
5. Caution
6. Confound
7. Comfort

We'll show how these themes appear and reappear throughout the *Apocalypse*.

---

77. Acts 2:42-46; 4:33.

Chapter 2
Keys That Unlock The Mystery

The Necessity Of Codes
Revelation reveals Christ. Unfortunately, few Christian readers today "see" Jesus as the Lord intended. Instead of reassuring (comforting) current believers, *Revelation* often frightens them. Imagine opening a package expecting to find a diamond, only to find gross, disgusting contents. Can we possibly find the Lord amidst such bizarre imagery? Why does *The Apocalypse* pose such peculiar, cryptic ciphers? For what purpose do such strange obscurities confront us?

While watching horror movies, few viewers feel love and goodwill. Yet *Revelation's* "scary" signs guided, enabled, and encouraged its original readers. How was that possible? And what made *Revelation's* outlandish characters and images necessary?

Suppose local authorities forbid Jesus' people to assemble in your city or town? Defying this no-worship ordinance brings severe penalties. Things get worse. A government leader orders all residents to publicly demonstrate their allegiance to him. All must declare loyalty to this despot. Unless you submit, you cannot purchase anything or travel anywhere. Comply or you face ridicule, possible arrest, and even execution.

Government officials enforce strict policies and physically mark those who conform. Authorities install surveillance systems to see whether you and your loved ones observe the ordinance. The powers that be can readily identify those who abide by their rules and the ones who do not. Choosing to worship God, most believers refuse to comply with this ungodly ordinance. As a result, many endure torture. Some suffer martyrdom.

Under these circumstances, would you wonder: Has God lost control? Is Satan winning? How long will this last? What about loved ones who died for their faith? Did they suffer in vain? Will God ever bring justice?

Chaos and **Conflict** reign. Additional news disheartens you. Some Christians in nearby cities lapse in their commitments to Jesus. They compromise their faith. Pride, greed, fear, and selfishness prevail among them. Some married couples no longer keep their vows. A few become openly involved in adultery and fornication.

Suppose that a Christian from another region becomes aware of your situation. That person knows that you question the Lord's apparent failure to resolve your distress. Your godly friend hopes to fortify your commitment to the Lord and to hearten you and your fellow believers. He/she does not advocate insurrection or civil disobedience. Rather, this person wants to remind you of God's faithfulness and his ultimate control. Because severe penalties loom for resisting government, your loved one writes carefully. Any paper or electronic trail that even hints of non-compliance might endanger you. Government agents might interpret such as evidence for sedition.

Common Codes
Your fellow Christians and you share numerous experiences. You've read many of the same books and have countless mutual friends. You have worshipped, sung together, endured similar hardships, and prayed together.

Single words or numbers often trigger recollections of common experiences. In other instances, your Christian friend recalls stories and events familiar to both of you. Those anecdotes, numbers, and experiences provide a code known only to you two.

An Oregon friend and his wife visited us in Iowa for several days. In high school, we shared many experiences. We had not seen each other for decades. During the visit, a mere word, name, picture, or sentence often elicited laughs or frowns. Codes we never consciously developed made interaction easy.

Couples usually share code words, sentences, songs, and even significant numbers. Today my wife noticed that the water in our cat's bowl was dirty. She said to me, "I need to change the cat's water." Was it a simple statement of her intentions? Hardly. She sent me a coded message. She really meant, "Would you please give the cat some fresh water?" I decoded the message and within minutes, the kitty drank from a clean dish. You, your friends, and loved ones likely communicate similarly. We use figurative language oftener than we recognize. Symbols familiar and precious to you and those close to you rarely mean anything to others.

Remember the precarious circumstances we described earlier? Your friend writes to remind you that Christ rules the world, not any government agent or agency. Faith and faithfulness to Jesus are vital. Not wanting to endanger you, your believing friend writes guardedly. Using symbols or codes you share, he/she composes a reassuring letter. Because of your common experiences, you easily decipher the hidden messages. What you clearly understand, though, makes little sense to anyone else.

First century and early second century Christians held numerous beliefs, experiences, history, writings, and knowledge in common. Those mutual matters provided codes for safe, symbolic communication. As we proceed, we shall identify the sources and the nature of these secret signs.

What Do Mortals Know?

Revelation employs not a single code, but many. For the protection of his faithful, Jesus sealed *Revelation's* mystery with numerous "locks." No "master key" to the Maestro's book exists. That's one reason *The Apocalypse* so vexes folks. Still, first-hand resources help us recognize symbols Jesus used. Spending time with Jesus and reading the letters his Apostles and their associates wrote greatly benefits us. Later we shall look at some of these "shared experiences" from the Gospels and other biblical sources. For now we need to consider one additional element.

In *Revelation* 4, John saw a door that opened into heaven. A trumpet-like voice ordered: *"Come up here, and I will show you what must take place after this."*[78] As an ordinary person straining to grasp the extraordinary, John faced special challenges. How can an earthbound, finite mind comprehend the Infinite, Ultimate, Supernatural Being, the Grand Designer, and Builder of Universes?

God exceeds us every way imaginable and in respects we cannot imagine. He is immortal. He is Spirit. Nothing limits God. His presence extends everywhere at the same time, and he knows everything—even prior to its occurrence.

Being material or whatever flesh is, space and time constrict us. In many ways our minds resemble airliners. First, we have limited capacity. Second, as airplanes suffer metal fatigue, time, and aging diminish our mental and physical faculties.

How does the infinite God communicate with us mortals? You know the difficulties of discussing complex subjects with children. To help them, you begin by using ideas and concepts they already understand and build on that foundation. As the children grasp each basic notion, you increase the complexity of your comparisons. No one understands algebra without first knowing how to read and to compute numbers.

We begin our comprehension of God by picturing human abilities and attributes. We see, hear, feel, touch, and think. God is said to do these things. But God is Spirit. Fleshly limitations don't confine or restrict him. Any comparisons we make, we must sketch cautiously.[79] Hardly anything we use to describe our Creator can be fully definitive.

---

78. 4:1b (NIV).

79. The word anthropomorphic (literally human form) describes this. Note Solomon's Temple dedication prayer (1 Kings 8). He understood that God is omnipresent, all-knowing, all-powerful spirit; he has no body or form as mankind. "Even the highest heavens cannot contain" him, Solomon acknowledged (v.27). Still, Solomon attributed

Comparing our growing ability to understand God with a child's increasing capabilities helps in some ways. That likening ultimately fails, though, for this reason. Adults and children share the same nature. As children mature, they begin grasping what reasonable adults comprehend. Though our knowledge of God should gradually increase over time, we shall never fully comprehend him.

God is immortal, all-knowing, Spirit. Other than his truth and goodness, nothing confines or restricts God.[80] Time, space, brain size, imperfect senses, limited abilities, and often pride, bind, and inhibit us.[81]

John beheld, felt, and heard abundant things. He "saw" God "seated" on his heavenly throne. Descriptions of that kind help us understand God's glory, his power, and his demands on us. Yet our scant capabilities, conceptions, and depictions of God always fail. Trying to comprehend the immensity and complexity of the billions of galaxies God created taxes the best of human minds. Fully grasping God's nature presents an infinitely greater task. No human representation begins to describe or to fully encompass his being.

John never attempted to draw a picture of God's form or substance.[82] He signified the Lord's presence and aura numerous ways.[83] Numbers provided certain information. Color descriptions created atmosphere. Yet John used none of the usual adjectives we utter when speaking of another being. No tall, short, medium build, brown eyes, or brown shock of hair. The Lord does not want us to picture him as a "mega hero" or "superhuman." He differs from us in every regard.

Were we created in God's image? Unquestionably. The *Book of Genesis* informs us so. The apostle Paul clearly explained that being in God's image has nothing to do with physical appearance, however.

---

many human (anthropomorphic) qualities to God: he hears, sees, forgives, promises, judges, and so on. Yet he does those things without having any physical nature or senses. God is not limited in any way.

80. We enlarge our views of God by reflecting on the varied ways he has equipped his creatures: bats-radar, dolphins-sonar, canine odor senses, and considering the immensity of space. Think of the intelligence necessary to conceive and create such things and other marvels in the Universe.

81. Current attempts by physicists to define gravity serve as an example. Newton's definition served well, but is now being discarded. Some of the views now presented might in another century seem laughable.

82. John maintained the usual Jewish reluctance to directly refer to God. Neither did he attempt to describe God in any way.

83. The throne on which the Lord sat indicates rule, majesty and supremacy. The fact that it is in heaven exalts him above all human authority and power.

Living in his "image" relates to thinking and acting morally, justly, and uprightly.[84]

How God Speaks To Us

When God communicates with human beings, he uses processes that our senses perceive. How did the Lord get John's attention in *Revelation* Chapter 4? Have you ever been awakened by a piercing trumpet sound? If so, you recall how the blast catches and fixes your consciousness. Even more impressive signals brought John to a full salute. Few things seize your mind like lightning and instantaneous, deafening, earth-rattling thunderclaps.

In *Revelation,* one significant human (anthropomorphic) description does appear. Chapter 5 opens by telling of the scroll in the Lord's "right hand." Seven seals fasten it, but do not just hide the scroll's contents. They likely also indicate the complexity of the subject matter. How intricate are *Revelation's* writings? They contain figurative, many faceted language. Sometimes a single word suffices as a sign. At times secret language lies buried within other symbols. Multiple emblems often hide in a single sentence.

Scenes sometimes recall *Old Testament* events. Among incidents evoked: the plagues of Moses, Israel's wilderness wandering, the three-and-half-year drought during Elijah's time, and *Zechariah's* olive trees.[85] Other symbols derive from nature (locusts) and a few from human imagination and folklore (dragons and beasts). Some signs evidently arose from "street talk"[86] and contemporary events.

Revelation's structure might be the book's greatest mystery. After the scroll's seventh seal opens, the story line seems to indicate the end time and Judgment. The narrative leads many readers to expect the finale. But the *finis* fails to occur. Instead, John sees another vision. At the conclusion of that visualization, readers again expect a conclusion. An additional vision occurs. That pattern continues. As R.C.H. Lenski noted, "*Revelation* reaches the end of the world in seven different places."[87]

---

84. Colossians 3:5-10.

85. Revelation 11:3-6 The OT background for the above can be found in Exodus 3-12, Exodus 32ff., Leviticus, Numbers, and Deuteronomy, 1 Kings 17, 18, Zechariah 4.

86. Revelation 13:3 NIV The head of the beast that "seemed to have had a fatal wound, but the fatal wound had healed," likely arose as a result of rumors that the despot Nero had returned from the dead; the so-called "redivivus theory." See Chapter 3, pages 75-77 for a fuller discussion.

87. *Interpretation of St. John's Revelation*. R.C.H. Lenski, Lutheran Book Concern, Columbus, Ohio, 1935, p 24.

Why does *Revelation* lead readers to expect the culmination, only to encounter repeated additional visions? None of the major interpretive views adequately explains this puzzle.

Weird Interpretive Devices

Scholars attempt curious interpretive devices. One method hopes to find *Revelation's* message by using every seventh letter in the book. Beginning with the first character, interpreters might count off seven letters. They list that seventh letter. They count off seven more and list that letter. After listing every seventh letter in the book, they arrange them in the order they appeared. Then interpreters try to "unscramble" words and messages from the assemblage of those seventh letters. Forget what the book appears to say. The narrative means little; it is only a "vehicle" carrying the message.

Schemes similar to this have been used to encode secret messages in other contexts. I doubt that *Revelation's* writer followed such an arrangement. In my view, that type of method seems amateurish—too simplistic.

The every-seventh-letter theory contains an inherent flaw. Consider the fact that John's original manuscript apparently does not exist. To prepare and produce our present *Revelation* (and other *NT*) texts, scholars reviewed and compared several different ancient Greek manuscripts (copies). None of those copies or manuscripts is a perfect text. How can we possibly depend on an every seventh-letter-message if we don't know which letter is the real seventh one?

In case you are now concerned that if we have none of the original texts, and only flawed copies exist, can we depend on the *NT's (*and *Revelation's)* reliability. Suppose you write me a lengthy, flawless ten-page letter. I treasure the contents of that letter and want to share it. I ask ten friends to make copies of it. Every one of them meticulously makes a handwritten copy of your letter. You understand the improbability of producing perfect copies of any lengthy handwritten document. As carefully as all of my friends copy your correspondence, each will likely make a few mistakes.

Common types of errors include word duplications, misspelled words, and skipped words and lines. In copying your letter, my friends make these and similar types of errors. In the meantime, the frequent reading and handling of your handwritten manuscript causes it to deteriorate. Your original letter falls apart or becomes unreadable. Only those flawed handwritten copies remain. Could we possibly reconstruct your letter? Lacking your handwritten manuscript, could we accurately regain your original message? I am confident we could.

Here's why I consider the *NT* text reliable. People working independently of one another will not likely err in the same way. Each person's errors will differ from the others. That being true, if we examine and compare five copies, we would have a good chance of recovering what you wrote in your original letter. Though no original manuscript of *Revelation* exists, copies from different sources are available to scholars. By comparing these later and numerous manuscripts, language experts can prepare reliable texts.

As we noted, these facts make the every-seventh-letter theory problematic. If one manuscript lacks a few words or suffers from duplicate or misspelled words, or other copying errors, the every-seventh-letter theory becomes suspect, doesn't it? To count every seventh letter, on which copy would you rely? Ample evidence shows that *Revelation* came encoded in ways other than the ones advocated in the seventh-letter and similar theories. In following chapters, we shall review *Revelation's* multiple codes.

Confusing Tree Etchings

If we recall what Jesus shared with us during his ministry here, *Revelation's* symbols seem not so odd. Comprehending them requires extra effort, but we can unravel them. Undoing the effects of all the weird interpretations that men and women inscribed over the centuries presents a far greater challenge.

Earlier I mentioned that interpreters scrawl all over the trees in *Revelation's* "forest." Much of this scribbling gives false directions. One method in particular leads thousands of people into dead-ends and cul-de-sacs. Possibly other interpreters recognize the problem and discuss it, but I rarely find recent critiques of this misguided approach. I refer to the tendency of interpreters to formulate theories by going from symbolic to literal instead of vice versa.

What do I mean? Religious teachers often devise schemes based on *Revelation's* symbols, rather than on Jesus' direct statements. A well-known example provides sufficient evidence for my reasoning. Many contemporary Christians expect that Jesus will return to earth and reign in the city of Jerusalem for a thousand years.

Jesus never spoke about doing that in the Gospels. How did that idea get started? It began with interpretations of *Revelation* 20. Some Bible teachers take literally the symbolic language in that chapter and then try to fit other *NT* statements into what they assume *Revelation* 20 teaches. In devising their theories, they often overlook or disregard other symbols in the chapter.

Hazards Of Interpretation

Many religious people also practice what I term selective symbolism. The interpretive views voiced by certain zealous nineteenth-century spiritual leaders in upstate New York serve as an example. On the basis of *Revelation* chapters 7 and 14, they predicted that only 144,000 people will attain heaven. Chapter 7:3 identifies the 144,000 as those who are sealed and in 7: 13 and 14 one of the four elders explained that the 144,000 clothed in white robes *"are the ones who come out of the great tribulation, and they have washed their robes and made them white in the blood of the Lamb."*[88]

Revelation 14:4 identifies these as "those who did not defile themselves with women." Literal acceptance of this verse means that all those virgins were males. Yet the leaders of the above religious group contend that "virgins" should be accepted figuratively. But they literally accept the number 144,000. They practice selective interpretation, don't they?

In *Revelation* 20, many "mainline" Christians accept the 1000 year reign literally. While they do that, they neglect other strongly symbolic messages in the chapter.[89] We err, I think, when we construct end-time theories based on *Revelation's* symbolic language, especially its numbers.

Not only do sincere Christians waste time conjecturing, they often neglect the strong **comfort,** which *The Apocalypse* originally taught. It seems more reasonable to first carefully examine what Jesus and his apostles said about the Last Day in their direct statements. Here's what Jesus said about the end-time in John's gospel:

> *Very truly I tell you, a time is coming and has now come when the dead will hear the voice of the Son of God and those who hear will live. For as the Father has life in himself, so he has granted the Son also to have life in himself. And he has given him authority to judge because he is the Son of Man. Do not be amazed at this, for a time is coming when all who are in their graves will hear his voice and come out—those who have done what is good will rise to live, and those who have done evil will rise to be condemned.*[90]

Jesus said nothing in the above about a literal reign in Jerusalem. He simply taught that at his return, all the dead will rise and go to their respective rewards. This scene accords with what he said in his *Matthew* 25 parables. When he returns in Judgment, Jesus will separate the sheep (good) from the goats (bad). Symbolism should be interpreted compatibly with direct statements, not vice versa. We shall later deal with Chap. 20's other symbols.

---

88. NASB.

89. In sermons based on Revelation 7 and 14, we examine these symbols in more detail.

90. John 5:25-29 NIV.

Confused By Angels[91]

Angels appear repeatedly in *Revelation*. In a trumpet-like-voice, the son of man (Jesus) ordered John to address a letter to each of the seven churches.[92] The son of man held seven stars in his right hand (1:16). Verse 1:20 identifies the seven stars as seven angels. The voice immediately told John to begin the first of seven letters to the selected churches: "To the angel of the church in Ephesus write." Using this same wording in Chapters two and three, he addressed the angels of the other six churches.

Jesus promised the faithful few in Sardis (one of the seven churches) that he would confess their names before "my Father and his angels."[93] Angels introduce visions and scenes. A few are called mighty angels.[94] The angel Michael appears. Jude[95] identified him as an archangel (a ruling angel). In *Revelation* 5, thousands upon thousands of angels praise God and the Lamb (Jesus).

The Greek word angel basically means "one who is sent." Translators sometimes render the word as messenger.[96] The Hebrew word translated angel often means messenger as well.[97] Edward White Benson aptly observed that the Greek word for the "sending" of the angel (*aposteilas*) in *Revelation* 1:2 is the word from which apostle comes. The term "describes the fullest powers given by a government to its emissaries or commissioners" and that it was "so used at Athens of certain commissioners."[98]

Benson thought the term **hierophant** appropriate for describing the angel's assignment. By referring to the angel as a **hierophant**, he meant one who could guide others through holy places and introduce

---

91. For further information about the subject of angels in Jewish literature, see *Everyman's Talmud*, Chapter II, III. Angelology, p – 47ff., Abraham Cohen, Schocken Books, New York, 1975.

92. Revelation 1:11.

93. Ibid 3:5.

94. 5:2, 10:1 (Greek, ischuo) able, powerful; see TDNT Vol. III, pp. 399-402, by Grundmann.

95. Revelation 12:7, Jude 9.

96. Cf: Matthew 11:10; Mark 1:2; Luke 7:24, 27 & 9:52; James 2:25.

97. Cf: Genesis 32:3; Joshua 6:17 for example Hebrew, Malak. See Young's concordance listings of "angel" and "messenger."

98. Edward White Benson — Margaret Benson, *An Introductory Study of the Revelation of St. John the Divine*, Nabu reprint. Originally published by Cambridge University Press, London, 1900, p14. In a footnote, Benson pointed to the word "epempsa" (sent). It indicates further precision in the sense of "the moving, so to speak, from place to place . . . the fullness and authority of the commission."

them to sacred secrets. Benson used that term as a title for his chapter on angels stating that "the Angel's work is the true counterpart of what men yearned after when they sought guidance through the mysteries that lay behind their life's experience."[99]

In 2013, my wife, our daughter Janice, and I visited London. A long-time friend arranged for us to visit the Parliament Building. Once we were inside, our friend's friend, an aid to a British government official, guided us through the lobbies, chambers, and back halls of the House of Lords. I do not know how much literal power he held, but he certainly seemed privy to the goings-on of both houses of Parliament. In a limited sense, he served as our personal hierophant. Many times while leading us, he beckoned with expressions similar to what the guiding angels said to John, "Come...I will show you... "[100]

Modern readers tend to picture angels as beautiful, winged women or handsome men. Those images did not originate in the *Bible*. Ancient artists created them. Recent popular films, literature, and misinformed preachers perpetuate these caricatures. Their misrepresentations add to the difficulty of understanding *Revelation's* message.

Are angels winged beings? The *Bible* describes three types of winged extra-terrestrial personalities. When God evicted Adam and Eve from Eden, he posted **cherubim** to prevent the couple's reentry. The word **cherub** (singular) means to "grasp" or "hold fast."

The Lord instructed Moses to fashion and place gold **cherubim** on the Ark of the Covenant's cover. That cover, also called the Mercy Seat, featured two **cherubim**, each with a pair of wings. **Cherubim** played a prominent role in Ezekiel's visions. Yet he described them as equipped with four wings and four different faces each.[101]

Only once does the *New Testament* refer to **cherubim**. The *Book of Hebrews* describes the Ark of the Covenant and the Mercy Seat (NIV, "atonement cover") with cherubim on it.[102] The slight information the *Bible* presents seems to indicate that God created cherubim to stand guard at significant places.

A second type of being is known as a **seraph**, plural **seraphim** (lit. burning or noble). Isaiah described **seraphim** as having six wings. They called "to one another: *"Holy, holy, holy is the Lord Almighty; the*

---

99. Ibid, p-15.

100. Revelation 4:1; 17:1.

101. The cherubim associated with the Ark of the Covenant had two wings, cf Exodus 25:18-20, I Kings 6:23-35. Ezekiel's cherubim had 4 wings, cf 1:4-14; 10:1-22. Ancient Near Eastern mythology featured similar types of images.

102. Hebrews 9:3-5.

whole earth is full of his glory."[103] Their praise to God resembles the tribute offered by the beings (translated "beasts," KJV, and "living creatures," NIV) in *Revelation* 4. Those living creatures were covered with eyes and also had six wings. Their other features, however, bring to mind the four-winged creatures in *Ezekiel*.[104]

The *Bible* records only two occurrences of winged "female" extraterrestrial creatures. Two winged women carry an evil woman in a lead-covered basket from Israel to Babylonia (or Shinar).[105] Who were these women? We know only that they had "wings of a stork" and that they carried a wicked female. Though *Zechariah* described them as winged-women, I doubt they were angels. The Law of Moses classed storks as unclean animals.[106]

Revelation 12:14 describes a woman, who gives birth to a male child. The dragon (Satan) threatened and pursued her after she gave birth. The woman was given "the two wings of a great eagle, so that she might fly to the place prepared for her in the wilderness" (NIV). As God protected Israel and carried her on eagles' wings, so he also carries and protects God's people in their "wilderness." This winged "woman" symbolizes God's church, not an angel or divine messenger.

The *Bible* consistently describes cherubim and seraphim as winged creatures, yet no passage describes any angel wearing or possessing wings. The prophet Daniel offered an earnest prayer of confession and the angel Gabriel came to him in swift flight. The account mentions no wings on Gabriel, however.[107] A few times, the Lord reminded Israel how he had assisted them: *"You yourselves have seen what I did to Egypt, and how I carried you on eagles' wings and brought you to myself."*[108] The Lord had "symbolic" wings. If his angels had them, no *Bible* verse references them.

---

103. Isaiah 6:1-7, verse 3b NIV.

104. Identifying and defining the living creatures, cherubim, and seraphim presents challenges beyond the scope of this study. Ezekiel himself seemed shocked to learn that the cherubim he saw in his vision of Jerusalem and the temple (that begins in Ezekiel 8) were the same living creatures he saw in his vision by the Kebar River in Babylon (Ezekiel 1). Note Ezekiel's comments and descriptions (10:15-22). We remain humbly aware that human expressions and definitions can never adequately explain other worldly objects and beings (including angels) let alone the Creator of all things. Also note Peter Craigie's notes in *The Daily Study Bible Series, Ezekiel*, Westminster Press, Philadelphia, 1983, p-73.

105. Zechariah 5:5-11.

106. Leviticus 11:19.

107. Daniel 9:20, 21.

108. Exodus 19:4 NIV. This text probably provides the background for understanding *Revelation* 12:14.

Angels often appeared as ordinary men. The Greek word for angel is consistently masculine. God's angels convey messages from him and sometimes act on his behalf. In both *Old* and *New Testaments*, angels often seemed indistinguishable from human males.[109]

The Angel Of The Lord

In *Genesis* 18, three men stood near Abraham's tent one afternoon. Abraham invited them to dinner. According to custom of his day, Abraham also provided water so they could wash their feet. He selected a choice fatted calf and ordered a servant to butcher the animal for the visitors' meal.

Abraham then asked Sarah, his wife, to bake bread for the men. Once the hosts prepared everything, Abraham served curds, milk, and veal to the three men. They ate a human-prepared meal. Abraham stood aside and watched them eat. After the meal, the "visitors" informed Abraham that his wife Sarah would have a baby boy in about a year.

Later in the chapter, the narrative identifies one of those "men" as the Lord—probably the "angel of the Lord." He told Abraham of his plans to destroy the cities of Sodom and Gomorrah. The beginning of Chapter 19 labels the other two men as angels, who are on their way to annihilate the wicked cities.

The "angel of the Lord" frequently appeared in the *Old Testament* voicing God's authority. At times during some accounts, the Lord or God speaks and later the angel of the Lord speaks or vice versa.[110] Many of the angels in *Revelation* spoke with God's authority and acted with his power. Distinctions between when the angel speaks-acts and when God speaks-acts are difficult to distinguish. In view of the OT examples we noted, this should not amaze us. Of most importance

---

109. The Gospels' descriptions of the angels at Jesus' resurrection show some variation. Matthew and Mark speak of one angel; Luke and John of two. Matthew described the lone angel as "like lightning, and his clothing, white as snow," (28:3 NRSV); Mark said merely that he was a "young man, dressed in a white robe," (16:5). Luke wrote that it was "two men in dazzling clothes," (24:4 NRSV; John revealed that Mary saw "two angels dressed in white," (20:12 NRSV). The variations demonstrate that there was no conspiracy among the disciples to create an air-tight story. If only one of the angels spoke, it is understandable that some witnesses would report seeing a single angel. Other than their apparel, nothing evidently distinguished angels from ordinary men. At times not even their clothes distinguished them.

110. For example this occurs in the appearance to Hagar (Genesis 16:7-14) and to Moses in Exodus 3 and 4.

stands the message the angels bring.[111] Identifying particular angels stays secondary.

One more thought about angels. In *Revelation* 22: 6, the angel reiterated his purpose, *"To show his (God's) servants the things that will soon take place."* John fell overwhelmed at the feet of the angel, who showed those things to him. He wanted to worship the angel, who guided him through the mysterious future and explained God's purposes. The angel quickly rejected John's adulation. *"Don't do that"* said the angel, *"I am a fellow servant with you and your fellow prophets and with all who keep the words of this scroll. Worship God!"*[112] The English word *worship* tends to be impersonal. Benson's translation of this verse speaks with sharp directness to us narcissistic human beings: "Adore God" says the angel, not any of his created messengers. Glory and honor to our Creator.

---

111. In Job 1:14, a messenger (Hebrew, *malak*, the word often translated angel) came to tell Job that the Sabeans had attacked and carried away his oxen and donkeys. The Sabeans also killed the servants attending them. Other messengers appear in quick sequence bringing more bad news. The messengers are incidental to the story. The news was important, not the messenger. I think it's probably wise to view Revelation's angels the same way. Rather than trying to identify each one, it's more vital to pay attention to the messages angels bring.

112. Revelation 22: 9 NIV.

Chapter 3

Sources Of And Keys To The Codes
In earlier chapters, we noted *Revelation's* countless codes and symbols. In the "son of man" vision (1:12-20), most readers recognize the figurative language. In other passages, the symbolism remains camouflaged. First century Christians easily decoded the disguises. Modern readers usually cannot.

For codes to be effective, the receiver(s) must be "on the same page" as the sender(s). The writers (senders) and the intended readers often share experiences or knowledge. Though *Revelation's* signs and codes seem foreign to us, the first century church could converse in them. We can become acquainted with them, too. Where did *Revelation's* seemingly bizarre symbols originate?

Numerous metaphors and references came from earlier Jewish literature. Allusions from these sources appear throughout the letter. The sayings of Jesus and the Apostles' teachings served as the basis for other symbols. References also came from contemporary history, the word on the streets, and very likely, whispered conversations among cautious believers.

Early Christians apparently knew these varied sources well. They recognized them as easily as my old friend and I recalled code words from experiences we shared decades before. What secret language(s) did the *Revelation* writer use? Also, how could the first recipients decipher those symbols?

1. The Old Testament
Many current Christians seem barely acquainted with the *OT*. Their knowledge appears limited to Scriptures they hear in Sunday sermons. Others hear Lectionary readings that many churches use. The creators of the Lectionary designed it to cover the *Bible* every three years. Sad to say, even Lectionary assignments for daily readings skip large segments of the *OT*. Some of the "neglected" sections give important clues to understanding *Revelation*.

Many sincere Christians regard the *OT* as outdated. They view it as an antiquated section of the Bible that no longer applies and read the *OT* only to look for predictions about the Messiah. Sunday school children hear a few *OT* stories and the names of Noah, Samson, David, Ruth, and Esther. Young people know of a few other heroes. Yet they hear almost nothing about many *OT* passages from which *Revelation* draws.

My first twenty or so readings of *Revelation* left me stumped and discouraged. As I continued my yearly "excursions" through the *OT*, however, certain *Revelation* symbols began making sense. Further *OT* reading and study created increasing excitement. More lights brightened, but I doubt I shall ever see all of the "dark corners." What I have discovered excites me.

B.F Westcott and F.J.A. Hort cooperated in preparing a Greek text of the New Testament. Their 1940 edition noted numerous *OT* quotations found in *Revelation*. In *The Apocalypse's* 404 verses, about two thirds of them (265) have at least one quotation or reference from the *OT*. Some verses contain more than one *OT* citation.

Westcott and Hort found 550 *OT* references in *Revelation*[113] I doubt whether they found all of them. *Revelation's* author drew symbols or references from most of the *OT* books. "He referred to the *Book of Daniel* in some 45 places."[114]

Other reasons make acquaintance with the *OT* vital. Unless we become familiar with the *OT*, we shall miss the point of many *NT* teachings. Jesus based his life and his doctrine on what "the Law of Moses, the Prophets and the Psalms"[115] taught in earlier times.

The author of the *NT Epistle to the Hebrews* compared Jesus and his actions with the Mosaic Law and the *OT* priesthoods of Melchizedek and Aaron. He contrasted Jesus' work with Israel's worship in the Tabernacle (including the sacrificial system). Israel's forsaking of its covenant with God also served as a backdrop in *Hebrews*. Significant portions of Paul's letters to the Romans, to the Corinthians, and to the Galatian churches make little sense unless one knows *OT* narratives and teachings.

Jesus' Apostles and other first century followers knew the *OT*. They committed much of it to memory. On the Day of Pentecost, Peter quoted extensive segments of the *OT*.[116] Stephen, the martyr, reviewed *OT* history in his defense before the Sanhedrin Court.[117] Examples of *New Testament* writers making *OT* citations are too numerous to mention here. The frequency with which *NT* writers alluded to *OT* events

---

113. The song in 15:3, 4 contains phrases from Psalm 111:2, 145:17; Jeremiah 10:7; Psalm 86:9, 99:3; Isaiah 66:23; and Psalm 98:2 in that order; amazingly John wrote it without a word processor or PC.

114. *The Apocalypse of St John*, Henry Barclay Swete, MacMillan and Company, London, 1909, 3rd Edition, p liii.

115. Luke 24:44 NIV, cf Matthew 5:17-48; 15:1-9.

116. See Acts 2, especially vss. 14-21; 25-36. Peter also referenced Balaam in 2 Peter 2:15, an example used in the warning given the church in Pergamum in Revelation 2:14.

117. Acts 6, 7.

and characters suggests that early Christians deeply immersed themselves in the *OT*.[118]

As he rode in his chariot, the Ethiopian treasurer read *Isaiah*.[119] Philip began with that section of Scripture and explained the Good News of Jesus to him.[120] Paul advised Timothy not to neglect public reading of the *OT* in the church where he preached.[121]

Those who interpret *Revelation* by "connecting its dots" with modern history often find themselves tied up and blinded in dark closets. They seem not to realize that the *OT* holds a huge "ring of keys" for *Revelation's* tightly sealed doors and complex locks.

Numerous *OT* references occur in *Revelation* Chapter 1. Although John's lampstand vision[122] does not contain the first references, it shows how the author drew on *OT* background. *Exodus* tells us that a golden lampstand with seven lamps stood in the Holy Place of the Tabernacle (and later the Temple).[123] In *Revelation* 1, John saw seven golden lampstands. The Chapter 1 "son of man" vision evidences rich *OT* background.[124]

Most standard Bibles supply *OT* reference notations. By following them, anyone can begin tracing their background. Nothing provides better information, however, than careful, thoughtful, steady reading through the *OT*. Some commentators point out the similarity of *Revelation's* structure with the warnings God gave Israel in *Leviticus*. Fascinating but informative parallels exist between the plagues, of which *Leviticus* 26 warns, and the afflictions unleashed in *Revelation* chapters 6-9.

These include:

- how the earth suffers for human disobedience;

---

118. Many, of course, learned those Scriptures in the Greek translation known as the Septuagint. Some may have learned them in other languages, for example Latin, and so on.

119. Chapters and verses were not inserted until centuries later. The eunuch was reading what is now identified as Isaiah Chapter 53.

120. Acts 8:26-40.

121. 1 Timothy 4:13.

122. Verses 12-20.

123. See Exodus 25:31-40; Zechariah 4:2, 3.

124. v. 13, see Ezekiel 1:26; Daniel 7:13 & 10:5; Isaiah 6:1
    v. 14, see Daniel 7:9
    v. 15, see Ezekiel 1:7 & 43:2; Daniel 10:6
    v. 16, see Isaiah 1:20 & 49:2; Judges 5:31.

- the use of sevens;
- the need for all to repent;
- the increasing misery mankind brings on itself by stubbornly refusing to humbly serve God.

Large sections of *Revelation* contain themes and expressions from the prophet Ezekiel (c.f. Chapter 26). *Ezekiel* forecasted the fall of the godless Mediterranean Sea power Tyre. In the same manner, *Revelation* predicted the destruction of Rome and probably all other proud, godless cities and nations.[125] *Revelation* 6 uses imagery from the plagues of Egypt. As you read *Genesis-Deuteronomy, Isaiah, Jeremiah, Ezekiel, Daniel, Joel, Zechariah,* and the *Psalms,* many of *Revelation's* seemingly odd references begin to make sense. You find notable, unmistakable connections between *Genesis* 1-3 and *Revelation* 20-22.

The author remarkably blended *OT* phrases. As H.B. Swete noted:

> *His (Revelation's writer) handling of these materials is always original and independent, and he does not allow his Old Testament author to carry him a step beyond the point at which the guidance ceases to lend itself to the purpose of his book.*[126]

2. Numbers

Numbers appear throughout *Revelation*. In a few instances, *The Apocalypse* appears to use raw numbers. But numerical symbolism makes it perilous to take any *Revelation* figure at face value. We cannot overemphasize this point. Failure to understand numerical imagery leads to gross misinterpretations. Whether the number is three, four, seven, ten, twelve, twenty-four, a thousand, or anything else, you can depend on it being symbolic.

Numerical values sometimes lie concealed in sentence structure. Chapter 1, verse 4 serves as a good example of this hiddenness. "Three" sometimes represents God. The Godhead is clearly the subject of verses 4 and 5. Those verses refer to God, Christ, and the Holy Spirit. The number "three," however, does not appear anywhere in them. "Threes" do appear figuratively, though, in the sentence structure and so does "seven."

Note how "three" refers to God. Verse one tells how God gave John the message of the book "to show his (God's) servants what must

---

125. Revelation 18, 19.

126. Henry Barclay Swete, *The Apocalypse of St John,* MacMillan and Co, London 1909, p cliv.

soon take place." So John addressed the letter "To the seven churches in the province of Asia: Grace and peace to you from him (God) 1) who is, and 2) who was, and 3) who is to come..." The three phrases refer to God. Next comes one phrase referring to the Spirit: "the seven spirits before his throne" (NIV footnotes "Or the sevenfold Spirit").

Finally, a second three-phrase reference applies to "Jesus Christ, 1) who is the faithful witness, 2) the firstborn from the dead, and 3) the ruler of the kings of the earth." Besides containing symbolic threes and a seven, this greeting stands out for other reasons that we shall discuss later.[127]

"Threes" hide in hymns of praise to God. It can't be accidental that the first hymn in Chapter 4 uses the word "holy" three times.[128] Next, the lyrics include three different references to the Divine: Lord, God, and Almighty. Third, the three-part phrase used in the greeting reappears: "who is, who was, and is to come."[129]

In 4:9 "the living creatures give 1) glory, 2) honor, and 3) thanks to him who sits on the throne." In verse 11, "three" appears in the types of adulation the twenty-four elders offer the one on the throne: "You are worthy, our Lord and God to receive *glory, honor,* and *power*,[130] for you created all things . . ." Later in the book, a heavenly multitude shouts "Hallelujah! (Literally, "Praise God") *Salvation, glory,* and *power* belong to our God . . ."[131] In Chapter 14: 6-13, the Lord sends three angels who fly in midair. The first angel proclaims the gospel and warns (every nation, tribe, language and people to fear God. The second angel announces Babylon's fall. The third angel warns all not to worship the beast or fear his image. The three messengers clearly came from God's throne.

Though threes expressed in phrases consistently appear linked to God, the number three does not always depict good. Threes in other contexts indicate woe and suffering. In Chapter 8 as the first of seven trumpets sounds, a third of the trees were burned up" (verse 7). As later trumpets sound, a third of the sea turned into blood, a third of sea creatures died, a "third of the ships were destroyed." In Chapter 16: 13, three evil spirits oppose God. Verse 19 of the same chapter tells of God's judgment on the city by means of thunder and severe earthquake. The city splits into three parts.

---

127. See the section on *Revelation's* **Music** later in Chapter 12.

128. 4:8.

129. For some reason, "is and was" are reversed here.

130. 4:11

131. 19:1.

"Four" seems connected to earth and creation. Four living creatures surround the heavenly throne.[132] When the Lamb appears, he is declared worthy to open the sealed scroll because his blood "purchased men for God from every 1) tribe, 2) language, 3) people, and 4) nation."[133] Chapter 6 introduces the well-known, "Four Horsemen of the Apocalypse." In Chapter 7, four angels stand at the four corners of the earth to prevent any harm until God's servants had been sealed.[134] The heavenly city is also laid out foursquare.[135]

"Seven" prevails as *Revelation's* most widely used number. As seven days comprise a week, "seven" consistently represents completeness. Chapter 1 includes seven churches in the province of Asia, seven lampstands, and seven stars. Chapters 4 and 5 reveal seven lamps blazing before God's throne. These are the seven spirits or sevenfold Spirit of God.[136]

The Lord assigned an angel to each of *Revelation's* seven churches. The scroll in God's hand was sealed with seven seals. There are seven plagues. Later seven angels blow seven trumpets and seven bowls contain God's wrath. Matthew's account of Jesus' Sermon on the Mount contains nine occurrences of "Blessed." *Revelation* uses "blessed" seven times. The "blesseds" never occur together, however. The Holy Spirit through John scattered them throughout the book.

Did you find "blessed" eight times in your translation? Chapter 1:3 (NIV) reads "blessed is the one who reads the words of this prophecy, and blessed are those who hear it and take to heart what is written in it. . ." Many translators take the liberty of supplying the second "blessed" because the sentence structure intimates it. The word *makarios* (blessed), however, appears only once in the Greek of verse 3.[137]

As we mentioned, symbols stand within symbols. Verses 4 and 5 of Chapter 1 (NIV) illustrate this:

> *John,*
> *To the seven churches in the province of Asia: Grace and peace to*

---

132. 4:6-11; the KJV unfortunately translated the word "zoa," living things, as "beasts." 5:6-14; 6:1-8.

133. 5:9 NIV.

134. 7:1-3.

135. 21:15,16.

136. For example see NIV footnotes regarding 1:4; 3:1; 4:5, 6.

137. Genesis contains numerous sevens, some of them hidden. Creation took seven days and sevens appear in the flood story, for example seven pairs of clean animals entered the ark (7:2); the rain would begin within seven days; there are seven Hebrew words in 1:1 and 14 in 1:2. Pharaoh's dreams had seven years of plenty followed by seven of famine (41:1-32). Seventy of Jacob's family went to Egypt (46:27).

> *you from him who is, and who was, and who is to come, and from the seven spirits before his throne, and from Jesus Christ, who is the faithful witness, the firstborn from the dead, and the ruler of the kings of the earth. To him who loves us and has freed us from our sins by his blood.*

Think of the Godhead consisting of Father, Son, and Holy Spirit. Then consider the sentence structure in the above. John wrote of seven spirits (or the seven-fold Spirit) before God's throne. Another seven appears in the sentence. Did you catch it? Recall the threes describing God: "who is, who was and is to come"? We also noted three phrases describing Jesus: faithful witness, firstborn from the dead, and the ruler of the kings of the earth. That makes a total of six. The single phrase concerning the Holy Spirit achieves the *seven*: "from the seven spirits before his throne." This seven refers to the Spirit's fullness or completeness.

The hymn lyrics in 5:12 (NIV) use a hidden seven to indicate the Lamb's full divinity: "In a loud voice they sang: 'Worthy is the Lamb, who was slain, to receive power and wealth and wisdom and strength and honor and glory and praise!'" For seven impressive reasons, the Lamb deserves acclaim. The next verse (13) tells us the Lamb merits every bit of the praise that God commands from all creation:

> *Then I heard every creature in heaven and on earth and under the earth and on the sea, and all that is in them, saying: 'To him who sits on the throne and to the Lamb be <u>praise</u> and <u>honor</u> and <u>glory</u> and <u>power</u>, for ever and ever!'*[138]

Consider another point about seven representing completeness.[139] Trusted people often abuse the confidence others place in them. Employees and volunteers who handle money for churches and agencies pilfer funds for years without being caught. No one suspects them because the losses occur gradually. A "trusted" person appears to have things in order. Some think this helps explain the dreaded number 666–close enough to deceive unsuspecting folks. If seven describes fullness, anything less than that is incomplete. Paul mentioned that Satan sometimes "masquerades as an angel of light."[140] The devil deserves the title "master of deceit." The Bible gives strong evidence for a fuller explanation of 666, which we shall address later.

---

138. V 13 The four underlined qualities illustrate the link of the number four with creation.

139. Sevens appear numerous times in the Pentateuch.

140. 2 Corinthians 11:14

The number seven involves another mystery. *Daniel* 12:7 predicts that a powerful future force will oppress the saints for "a time, times and half a time." Most interpret this as a year, two years, and half a year, or three and one half years. You need only second or third grade math to recognize that three and one half are half of seven. Three and a half years also compute to 42 months or 1,260 days. All likely symbolize the same concept — a limited period of time totally controlled by God. I emphasize *symbolize* because literally interpreting any *Revelation* number eventually proves foolhardy. Biblical usage of the terms leads me to conclude that if seven represents completeness, three and a half falls considerably short of fullness.

Add one more detail about three and a half. The contexts in which *Revelation* uses the number (or its equivalents 42 months or 1,260 days) indicate a period of extreme testing under God's control.[141] This point remains consistent and vital. Everything happens under God's management. Nothing occurs beyond his jurisdiction.[142] At all times, Satan and the forces of evil operate subject to our Sovereign Lord's control and his judgment.

The number **ten** represents completeness in varied contexts—good and bad. Human beings normally come from the womb with ten fingers and ten toes. Is it any wonder that in current society, ten symbolizes absolute feminine attractiveness? The Lord afflicted Egypt with ten plagues and gave Israel Ten Commandments.[143] A tithe is a tenth.

Revelation's "tens" seem representative of the whole in terms of history and power. In Chapter 13, the beast out of the sea "had ten horns and seven heads, with ten crowns on its horns."[144] In Chapter 17, the beast on which the prostitute sat possessed ten horns. Those horns

---

141. See 11:1 6 & 12: 1-13:1.

142. In Matthew's genealogy of Jesus (chapter 1:1-17), he counted fourteen generations from "Abraham to David, fourteen from David to the exile to Babylon, and fourteen from the exile to Christ." It's difficult to reconcile Matthew's fourteens with the genealogy found in 1 Chronicles 3. Compare verses 10-16, Solomon through Zedekiah. The chronicler listed 16 generations from Solomon through Josiah. Because Josiah's successors had incomplete reigns it is hard to consider each of them as a generation. Matthew also skipped a few descendants after the exile. Note the omission of Pedaiah, for example verses 17 & 19. Matthew's reasons for deleting some from his list so he could count the fourteens are the subject of another study. It is intriguing, however, that the total of Matthew's three fourteens is 42. Did Matthew intimate that this was typical of a period under divine guidance—3 ½ years, 42 months, 1,260 days?

143. Exodus 7-12; 20.

144. v. 1.

represent ten kings "who have not received a kingdom, but who for one hour will receive authority along with the beast."[145]

Chapter 20 tells of Satan's "binding" for a thousand years: 10x10x10 = 1,000. Rather than seeing 1,000 as a specific period of time, I think it better to view the number as symbolic of human history—ten times ten times ten. For the same duration, the priests of God and of Christ reign with the Lord.[146] Ten relates to human history and events that occur within it.[147] God is Alpha and Omega, beginning and end of all creation.

Twelve usually appears in reference to God's covenants with his people. "Twelve" occurs throughout the Bible: twelve tribes of Israel, two times twelve (24 courses) of priests, Twelve Apostles, and 24 elders are seated around God's throne.[148] The number of the sealed or redeemed is 144, 000 (12 x 12,000).[149] The city of God has twelve gates, each bearing the name of an Israelite tribe.

By ancient and modern standards, the city was huge. The New Jerusalem (Chaps. 21 and 22) measured twelve stadia by twelve. The city also included vast airspace; 12 stadia high (12 stadia = 1,400 miles). Its protective wall measured 144 cubits (about 200 ft.) thick. The city's enclosure included twelve foundations, each one a different type of stone. Finally, every month the Tree of Life bore a different fruit.

Despite the fact that *Revelation* uses extensive metaphorical numbers, some interpreters cling to a literal thousand year earthly reign by Christ. Others think that only 144,000 persons will be saved. We shall comment more on this subject in later chapters. Though 40 appears throughout the *OT*, for some reason *Revelation* does not use the

---

145. v. 12 NIV Twenty years ago many Continuous-Historical and Futurist interpreters thought the "beast" was the European Common Market and the ten kings represented the full membership (ten) the members were trying to attain. At the present, the European Common Market hardly seems a threat. Many of its vaunted members teeter on bankruptcy. Those who try to interpret *Revelation* by connecting it with specific current events do so at great risk.

146. v. 6.

147. Genesis often uses tens. Its author divided it into ten sections. In chapters five and eleven, ten names appear in the genealogical records, for example, in Chapter Five, from Adam to Noah.

148. *Revelation* 4:4.

149. *Revelation* 7 lists 12 tribes of Israel x 12,000 from each tribe. The redeemed are the true "Israel" and will inhabit the New Jerusalem (see *Hebrews* 12:12-29 and *Revelation* 21, 22. The number 12,000 is most likely another symbol of completeness in respect to God's covenants with his people. The tribes of Dan and Ephraim are lacking from the list in *Revelation* 7. Dan never took control of its original tribal area (see Judges 18) and Ephraim led the northern ten tribes in rebellion against God that led to the Assyrian captivity and loss of their nation (see Hosea 4-12).

number. It uses 42 as in three and a half years, and 144,000, a multiple of 12. Yet never 40.[150]

3. Music

Music indicates a society's moods, fears, and passions. Nearly every decade of recent American history can be identified by its songs. OT psalms reflected societal changes as well as the personal ups and downs of the writers. Compare the varying frames of mind expressed in the first ten psalms, all of which are attributed to David.

The music we sing, play, and hear changes with our moods. Sometimes music alters our spirits. We tend to sing or play according to how we feel at the moment. *Revelation's* songs communicate varying states of mind. The stanzas not only convey emotion, they transmit theologically rich, usually straightforward, factual information.

Revelation's lyrics tell its "story's" progression. I use the term "music" broadly for the songs, shouts, complaints, and some angelic announcements in *Revelation*. Though not always identified as songs, the sections to which I refer relate their messages poetically. We can usually recognize these musical interludes because the NIV, NRSV, and many modern translations show or indent them.

These lyrical sections seem to serve as "a self-guided tour" through the book. They dependably and consistently yield clues to the meaning of *Revelation's* narrative. Often they reveal the plot.[151] As a prime example, many interpreters consider *Revelation* 12 a prehistory event when God cast Satan out of heaven. The song found in verses 10-12 indicates otherwise. Jesus' work on the cross caused Satan's fall. God's people overcome, "by the blood of the Lamb and by the word of their testimony." As Peter noted:

> "Be alert and of sober mind. Your enemy the devil prowls around like a roaring lion looking for someone to devour. Resist him, standing firm in the faith, because you know that the family of believers throughout the world is undergoing the same kind of sufferings."[152]

Follow the story line. "Listen" to *Revelation's* music. This book's last chapter will include a narrative based on *Revelation's* songs and voices from God's throne.

---

150. Most NT references apply to someone's age or when various speakers recall OT events. According to my count, the number seven curiously appears forty times in *Revelation*. Our mathematician friend Kathy Wankum noted that 3,600 x 40 equals 144,000. She has been of inestimable help in reading the manuscript and challenging my logic at times. Kathy also corrected many of my grammar gaffes.

151. Examples include: 4:11; 5:12,13; 11:15-18; 12:10-12.

152. 1 Peter 5:8, 9 NIV.

4. Other New Testament Writings; Jesus' And The Apostles' Teaching

Revelation's codes also include references to the life and teachings of Jesus as the Gospel writers recorded them. The Apostles John and Matthew heard, saw, and experienced firsthand. Mark likely got much of his information from Peter in their personal conversations.[153] Early church people probably memorized numerous sayings of Jesus and the stories about his life.

Beginning in *Revelation* 1, Jesus becomes strongly evident. In the expressions "word of God"[154] and "the testimony of Jesus,"[155] we see *Revelation's* kinship with John's other writings. The Son of Man vision in Chapter 1 resembles the Gospels' transfiguration scenes.

Belief in Jesus' death, burial and resurrection form the basis for *Revelation's* message of hope. The use of the "blessed are" statements shows the author's familiarity with the Sermon on the Mount. he certainly knew Jesus' teachings concerning Jerusalem's destruction and the end time as *Matthew* 24, *Mark* 13, and, *Luke* 21 describe them.

Often in the Gospels, Jesus appealed for his hearers to listen, "he that has ears to hear, let him hear,"[156] or as the NRSV translates, "Let anyone with ears, listen!" John never repeated the phrase in his gospel. *Revelation*, however, uses a similar phrase in each of the letters to the seven churches.[157] Though placed in differing parts of the seven letters, *The Apocalypse's* phrasing, "He who has an ear, let him hear what the Spirit says to the churches" (NIV) never varies. A like appeal but with slightly different wording appears in *Revelation* 13:9.

Additionally, *Revelation's* writer used numerous symbolic references and ideas taught by the Apostles and evangelists in the Epistles and the *Book of Acts*. Whether they read it or heard it from teachers or evangelists, most first century believers probably knew the information related in *Acts* and the Epistles.

The amount of instruction early Christians received concerning doctrine and Christ-like lifestyles far exceeded what most present day converts are taught or acquire. The writers of the Epistles constantly reminded their readers of things they already "learned" or "heard."[158]

---

153. On the basis of Mark 14:51, 52, numerous scholars think Mark personally experienced at least one terrifying and embarrassing moment as a young disciple.

154. Cf John 1:1, 2 ; 1 John 1:1.

155. Cf John 21:24; 1 John 5:7-9.

156. Matthew 11:15, Mark 4:9, Luke 8:8 for example.

157. Revelation 2:7, 11, 17, 29; 3: 6, 13, 22.

158. Cf 1 Corinthians 1: 5, 6 ; 2: 1-3; Galatians 1:6-2:10; Ephesians 4: 17-32; Philippians 1: 3-6; Colossians. 1:3-8; 1 Thessalonians 1: 5, 6, 8; 2: 2, 9 ; Hebrews 2:1-4; 1 Peter 1:3-25;

Many of those facts are crucial to understanding *Revelation* 20. For some reason, many interpreters never connect the first death and resurrection in Chapter 20 to dying with Christ and being raised with him in baptism (*Romans* 6:1-14 and *Colossians* 2:12).

5. Jewish, Greek And Roman History

One must also understand *The Apocalypse* in the light of first century Roman Empire events, particularly in what is now Western Turkey. Emperor worship ominously evolved. At the dawn of the first century, its embryonic stage began when Octavian took on the title Augustus, "the revered one." Worship of Rome's leaders waxed and waned, but forcefully progressed.

Modern scholars differ in their opinions of whether Emperor Nero torched Rome and then blamed Christians for the big blaze. Two facts no one disputes. First, Nero felt no compunctions about killing— even his stepbrother, two wives, his mother, and eventually Seneca, his tutor. Second, Nero plundered Italy and the provinces in order to finance his building programs, his provisions of free grain to the populace, and the public spectacles he held.

During Nero's reign, revolts began in Judea, but Nero committed suicide before the uprisings resulted in the destruction of Jerusalem and the Temple. As *Matthew* 24 records, Jesus predicted the unrest and the misery that ensued. Many Jews and Christians fled Israel during the upheaval. Both Paul and Peter probably suffered their executions during Nero's rule. The atmosphere created by Nero brought unsettling fear. Rumors spread that he would return from the dead giving rise to the so-called *Nero redivivus* theory. We shall later look at *Revelation's* references to the disquieting belief that the fearsome despot either did not die or somehow revived from death.

When citizens of Rome acknowledged Roman Emperor Domitian (81-96 AD) as *dominus et Deus* (Latin for Lord and God), tension increased. In Greek that title reads *kurios kai theos* (Lord and God). No wonder *Revelation* begins with reassuring words to beleaguered Christians. "I am the Alpha and the Omega," says the Lord God, "who is, and who was, and who is to come, the almighty."

In his public appearances, Domitian claimed divine status. God reminded *Revelation* readers that he, the Lord, is no mere mortal. God is first, last, and everything in between. He not only is past, and present, he will judge everyone's future.

The word translated "almighty" in *Revelation* 1:8 is *pantocrat* (ruler of everything). The combining form "crat" appears in many English words. Examples include autocrat (a ruler with unlimited powers or a domineering person) and plutocracy (government by the wealthy). In

---

2 Peter 1:12-15, 1 John 2:3-14.

Latin, almighty is *"omnipotens."* The Lord was not and is not limited to overseeing only the ancient Roman Empire. Our Creator controls all nations for all time.

The heavens thunder the proclamation: "You are worthy, our Lord and God, to receive glory and honor and power, for you created all things, and by your will they were created and have their being."[159] As H.B. Swete noted, Jesus also stated, "I am the Alpha and the Omega, the First and the Last, the Beginning and the End." The cryptic message for Jews signaled Jesus' divinity. They regarded God as Aleph–Tau, the first and last letters of the Hebrew alphabet.[160] The **Creator** supplied **Comfort** to those encountering **Conflict** in **Chaos**.

Other communications need unraveling. We must also answer this question: Why does *Revelation* arrive at what seems like a finale more than once only to present additional puzzles or mysteries in a continued narrative?

---

159. Revelation 4:11 NIV.

160. See H.B. Swete, *The Apocalypse of St. John*, pp. lxxiii-xciii for a fuller development of the Emperor worship topic. Compare Isaiah 44:6 and 48:12 with Revelation 22:13 NIV.

Chapter 4

Faith Under Pressure

In many American communities, attending church brings one status. In the first century Roman Empire, few Christians gained full social acceptance. Professing Christ usually brought jeopardy. From the beginning, the Christ's followers faced powerful resistance from the Jewish establishment. As the church extended into Gentile regions, it encountered opposition from other forces that felt threatened by Jesus' teaching.[161] Later pronouncements concerning veneration of Rome and its Emperors put increasing pressure on believers.

Christians currently contend with fierce antagonism in many countries as well as from some unbelievers in this nation. In the first and second centuries AD, believers faced similar animosity. Religious, social, and governmental censure tested their faith. Arrest, imprisonment, and torture loomed for believers and their families. They did not know when hostile authorities might bang on their doors.

In his Parable of the Sower, Jesus described what would happen to his followers when subjected to persecution.[162] Topics folks discuss while sitting comfortably in Sunday school suddenly become gut-wrenchingly personal—far more than pros and cons for a *Bible* class debate. Disciples not rooted in faith disappear from the fold.[163] Committed believers suffer perplexity. When foes of Christ act cruelly, the faithful begin asking:

- Is God able to help me in the real world?
- Is the invisible God more powerful than these intimidating visible authorities?
- Does God rule the Universe?
- Or is some dictator, president, or prime minister ultimately more potent?

Pressured belief makes one ponder: Is Jesus really God's faithful, true witness? Or was Mohammed, Buddha, or someone else God's authentic prophet? If Jesus is God's only Son, what proves his identity?

Other questions arise. Does God participate in the present? Does Jesus' Spirit actively intervene in the world? Can I feel assured that

---

161. For example, Paul's encounter with the shrine makers' guild in Ephesus, Acts 19:23-41.

162. Matthew 13:1-23.

163. Ibid. v. 21.

the Spirit stays alongside me as Jesus promised?[164] If authorities break down our doors, can my family and I feel the Lord's comforting presence? Or must we await the Judgment before we see God act?

Persecution prompts other uncertainties. Jesus warned his disciples about being ashamed of him.[165] In the first few centuries, death-threats often vexed believers. Some Christians cowered in the face of ridicule. How many of us would confess Jesus while staring at a menacing machete or a brandished gun barrel? What about those believers who succumbed to fear and silenced their witness? Should they be readmitted to the fold if persecution ends and they want to be a part of Jesus' church again?

Other dilemmas arise. How will God judge churches and individuals who weaken and compromise with the world's principles? The Apostle Paul harshly admonished the Corinthian church for tolerating immoral practices within their numbers.[166] Many church leaders now openly advocate behavior the Apostles labeled as corrupt. Paul later warned Christians in Rome about being conformed to the world.[167] The letters to the Seven Churches (*Revelation* Chapters 2 and 3) strongly condemned those who compromised with the immoral behavior around them rather than follow Christ. Jesus himself enumerated numerous practices that render us "unclean."[168]

The *Acts of the Apostles* and the Epistles[169] inform us that first century followers of Jesus faced the challenges of decadence, halfhearted commitment, lack of faith, and other doubts we might never know. The intensity and urgency of the tests for believers we enumerated above led to the authoring of *Revelation*.

The book's letters to the Seven Churches make it clear. Not all early Christians felt fully committed to Jesus. Loss of fervor crippled some churches. Moral depravity took its toll on others. So did greed and fear. Every student must consider these facts when attempting to understand *The Apocalypse*. Also, the historical and topographical features of each *Revelation* city that scholar E.M. Blaiklock provided give us

---

164. John 16:5-16.

165. Luke 9:26 -The church had to deal with those who renounced Christ in the face of death, only to later repent of that weakness. Should those who denied Christ under those circumstances be re-admitted to fellowship?

166. 1Corinthians 6: 9-11.

167. Romans 12:1, 2.

168. Matthew 15:15-20.

169. Galatians 5:19-21.

insights into the symbolism found in the letters to the Seven Churches. We shall later review a sampling of those correspondences.[170]

Revelation's cryptic warnings prove God's displeasure with indifference and tepid faith. Many of John's contemporaries gave in to the world. Neglecting Jesus' standards can be costly. To describe the sins, the potential punishments for committing them, as well as the rewards for those who remained faithful, John used secret language. He employed a code that drew on *OT* events, Jesus' teachings, and contemporary occurrences.[171] As we noted before, these various themes served as the background for *Revelation's* hidden messages. The teachings, warnings, and promises in the book remain applicable until Jesus returns. Tests of trust brought on by persecution occasioned the book. So did waywardness, hypocrisy, greed,[172] and flagging faith. The Lord intimately knows human hearts and actions.

- God sternly warned the readers about denying the faith.
- Immorality brings serious consequences.
- He rewards those who remain staunchly faithful to the end.
- God's **Conviction** and **Comfort**.

Those who already lost their lives because of their faithful witness remain safe in the Lord's care. As Paul consoled Christians in Rome, nothing can "separate us from the love of God that is in Christ Jesus our Lord."[173]

- In the Judgment, God will punish all evildoers.
- Lapses in trusting God and failure to lovingly deal with our fellow travelers disqualify us from the Lord's approval on the Last Day.

The Journey

NT writers often compared the church in the world to Israel's years in the wilderness. The Church treks an arduous road to the Promised Land.[174] As God led Israel through waterless, food-scarce terrain, he

---

170. *The Cities of the New Testament*, E.M. Blaiklock, for example to Smyrna, Pergamum, Thyatira, Laodicea, and so on.

171. I suspect that in order to survive now, Christians in Iran, Egypt, China, and similar areas likely have developed their own codes.

172. Cf 2 Peter 2:1-3.

173. Romans 8:37-39.

174. 1 Corinthians 10: 1-22; 2 Corinthians 3:1-18; Galatians 3, 4. The author of Hebrews warned first- century Christians about faith lapses using the example of Israel's "wilderness" failures. See Hebrews 3 and 4.

leads us. We pilgrims sometimes similarly slog and wander through places not fit for permanent habitation. The Lord uses this "trip" as our faith-fitness-test.

Paul's warnings to the Corinthians send strong signals to us and our contemporaries.[175] All the Israelites, Paul noted, were immersed as believers were. The Twelve tribes ate and drank divine food and water. Christ accompanied the Israelites on their journey from Egypt and through the desert to the Promised Land. He escorted first century believers. He remains always with us.

Despite Divine help and presence, Israel flunked. They miserably failed their idolatry and adultery tests. As a result, the Lord scattered their bodies over the desert. Some Israelites thought God's actions "unfair" and they grumbled. Those murmurers paid a mortal price.

Many tend to misread Paul's conclusion. The Apostle assured the Corinthians that God does not tempt us beyond our ability to withstand. Most of us apply that principle only to occasional suffering we endure. The Scripture likely pertains to that. But the context of Paul's statement mandates that we regularly self-examine our ethics and readjust them to the Lord's way.

Temptations to follow the majority in its lifestyle remain as strong as they tugged in the first century.[176] Satan always beguiles with fleshly wiles. He also pressures us through the deceptive device of society's calls for conformity. Those who create temptations for others and those who succumb to the lures will all answer to God. Christians must pray that they can resist the intense pressures societies exert.

Monuments In The Desert

One other "travel" subject requires our attention. Jesus taught us not to try building permanent homes here.[177] His parables consistently remind us of our caretaker status. God the landowner owns the Cosmos.[178] Only presumptuous tenants attempt to build on or alter another's property.

When leading Israel to the Promised Land, the Lord ordered them not to construct anything permanent in the desert. The Israelites resided in tents. Following the Lord's instructions, they assembled a portable house of worship appropriate for pilgrims. God wanted no wilderness memorials.

Jesus reminded us of our temporary occupancy. Despite his warnings to the contrary, we keep trying to build long-term "residences,"

---

175. 1 Corinthians 10:1-13.

176. Matthew 7:13, 14.

177. John 14:1, 2 for example.

178. Matthew 20:1-16; 21:33-46; 25:14-30; Luke 16:1-15; 19:11-27 for example.

which clutter urban and rural country sides. Even Jerusalem's beloved Temple fell to decay, disrepair, and war.[179]

NT writers often pointed to Israel's fitness failure. Church leaders rarely heed the lessons. Present day believers spend massive amounts of time, energy, and resources constructing big, impressive, occupant-friendly worship shrines. They dedicate comparatively meager amounts to telling the Good News.

Christians erect monuments in the form of church buildings, cathedrals, grottos, and elaborate university campuses all over the globe. These structures and institutions mostly commemorate creatures, not the Creator.[180] How might the Holy Spirit express his displeasure with our generation of materialistic, monument-builders?

Misreading *Matthew* 24, *Mark* 13, And *Luke* 21

Imagine that you teach kindergarteners or first graders. You plan to show your class how to add fractions. You begin with the basics: two halves make a whole; two quarters make a half. You expect your students to quickly grasp the lesson.

Something unexpected happens. You discover that your task exceeds simply teaching new information to immature brains. Nearly every student has learned an incorrect method of adding fractions. Some are convinced that ½ and ½ equal 1/4. Before you progress further, you must undo the error they previously learned. Not until they "unlearn," can you teach them the truth.

A similar situation currently makes teaching the Bible difficult. False teachers have "pressed" massive amounts of misinformation into the minds of believers. We earlier talked about the graffito-covered trees in the woods. The "forest" isn't just mystifying and befuddling. The graffito and scribbling of pseudo teachers blot and obscure the true road signs that seekers need for safe travel.

Modern interpretations of Jesus' comments in *Matthew* 24, *Mark* 13, and *Luke* 21 illustrate my point. These Scriptures tell of conversations between Jesus and his disciples. Questions began as they viewed the Jerusalem Temple and its nearby buildings.

---

179. The Babylonians destroyed Solomon's Temple in 586/587 BC. The Romans destroyed the "Second" Temple in 70 AD (it was actually the third temple; the OT books Ezra, Nehemiah, Haggai, and Zechariah inform us of a Temple built after the return from Babylonian Captivity). In the meantime, numerous restoration projects took place, for example Josiah's circa 620 BC. Three facts should give church building advocates pause. Heaven contains no temple; God and the Lamb are its temple (21:22). The Lord didn't allow David to build a permanent structure. Third, the Temple became a divisive idol and shrine, which prompted many ungodly actions.

180. "The Lord of heaven and earth . . . does not live in temples built by human hands," Acts 17:24 NIV.

In about 20 BC, King Herod the Great started work on the splendid edifice. He chose a prominent hill (ridge) on the east side of Jerusalem. The Kidron Valley to its east lay between the Temple Mount and the Mount of Olives. Temple construction continued for decades finally reaching completion in 64 AD.

Scholars estimate that the Temple equaled about fifteen stories in height. The first-century writer Josephus noted that the "front was all of polished stone."[181] The building's use, stunning size, décor, and location made it "hallowed" ground to most Jews.

Compare the accounts in the three gospels (see the chapters listed above). In about 30 AD, Jesus and a group of his followers walked the Temple area. The disciples commented on the buildings' magnificence. The splendid sights probably stirred their national and religious pride. Jesus' statement in response must have "rocked" them: "Not one stone will be left on another."[182]

Jesus and his small band left the city, descended into the Kidron Valley, and then continued east. They ascended the ridge known as the Mount of Olives from which the Temple Mount looks so impressive. When Jesus sat with his disciples, they began questioning him about the Temple's destruction. Tell us," they said, "when will this happen, and what will be the sign of your coming and of the end of the age?"[183] The disciples asked about three different events. Unless we remember this trio of inquiries, our simple math might confound us more than an Einstein equation.

Examples Of Misinterpretation
Before Jesus answered the disciples' questions regarding the Temple's destruction, the signs of his coming, and the end of the age, he erected a huge caution sign. "Watch out that no one deceives you," he warned.[184] Many interpreters "speed" past that important signal, not looking left or right. I refer to both teachers and students who ignore or forget the three different questions the disciples asked. Doing that creates greater hazards than disregarding end-of-road-barriers. Neglecting those queries explains why religious folks often speed on highways to nowhere. How have people been deceived? Since Jesus'

---

181. *Antiquities of the Jews,* Book xv, 5, *Life and Works of Flavius Josephus,* trans. William Whiston, The John C. Winston Co. Philadelphia. Foundation stones were massive: 37'x12'x18'.

182. Luke 21:6, Cf. Matthew 24:2 & Mark 13:2.

183. Matthew 24:3 NIV.

184. Ibid, v. 4 NIV.

time, many teachers have claimed to be Jesus, the Messiah, or even God himself. Too often, naïve folks take such imposters seriously.[185]

Next, Jesus listed ongoing events that continually and frequently interrupt life. These include wars, earthquakes, famines, and civil strife. Jesus regarded them as the beginning of birth pains, but not necessarily portents of the end. They signal nothing other than the constant recycling of testing and of human misery.

For many years, I taught a Bible study at a Los Angeles home for unwed mothers. Through the 1970s and 80s, various charities operated similar facilities. The home where I taught housed about seventy or eighty girls. Clients usually stayed from early pregnancy through delivery and placement of the child. Ages of the girls ranged from twelve to nineteen. Many of them told me of being in the hospital the prior week because of "a false alarm." False labor pains often came weeks before the baby was born.

Paul reminded Roman Christians that the creation goes through its own birth pains.[186] When "delivery" will come, God only knows. However well-educated or knowledgeable they claim to be, preachers do not know the date or time. Is there a way to identify bogus prophets? It is almost as if Jesus said, "It's easy." Consider anyone predicting the world's imminent end as a false prophet. Jesus warned us not to heed such people.

In *Matthew* 24:9-14, Jesus also predicted another vital fact. His followers would face hatred, humiliation, and persecution. That opposition would cause many believers to lose their faith. Their love would turn frosty.

Faith-tests tend to be long-term, not climb-the-rock-and-ring-the-bell-once demonstrations. Jesus called for perseverance. He noted that before the end would come, his Word would go out to all of the nations. That task remains formidable. Each generation brings new billions who need to hear the Gospel.[187]

An Important Transition
Verses 4-14 of *Matthew* 24 include Jesus' general warnings, statements, and predictions. He did not want his disciples led astray by false claims, rumors, and those types of events that recycle through history — earthquakes, famines, wars, and so on.

---

185. During our 34 years in California, we met men who made these claims, and some women who acted as if they were gods.

186. Romans 8:22-25.

187. The Internet makes it doable.

In verse 15,[188] Jesus returned to the main subject. This related to the disciples' original inquiries about the Temple's devastation. Concerning that cherished edifice, Jesus said: "Not one stone will be left on another." An important transition occurs here. Unless we remain wary at this point, we run through a vital "stop sign." In verse 15, Jesus gave several clues so his followers would know when the Temple's destruction was imminent. Each gospel writer added details that help us identify the event. Matthew recorded Jesus' statement this way:

> So when you see standing in the holy place "the abomination that causes desolation," spoken of through the prophet Daniel—let the reader understand—then let those who are in Judea flee to the mountains.[189]

Jesus apparently referred to *Daniel 9:25-27*. *Daniel 9* is difficult to translate and we must cautiously interpret it.[190] The references to putting an end to sin, bringing everlasting righteousness, and anointing the most holy (verse 24) seem to predict Jesus' sacrificial work and his establishment of a new covenant. Jesus apparently is the Anointed One in verse 25.

Some interpreters add more puzzlement by taking literally the numerous sevens that appear in the passage. Few agree on how to apply the sevens. Computing figurative numbers in prophecies is riskier than taking the sum of the numbers in any mathematical equation with disregard for the symbols contained in the problem.[191]

Interpreters compound the confusion by combining *Daniel 9* with figurative language from *Revelation* 20. Then they begin calculating. As a result they have created theories about a so-called "Tribulation" and a literal thousand year reign by Jesus in Jerusalem. These theories contain more variations than a dozen improvisation solos in a jazz band presentation. They trigger more false alarms than a convention of pyromaniacs could conjure.

---

188. Cf Mark 13:14; Luke 21:20

189. Matthew 24:15, 16 NIV; cf Mark 13:14.

190. I refer readers to comments by A.R. Millard in the *New International Bible Commentary*, pp. 847-870 especially remarks on Daniel 9:25 re: the interpretive translation found in the NIV. Trying to make specific calculations based on this verse is trickier than pitching a tent on a glacier. Earlier versions of the NIV misguidedly lent credence to the tribulation theory by printing the paragraph heading starting in Luke 21:5 **"Signs of the End of the Age."**

191. For example, the volume of a sphere: **$4\pi r^3$**; no one would multiply four times three in the numerator (the part **3** above the line) in this equation disregarding the symbols for π, radius, and so on.

Heeding a few simple rules of interpretation helps us avoid the fright and embarrassment of the bogus clamor. Jesus warned us not to be agitated by such reports. What Daniel had completely in mind, we shall leave to speculators.

In *Matthew* 24: 27, Jesus spoke of the "abomination that causes desolation." he did not leave us clueless as to what that phrase signifies. *Luke* 21:20-22, in fact, makes evident what Jesus meant by that desolating abomination:

> *When you see Jerusalem being surrounded by armies, you will know that its desolation is near. Then let those who are in Judea flee to the mountains, let those in the city get out, and let those in the country not enter the city. For this is the time of punishment in fulfillment of all that has been written (NIV).*

During his Triumphal Entry (see Luke 19), the crowds honored Jesus by shouting praises to God: "Blessed is the king who comes in the name of the Lord!" This acclaim offended some of the Pharisees. "Rebuke your disciples!" they insisted. "If they keep quiet the stones will cry out," Jesus replied.[192]

What Jesus did and said next appears unnoticed by many tribulation interpreters. As he viewed Jerusalem, Jesus wept. He foresaw what would happen to the proud city in a few decades: "If you, even you, had only known on this day what would bring you peace — but now it is hidden from your eyes," (Luke 19:42 NIV).

Most Jews of the time chafed at the Roman occupation of their country. Many worked secretly (some overtly) to overthrow the government.[193] Jewish leadership made numerous efforts to entrap Jesus in their schemes to topple Caesar's government. They often used "gotcha" questions calculated to get him in trouble with the godless foreigners from Rome. In the Sermon on the Mount, Jesus counseled his countrymen to help create peace. He advised them to forgive their enemies, go the second mile, and rejoice in persecution.

Despite Jesus' advice, resistance to Rome festered. Caesar sent troops to quell the defiance. This only fired the zealots' opposition and confrontations. Open rebellion began in 66 AD leading to disaster. In response to increasing agitation, the Roman General Titus advanced on Jerusalem. Jesus foresaw the unequaled distress the city would suffer. He predicted the horrible truth.

---

192. Verses 38-40 from NIV.

193. The different Jewish sects mentioned in the New Testament reflect the varying attitudes toward resistance or cooperation with the Romans. Zealots intensely resisted. Herodians evidently cooperated with members of King Herod's dynasty, who were vassals of the Roman Imperial government, cf Mark 3:6; 12:13.

> The days will come upon you when your enemies will build an embankment against you and encircle you and hem you in on every side. They will dash you to the ground, you and the children within your walls. They will not leave one stone on another, because you did not recognize the time of God's coming to you.[194]

Titus began his siege in the spring of 70 AD. Many Jews were on their way to Jerusalem to celebrate Passover. Titus drove the pilgrims forward. General Titus's actions placed an immediate strain on city food supplies. The Romans built siege towers erecting those multistoried constructs strategically near the city. Equipped with drawbridges and battering rams, the towers enabled the Romans to penetrate Jerusalem's walls.

Titus surrounded the city with his troops. He cut off food supplies. Starvation ensued. To avoid the plague, the Jews dropped the bodies of the dead over the walls. Some Jews resorted to cannibalism. The Romans crucified up to 500 fugitives a day within sight of the city. Many Jewish prisoners were forced to fight as gladiators in the arenas. In July of that year, priests ceased making sacrifices at the Temple.

The Romans razed and torched the city. On August 6, troops stormed the Temple. Titus ordered his troops not to destroy that Jewish holy place. Soldiers recklessly burned it anyhow. As Jesus predicted, the great building stones were upended. The Romans triumphantly took 700 prisoners to Rome, including two rebellion leaders.

During the summer of 2013, my wife, other family members, and I toured the Roman Forum. The Arch of Titus stands near the entrance to the ancient market and meeting place. The monument was erected in honor of Titus' conquering of Jerusalem. Reliefs on the memorial depict Temple articles carried back to Rome by victorious troops. These include the Table of Showbread and the seven-branched candelabrum, the two main furnishings in the Temple's Holy Place.

Short-term and long-term events and effects indicated the loss of Jerusalem and the beloved Temple. Women and children suffered horribly. The Temple has never been rebuilt. Jews control only the lower part of its Western wall today. Many refer to that portion as the "Wailing wall." Two Moslem mosques sit atop the former Temple Mount. The horrible 70 AD event surely constituted the "abomination that causes desolation."

The above facts demonstrate another truth Jesus predicted about Jerusalem's fall: it "will be trampled on by the Gentiles until the times of the Gentiles are fulfilled."[195] Jerusalem residents and subsequent

---

194. Luke 19:43, 44 NIV.

195. Luke: 21:24 NRSV.

generations paid a great price for disregarding Jesus' teaching, predictions, and advice. Jerusalem's destruction took place during the lifetime of many of those disciples.

Comprehending what Jesus taught them in the three Gospel accounts is admittedly difficult. When we keep in mind the disciples' questions, though, Jesus' predictions become clearer. Following Matthew's gospel (Chapter 24) as we have so far, we can summarize Jesus' prophecies this way:

Verses 3-14 include warnings about misinterpreting signs, "Watch out that no one deceives you," many will claim to be the Christ; wars, famines, and earthquakes will take place throughout ages to come. Disciples must persevere through the **Chaos** presented by prevailing wickedness and love grown cold.

Verses 15-28 refer to the warning and alert signs of Jerusalem's destruction, advice about fleeing, hints of the suffering, and cautions about being taken in by pseudo-Christs and false prophets. Note that in verses 3-28 (and the parallel verses in *Mark* and *Luke*) Jesus seemed to deal with concerns of his contemporaries. Thus he consistently used the second person pronoun "you."

Referring to those affected by his return as Judge in *Matthew* 24:30, however, Jesus used the third person pronoun "they."[196] We can reasonably infer that Jesus used the second person (you) in reference to events the disciples would experience, and the third person (they) to a future generation that would be alive when Judgment Day arrives. His return would not be immediate.

Beginning in *Matthew* 24:33, Jesus asked his disciples to remember how fig trees reflect the changing seasons. He spoke of summertime signs; tender twigs and leaves coming out—signs they would soon see. So also would they behold the events leading to Jerusalem's destruction. They could interpret those signs.

The disciples could not nor could any human being foresee, however, the precise date the Son of Man will return. That could occur at any time, of course, but other events would take place first. Readiness remains the key (at an hour you do not expect).[197] The fact that everyone will be held accountable should sober us. "Who then is the faithful and wise servant?"[198] All generations need to stay mindful of these truths.

---

196. Mark 13:26 (NIV) reads "Men will see the Son of Man coming in the clouds." Luke used the third person pronoun "they" in agreement with Matthew.

197. Matthew 24:44.

198. Ibid. v 45 NIV.

One word found in *Matthew* 24:29 appears to stand in the way of my interpretation: "*Immediately* after the distress of those days, 'the sun will be darkened and the moon will not give its light...'" Did Jesus intend us to understand that directly after Jerusalem's fall, signs of his return to earth would appear in the heavens?

Jesus quoted from two different sections of *Isaiah*: 13:10 and 34:4 (written circa 700 BC). Most OT prophecies served a dual purpose. First, they usually foretold an immediate fulfillment that their contemporary hearers and readers would witness. The messages carried a secondary application for the end of the age (or the time of the Messiah).[199]

Isaiah directed his words in Chapter 13 to Babylon. The prophet intended the Chapter 34 message for the ancient kingdom of Edom. Darkened sun and a moon of blood have long symbolized the rise and fall of nations. People recall frightening events as "dark days." The year 1942 was certainly that for citizens of the United States. During that time, many Americans wondered (some doubted) whether this country would recover from the attack on Pearl Harbor and Hitler's advances in Europe, the North Atlantic, and North Africa.

In *Matthew* 24: 29, Jesus probably predicted the rise and fall of many tribes and nations following the fall of Jerusalem. World powers continue to rise and fall. Hardly any great power remains dominant for more than a few centuries. The Vandals, Goths, and Visigoths caused the Romans many dark days and moons of blood.

The four-letter Greek adverb "tote" (τότε) usually translated "at the time" or "after that" in verse 30 lends credibility to my theory. Note the context in which "tote" appears in 2 *Peter* 3:6. In verse 5, Peter referred to the creation "formed out of water and by water (NIV)." Next Peter wrote of the world "at that time" being deluged by water, referring to Noah's flood. Millennia intervened between the two events (the creation and the flood). In *Matthew* 24: 36, Jesus warned about human readiness for the Judgment. His return will be sudden. In Noah's time, no one believed a flood was coming. The Son of Man's return will find most folks unprepared. Wise servants remain vigilant and work hard. They know they must reckon with the Lord at his reappearance.

In reference to verse 34, some understand Jesus' comment to mean that that all of the events he predicted would shortly occur: "Truly I tell you, this generation will certainly not pass away until all these things have happened." Was Jesus mistaken about his second coming and return for the Judgment? His comments as he carried the cross give us perspective.

---

199. See Hebrews 1:1, 2, esp. verse 2: "But in these last days he has spoken to us by his Son..." NIV.

Luke's Gospel informs us of the miserable manner authorities treated Jesus. They seized Simon of Cyrene and forced him to carry Jesus' cross. Numerous people followed the wretched procession. As many women wailed loudly, Jesus spoke to them: "Do not weep for me; weep for yourselves and for your children. For the time will come when you will say, 'Blessed are the barren women . . .'" Jesus foresaw the terrible days only decades hence; Jerusalem's families would suffer horribly at the Romans' hands. *Luke* 23:41 is especially telling. Still addressing those weeping women, Jesus declared: "If men do these things when the tree is green, what will happen when it is dry?" Compare the green-dry contrast Jesus predicted in *Matthew* 24: 32-34 NIV:

> *Now learn this lesson from the fig tree: As soon as its twigs get tender and its leaves come out, you know that summer is near. Even so, when you see all these things, you know that it is near, right at the door. Truly I tell you, this generation will certainly not pass away until all these things have happened.*

Three pieces of evidence indicate that in this fig tree parable, Jesus once again spoke of Jerusalem's destruction, not the end of the world. First, his passion and suffering at the cross occurred when the tree was green. Already in 30 AD, the beginnings of Israel's rebellion and insurrection were taking place. By 70 AD, Israel's insurgence tree was incendiary-dry and aflame. Imagine the burden, sorrow, and dread of mothers, whose children starved and died as Roman troops cut off food-water supplies, invaded the city, then ransacked, pillaged, and raped.

Second, note Jesus' pronouns. He did not use the vague, third person, plural "they" of a distant age. It was "when you see all these things happen." The "fall" occurred in the lifetime of many present when Jesus spoke in *Matthew* 24. Their generation had not passed.

Third, we must remember the queries that led to Jesus' teaching as recorded in *Matthew* 24, *Mark* 13, and *Luke* 21. The disciples' first question related to the Temple's destruction, not the end of the age. End-time inquiries were secondary. Despite that order, in all three gospels, the earlier NIV translators labeled the portions dealing with the issues: "Signs of the End of the Age." *Chaos* was/is at its zenith.

In the next chapter, we shall deal with evidence (or lack of it) for the so-called Rapture.

Chapter 5
Tribulation And Rapture

Is There Or Isn't There A Rapture?
Do "end time" rumors keep you on edge? Do you fear being left behind at the so-called "Rapture?" Are you anxious about having to endure the "Great Tribulation"? Thoughts of facing such happenings worry many.

Speculation about the "Rapture" and the "Great Tribulation" generates lots of attention. The two theoretical events come joined at the hip. In many Protestant churches, they dominate conversations. In this chapter, we examine: "What does the *Bible* teach about these subjects?"

Rapture advocates literally interpret a symbolic scene in *Revelation* 20. Though Jesus spoke concerning a resurrection of the just and unjust[200] on Judgment Day, advocates of the Rapture and Great Tribulation espouse certain events occurring prior to the Judgment. They expect a series of incidents resulting in the faithful being bodily transported to heaven[201] while the others are left on earth. Supporters of the theory include many prominent Bible teachers and preachers. The "Rapture" is an essential doctrine of the "Great Tribulation" theory.

Though numerous believers uphold the "Rapture" doctrine, note this curiosity about the word "rapture." The term does not appear in the King James Version or in most English translations. You will not find "rapture" listed in either Young's or Strong's concordance, or even in the NIV Study Bible concordance. Nonetheless many televangelists and popular preachers strongly advocate these two interdependent doctrines.

Opinions differ over when this "Rapture" will take place. Most link it to a period of "great tribulation."[202] Those who teach "pre-tribulation" think that the rapture will occur before the "tribulation." Thinking that the "tribulation" will last seven years, mid-tribulation believers teach that the church will be on earth for three and a half years (the first half of the "tribulation"). Then the "Rapture" will take place. After the Rapture, the severest of the suffering will take place.

Recent publishers of the New International Version help promote the Rapture theory in two ways. First, some editions of the NIV print

---

200. See John 5:24-30.

201. The word rapt refers to being lifted by supernatural force, for example, Elijah (see 2 Kings 2:9-12.)

202. The linking of two Greek terms, *mega* (much or great) and *thlipsis* (suffering), appears only in Revelation 7:14. It appears in this order ἐκ τῆς θλίψεως τῆς μεγάλις, literally "out of the suffering, the great".

the following bold heading for *Revelation* Chapter 20: **The thousand years**. The 2011 edition of the *NIV Study Bible* listed "The Great Tribulation" under both its **Index to Topics** [203]and its **Index to Notes**. The two sites list some of the same Scripture references, but they are not duplicates.[204] The NIV concordance[205] in that same 2011 edition lists only one reference to the Tribulation, *Revelation* 7:14.[206] In that single Scripture, the expression "great tribulation" can be found in the NIV.

The 2011 edition does not list the word "Rapture" in either the **Index to Topics** or its **Concordance**. It is found in the **Index to Notes** under the title "**Rapture, The.**" These Scriptures are included in that listing: 1 *Corinthians* 15:52; 2 *Corinthians* 12:2-4; 1 *Thessalonians* 4:17; *Revelation* 4:1. My 1995 edition of the *NIV Study Bible* also does not include "Rapture" in its **Index to Subjects** but does include **Rapture** in its **Index to Notes** section. Both editions also list "Premillennialism" in their note sections with one Scripture: *Revelation* 20:2. The term premillennial means pre-1000 or before the presumed earthly thousand year-reign of Jesus.

Post-Tribulationists teach that the Rapture will not happen until after the completion of the "Great Tribulation." As we wrote earlier, proponents of rapture and tribulation base their theories on literal interpretations of *Revelation* Chapter 20.

Does the *New Testament* tell of "rapture"? It nowhere uses that precise term. Jesus certainly warned that at his return, two men will be in a field, "one will be taken and the other left."[207] But in what context did Jesus teach about that type of event?

Many Christians thought that following his ascension, Jesus would almost immediately come back and take believers to heaven with him. Years passed. Numerous Christians died of natural and accidental causes. Some died as martyrs. Believers who expected Jesus' speedy return became troubled about the "delay."

Surviving Christians wondered about their believing loved ones who had died. At Jesus' return, would they be left in the grave and miss heaven? In 1 *Thessalonians* 4, Paul assured Christians of the following sequence of events.

---

203. See pp. 2235 and 2338.

204. The **Index to Topics** lists Revelation 7:14; Isaiah 24: 1-20; Daniel 12:1; Matthew 24:15-28; Daniel 9:24-27; Revelation 13:11- 17; Revelation 14:8; Revelation 18:1-24; Matthew 24:22. The **Index to Notes lists:** Matthew 24:16; Matthew 24:21; Matthew 24:22; Matthew 25:31-46; Revelation 7:4; Revelation 7:9 and Revelation 7:14.

205. The concordance was created by John R. Kohlenberger III.

206. See p. 2498.

207. Matthew 24:40 NIV. Verse 41 refers to two women experiencing a similar type of experience that would separate them as were the two male field-workers.

At Jesus' reappearance:

> *The Lord will descend from heaven with a loud command;*
> *There will be the voice of an archangel;*
> *God's trumpet will sound a call;*
> *The dead in Christ will rise first;*
> *After that those still alive will rise to meet the Lord in the air.*
> *Those who had already fallen asleep (died) in Christ and those still alive will be forever with the Lord.*[208]

Paul comforted believers in Thessalonica by reminding them of these facts.

Tribulation proponents teach that the events in this passage describe the "Rapture." In their view, the Lord will reign in Jerusalem 1,000 years. During that time, the rest of the earth (those not "raptured" then) will undergo this tribulation or period of great suffering. Following that there will be further judgment for those who remain on earth after the Rapture. *Tribulation* people base most of their theory on their interpretations of *Revelation* 20.

Many believers overlook or ignore an important body of teaching. I refer to the *New Testament* comparison of baptism to death.[209] Paul keenly reminded the Roman and the Colossian churches of that first death.[210] Later we shall see how that neglect has shaped interpreters' conclusions in *Revelation* 20.

Did Jesus Teach The "Tribulation" And "Rapture"?

Numerous authors and preachers teach that the earth will undergo a period of tribulation in the last days. All Christians should know what the New Testament teaches about this term. Tribulation (*thlipsis*, θλῖψις in Greek) appears twenty times in the *NT* King James Version. The verb form *thlibō* originally meant to "press," "squash," and "hem in." If you are intensely pressed, squashed, or "hemmed in" for any duration, you are likely suffering, aren't you?

New Testament translators after the KJV (1611) often used the word afflict or affliction to convey the meaning of *thlipsis* (tribulation). Those not familiar with *NT* Greek can easily refer to a Cruden's, Young's, or any other complete concordance to find the *New Testament* occurrences of the term.

---

208. 1 Thessalonians 4:13-18 (a summary).

209. Romans 6:1-14; Colossians 2:12. The post-apostolic practice of sprinkling for baptism dilutes and weakens the powerful representation of baptism as a death.

210. Ibid.

Tracing the NT usage of tribulation *thlípsis* leads to noteworthy facts. In *Matthew* 13, the term appears when Jesus explained the parable of the sower.[211] Jesus connected affliction (tribulation) with persecution (v.21). The NIV translates it as pressure applied to the "seed" sown on rocky ground. Because he/she "has no root" in Christ, in tribulation (persecution) the person quits.

Thlípsis appears again in *Matthew* 24: 21; this time followed by the word *mega* (great).[212] Jesus spoke of the great "distress" (NIV) that believers will suffer when the "abomination that causes desolation, spoken of through the prophet Daniel"[213] takes place. When Jesus described the suffering pregnant women and nursing mothers would have to endure during the destruction of the Jews' beloved city, *Luke*, in his gospel, used the term "horrible" (woe!).[214] In an earlier chapter, we presented ample evidence to show that those predictions referred not to the end time, but to Jerusalem's ruin in 70 AD.

Jesus described the grief, weeping, and other suffering ahead for his followers. *John* 16 concludes with Jesus announcing, "In this world you will have trouble (*thlípsis*), but take heart! I have overcome the world."[215]

The *Book of Acts* tells Paul's conversion and mission efforts. From the first, he suffered rejection even from believers. He encountered persecution and nearly died from the stoning he received in Lystra. He and Barnabas prepared others for that kind of treatment as they left the area: "'We must go through many hardships (*thlípsis*) to enter the kingdom of God,' they said."[216] The word preceding *thlípsis* translated "many" indicates both frequency and intensity.

Thlípsis appears at least four times in *Romans*[217], twice in both *Second Corinthians*[218] and *Second Thessalonians*,[219] and once in *Ephesians*.[220] Paul mostly used the term to describe his own suffering. But he also

---

211. Matthew 13:1-23.

212. Though in English modifying adjectives (for example great) rarely follow a noun, this occurs commonly in Greek.

213. Matthew 24:15.

214. Luke 21:23 -The term translated as woe is Greek- οὐαί, pronounced ooai, likely an onomatopoeic word.

215. John 16:33 NIV.

216. Acts 14:22 NIV

217. 2:9, 5:3, 8:35, 12:12.

218. 1:4, 7:4.

219. 1:4, 1:6.

220. 3:13.

reassured Christians that on the Last Day, God will bring affliction *thlipsis* on evil people.[221] The word appears five times in *Revelation*. John reminded his readers (1:9) that he was a companion and brother in their tribulation. The Lord encouraged the people in Smyrna by telling them he knew of their "works and tribulation" (2:9). He informed them that their tribulation would last ten days (v. 10).

In a warning similar to those Paul issued in *Romans* and *2 Thessalonians*, the Lord cautioned the church in Thyatira (2:22) that those who persisted in following the adulterous, immoral, and idolatrous behavior of Jezebel would find themselves in a miserable bed—one of *thlipsis mega*.[222]

The last instance of *thlipsis* occurs in *Revelation* 7:14. It follows the appearance of "a great multitude from every nation, tribe, people and language, standing before the throne and in front of the lamb." They wear white robes and the sing loud praises to God. One of the 24 elders asked John a rhetorical question:

> *"These in white robes—who are they and where did they come from?"*
> *I answered, "Sir, you know."*
> *And he said "These are they who have come out of the great tribulation; they have washed their robes and made them white on the blood of the Lamb."*[223]

In Greek, the term *thlipsis* is followed by the word mega as in the instances already shown. The only difference is that in *Revelation* 7:14, definite articles appear prior to both *thlipsis* and mega.[224]

The above data illustrate how the "Tribulation" theory rests on weak evidence. Jesus warned that all his followers will face tribulation (*thlipsis*). Paul advised us that anyone entering the kingdom encounters fierce pressure (tribulation). Every member of the kingdom must have his/her robe washed in the blood of Jesus. To base a theory of the end-time on such fragile Scripture support seems questionable.

Two facts bother me.

- First is the editing done by the usually scholarly *NIV Study Bible, 2011 Edition*. Under "Index to Topics" (page 2185), it defines **The Great Tribulation** this way—"A time of distress

---

221. Romans 2:9 and 2 Thessalonians 1:6.

222. Revelation 2:22 Greek, θλίψιν μεγάλην.

223. Ibid 7:13, 14 NIV.

224. The definite articles are similar to the English "the." Refer to Schlier in *TDNT* Vol III, pp. 139-148. Also note "afflictions" in *Young's Concordance*, 2 Corinthians 8:2 "in much testing of affliction."

at the end of the world." The editors noted that the only use of the term, **Great Tribulation** occurs in *Revelation* 7:14. But from there, they draw many inferences connecting tribulation with the *Daniel* 9 passage. We discussed them in chapter 4. The 2011 NIV also lists *Matthew* 24:15-28. We presented evidence indicating that in those verses, Jesus referred to the destruction of Jerusalem, not the end time.

- The *NIV Study Bible* editors also list *Revelation* 13:11-17, 14:8, and 18:1-24. All refer to suffering inflicted on believers by Babylon (probably Rome). Not one of those passages uses the word "tribulation." The Roman Imperial government (the first through the third centuries AD) inflicted that suffering on believers long ago.

- The NIV translation uses the word "tribulation only in *Revelation* 7:14. The expression there could just as easily be translated as affliction or persecution.

Since Jesus' ascension, believers have undergone persecution-affliction-tribulation. In *Acts* Chapters 2-9, author Luke described the pressure the Apostles and the fledgling church faced. Saul of Tarsus bore the responsibility for much of the early persecution believers endured. Within a few decades, Saul (Paul) underwent his own multiple, intense *thlipsis* for Jesus' sake. He wrote the church in Rome that "suffering (*thlipsis*) produces perseverance." He itemized to the church in Corinth (*2 Corinthians* 11:23-33) the *thlipsis* he experienced to that date (circa 55 AD).

Few have suffered greater or more prolonged tribulation than Paul did. But he was not the only one who had endured it. Christians in various parts of the world suffer similarly today. We best understand that the great tribulation began when the church was first established and will continue to the Judgment Day. Later we shall take a closer look at the interpretations of *Revelation* Chapters 7[225] and 20 that provide the fuel for the theories of the millennium and the so-called Great Tribulation.

Keep first century circumstances in mind. Christians faced increasing disapproval from the Roman government. Many believers died for professing their faith. As Jesus predicted, the love of some grew cold. Fear of ridicule displaced firm belief. Followers of the Lamb succumbed to fear of losing limbs, shelter, and life. Others yielded to both blatant and subtle temptations that plague God's people in every age. With lustful, alluring arms, and promised ecstasies, immorality enveloped them.

---

225. See chapters 10-12.

Faced with a bewildering multitude of pagan influences and pseudo-Christs, not a few believers began questioning whether Jesus was God's true Messiah (Christ). Was the man of Nazareth God's faithful and true witness?

Present day Christians struggle with similar doubts, fears, and temptations. One of the most subtle pressures we face strained the faith of first century Christians and may be the most lethal of all the church's foes. The *Revelation* writer knew the potency of that pressure and he continually addressed it. Somehow many preachers seem unaware of continuing *thlipsis* (affliction) and actually contribute to the enemy's cause.

The issue: God's control of history and world events. First century Christians saw the Roman government's unequalled power. Visibly, palpably, believers witnessed the Roman army's grip and the government's increased authority and interference into life. From the British Isles to India, the great "crat" Caesar's legions spread constrictive tentacles. How could an invisible God rival the Roman monster's supremacy?

Christians seem always to ask the same about contemporary powers. Current disciples spend vast amounts of time, money and energy trying to change their nations' governments. They forget that Jesus advised his contemporaries not to work against world rulers but to love everyone and keep telling Jesus' Good News.

That's what Jesus meant by going the second mile and agreeing quickly with your adversary. God's kingdom is not of this world. Most of Jesus' contemporaries tried to resist Roman authority rather than to trust the forgiving, loving approach he taught and practiced. Though God seems invisible to human eyes, throughout history his truth borne by believers presents strong confirmation of his powerful, loving, wise existence.

Present day Christians fret about the United States government as well as the regimes of China, Russia, Iran, North Korea, Syria, Pakistan, India, and so on. The combined might of all past, present, and future world governments stands less than a gnat's chance against the Creator of the Cosmos. *Revelation* begins by declaring that Jesus rules supreme over the kings of the earth (1:5, 8). The almighty Pantocrator[226] (ruler of all) reigns forever. This directly contested the Emperor's puny claim.

The Church constantly finds itself in **Conflict** with the world. God's people would be wise to follow the example of church leaders in *Acts* 4. Authorities ordered the Apostles not to teach anything further about Jesus. Faced with threats, the church hired no attorneys

---

226. Greek, ὁ παντοκράτωρ.

or attempted to influence no politicians. The Apostles simply asked God for boldness to continue their witness. Even today God answers disciples' prayers. If believers focused their energy and used their opportunities to tell Jesus' good news, the Church would more readily see and benefit from God's power.

Of Cartoons, Codes, And Complexity
For many years, I taught a Bible study for business and professional people in Los Angeles. Attendees came from a range of backgrounds. Few of them came from a typical protestant Christian upbringing. One day before we began our study, a very successful business woman said she wanted to inquire about a matter. She read extensively and she endured life-threatening moments that make the plots of popular novels and movies. This friend moved comfortably among elite people in the city. She knew the inner-workings of government as well as the actions of wealthy citizenry. She experienced life's extremes — bad and good.

My friend posed what she considered a rational question. Her body language and her eyes indicated significant concern. One, she felt deeply frustrated dealing with those close to her. Second, she bore great anguish over the realization that despite her strong efforts to make things better around her, she saw little improvement taking place. In fact conditions seemed to worsen. The world and even her own community were already tucked away in the proverbial perdition "hand basket."

"Who is more powerful: God or the devil?" she asked. From her observations of family, society, and world events, the battle seemed: "No contest. The devil appeared to win round after round." The frustration and discouragement among many Christian friends tells me that they, too, have arrived at the same "logical" conclusion as my late friend. Many believers in first century Asia Minor similarly pictured Satan ready to score a huge knockout punch.

A Brief Review Of Why John Wrote Revelation.
Many first-century Christians in Asia Minor (Western Turkey) faced severe tests of faith.

- Worldly practices and standards in the area took their toll on Christians' morals.
- Persecution and other trials caused some to doubt God's purpose and control.
- Was God the true ruler? Was he more powerful than Rome's Emperor?

- Was Jesus the real king?
  - Will right ever prevail?
  - When will suffering and persecution end?

In cryptic form, the Lord revealed a series of visions to John. Their purpose:

- Confront Christians who were succumbing to fleshly temptations;
- Encourage doubting Christians;
- Counsel all to remain faithful to the finish;
- Assure believers of God's surpassing power and that he will in time justly judge all the earth's past, contemporary, and future rulers;
- Jesus, who is fully God, is King of all kings and Lord of all lords.

Revelation interpreters must keep the above points in mind.

Uncertainty concerning their future dogged early believers. Beleaguered by Rome's seeming invincibility, many grew discouraged. Fear of crucifixion, beheading, or stoning understandably troubled them. For various reasons, some doubted Jesus' identity as God's Son. Greed took its toll on the church. So did immorality. Apparently some eagerly "jumped into bed with Jezebel" lured by her idolatrous practices. Through the writer John in *Revelation,* the Holy Spirit addressed this assortment of faith failures.

For good reason, targeted readers could understand *Revelation's* figures of speech and parables. The symbolic language came mostly from the *Old Testament,* from Jesus' teaching, and the common trials first century Christians faced. While precisely prescribing what believers needed, *Revelation's* figurative style protected its recipients. Non-Christian authorities did not understand the Holy Spirit's cryptic language. To them the book would have read like gibberish. The *Apocalypse's* virtually unbreakable code made treason charges against believers difficult to prove.

Can we now unscramble the book's meaning? Nearly two millennia have elapsed. Most interpreters seem to miss various key elements. We begin our understanding of *Revelation* using perspectives moviegoers and playgoers should easily grasp.

Developing Our Interpretive Theory

Let's lay the groundwork for this view. You possibly saw the movie, *The Sound of Music.* The film opened with breathtaking views of the Austrian Alps. As she sang the title song, cameras gradually brought us closer to Julie Andrews. Subsequent scene changes included the nunnery, the von Trapp mansion, the Austrian village, the amphitheater where the villagers performed, and the convent graveyard. As the story line progressed, each time-frame required several scenes. In many instances, the filmmakers wanted us to understand that what we saw in one scene took place at approximately the same time as the events in the next part.

Books, stage plays, movies, television presentations — all types of dramatic presentations — give us overviews (birds-eye views) and sometimes close-up shots. We also get viewpoints from different perspectives. Writers and producers script scenes to let us know that events in multiple locations sometimes occur simultaneously. After viewing an episode in one location, we see something happening at the same moment in another place.

The convent scene, for instance, leads viewers to conclude that the Julie Andrews character will not succeed as a nun. Meanwhile at the von Trapp mansion, it becomes apparent that the children need an understanding governess or mother.

Those familiar with old Western movies know their stereotypical sequence. Opening scenes often show bad guys burning a rancher's home and threatening his daughter. In town at the same time, the crooked banker schemes with the local sheriff and their henchmen to repossess the rancher's land. These settings support the fact that, unknown to most local residents, the railroad will be coming to town. Land values will dramatically increase. This sequence of revolting events makes another character necessary. Concurrently with the other scenes, a good-guy gunslinger rides into town. Though the film displays the events in sequence, viewers easily understand that some occur simultaneously.

In 1 Samuel 25, the writer used this method as he told the story of David, Nabal, and Abigail. David, a fugitive at the time, and his six hundred men were hiding from Saul, who intended to kill him. David fled to the Negev, the extreme southern part of Israel.

Brigands frequented this border-wilderness area. The narrator introduces us to Nabal, a wealthy, but surly landowner, who lived near Carmel in the Negev with his beautiful, discreet, wife Abigail. Nabal enjoyed large holdings and numerous livestock: three thousand sheep and a thousand goats. His farm-ranch likely included sizable vineyards and numerous fig trees. By David's orders, his men kept Nabal's property and animals secure from bandits.

Feeding six hundred armed men and some of their families required substantial planning and effort. David sent some of his men to Nabal with instructions to first give Nabal a cheery and positive blessing. Next, David wanted them to remind Nabal that for some time, his men protected Nabal's personnel and holdings. Now at sheep shearing (a festival time), would Nabal spare some food for David's men?

Nabal nastily refused the request. When David's messengers returned with the bad news, he ordered four hundred of his men to arm themselves and leave for Carmel in order to avenge Nabal's insult.

In the meantime, back at Nabal's ranch, one of Nabal's servants informed Abigail of Nabal's gruff, insulting treatment. He also told her how well David's men had treated Nabal's shepherds. The servant feared that Nabal's churlishness endangered everyone. He asked Abigail to consider what she could do.

Simultaneous scenes now unfold. As David's men readied their swords and battle gear, Abigail hurriedly rummaged her pantries to find "peace offerings." She loaded bread, wine, dressed sheep, raisin cakes, and pressed figs onto numerous donkeys and sent them in David's direction. Riding her personal donkey, Abigail accompanied the animal convoy.

The two parties convergence:

> As she came riding her donkey into a mountain ravine, there were David and his men descending toward her, and she met them. David had just said, "It's been useless—all my watching over this fellow's property in the wilderness so that nothing of his was missing. He has paid me back evil for good. May God deal with David be it ever so severely, if by morning I leave alive one male of all who belong to him!"[227]

Similar sequential scenes depicting simultaneous and overlapping events happen in *Revelation*. Setting changes occur throughout the book. Time progresses through the individual scenes. Numerous concurrent-parallel sections take place. The book features wide-sweeping, birds-eye views of history and also close-ups.

A few interpreters have grasped the concept. These include Edward White Benson and his daughter Margaret,[228] as well as S.L. Morris.[229] Benson died before he completed his work. His daughter Margaret later organized much of his material and published it. Benson noted what he called Acts and Scenes in *Revelation*, but hesitated to call it a true drama.

Influence Of Greek Culture And Dramas

227. 1 Samuel 25:20-22.

228. Benson, Edward White and Margaret Benson, *The Apocalypse, an Introductory Study of the Revelation of St. John the Divine*. Note the **Introduction**, especially page 6.

229. Morris, S.L., *The Drama of Christianity*, paperback edition, issued 1982 by Baker Book House from the 1928 edition of the Presbyterian Committee of Publication.

S.L. Morris evidenced less hesitancy in making the theatrical comparison. In fact he titled his work, *The Drama of Christianity*. Morris saw parallels between *Revelation* and Greek dramas: "with various parts, its different actors and, at regular intervals, its chorus singing its heavenly anthems, in which more specifically is revealed its spiritual purpose-Consolation."[230] Morris observed that *Revelation* was:

> ...*written in the age of the Greek drama, a period characterized by the use of parables, pageants and panoramas. Sophocles, Euripides and Thucydides were masters in the use of the dramatic art for presenting their thoughts in a popular method to insure a hearing and acceptance by the common people. John may not have been familiar with these Classics; but in the school of Christ he had been taught, by means of parables, the use of the dramatic method in story form-which presented the concrete truth-for example, in the parable of the "prodigal," or in the character of "Dives," so strikingly, as to be living illustrations speaking through the ages. The age in which he lived, and the Spirit of God which inspired him, influenced John to write in simplest form the greatest drama in all human history, as will be seen by future study of his Revelation.*[231]

The synoptic gospels feature numerous parables of Jesus. Sometimes all the hearers grasped the meanings. On other occasions, Jesus meant only his disciples to understand them. Why should we be amazed if a book written to believers under the duress of persecution should be composed largely of parables presented similar to theatrical scenes?

Morris noted other similarities between Greek dramatic presentations and *Revelation*. They include: prologue, acts, scenes, interludes, plot, counterplot, choruses, temporary defeat, the triumph of right at the conclusion, and epilogue. Actors enter and exit. "The acts consist of seven Panoramas. The period of time covers the entire Christian Dispensation. The Interlude with its significant chorus occurs regularly and unfailingly in each separate panorama."[232]

Do historical, linguistic, and archaeological evidence support Morris's theory? Space hardly exists to fully investigate these concerns. But ample evidence shows substantiation for Morris's theory. Twice in

---

230. Ibid, p. 20.

231. Ibid, I think we can safely assume Morris knew that the parables of the prodigal son, the rich man and dives, and so on, to which he alluded came from the Gospel of Luke, not John's Gospel. Though John did not include them in his gospel, he probably would have heard them many times from Jesus.

232. Ibid, p. 21.

Acts 19, Luke used the Greek word "theatre" to describe the location of the near-riot in Ephesus.[233] Paul's ministry there upset the silversmith guild because they thought the rise of Christianity would reduce sales of the souvenir temple shrines they made.

To describe the mockery suffered by Christians, the *Book of Hebrews* author used a verb form of the word "theatre.[234] Believers became "a theater, or a set upon a stage for all to look upon."[235] Use of the terms tells us that information about the theatre was well known by the time of *Revelation's* writing.

The Greeks and Romans built amphitheaters all over the Mediterranean area. According to Josephus, Herod the Great constructed an amphitheater in Jerusalem.[236] The comparison of *Revelation* with Greek drama gains substantiation from the fact that in *Acts* 19, the near-riot took place in a theatre. The Ephesians possessed a huge theatre even by modern standards. Some think it accommodated more than 25,000 persons. Hollywood's Greek Theatre seats about 6,000. Citizens of all seven *Revelation* cities enjoyed theatres having extraordinary acoustics. Performances were popular. Even had they not attended, most residents would have been familiar with the huge facilities. Whether, in 1928, Morris knew all the archaeological evidence, I do not know. The ancient Greeks or Romans built at least 26 theaters in Asia Minor and Ionia (Turkey).

What did *Revelation's* "theater" depict? As did Greek tragedies, *Revelation's* scenes include the effects of wars, famine, and plagues. The *Apocalypse* portrays the outlook for God's church as well as the future of Rome and other evil empires, the devil's prospects, and death's demise. The apparent theme or thesis of the book accords with what Jesus said in John's Gospel: "In this world you have trouble. But take heart! I have overcome the world."[237]

In every age the Lord expects behavior consistent with loving belief in his overpowering victory. Will God's people give up doubt, hate, pride, greed, vengeance, and immoral behavior? When Jesus returns and brings that new city and home, will we have our reservations in order?

---

233. Acts 19:29 and 31.

234. Hebrews 10:33 NIV "Sometimes you were publicly exposed to insult and persecution; at other times you stood side by side with those who were so treated." It is as though they were put on a theater stage to be publicly mocked and tormented.

235. Robert W. Ross, *The Wycliffe Bible Commentary*, Charles Pfeiffer and Everett F. Harrison, eds., Moody Press, Chicago, 1962, p 1421.

236. *The Life and Works of Flavius Josephus*, "Antiquities of the Jews," Book XV, Chapter 8, transl. William Whiston, The John C. Winston Company, Philadelphia, p. 463

237. John 16:33 NIV.

Verses from *Revelation* Chapter 7 consistently rank among the best-known and loved of all the Scriptures. Grieving families find consolation in the lyrics the twenty-four elders sang in this passage:

> *They are before the throne of God and serve him day and night in his temple; and he who sits on the throne will shelter them with his presence.*
>
> *Never again will they hunger; never again will they thirst.*
>
> *The sun will not beat down on them nor any scorching heat.*
>
> *For the Lamb at the center of the throne will be their shepherd; he will lead them to springs of living water.*
>
> *And God will wipe away every tear from their eyes.*[238]

Morris, Benson, and others researched massive amounts of material. They helped uncover valuable insights. Recent archaeological discoveries center on an area of Greek influence called the Decapolis, literally ten cities. According to Matthew, folks from the Decapolis were among the large crowds that followed Jesus early in his ministry.[239]

Mark's Gospel refers twice to the region.[240] One passage describes the violent, uncontrollable man who lived among the tombs from whom Jesus cast the legion of demons into the swine. That demoniac evidently came from one of the cities. After Jesus freed him from demon-possession, the man wanted to follow the Lord. Jesus refused his offer, instead advising him to, "Go home to your family and tell them how much the Lord has done for you, and how he has had mercy on you." The result: he "began to tell in the Decapolis how much Jesus had done for him."[241]

---

238. Revelation 7:15-17 NIV.

239. Matthew 4:25.

240. Because of similarity in the names of the two cities, later scribes making copies of the gospels apparently confused the two cities when identifying the home city of the demon-possessed man. In his *Natural History* (5.16.74), the Roman scientist-historian, Pliny the Elder listed ten cities he identified as constituting the Decapolis. Gadara and Gerasa were among them. At Gerasa, (modern Jerash) extensive ruins of the Greek and Roman era have been unearthed. The origin of the ten likely occurred after Alexander the Great conquered the area (circa 320 BC) and came under Roman control about 60 BC. Some variation occurs in the names of the cities involved and in the total number of them as well.

241. Mark 5: 20 NIV.

Mark's second reference to the Decapolis described when, from Galilee, Jesus traveled northwest to the area of Tyre and Sidon. Then, as Mark records, Jesus went to the Decapolis where he preached and performed miracles.[242]

These and other facts lead me to think that Greek influence on Israel was stronger than generally supposed. The fourth-named apostle in all lists was Philip. Philip's (Greek) name means "horse-lover."[243] The Gospels identify Philip's home as Bethsaida, located on the northern shore of the Sea of Galilee, east of the Jordan River. Areas of the Decapolis extend from the eastern and southern shores of the Sea of Galilee.

Maps show Beth-Shan (Scythopolis),[244] the only city in the Decapolis group located west of the Jordan, barely a dozen miles from Nazareth. In 1980, my wife and I visited the ruins of the impressive amphitheater in that city. We can reasonably assume that Jesus spoke Greek in addition to Hebrew and Aramaic. No language barrier apparently existed when Jesus and the demon-crazed man conversed. Because of the fellow's background, he likely spoke Greek.

Despite the similarities of dramatic presentation, we should not regard *Revelation* as just another Greek tragedy or comedy. Though powerful and exceptional, Greek and Roman gods were half-human in behavior. Neither God nor the Lamb of God (Son of God) suffers weakness or gives in to human whims and frailty. As we explore scene after scene *of Revelation's* drama, God's powerful rule unfolds. Christ the Son prevails over all obstacles and foes. Later, we shall present further evidence supporting our theory of simultaneous scenes.

---

242. Mark 7: 31.

243. The name of Peter's brother, Andrew, is also Greek.

244. The ancient city of Beth-Shan (sometimes spelled Beth-Shean, cf 1 Samuel 31:1-13) was re-founded and renamed Scythopolis in Hellenistic times. See article by T.C. Mitchell entitled "Beth-Shean" in the *New Bible Dictionary*, 1965 edition, pp. 145, 146. My wife and I visited Beth-Shan in 1980 and took numerous photos of its large amphitheater.

Chapter 6

Let The Play (the Unveiling) Begin
Why does *Revelation* differ so from other *New Testament* books? In the next few pages, we shall review one distinction. We'll also trace a similarity between *Revelation*'s structure and Jesus' teachings as the Gospels record them. Many interpreters seem to miss a significant resemblance.

During the last week of his ministry, Jesus told numerous parables. He ended them with a pronouncement of woes on those who refused to listen. Then Jesus walked away from the Temple area.[245] We already discussed how, as he left, the Apostles commented on the Temple's magnificence. Jesus shocked them by saying that the imposing structure would one day be dismantled stone by stone. They wanted to know when that disaster would take place. Would any signs precede the occurrence? The disciples hoped for a "heads-up" prior to the fearsome event.

Jesus furnished the disciples ample portents that would come before the destruction of their beloved Temple. Imagine seeing a giant crane-truck drive in front of the building you presently occupy. The huge vehicle comes equipped with a wrecking ball. Dump trucks follow the crane-truck. Hard-hatted workers begin to set up barriers and block nearby streets. Would you think your building might be in jeopardy? To observant followers of Jesus, seeing armies gather around Jerusalem[246] should have been a wrecking-crew-like sign.

Jesus also forewarned how Jewish society would crumble. He foretold other events that would rock the world, stress believers, and continue to pressure them until his return for Judgment. Precisely as Jesus predicted, the Romans obliterated the Temple a few decades later. As the disciples carried out his Great Commission[247] to the non-Jewish world, other events unfolded according to Jesus' forecasts in Matthew 24, Mark 13, and Luke 21. None of what Jesus predicted should take believers by surprise.

The church began with a Jewish core. In fulfillment of Jesus' command to "Go teach all nations," the church fleshed out embracing people of every land, ethnicity, and language. New generations of be-

---

245. See Matthew 21-24.

246. Luke 19:41-44; 21:20.

247. Matthew 28:18-20.

lievers faced the trying circumstances Jesus described to his original disciples.

Speaking to Jewish people about Jesus required a certain focus. Jesus' disciples pointed out *Old Testament* predictions of the Messiah and the signs that signified his appearance. Jesus' proved himself to be God's long-awaited Messiah or Christ.

Declaring Jesus' qualities amidst polytheistic cultures (people who believed in many gods), however, required different messaging.[248] Escalating emperor worship in significant parts of the Roman Empire further affected the Church's testimony about Jesus.

Good leaders anticipate challenges and help their followers prepare for them. Jesus readied his disciples by stages. He began by sending his first disciples on a limited mission to Jewish people within Israel's boundaries. Their task: announce the imminence of God's kingdom. As he clearly stated, "Preach this message: 'The kingdom is near.'"[249] Jesus outlined the methods and scope of their task. He warned them of adversities they would face and he instructed them how to deal with them.

As you will remember from our review of *Matthew* 24, Jesus described what future disciples would encounter as they obeyed his Great Commission. Following his instructions, believers took Jesus' news to distant lands. As they did, circumstances constantly evolved. New situations and questions arose. The Master of all things did not want his people caught off guard by ever-changing conditions. Toward the latter part of the first century, the situation demanded additional instructions. Thus *The Apocalypse* begins:

> *The revelation from Jesus Christ, which God gave him to show his servants what must soon take place. He made it known by sending his angel to his servant John, who testifies to everything he saw — that is, the word of God and the testimony of Jesus Christ.*[250]

Those who read, hear, and take to heart what *The Apocalypse* reveals will be enabled, strengthened, and made happy because "the time is near." The Kingdom's completion and the condemnation of those who reject Jesus draw closer. That did not mean that all the events predicted would immediately occur; only that the unfolding would start soon. The budding of *Revelation's* events began immediately. The

---

248. The difference is evident in the Book of Acts. Paul's sermon to the Gentile scholars in Athens (chapter 17) did not have the same emphasis as his earlier sermons in the synagogues (chapters 13 and 14). In Athens, he could not assume that his hearers knew about *Old Testament* predictions.

249. See Matthew 10.

250. Revelation 1:1 NIV.

process continues: unfurling, progressing, and evolving. The development will continue until Jesus returns in the Judgment.

A Word To The Audience About *Revelation's* Author

John did not really conceive *Revelation*. Acting as an imbedded secretary or reporter, John wrote only what he saw and the Lord told him to say.[251] Seven churches in Asia Minor (what is now western Turkey) initially received the letter which correspondent John wrote.

True, reliable witnesses are traditionally difficult to find. *Revelation's* first comments regarding Jesus tell of his (the Christ's) credibility. Only Jesus fully and truthfully witnesses for God. He alone "came from heaven"[252] — from God. No one else has fully conquered the devil and death.[253] Only Jesus has come back from death never to die again.[254] All history's arrogant kings and pompous presidents will one day be on their knees declaring Jesus to be their tsar-rajah-chief-ruler — God's only true prophet.[255]

In contrast with present heads of state, Jesus possesses all-encompassing authority. His rule extends to every past, present, and future person. No one in any mountain, plain, valley, cave, outer space, or submarine location of the world qualifies for exemption. Jesus' control extends to other universes and beyond. *Revelation* was written from Jesus (Chapter 1, verse 4) and to him (verses 5 and 6). Jesus not only accurately foresees the future. He manages human history from beginning to end. He is Alpha to Omega (A to Z) and Aleph-Tau.[256] As the one and only from the Father, Jesus uniquely witnesses and exclusively portrays truth.[257]

From Book to Stage

Another fact adds difficulty to comprehending *Revelation*. The book begins as a literary work, but shifts to scene changes as in a stage drama or movie. The transition should not amaze us. Chapter 1, verse one clearly indicates the change when it reads "The Revelation of Jesus

---

251. Or an "amanuensis."

252. John 3:13.

253. Hebrews 2: 14-18; 4:15.

254. Romans 6:9.

255. Philippians 2:5-11.

256. First and last letters of the Hebrew Alphabet; see Isaiah 41:4.

257. God refers to himself as "first and last" three times in Isaiah: 41:4; 44:6; and 48:12. In Revelation 1:8, he is Alpha and Omega (first and last letters of the Greek alphabet). Jesus' reference to himself as "first and last" (Revelation 1:17 and 2:8), strongly denotes his full divinity.

Christ, which God gave him to **show** his servants what must soon take place..."

This "showing" required different methods of illustration. During his ministry, Jesus used both plain language and stories to illustrate our relationship with God and accountability to Him. Jesus invited people to imagine various scenes: farmers planting and harvesting, fishermen sorting their catches, shepherds at work, stewards held responsible for their farming and ranching operation oversight, and so on. Among Jesus' most famous parables are the agrarian stories: the Prodigal Son and the Shrewd Money Manager. Those mental pictures adequately fitted Jewish residents in Israel. *Revelation* required imagery, however, for people of a different background. *Revelation's* mostly city folk recipients didn't so easily "dig" the agricultural scene.

When we moved from Los Angeles to rural Iowa, the regional and cultural differences impressed us. Preparing sermons has always been hard work for me. From the start, I began keeping all my notes. Soon I started saving complete manuscripts of nearly all my sermons. When I tell Iowans how much time I spend getting a lesson ready to preach, people often ask me: "Can't you just pull an old sermon out of the file?" Very rarely can I prepare a sermon that easily. Rural Iowans differ in backgrounds and interests from Southern Californians. Not many Angeleños would have wanted to discuss corn and soybean yields — or the hourly prices of those commodities per bushel.

The basic needs of people remain unchanged from the days of Adam and Eve. But day to day interests vary widely according to culture, region, and era. The reach of the Gospel into Asia Minor required a new type of messaging. Jesus used numerous agricultural illustrations in the Gospels. Yet, in the letters to the seven churches of Asia, the only "agricultural" reference pertains to the Tree of Life in *Revelation* 2:7.[258] Imagery clearly designed for its contemporary readers and hearers came from numerous sources.

Show And Tell

Does the book present a gradual unfolding of actual history as many contend? Does a chronological story begin in Chapter two, four, or six and end in Chapter 22? Can we connect actual historical events with any of *Revelation's* scenes? Is there a reference to a millennium? My answer is a probable "no" to the first two questions. The answer to three is, "possibly."

---

258. Later chapters include general references to food supplies as in 6:5,6 ; to grass, plants and trees in 9:2-5; the harvests in Chapter 14: 14-20. But the great city appears to be the main target of God's wrath: see chapters 11-18. The New Jerusalem replaces the doomed Babylon the great. In *Revelation*, Jesus speaks mostly to urban dwellers, not to farmers or ranchers.

Revelation's sequential scenes often portray simultaneous events. They generally cover the period that began with Jesus's first appearance in the flesh and end with his Second Coming harvest. The scenes address age-old questions: What is the meaning of wars, earthquakes and plagues? Does God currently warn people about their behavior? Do they listen? How should the church deal with persecution? Will God ever judge evil? What is heaven like? How will God deal with hostile governments? Most of *Revelation's* colorful passages cover Jesus' first advent to his second. Whether they present a gradual unfolding of history to which historical events can be connected remains for later discussion.

Can I give evidence for my theory? Yes, plenty of it. During his ministry, Jesus taught that his kingdom would soon begin.[259] Matthew 13 includes parable after parable Jesus told concerning the kingdom. His story of the sower informed his followers of the tests they would face as well as the need to prepare their own hearts to receive God's word. The parable of the weeds helped followers see that they needed to patiently deal with hypocrites and allow God to be the final judge.

The mustard seed and yeast parables advised followers that kingdom growth will not be spectacular or resemble a "Christian" rock concert or a mega-church service. God's Kingdom progresses often quietly. Sometimes we barely discern its growth.

The hidden treasure and the pearl of great price stories (*Matthew* 13: 44, 45) indicate joy at finding something valuable. The parable of the fishing net reminds that we must try to reach all types of people and that God will be the ultimate judge and punisher of evil. Much as a crystal refracts light into separate colors, each parable emphasizes different aspects of the Kingdom.

Considering the assorted *Matthew* 13 examples, why should we be amazed by *Revelation's* sequence of varied scenes? As happened in Jesus' parables, time intervals often overlap. *Revelation's* passages treat similar and additional themes but as we noted, to a more cosmopolitan audience. We will also see that *Revelation* includes numerous vistas designed to reassure believers.

Let's return to Chapter 1, verse 1 of *Revelation* and its evidence for my theory: "The Revelation of Jesus Christ, which God gave him to **show** his servants what must soon take place." The Greek word *deiknuma* translated "show" indicates what is to come. Tracing the usage of the term translated "show" by *New Testament* writers illustrates my point. Matthew used the word *deiknuma* in his account of Jesus' temptation by Satan. In his third attempt to lure Jesus, "the devil took

---

259. Mark 9:1.

him to a very high mountain and *showed* him all the kingdoms of the world and their splendor."[260]

The Gospel accounts emphasize what Jesus saw. Did he see the palatial structures of Greece, Rome, and Egypt and the remnants of once dominant kingdoms in the Tigris and Euphrates Valleys? Did he also see the pompous human inhabitants of those artfully detailed, majestic buildings and the miserable souls who labored and slaved so the elites could enjoy opulence? Did Jesus also glimpse future kingdoms? Did he tour the creaky halls of the Kremlin and freshly-painted DC White House walls? Perhaps someday, we shall know the answers. More likely the splendor of God might so overwhelm us, we won't even care about the decayed planet we once treasured. Back to our point; Secretary John received instruction: "What you see, write in a book."[261] This statement clearly emphasizes the visual. Sets in stage plays usually convey vital non-verbal info. *Deiknuma* suggests that the scenes and signs John saw expressed formidable messages.

Modern readers often miss the Bible's strong imagery. A Sunday morning Bible class I visited in another state was studying *Proverbs*. A former missionary effectively led the discussion. In *Proverbs* 6, however, it seemed neither he nor any member saw (grasped) the scene the Scripture intends in verse five. The *Proverbs* author sought to impart wisdom to his son. Chapter 6 deals with a situation nearly every adult faces at some point: How do you help someone who begs for financial assistance?

Relating my Hollywood ministry experiences would fill hundreds of pages. One very persuasive fellow attended church several weeks with his wife. Both seemed personable and well-groomed. He called our house one night explaining that he had been falsely charged and arrested. He thought we should help secure his bail bond by mortgaging our house. He insisted on his innocence, of course, swearing he would repay us as soon as he was proved not guilty.

Irresponsible people make promises like that every day. You see them featured on TV judge and courtroom programs. Many of us get "conned" into cosigning or assisting at least once. I wavered over the decision until I consulted a few experienced people. Their wisdom proved sound. He was guilty of drug-dealing. We never saw or heard from him or his "respectable" appearing wife again.

The writer of *Proverbs* warned his son about co-signing, making a "pledge for another." In the event his son had already "shaken hands," sealed the deal, the father urged him to make every effort

---

260. Matthew 4:8 NIV.

261. Revelation 1:10. My literal word for word translation. Here the word "Blepo" is a frequently used word for see.

to free himself from the agreement. Barely a week after sitting in the Bible class studying *Proverbs* 6, I stood talking with an Iowa neighbor in a nearby wooded area. He had just gotten out of his tractor and walked to where I stood. A deer bolted from behind one of the trees, crashed through some brush, and disappeared out of sight in seconds. The picture presented in *Proverbs* 6:5 instantly took on new meaning for me: If you have co-signed for a debt, "Free yourself like a gazelle from the hand of a hunter."

Scenes As On A Theater Stage

In *Matthew* 24, *Mark* 13, and *Luke* 21, Jesus taught his disciples what the future held for them. Sometimes natural events, such as, earthquakes result in suffering and uncertainty. Often the insecurity and anxiety believers feel can be attributed to human causes: civil upheavals, famines, wars, and persecution. *Revelation's* scenes made similar predictions to Jesus' followers in a different time and place. The new circumstances (a pagan society that promoted emperor worship) required symbolic language. *Revelation* presents its message in pictures intended to warn, to encourage, and remain true to the Lord. Each scene that depicts a warning about suffering is followed immediately with reassurance of God's care. But we must remember to use the proper codes to interpret those depictions. What lessons do they teach? One notable one: when people defy God's laws, human suffering nearly always results. We shall next review some helpful perspectives and insights.

Revelation Basics And Definitions

Unless you come from Turkey or Greece, are a geography buff, or are an avid historian, you might not have heard of the Dodecanese. A group of twelve islands off the southwestern shores of Turkey bears that name. Control of the Dodecanese has switched many times. Though Greece now controls them, the Romans ruled those isles in the first century.[262]

The title Dodecanese might not seem familiar, but the names of two landmasses in them might chime your memory bells. The ancient wonder known as the Colossus brought fame to Rhodes, the Dodecanese's chief island. Many Bible readers recognize the name of a second island in the group — Patmos. John tells us that he wrote *Revelation* while on that thirteen-square-mile rugged islet of volcanic hills which rises from the Aegean Sea floor.

Authorities banished John to Patmos because of his public confession of faith in Jesus. He and many others suffered severe distress because they openly made Christ their King. John was an elder

---

262. The name Dodecanese comes from the Greek word for twelve (δώδεκα). The word appears, for example in Matthew 10: 1.

(presbyter) in the Ephesus church. Ephesus emerged as a principal city in western Turkey, a region the Romans called Asia Minor.

On the "Lord's Day," John was in Spirit.[263] When used as a possessive of "day," the Greek word for Lord, *kurios*, changes its form to *kuriakē*. Through gradual stages, *kuriakē* became our English word "church." You will recognize the connection in the Middle English, *chirche*, and Scottish, *kirk*, as in "Wee Kirk of the Heather."

When John referred to the Lord's Day (*kuriakē*), he likely meant the day we call Sunday. Jesus' resurrection took place on the first day. Recalling Jesus' suffering and his rising from the dead, his followers assembled on that day, to share fellowship (communion).[264] Usage of the word "church" unfortunately evolved so it now usually refers to a building dedicated to worshiping. The Greek word *ecclesia* is commonly translated into English as church. No New Testament writer ever used the term *ecclesia* to denote a building or place of worship. In first century usage, "*ecclesia*-church" referred to an assembly, a gathering of people. In fact Luke termed an assembled mob in Ephesus as "the *ecclesia*."[265]

While John was in-Spirit that first day of the week, he heard an authoritative command spoken with the sharp clarity of a trumpet. That voice ordered him to "write what you see." John received no set of written instructions as Moses did on Sinai. The Spirit directed him to write what he (saw) observed.

The Lord presented numerous visions and scenes which John described in this book we call *Revelation*. John portrayed them as he saw them. He wrote as a secretary should, not as reviewer or critic. What John penned in his book or scroll, the Lord instructed him to send to seven churches located on the nearby mainland.

John turned to see the source of the voice. He first saw seven golden lampstands.[266] The first biblical mention of a lampstand with seven lamps occurs in *Exodus* 25. Those lamps provided light in the Holy Place of the portable worship structure called the Tabernacle. What happened to the original lampstand remains a mystery.

When Solomon constructed the Temple in Jerusalem (circa 950 BC), he furnished the first permanent worship building with ten lampstands.[267] After the Babylonians destroyed that structure in 586 BC,

---

263. Verse 1:10 — In this verse, there is no article (the equivalent of "the") before the word Spirit.

264. 1 Corinthians 11:20.

265. Acts 19:32.

266. The KJV mistakenly called them "candlesticks."

267. 1 Kings 7:49.

they likely melted the pure gold lampstands and used the precious metal for other purposes.

After the Jews' return from Babylonian captivity (circa 536 BC), builders provided a new lampstand for the Temple, which accommodated seven lamps. In a vision, Zechariah the prophet saw a light stand being perpetually supplied with oil from two olive trees through pipes that stood beside the stand.[268] About 170 BC, Antiochus Epiphanes, "arrogantly entered that Temple's sanctuary and took the golden altar, the lampstand for the light, and all its utensils . . . taking them all he departed to his own land."[269]

When Herod the Great reconstructed what is known as "the Second Temple," he evidently furnished a new lampstand with seven lamp holders. That apparatus also stood short-term. In 70 AD the Romans destroyed Herod's Temple and Jerusalem. The Roman General Titus removed that lampstand and took it home to Rome. As we noted before, the Arch of Titus in the Roman Forum memorializes that event. The scenes depicted on the monument include the seven-lamp-stand menorah or candelabrum.

What did the lampstand in John's vision denote? The *NT Book of Hebrews* tells us that the earthly temple, including its furnishings and offerings, was merely a "copy and shadow of the heavenly sanctuary."[270] John's vision indicated that all the lost lampstands, including the one Titus seized and took to Rome, stood as mere models—puny ones. The prototype lampstand remained intact "in heaven." John saw Jesus standing among the seven lampstands—a vision emphasizing Jesus' continuing presence, his power, and his authority. That positive predictive-reminder surely encouraged John and first century readers of *Revelation*.

What God decides, human power cannot alter an iota. Furthermore, as Jesus reminded his apostles: *"It is not for you to know the times or dates the Father has set by his own authority."*[271] God acts in his own time, not according to human agendas and appointments. Next, John saw the "Son of Man" standing amidst the lampstands. At that time, the seven lampstands represented the seven churches of Asia. That group of churches probably signifies Jesus' beloved church throughout the eras. Jesus promised the disciples that he would be with them "to the very end of the age."[272] He oversees today's churches with

---

268. Zechariah 4:1-3.

269. 1 Maccabees 1:20-24a.

270. Hebrews 8:5 and 9:23 RSV.

271. Acts 1:7 NIV.

272. Matthew 28:20.

the same authority. Compared to Jesus, present world superpowers resemble rickety toy soldiers.

Old Testament descriptions of the Tabernacle and the later Temples tell of a one piece lampstand having seven-branches.[273] The *Revelation* 1:12 vision describes seven individual lampstands, which seem to indicate that the Lord holds each church accountable for its witness to Jesus. The scholar F.F. Bruce noted that difference.[274]

The Letters to the Seven Churches in Chapters 2 and 3 strongly make that point. That truth should cause church leaders to tremble. God holds every church accountable for its witness to the risen Jesus, for the morality of its members, and its faithfulness to the truth of God's word.

The vision of Christ in Chapter 1 gives a sampling of the various signs and keys. This and other images, descriptions, and statements in *Revelation* harmoniously string, lace, mix, and blend *OT* scenes and phrases. These include:

- The Creation (Genesis) and events in the Garden of Eden;
- The experiences of the patriarchs Abraham, Isaac, Jacob, Joseph, and his brothers;
- Israel's deliverance from Egypt, its covenants, wilderness-testing and Moses' leadership (Exodus-Deuteronomy);
- The nation's (Israel's) disobedience (Joshua, Judges, Books of Samuel, Kings, and Chronicles);
- Themes and references associated with the nation of Israel:
    - the Ark of the Covenant;
    - numerous Temple furnishings;
    - the reign of David;
    - the prophet Elijah;
    - the writing prophets, and their visions (Isaiah, Jeremiah, Ezekiel, Daniel, and most of the twelve minor prophets);
- The *Psalms* and other OT writings, such as *Job, Proverbs, Ecclesiastes*.

Revelation's symbolism derives not just from the *OT*. Sizeable segments come from Jesus' life, his direct teachings, and his Gospel

---

273. Exodus 25:31-40; Zechariah 4:1-3.

274. Bruce, F.F., Gen. Ed. *New International Bible Commentary*, Zondervan, Grand Rapids, 1979, p. 1599.

parables. We also find references in *Revelation* to the instructions and actions of his Apostles in *Acts* and in the epistles.

The Book Of Prophecy

About 600 BC, the Lord revealed mystifying phenomena to the *Old Testament* prophet Daniel. In the *Theological Dictionary of the New Testament*,[275] Gottlob Schrenk pointed to the differences between Daniel's prophecy concerning the end times and the instructions John received in *Revelation*. Daniel wanted to know when the things revealed to him would occur. The Lord allowed him to say little about the future events he saw. "But you, Daniel, roll up and seal the words of the scroll until the time of the end. Many will go here and there to increase knowledge."[276] This information troubled Daniel and he wanted to know how long before they would happen as well as their outcome. The Lord replied: "Go your way, Daniel, because the words are rolled up and sealed until the time of the end."[277]

In contrast to the instructions Daniel received, the trumpet-like voice ordered John: "Write on a scroll what you see and send it to the seven churches . . ." The word the NIV translates as "scroll" is biblion, from which our word Bible comes. Scholars discuss whether biblion here consisted of a codex (leaves bound together in modern book form) or a scroll. The context seems to signify a scroll similar to what Daniel saw.

The word translated "see" likely carries greater significance than the form of the book. In this case, "see" translates a present active participle indicating "what John was seeing and would be seeing." John saw many scenes and he described them in *Revelation*. The Lord ordered him to send the complete information to the seven churches.

The "Last Days" And The "Day Of The Lord"

Isaiah the prophet declared that "In the last days the mountain of the Lord's temple will be established as the highest of the mountains. . ."[278] Since my first preaching days, people have asked, "Are we living in the last days?" Some of them were not asking my opinion. They were telling me: "We are in the last days!" they insisted. The signs were unmistakable, they reasoned:

- Frequent earthquakes;
- Wars in the Middle-East;

---

275. TDNT, Vol. I, p. 618.

276. Daniel 12:4 NIV.

277. Ibid, v 9.

278. Isaiah 2:2 NIV.

- Moral decay;
- Various international events.

These events prove it, they opined; they clearly point to "the last days!" Decades of investigating the supposed "last day" signs and Bible prophecies, which includes consulting numerous authoritative sources, researching meanings of Hebrew and Greek terms, and examining the evidence, leads me to definite conclusions. Five words accurately describe my findings and give my answer to the question: "Are we living in the last days?"

- The first of the five words is "Yes;" (we are living in the last days).
- The second word is "No;" (we are not living in the last days).
- Words three, four, and five are "I don't know."

I admit to occasionally being evasive and flippant. By answering this way, I am being neither.

I stand by all the answers: "Yes," "No," and "I don't know." Consider them.

1. Yes — The Bible clearly says that we live in the last days. But what are the last days?

Isaiah lived and prophesied about 700 BC. By last days, he likely referred to an era introduced by Christ, the Messiah. As Isaiah looked into the future, he knew little of coming events. We "enjoy" the advantage of 2,700 years of history, which Isaiah lacked. Looking back or forward in time, it's hard to keep perspective, isn't it? If you've ever talked to kids, you know how time gets skewed. Our children used to ask me questions like, "Dad, when you were young, did people have cars?"

Gaining proper perspective on past events in the Bible presents an equal challenge. Some people carry the notion that *OT* characters such as Noah, Abraham, and Moses knew one another. That compares to our kids assuming that Christopher Columbus became one of my childhood buddies.

Recall Noah, who built the ark and saw the great flood. He and his family built that giant ship and floated for months. After the water receded and he debarked, he sacrificed animals to God. Noah planted a vineyard, made wine from his first grape crop, and got a little tipsy. G.K. Chesterton wrote these lines about Noah's experience:

"And Noah, he often said to his wife when he sat down to dine, 'I don't care where the water goes, if it doesn't get into the wine.'"

Noah preached, constructed, floated, and got drunk, but he never while inebriated, collided camels with Abraham. Their chances of knowing each other equal your or your friend's acquaintance with a Pilgrim or a Native American at the first Thanksgiving dinner. Abraham preceded Moses by an additional four hundred years.

We have the same difficulty looking ahead in time. In some respects, trying to foresee the future compares to viewing the heavens. When you look at distant objects, it's hard to tell how far apart they are. Without a telescope and science books, would you know that the stars are farther away than the planets? Look at the sky tonight and you'll see countless twinkling stars. Find two stars that appear to be close to each other. Light years (millions of miles) likely separate them.

I mentioned earlier my backpacking ventures with some Hollywood church friends. They were experienced backpackers; I was a novice. On my first trip, we hiked into California's Sierra Nevada Mountains on a challenging trail with endless switchbacks. After an arduous climb, we arrived at our first camp site. A sign told us the gap we ascended, Duck Pass, exceeded 10,000 feet in height. Near Duck Lake that first night, I prepared dinner — a freeze-dried meal to which I added water. Instructions said to boil entree for several minutes.

Cooking food in the mountains takes much longer than required at sea level, as you know. For every 550 feet of height above sea level, water's boiling point goes down one degree Fahrenheit. Our tuna casserole came to a boil about 194 degrees. I thought it might have to cook until the "Last Day" to get done.

As we sat down to dine on our not-quite-done "feast," we surveyed the blue waters of Duck Lake. Contrasted with our subpar repast, snowcapped mountains at the far end of the lake captivated us. Tomorrow, we said, we'll explore them. The next day we hiked along the edge of the lake — two, three miles — perhaps more, to the opposite end of the lake from where we camped. How near did those mountains look? They seemed almost as distant as they did the night before. Gaining perspective on faraway objects, involving time or space poses immense difficulty.

For Isaiah "last days" meant that the Messiah would come in the future. When the Messiah came, he would rule. That tells the context of Isaiah's "last days:" "The mountain of the Lord's temple will be established as chief among the mountains; it will be raised above the hills, and all nations will stream to it." When Isaiah wrote about "last days," I doubt he had in mind the "final day" or days. He meant the era of the Messiah's rule. How sure can we be of that opinion?

Isaiah was not alone in his prophecy of the "last days." About two hundred years later, the prophet Joel (2:28-32) similarly predicted those days.[279] Both Isaiah and Joel wrote about the Messiah's era, not necessarily the final days of history. Remember the events on the Day of Pentecost following Jesus' resurrection and ascension? The Holy Spirit came on the disciples with a sound resembling a windstorm. Though the Apostles spoke in their native Aramaic, people heard them in a dozen different languages. Some bystanders thought they were drunk. Peter said: Impossible! Jerusalem's bars are not even open yet. Those are not his exact words, but you get the idea. This fulfills, said Peter, what the prophet Joel predicted: "In the last days it will be," God declares, "that I will pour out my Spirit upon all flesh, and your sons and your daughters shall prophesy . . ."

Jesus promised that after his ascension, he would send the Holy Spirit. In other words, the Holy Spirit will come on people in the "last days." The "last days" do not necessarily designate the final days of history. They refer to the time of the Messiah's (Christ's) rule during which God's Spirit indwells his people.

The Book of Hebrews confirms this truth about the expression, "the last days":

> *In the past God spoke to our ancestors through the prophets at many times and in various ways, but in these last days he has spoken to us by his Son, whom he appointed heir of all things and through whom also he made the universe.*[280]

The writer of Hebrews declared that he was living in the last days 2,000 years ago. The Day of Judgment remains hence—no one but God knows how far away. By "last days," the Hebrews author meant that he and his contemporaries lived in the time of Jesus, the Messiah, not necessarily the final day.

Exceeding the importance of whether we live in the end times is the fact that "In these last days he (God) has spoken to us by his Son." The takeaway for us is: if we're not listening to Jesus and doing what he says, we err terribly. Why? Because all will be judged by the standard Jesus demonstrated. The author of *Hebrews* wrote about living in the last days 2,000 years ago. We still live in the Messiah's era. During these "last days," he is fully in charge.[281]

2. Consider my second answer—"**No.**"

---

279. Acts 2:17 NRSV. Joel used the term "afterward," but the Apostle Peter explained that Joel was referring to the last days.

280. Hebrews 1:1, 2 NIV.

281. For a fuller discussion of last days, you may want to consult the *Theological Dictionary of the New Testament*, Vol. II, pp. 943-953, articles by Gerhard Delling.

Many preachers make a living — some have gotten rich — convincing people that we live in the last days. They rouse people to anxiety and uneasiness. False preachers predicted similarly in the Apostles' time. Christians were confused about the "Day of the Lord," Jesus' Second Coming. When people think Jesus' return imminent, they get agitated and do crazy things. For that reason, Paul wrote to the Thessalonian church. Thinking that event had already come, many Thessalonians fretted that they had missed out. Some first century Christians there evidently quit their jobs and lived off of hard working brothers and sisters. In his next letter, Paul bluntly cautioned: "Such people we command and urge in the Lord Jesus Christ to settle down and earn the food they eat."[282]

Paul informed them of this principle in his first epistle:

> *Make it your ambition to lead a quiet life: You should mind your own business and work with your hands, just as we told you, so that your daily life may win the respect of outsiders and so that you will not be dependent on anybody.*[283]

Paul wanted the Thessalonians to trust Jesus, not be unsettled or agitated by false reports. The expression "settle down" refers to being tranquil or at peace from within. Twenty-first century people seek temporary escape. They take pills, eat, drink, gamble, escape into video games, and brain-numbing music. When their short fixes end, their anxiety worsens.

Lasting peace and tranquility come from trusting Jesus' promises. The truth of his word calms our fears. We work and take care of our day-to-day responsibilities, becoming increasingly confident that the Lord knows the right way. Through the centuries, numerous preachers and prophets unnecessarily troubled people by predicting the Last Days. They pointed to all the "sure" signs:

- Earthquakes — they constantly take place;
- Wars — they are repeatedly waged;
- Trouble in the Middle-East – It's never ending.

Those prophets lie silenced in the graves.
The world continues.
Pardon the pun but they were all dead wrong about the "last days." They all belonged in the "No!" category. They wait for the Last Day — the Day of Judgment.

---

282. 2 Thessalonians 3:12. NIV.

283. 1 Thessalonians 4:11, 12 NIV.

Now, about the last three words of our previous answer concerning living in the last days.

3. The "**I don't know**" part needs only brief comment. Jesus said, "No man knows the day or the hour." When he lived here in the flesh, he did not even know the time of his return. We do not know whether we live in the very last days because Jesus told his disciples: "So you also must be ready because the Son of Man will come at an hour when you do not expect him."[284] His arrival will occur when no one anticipates him. Those who busily do the Lord's work will be joyful at his return time. If on your job you conscientiously fulfill your assignments, you will be happy to see the boss any time he or she shows. If you have coworkers who cheat, steal, and abuse the other employees, you will be especially happy when the boss arrives.

> *Who then is the faithful and wise servant, whom the master has put in charge of the servants in his household to give them their food at the proper time? It will be good for that servant whose master finds him doing so when he returns.*[285]

We do not know when the last day will come. Those who work and serve contentedly in the Lord need not fear. It will be a glad day. As the early Christians yearned:
"Come, Lord Jesus!"

---

284. Matthew 24:44 NIV.

285. Ibid, 45, 46.

Chapter 7

Basics For Our Interpretive View

False prophets continually try to predict historical events based on *Revelation's* symbolic narrative. Failure inevitably exposes them. Hoping to gain an economic advantage in the 1950s, several western nations began forming the European Common Market. Many *Revelation* interpreters warned that the venture signified grim fulfillment of a "prophecy" in Chapter 17. This graphic section features a woman sitting on a scarlet, seven-headed, ten horned beast covered with blasphemous names (v. 12).

Those analysts claimed Chapter 17 foretells an eventual block of ten nations that will cooperate and coordinate as one. Many Continuous-Historical View supporters considered the ECM a literal fulfillment of 17:12: *"The ten horns you saw are ten kings who have not yet received a kingdom, but who for one hour will receive authority as kings along with the beast" (NIV)*. These conjecturers produced a spate of books that prophesied doom once the Common Market reached a dreaded ten-nation total. Anxious acquaintances of mine purchased those tomes and urged me to read them.

Subsequent events prove such prognostications balderdash. That economic league of countries never attained the power the "prophets" fretfully presaged. In the teens of the twenty-first century, the much feared ten-nation economic league eventually grew to twenty-plus members. So much for the significance of the "ten-king-fulfillment." Not only that, though the European Union (as it is now called) gained popularity, the EU never attained the world domination, which distressed those twentieth-century "prophets."

Humans foretell at great risk. Successive generations continue to prove that only one faithful, true witness exists—Jesus, the Son of God. He correctly predicted: "False prophets will appear... to deceive if possible, even the elect."[286] If God allows history to continue, new misguided diviners will arise from the previous pseudo-prophetic stubble.

Revelation forecasts wars, but foretells no specific conflicts, except the continuous battle against Satan, evil, and death. Aside from the fall of Rome and the Last Day (Judgment), we do not attempt to connect *Revelation's* scenes with historical events. We shall later explain how we understand the prophecy concerning Rome's fall.

---

286. Matthew 24: 24 NIV. The Common Market is currently known as the European Union.

We previously noted how early disciples of Jesus endured **chaotic** conditions. **Christ's** followers faced Roman government disfavor and aggression, which influential trade guilds, and hostile Jewish leaders helped generate. In addition to those challenges, intense greed and blatant moral laxness in their societies **conflicted** many believers. In the region the Romans called Asia, Christ's people endured tribulation and temptation. In the midst of the ensuing **chaos** and uncertainty, God's Holy Spirit revealed the risen Jesus, his true and faithful witness, to the Seven Churches of Asia.[287]

The Holy Spirit Designed *Revelation* To Encourage First Century Believers

Revelation came about because our forefathers in the faith needed cautions, reassurances, guidance, and support. In that sense, one can label *Revelation* a Preterist or past book.[288] The Spirit knew, of course, that most of the target audience would persevere and produce new generations of believers. The Lord also foresaw as far as two millennia later, and perhaps beyond, Christians would need "substance" for their hope.

Immoral pagan societies typically exert intense, corrupt pressures on godly people. About 1800 BC, Sodom's climate and its apparent healthy economic conditions appealed to Abraham's nephew Lot. His disregard for the city's rampant depravity led to Lot's undoing.[289]

During the early fifties of the first century, government policies created trouble for unmarried Christians in Corinth (now Greece). The Holy Spirit moved the Apostle Paul to write the following to those apparently young believers: "Because of the present crisis, I think it is good for a man to remain as he is."[290] To what conditions did Paul evidently refer?

For decades prior, Israel suffered severe unrest. When Jesus arduously made his way to Calvary:

> *A large number of people followed him, including women who mourned and wailed for him. Jesus turned and said to them, "Daughters of Jerusalem, do not weep for me; weep for yourselves and for your children. For the time will come when you will say, 'Blessed are the childless women, the wombs that never bore and the breasts that never nursed!'*

---

287. Present western Turkey.

288. Some Preterists believe that everything predicted in The Apocalypse has already been fulfilled. We do not subscribe to that view.

289. Genesis 13 tells the reasons for Lot's choice of residence in Sodom; Genesis 14, 18, 19, and 2 Peter 2:4-10 relate Lot's conflict.

290. 1 Corinthians 7:26 NIV.

> Then 'they will say to the mountains, "Fall on us!" and to the hills, "Cover us!"
>
> For if people do these things when the tree is green, what will happen when it is dry?"[291]

Jesus foretold the miserable circumstances his contemporaries' seditious actions were creating. He advised them to forgive the Roman occupation troops.[292] Instead, defiant activities increased. In his *Wars of the Jews*, Josephus recorded Israel's stubborn resistance.

Before the rebellion became open and widespread, Claudius (41-54) expelled all Jews from Rome. He also reprimanded some Jewish agitators in Alexandria (now Egypt). Claudius's actions against Jews and subsequently Christians brought calamitous effects for believers. The Emperor's decree severely increased instability and uncertainty for Jews not only in Israel, but throughout the Roman Empire. Some experts question whether Claudius gave his order with Christians in mind. Yet because the majority of Christians then came from a Jewish background, they felt the edict's effects.[293]

To Corinthian believers contemplating marriage, Paul gave timely advice. He seemed to say that under the current circumstances, young people would save themselves considerable misery if they delayed marrying and having children. Dire conditions for Christians didn't soon ease. Nero's (54-68 AD) later policies produced appalling effects. In fact, Roman government disapproval remained in place until the early fourth century.

As Adam and Eve famously demonstrated, tests and enticements arise even in quiet, secluded gardens. Bible and secular history confirm that lustful lures exist in rural areas; they multiply, however, in major cities. Inhabitants of the port city Corinth rampantly courted, coaxed, and harassed Christians. During the first century AD, Jezebel-style inducements enticed believers in Thyatira.[294] Greed, pride, and the need for status caused many in the Laodicean church to stumble. Succumbing to those appeals negatively affected the Ephesus church, too.[295]

In Second Corinthians, Paul advised believers:

---

291. Luke 23:27-31 NIV.

292. Jesus suggested that when Roman soldiers forced them to carry their luggage one mile, his contemporaries should cheerfully offer to carry the burden an extra mile. See Matthew 5:41.

293. The disciples, Aquila and Priscilla left Rome because of Claudius's order. See Acts 18:1, 2.

294. I Kings 16:31; 21:25; 2 Kings 9:7 give examples of Jezebel's evil influence.

295. These were three of Revelation's seven cities.

> *"Therefore, Come out from them and be separate", says the Lord. "Touch no unclean thing, and I will receive you." And, "I will be a Father to you, and you will be my sons and daughters," says the Lord Almighty.*296

Paul quoted these lines from the prophet Isaiah (eighth century BC). A century after Isaiah, the prophet Jeremiah likewise cautioned his countrymen about conforming to Babylonian morality. Similar warnings reverberate in *Revelation* 18: 4: *"'Come out of her my people,' so that you will not share in her sins, so that you will not receive any of her plagues. . ."*297 The Lord and Savior Jesus held those past people (first century believers) accountable. He also reckons us and future generations responsible for our actions.

The conduct of our lives matters. Godliness majors as a theme in every *Bible* book. Many present believers deceive themselves into thinking that "enlightened" modern folks know better than their "ancient" counterparts. The *Bible* warns against being misled by that lie. *Revelation* **convicted** readers of their waywardness. Our holy God required past folks to live virtuously. He demands holiness from present and future people. On the Judgment Day, all will account to Him.

Paul warned young Corinthians about marriage, not because he hated women, as some allege. He foresaw that the coming societal turmoil would create such instability that couples would be bringing children into dangerous circumstances. Had 1930s European Jewish leaders foreseen what Nazi Germany would later do to their children, they would have undoubtedly warned young couples not to marry and to form families. Young Ukrainians and possibly citizens of other southern European countries may now face similar challenges.

Revelation's Focus On The Future

Revelation's storyline continually moves readers in the direction of a well-planned conclusion. As *Revelation* 10:5-7 NIV illustrates, history progresses toward a Divinely-planned **finale** (Greek, τέλος pronounced telos):

> *Then the angel I had seen standing on the sea and on the land raised his right hand to heaven. And he swore by him who lives for ever and ever, who created the heavens and all that is in them, the earth and all that is in it, and the sea and all that is in it, and said, "There will be no more delay! But in the days when the seventh angel is about to*

---

296. 2 Corinthians 6: 17, 18 NIV. The quotation marks in this NIV passage seem questionable.

297. NIV — The original warnings and descriptions of particular sins can be found in Leviticus 18, 19. God's laws of morality have never changed, relaxed, or evolved. See Acts 15:1-29 and Matthew 15:1-20.

sound his trumpet, the mystery of God will be accomplished,[298] *just as he announced to his servants the prophets."*

The *Genesis* to *Revelation* narrative traces the Lord's past and present actions in moving history toward the completeness God intends. "Telos" and related terms convey the concept of maturing, growing, and transpiring to a certain culmination, which only our Creator foresees. No human effort can derail, inhibit, or hinder his design.[299]

Jesus' simile of the vine and the branches clearly shows that he expects results from us.[300] When we sow beans in the spring soil, we envisage those seeds germinating and producing green plants, which will yield pods. God advances history in the direction of a similar goal. He judges us on our "fruit" production.

The Apocalypse deals with the past and foresees the future that God arranged for his **Creation**. Angels warn of Judgment and punishment for those who alter, modify, or revise God's word. Encouragement to endure resounds. *Revelation's* last chapters describe Heaven or Paradise and the joy of entering the high-walled New Jerusalem.

When Jesus sent the Twelve on their first evangelistic effort, he forewarned them of fierce opposition. Note how he urged them to hang tough: *"You will be hated by everyone because of me, but the one who stands firm to the end will be saved."*[301] The word translated "end" is that same term, telos. Every one of the Seven Churches received a similar warning-encouragement: "To the one who overcomes."[302] Unless we persevere, we shall not enjoy God's harvest, when he brings all things to their completion or finish.

Revelation's Strong Symbolism And The Antichrist

The Spirit concealed *Revelation's* scenes in symbolism. As we discussed, this figurative language **confounded** hostile authorities. Nonetheless some of the letter's expressions spoke quite directly. Non-believers might not recognize the straightforward speech, but Jesus' first century followers probably could not miss his references. One quick ex-

---

298. The words "accomplished" NIV, "finished" KJV, fulfilled, NRSV are translations of a verbal, passive past tense form of telos, indicating that God makes all happen according to his purposes.

299. Understand that my reference here to "past and present" applies to what God has revealed about himself in Scripture. I intimate nothing beyond that.

300. John 15:1-17.

301. Matthew 10:22 NIV. The NIV undergoes constant revision, so later editions will vary from earlier ones.

302. Compare the letters in Revelation 2 and 3.

ample: In *Revelation* 2:2, the Lord commended the Ephesus church: "I know that you cannot tolerate wicked people, that you have tested those who claim to be apostles but are not, and have found them false," (NIV). Probably writing from Ephesus, John, the Apostle, earlier warned God's churches:

> *Test the spirits to see whether they are from God, because many false prophets have gone out into the world. This is how you can recognize the Spirit of God: Every spirit that acknowledges that Jesus Christ has come in the flesh is from God, but every spirit that does not acknowledge Jesus is not from God. This is the spirit of the antichrist, which you have heard is coming and even now is already in the world.*[303]

Area church leaders likely knew what John meant about testing. John clearly identified the spirit of the antichrist—anyone who denies that Messiah Jesus came in human flesh. Shortly after the first century, many "believers" and church leaders began distorting the warnings. False prophets still mislead God's people. Pseudo-prophets continually alarm the church with silly warped messages about the identity of the antichrist. The "antichrist" refers to false teaching, not the ruthless, lawless, rebellious ruler "who sets himself up in God's temple, proclaiming himself to be God."[304]

Pondering the Christ-Messiah: *"The revelation of Jesus Christ, which God gave him to show his servants what must soon take place."*

The opening sentence of *Revelation* states intention and content. The book begins as a narrator might announce what will transpire on stage as a play opens. *Revelation* opens the curtain on Jesus, but not just the historical Jesus of Nazareth. Words two and three in Greek are "Jesus Christ." Christ indicates not a family name or simply a title. As many believers know, Christ is the Greek equivalent of the *Old Testament* (Hebrew term) Messiah, an anointed one.

Revelation's letters and visions reveal that the Christ-Messiah is the Lamb who was slain. He is **Alpha and the Omega, First and Last, Beginning and End**, expressions which the *OT* uses to describe only God. *Revelation* reveals the Divine Messiah-Christ, who controls the Cosmos and rules history. All creation will be completed-fulfilled in him. H.B. Swete aptly stated, "The book is a Divine revelation of which Jesus is the recipient and the giver."[305]

---

303. 1 John 4:1b-3 NIV.

304. 2 Thessalonians 2:4 NIV. For the context, see verses 2:1-12.

305. *The Apocalypse Of St.John,* Henry Barclay Swete, MacMillan and Co. London, 1909, p. 1.

The term translated "show" (verse 1) often indicates a pointing to or and exhibiting of something.[306] The imperative mood of "show" (δείξαι) stresses the importance of the "displaying." *Revelation* introduces Jesus Christ as the great protagonist, the lone luminary of the cosmic show. At his Second Coming, Jesus will completely disclose his identity-*"'Look, he is coming with the clouds,' and 'every eye will see him, even those who pierced him' and all peoples of the earth 'will mourn because of him.' So shall it be! Amen."*[307] When history's final curtain closes, creation will acknowledge, appreciate, and applaud him. Those not joining in admiration will whimper and remorsefully lament.

We cannot overemphasize the *OT's* importance as a key to understanding *Revelation's* code. Both Eb. Nestle and H.B. Swete remarked on use of the expression "take place," (Greek - δεί γενέσθαι), in the *Septuagint* version of Daniel 2:28.[308] In case you forgot, this was the popular Greek translation of the *Old Testament* in Jesus' time. Many *New Testament* authors quoted from the *Septuagint,* also known as the *LXX*.

King Nebuchadnezzar wanted his wise men to interpret a strange dream that disrupted his sleep one night. His demand created a scary future for the wise men because the king couldn't recall what he dreamt. No prophet can interpret a dream without knowing the details of the dream, they protested. The monarch accused them of trying to buy time and he scheduled the execution of his whole advisory board, which included Daniel and the famous Shadrach, Meshach, and Abednego. *Daniel* 2:28 records the interpretation the Lord revealed to Daniel. As the English translation of the *Septuagint* reads:

> *There is a God in heaven revealing mysteries and he has made known to king Nabuchodonosor what things* <u>must come to pass</u> *(Greek - δεί γενέσθαι) in the last days.*

The HOLY SCRIPTURES according to the Masoretic (Hebrew) *Text* renders the phrase "what shall be."[309] Those ancient translators who produced the Greek *Septuagint* used the phrase: "must come to pass." Thus Hebrew scholars of both ancient and modern times agree that God's

---

306. For a fuller discussion of the word, see the term δείκνυμι in *The Theological Dictionary of the New Testament,* J. D. Douglas, General Editor, Volume II, pp. 25-33, article by Heinrich Schlier.

307. Revelation 1:7 NIV.

308. *The Septuagint with Apocrypha: Greek and English,* Sir Lancelot C.L. Brenton, Hendrickson Publishers, Peabody MA, 1986, p. 1051. The word translated "revealing" is a form of *apocalypse,* ἀποκαλύπτων.

309. *The HOLY SCRIPTURES according to the Masoretic* (Hebrew) *Text,* The Jewish Publication Society of America, Philadelphia, 5707-1947, p.1009.

designs always reach fulfillment. As builders shape and construct according to blueprints, the future of the Cosmos will result precisely as God purposed in the Creation. "In the beginning God created." his telos (finish) will come about as he wills.

How God's Kingdom Grows

We should not overlook the context of the expression "take place." In the above *Book of Daniel* passage, Babylon's King Nebuchadnezzar's dream involved an awesome statue, which a mighty, earth-sized rock ultimately destroyed. With God's help, Daniel interpreted the king's dream: Nebuchadnezzar's kingdom would fall to a second kingdom, which would fall to a third, which would eventually be replaced by an indestructible kingdom. That fourth dominion Daniel understood as God's kingdom, which Jesus presently rules.

As Christ demonstrated during his thirty some years on this planet, the kingdom of God is "within you."[310] Wherever human beings allow God's principles to fully guide them, the Kingdom exists. The Kingdom began its development in Christ and grows each time a person completely commits her/his life to God in Christ. When Daniel prophesied about coming world events, human decisions, and actions, he indicated God's plan as already in motion.

We cannot assume from the phrase, "what must soon take place," that everything prophesied would immediately occur. Jesus compared the Kingdom to the way yeast works in bread dough. As soon as the baker mixes the yeast with the other ingredients, the process begins. To a hungry soul, full leavening seems to take forever. Impatience, disobedience, and failure to understand God's playbook and plans gave rise to this perplexing book *Revelation*. Daniel fixed no dates; neither did Jesus nor any *New Testament* writer predict precise day, month, and year for the Kingdom's beginning. The inspired writers mentioned types of events, but specified no times for their occurrence.[311]

Attention, Servants Of God!

One additional word in *Revelation* 1:1 deserves attention. While speaking of the Kingdom, Jesus frequently compared us world inhabitants to **servants**:

> *He went on to tell them a parable, because he was near Jerusalem*

---

310. Luke 17:21 See *The New Testament: A Translation in the Language of the People*, by Charles Williams, Moody Press, Chicago, 1950.

311. Israel stayed a predicted seventy years in captivity and Jesus spent three days in the grave, (cf Daniel 9:2 Matthew 20: 19). To my knowledge, no date was prophesied for the beginning of either event.

> *and the people thought that the kingdom of God was going to appear at once. He said: "A man of noble birth went to a distant country to have himself appointed king and then to return. So he called ten of his servants and gave them ten minas. 'Put this money to work,' he said, 'until I come back.'*
>
> *"But his subjects hated him and sent a delegation after him to say, 'We don't want this man to be our king.'*
>
> *"He was made king, however, and returned home. Then he sent for the servants to whom he had given the money, in order to find out what they had gained with it.*
>
> *"The first one came and said, 'Sir, your mina has earned ten more.'*
>
> *'Well done, my good servant!' his master replied. 'Because you have been trustworthy in a very small matter, take charge of ten cities.'"* [312]

This parable and Jesus' other life-stories reflect a vital truth: we reside on this planet as temporary, undeserving tenants. Through our Creator's generosity and by his mercy, we live on his property. We servants rarely thank him. We seldom appreciate or comprehend the tests and challenges he arranges to prove our loving allegiance and gratitude. Most of our fellow tenants practice never-ending disenchantment with him and displeasure with others. We all struggle to let God completely control us. Yet when we permit him to fully rule us, we begin to realize the marvelous advantages he furnishes. Life improves infinitely when we acknowledge our condition and submit as servants to God's rule in Christ.

Other Vital Observations On The *Apocalypse-Revelation*

The Gospels record how the Apostles and other contemporaries witnessed Jesus successfully handling life-situations. *Revelation* shows him controlling not only present, but coming events. The book states these truths in language recognizable to believers but **confounding** to those not acquainted with God's word. In *Revelation*, letters, messenger-angels, and visions present Christ in various roles, situations, and achievements.

The prologue (vv.1-3) tells the benefits of reading, hearing and taking the writing to heart "because the time is near." The word translated time does not suggest chronological time, but the right moment. Our **Creator** acts according to his purposes. Wise teachers and professors usually understand the appropriate times to test their students.

---

312. Luke 19: 11b-16 NIV.

The chosen moments often catch pupils unprepared, especially those who pay scant attention to the instructors.

To a Roman court prosecutor, the Prologue possibly sounded as if the writer might openly confess treason. Yet the subsequent language likely seemed nonsensical:

> *John,*
> *To the seven churches in the province of Asia: Grace and peace to you from him who is, and who was, and who is to come, and from the seven spirits before his throne, and from Jesus Christ, who is the faithful witness, the firstborn from the dead, and the ruler of the kings of the earth. To him who loves us and has freed us from our sins by his blood, and has made us to be a kingdom and priests to serve his God and Father—to him be glory and power for ever and ever! Amen.*
>
> *"'Look, he is coming with the clouds," and "every eye will see him, even those who pierced him"; and all peoples on earth '"will mourn because of him." So shall it be! Amen. 'I am the Alpha and the Omega,' says the Lord God, 'who is, and who was, and who is to come, the Almighty.'"*[313]

Multiple symbols appear in this greeting that we shall later discuss in greater detail. For now, note how the sentence structure reveals the Godhead:

- **God,** *"who is, and who was, and who is to come."*
- **The Holy Spirit,** *"the seven spirits before his throne."*
- **The Son,** *"Jesus Christ, who is the faithful witness, the firstborn from the dead, and the ruler of the kings of the earth."*

The sentence also reveals seven divine characteristics:
"Who is,
who was,
who is to come.
(three phrases)

"Seven spirits before his throne." (one phrase)

"Faithful witness,"
"firstborn from the dead"
"ruler of the kings of the earth."
(three phrases)

---

313. 1:4-7 NIV

Sevens dominate the book. Seven phrases refer here to the Godhead. More than fifty "sevens" appear in the book. Seven often describes God's attributes and his purposes. Many have noted the grammatical inconsistency in the phrase: *"who is, and who was, and who is to come."* "Is" and "was" are forms of the verb "to be." "Is to come" indicates change to a different verb. One would expect the phrase to read "and shall be." [314] The warning of accountability prevails over grammatical form. Thus the admonitions:

> *Look, he is coming with the clouds, and every eye will see him, even those who pierced him; and all peoples on earth will mourn because of him. So shall it be! Amen. "I am the Alpha and the Omega," says the Lord God, "who is, and who was, and who is to come, the Almighty."*[315]

Almighty is Pantocrator. The **Creator**-ruler of the Cosmos makes no empty threats. All will mourn when the Christ–Messiah becomes visible. The Spirit inextricably links the Messiah-Christ to God. Through his life, death and resurrection, the Messiah confirmed himself as God's true and faithful witness. Only he successfully defeated death. He remains sovereign over all earth's rulers.

> *I, John, your brother and companion in the suffering and kingdom and patient endurance that are ours in Jesus, was on the island of Patmos because of the word of God and the testimony of Jesus. On the Lord's Day I was in the Spirit, and I heard behind me a loud voice like a trumpet, which said: "Write on a scroll what you see and send it to the seven churches: to Ephesus, Smyrna, Pergamum, Thyatira, Sardis, Philadelphia, and Laodicea."*
>
> *I turned around to see the voice that was speaking to me. And when I turned I saw seven golden lampstands, and among the lampstands was someone like a son of man, dressed in a robe reaching down to his feet and with a golden sash around his chest. The hair on his head was white like wool, as white as snow, and his eyes were like blazing fire. His feet were like bronze glowing in a furnace, and his voice was like the sound of rushing waters. In his right hand he held seven stars, and coming out of his mouth was a sharp, double-edged sword. His face was like the sun shining in all its brilliance.*
>
> *When I saw him, I fell at his feet as though dead. Then he placed*

---

314. Most Revelation's original readers were probably familiar with the Aramaic language, which many Jews spoke in Jesus' time. These irregular grammar sections are often referred to as solecisms, to "speak incorrectly." Some refer to these peculiarities as Aramaicisms.

315. 1:7, 8 NIV.

> his right hand on me and said: "Do not be afraid. I am the First and the Last. I am the Living One; I was dead, and now look, I am alive for ever and ever! And I hold the keys of death and Hades. Write, therefore, what you have seen, what is now and what will take place later. The mystery of the seven stars that you saw in my right hand and of the seven golden lampstands is this: The seven stars are the angels of the seven churches, and the seven lampstands are the seven churches."[316]

As the Spirit assigned him, Secretary John addressed the letter to seven churches. John revealed his location (Patmos Island). he also identified himself as *"your brother and companion in the suffering and kingdom and patient endurance."* The NIV translates the Greek word *thlipsis* (θλίψει) as suffering. A definite article precedes suffering. God's people suffer constant tribulation. *Thlipsis* began when Jesus first came to this planet. God's people endure *thlipsis* until Jesus appears to judge all the earth's inhabitants. That a great tribulation will precede the final day rests on a vast myth false prophets perpetuate.

John also wrote that he was a companion in the kingdom. Concerning what Jesus accomplished for us, Paul earlier assured the church in Colossae:

> For he has rescued us from the dominion of darkness and brought us into the kingdom of the Son he loves, in whom we have redemption, the forgiveness of sins.[317]

When we repent and accept Christ's forgiveness, we become the redeemed, who enjoy the honor of citizenship in God's Kingdom. For those who renounce greed, lust, power, and other selfish enticements, giving total allegiance to King Jesus, the Kingdom becomes present reality. The kingdom will not be complete, of course, until the King gathers all the elect home.

Revelation 1 reveals additional truth pertinent to our interpretive theory. When John heard the trumpet-like voice, he turned to see God's Messiah in other symbolic settings. For John's contemporaries, lampstands well-known in the *Old Testament* took on new connotations. During his ministry, Christ repeatedly reminded his disciples to spread the light of his message. Jesus expected the seven churches to carry out this vital assignment. In a larger context, the lampstands likely represent all God's churches for all time. Because new generations continue to be born, Jesus' disciples must continually advance his message to all their contemporaries. The one *"like the son of man"*

---

316. Revelation 1: 9-20 NIV

317. Colossians 1:13 NIV.

among the lampstands reveals Christ's intimacy with his churches. He remains with us "always, to the very end of the age."[318] These images hark back to visions the prophets Ezekiel and Daniel saw six hundred years prior.[319]

"*Out of his mouth came a sharp, double-edged sword.*" This phrase described the word of God in *Hebrews* 4:12. The Messiah-Christ stands alone as First and Last (as God). He holds the keys of death and Hades, as only God does. He orders John to write: "*What you have seen, what is now and what will take place later.*" Note the similarity of this sequence of phrases to the one which describes God: "*who is, and who was, and who is to come.*" Jesus, the Son of Man, holds the stars in his right hand. He unmistakably identifies those stars as "the angels-messengers" of the seven churches.

The Letters To The Seven Churches

We can trace the existence of *Revelation's* seven churches to the evangelism of Paul and his coworkers. The author of *Acts* recorded that "all the Jews and Greeks in the province of Asia heard the word of the Lord."[320] On his third missionary journey, Paul spent about three years in Ephesus, the leading city in the area. On his return trip from Macedonia and Achaia (Greece), he met with the Ephesus church elders at nearby Miletus.[321] Paul foresaw that "savage wolves" would attempt to destroy the church and persons from their own numbers would arise and distort the truth. Colossae and Laodicea lay about a hundred miles east of Ephesus. The Apostle corresponded with churches in both cities requesting them to share their letters with each other. The letter to Colossae is preserved in the *NT*. The Laodicean church received harsh criticism in *Revelation's* seventh letter;[322] Colossae got no mention.

Years after Paul met with the Ephesus elders, he sent his understudy Timothy to the city. He gave Timothy the challenge of dealing with false teachers and other opponents of God's truth. Paul wrote two letters (1 and 2 *Timothy*) to the young preacher outlining church organization, doctrines, and the behavior expected of believers. Only a minority of present day churches follow the prudent guidelines Paul supplied in his correspondence with Timothy, and also Titus, who at the time worked on the island of Crete. The failure of modern church

---

318. Matthew 28:20 NIV.

319. See Ezekiel 1: 26; 8:2; 9:2; Daniel 7:9; 10:4-6.

320. Acts 19:10 NIV.

321. See Acts 18, 19.

322. Revelation 3:14-22.

leaders to comply with Scriptural expectations should make them tremble.

The same types of symbols appear in *Revelation's* letters to the Seven Churches as in other parts of the book. The Lord candidly directed commendation and condemnation of each church. Each letter shows intimate familiarity with the targeted city and believers in it. Readers acquainted with the *OT* can easily decipher most of the Lord's messages to Ephesus, Smyrna, Thyatira, and so on. As Charles Erdman observed, each letter follows the same seven-part outline. In most letters, author Jesus shared some aspect by which he revealed himself in Chapter 1. In the Ephesus letter, the Lord "holds the seven stars in his right hand and walks among the seven golden lampstands." Compare this characterization with the description in the Chapter 1 vision:

> *The mystery of the seven stars that you saw in my right hand and of the seven golden lampstands is this: The seven stars are the angels of the seven churches, and the seven lampstands are the seven churches.*

In all seven letters, the Lord declares: *"He who has an ear, let him hear what the Spirit says to the churches."* Jesus made similar appeals in the Gospels.[323] Concluding words of all seven of *Revelation's* letters include a promise to the one who overcomes, which translates the Greek word for victory in participle form. H.B. Swete observed: "the present participle here is timeless."[324] That term (*nike*) refers to a person who is victorious or who conquers. In this case, the word denotes those who endure to the end by trusting Christ, God's true, faithful witness.

Because others have detailed numerous aspects of the seven letters, we shall include only information in them necessary to explaining our interpretive view. If God permits, we shall however accompany this volume with sermons that deal with the Seven Churches and will include sermons on the contents of *Revelation* 4 and 5.

---

323. For example Matthew 11:15 and 13:9.

324. H.B. Swete, *The Apocalypse of St. John*, p. 29 (νικῶντι).

Chapter 8
The Interpretive View On Stage

Reviewing The Keys
We promised a unique, plausible perspective of *Revelation*. This view overcomes the limitations of the four traditional interpretations. The keys we previously presented all come into play: the *Old Testament*; numbers; music; Jesus' direct teachings and his Gospel parables; his death, burial, resurrection, and ascension; the *New Testament* Epistles, particularly *Ephesians* and *Colossians*. As we shall show, the Holy Spirit symbolically used even baptism.

The Stage Is Set And The Curtain Opens
Whether portrayed on stage or screen, most theatrical productions fix on past events. Fairy tales, tragedies, mysteries, or comedies predominantly base their narratives on bygone occurrences and experiences. By their very nature, lampoons, satires, and spoofs mock previous events and the characters involved. *Revelation* makes use of historical figures and incidents. Yet *Revelation* often recasts known symbols and facts from past happenings to foretell a course of affairs to soon unfold. *The Apocalypse* pulls the curtain on forthcoming events.

The Lord leaves no unfinished business. He alone knows the future and accomplishes all his plans. He concludes courses of action only he foresees. Thus *Revelation* 21:5, 6 read:

> And he who sits on the throne said, "Behold, I am making all things new." And he said, "Write, for these words are faithful and true." Then he said to me, "It is done. I am the Alpha and the Omega, the beginning and the end. I will give to the one who thirsts from the spring of the water of life without cost."325

The Apocalypse's opening states the production's purpose:

> The revelation of Jesus Christ, which God gave him to show to his bond-servants, the things which must soon take place; and he sent and communicated it by his angel to his bond-servant John.

This drama's playwright possesses qualifications beyond those of all history's dramatists combined. The Cosmos Creator and Controller

---

325. (NASB) Greek ἡ ἀρχὴ καὶ τὸ τέλος referring to Jesus. Both John's gospel (verse 1) and John's First Epistle (verse 1) use the term ἀρχὴ beginning. I think it logical to infer that what God created or began in the beginning he will bring to the conclusion telos (τέλος); the end or fulfillment he originally foresaw. We win only by working according to God's will in Christ.

scripted the entire spectacle. *Revelation's* multi-scene drama presents numerous symbolic-prophetic vistas. A narrator explains the purpose, makes the basic message clear, and identifies the target audience. Co-hosts (commanding voices and mighty angels) introduce varied subsequent sites, sights, and spectacles. God guides this host of components toward his preset finish.

About The Play

Some might call *The Apocalypse* a "morality play," but the actors do not spout platitudes or typical Sunday morning clichés. Bizarre, frightening motifs and disgusting signs come into view. We already explained reasons for these peculiar metaphors. The drama addresses leaders and members of seven churches that likely represent God's worshipers of all eras and places. The selected churches face numerous immediate trials: intense persecution; temptations to gross immorality and greed; societal rejection; difficult-to-identify false teachers; and pseudo believers. In addition, loss of focus and hostile human authorities continually challenge believers. During his earthly tenure, Jesus met and won victories over all evil forces. Though destined to encounter formidable tests, we participants win by resolutely trusting God and persistently modeling Jesus' lifestyle. To receive their victory awards, members of the seven churches must endure faithfully with Christ to the finish.

As *Revelation's* first chapter affirms, Jesus the Lamb walks among them and he intimately knows each congregation's, and each individual's challenges, weaknesses, and strengths. He remains alert to their needs. Jesus also requires watchfulness. In the same way he ascended, he will suddenly return with the clouds.[326] "When the Son of Man comes, will he find faith on earth?"[327]

Revelation's Format And Style

As occurs in some plays, *Revelation's* narrators (messengers-angels) appear on stage to announce and describe the settings. Scenes in the developing plot portray various world conditions and how the "players" react to them. *Revelation* 6's unfolding sections resemble the previews Jesus gave the disciples in *Matthew* 24 (also *Mark* 13 and *Luke* 21). Jesus counselled the Twelve to expect wars, earthquakes, famine, suffering, and human hostility.

Revelation's successive visions or scenes do not necessarily predict events chronologically. Because they fail to recognize the numerous simultaneous scenes *The Apocalypse* depicts, interpreters often stray. To explain, I offer the following:

---

326. Revelation 1:7; Matthew 24:30; Acts 1:9-11; 1 Thessalonians 4:13-18.

327. Luke 18:8 NASB.

First, plays, movies, TV dramas, and so on often present simultaneous events in the same act. For instance, audiences might see a scene with characters said to be in a certain location occurring on Saturday, at one PM. In the next scene, characters in another part of the city, or perhaps miles distant, deal with events at the same moment as those in the previous scene (Saturday, at one PM).[328] As we shall show, *Revelation* presents numerous concurrent happenings.

That *Revelation* might portray events in this manner apparently does not occur to many interpreters. We earlier treated how the writer of *1 Samuel* movingly dealt with simultaneous events in an incident that involved David, the wealthy but churlish Nabal, and Nabal's astute wife Abigail.[329] The Bible gives other memorable examples of coinciding events. In Genesis 18, three strangers arrived at Abraham's tent one sweltering day. Only after Abraham and Sarah welcomed them and fed the trio did the old patriarch learn their identities. The lead stranger was the Angel of the Lord; the other two, "ordinary" angels. While Sarah eavesdropped, the Angel of the Lord (God) informed Abraham that Sarah would finally become pregnant. Concurrent to his visit with the couple, the Lord planned to destroy Sodom. The two "regular" angels set out toward Sodom to relocate Lot and his family who resided there. As the angelic duo left the camp, the Lord conversed with Abraham informing him of his intention to annihilate the sin-filled city.

We noted, too, how the Gospels provide a second and perhaps stronger reason to conclude that we should not assume *Revelation* always chronologically lists its scenes and visions. In *Matthew 13*, Jesus told numerous parables concerning the Kingdom. His parable of the Sower inspires countless sermons even today. During this seed-planting story, Jesus commented on the various circumstances with which people receive news of his Kingdom. Some refuse all information about God's word: "Not interested; it's for the birds." Some joyfully receive the Good News, but at the initial faith test, give up and go back to their old ways. Others buy into Jesus' way and at first follow, but when persecution and suffering result from their belief in God, "they're out of there." The majority of church folks likely belong in the next category: Worry and greed "choke the word" making it unfruitful. Nonetheless, some faithful believers hear, understand, and pro-

---

328. Modern TV and movies now often present these using split screens.

329. 1 Samuel 25.

duce fruit for the Lord. *Matthew* 13:9 records Jesus' caution: "He who has ears, let him hear."[330]

The multiple parables in *Matthew* 13 cover the same time period — first to second Advent. Each addresses a different aspect of God's kingdom. In the Tares and Wheat section (verses 24-30), Jesus advised against trying to weed hypocrisy from the church. The parable of the Mustard Seed (31, 32) cautioned his disciples about despising humble beginnings. The brief Leaven section (verse 33) intimates the quiet power of growth when Kingdom members experience their Christ-inspired life change. Jesus covered further subjects when speaking of the Hidden Treasure (verse 44), the Costly Pearl (verses 45, 46) and the fishing Dragnet (verses 47-50).

Luke's gospel successively links several lengthy parables that cover wide ranging aspects of the Kingdom.[331] Most of these stories apply to the conduct of our lives here — how we servants of God treat one another, how we use our gifts, whether we accept the authority of God's Son, and our preparation to give an accounting when Judge Jesus returns. Considering Jesus' treatment of diverse matters in consecutive Gospel stories, we should not be amazed that *Revelation's* visions and scenes cover varied themes. Many apply to the same general time period.

Questions Pleading For Answers

As Jesus' comments, teachings, and parables often provoked questions, numerous *Revelation* scenes also beg for immediate answers. So *Revelation* 6's opening of the first four seals reminds us of Jesus' *Matthew* 24 prediction of wars, rumors of wars, famines and earthquakes. First century Christians hoped to see a Kingdom of peace and righteousness. Instead they suffered uncertainty and intense persecutions. Opening of the fifth seal addresses the quandary:

> *When he opened the fifth seal, I saw under the altar the souls of those who had been slain because of the word of God and the testimony they had maintained. They called out in a loud voice, "How long, Sovereign Lord, holy and true, until you judge the inhabitants of the earth and avenge our blood?"*
>
> *Then each of them was given a white robe, and they were told to wait a little longer, until the full number of their fellow servants, their brothers and sisters, were killed just as they had been.*[332]

---

330. We earlier noted the similarities between this warning and those given the churches *in* Revelation 2 and 3.

331. See Luke chapters 12-20.

332. Revelation 6:9-11 NIV.

Addressing this martyr scene in *Revelation* 6:9, the late Tübingen scholar, Otto Michel observed: "As the blood of sacrificial beasts flowed out of the foot of the altar of burnt offering in Jerusalem, so the blood of martyrs flowed out at the foot of the heavenly altar."[333]

In the same manner God tested the Israelites on their way to the Promised Land, his plan for us sometimes includes suffering during our heavenward journey.[334] Throughout these trials, we wait on God's righteous judgment. As it describes God's wrath against evil, the sixth-seal-opening appears to bring hope. Undoing of the seventh seal, however, must await explanations of other questions and concerns. Thus *Revelation* presents scenes depicting God's just actions toward evil in different contexts (such as, the blowing of the Seven Trumpets by God's seven angels in chapters 8 and 9). In fact an attention-grabbing delay occurs (heaven's silent half hour in 8:1).

The four winds of judgment will not blow until God identifies and seals his servants. Several OT passages provide background and understanding for the *Revelation* 7 scenes.[335] Do these passages describe events of the past, the present or the future? Judging by the answer Jesus gave the skeptical Sadducees concerning the resurrection, I think we can safely assume the *Revelation* 7 scenes include the faithful of every era, (those in the grave and those not yet born). Jesus said:

> *Are you not in error because you do not know the Scriptures or the power of God? When the dead rise, they will neither marry nor be given in marriage; they will be like the angels in heaven. Now about the dead rising—have you not read in the Book of Moses, in the account of the burning bush, how God said to him, "I am the God of Abraham, the God of Isaac, and the God of Jacob"?*
>
> *He is not the God of the dead, but of the living. You are badly mistaken.*[336]

He who Created time, space, and life can speak of things not yet occurring as having already happened. Because God will command from the dead at Jesus' return, Abraham, Isaac, Jacob, and all of Abraham's children, "He is not the God of the dead, but of the living." Anyone who doubts our **Creator's** power and authority errs eternally.

---

333. Otto Michel, *TDNT* Vol. VII p - 935.

334. Deuteronomy 4:34; 7:1-8:5; 29:1-9.

335. These include: Jeremiah 13:8-11 and 49:36; Ezekiel 7:2 and 9:1-11; Daniel 7:2.

336. Mark 12:24-27 NIV   Earlier NIV versions of this passage lack the modifier *burning*. In Chapter 12, we shall look at these Revelation 7 events in greater detail.

Themes of most sections in *Revelation* fall under the category of one or more of **Seven Cs:**

1. **God as Creator-Controller**
2. **Christ, the slain Lamb**
3. **Chaos caused by disobedience**
4. **Conflict God's people feel as a result of chaos**
5. **God Convicts believers of his truth and might**
6. **God Confounds the disobedient**
7. **God Comforts the faithful**

Sorting Revelation 7's Scenes
My **New American Standard Bible** divides *Revelation 7* into three sections. Editors labeled the first three verses: *An Interlude;* verses 4-8: *A Remnant of Israel—144,000;* verses 9-17 they call: *A Multitude from the Tribulation.* In Chapter 7, **The New International Version,** verses 1-8 carry this heading: *144,000 Sealed.* The balance of the chapter falls under the heading, *The Great Multitude in White Robes.* These particulars illustrate the broad extent of interpretation that occurs even among those who print Bibles. No original Bible manuscript carried these headings and none contained chapters and verses.

The Chapter 7 scenes (visions) give the Lord's answer to the pleas of those killed because they witnessed to Jesus' reappearance from the grave (see the opening of the fifth seal in 6:9-11). Beginning with the first murder (*Genesis* 4:1-12), innocent blood pleads for vengeance. Many first century followers laid down their lives rather than follow society's demands and the government's directives not to speak of Jesus' resurrection. As Jesus, the Lamb slain opens the fifth seal, we hear the victims' pleas for justice. Because God's salvation plan advances, he requests the martyrs to rest and he supplies them with white robes of Jesus' righteousness.[337]

---

337. In verse 9, the Greek word translated by the NIV "those who had been slain" (ἐσφαγμένων) is a perfect middle or passive participle, which is very difficult to translate into English. The middle form of this participle seems to indicate some participation on the part of the martyrs. As the wording confirms, their bold testimony to Jesus' resurrection precipitated their deaths: "because of the word of God and the testimony they had maintained."

Revelation 7 helps us pinpoint these righteous ones. The *144,000* and the *multitude* scenes likely depict not two separate groups, but the saved from two different perspectives. First, they constitute the true Israel; 12 thousand from each of Israel's twelve tribes (the twelves symbolizing the fullness or completion of God's plan).[338] When Paul testified before Governor Festus and King Agrippa, he related how the truth about Jesus' resurrection from the dead affected him. The Apostle spoke of the hope God's promise to Israel provided: "This is the promise our twelve tribes are hoping to see fulfilled as they earnestly serve God day and night...

Why should any of you consider it incredible that God raises the dead?"[339]

The second perspective lets us know that God's Kingdom (the true children of Abraham) includes multitudes from every nation, tribe, people, and language (7:9).[340] Wearing white robes and holding palm branches, they stand before the throne loudly declaring: "Salvation belongs to our God, who sits on the throne, and to the Lamb."[341] They join all creation in giving seven-fold (praise, glory, wisdom, thanks, honor, power and strength) reverence to God forever. One of the elders asked John the multitude's identity. When John defers to him, the elder reveals that they have come out of the "great tribulation," they've "washed their robes and made them white in the blood of the Lamb." They wholeheartedly believed in Jesus Christ, the world's Savior.

Jesus early and strongly hinted at the Gentiles' salvation when he shocked and offended fellow Nazarenes in the synagogue of his youth declaring:

> *I assure you that there were many widows in Israel in Elijah's time, when the sky was shut for three and a half years and there was a severe famine throughout the land. Yet Elijah was not sent to any of them, but to a widow in Zarephath in the region of Sidon.*
>
> *And there were many in Israel with leprosy in the time of Elisha*

---

338. In Romans 3, 4; 9-11 and in Galatians 3-5, Paul identifies true Israel (the sons of Abraham) as those who accept Christ and serve the Father through him (see Galatians 3:26-29). Note also that James addressed his letter to the: "Twelve tribes scattered among the nations," (James 1:1 NIV). These become children of Abraham because they manifest the same type of faith Abraham did (see Romans 4:13-15).

339. Acts 26:7, 8 NIV.

340. Jesus: "I have other sheep that are not of this sheep pen," John 10:16 NIV. He also taught in Gentile areas, for example the Decapolis and the regions of Tyre and Sidon. Isaiah prophesied this: 42:1-9, 49:1-7, 55:1-13, 60:1-22, 66:18-21. Instructing him that he wanted the Gentiles to repent, the Lord took Jonah "to the depths."

341. Revelation 7:10 NIV.

> the prophet, yet not one of them was cleansed—only Naaman the Syrian." All the people in the synagogue were furious when they heard this. They got up, drove him out of the town, and took him to the brow of the hill on which the town was built, in order to throw him off the cliff.[342]

In speaking of the widow near Sidon, and Naaman the Syrian general, Jesus affirmed that he personally fulfilled the *Isaiah* Chapter 42 prophecy. He, God's servant, in whom God delights (verse 1) will "be a covenant for the people and a light for the Gentiles" (v. 6 NIV). *Isaiah* extended the Lord's invitation to all people everywhere: "Turn to me and be saved, all you ends of the earth; for I am God, and there is no other" (45:22 NIV).

Isaiah's prophecy specifically helps us understand the *Revelation* 7 scenes:

> And now the LORD says— he who formed me in the womb to be his servant to bring Jacob back to him and gather Israel to himself, for I am honored in the eyes of the LORD and my God has been my strength—he says: "It is too small a thing for you to be my servant to restore the tribes of Jacob and bring back those of Israel I have kept (scene 1). I will also make you a light for the Gentiles that my salvation may reach to the ends of the earth (scene 2)."
>
> This is what the LORD says— the Redeemer and Holy One of Israel—to him who was despised and abhorred by the nation, to the servant of rulers: "Kings will see you and stand up, princes will see and bow down, because of the LORD, who is faithful, the Holy One of Israel, who has chosen you."[343]

Jesus, the Lamb, the servant, restores the *twelve* tribes of Israel; he also brings Gentiles from the ends of the earth (every nation, tribe, language, and people) that all may be one in God's Kingdom. Paul wrote the Ephesus church (the first of *Revelation's* seven churches) about cryptic knowledge God revealed in Jesus: "This mystery," wrote Paul, "is that through the gospel the Gentiles are heirs together with Israel, members together of one body, and sharers together in the promise in Christ Jesus."[344]

The second scene fully answers the question: "From where do all the Gentile saved come (those in white robes)?" "Every nation, tribe,

---

342. Luke 4:25-29 NIV.

343. Isaiah 49:5-7 NIV <u>Underline</u> emphasis mine.

344. *Ephesians* 3: 6 NIV.

people and language . . ."[345] In God's Kingdom, birthright, privilege, and ethnicity account to nothing. You likely learned the Greek word for "tribe" in junior high science class, if not before. The English word phylum derives from the Greek term (phulās-φυλῆς) translated as tribe. Phylum means, "descended from." If the presence of any tribe (phylum) people, nation, or language troubles us now, we shall not be comfortable in heaven.

Jesus died once for all. By his death on the cross, he qualified all believers, but we must keep our "membership" active. As Jesus wrote the church in Smyrna: "Be faithful, even to the point of death, and I will give life as your victor's crown"[346] (a victor's wreath). The section marked Chapters 6 and 7 of *Revelation* **consoled** believers undergoing great tribulation. Their agony evidently led some of them to doubt God's control of world events.

Revelation 6 concludes with judgment ready to fall on frightened unprepared kings, commoners and all classes of people in-between. Chapter 7's beginning scene somewhat resembles visions Ezekiel saw in his prophecy (especially *Ezekiel* 9). In the prophet's day, Israel crassly rebelled against God. Though the Lord delivered them from Egyptian slavery, cared for them during an arduous journey, and led them to a fertile land they did not cultivate and to cities they did not build, Israel soon rejected God's loving care. Most Israelites began serving the idols the previous inhabitants of the land so repulsively and lasciviously worshiped.

At some point, the Lord draws the line. He repeatedly warned Israel of disobedience's consequences giving them numerous chances to repent. Only a few did. In a "virtual" vision of temple activities, the Lord showed Ezekiel Israel's detestable behavior. Concerning the prophet's countrymen, he said: "I will deal with them in anger; I will not look on them with pity, or spare them. Although they shout in my ears, I will not listen to them." As he devastated the stubborn Egyptians on Passover night, the Lord punished Israel's unrepentant idolaters. The narrative continues in *Ezekiel* 9:

> Then I heard him call out in a loud voice, "Bring near those who are appointed to execute judgment on the city, each with a weapon in his hand." And I saw six men coming from the direction of the upper gate, which faces north, each with a deadly weapon in his hand. With them was a man clothed in linen who had a writing kit at his side. They came in and stood beside the bronze altar. Now the glory of the God of Israel went up from above the cherubim, where it had been,

---

345. *Revelation* 5:9 NIV.

346. *Ibid* 2:10c.

> and moved to the threshold of the temple. Then the LORD called to the man clothed in linen who had the writing kit at his side and said to him, **"Go throughout the city of Jerusalem and put a mark on the foreheads of those who grieve and lament over all the detestable things that are done in it."**347

The Lord intended to punish the inhabitants of Jerusalem, but he exempted the faithful few. Before the destroying agents began their work, God wanted the righteous ones clearly marked. We should interpret *Revelation* 6 and 7 with this *Ezekiel* background in mind. Also pertinent to understanding the meaning of this section, note *Exodus* 13:6-9 (NIV), which contains part of Israel's instructions prior to their leaving Egypt. The Lord ordered his people to bear an identifying mark. Strict Passover observance provided part of the signage.

> *For seven days eat bread made without yeast and on the seventh day hold a festival to the LORD. Eat unleavened bread during those seven days; nothing with yeast in it is to be seen among you, nor shall any yeast be seen anywhere within your borders. On that day tell your son, "I do this because of what the LORD did for me when I came out of Egypt."* **This observance will be for you like a sign on your hand and a reminder on your forehead that this law of the LORD is to be on your lips.** *For the LORD brought you out of Egypt with his mighty hand.*

In Ezekiel's day, a small remnant retained their seal or mark by keeping Passover and other laws.

Deuteronomy 6 (verses 3-8 NIV) shows us that Israel's faithful keeping of the Lord's commands and ordinances, and teaching their children to do the same, equaled having signs on their hands and foreheads:

> *Hear, Israel, and be careful to obey so that it may go well with you and that you may increase greatly in a land flowing with milk and honey, just as the LORD, the God of your ancestors, promised you. Hear, O Israel: The LORD our God, the LORD is one. Love the LORD your God with all your heart and with all your soul and with*

---

347. Ezekiel 9:1-4 NIV **Bold** emphasis mine. In verse 4, the Septuagint used the word (σημεῖον) pronounced sāmíon, where the Hebrew used ת, pronounced tau. Some scholars think the original mark was simply the Hebrew letter "tau," the last letter of the Hebrew alphabet. As first written, the tau looked similar to a cross. We should probably understand this mark as an unmistakable identifying sign. The word sāmíon appears repeatedly in the New Testament as "miracle" and "sign." John used it in Revelation 15:1. For more info on the term, see article by Karl Heinrich Rengstorf in *The Theological Dictionary of the New Testament*, Vol. VII, pp. 200-269.

all your strength. These commandments that I give you today are to be on your hearts. Impress them on your children. Talk about them when you sit at home and when you walk along the road, when you lie down and when you get up. ***Tie them as symbols (samion) on your hands and bind them on your foreheads.***

What seals, signs, and marks do Christians now wear?

When you believed, you were marked in him with a seal, the promised Holy Spirit, who is a deposit guaranteeing our inheritance until the redemption of those who are God's possession—to the praise of his glory.[348]

In *Ephesians* 1:13 and 4:30, as well as in *2 Corinthians* 1:21, Paul referred to the seal of the Holy Spirit. By direct teaching and example, the NT shows that God gives his Spirit as a seal of salvation's guarantee to those who believe in Christ, repent of their sins, openly confess Christ and are baptized into Christ.[349]

Years ago, I attended the funeral of a Los Angeles neighbor, who once served in the Latvian military. Latvia (located in Northeastern Europe) was once part of the USSR. Our family did not know the deceased well, but we became acquainted and often chatted with his pleasant college aged son. To close the funeral service, several associates, who decades earlier served with the departed in the Latvian army, gathered near his casket. Facing change and their former comrade's death, those men found meaning by ardently singing about their homeland. In full military uniform and with patriotic fervor, they stood singing the Latvian national anthem — in their language.

As I sat watching, I felt in a time-culture warp. Decades old Latvian loyalty seemed light years distant from Los Angeles of the time. To some, these *Revelation 7* scenes might seem equally odd and out of place. A multitude clothed in white robes and holding palm branches stands before God's throne. Unless they attend toga parties, few American Christians dress that way now.

What would seem odder to you: seeing a throng of folks in white robes waving palm branches or attending a funeral where several men wearing forty-year-old foreign military clothes sing an unfamiliar hymn?[350] A vital difference exists between the two scenes. How so? Decades old army uniforms belong to a past that will never return. Yet white robes and palm branches could symbolize your future.

---

348. Ephesians 1:13b, 14 NIV.

349. Acts 2:38, 39.

350. To the best of my memory, it was the Latvian National Anthem or Hymn.

The first recipients of *Revelation*, those dedicated Latvians, we, and our contemporaries all share something in common. The world might change, but death never quits. The grave skulks from millions of dark places and not once fails its grim undertaking.

We keep looking for meaning and hope. Finding them permanently always seems to elude us. As folks anxiously quest for life answers, hope ebbs and flows according to the news current at the time. A 2015 issue **of USA Today** headlined this statement: "Many Gen Xers (Folks 35-48) say future looks less than rosy."[351] According to a 4-22-15 Rasmussen poll, only 37% of likely American voters thought America's best days are in the future. "But 45% . . . think the country's best days have come and gone." Eighteen percent were not sure. Some thought this country deserves no future. At the time of this writing, many Christians feel angst and anger; only months ago, most of them felt highly optimistic.[352]

When John wrote *Revelation*, Christians faced bleak prospects. Some wondered whether any reason existed to hope. To bolster Christians in those grim circumstances, the Lord delivered the *Revelation* to John. Nothing equals the book's hope promise. Naught comes even close. How does *The Apocalypse* give us lively confidence? From the start of this country, Christianity enjoyed being the majority religion.[353] When the church began, Christians never held a majority anywhere. For the first few centuries, Christianity remained an illegal sect. Opponents fiercely hassled and killed many of Jesus' followers.

We earlier labelled *Revelation* a believer's survival manual. The book's symbolic language seems unconventional and out-of-place to us. Yet the peculiar images like white robes, palm branches, and so on hide powerful secrets. Properly understanding those mysteries benefits us, brings hope, and makes us strong. How?

- We gain information about the future.
- We learn how to live powerfully.
- We find clear-cut purpose.

The Seven Seals Reveal Future Vitals

Opening the first four seals reveals how wars, civil strife, famine, and death will continue. Events such as these do not portend the end. They trouble every generation; earth sciences and history confirm their nearly perpetual occurrences. In all eras, innocent folks apprehensively ask:

---

351. *USA Today*, Tuesday, May 5, 2015, Section 4B by Charisse Jones.

352. Due to the 2020 Covid-19 pandemic.

353. I use the term in a broad sense.

- "How long will evil and uncertainty prevail?"
- "When will the Lord bring justice?"

The fifth seal opening notes these persistent, anxious queries of God's people:

The Lord's answer: "Be patient and trust Him."

The sixth seal opening gives a preview of happenings when the Lord brings justice: Few folks will be ready.

- Most never acknowledge God as their Creator.
- Neither do they ever thank Jesus for dying to save them or live to praise him.

Suppose pollsters asked the world's inhabitants how often they praised and honored God for being the Universe Creator. What percentage would say they praise God at least once a day?

How many times a year would a typical marcher or protester thank anyone for anything? How might the typical college student or athlete answer the above questions?

Do you wonder what percentage of church goers can say they daily praise and thank God?

- What percentage of believers shares Jesus' resurrection good news with others?
- How many actively work on modeling their lives after Jesus?
- How many feel obligated to help others beyond their own families or friends?
- How many assume that life's primary purpose is to achieve happiness?

From time to time some might ask, "How did life get here?" Do they ever ask "Why are we here?" Or are they satisfied with the answers of so-called learned people—"It's just a big cosmic accident." Those who publicly praise God embarrass so called sophisticated people. Thus the saying: "Don't talk religion or politics": except people do talk politics. In the world's view however, only "fanatics" and "fundamentalists" talk about God.

Folks routinely make gods of men and women and honor them, however. Contemporaries idolize NBA and NFL players, musicians and actors, politicians, preachers, and newscasters. In practice, some in our society reason:

> *It's okay to idolize people.*
> *Exalting God is not okay.*

Elitists and reporters often venerate the human gods for being slick, wily, and deceptive. Even when they lie, cover up, and hoodwink us, the intelligent "deserve" admiration and honor. Some idolize high IQs—even when the idols possessing the gift deceive them. God, who created human brains, speaks truth to us, rebukes and corrects us, lifts us up, and helps us.

Jesus stated the highest life-objective: "Let your light shine before others, that they may see your good deeds and glorify your Father in heaven."[354] We humans want others to see our good deeds so they will admire us and say nice things about us. Jesus advised us to do good things but always to glorify God. Luke's Gospel describes a crippled woman, who suffered back problems for 18 years. Jesus "put his hands on her, and immediately she straightened up and praised God."[355] When Jesus performed miracles, he ordered people to praise and thank God. When many human gods help someone, they demand "under the radar" donations and expect top billing. Peter advised:

> *Whoever speaks must do so as one speaking the very words of God; whoever serves must do so with the strength that God provides, so that God may be glorified in all things through Jesus Christ. To him belong the glory and the power forever and ever. Amen.*[356]

Emperor Domitian (81-96 AD) enacted himself to be god. "He informed all provincial governors that government and pronouncements must begin: 'Our Lord and God Domitian commands ...'"[357] Of course Christians could not and would not bow to anyone except God. True believers honor no one but God in Christ.

The Lord accepted the prayers of a Roman centurion named Cornelius and told him to send for the Apostle Peter. When Peter and several witnesses[358] arrived at the centurion's house:

> *Cornelius was expecting them and had called together his relatives and close friends.*
>
> *As Peter entered the house, Cornelius met him and fell at his feet in reverence.*

---

354. Matthew 5:16 NIV.

355. Luke 13:13 NIV.

356. 1 Peter 4:11 NRSV.

357. William Barclay, *The Revelation of John*, Vol. 1, DSBS, p. 19.

358. Peter's examples of using multiple witnesses in Acts 10 and 11 illustrate their necessity.

> But Peter made him get up. "Stand up," he said, "I am only a man myself."[359]

Neither the Apostle Peter nor the Apostle Paul accepted that kind of honor or recognition. None of God's angels permitted it. They consistently deferred to God. In spite of the specific warnings Jesus gave, religious leaders seem to covet special titles and apparel that enhances their dignity.

Jesus warned religious leaders about using titles. You judge whether we listen and heed him.

> *They love to be greeted with respect in the markets. They love it when people call them 'Rabbi.' "But you shouldn't be called 'Rabbi.' You have only one Teacher, and you are all brothers. Do not call anyone on earth 'father.' You have one Father, and he is in heaven. You shouldn't be called 'teacher.' You have one Teacher, and he is the Messiah. The most important person among you will be your servant. People who lift themselves up will be made humble. And people who make themselves humble will be lifted up.*[360]

Only God deserves reverence. Facing Emperor Domitian's demand that people honor him as Lord and God, Christians refused. Persecution intensified. Some believers received the death penalty. As we have seen, the faithful kept asking, "Lord how long will evil prevail?" "How long will righteous people have to suffer?" The Lord answered two ways:

- First, be patient; wait for him to act justly; human judgment rarely results fairly.
- Second, <u>be separate.</u> Do not take part in the world's evil.

Then the Lord began punishing evil.

God's wrath against evil created a quandary. Suppose pirates begin boarding ships, killing some folks, and taking others prisoner. The Lord then decides to punish the pirates. If the Lord sinks the pirates' ship, what about the innocent prisoners on board? Many felt that type of conflict about God's judgment on evil societies: "What will happen to the good people in their midst?" Before we deal with this question, we need a brief review.

---

359. Acts 10: 24b-26 NIV.

360. Matthew 23:7-12 NIRV Accessed through sermoncentral.com/bible

Briefly Reviewing *Revelation* 7's Scenes.

    A) God puts his seal on the righteous. When we turn away from sin, make Jesus our Lord, and are baptized into Christ, God seals us with his Holy Spirit.[361]

    B) From what background do the sealed folks come?
        The first scene: 12,000 from each of the tribes of Israel, totaling 144,000 represent Jesus' Church, the true Israel.

    C) The next scene shows that the true Israel, Abraham's seed come from every nation and tribe and people and language.

Then as now, athletes had to cross the finish line to qualify for the prize. In the same way that sports' winners today hold up trophies, back then, white robes and palm branches signified victory.[362] Victors crossed the finish line — some dying as they traversed it. The Bible repeatedly refutes the idea that once saved you can't be lost. To cross the finish line in Christ, we must faithfully complete the course.

    D) Now we can appreciate the third scene. The heavenly throng praised God:

"Salvation belongs to our God, who sits on the throne, and to the Lamb." All the angels were standing around the throne and around the elders and the four living creatures. They fell down on their faces before the throne and worshiped God, saying: "Amen! Praise and glory and wisdom and thanks and honor and power and strength be to our God for ever and ever. Amen!"[363]

You probably noticed the seven types of tribute offered to God, the Creator prior to the above "Amen!" Sevens nearly always express completeness.

In the next chapter, we shall cover two major questions:
    What are signs?

    What is sealing?

---

361. Acts 2:38; 2 Corinthians 1:21, 22; Ephesians 1:13,14.

362. See William Barclay, *The Revelation of John*, Vol. 2, pp. 26, 27.

363. Revelation 7:10-12 NIV

Chapter 9

Signs And Seals

What Are Signs?
Picture yourself driving a tight-curved mountain road in a country whose language you barely comprehend. At every turn, new, unfamiliar signs confront you. The farther you travel, the greater your confusion. To most readers, trying to maneuver through *Revelation* resembles that vexing venture.

English readers encounter additional challenges. Translators inconsistently render important terms. In English versions, uneven interpretation begins in the latter part of Chapter 1, verse one, in the case of a Greek verb meaning to "indicate, predict, signify, or give a signal."[364] The NIV reads "He made it known by sending his angel. . ."[365] The NASB renders the phrase: "He sent and communicated it." The TEV provides: "Christ made these things known to his servant John by sending his angel to him." The KJV translates the phrase: *"He sent and signified it."* What can we make of this wide interpretive variation in the verb's basic meaning? On one detail at least, all these versions agree. They correctly translate the main verb as past tense.[366]

In the present tense, the Greek word in question is pronounced *sāmaino;* a verbal form of the noun *sāmeion*. Sāmeion appears many times in the Gospels, usually, but not always, translated as *sign*. "The term *sāmeion* simply denotes something which may be perceived and from which those who observe it may draw assured conclusions."[367] A notable exception to this "general rule" rears itself already in *Revelation* 1:1. Not all who observe the "phenomenon" or "thing" draw the "assured conclusion." The translation variations we noted prove the point. When we drive near intersections and see large red, octagonal markers with the lettering STOP, most of us draw the reasonably assured inference. Those lacking knowledge of English and acquain-

---

364. Sources: Gary Alan Chamberlain, *The Greek of the Septuagint, a supplemental lexicon*, Hendrickson Publishers, Peabody, MA, 2011 and *Barclay M. Newman, Jr., A Concise GREEK-ENGLISH DISTIONARY of the NEW TESTAMENT*, United Bible Societies, London, 1971.

365. The NRSV reads similarly.

366. The term is ἐσήμεν, Greek aorist (past) of σημαίνω.

367. Karl Heinrich Rengstorf, *TDNT*, Vol. VII, p 232.

tance with international symbols might blast through the intersection. Nonetheless, most of us know that the sign means "halt."

In New Testament usage, *sāmeion* sometimes conveys hiddenness. For instance, in a verbal form similar to the one found in *Revelation* 1:1, *sāmeion* appears three times in John's Gospel. To a crowd of people who just heard some strange phenomena, Jesus declared, as the NIV translates:

> Now is the time for judgment on this world; now the prince of this world will be driven out. And I, when I am lifted up from the earth, will draw all people to myself."
> He said this to show the kind of death he was going to die.[368]

For a while after his resurrection, the Apostles didn't fully understand that Jesus' sign referred to his crucifixion.[369] In the above instance, "give a hint" probably better conveys the mystery involved than "show." The KJV more correctly translates "signify" here. Even that term, however, doesn't adequately intimate the stark hidden message involved. Later generations benefit from the insights the disciples gained from Jesus' post-resurrection appearances and explanations.[370]

Early believers surely comprehended *Revelation's* signs. The enemy did not. As we try to gain fuller understanding of the book's imagery, we face formidable yet doable tasks. Confusion caused by the widespread inconsistency in translating sāmeion (sign) poses significant challenges. Note the following examples:

- The KJV renders *sāmeion* as *wonder* in *Revelation* 12:1 and 3 and 13:13, 14.[371]
- The *Revelation* 13 verses in question refer to *sāmeions* performed or displayed by the "beast from the earth."

---

368. John 12: 31-33 NIV. In John 21: 19, when Jesus referred to Peter's future, the NIV translated the verb *sāmaíno(n)* as "<u>to indicate</u> the kind of death by which Peter would glorify God."

369. Luke 23:55-24:12 emphasizes the difficulty with which the women, and even more so the Eleven, comprehended Jesus' statements about his impending crucifixion and resurrection. Note especially Luke 24:7and John 20:1-10. Matthew 12 records the exchange between Jesus and his critics regarding signs (*sāmeions*).They wanted him to perform one. He replied that they would receive only the *sign* of the prophet Jonah, who spent three days inside the great fish. To us now, that event clearly signified Jesus' death, burial, and resurrection. At the time, his critics and also his followers seemed clueless.

370. Matthew 28, Luke 24, John 20 and 21, as well as several passages in Acts provide significant clues.

371. In Revelation 13:13 *sāmeia* (the plural form) and megâla.

- In *Matthew* 24:3, when the disciples asked Jesus the *sign* of his coming, the term *sāmeion* appears.[372] When Jesus referred to the *signs* and *wonders* associated with false prophets (24:24), the KJV interestingly translated sāmeia (plural) as *signs*, but *wonders* in that verse is their rendering of the Greek term *terata*.[373]

The KJV also translates *sāmeion* in numerous instances as *miracle(s)*.[374] *Sāmeion* can at times be understood that way. Herod evidently hoped to witness some type of wonder or miracle when he asked to see Jesus (*Luke* 23:7, 8).[375]

In the well-known water to wine event his gospel relates, John used the noun sāmeion.[376] The NIV 1978 edition illustrated not only translation inconsistency, but also failure to appreciate a vital truth about the word **sign** as John and other biblical writers used *sāmeion*. In *John* 2: 11, the NIV translated: "This is the first of his *miraculous signs*, Jesus performed in Cana of Galilee." In this verse, no adjective in the original modifies signs (*sāmeiōn*).[377]

By adding the modifying word "miraculous," translators focused attention on the water to wine miracle rather than on the larger significance of this event. To what do I refer? This liquid transformation dramatized Jesus' superiority over every law, custom, teaching, and occurrence connected with Moses, any other *OT p*erson, or anything previous to Jesus. If the NIV translators wanted to emphasize something in verse 11, they should have accentuated the word "revealed."[378]

---

372. The KJV reads: "What shall be the sign of thy coming, and of the end of the world?" The NIV renders: "What will be the sign of your coming and of the end of the age?"

373. Matthew 24:24, 25 NIV reads: "For false messiahs and false prophets will appear and perform great (megâla) signs and wonders to deceive, if possible, even the elect. See, I have told you ahead of time." Early NIV versions read *miracles* instead of *wonders* here.

374. See also, Revelation 13:14; 16:14; 19:20; as well as Luke once, John-13 times, Acts-5 times for example 15:12. In 2 Thessalonians 3:17, both the NIV and NASB translate *sāmeion* as *distinguishing mark*; the KJV renders it *token*.

375. The term *sāmeion* appears in the *Septuagint*, 2 Chronicles 32:24. Referring to King Hezekiah's miraculous recovery, Sir Lancelot Charles Lee Brenton translated as follows: "In those days Ezekias was sick even to death, and prayed to the Lord: and he hearkened to him and gave him a sign."

376. John 2:11.

377. This is the plural genitive (possessive) form of the word here; a definite article precedes it.

378. Later editions show the term *miraculous* eliminated in verse 11 and placing emphasis on the larger, more vital theme.

To describe the totality of his manifestation to his Apostles (verses 6-19), Jesus used the first person form of the verb they translate as *revealed* (John 17:6).[379] That verb appears in some of Jesus' post-resurrection appearances (John 21:1 and 14).[380]

In *John* 3, sāmeiōn appears when Nicodemus questioned Jesus. In *John* 3: 2, the 1978 version reads: "For no one could perform the miraculous signs you are doing if God were not with him." In more recent NIV editions, the first phrase reads: "For no one could perform the signs you are doing . . ." Here, in the Greek text, the modifier *dunatai* (δύναται) precedes the plural form *sāmeia*. The term *dunatai* intimates *power* or *strong* as evidenced in the English word dynamite, which derives from a related word.

Jesus' mild rebuke of the royal official, whose son was dying (John 4:46-54) gives us important clues concerning the meaning and intention of signs. Because the Greek verb translated *believing* is second person plural form, we can assume that Jesus addressed the official plus his fellow Israelite citizens.[381] The NASB more accurately translates: "Unless you *people* see signs and wonders, you *simply* will not believe."[382]

Jesus performed signs not only to demonstrate extraordinary, miraculous ability. Those events authenticated his identity as the one and only Christ-Messiah of God. Jesus' *sāmeia* should help true seekers strongly believe God's incarnation in Christ. The Lord sent Abraham, Moses, Elijah, and other prophets as his agents. Meet Christ and you see the Father.[383] The conversations between Jesus and the crowds he drew when he fed the five thousand confirm that Jesus primarily performed these signs to validate his divine presence:

> When they found him on the other side of the lake, they asked him, "Rabbi, when did you get here?"
>
> Jesus answered, "Very truly I tell you, you are looking for me, not because you saw the signs I performed but because you ate the loaves and had your fill. Do not work for food that spoils, but for food that endures to eternal life, which the Son of Man will give you. For on him God the Father has placed his seal of approval."[384]

---

379. The aorist verb ἐφανέρωσα appears here meaning literally "I manifested."

380. That verb φανερόω is pronounced phaneróō, meaning to make known, evident, or plain.

381. Verse 48, πιστεύσητε.

382. Ibid.

383. John 10:30; 14:9.

384. We shall deal with the word translated *seal* later in this chapter.

> *Then they asked him, "What must we do to do the works God requires?"*
>
> *Jesus answered, "The work of God is this: to believe in the one he has sent."*
>
> *So they asked him, "What sign then will you give that we may see it and believe you? What will you do? Our ancestors ate the manna in the wilderness; as it is written: 'He gave them bread from heaven to eat.'" Jesus said to them, "Very truly I tell you, it is not Moses who has given you the bread from heaven, but it is my Father who gives you the true bread from heaven. For the bread of God is the bread that comes down from heaven and gives life to the world."*
>
> *"Sir," they said, "always give us this bread."*[385]

The above conversation tells us that the Lord used signs as guides for true seekers to identify truth and confirm belief. The crowds sadly thought only of their immediate needs — free food.

Signs enabled sincere inquirers to find and know Jesus. For genuine Kingdom seekers, signs constituted Jesus' valid credentials. He informed an amazed crowd, and also his skeptics: "If I drive out demons by the finger of God, then the kingdom of God has come to you."[386] Such abilities as enabling the blind to see and other astounding works, the OT connected only with God himself.[387] Jesus prevailed over earth's most deadly, sinister powers. His authority over demons provided imposing, unambiguous evidence of the truth that in Christ, God manifested himself in the flesh.

Acts 2 reports that on the Day of Pentecost, people came running and wondering about the meaning of the language phenomena they just witnessed. Peter explained that they were seeing "Last Days" events the prophet Joel predicted. The happenings included wonders (*terata*) "in the heaven above and *signs* on the earth below (Acts 2:19 NIV)." Peter linked these events to the resurrection of Jesus, the man from Nazareth. Only weeks before, many of those assembled demanded Jesus' crucifixion. They called for his execution in spite of the fact that God fully accredited (proved Jesus' identity among them) as Lord and Christ.

Jesus attested his Divine identity "by miracles (*dunamoi*), wonders (*terasa*) and signs... (*sāmeion*) as you yourselves know." "But God raised him from the dead," said Peter. [388] Whether the people

---

385. John 6: 25-34 NIV.

386. Luke 11:20 NIV.

387. Isaiah 42:5-9.

388. Acts 2:22 and 24 NIV.

got caught up in mob violence, worries about political instability, or greed, the Holy Spirit held them accountable.

We face the same reckoning for not seriously considering the extraordinary evidence God's Word presents that Jesus is God's one and only Son. In verse 36 (NIV), Peter summarized the case for God's verification. The word *assured* (*aspholōs*) means to prove beyond all doubt: "God has made this Jesus, whom you crucified, both Lord and Messiah."

Revelation's signs help us see Jesus' divine comforting, consoling, encouraging presence in the hostile turmoil of past ages, uncertainties of this present age, and any future ages. God dominates and overcomes every real and imagined foe. In human flesh just like ours, Jesus personified the Lord; "God was reconciling the world to himself in Christ."[389] Jesus exemplified, characterized, and embodied God's "faithful and true witness."[390]

English speaking students unacquainted with Greek, but wanting to further explore the translation variation matter, can trace the usage by consulting parallel Greek-English Bibles, or by checking complete concordances that list the Greek origins of words. To trace all the inconsistent renderings requires a study in itself.

Don't let this inconsistency discussion dismay or discourage you. Though translators vary in the way they describe the signs that point to the objects, the keys we previously discussed help identify the items themselves. *Revelation* 12:1-3 well illustrates my point. The NIV 1978 edition translated as follows:

> *A great and wondrous sign appeared in heaven: a woman clothed with the sun, with the moon under her feet and a crown of twelve stars on her head. She was pregnant and cried out in pain as she was about to give birth. Then another sign appeared in heaven: an enormous red dragon with seven heads and ten horns and seven crowns on its heads.*

Only the word *mega* modifies the word *sāmeion* (sign) in the original. Later editions of the NIV correctly dropped the word "wondrous." The NIV also made curious gender changes in respect to the child and the dragon. In Greek, child is neuter and dragon male.

To our original point; unceasing speculation centers on the phrase: *"a woman clothed with the sun with the moon under her feet and a crown of twelve stars."* We shall discuss this scene further in a later chapter, but

---

389. 2 Corinthians 5:19 NIV.

390. John 18:37; Revelation 1:5, 3:14. See Edward White Benson's Essay V, *THE APOCALYPSE, an Introductory Study of the Revelation of St John, the Divine*, MACMILLAN AND COMPANY, London, 1900, reprint by NABU, pp 139-142.

Joseph's dream, which is familiar to many *Old Testament* readers, helps us identity the "woman."[391]

A different but equally curious translation variation occurs in *Revelation* 15:1 and 2. John wrote, as I literally translate;

> I saw another sāmeion out of heaven, great (mega) and <u>astonishing</u>, seven angels, having the seven final plagues (they complete God's anger), when I saw a sea, clear as glass mingled with fire. And the ones victorious over the beast and over his image and over the number of his name, <u>standing upon the glassy sea</u>, having harps of God . . .[392]

The NIV, NRSV, TEV, and many other translations read "standing beside the sea." Because Matthew twice used nearly the same wording found here when he described Jesus walking on the Sea of Galilee, the "standing beside" rendering seems inconsistent.[393] In all three instances, the preposition *epi* (ἐπὶ) precedes the word for sea. The prefix *epi* appears in dozens of English words nearly always connoting *over* or *upon*. **Epidermis,** (literally, *over skin*) for example, is an English word of Greek origin. In contrast, when Jesus walked by the sea, as in *Mark* 1:16 and *Matthew* 4:18, the Gospel writers chose another familiar preposition, *para*. A paramedic comes beside or alongside you to treat you.

The *OT* background for the sea scene comes, of course, from *Exodus* 15. Using Moses as his human agent, God parted the waters allowing the Israelites to escape across the temporarily dry sea bed. When the Egyptian army pursued, the Lord locked the Egyptian's chariot wheels and collapsed the interim sea walls drowning Pharaoh's troops. On the far side of the sea, Moses' sister Miriam played her tambourine "and all the women followed her, with tambourines and dancing,"[394] praising the Lord for delivering them.

Walking on water outclasses descending to the sea floor and ascending on the far side with water piled high on your left and right.[395]

---

391. Genesis 37: 9,10.

392. The word I translate <u>astonishing</u> is the neuter, nominative, singular of thaumaston (θαυμαστόν) = marvelous, wonderful; extraordinary, astonishing-See Barclay M. Newman, Jr., *A Concise GREEK-ENGLISH DICTIONARY of the NEW TESTAMENT*, United Bible Societies, London, 1971, p. 82.

393. Matthew 14:25, 26.

394. Exodus 15:20 NIV.

395. In 1 Corinthians 10:1-10, Paul warned the Corinthian church of lapsing into sin. He noted that the Israelites were immersed in the sea—water on both sides and the

The *Revelation* scene builds further on Israel's *Exodus* experience. The saved Israelites sang the Song of Moses. The *Revelation* saved also sing the Song of Moses the servant of God but add the Song of the Lamb. The sea no longer threatens. I suspect that as the Israelites hastened across the sea bed with huge water walls on each side, they nervously eyed those "walls" for "cracks." In contrast, by faithfully following the Lamb, the *Revelation* saved stand securely on the surface of the placid, peaceful, crystal, sea praising the Lord God Almighty for his great and marvelous deeds (15:3).[396]

When attempting to decipher *Revelation,* most Christians know an important truth about signs, but somehow often forget it. Signs point us to the real and sometimes warn us of the actual, but they are not the reality. While driving the countryside, Iowan's frequently see yellow road signs featuring a black image depicting a farmer on a tractor. The signs indicate that a farmer driving a tractor might be on the road a short distance ahead. The farmer could be in town when you drive the area. The sign makers simply use a recognizable image to warn us of potential danger to the farmer and to drivers. Virtually everybody understands this concept yet many *Revelation* interpreters apparently neglect it. To what truths do the signs guide, warn, encourage, or lead us? Using one of our previously discussed keys usually helps us discover the answers. Often, an *OT* occurrence, teaching, or person, provides the clue. Oft-times, too, Jesus' teachings or sayings afford the key. Frequently *NT* and *OT* references combine to help us understand the sign(s).

What Does Seal Mean? What Is A Seal?
Few English words derive from the Greek term for seal. Whether the word *sphragistic* ever earned its way into the National Spelling Bee, I don't know. My computer word-spell did not recognize the term. In

---

cloud overhead constituted baptism (immersion). Nonetheless many of the saved Israelites grumbled and the Lord scattered their bodies over the desert. As far as the path through the sea, being more efficient, walking on a glassy sea also fits the Isaiah prophecy that John the Baptist echoed: "Every valley shall be filled in, every mountain and hill made low . . ." (Isaiah 40:3-5 and Luke 3: 5 NIV).

396. In Zechariah 10:11, the prophet wrote of a future time when God's people "will pass through the sea of trouble; the surging sea will be subdued" (NIV). See also Isaiah 51:9-11. Verse 9 refers to Rahab (Rahab means tumult) being cut to pieces and the sea monster pierced through. Contrast the placid "sea of glass" in Revelation 15: 2. Though fire might ordinarily be fearsome, Daniel's three friends suffered no ill effects from the fiery furnace (Daniel 3:8-30). In fact, by faith they quenched the lethal fire (Hebrews 11:34). The mix of fire and water in Revelation 15 seems eternally distant from the lake of fire awaiting those who resist God (20:10 and15).

some U.S. regions, folks once peddled grayish-yellow aluminous earth they called Lemnian bole. Vendors labelled the product *sphragide*. They coined that term *sphragide* because promoters packaged the product in sealed envelopes. My word-spell did not recognize *sphragide* either. Otherwise the Greek term for seal made little headway into this country's speech.

The verb *sphragidzo* (σφραγίζω) and the noun *sphragis* express a range of related ideas including inscription, impression, seal (as with a signet ring), and seal up.[397] In verse 3:33 of John's gospel, he used the past (aorist) form of the verb. The NIV translates the term as *certified*. The issue relates to Jesus' witness of the father: Whoever accepts it certifies God's truth. The KJV reads: "He that hath received his testimony hath set to his seal that God is true." *Seal* refers to the credibility Jesus gave to his message.[398] In *John 6:27*, Jesus said: "Do not work for food that spoils, but for food that endures to eternal life, which the Son of Man will give you. For on him God the Father has placed his *seal* of approval (NIV)." In *Matthew 27:66*, though, *seal* clearly represents something tangible (a visible marker):

> *The next day, the one after Preparation Day, the chief priests and the Pharisees went to Pilate. "Sir," they said, "we remember that while he was still alive that deceiver said, 'After three days I will rise again.'*
>
> *So give the order for the tomb to be made secure until the third day. Otherwise, his disciples may come and steal the body and tell the people that he has been raised from the dead. This last deception will be worse than the first." "Take a guard," Pilate answered. "Go, make the tomb as secure as you know how." So they went and made the tomb secure by putting a **seal** on the stone and posting the guard.*[399]

Gottfried Fitzer reviewed use of the word σφραγίζω (*sphragistic*) as in *Revelation 5: 1* and subsequent verses. His comments deserve noting: "The opening of the seven seals successively carries events forward..." "The ancient custom of providing something with a sign of ownership" is in play.[400]

---

397. The Septuagint extensively used these terms. See Bernard A. Taylor, *ANALYTICAL LEXICON to the SEPTUAGINT; expanded edition*, Hendrickson Publishers, 2009, p. 526. Examples of the Septuagint use of the term appear in the *Book of Esther* 3:10, 8:8 and 10, for example.

398. Scholars disagree on whether John the Baptist speaks here or whether the Apostle John gives commentary.

399. Matthew 27:62-66 NIV Though seal often indicates ownership, Matthew's use of it appears to be a notable biblical exception.

400. Gottfried Fitzer, *TDNT*, Volume VII, pp. 950, 951.

Recall our music key? Once the slain Lamb took the book out of God's hand (Chapter 5), the new song begun by those near the throne informs us:

> *"You are worthy to take the scroll and to open its seals, because you were slain, and with your blood you purchased for God persons from every tribe and language and people and nation. You have made them to be a kingdom and priests to serve our God, and they will reign on the earth." Then I looked and heard the voice of many angels, numbering thousands upon thousands, and ten thousand times ten thousand. They encircled the throne and the living creatures and the elders.*[401]

Jesus displayed abundant power and authority by redeeming and presiding over folks from every tribe, language, people, and nation. In fact, according to 5:13, 14, the Lamb receives and shares equal worship praise with God.

Sphragidzo also plays prominently in our relationship with God. As *Ephesians* explains:

> *In Him, you also, after listening to the message of truth, the gospel of your salvation—having also believed, you were sealed (**sphragidzo** in aorist-past tense form) in him with the Holy Spirit of promise, who is given as a pledge of our inheritance, with a view to the redemption of God's own possession, to the praise of his glory.*[402]

On the basis of our repentance, confession of his Christ, and resolve to be kingdom-subjects (letting God rule our lives), God seals us with the Holy Spirit at baptism. The Holy Spirit's presence signifies God's authority over us and marks us as guaranteed heirs with Christ.[403]

Images, Marks, And The Mark Of The Beast

Images

The word *eikon*[404] originally referred primarily to a face on a coin. I bought two one-dollar coins with Susan B. Anthony's image on the

---

401. Revelation 5:9-11 NIV.

402. Ephesians 1:13, 14 NASB The NIV renders the single term ἐσφραγίσθητε "marked in him with a seal," leaving readers the impression that there are two separate terms here. The aorist form also indicates a one-time occasion of sealing at baptism (see Acts 2:38, 39).

403. For further info on these points, see 2 Corinthians 1:22; Ephesians 4:30; 2 Timothy 2:19.

404. Many scholars pronounce the diphthong epsilon-iota (e and i with a long i sound. The "e" is dropped in English.

obverse of those silvers. In the late '70s, officials thought the SBA coins would be popular. For some reason, the public "skirted" them. Some "gold" coins bear George Washington's image.[405] On the coins I possess, George is not smiling. Did his teeth hurt or did he foresee his country's future? From ancient times, the image struck on coins represented a significant person or supposed god. They called such coin-images *eikons*.[406]

Graven images (depictions of kings or gods) were also "eikons."[407] In the *"Seventy" (Septuagint)* version of *Daniel* 2, King Nebuchadnezzar erected a ninety-foot-tall image (eikon) of himself and commanded all people to bow and worship it. *Revelation* Chaps. 13-15 describe a similar circumstance regarding the beast "out of the earth."

> *It exercised all the authority of the first beast on its behalf, and made the earth and its inhabitants worship the first beast, whose fatal wound had been healed. And it performed great signs, even causing fire to come down from heaven to the earth in full view of the people. Because of the signs it was given power to perform on behalf of the first beast, it deceived the inhabitants of the earth. It ordered them to set up an image in honor of the beast who was wounded by the sword and yet lived. The second beast was given power to give breath to the image of the first beast, so that the image could speak and cause all who refused to worship the image to be killed. It also forced all people, great and small, rich and poor, free and slave, to receive a mark on their right hands or on their foreheads, so that they could not buy or sell unless they had the mark, which is the name of the beast or the number of its name.*[408]

Whether the image (*eikon*) in this section refers to a coin image or an actual idol is difficult to conclude. Believers faced both types of test. Images of Emperors on coins were commonly minted in the first century. Later rulers created full images of themselves and expected folks to reverence them. Caligula 37-41 AD erected his image in the Jerusalem Temple's Holy of Holies. Decades later, in a letter to Emperor Trajan, Pliny the Younger wrote of the testing procedures he followed when those accused of being Christians came before him.

> *Any information was presented to me without any name subscribed,*

---

405. Both coins are mostly copper. The SBA is covered with nickel, the GW with manganese brass. The SBA's melt value on 7-22-16 was .0435471.

406. Greek εἰκών

407. For a fuller discussion, see *TDNT*, Vol. II, G. Kittel, pp. 381-397.

408. Revelation 13: 12-17 NIV.

containing a charge against several persons. **Those who denied they were, or had ever been Christians, who repeated after me an invocation to the gods, and offered religious rites with wine and frankincense before your statue, which I had ordered to be brought for that purpose, together with those of the gods, and even reviled the name of Christ** — *whereas there is no forcing, it is said, those who are really Christians into a compliance with any of these articles* — *I thought it proper to discharge them. Some among those who were accused by a witness in person at first confessed themselves Christians but immediately after denied it. True, they had been of that number, but they had now (some three years, others more, and a few as much as twenty-five years ago) forsaken that error.* **They all worshipped your statue and the images of the gods, throwing out imprecations at the same time against the name of Christ.** *(emphasis mine)*

The above letter indicates that willingness to bow in deference to the Emperor's statue and images of prominent Roman gods evidenced obedience to the Roman government. Apparently the Emperor's statue also provided refuge for those fleeing for protection from certain charges as Pliny's letter LXXIV shows:

> TO THE EMPEROR TRAJAN
> *I received a letter, Sir, from Apuleius, a soldier now in garrison at Nicomedia, informing me that one Callidromus being arrested by Maximus and Dionysius, bakers to whom he had hired himself,* **fled for refuge to your statue;** $_2$ *that being brought before a magistrate, he declared he was formerly slave to Laberius Maximus, but being taken prisoner by Susagus in Mœsia, he was sent as a present from Decebalus to Pacorus king of Parthia, in whose service he continued several years, from whence he made his escape and came to Nicomedia.*[409]

Colossians 1:15 NIV reads: "The Son (Christ) is the image (eikon) of the invisible God."

The *Book of Hebrews* adds: "the Son radiates God's own glory and expresses the very character of God, and he sustains everything by the mighty power of his command."[410] How can you make an image of something invisible? The answer: When Christ came in the flesh, the

---

409. William Melmoth's translation, which I earlier cited, contains this footnote: "Statues of the emperor gave sanctuary," Volume III, p 153.

410. Hebrews 1:3a NLT — Accessed through sermoncentral.com/bible

eternal God, whom no one has seen, became reachable and personal to every human.

Jesus changed everything. All individuals can access God in and through Christ. To reach and speak with God, no one needs a priest, clergyman, or any professional religious person: "For there is one God and one mediator between God and mankind, the man Christ Jesus . . ."[411] These descriptions and clarifications are vital:

- Christ "radiates God's . . . glory and expresses the very character of God."
- "In Christ all the fullness of the Deity lives in bodily form."[412]

Christ differs from every other prophet, guru, and religious leader. He was God in human form, living for a while in the Cosmos he created, dealing with the very human beings he formed. Beginning in Chapter 5, *Revelation's* songs affirm and build on these truths about Jesus, the slain Lamb.

Marks

In the 1970s and '80s, zealous religious writers and preachers incited anxiety, indigestion, and fear by predicting that government agencies would mark folks with the *sign of the beast*. These presumed "experts" conjectured indelible body marks or electronic implants that enabled evil governments to identify and control citizens. They based their fervent speculation on this section of *Revelation* 13:

> Then I saw a second beast, coming out of the earth. It had two horns like a lamb, but it spoke like a dragon. It exercised all the authority of the first beast on its behalf, and made the earth and its inhabitants worship the first beast, whose fatal wound had been healed. And it performed great signs, even causing fire to come down from heaven to the earth in full view of the people. Because of the signs it was given power to perform on behalf of the first beast, it deceived the inhabitants of the earth. It ordered them to set up an image[413]in honor of the beast who was wounded by the sword and yet lived. The second beast was given power to give breath to the image of the first beast, so that the image could speak and cause all who refused to worship the image to be killed. It also forced all people, great and small, rich and poor, free and slave, to receive a mark on their right hands or on their

---

411. 1 Timothy 2:5 NIV.

412. Colossians 2:9 NIV.

413. εἰκόνα

> *foreheads, so that they could not buy or sell unless they had the mark, which is the name of the beast or the number of its name. This calls for wisdom. Let the person who has insight calculate the number of the beast, for it is the number of a man. That number is 666.*[414]

Every person bears unique inherited and acquired body spots. In my youth, I heard folks talk about birthmarks. Some joked about them. This *Revelation* 13 scene relates little to childhood stories, songs, or individual blemishes. Whether a government or some enemy might mark us, I cannot say. Yet each of us carries a definite indicator. Other people might not recognize the feature on us, but the Lord and the devil do.

Of the two opposite designations, God destined no one to bear one brand or the other. We choose the type we display. We can also change our marks. How do we get these features? Who marks us? How can we switch marks? Answers to these questions come from various parts of the *Bible*. *Revelation* delivers figurative messages through numbers, visions, dreadful images, and war references. *Chapter* 13 focuses on two symbolic beasts that represent the devil's agents.[415]

The first beast (Greek *therion*) emerged from the ocean or sea.[416] The verses above say a second beast (also a *therion*) came "out of the earth." This next *theríon* or beast looked like a lamb yet wore two horns. Though appearing innocent, he spoke like a dragon. This second beast carried the authority of the first beast (v.12). His purpose: make people on earth worship the first beast.

What or who was the first beast? The verse 12 phrase, "Whose fatal wound had been healed" offers a clue. Most scholars assume this first beast with the cured wound refers to Nero Caesar. Nero ruled Rome from 54-68 AD. In 64 AD, a tremendous fire destroyed much of the city. Rumors spread that Nero started the blaze. Whether or not he torched Rome, Nero blamed Christians for the pyrotechnics. Numerous followers of Jesus suffered because of Nero's false accusations. The mention of Nero's name made many Christians tremble. Both Paul and Peter likely died during the last part of his

---

414. Verses 11-18 NIV.

415. The word translated beast refers to an animal. The Greek word is theríon (θηρίον). Most rural people routinely deal with a person who practices theriatrics. *Therí* refers to an animal of some kind. A theriatric practices veterinary medicine. *Therí* also occurs in a different context. Some movies feature therianthropics, animal men, for example **werewolfs.** Therianthropics **refers to humans taking animal form.** Theríon simply refers to an animal of some kind— some type of beast— even a snake.

416. Revelation 13:1-10.

reign. After Nero committed suicide in 68 AD, rumors circulated that he either didn't die or that he came back from the dead. For decades those two possibilities activated fear.

In 1945, Adolph Hitler and Eva Braun (his mistress-wife) presumably committed suicide; their bodies burned beyond recognition. Reports persisted for years that Hitler and Eva escaped alive to Argentina or somewhere in South America. Imagine the terror Hitler's name created among Jews, Poles, Russians, and others who survived the holocaust. Nero never reappeared. Emperor Domitian began ruling Rome in 81 AD, however, and renewed Nero-like persecutions. The revived fiery oppressions resembled a "resurrection" of Nero — as though his "fatal wound had been healed."

Assaults on believers developed on an additional front. Throughout the first century, Rome's rulers progressively exalted themselves. Our yearly calendars display a month named for Julius Caesar and another month for Octavius, who took the name Augustus, which means "inspiring awe and reverence."[417] Later in the first century, Rome's rulers began referring to themselves as gods. Their representatives used various ruses to promote emperor-worship. One ploy involved deceiving folks into thinking those reigning possessed divine powers. Paul predicted these efforts in 2 Thessalonians:

> *The coming of the lawless one will be in accordance with how Satan works. He will use all sorts of displays of power through signs and wonders that serve the lie, and the ways that wickedness deceives those who are perishing. They perish because they refused to love the truth and so be saved.*418

What Do *Revelation's* Two Beasts Symbolize And What Is The Mark Of The Beast?

The first beast likely represents authoritarian power vested in the emperors. The second beast probably symbolizes the state's intrusion into and control of religion. During the first century AD, emperor-worship stunningly escalated, especially in eastern parts of the Empire, location of *Revelation's* Seven Churches. Note *Revelation* 13: 14: "It (the second beast) ordered them to set up an image in honor of the beast..." And "(15) cause all who refused to worship the image to be killed."

---

417. That's one reason I deplore attaching the term "reverend" to my name. No created being deserves that honor.

418. 2:9, 10 NIV I suspect that public portrayals of the Emperors' miraculous powers included scenes that depicted them surviving even death by sword. Consider the fright moviegoers underwent which was created by the staged recovery abilities of Frankenstein's monster and Freddie Kruger.

Some regions of the Roman Empire required Emperor-allegiance before citizens could buy or sell anything.

Verses 16-18 of Chapter 13 tell us that authorities required people to worship the sovereigns. The second beast forced everyone, small and great, rich and poor, free and slave:

> *to receive a mark on their right hands or on their foreheads, so that they could not buy or sell unless they had the mark, which is the name of the beast or the number of its name. This calls for wisdom. Let the person who has insight calculate the number of the beast, for it is the number of a man. That number is 666.*

To what does this marking refer, and who is 666? Instead of texting, playing computer games, and tweeting in those days, many people played Gemátriah. What is Gemátriah? Because the ancient Hebrew language lacked numbers, folks represented numerals by using the letters of the alphabet. Aleph, the first letter equaled one; Beth, two; Gimel, three, and so on. The tenth Hebrew letter Yod represented ten. The following letter, Kaph=twenty, and next, Lamedh=thirty, and so on. Archaeologists confirmed the use of this ancient game when they uncovered an ancient inscription which read, "I love her whose number is (such and such)." If you similarly assigned numbers in English, the following names would share these numerical qualities: Jim=59, Lorraine=335, Roger=252, Beverly=1232. Aramaic, a sister language, used the same letters as Hebrew. Assign numerical qualities to each letter of the Aramaic alphabet using the above method, and Nero Caesar's name computes to 666. In fact one of the Dead Sea Scrolls contains an example of this usage.[419]

Computations similar to the above may explain 666, but other possibilities exist for the meaning of the much-feared triple-six. Recall the placement of the beast's mark? The beast forced all: "... **to receive a mark on their right hands or on their foreheads...**" Most people are right- handed, so that hand appears more prominently. Foreheads typically offer lots of empty face space. Marks placed on other parts of human bodies are far less discernible. These truths and a pair of OT readings suggest other insights into **mark** placement. First, from Deuteronomy:

> *Hear, O Israel: The LORD our God, the LORD is one. Love the LORD your God with all your heart and with all your soul and with all your strength. These commandments that I give you today are to*

---

419. Some refer to this type of computation as a cryptogram. See Carroll Gillis, *Revelation: an Exposition,* Sunburst Press, Pacoima, CA 1989, pp. 141-148, for a fuller explanation of this method and interpretation.

> be on your hearts. Impress them on your children. Talk about them when you sit at home and when you walk along the road, when you lie down and when you get up. **Tie them as symbols on your hands and bind them on your foreheads.**420

Exodus 13 reads similarly but primarily pertains to Passover celebrations, when the Lord required Israelites to eat yeast-free food for a week. The Mosaic Law obliged them to clear all traces of yeast from their homes. If you celebrated a seven day holiday and ate unleavened bread and super-flat, crusty pancakes, your kids would ask, "Why are we doing this?" If you have children and you dedicate your Sundays to God, they probably already question:

"Why do we have to be different?"

"Why do we have to go to church?"

"Why can't we sleep in Sundays or watch football or play soccer like everyone else?"

The Lord prepared obedient Israelite parents with the proper and reasonable answer:

> *On that day tell your son, "I do this because of what the LORD did for me when I came out of Egypt." This observance will be for you like a sign on your hand and a reminder on your forehead that this law of the LORD is to be on your lips.*421

> *Tie them (God's laws) as symbols on your hands and bind them on your foreheads.*

Israel's feast celebrations and faithful Law of Moses observances marked them as God's people—those who obeyed God, loved God and regularly credited and thanked God for giving them so much. These *OT* references strongly resemble the **mark *or* sign**, don't they?

Unfortunately, most of the Israelite leaders and population refused to put the Lord first. They wanted to live as their neighbors did. Worshiping God cut into their fun and making-money-time. The Israelites quit their marriage vows and became greedy, ungrateful, proud, and arrogant.[422] They disavowed the thought of loving and respecting one

---

420. Deuteronomy 6: 4-8 NIV.

421. Exodus 13:8, 9 NIV This commandment later gave rise to the use of phylacteries and other devices containing scripture, which some proudly wore as "signs" of their righteousness (Matthew 23:5).

422. The Lord ordered Jeremiah (17:19-27) to stand at Jerusalem's gates and warn merchants, farmers, and so on not to violate the Sabbath, reminding them that they might lose their nation. Jeremiah's contemporaries refused to heed the warnings. After the Exile, Nehemiah confronted the same greed among his countrymen (13:15-22).

another. Rejecting obedience to God; they snubbed the Lord's way, and forgot all he did for them.

The *OT* prophets reminded Israel's people of their errors and the consequences of disobedience. The majority declined to act as God required. Nearly the whole country stopped worshipping the Lord. Honoring their Creator took too much time and interfered with their fun and games. They chose greed and pleasure.

Contemporary society similarly emphasizes money, various forms of alcohol consumption, partying, loud music piped through the latest earbud gadgets, phone gizmos, electronic games, movies, sports, worrying, and other forms of self-focus.

The prophet Jeremiah lived and actively served God in Israel's final days. During the time that the powerful Babylonians were overrunning and destroying Jerusalem, Jeremiah wrote the book that bears his name. Through Jeremiah and the earlier prophet Isaiah, the Lord warned the leaders and the people of disastrous outcomes. Nobody listened.[423] The same concerns that obsess us preoccupied them. They savored the similar leisure forms that fixate modern society. The Lord finally said: You are on your own. Your greed, ingratitude, pride, and refusal to listen will bring catastrophic consequences. *Ezekiel 9* describes the Lord's withdrawal from Israel. Verse four of that chapter tells that the Lord sent a messenger, telling him: "Go throughout the city of Jerusalem and put a mark on the foreheads of those who grieve and lament over all the detestable things that are done in it."[424]

The Holy Spirit's Marks

Does marking still occur? Yes. We wear either the world's mark or God's. How does one know whose mark he/she bears? When we repent of sin, confess Christ, and are baptized into him with intentions of living for him, the Lord marks us with his Holy Spirit. As we earlier quoted from Ephesians:

> *And you also were included in Christ when you heard the message of truth, the gospel of your salvation. When you believed, you were marked in him with a seal, the promised Holy Spirit, who is a deposit guaranteeing our inheritance until the redemption of those who are God's possession—to the praise of his glory.*425

---

423. Isaiah 55: 2 contains strong appeals to listen. Isaiah 3 records stunning parallels with current (21st century) society. In case you agree with American society's current reform and empower movements, read Isaiah's description of Israel's late eighth century trends.

424. Verse 4, NIV.

425. 1:13, and 14 (NIV); see also Acts 2:38, 39 and 1 Corinthians 12:12,13.

God places his seal, the Holy Spirit, on his people who believe and obey. God marks us, but he also warns that we can lose his Holy Spirit mark:

> *And do not grieve the Holy Spirit of God, with whom you were sealed (marked) for the day of redemption. Get rid of all bitterness, rage and anger, brawling and slander, along with every form of malice.*426

When we rid ourselves of bitterness, rage, anger, and so on, the Holy Spirit remains with and in us. Certain types of sincere behavior and demeanor enable others at times to recognize God's mark on us. Thus verse 32 NIV advises: "Be kind and compassionate to one another, forgiving each other, just as in Christ God forgave you." When we stop loving God and allow hate to control us, as happened in Ezekiel's day, God exits. We cannot continue to grieve the Holy Spirit. Only you and the Lord really know whether God's Spirit marks your hand and forehead.

Young's Analytical Concordance to the Bible shows the "mark of the beast" occurring eight times in *Revelation*. Young followed the King James Version in which the word *mark* appears that number of times. *Karagma* (χάραγμα), which refers to an etching or an engraving, is the Greek term. In the Greek text of *Revelation*, however, *karagma* appears only seven times. Young's parenthesis in 15:2 indicates that *karagma* there is only intimated. No major Greek manuscript includes the word in that verse; neither does the Nestles text nor Westcott and Hort. The sole other *NT* usage of *karagma* appears in *Acts* 17:29: "Being then the children of God, we ought not to think that the Godhead is like unto gold, or silver, or stone, *graven* by art and device of man" (ASV).427 Paul's usage of the term here helps us perceive the inscribed or etched concept. On the one hand, the Holy Spirit doesn't appear to be an impulsive or slam-bam scratch. No one shapes an image with a few whacks. On the other hand, the beast's *karagma* type mark requires a period of whittling or etching resulting from continued giving in to Satan's wiles.

Jesus fully resisted the devil's cleverest temptations then came back from the dead after wrath-filled enemies executed him. In accomplishing these extraordinary feats, Jesus destroyed Satan's superpower status. Unwavering belief in Jesus' moral perfection and his return from death alters our life-perspective. Appalling news headlines seem less ominous. When we trust Jesus' identity, power, and authority, fear of death fades.

---

426. Ephesians 4:30, 31 NIV

427. The form used in this verse is χαράγματι

Recall how Satan tried to tempt Jesus by taking him to a high mountain and showing him all the kingdoms of the world and their splendor.[428]

> "All this I will give you," he said, "if you will bow down and worship me."
> Jesus said to him, "Away from me, Satan! For it is written: 'Worship the Lord your God, and serve him only.'"[429]

Cash, power, and popularity daily entice us from Jesus' high moral standards and his complete, loving devotion to God. Too often we succumb to Satan's inducements. None of us repels temptation completely as Jesus definitively and resolutely did.

---

428. Δόξαν splendor or glory.

429. Matthew 4:8-10 NIV.

Chapter 10

Selected Scene Subjects In Chapters 8-19

Revelation Chapter 8 — The Half-Hour Of Silence

> When he opened the seventh seal, there was silence in heaven for about half an hour.
>
> And I saw the seven angels who stand before God, and seven trumpets were given to them. Another angel, who had a golden censer, came and stood at the altar. He was given much incense to offer, with the prayers of all God's people, on the golden altar in front of the throne. The smoke of the incense, together with the prayers of God's people, went up before God from the angel's hand. Then the angel took the censer, filled it with fire from the altar, and hurled it on the earth; and there came peals of thunder, rumblings, flashes of lightning and an earthquake. [430]

The above tells the opening of seal seven on history's great scroll. Readers expect finality. Instead there was about half an hour of silence in heaven. Hush sometimes follows disasters. Violent traffic accidents shock us with shrieking of brakes, metal crashing, breaking glass, steaming radiators, steamed people cursing and moaning, and car horns blaring. At times catastrophe leaves stunning stillness. In the 1971, Los Angeles early AM earthquake, we felt as though four giants picked up the corners of our house and violently shook it. To the west, electrical transformers exploded, temporarily lighting the darkness. Because power shut down, dark prevailed till dawn. Eerie quiet ruled broken only by occasional aftershocks.

Chapter 8's sudden stillness of heaven occurs prior to catastrophe. Quiet comes from the realization that God's messenger force (seven attendant angels) stand ready to bring ruin on a third of the world's population. That well known *Habakkuk* 2:20 passage alerts: "The Lord is in his holy temple; let all the earth be silent before him" (NIV). The ancient *Septuagint* translators used a word meaning "reverence" or "be moved with fear." Zephaniah the prophet warned similarly: "Be silent before the sovereign Lord . . . (1:7 NIV), where the *Septuagint*

---

430. *Revelation* 8:1-5 NIV.

uses a form of the same verb.[431] This moment looms more sobering than any war declaration by a major world power. God set the time to punish those combatting his saints. His punishing angels prepare their assault in response to the prayers of God's suffering servants. Recall the persistent widow parable (*Luke* 18:1-8) and the pleas of Jacob's descendants enslaved in Egypt (*Exodus* 2:23-25).

> *Then the seven angels who had the seven trumpets prepared to sound them.*
>
> *The first angel sounded his trumpet, and there came hail and fire mixed with blood, and it was hurled down on the earth. A third of the earth was burned up, a third of the trees were burned up, and all the green grass was burned up.*
>
> *The second angel sounded his trumpet, and something like a huge mountain, all ablaze, was thrown into the sea. A third of the sea turned into blood, a third of the living creatures in the sea died, and a third of the ships were destroyed.*
>
> *The third angel sounded his trumpet, and a great star, blazing like a torch, fell from the sky on a third of the rivers and on the springs of water—the name of the star is Wormwood. A third of the waters turned bitter, and many people died from the waters that had become bitter.*
>
> *The fourth angel sounded his trumpet, and a third of the sun was struck, a third of the moon, and a third of the stars, so that a third of them turned dark. A third of the day was without light, and also a third of the night.*
>
> *As I watched, I heard an eagle that was flying in midair call out in a loud voice: "Woe! Woe! Woe to the inhabitants of the earth, because of the trumpet blasts about to be sounded by the other three angels!"* (8:6-13 NIV)

Numerous times, God has responded to his imploring saints and destroyed earthly powers that exceeded certain bounds. The destruction of the Third Reich might be an example. Contemporary ungodly nations-states might suffer the same fate. God sets the times and seasons for these actions; not human "experts" or "authorities."

Revelation 12 — The Sun, Moon, 12 Stars, And The Dragon
Why do so many interpreters fail to consider the most simple and biblically-based explanation for the meaning of *Revelation* 12's "mega

---
431. Both verbs from εὐλαβέομαι, according to Bernard A. Taylor to be "cautious", "afraid" ,"fear" , "honor", "reverence"; Habakkuk -εὐλαβείσθω (present middle or passive third person singular); Zephaniah — εὐλαβεῖσθε (pres m/p 2nd person plural).

sign?" H.B. Swete noted the similarity between the *OT* references and this much argued scene, but did not seriously consider it.[432] Though Eb. Nestle found numerous *OT* references, citations, and quotations in *Revelation*, my parallel Latin-Greek Nestles text shows no *OT* allusion for 12:1. In verse 2, Nestle cited *Isaiah 66:7* and *Micah 4:2*. These two prophetic verses give stunning information for understanding this sign, yet Nestle gave no *OT* references for verse one. Westcott and Hort listed hundreds of *OT* quotations and references in their 1940 Greek text edition, but listed nothing for this verse.[433]

What did this mega scene signify? Was this unusually dressed pregnant woman actually in paradise? Do you suppose most believers expect to see this sort of spectacle in heaven? What does this pained, prenatal lady portray?

When Jesus and the Apostles urged familiarity with the Scriptures, they meant the *Old Testament*. Most *New Testament* writers assumed that their readers thoroughly knew the *OT*. Even though the churches he addressed had strong Gentile representation, Paul made repeated *OT* references in *Romans* and *1 Corinthians*. *Revelation* uses abundant *OT* sources, narratives, and quotations.[434] Think of the names Balaam, Jezebel, David, and Judah, which appear in the letters to the seven churches. Strong evidence leads us to conclude that returning to Eden emerges as one of *Revelation's* clear-cut subthemes.[435]

With these facts in mind, note Joseph's *Genesis* 37 dreams. Joseph son of Jacob and Rachel had eleven brothers. He earlier told his family a dream about them binding sheaves of grain out in the field. Joseph's sheaf stood and the sheaves gathered by all the other brothers came and bowed to his. Grasping the dream's gist doesn't require higher education.

> *Then he (Joseph) had another dream, and he told it to his brothers. "Listen," he said, '"I had another dream, and this time the sun and moon and eleven stars were bowing down to me." 10 When he told his father as well as his brothers, his father rebuked him and said, "What is this dream you had? Will your mother and I and your brothers actually come and bow down to the ground before you?"*[436]

---

432. See H.B. Swete, THE APOCALYPSE OF ST. JOHN, p. 147.

433. Brooke Foss Westcott and Fenton John Anthony Hort, THE NEW TESTAMENT IN THE ORIGINAL GREEK, New York, THE MACMILLLAN COMPANY, 1940, p 615.

434. These include the Exodus, wilderness journey, Temple construction, and so on.

435. Revelation 2:7; 22:1-6.

436. Genesis 37: 9, 10 NIV.

Not realizing Joseph would one day be second in command of the earth's most powerful nation, the implications of his son's dream distressed Jacob. Despite God's promises to him, neither could Jacob foresee that his descendants would become the nation of people through whom God's Messiah or Christ would come. Jacob, his wife Rachel, and his twelve sons help us understand this heaven-sign in *Revelation* 12.[437]

Context is vital to this scene. The chapter and verse separations in most Bibles help us locate particular sayings and incidents. These "helps" also mislead readers, however, concerning related incidents and circumstances. Without context, folks get lost unnecessarily in deep, dark speculation forests. The *Bible* perpetually warns us about those who lead us astray.

Consider the setting (context) for this *Revelation* 12 passage. Opening of the last of the seven seals brought one half hour of silence. After intense, powerful sights, prolonged quiet increased the dramatic tension. Recall the major source of unresolved tension? How long must the faithful suffer injustice and unpredictable turmoil? When will God play his strong hand?

God's people are not yet home and will not reach "home" in this world. Like Israel on its way from harsh Egyptian slavery, trudging through a wilderness of testing, God's church makes its way through present uncertainty. The strongest nation on earth at the time considered Jesus' followers enemies of the state. Though local Roman officials didn't always enforce the religious bans, Christians never gained legal status until Constantine's time, nearly three hundred years after Jesus. For witnessing to Jesus' resurrection, first century believers faced death. Sixty years after Jesus, persecution intensified, especially in Asia (western Turkey). At what point of suffering or lack of immediate reward for your godly efforts, would you be tempted to say, "Enough," "I quit," "I can't take any more"? Would you doubt God's plan? To spare your family or to gain approval of your neighbors, might you want to compromise?

How many contemporary readers view *The Apocalypse* as a book of encouragement? Unless we see *Revelation's* strong hope and victory emphasis, we shall be lost in the weeds and woods. Recall when Moses sent twelve spies into the Promised Land to scope it out? Only two of the twelve (Caleb and Joshua) returned confident in God. Caleb and Joshua saw the potential and they trusted the Lord's power to attain occupation of the land. *Revelation* helps us see the Promised Land and gives us glimpses of God's eternal power. Numerous scenes of Israel's journey cheer us and provide hope. Realizing that expectation

---

437. The sons were not all Rachel's. Jesus was born of Judah's descendants. Judah's mother was Rachel's sister Leah. See Genesis 29:14-35.

depends on our choice to purely, faithfully, obediently trust God and follow Jesus, the Lamb slain.

Readers can see how Jacob's family provides background for this great *Revelation* 12 section. Jacob's sons, Israel's twelve tribes, spent centuries looking for a solution to their mistakes. The sun, moon and stars likely represent Israel as God's people. They kept looking for a rescuer, a Messiah who would rule justly. God did not immediately answer Israel's wishes and prayers. For centuries they longed and endured; they also sinned grossly by disobeying God. Jesus, the Messiah's, arrival was painful. Mary dealt with the awkwardness of a pregnancy induced by the Holy Spirit. Joseph faced serious embarrassment.[438] When we Christians suffer persecution, we need to know we are part of God's long-term plan to save all people. This Chapter 12 "woman" sign reminds us how God uses us believers in his grand design. In the Lord, our work becomes meaningful. God involves us in his winning strategy that began in creation and ends when he finishes history.

> *(12:3, 4) Then another sign appeared in heaven: an enormous red dragon with seven heads and ten horns and seven crowns on his heads. Its tail swept a third of the stars out of the sky and flung them to the earth.*

We do not expect to see this sort of sight in heaven, either. "Enormous" translates the Greek word *mega*. The *dragon*, of course, is a sign, not the full reality. This scene resembles a cartoon designed to convey truth of Satan's ugly potency.

The dragon possesses seven heads, but ten horns. John did not tell us the positions of the dragon's horns though they signify his destructiveness throughout the course of human history. Seven heads probably intimate his extensive super-craftiness. The sweeping tail that fells stars likely shows his capability of bringing down nations. Red makes him frightening and ghastly.

Each of the dragon's seven heads wears a diadem. Only God or those pretending to be God wear diadems. Faithful Christians will receive victory crowns or wreaths; not kingly crowns.[439] Verse 9 identifies the dragon, serpent, devil, Satan. All humans know of his power first-hand.

---

438. See Matthew 1:19. Though Mary's pregnancy caused by the Holy Spirit did not seem credible to Joseph, he did not want to publicly humiliate or disgrace her.

439. These are "stephanoi" crowns-wreaths of the type awarded then to victorious athletes.

Revelation 13 — Looking Anew At 666

For many years, the arguments some presented concerning the identity of the beast persuaded me that the mark of the beast, **666**, referred to Nero. Evidence based on the alphabet related symbolism called Gemátriah seemed adequate. *Old* and *New Testament* data now point me in a different direction. The particulars that support my new conclusion appear in the following paragraphs.

Scholars estimate that Rome's first century AD population exceeded one million. Some reckon that the city's vast populace annually consumed on average 600 pounds of wheat per person. The emperors learned to regulate and subsidize grain prices to keep the metropolis happily fed. Massive fleets of merchant and government ships regularly transported grain from Egypt to Rome.[440]

That city's government controlled a huge area surrounding the Mediterranean Sea. Rome's borders extended north to the Danube in Central Europe and west to Spain and the British Isles. The Empire controlled much of North Africa (Egypt was long known as Rome's bread basket). Legions conquered east as far as the Caspian Sea.

Because Rome lies inland, the city depended on ports such as Puteoli,[441] (north of modern Naples) and Ostia (much closer to Rome) to supply its vast needs and incalculable wants. Those harbors proved inadequate for the burgeoning commerce. In about 44 AD, Claudius Caesar began construction of a complex known as Portus at the mouth of the Tiber River, which flows through Rome. Portus' grand design included an intricate, extensive network of canals, distribution centers, warehouses, and splendid government buildings.[442] Planners created an impressively efficient system for moving and transferring goods to intended destinations. Emperor Trajan (ruled 98-117 AD) completed the mammoth project. His armies also conquered significant previously held Parthian territory in the East.

By land and sea, Rome imported and exported increasing quantities of foods, wares, treasures, curiosities, and tribute. Rome imposed burdensome import and export duties, taxes, and tariffs.

> *The Roman emperor Vespasian, a military commander who came to power after the profligate Nero committed suicide, was anxious to restore the Roman state to solvency. Virtually everything was taxed,*

---

440. In Acts, Luke refers to numerous merchant ships that transported Paul to and from various Mediterranean ports.

441. The ship that transported Paul and company from Malta to the mainland docked at Puteoli (Acts 28:13-16). Air mile distance from Rome =112, by road =142.

442. For more information on Portus, see **Rome's Imperial Port** by Jason Urbanus, "Archaeology Magazine," March/April 2015, pp.26-33.

*even Rome's public urinals. When his finicky son Titus protested that this tax was beneath the dignity of the state, Vespasian took a handful of coins obtained from its source and held them up to his nose, "Non olet! (It does not smell!)*443

Revelation 18 itemizes wide arrays of goods shipped to and from the city. Maximum profit greased the efforts' productivity. These factors prompted God's woes on the city (18:3-24) "glittering with gold, precious stones, and pearls."

Rome's government made two demands of their conquered foes; maintain peace and pay taxes. Recall how in Jesus' day, coinage used in Israel bore Caesar's image or *eikon*?[444] Each time Jewish citizens bought something or paid taxes, their purchasing coins reminded them of foreign rule. The chief priests, rulers, and Pharisees, who so guardedly secured the inner Temple courts from the presence of Gentiles, likely carried images of the hated rulers in their coin purses as they entered the pristine "holy" gates.

Computer owners world-wide know how icons represent rife greed, which Paul labeled as idolatry.[445] The later requirement to offer incense to the Emperor's image (*eikon*) before he/she could buy or sell anything linked difficult monetary decisions with the choice between God and ruler (or mammon-wealth). Jesus taught that we cannot serve both.

Luke's Gospel includes Jesus' comments on the Pharisees' and Sadducees' love of money. The well-known parable about the rich man and Lazarus probably teaches more about preferring wealth over serving God than the story tells of the "soul's" state between death and the Judgment.[446] Past and present church leaders often turn blind eyes to avarice. Compare the numbers of church members, who have been dis-fellowshiped for greed with those "cut-off" for immorality.[447] Yet note the compelling cautions in *Luke* 12 and *Colossians* 3:5.

Revelation's letters to the seven churches warn against the Nicolaitans and those who "hold the teachings of Balaam." Both references symbolize selfish desire for riches.[448] Big money motivated Balaam

---

443. Lance Davidson, *The Ultimate Reference Book: The Wit's Thesaurus,* Avon Books, New York, 1994 p. 262.

444. Matthew 22:15-22. The word translated image is eikon (εἰκών).

445. Colossians 3:5.

446. Note the context of Jesus' rich man and Lazarus parable in Luke 16.

447. I've heard of no such instances.

448. Nicolaitan means "power over the people;" Greek nikos=victory and laos=people. In Hebrew "bala" means to swallow down, devour or destroy.

and led the proud Laodicean church to boast.[449] Present church leaders rarely identify, as Peter so clearly did, those whose who "have a heart trained in greed . . . forsaking the right way, they have gone astray, having followed the way of Balaam, the son of Beor, who loved the wages of unrighteousness."[450]

The Holy Spirit supplied John with various combinations of both *Old* and *New Testament* instances to describe Rome's glaring transgressions and to pronounce the perverse city's eventual fall. As in all of *Revelation*, OT wording, references, and phrasing weave through Chapters 16-19. The section recalls numerous arrogant, materialistic prototypes of Rome. The city became the re-embodiment of Egypt's slave owning pharaohs; the proud ancient naval power Tyre; merciless Nineveh; magnificent, corrupt Babylon, and hosts of nearby ungodly enemies of Israel.[451] Add Jerusalem's covetous, haughty priestly class and Israel's false prophets.

Historic evidence indicates voracious, rampant greed in Roman customs and practices.[452] These fused with scandalously immoral behavior that saturated first-century Roman society. Roman decadence, especially in its elite and ruling class became legendary and needs little further comment.[453] Emphasis on power, splendor, wealth, and debauched behavior rivalled King Solomon's conduct, which the writer of 1 Kings sadly chronicled:

> *King Solomon . . . loved many foreign women besides Pharaoh's daughter—Moabites, Ammonites, Edomites, Sidonians, and Hittites. They were from nations about which the LORD had told the Israelites, "You must not intermarry with them, because they will surely turn your hearts after their gods." Nevertheless, Solomon held fast to them*

"Am" means "the people." "Balaam" therefore denotes to destroy the people or conquer the people. The Balaam reference seems aimed at believers of Jewish background; Nicolaitan to Gentiles.

449. Revelation 3:14-22. See Numbers 22-25 for the Balaam account.

450. 2 Peter 2:15 NASB.

451. See Exodus 1-14; Isaiah 19-25; Jeremiah 25; Ezekiel 26-32; Daniel 7; Joel 1-3; Nahum 1-3; Zephaniah 2, 3; for example, as well as references to Balaam in Numbers and Jezebel in 1 and 2 Kings.

452. See remarks on Roman society by H.H. Harper in his preface to *The Letters of Pliny*, translated William Melmoth, (ed. Clifford H. Moore, The Bibliophile Society, Boston, MDCDXXV, pp. ix-xxviii).

453. For specifics of Rome's conquests, excessive taxation, and their effects, consult Barry Cunliffe's *Europe Between the Oceans: 9000 BC – AD 1000*, Chapter 11, "The Interlude of Empire: 140 BC-AD 300," Yale University Press, New Haven and London, 2008.

in love. He had seven hundred wives of royal birth and three hundred concubines, and his wives led him astray. As Solomon grew old, his wives turned his heart after other gods, and his heart was not fully devoted to the LORD his God, as the heart of David his father had been. He followed Ashtoreth the goddess of the Sidonians, and Molek the detestable god of the Ammonites.

So Solomon did evil in the eyes of the LORD; he did not follow the LORD completely, as David his father had done. On a hill east of Jerusalem, Solomon built a high place for Chemosh the detestable god of Moab, and for Molek the detestable god of the Ammonites.

He did the same for all his foreign wives, who burned incense and offered sacrifices to their gods. The LORD became angry with Solomon because his heart had turned away from the LORD, the God of Israel, who had appeared to him twice. Although he had forbidden Solomon to follow other gods, Solomon did not keep the LORD's command.[454]

Consider some curious similarities between Solomon and Rome's emperor Domitian (Emperor from 81-96 AD, approximate time of *Revelation's* writing):

1. *1 Kings* 10 detailed King Solomon's splendor and pomp. He lavishly flaunted gold objects to such an extent, "silver was considered of little value" (verse 21). Trading ships regularly sailed to and from distant foreign ports returning with rare objects such as peacocks, ivory, and apes. Solomon gained notoriety from his lucrative import-export business (verses 28 and 29). He sat on a throne of ivory covered with fine gold. Solomon exceeded all the kings of the earth in riches and wisdom.
   In Solomonic fashion, but on a far grander scale, Rome proudly reveled in its escalating wealth and power. Predicting Rome's fall (figuratively referring to it as Babylon, which was destroyed centuries earlier), in *Revelation* 18: 2, 3, the angel from heaven shouted: "Fallen! Fallen is Babylon the Great! . . . The kings of the earth committed adultery with her and the merchants of the earth grew rich from her excessive luxuries."[455]

2. Solomon perfected the art of taxes, tariffs, import, and export duties (*1 Kings* 10: 26-29). The infidelity of Solomon's

---

454. 1 Kings 11: 1-10 NIV.

455. The Book of Daniel relates how Babylon's King Nebuchadnezzar (or Nebuchadrezzar) emphasized and gloried in the same type of splendor but then lost his kingdom.

father David lay behind the Lord's prophecy through Nathan the prophet to break Israel's kingdom apart. Solomon's son Rehoboam's unwise decision not to lower his father's oppressive taxes, however, led to the actual permanent division between Israel's northern and southern kingdoms and their eventual demise.[456]

Immediately after the *Revelation* 13:17 (NASB) reference to the mark "of the beast and the number of his name," John wrote (v. 18): "Here is *wisdom*. Let him who has understanding calculate the number of the beast, for the number is that of a man; and his number is six hundred and sixty six."

Both *1 Kings* 10:14 and *2 Chronicles* 9:13 specify the weight of the gold that Solomon received yearly as 666 talents, not including the revenues from merchants, and traders, and so on.[457]

For first-century Christians, the connections between Solomon and Rome's Domitian likely seemed clear. They easily interpreted the links which we shall present. Most twenty-first century Christians lack familiarity with the *OT* that *NT* writers assumed present among first century Christians. Scarcity of acquaintance with the *OT* contributes greatly to modern church members' incomprehension of the numerous *OT* allusions in *Romans, 1 Corinthians, Galatians, Hebrews, 2 Peter,* and *Jude.* Matthew's Gospel constantly refers to Jesus fulfilling predictions of *OT* prophets. Political leanings, social pressure, and monetary cravings tend to blind us as to what happened with many of Jesus' fellow countrymen.[458]

Link A -Three different Gospels cite Jesus' mention of Solomon's wisdom: The Scribes and Pharisees demanded that Jesus offer a sign of his godly authority. Part of his response included the fact that the Queen of Sheba "came from the ends of the earth to hear the *Wisdom* of Solomon

---

456. 1 Kings 12:1-24.

457. As 1 Kings 10 indicates, Solomon had a curious affinity for sixes. Six hundred bekas of gold went into each of the two hundred shields for his "Palace of the Forest of Lebanon," (verses 16, 17). His throne had six steps with twelve lions at each end of those six steps, (verses 18-20). Note also the penchant for sixes in verses 10: 26-29.

458. For that reason, few connected the idea that the Messiah would be a suffering servant. Cf. Isaiah 52-54; Luke 24:25-27 (Even Jesus' disciples struggled to accept the thought); Acts 3:18, 19; 17:3. Peter plainly told us that we should be ready to suffer with Christ (1 Peter 2:11-25; 3:8-5:11).

and behold something greater than Solomon is here."⁴⁵⁹

In *Revelation* 4's heavenly scene, the four living creatures and 24 elders laid their crowns before the throne saying: "You are worthy, our Lord and God, to receive glory and honor and power, for you created all things, and by your will they were created and have their being."⁴⁶⁰ Once Jesus the Lamb took the scroll from the right hand of the One on the throne, every creature in heaven and earth joined the living beings, elders, and angelic host loudly singing: "Worthy is the Lamb, who was slain, to receive power and *wealth* and *wisdom* and strength and honor and glory and praise!"⁴⁶¹ Note the word order of the reasons for praising God and *the Lamb* and the added qualities of *wisdom* and *wealth*.

The similar qualities appear in *Revelation* 7:12 after those who come out of the great tribulation cry in a loud voice: "Salvation belongs to our God, who sits on the throne, and to the Lamb." The mighty throng "fell down on their faces before the throne and worshiped God, saying: 'Amen! Praise and glory and *wisdom* and thanks and honor and power and strength be to our God forever. Amen!" Here, word order changes. As we already referenced, *wisdom* appears in 13:18. *Wisdom* reappears in Chapter 17:8-11:

*The beast, which you saw, once was, now is not, and yet will come up out of the Abyss and go to its destruction. The inhabitants of the earth whose names have not been written in the book of life from the creation of the world will be astonished when they see the beast, because it once was, now is not, and yet will come. ⁹"This calls for a mind with wisdom. The seven heads are seven hills on which the woman sits. ¹⁰ They are also seven kings. Five have fallen, one is, the other has not yet come; but when he does come, he must remain for only a little while.*⁴⁶²

What makes these additions of *wisdom* so significant?

Before we deal with this question, consider opinions (2020) posted on wikipedia and also appearing on the biblicalarcheaology.org website, and other sources, which question the long-held view that Domitian fiercely persecuted Christians. Pointing to Brian W. Jones's

459. Matthew 12:42 NASB and see Luke 11:31. Wisdom is *sophia* (σοφία(ν)) as in Revelation 13.

460. Verse 11 NASB.

461. 5:8-12 NIV.

462. 17:8-10 NIV.

research, Mark Wilson referred in **Biblical Archaeology Review** to a critical biography Jones wrote of Emperor (81-96 AD) Domitian of Rome. Both Jones and Wilson strongly opine that the tradition concerning Domitian's fierce opposition to Christians grew out of "fake news" generated by ancient writers. This false narrative occurred despite no evidence, Wilson claimed:

> "From a frail, almost non-existent basis, it gradually developed and grew large."2 ...No pagan writer of the time ever accused Domitian ...of persecuting Christians. Pliny, for example, served as a lawyer under Domitian and wrote in a letter to Trajan (r. 98–117 C.E.) that he was never present at the trial of a Christian (Letters 10.96.1)... Jones concludes, "No convincing evidence exists for a Domitianic persecution of the Christians."463

The allusion to "fake news" and "alternative facts" seems peculiar to me. In the letter to Trajan cited by Jones, Pliny unquestionably wrote:

> "Having never been present at any trials concerning those who profess Christianity, I am unacquainted with the measure of their punishment or how far it is proper to enter into an examination concerning them."464

Yet further reading of Pliny's letter to Trajan indicates that several Christians, former believers in Christ, and those alleged to be Christians previously appeared before Pliny.

He at times matter-of-factly dispatched some to death (administering capital punishment) and released others depending on whether the accused denied faith in Christ and willingly offered incense to the Emperor's statue. So you can read the facts yourself, included first, is not only the balance of Pliny's letter to Emperor Trajan, but second, Trajan's response.

> In the meanwhile, the method I have observed towards those who have been denounced to me as Christians is this: I interrogated them whether they were Christians; if they confessed I repeated the question twice again, adding the threat of capital punishment at the same time; when, if they still persevered, I ordered them to be immediately punished; for I was persuaded, whatever the nature of their opinions

---

463. www.biblicalarchaeology.org by Mark Wilson May 31, 2020. Alternative Facts: Domitian's Persecution of Christians, **Was Roman emperor Domitian really the great persecutor of Christians?**

464. As translated from the Latin original by William Melmoth for the Bibliophile Society circa 1920. Book III, pp. 167-169.

might be, a contumacious and inflexible obstinacy deserved correction. There were others also brought before me, possessed with the same infatuation; but being citizens of Rome / I directed them to be carried thither.

These accusations spread (as is usually the case) while the matter was actually under prosecution and several instances of the same nature occurred. An information was presented to me without any name subscribed, containing a charge against several persons. Those who denied they were, or had ever been Christians, who repeated after me an invocation to the gods, and offered religious

> Foot note in the original "A Roman citizen had the right of appeal to Rome as St. Paul appealed to Caesar." Acts XXV. 11" [167]

rites with wine and frankincense before your statue, which I had ordered to be brought for that purpose, together with those of the gods, and even reviled the name of Christ — whereas there is no forcing, it is said, those who are really Christians into a compliance with any of these articles — I thought it proper to discharge them. Some among those who were accused by a witness in person at first confessed themselves Christians but immediately after denied it. True, they had been of that number, but they had now (some three years, others more, and a few as much as twenty-five years ago) forsaken that error. They all worshipped your statue and the images of the gods, throwing out imprecations at the same time against the name of Christ. They affirmed, however, the whole of their guilt or their error, was that they met on a certain stated day before it was light, when they sang in alternate verses a hymn to Christ, as to some god, binding themselves by a solemn oath, not for the purposes of any wicked design, but never to commit any fraud, theft or adultery, never to falsify their word, nor deny a trust when they should be called upon to deliver it up; after which it was their custom to separate, and then reassemble to eat a meal- but a meal of a common and innocent kind.' From this practice, however, they had desisted after the publication of my edict, by which, according to your orders, I had forbidden the

> This was the Christians' answer to the charges brought against them that they murdered children and drank the blood and committed other crimes. The meal here referred to was the agape. [168]

> meeting of any associations. I judged it so much the more necessary to extort the real truth by putting two female slaves to the torture, who were styled deaconesses; but I could discover nothing more than an absurd and excessive superstition.
>
> I thought proper therefore to adjourn all further proceedings in this affair, in order to consult with you. For it appears to be a matter highly deserving your consideration; more especially as great numbers must be involved in the danger of these prosecutions, this inquiry having already extended, and being still likely to extend, to persons of all ranks and ages, and even of both sexes. For this contagious superstition is not confined to the cities only, but has spread its infection among the country villages. Nevertheless it still seems impossible to remedy this evil and restrain its progress. The temples at least, which were once almost deserted, begin now to be frequented; and the sacred solemnities, after a long intermission, are again revived; while there is a general demand for the victims, which for some time past have met with but few purchasers. From hence it is easy to imagine what numbers might be reclaimed from this error, if a pardon were granted to those who shall repent.

The complete text of the letter indicates that Jones and Wilson misread or should have read further into Pliny's letter. Only they and the Lord fully know their motives.

What can we conclude from Pliny's statement that he'd been present at no trials of Christians and his further statements about torture and executing those he found guilty? Why this seeming contradiction? I find the discrepancy rooted in what may be an unfortunate translation of the Latin word *cognitionibus* (root, cognition, dative case). According to *Cassell's Latin Dictionary*, the word can be understood as a legal inquiry, but the primary meanings are along the lines of *getting to know, study, acquaintance*.

On the basis of this evidence, Pliny seems to indicate that he never asked Christians why they believed in Jesus. In other words, what was the substance of their faith in Jesus, the Jew? Pliny dealt only with the question of the illegality of this new religion, which gave no regard to the traditional Roman gods and did not acknowledge the Emperor's divinity. Why else would Pliny keep a statue of Rome's supreme ruler at hand in order to apply the test?

Three *NT* examples support my theory. First, in *Acts* 23, Luke records the accusations of the Sanhedrin Court against Paul and the plot by forty men to kill the Apostle. The Jerusalem based Roman commander held Paul in custody. The conspirators went to the chief priests and elders telling of their vows and stating: "Now then, you and the Sanhedrin petition the commander to bring him before you on the pretext of wanting more accurate information about his case. We are ready to kill him before he gets here."[465] At Paul's defense (*Acts* 22), the Apostle explained why he converted from being a strict, rabid Pharisee to faith in Jesus of Nazareth, whom he'd been persecuting. Jesus' appearance to Paul on the Damascus road comprised much of the Apostle's case. My *Nestle's NOVUM TESTAMENTUM GRAECE ET LATINE* uses the Latin terms *certius cognituri de eo* where the English translates "more accurate information about his case."

Second, *Acts* 18 tells of Paul's year-and-a-half mission stay in Corinth. A radical Jewish element there took Paul to court (Latin-*tribunal*). Gallio presided as proconsul of Achaia. When Paul's opponents brought the charge of persuading people to worship God in ways contrary to the law,[466] Gallio viewed the matter as a disagreement over Jewish law (the Law of Moses). Because Judaism was legally practiced all over the Empire, Gallio showed no interest in getting involved in Mosaic Law intricacies stating:

> *"If you Jews were making a complaint about some misdemeanor or serious crime, it would be reasonable for me to listen to you. But since it involves questions about words and names and your own law — settle the matter yourselves. I will not be a judge of such things."* So he drove them off.[467]

In the verse 15 reference to "your own law," the Latin reads *lege vestra*, for example. "your (Jewish) legal matters." I will not be a judge (*Iudex*).

Acts 25 relates Paul's appearance before the Roman governor Festus. Festus asked Paul: "Are you willing to go up to Jerusalem and stand trial before me there on these charges?"[468] For trial, the Latin version uses the term *iudicari* (a court of justice). According to *Cassell's Latin Dictionary*, the usual words for trial are *iudicium* and *quaestio*, not *cognitio*; which can be used, however, for a legal inquiry or investigation as was conducted to examine the origins of Paul's radical life-change. Considering these facts, I think we can reasonably assume

---

465. Acts 23:15 NIV.

466. Verse 13.

467. Acts 18:14, 15 NIV.

468. Acts 25:9 NIV.

that Pliny adjudicated many trials of Christians. What he never bothered to do was to question any of them why they believed in Jesus. On the basis of their confession of faith in Christ, he presumed them guilty, so he gave them opportunity to renounce their belief, which evidently some did rather than to suffer execution.

Link B- The Wisdom Connection Between Solomon And Domitian

Solomon's wisdom included extraordinary philosophic, poetic, and musical abilities as well knowledge of plant and animal life.[469] If he wrote *Proverbs*, which I think he did, he realized that true wisdom derives from consulting, honoring, and obeying God at every life juncture. All the adulation Solomon received caused him to forget that God gave him his wisdom. By Jesus' time, Solomon's wisdom became legendary among the Jews and subsequently early Christians, too. In pointing to Israel's experiences, Paul wrote the Corinthian church, which apparently included many Gentiles: "These things happened to them as examples and were written down as warnings for us."[470]

Human wisdom leads to pride and the idolatry that worships and exalts human stars and heroes. Earlier in *1 Corinthians*, Paul made it clear that Christ: "became to us wisdom from God, and righteousness and sanctification and redemption."[471] Scripture denounces the wisdom of the age, which the Greeks so prized and the Romans cherished.

What seems not so evident was Domitian's quest for wisdom. He zealously worshipped the Roman goddess Minerva, goddess of wisdom (Greek, Athena). In his bedroom, the Emperor kept a personal shrine of Minerva. In at least four reverse types, Minerva appeared on coins minted with Domitian's image on the obverse side. He also named a legion after the wisdom goddess. Is it any wonder that the writer of *Revelation* asks readers to stop and think with the phrase: "This calls for wisdom."?[472]

Emperor Trajan's reply provides support for our conclusion. His letter, which follows, indicates his approval of Pliny's policies. Roman law clearly prohibited belief in Christ. If evidence presented confirmed that one practiced Christianity, the accused could refute the charge with a verbal denial and willingness to invoke the legal Roman gods.

---

469. 1 Kings 4:29-34.

470. 1 Corinthians 10:11 NIV.

471. 1 Corinthians 1:30 NASB.

472. Minerva"f. goddess of wisdom and patroness of arts and sciences," *Cassell's Concise Latin-English Dictionary*, p 141, ASA, "Identified with Greek Athena," *Columbia-Viking Desk Encyclopedia* p. 1179.

XCVII
TRAJAN TO PLINY

The method you have pursued, my dear Pliny, in the proceedings against those who were denounced to you as Christians, is extremely proper; as it is not possible to lay down any fixed plan by which to act in all cases of this nature. But I would not have you officiously enter into any inquiries concerning them. If indeed they should be brought before you, and the crime is proved, they must be punished; with the restriction however that where the party denies himself to be a Christian, and shall make it evident that he is not, by invoking our gods, let him (notwithstanding any former suspicion) be pardoned upon his repentance. Information without the accuser's name subscribed ought not to be received in prosecutions of any sort, as it is introducing a very dangerous precedent, and by no means agreeable to the equity of my government.

To Trajan, inquiring further would have only led to more legal uncertainty as judged by Gallio in Acts 18 and later voiced by Governor Festus and King Agrippa. Festus voiced his dilemma that came about when the Jewish chief priests and elders appeared before him in Jerusalem.

When his accusers got up to speak, they did not charge him with any of the crimes I had expected. Instead, they had some points of dispute with him about their own religion and about a dead man named Jesus who Paul claimed was alive. I was at a loss how to investigate such matters; so I asked if he would be willing to go to Jerusalem and stand trial[473] there on these charges.[474]

This incident likely took place about 59-60 AD, sometime before Nero's tirades began. Nonetheless it reflects the quandaries inherent when someone attempts to judge the worship practices of a religion different from the judge's. Imagine a typical American protestant trying to understand Hindu beliefs. If Hinduism were illegal, how well would a prosecutor of another religious persuasion understand the intricacies of Hindu worship or why adherents believe as they do?

Though Trajan approved of executing believers in Christ, his sense of fairness far exceeded that of many who claim standing in our present society. Numerous media sources, including major newspapers, television networks, and social media regularly report information from anonymous sources in efforts to publicly "convict" innocent

---

473. Latin- *iudicari*.

474. Acts 25:18-20 NIV.

people. Trajan refused to tolerate such destructive nonsense: "Informations (sic) without the accuser's name subscribed ought not to be received in prosecutions of any sort, as it is introducing a very dangerous precedent, and by no means agreeable to the equity of my government."

In respect to the Domitian's intolerance of Christians, imagine the horror Christians must have felt during his reign as suggested by an *Encyclopedia Britannica* writer: "It seems certain that cruelty and ostentation were the chief grounds of his unpopularity, rather than any military or administrative incompetence."[475] Domitian "wore triumphal dress in the Senate; and he presided, wearing Greek dress and a golden crown, over four yearly games on the Greek model, with his fellow judges wearing crowns bearing his own effigy among effigies of the gods. According to Suetonius, a grave source of offense was his (Domitian's) insistence on being addressed as *dominus et deus* ("master and god")."[476] The well-known hymn, "Holy, Holy, Holy" is based on a scene in *Isaiah* 6, which *Revelation* 4:8 recalls. Notice the parallels between the title Domitian claimed and the praise to Almighty God in the Latin Version of *Revelation* 4:8: "*Dominus Deus.*"

Domitian died rather abruptly in 96 AD.[477] his successor, Nerva reigned only two years. Nerva's adopted son Trajan succeeded him. Pliny would have been 34 years old when Domitian died; relatively young for a person with such major responsibilities. Considering the rapid changes occurring in Rome's leadership, his letter to Trajan probably reflected Pliny's uncertainty about continuing policies and guidelines previously established by Domitian.

During his reign, Domitian unhesitatingly and unmercifully persecuted Christians. He portrayed himself as a god. He revered the goddess Minerva, the Roman deity of wisdom, the quality that made Solomon famous. Both Solomon and Domitian associated themselves with wisdom and greedily accumulated treasures from near and far. Early Christians commonly read or heard the *OT* and would have been well acquainted with its narratives. Two different *OT* writers specifically listed the amount of Solomon's annual income from trade as 666. This evidence convinces me that 666 was most likely Emperor Domitian, but in later times could have represented any greedy ruler claiming

---

475. www.britannica.com *Domitian: Roman emperor,* By Guy Edward Farquhar Chilver, Professor of Classical Studies, University of Kent at Canterbury, England, 1964–76. Author of "Vespasian" in Oxford Classical Dictionary.

476. Ibid.

477. His wife and some prominent Roman leaders became dissatisfied with his cruelty and the way he confiscated property. They arranged Domitian's death in 96 AD.

divinity while at the same time forbidding worship of the only God and Father of our Lord Jesus Christ.

Chapter 11

Revelation 20 — Verse By Verse Interpretation

Don't Let Symbolism Fool You

In Chapter 20, major controversy centers on the binding of Satan (dragon-serpent-devil). In some people's minds, *Revelation's* chain symbolism creates images of physical restraint. We control our fellows with handcuffs, prison bars, walls, drugs, and isolation. How do you *bind*, however, an evil force-mind-spirit capable of tempting every living human being simultaneously and continually? What does *Revelation* 20 teach us? Too few interpreters apparently recognize the symbols involved. This section requires us to draw from several OT and NT[478] sources. In verses 1-6 of Chapter 20, NT imagery dominates.[479]

Keep in mind two vital truths. First, the Lord did not intend *Revelation* as a continuous-historical account. As we have noted, Jesus spoke of God's kingdom from several different aspects. His kingdom parables met numerous questions and needs. In the same way, the scenes John saw in *Revelation* help provide answers to the thorny questions God's people ask when they suffer for their faith.

H.B. Swete's introduction to Chapter 20 lends support to the interpretive view we advocate. Swete explained the setting:

> "The formula καὶ εἶδον ("I saw") does not, like μετὰ ταῦτα εἶδον ("after this I saw") determine the order of time in which the vision was seen relatively to the visions which preceded it, but merely connects it with a series of visions which for whatever purpose the writer has seen fit to bring together in this part of his book."[480]

---

478. By NT I refer to the apostolic letters already in the possession of churches, for example Ephesus, as well as the personal teaching by Paul, John, other witnesses of Jesus and his teachings in the area. Note Acts 2:42; 4:33; 8:4.

479. Because Chapter 20 contains no praise or comments other than the one beatitude, and controversy surrounds it, we treat this chap. separately.

480. H.B. Swete, THE APOCALYPSE OF ST JOHN, p. 259.

He correctly concluded that Chapter 20's scenes do not chronologically follow Chapter 19's events. Rather, in the midst of tests, Chapter 20 assures the security of believers.[481] In the chaos Christians then faced, the writer purposed to comfort them by ringing their memory bells of the Creator's and his Christ's supreme rule over all evil forces. In symbolic style, he reminded believers that their previous actions helped secure their future. Earlier Scripture signs provide the needed clues.

The visions John saw alternated between **cautioning** and **comforting**. Based on God's dealings with **chaos** in former times, and also Jesus' teachings and life, *Revelation's* scenes informed the churches of joyful results based on their faith-actions. Yet the Lord cautioned believers not to become involved in the world's idolatry, immorality, greed, fear, and hate.

On his first earth assignment, Christ dealt the devil a stunning blow. At his Second Coming Judgment, Jesus, the Lamb and "King of kings" will wholly punish Satan and his agents. The Lord's people must share this Good News as they loyally endure persecution perpetrated by scoffers and spiteful unbelievers. Confidently and patiently awaiting his Judgment, believers glorify God, while proclaiming Christ's death and resurrection. *Revelation's* written accounts and figurative scenes supplied "signed" information to encourage and assist Christ's followers during present as well as future fiery persecution and chaos. The disagreement surrounding Chapter 20 requires us to treat much of it verse by verse.

Revelation 20:1 NASB
"*Then I saw an angel coming down from heaven,
holding the key of the abyss and a great chain in his hand.*"

Some interpreters attempt to distinguish angels from Jesus the Son as a hard and fast rule. Both *OT* and *NT* precedents and the context lead us otherwise. When Abraham sent Hagar, Sarah's handmaiden away, Hagar found herself and her son in a desperate situation. Hagar wandered in desert-like conditions with limited water supply. Fearing doom for herself and son Ishmael, Hagar began weeping. The *Genesis* narrative tells God's response: "God heard the boy crying and the angel of God called to Hagar from heaven." Genesis 21:18 reads: "Arise, lift up the lad and hold him by the hand, for I will make a great nation of him. Then God opened her eyes and she saw a well of water."

---

481. From the latter part of the quotation above and his later extended comments, Swete seemed not to fully grasp the "purpose" of Chapter 20's content.

Distinguishing between God and the angel of God isn't doable.[482] In Egypt, Jacob wanted to bless Joseph's two sons (*Genesis* 48). The fact that Jacob chose second-born Ephraim over first-born Manasseh frustrated Joseph. Jacob's references to God evidence the difficulty in differentiating God from his "Angel in biblical accounts." Verses 15 and 16a illustrate the complexity we face in descriptions or characterizations of our Creator:

The God before whom my fathers Abraham and Isaac walked,
The God who has been my shepherd all my life to this day,
The angel who has redeemed me from all evil... 483

When we read about an angel-messenger from heaven, we should probably consider context and other signs before we draw identity conclusions.

The phrase: *"I hold the keys of death and Hades"* appeared in *Revelation* 1:18 as part of the "Son of man" (Jesus) self-description.[484] If Jesus' authority includes holding keys to death and Hades (the grave), he can lock and unlock anything. Consider, too, that in Luke's account of the Gerasene[485] demoniac, the demons begged Jesus not to send them immediately to the *abyss*.[486] The demons recognized Jesus' power to banish them there. Third, Mark's gospel told how the demoniac broke *chains* the locals used in efforts to bind the possessed man prior to this incident.[487]

---

482. Genesis 21:9-20 NASB. The well-known *Isaiah* passage: "For to us a child is born, to us a son is given," should alert us against assuming that no angel passage ever applies to Jesus. Note the NIV phrase reading: "And he will be called Wonderful Counselor, Mighty God..." Verse six in an English translation of the *Septuagint* reads: "And his name is called the Messenger (angel) of great counsel" (megales boulâs angelos; Greek –Μεγάλες βουλής ἀγγελος). Hardly any Christian disputes that this *Isaiah* prophecy applies to Jesus. Nonetheless the *Septuagint* here refers to Messiah as a messenger-angel.

483. NASB In addition to the earlier cited example in Genesis 18, see also Genesis 22:11-15 and Judges 2:1-5; 6:1-40. The Hebrew word *malak* appears in these instances. At times *malak* is also translated as messenger or agent.

484. Similarly, Chapter 10 opens with a "mighty angel coming down from heaven... robed in a cloud with a rainbow above his head...his face like the sun..."Compare these phrases with 1:16 and Jesus' face at his transfiguration
(Matthew 17:1-3).

485. Some earlier versions read Gadarene; for various reasons, confusion exists over the city's location and its name.

486. Matthew's account (8:31) tells us that on that occasion, Jesus actually encountered two demon-possessed men.

487. Both here in Revelation and in Mark, the word *chain* translate the Greek term "halusis" (ἄλυσις).

Revelation 20:2 NASB
"And he laid hold of the dragon, the serpent of old, who is the devil and Satan,
and bound him for a thousand years..."

Because this "laid hold" is in past (aorist) tense; this action likely already occurred. Various NT writers used the Greek verb *krateo* (κρατέω) translated *laid hold* or *seized* in a metaphorical sense.[488] This point is vital because *Revelation* uses its symbolic dramatic scenes to *show*[489] us what has and will take place. Very reluctantly should we literally interpret passages such as this one.

Before we proceed, we should ask those who think this scene describes actual events why they construe this particular section literally when so many prior scenes are clearly symbolic? Such picking and choosing diverts us on detours to nowhere. In *Revelation* 17, John told what happened when an angel took him "in Spirit" to a desert: "I saw a woman sitting on a scarlet beast, full of blasphemous names, having seven heads and ten horns."[490]

Ordinary people do not expect to see similar living things. They observe fearsome, ugly beasts in zoos and aquariums. Hideous looking creatures presently inhabit deep sea realms. Few animals that roamed the planet eons ago would have made cuddly pets. Pick the horrid primeval or current creature of your choice. No past or present beast equals this description in *Revelation* 17:3: red; covered with — blasphemous names; seven heads and ten horns. To my knowledge, no one literally interprets this scene. First century Christians surely knew that this figurative language pointed to Rome.

- Red with the blood of martyrs.
- Emperors blaspheming, boasting to be gods.
- Built on seven hills.
- Ten horns indicate its power and likely that of its successors.

Chapter 17 continues:

The woman was clothed in purple and scarlet, and adorned with gold and precious
stones and pearls, having in her hand a gold cup full of abominations and of the unclean

---

488. For example Mark 7:3,4,8; Luke 24: 16; Revelation 2:14, 15 NIV.

489. Recall the word show (δεῖξαι) from 1:1.

490. 17:3b NASB.

> *things of her immorality, and on her forehead*
> *a name **was** written, a mystery,*
> *"BABYLON THE GREAT, THE MOTHER OF HARLOTS*
> *AND OF THE ABOMINATIONS OF THE EARTH."*[491]

The entertainment world has cast a plethora of women to play vile prostitutes. Because young women ambitious for stardom constantly emerge, in some cases, film producers might have had to "bind" harlots to keep them away from filming locations. Yet finding an actress or a rodeo queen capable of riding such a beast as described here surpasses even Hollywood's ability.

Scholars agree that Chapter 17 and most other parts of *Revelation* are symbolic. Why do so many regard Chapter 20's vision literally, but not *Revelation's* other visions? Most interpreters agree on the symbolism of numbers such as 144,000. Yet many of those same scholars assume the literalness of Chapter 20's 1,000. They also interpret the "binding" of Satan as non-symbolic. Construing in this manner, they sidestep and overlook Chapter 20's reassuring and emboldening symbols.

Several *NT* examples illustrate how Jesus bound-laid hold-seized-arrested Satan.

- By resisting his temptations, Jesus limited the devil's power.
- Jesus cast out and controlled Satan's messenger-angels.[492]
- He overcame death, the penalty human beings pay for yielding to the devil.[493]

Other *New Testament* usage attests that *bound* does not necessarily mean Jesus rendered Satan totally confined or helpless. In a synagogue, Jesus healed a woman crippled by an evil spirit. For 18 years, she walked stooped; could not "unbend" her back. Putting his hands on her, Jesus healed her. *"Immediately she straightened up and praised God."* As this incident took place on the seventh day, the synagogue ruler criticized Jesus for violating the Sabbath. After exposing the hypocrisy involved, Jesus said (*Luke* 13:16 NIV): *"Should not this woman ... whom Satan has kept bound for eighteen long years, be set free on the Sabbath day from what bound her?"* The Greek term "édasen" (ἔδησεν) appears in both accounts (*Luke* 13:16 and *Revelation* 20:2). Though "bound," bent over, this lady still walked and got around. Based on *NT* terms

---

491. Ibid verses 4, 5.

492. See Luke 11:14-26. "Edasen" is an aorist (past) tense form of *deo* (δέω) which mean to bind or compel. The word even defines "the binding" involved in marriage vows (1 Corinthians 7:27).

493. Hebrews 2: 14, 15 Later in this chapter, we treat these verses more fully.

used for *bound*, we cannot conclude Satan's complete confinement.[494] We couldn't resist him if the devil were not bound now. Paul, in fact, instructed the Ephesian church how to repel the evil one: *Finally, be strong in the Lord and in the strength of his might. Put on the full armor of God, so that you will be able to stand firm against the schemes of the devil.*[495]

Revelation 20:3 NASB

...and he threw him into the abyss, and shut it and sealed it over him, so that he would not deceive the nations any longer, until the thousand years were completed; after these things he must be released for a short time.

If the "angel" threw Satan into the abyss, which was then shut and sealed, does that contradict the limited idea of binding or restricting we discussed? After the debate about whose name Jesus used to cast out demons, he declared:

> *If I cast out demons by the finger of God, then the kingdom of God has come upon you. When a strong man, fully armed, guards his own house, his possessions are undisturbed. But when someone stronger than he attacks him and overpowers him, he takes away from him all his armor on which he had relied and distributes his plunder.*496

When Jesus resisted the devil's temptation and cast out his underlings, he clearly overpowered- subdued[497] the evil one and his operation. Satan continues his roaring-lion lurking, but Jesus alerted his followers to the devil's devices. Standing firm in Christ enables believers to resist Satan.[498] Depending on Jesus, following his example, and doing God's will lead us to victory.

As for the word *shut*, Matthew used the term translated *shut* metaphorically for hinder or block. This occurred when Jesus accused the law teachers and Pharisees of shutting God's kingdom in ordinary people's faces.[499] Many believers worry, because to them, Satan doesn't appear to be bound now. He still deceives folks. Those who follow God's will in Christ, however, should not be fooled. God allows

---

494. Matthew used a different word stem (*krat*) for *bound* or *laid hold of* when the mob seized Jesus in Gethsemane, 26: 48 and 50. They controlled Jesus, but he evidently walked wherever the mob directed him.

495. Ephesians 6:10, 11 NASB; the Greek word translated *schemes* here is *methodias*.

496. Luke 11: 20-22 NASB.

497. The verb here is form of nikao-conquer.

498. 1 Peter 5:8, 9.

499. Matthew 23:13.

the tempter to remain in order to test his people. In our day to day decisions, God put us through tryouts. As Paul wrote the Corinthians:

> *"Another reason I wrote you was to see if you would stand the test and be obedient in everything. Anyone you forgive, I also forgive. And what I have forgiven — if there was anything to forgive — I have forgiven in the sight of Christ for your sake, in order that Satan might not outwit us. For we are not unaware of his schemes."*[500]

Jesus bound the devil. God's "trust" testing includes the forgiveness exam. If we forgive as Jesus did, and follow his example of obeying God, Satan will not outwit us. The last phrase above contains two negatives. Reading them positively instructs us: "We are aware of Satan's schemes." If you know a crook's methods ahead of time, he/she should not deceive you and take your money. When we model Jesus' teaching and actions, we usually elude Satan's hoodwinks.

Misuse of the word *abyss* leads people in abysmal directions. Keep in mind *Revelation's* purpose. The Lord meant for this symbolic book to **caution** and **comfort** believers and at the same time **confuse** hostile authorities. How unfortunate that for centuries, many Christians have attempted to literally understand *Revelation's* signs. As a result, believers busy themselves and alarm millions with baseless theories. H.B. Swete apparently failed to see the rich figurative language in this scene.[501] So did/do most of the authors I have read.

Caution, The "Deep" Subject *Abyss* And Two Hard Realities Adam And Eve Learned

We insert this caution. Wariness includes <u>being careful not to assume</u> the meanings of terms such as "the deep," "the pit," and "abyss." Sometimes knowing etymologies of terms assists us in understanding biblical words. A term's origin, however, does not always reflect its later usage.[502] To some contemporaries, "abyss" in the Bible routinely brings to mind concepts from ancient Persian and Greek mythology.[503] Trace usage of the Hebrew term pronounced *tehom* in the *OT*, which

---

500. 2 Corinthians 2:9-11 NIV.

501. Swete, *"The APOCALYPSE OF ST JOHN*, pp 259-262.

502. *Car* derives from the Middle English term *carre*, which likely described a curtain covered litter with poles for carrying a single (possibly two) very rich or important occupant, and later animal-drawn two and four wheeled chariots or carriages. *Cars*, you recall, were originally "horseless carriages."

503. For example Concerning ἄβυσσος (abyss) Joachim Jeremias wrote: "A description of the underworld as a) the 'place of imprisonment for disobedient spirits' . . . and b) the realm of the dead." Jeremias also asserted that in the NT, abyss refers to a "prison of spirits." *TDNT*, Vol. I, pp. 9, 10.

the KJV translated as either *the deep* or *depth*.[504] The *KJV* similarly renders the Greek term *abyss* as "the deep" or "the bottomless pit." Many OT occurrences of "the deep" refer to ocean depths, some to subterranean water sources, and several refer to the waters that first dried for the Israelites and then swept over the Egyptian army. In *Job* 41:32, the author used *tehom* when the Lord questioned Job about various mysteries beyond human conception. Picturing God poking fun at human fear of the leviathan (likely a crocodile) causes a chuckle.[505] From its usage in the *Septuagint*, one can hardly regard the word *abyss* as a place of demon habitation.

Associations of disaster and devastation connected with death and the grave enable us to better understand *abyss*. The term suggests the same mystery and fear death creates in us humans. Recall the *Luke* 11 account of Jesus expelling Satan's underling demons. Jesus' opponents accused him of casting out demons by Beelzebub's (the prince of demons) power. Using perfect logic regarding a divided house or kingdom, Jesus replied: Why would a king kill his own troops? Alluding to God's inestimably superior power, "If I by God's finger drive demons out, God's rule has befallen you,"[506] Jesus explained how his godly power affected Satan:

For when a strong man like Satan is fully armed and guards his palace, his possessions are safe—until someone even stronger attacks and overpowers him,
strips him of his weapons, and carries off his belongings.[507]

In Eden, Adam and Eve disobeyed God and succumbed to Satan's lies. The Lord warned them that violating his word brought death. For their defiance, the couple faced two immediate effects. First, they felt shame and tried to hide their guilt. The Lord designed human beings to obey his instructions. Pride leads us to act otherwise. Contemporary

---

504. See a complete concordance for example Young's or Strong's for listings of the terms. The Septuagint often translated Hebrew tehom as abyss (ἄβυσσος).

505. The great "Hallelujah" — *Praise the Lord,* Psalm 148 encourages all creation to praise and exalt God, our Creator. Verse 7 of Psalm 148 ends with the Hebrew term *tehom,* the *Septuagint* with the plural of abyss (abussoi), which the KJV translated as "deeps" and the NIV "ocean depths." See also the "deep" reference in Psalm 36:6. On his deathbed, Jacob blessed Joseph, Genesis 49:22-26. In verse 25, English translations tend to follow the Masoretic text by translating the Hebrew words *baracat tehom* "blessings of the deep." The ancient Septuagint translators for some reason avoided or skipped that phrase. Could they not harmonize the *deep* and *blessings*?

506. My translation of Luke 11:20.

507. Luke 11:21, 22 New Living Translation.

mental health professionals tend to exclude God from their therapies. Mind analysts can make people feel temporarily good, but unresolved guilt usually leads to depression. Drug dependency cycles often result. Jesus' visit to our planet brought new reality for the devil. Since then, by confessing wrongs, accepting Christ's forgiveness, changing behavior, and doing God's will in Christ, all can find healing.[508]

Adam and Eve experienced death's imminence, a second hard reality. After their eviction from the garden, the cherubim and the flashing, flaming sword forever prohibited the couple's access to the tree of life.[509] In his letter to the *Romans,* Paul pointed out how Adam and Eve introduced sin into the world and death to all, "because all sinned." Death ruled until Jesus' resurrection. Thus:

> *For if by the transgression of the one, death reigned through the one, much more those who receive the abundance of grace and of the gift of righteousness will reign in life through the One, Jesus Christ.*510

Numerous mental health experts and even some ministers seem to brush off fear of death's effects on the human psyche (or soul). The writer of *Hebrews* correctly perceived how death-fright enslaves folks. Some remain in denial till their last breath. Jesus overcame mortality's threat and the fear surrounding it:

> *Because God's children are human beings — made of flesh and blood — the Son also became flesh and blood. For only as a human being could he die, and only by dying could he break the power of the devil, who had the power of death. Only in this way could he set free all who have lived their lives as slaves to the fear of dying.*511

---

508. In Luke 11:24-26, Jesus referred to the need for doing God's will: "When an evil spirit leaves a person, it goes into the desert, searching for rest. But when it finds none, it says, 'I will return to the person I came from.' So it returns and finds that its former home is all swept and in order. Then the spirit finds seven other spirits more evil than itself, and they all enter the person and live there. And so that person is worse off than before" (NLT). It's not enough to quit doing wrong. In all phases of life, we must fill the "empty time spaces" by doing the works of God, glorifying and honoring him through Christ.

509. Genesis 3:21-24.

510. Romans 5:14, 17 NASB The verse 14 form is ἐβασίλευσεν (ebasīleusen), an aorist or past tense form; literally, "through one person's sin, death became king." The stem basileus means king. The v. 17 word *reign* is βασιλεύσουσιν (basileūsousin); third person plural future—the new reality created. Jesus proved his kingship over the devil and over the grave by his perfect life, his death, burial, and resurrection to indestructible life.

511. Hebrews 2:14, 15 NLT — Accessed through sermoncentral.com/bible.

Since Satan worked his first wile, death-dread persists. To devilish extremes, it affected the world-wide Covid-19 crisis. Jesus brought death's remedy. Before he died on the cross, Jesus announced how he would first limit and then eliminate mortality: "the prince of this world now stands condemned."[512] The scarred Lamb's resurrection powerfully attested his triumph over Satan. Readers should consider these facts when trying to interpret *Revelation* 20's signs.

Ancient fables confuse the *abyss* subject. The Apostle Paul cautioned his two famous understudies not to pay attention to myths.[513] *New Testament* authors used numerous Greek terms of mythological origin, but gave them the Lord's unique meaning. The term *nike* serves as good example. Few contemporary believers and likely not all ministers know that *nike* was the Greek goddess of victory. In Ephesus and other cities, artisans carved and shaped numerous stone images of the supposed goddess. To my knowledge, no hint of that idol emerges in Scripture. Yet the *New Testament* employs *nike*, the term of mythological origin nearly thirty times as *victory, win, overcome*, and so on. The Apostle John frequently used *nike* in verb and noun forms. *Nike* as "overcome" appears six times in *1 John* and twice that number in *Revelation*. Jesus assured: "Be of good cheer, I have overcome (*nikied*) the world."[514]

Abyss appears in *Revelation* 9: 1, 2, 11; 11:7; 17:8; 20:1, 3. On the basis of info we've reviewed and its usage in *The Apocalypse*, we should probably understand *abyss* as representing the fearsomeness of death and the grave. Jesus' manifestation in the flesh dealt the devil his initial blow. At the Lord's Second Coming, he destines Satan for the *"lake of fire."* Though NT writers warned against following myths, many interpreters seem satisfied to let the devil "reside temporarily" in a "place" Greek mythology made famous.

Research on *abyss* led me to matters I didn't anticipate. Perhaps other Greek students have come across this curiosity regarding the term. The Greek word *bussos* (βύσσος) refers to fine linen, which wealthy people then regularly donned. The rich man in Jesus' *Luke* 16 parable dressed in *bussoi* (plural form) for every-day apparel. According to the *Septuagint* version, upon his promotion, Joseph received a *bussos* from Pharaoh (*Genesis* 41:42).[515] *Revelation* 19 tells of a vast multitude giving

---

512. John 16:11 NIV; see also John 12:31; 14:30.

513. See 1 Timothy 1:4, 2 Timothy 4:4, Titus 1:14.

514. John 16:33 KJV.

515. This was likely a far more expensive piece of attire than his "coat of many colors" (see Genesis 37).According to the LXX of 1 Chronicles 15:27, David wore a linen ephod (bussina) when accompanying the Ark of the Covenant to Jerusalem. The term appears twice in this verse. The English translation, LXX version of Esther 8:15 reports

thunderous praise because the bride (the Church) had readied herself. "'*Fine linen,* bright and clean was given her to wear.' (*Fine linen* [*bussos*] stands for the righteous acts of God's holy people.)"[516] In contrast, The Lord scolded the Laodiceans:

> Because you say, "I am rich, and have become wealthy, and have need of nothing," and you do not know that you are wretched and miserable and poor and blind and naked, I advise you to buy from me gold refined by fire so that you may become rich, and white garments so that you may clothe yourself, and that the shame of your nakedness will not be revealed; and eye salve to anoint your eyes so that you may see.[517]

When converting words from Greek to English, a lone upsilon (υ) nearly always becomes a *y (bussos=byssos).* In both English and Greek, placing an "a," (in Greek, an alpha-α) prior to the word usually negates the term. The most familiar example: an "a" added to theist, a believer in God, becomes the word atheist, a nonbeliever.[518] Possibly you have noted that addition of the alpha (a) to bussos-byssos — abyssos is never translated to mean "no clothes." Greek dictionaries usually identify abussos as "home of demons and evil spirits."[519] Complete study of this matter far exceeds my ability and of this work. Yet biblical and extra-biblical evidence lead me to conclude that the usual mythological assumptions about *abyss* lack credibility for believers.[520] We must heed warnings concerning involvement with myths. In addition, if *abyss* means "home of demons," those who inhabited the Gerasene demoniac didn't want to go *home.*[521]"

---

that Artaxerxes rewarded Mordecai (Mardochæus) with a "diadem of fine purple linen" (bussinon=βύσσινον).

516. 19:8 NIV Swete considered the expression edotha (given) a Revelation keynote because it "occurs some twenty times in cc.vi. — xx." THE APOCALYPSE OF JOHN, p 247.

517. Revelation 3:17, 18 NASB The word naked translates "gym" (γυμνός) and "clothes" himatia (ἱμάτια).

518. Jesus rebuked Thomas for his skepticism: "Do not be unbelieving (ἄπιστος), but believing (πιστός), (John 20:27).

519. For example Greek-English DICTIONARY of the New Testament, by Barclay, p 1. Other scholars connect it linguistically with Bathos, deep water.

520. Swete mentions the possibility that the alpha in front of the bussos may be "intensive" for example, indicating a really deep or "bottomless" hole.

521. See Luke 8:31. Jesus might not have granted the evil spirits' wish. They possibly perished with the swine. The word translated "drowned" (NIV and NRSV) is related to the word for strangled or choked (a form of πνίγω). Variants of this term appear in

Greek myths concerning Hades, Tartarus, and soul have made detrimental inroads into Christian thought. Paul's reference to *abyss* in Romans 10:7 appears to indicate "the realm of the dead," a subject of long standing mystery. The Hebrew term *sheol* seems related to a Hebrew verb *sha'al* meaning "to ask."[522] When loved ones die, children always wonder, "Where are they now?" It seems reasonable to identify the devil's abyss-banishment as meaning that Jesus exposed him **as a liar and chief perpetrator of all other evil, deceitful activities, who faces impending death.**

The Devil's Desert Work

Jesus limited Satan to a *deep water place* of God's truth as opposed to the anhydrous, waterless places where the devil does his best work. Recall the wilderness, desert area where the devil tempted Jesus. Also, the angel mentioned in Chapter 17:1 carried John "in spirit into a wilderness," where he saw the great harlot and the ugly scarlet beast (v.3). Jesus brought water and light. In essence, Jesus "defrocked the devil"; removed his angel of light disguise and informed Satan of his total-disaster future. Jesus fully notified his followers of his effective binding job. Those who "fall" for myths apparently don't properly read Jesus' signs. As D.W Gooding perceived:

> *"The great psychological and theological terms of the New Testament, must be understood, not merely (often not at all) in their pagan sense, but in the light of the Hebrew words that they represent in the LXX."*[523]

Jesus' parable of the sower, for example Mark 4:19: "Worries of this life, the deceitfulness of wealth, and the desires for other things come in and *choke* the word." We now reside in Iowa, but I learned from the internet, not from local farmers, that pigs swim excellently. In footnote 27, we related Jesus' Luke 11 comment regarding unclean spirits that have been cast out of humans. The demons go through *waterless* or *desert places* (the Greek word is *anhydrous*, lit. "no water" looking for a home. As we have seen, most OT references to the deep indicate abundant water. The thought of being lost at sea or drowning fosters frightening nightmares to most folks. Jesus' action possibly caused the demise of both animals and evil spirits. The *Septuagint* interestingly connects fine linen (bussos) and no clothing in the Ezekiel 26, 27 prophecy of woe for Tyre and its coastal neighbors.

522. *Hades* is usually regarded as the Greek equivalent of the Hebrew term *Sheol*=the grave or "world of the dead." When trying to interpret Scripture, very cautiously should Christians rely on Greek mythological understanding of these and related terms. Paul based this Romans passage on Deuteronomy 30:11-14. This OT reference follows the question about ascending into heaven with the contrast and challenge: "Nor is it beyond the sea, that you should say, 'who will cross the sea for us to get it for us ...'" NASB. Biblical references to *abyss-the deep* often include "mega water," for example Genesis 7:11; 8:2; Jonah 2:5, 6. The famous "down to the sea" section (verses 23-32) of Psalm 107 shows a connection between bathos and abyss in the Septuagint.

523. **TEXT AND VERSIONS, The Septuagint,** Significance. D.W. Gooding, *The New BIBLE Dictionary*, p. 1261.

With Gooding's observation in mind, note earlier references to the *abyss* that appear to contradict the understanding we take. *Abyss* first appears in *Revelation* 9:1, 2, and 11. With the opening of the seventh seal (8:1), John saw the seven angel-messengers who stand before God. Each of the seven received a trumpet. Trumpet blasts warned of significant events (recall Jericho in Joshua 6).[524] The sounds and effects of the first four trumpets described God's devastating response to the martyrs' prayers. Symbolism here largely comes from events of the Exodus as found in the *Pentateuch* and the prophets; *Jeremiah*, *Ezekiel*, *Amos*, and *Zechariah*. The earth and creation suffer dreadful, but limited woe.

Revelation 9 begins with the fifth trumpet blast. God fully directs his wrath toward human sinfulness and rebellion against Him, "those who do not have the seal of God on their foreheads" (9:4). The "sealing" resembles that described in *Ezekiel* 9. The devastation that beset Israel and Judah in response to their ungodliness, however, echoes the locust invasion featured in *Joel*. Recall, too, the Lord's destruction of Sodom and Gomorrah in *Genesis* 19. This possibly reflects the dry, depleted desert of mankind apart from Jesus, the living water.[525] Due to rejection of God, many of this country's once proud cities are quickly becoming inhospitable wastelands.

Continuing the near "bottomless" subject *abyss*, three passages from the *Septuagint* help us see the contrasting results of obeying and disobeying God. Before and after contrast starkly.

Prior to human disobedience, well-watered, Eden-like circumstances exist. Afterward, parched, desolation prevails.

1. Genesis 2 tells of the river-watered garden God planted in Eden. Trees bore abundant easy-pick fruit. The tree of life stood in the midst. God evicted the first couple after their disobedience informing Adam that he would work up a sweat tilling (likely with pick, plow, and shovel) the ground and bending low to harvest the earth's herbs. He would even sweat while he ate—all this until he returned to the dust.

2. <u>Genesis 13:10:</u> Before — "And Lot, having lifted up his eyes observed all the country round Jordan that it was all watered before God overthrew Sodom and Gomorrah as the garden of the Lord." After — Genesis 19:28 – "And he (Abraham) looked toward Sodom and Gomorrah, and towards the surrounding country, and saw, and behold a

---

524. The Lord reviewed Israel's multiplying sins to Isaiah; then commanded him to "Raise your voice like a trumpet, and declare to my people their transgression. . ." Isaiah 58:1a NASB.

525. See John 4:1-42.

flame went up from the earth, as the smoke of a furnace."
3. <u>Joel 2</u>: The warning, the punishment of consuming fire, and the result (see verses 1-3):
Before – "The land is like the garden of Eden before them (the fiery locust invasion)."
After – "A desolate wilderness behind them."

Knowing that he and his minions abhor and reject the water of life, should we wonder that a *lake*[526] *of fire* awaits Satan's and his allies? Conversely, to those who thirst, he who is alpha and omega, beginning and end (telos) will give "the spring of the water of life without cost."[527]

We earlier cautioned against trying to understand God's nature or his eternity using human reason and logic. Jesus reminded: "God is Spirit." he exists beyond (outside) creation. He spoke the cosmos into existence. Physical laws and principles do not limit him. Our minds tend to picture things in accordance with what we experience and can measure. We conceive heaven as above us—up, and Satan's habitation down—in the deep. Though *Bible* writers used these terms, they also informed us that the living God created all things and that he exists separate and apart from his Creation.

In *Revelation*, the Lord informs us of transformed life: "Behold, I make all things new." That word "new" indicates something which never existed before. The world to come will not just be a refurbished and improved earth. Those who *overcome* in Christ and gain entrance into the New Jerusalem will experience life on an unimaginably different plane. If you escaped all gravitational forces of our solar system and found yourself in outer space, which direction would you head to find heaven? Up and down, deep and high would have no meaning. We must remain wary of language that attempts to logically or idealistically describe God or the afterlife.

Some qualities of the new life, *Revelation* makes unmistakable. Absent will be death, mourning, crying, and pain. Those now disobeying God and denying his Christ won't be in residence: such as the cowards, unbelievers, immoral persons, sorcerers, idolaters, and all liars.[528]

---

526. Revelation nearly always uses the term *thalassa* (θάλασσα) for sea. In reference to the burning lake of punishment for the devil and his followers, the term limna (λίμνη) appears. For some reason, Luke used both terms in his gospel. In 5:1, 2, he used *limna*; also in Chap, 8, when describing the demons into the swine incident. In his Chap. 17:2 and 21:25 references to "sea," Luke used *thalassa*. In Luke, the NASB translates *limna* as lake.

527. Revelation 21:6 NASB; in Deuteronomy 8:7 NASB, God promised Israel that he was taking them to a land with flowing brooks, fountains, and streams.

528. Revelation 21:8.

Both 2 *Peter* 2:4 and *Jude* 6 refer to the *abyss-the deep* as a location where the Lord confines unfaithful angels (presumably evil-spirits-demons) until God's decisive Judgment. If any future earth inhabitants should travel into "deep space," they will never come across the *abyss*. We know of that realm only through the *Bible's* symbolic language. Both 2 *Peter* 2 and *Jude* 6 forcefully warn that God justly punishes all forms of disobedience and idolatry.

Jesus soberly alerted us to two afterlife matters. From my perception, ministers seem rarely to discuss the duo. When he healed the non-Israelite centurion's servant from a distance, Jesus remarked on the centurion's faith. In contrast with the military officer's remarkable belief, and probably also his profound empathy for his servant, Jesus advised: Many will arrive and dine at the table with Abraham, Isaac, and Jacob in the kingdom of heaven. "But the sons of the kingdom (those who consider themselves entitled by denomination, birth, race, prestige, social connections, success, and so on) will be cast out into the outer darkness; a place of weeping (bitter crying) and gnashing of teeth."[529]

Jesus made another difficult statement in his marriage feast parable. Almost none of the guests the king invited to his son's wedding showed. Farming and "taking care of business" overly occupied them. The non-appreciation and neglect of those who rejected his invite enraged the king and he punished them.[530] The monarch ordered his servants to give a general invitation to people of all backgrounds — good and evil. Guests filled the wedding hall. In viewing the attendees, the king saw a man not dressed in wedding clothes. "Friend, how did you come in here without wedding clothes?" he asked. The man was dumbstruck. As you probably know, marriage hosts then provided garments for all guests. Because they usually travelled long distances and lacked modern conveniences, invitees would arrive sweaty, smelling like animals, and street filth. The speechless guest had no regard or respect for the gracious host or the others in attendance. he didn't even bother to change into the free, clean garment. He, too, found himself cast into outer darkness that is away from God and the light of his presence.[531]

---

529. Matthew 8:12 NASB.

530. I understand that it was customary at the time to issue invitations early and then notify again early on the wedding day. Those too busy that day had earlier sent RSVPs saying they would attend. No one appreciates "no-shows." The wedding day celebration of God's one and only Son came at unimaginable expense.

531. Matthew 22:1-14.

Revelation 20:4 NASB

*Then I saw thrones, and they sat on them, and judgment was given to them. And I **saw** the souls of those who had been beheaded because of their testimony of Jesus and because of the word of God, and those who had not worshiped the beast or his image, and had not received the mark on their forehead and on their hand; and they came to life and reigned with Christ532 for a thousand years.*

In respect to thrones and judgment, Jesus promised his disciple-dozen that they would sit on twelve thrones judging the twelve tribes of Israel.[533] The Twelve must have repeated the promise to early Christians. Thus when folks in the Corinthian church acted immaturely, Paul asked them: "Do you not know that the saints will judge the world?"[534] Paul addressed both Corinthian letters "to the saints" — meaning all church members. The idea of sainthood as descriptive of exceptional disciples was then unthinkable. The word saint or holy means someone set aside for service to God, as all Christians should be.

Paul scolded the Corinthian church because they sued one another in human courts instead of resolving their differences. "Can't people in the church help resolve and judge these matters?" asked Paul. These issues constituted tests for God's people. Tests for what? God's people undergo "judging" exams to qualify them for greater assignments later as magistrates. Paul explained:

If any of you has a dispute with another, do you dare to take it before the ungodly for judgment instead of before the Lord's people? Or do you not know that the Lord's people will judge the world? And if you are to judge the world, are you not competent to judge trivial cases? Do you not know that we will judge angels? How much more the things of this life![535]

---

532. Swete saw in the rare mention of Christ here as well as in Revelation 11:15 and Revelation 12:10 "a reminiscence of Psalm 2:2. "The Lord's Anointed against Whom the kings of the earth conspired has triumphed over his enemies and his victory ensures that of those who have fought on his side," (Swete, p. 262, 263). The use of the word "those" (οἵτινες) intimates that this is a select group. Indeed they willingly suffered for their public allegiance to King Jesus.

533. Matthew 19:28-30.

534. 1 Corinthians 6:2a NIV.

535. 1 Corinthians 6:1-3 NIV.

Though we merely "practice judge" now, we are already judges. *New Testament* teaching forbids condemning unbelievers' actions.[536] We do practice drills by prayerfully, humbly maintaining peace and order within the church. By following Jesus' advice,[537] we can properly judge and avoid most divisive actions. At the same time they failed their judging tests, the Corinthians allowed some church members to openly act despicably and immorally.[538]

In respect to judging, probably all of those who had been beheaded for their faith sat in a courtroom and heard a magistrate pronounce a "guilty verdict" on them. Their surviving loved ones would be consoled knowing that their dead loved ones will judge evildoers in God's court. Those martyred for their faith made no compromises with the world. They refused to worship the beast of Rome, his money, or the status he conferred on those who received his mark. "They had not worshiped the beast or his image and had not received his mark on their foreheads or their hands."

To clarify the phrase: "They came to life and reigned with Christ a thousand years," we connect it with the next verses.

20:5, 6 NASB:
The rest of the dead did not come to life until the thousand years were completed. This is the first resurrection. Blessed and holy is the one who has a part in the first resurrection; over these the second death has no power, but they will be priests of God and of Christ and will reign with him for a thousand years.

This imagery made perfect sense to those in Christ, yet surely baffled Roman authorities and still puzzles many. Early Christians received careful, detailed instructions about Jesus and how to follow him. Paul repeatedly reminded believers of the fundamentals they learned earlier. Note this memory jog in *1 Corinthians* 15:

> "*Now, brothers and sisters, I want to remind you of the gospel I preached to you, which you received and on which you have taken your stand. By*

---

536. See 1 Corinthians 5:12, 13. Many Christians practice the precise opposite of what these verses advise.

537. Matthew 18:15-18 "If your brother sins, go and show him his fault in private; if he listens to you, you have won your brother. But if he does not listen to you, take one or two more with you, so that BY THE MOUTH OF TWO OR THREE WITNESSES EVERY FACT MAY BE CONFIRMED. If he refuses to listen to them, tell it to the church; and if he refuses to listen even to the church, let him be to you as a Gentile and a tax collector. Truly I say to you, whatever you bind on earth shall have been bound in heaven; and whatever you loose on earth shall have been loosed in heaven" NASV. See also Galatians 5:13-6:18.

538. See 1 Corinthians 5, 6.

> *this gospel you are saved, if you hold firmly to the word I preached to you. Otherwise, you have believed in vain.*
> *For what I received I passed on to you as of first importance: that Christ died for our sins according to the Scriptures, that he was buried, that he was raised on the third day according to the Scriptures. . ."*[539]

"Jesus' University" strongly emphasized the basics above. "Students" received no training on whether to be liberal or conservative. They did not choose their denomination or philosophy.

- They learned that Jesus the Word, Creator of all things visited this planet — entered history and participated in a life-battle as each earth-born human must.
- While here, he taught and showed people how to honor God and to live righteously.
- Jealous religious leaders rejected him, falsely accused him, and killed him.
- Jesus came back from death.
- He presented overwhelming evidence of his power over life's most fearsome foe.
- Jesus returned to God promising to raise believers from their burial places on history's final day; he will then fairly judge every person's deeds by our Creator's standards.

Not only must we believe the truth of Jesus' death, his burial, his resurrection, and his return for Judgment, God requires that we love, trust, unite with, and follow his Son. His people do not blindly idolize newscasters, educators, scientists, sports heroes, politicians, preachers, or any earth-based philosophy. They exclusively, devotedly worship only the Universe Creator and his Anointed One.

When Jesus said: "Take up your cross and follow me," he warned that heaven's highway requires total commitment. No easy lifts. People who carried crosses nearly always died on them. Liken it to carrying all the rifles and ammunition for the firing squad assigned to end your life.

Hate, anger, and vengeance fiercely propel the world's "big wheels." God's people end their bitterness by sundown every evening, forgiving and letting go.[540] Lust, pleasure, and greed grease the world's social circles. God's people die to self, follow Jesus, and live to please God as Jesus modelled for us. The world continually reaches for more gold, additional power, and all-encompassing control. God's people

---

539. 1 Corinthians 15:1-4 NIV.

540. Ephesians 4: 26 NIV "Do not let the sun go down while you are still angry."

fully trust him today and each day he grants. Anxiety about tomorrow signifies non-faith. The world sneers at wedding vows. God's people practice faithfulness and purity. Earth pursues pleasures. God's folks gratify him, tell his Good News, and humbly serve others.

Some religious folks try to stuff God into a pint-sized box and take him out for an hour on Sunday — if nothing else more strongly beckons. God's people constantly exalt him in Christ. They boldly share God's good news never fearing sneering neighbors, the politically-correct-crowd, or disapproving government officials.

First-century Roman Empire edicts, you recall, forbade Christianity. To buy or sell in many cities, one had to offer incense and prove allegiance to the Emperor. Citizens who complied were marked okay. Government wrath usually came sharply down on the necks of those who refused to submit. Not surrendering their morality to the world, many early believers yielded their mortality for Christ. This present generation and subsequent ones may likely face choices first century Christians encountered. Early twenty-first-century social trends and governmental actions do not bolster belief in Jesus, Christ, God's Son.

Two Deaths And Resurrections

Though many interpreters seem not to perceive the signs, the references to first and second resurrections and power over the second death were meant to comfort believers. Bible allusions give ample info to grasp these symbols. Most Christians likely know what Jesus told the Jewish leader, Nicodemus. On his covert night visit, this religious bigwig besieged Jesus with questions about God's kingdom. Christ emphatically told Nick: "Unless one is born again he cannot see the kingdom of God."[541] If you aren't dead, or close to it, why would you need to be "born again"? Scripture clearly reveals rebirth as the first death and resurrection:

> *Do you not know that all of us who have been baptized into Christ Jesus have been baptized into his death? Therefore we have been buried with him through baptism into death, so that as Christ was raised from the dead through the glory of the Father, so we too might walk in newness of life. For if we have become united with him in the likeness of his death, certainly we shall also be in the likeness of his resurrection, knowing this, that our old self was crucified with him, in order that our body of sin might be done away with, so that we would no longer be slaves to sin; for he who has died is freed from sin.*
>
> *Now if we have died with Christ, we believe that we shall also live with him, knowing that Christ, having been raised from the dead, is never to die again; death no longer is master over him. For the death*

---

541. John 3:3 NASB.

that he died, he died to sin once for all; but the life that he lives, he lives to God. Even so consider yourselves to be dead to sin, but alive to God in Christ Jesus.[542]

About thirty years prior to *Revelation*, Paul wrote the following to the disciples in Ephesus, the first of *Revelation's* churches:

But God, being rich in mercy, because of his great love with which he loved us, even when we were dead in our transgressions, made us alive together with Christ (by grace you have been saved), and raised us up with him, and seated us with him in the heavenly places in Christ Jesus . . .[543]

Paul also reminded Colossian believers of their first death and resurrection: "When you were dead in your transgressions and the uncircumcision of your flesh, he (the Lord) made you alive together with him, having forgiven us all our transgressions."[544] Paul defined rebirth (what made the Colossians alive): "Having been buried with him (Christ) in baptism, in which you were also raised up with him through faith in the working of God, who raised him from the dead." These citations explain our first death and resurrection. In baptism, we renounce the world, die to our old lifestyle, and join-unite with Christ in his death, burial, and resurrection.

The post-apostolic practice of baptizing sinless babies unhappily robs believers of a signal experience in Christ. Because "the kingdom of heaven is near," John the Baptist called for repentance and changed behavior consistent with a godly life.[545] Upon people's confession of their wrongs, John baptized them in the Jordan "for the forgiveness of sins."[546] After John's imprisonment, Jesus preached the same message and also baptized.[547] Note that the Colossians made their decisions

---

542. This passage (Romans 6:3-11 NASB) reveals that there is no such thing as an unbaptized Christian. As Peter insisted in Acts 2:38, "Repent and be baptized, every one of you, in the name of Jesus Christ for the forgiveness of your sins," NIV.

543. Ephesians 2:4-6 NASB.

544. Colossians 2: 12, 13 NASB Colossae was a short distance from Laodicea, last named of the Seven Cities.

545. Matthew 3:1-10.

546. Mark 1:1-5.

547. Matthew 4:17; Mark 1:14, 15: and John 4:1, 2 Jesus' disciples performed the actual baptisms, likely for two reasons: 1) the sheer volume of candidates; 2) if Jesus actually immersed folks, they might have bragged that their baptism was of greater value because Jesus himself performed it. Which person actually immerses another is

based on their belief in Christ: "Having been buried with him (Christ) in baptism, in which you were also raised up with him through faith in the working of God." They chose to give their lives to Jesus; their parents didn't try to decide for them.

The teachings of some reformers and prominent preachers lead folks astray from the pivotal step baptism held in *New Testament* times. Rather than letting Scripture speak to them and guide them, folks obey a church policy or a certain reformer's tradition. Many scoff at baptism's importance saying that those who practice the rite believe in "water salvation." Yet Peter declared that the flood waters in Noah's time symbolized "baptism that now saves you also—not the removal of dirt from the body, but a clear conscience toward God. It saves you by the resurrection of Jesus Christ . . ."[548]

We err when we consider baptism as a mere symbol. God expects us to put away the old proud person and yield our lives to him. In baptism's water, we die to our old, vain, disobedient self. If you think I overstate the case for adult baptism by immersion, prayerfully consider the Scriptures we list. Note also the case of Naaman the leper (2 Kings 5:1-15). Should we follow the counsel of preachers who deem baptism unnecessary or should we adhere to God's word.[549]

Some speak of Paul's *conversion* on the Damascus road, yet *Acts* 22: 16 states that Paul remained unforgiven until his baptism. In fact, God's select spokesman, Ananias, reprimanded Paul for delaying the matter: "What are you waiting for? Get up, be baptized, and wash your sins away..." (NIV).

As the *Acts* texts indicate, folks were baptized as soon as they learned what God's Word requires of those who hear and believe in Christ.[550] No one encouraged them to wait for a special baptism Sunday when multiple baptisms take place.[551] To grasp *Revelation* 20's

---

immaterial. What matters is the candidate's belief of his/her own need to die to self, become one with Christ's death, burial, and resurrection, and to openly submit to Jesus' management and kingship.

548. 1 Peter 3:20, 21 NIV.

549. Matthew 28:18-20; Acts 2:38, 39; 8:12, 13; 8:26-40; 10:34-48; 16:14, 15, 16- 40 ; 19:1-5; 22:1-16; 1 Corinthians 12:12, 13.

550. Acts 2:41 NIV "Those who accepted his message were baptized, and about three thousand were added to their number that day." Acts 10:34-48, Cornelius, his relatives, and close friends; Acts 16:11-15 Lydia and her household baptized immediately; Acts 16:16-34 The Philippian jailer and his family came to believe and were baptized the same hour of the night.

551. See Matthew 8:11; Luke 13:23-30. The well-known "thief on the cross" argument pointlessly depends on an incident that occurred prior to Jesus' death and resurrection. Abraham, Isaac, and Jacob weren't baptized either, but Jesus promised their presence at the kingdom feast.

symbols, no one needs to cut, slice, and do mathematical gymnastics with Daniel's prophecies. The NT provides abundant symbolic references and also renews OT warnings about taking exceptions to God's commandments. The Lord mandates absolute obedience.[552]

Baptism contains symbols, but full obedience to God's commands brings a new relationship. Marriage ceremonies generally include considerable symbolism — fathers giving daughters to be married, exchanging rings, unity candles, and so on. The service, however, should also help the couple feel married. In addition, bride and groom publicly state their life-commitment to each other. They vow oneness in the presence of God and witnesses. Former suitors, parents, and those who find either party attractive should respect those solemn oaths. Alongside the visible commitment to King Jesus, baptism visibly affirms our intention to obey Christ and to quit ungodly actions.[553]

Vanity probably reigns as chief impediment to adult immersion: "I don't want to look foolish." If we object for that reason, human pride still "strangles" us. Martin Luther said: "The old man does not die easily." "Neither does the 'old woman,'" we might add. Knowing the need to complete God's will, Jesus provided a perfect example for us. He insisted that John baptize him as an adult: "to fulfill all righteousness."[554]

Expectation of the second resurrection formed the basis for the assurance Paul gave believers who mourned the loss of loved ones in Thessalonica:

> *But we do not want you to be uninformed, brethren, about those who are asleep, so that you will not grieve as do the rest who have no hope. For if we believe that Jesus died and rose again, even so God will bring with him those who have fallen asleep in Jesus. For this we say to you by the word of the Lord, that we who are alive and remain until the coming of the Lord, will not precede those who have fallen asleep. For the Lord himself will descend from heaven with a shout, with the voice of the archangel and with the trumpet of God, and the dead in Christ will rise first. Then we who are alive and remain will be caught up together with them in the clouds to meet the Lord in the*

---

552. Deuteronomy 4:2; 5:31, 32; Joshua 1:7, 8; John 14:15, 21; 1 John 3:23, 24; 5:2-5; 2 John 6; Revelation 22: 18, 19. Ananias and Sapphira paid dearly for misrepresenting their offering (Acts 5:1-16).

553. Acts 19:1-20 illustrates powerful public conversions in Ephesus.

554. Mark 1:10 tells us that John baptized Jesus "in the Jordan." Mark and Matthew relate that the Holy Spirit descended on Jesus as a dove as he came up out of the water, cf Matthew 3:16 Baptism means immerse in Greek.

> air, and so we shall always be with the Lord. Therefore comfort one another with these words.555

At his Second Coming, just as Jesus triumphantly arose, loved ones "who have fallen asleep in Jesus" will rise from their graves.556 **Blessed and holy is the one who has a part in the first resurrection; over these the second death has no power** . . . (that's why the references to their having "fallen asleep"). When so many church leaders since the Reformation reject baptism and its place in conversion, no wonder folks misunderstand the first and second resurrections. Though human theories teem concerning this beatitude's meaning, we see how *NT* references easily clarify it.

Ancient Greek thought infiltrates current Christian teachings to a great extent. This Hellenistic intrusion blinds folks to the connection between baptism and the first resurrection. Current views of the word *psyche* or *soul* supply evidence of the Greek influence to which I refer. The KJV rendering of Genesis 2:7 increases the confusion: "And man became a living soul." Many believers and their leaders follow Plato's idea of the soul's immortality rather than to accept Scripture's teaching. Recall the Lord's warning to Adam about eating from the forbidden tree: "when you eat of it, you will surely die."557 he wasn't telling Adam that his body would die, but his soul would survive. He plainly said: "You will die." In *Ezekiel*, the Lord explained: "The soul who sins will die."558 Using biblical language, one cannot differentiate between life that God gave humans and what he gave animals. The Genesis narrative described the great flood's effects:

> *All flesh that moved on the earth perished, birds and cattle and beasts and every swarming thing that swarms upon the earth, and all mankind; of all that was on the dry land, all in whose nostrils was the breath of the spirit of life, died. Thus he blotted out every living thing that was upon the face of the land, from man to animals to creeping things and to birds of the sky, and they were blotted out from the earth; and only Noah was left, together with those that were with him in the ark.*559

---

555. 1 Thessalonians 4:13-18 NASB.

556. Daniel foretold that in the end time, "many of those who sleep in the dust of the ground will awake, these to everlasting life arise: Daniel 12:1, 2 NASB.

557. Genesis 2:17 NIV.

558. Ezekiel 18: 4 NASB.

559. Genesis 7:21-23 NASB.

According to Scripture, God gives life and he takes it away. How do we human beings differ from animals? Our Creator holds us accountable for our use of his life-gift. God's grace gives us the prospect of life anew through Christ's sacrifice. Persian and Greek philosophers fantasized the immortal-soul idea, which many contemporaries assume. Moderns have "buried" the Resurrection as a meaningless afterthought. Many Christians suppose that the "souls" of all deceased persons enter heaven at death or go to an intermediate place called hades (*sheol*) to await judgment. Resurrection, the focal point of first century testimony, became a pagan-permeated spring fertility fete. Jesus and his Apostles taught resurrection.

Daniel and Jesus prophesied resurrection on the Last Day, not a soul's immortality.[560] *Acts* 4:2 (NASB) relates the religious elites "being greatly disturbed because they (Peter and John) were teaching the people and proclaiming in Jesus the resurrection from the dead." "And with great power the apostles were giving testimony to the resurrection of the Lord Jesus, and abundant grace was upon them all."[561] The Corinthians lost sight of the Resurrection's importance. Paul clearly stated to them that at "the last trumpet . . .the dead will be raised imperishable, and we will be changed...this perishable must put on the imperishable, and this mortal must put on immortality..."[562] What does this next phrase mean?

Revelation 20:6 NASB
"they will be priests of God and of Christ and will reign with him for a thousand years."

Kingdom and priesthood matters have long bewildered believers. Jesus' contemporaries struggled with the issue. A muddle of "dark matter" concerning priesthood and God's kingdom persists today. Translators bear responsibility for some, but not all the present puzzlement surrounding this verse.

Scripture helps us undo kingdom and priesthood misconceptions. Begin in the *Book of Exodus* when the Lord brought Israel from Egypt. He told those long-enslaved people his plans:

> *And now if ye will indeed hear my voice and keep my covenant, then ye shall be to me a peculiar people above all nations; for the whole*

---

560. Daniel 12:1, 2; John 5:25-29.

561. Acts 4:2, 33 NASB.

562. In 1 Corinthians15, Paul dealt at length with the resurrection, which some in Corinth doubted, likely due to Greek influence. Quotations above are from verses 52-54. Why some prefer to accept a theory of the afterlife based on Revelation symbolism, rather than the straightforward language in the Gospels and Epistles baffles me.

> *earth is mine. And ye shall be to me a royal priesthood and a holy nation.*[563]

Obedience would gain and retain for Israel a special relationship with the Creator. This exclusive bond depended on them placing themselves under God's rule. Becoming a kingdom (basileios-βασίλειος) "royal" priesthood required listening to him, obeying his commands, and setting themselves apart to serve him, their Creator. That obedience would make them *a holy nation*. Israel never held God as king (separated themselves as a highly principled, God-managed people) for any extended period. They replicated the golden calf incident repeatedly over the centuries.[564] As the books of *Ezra* and *Nehemiah* record, greed also consumed Israel. Profit became so vital they couldn't wait for the Sabbath to end.[565] Their continual lapses into immorality ruined their "holy" priesthood.

Isaiah[566] prophesied an end-time when people of all nations and languages would see God's glory. Some would serve as priests in a special relationship with God as *Levites* did during the Mosaic Covenant times. "They will proclaim my glory among the nations," said the Lord.[567]

The rendering of significant terms in some versions hinders understanding. In the following, compare usage of the stems ἱερ (priest) and βασιλε (king-royal). To clarify how Greek readers and listeners would have seen and heard these terms I underlined the Greek words for priests, and kingdom-royal-reign. These latter three all come from the same word stem.

English readers likely don't perceive the linguistic connection that Greek readers and/or listeners quickly grasped. Many current believers seem not to appreciate that God's people serve in a holy, kingly, priesthood. As *Exodus* 19:6 illustrates, God meant for Israel to be kingly priests. They miserably failed. *Isaiah* (61:6) foresaw an age when all God's people would be his priests. Peter reminded the church of what Jesus made possible: "You are kingly priests." *Revelation* 5:10 also speaks to what Christ accomplished. Note the comparisons:

<u>Exodus 19:6</u>	Ὑμεῖς δὲ ἔσεσθέ μοι βασίλειον ἱεράτευμα καὶ ἔθνος ἅγιον
English pronunciation:	humeís de ésthesthé moi basíleion hieráteuma kai éthnos hágion

---

563. Exodus 19:5,6 *THE SEPTUAGINT WITH APOCRYPHA: GREEK AND ENGLISH*

564. Cf Exodus 32, numerous examples in Judges, 1 and 2 Kings, 1 and 2 Chronicles, and The Prophets.

565. Nehemiah 13:15-29.

566. Moses lived circa 1300-1400 BC and Isaiah circa 730 BC.

567. Isaiah 66:18-24, verse 19 (latter part, NIV).

Septuagint Translation: "And <u>ye shall be to</u> me a <u>royal priesthood</u> and a holy nation"

<u>Isaiah 61:6 in Sept.</u>[568]   Ὑμεῖς δὲ <u>ἱερεῖς</u> Κυρίου κληθήσεσθε
English pronunciation: humeís de <u>hiereîs</u> kuríou klāthāsesthe
Septuagint Translation:[569]   "But <u>ye shall be</u> called <u>priests</u> of the Lord"

<u>1 Peter 2:9</u>[570]   Ὑμεῖς δὲ γένος ἐκλεκτόν, <u>βασίλειον ἱεράτευμα</u>, ἔθνος ἅγιον
English pronunciation: humeís de génos eklektón, <u>basíleion hieráteuma</u>, éthnos hágion
NASB translation   "But you are A CHOSEN RACE, a royal PRIESTHOOD, A HOLY NATION"

<u>Revelation 1:6</u>
English pronunciation:
NASB translation
καὶ ἐποίησεν ἡμᾶς <u>βασιλείαν, ἱερεῖς</u> τῷ θεῷ
Kai epoíāsen hāmás <u>basileían hiereís</u> tō theō
"And he has made us to be a <u>kingdom, priests</u> to his God"

<u>Revelation 5:10</u>

Eng. pro:
καὶ ἐποίησας αὐτοὺς τῷ θεῷ ἡμῶν <u>βασιλείαν</u> καὶ <u>ἱερεῖς</u>, καὶ <u>βασιλεύσουσιν</u> ἐπὶ τῆς γῆς.
kai epoíāsas autoús tō theō hāmōn <u>basileían</u> kai <u>hiereís</u> kai <u>basileú</u>sousin epí tās gās. NASB translation: "You have made them to be a <u>kingdom and priests</u> to our God; and <u>they will reign</u> upon the earth."[571]

<u>Revelation 20:6</u>
ἀλλ' ἔσονται <u>ἱερεῖς</u> τοῦ θεοῦ καὶ τοῦ χριστοῦ, καὶ <u>βασιλεύσουσιν</u> μετ'αὐτοῦ τὰ χίλια ἔτη Eng. pro: al esontaí <u>hiereís</u> tou Theou kai tou Christou kai <u>basileú</u>sousin met' autoú ta chília etā NASB translation "they will <u>be priests</u> of God and of Christ and <u>will reign with</u> him for a thousand years."

---

568. When he began his ministry, Jesus read from this Isaiah passage in the Nazareth Synagogue (Luke 4:18 ff.).

569. See also Isaiah 66:21.

570. According to Nestlé's Greek text. In the present tense, when Peter wrote this about 64 AD.

571. In this Chapter 5 scene, we see Jesus as the Lamb.

The verse (20: 6) future tense reflects the effects of Jesus' sacrifice for sin and victory over death during his earth-visit. This scene signifies that the generations of believers who faithfully endure serve as *priests* and belong to God's *kingdom* during the "thousand years," for example, until Jesus' second coming for Judgment. 10 x 10 x 10 =1,000 symbolizes a long, God-controlled period.

Jesus predicted that his Kingdom would soon "come with power."[572] He also promised Peter that he (Peter) would possess keys of the Kingdom.[573] In Jesus' conversation with Pilate, he confirmed his kingship: "Certainly I am a king. For this very purpose I was born."[574] The Apostles didn't realize it or foresee it at his ascension, yet Jesus' kingdom became humanly and powerfully visible on Pentecost.

By the Spirit, Peter made Jesus' kingship public when, in Jerusalem, he declared to the Jerusalem crowd: "God has made this Jesus, whom you crucified, both Lord and Christ." Christ means anointed, of course (as priest and king). The *Book of Hebrews* emphasizes Jesus' anointing as High Priest forever in the order of Melchizedek. Melchizedek held title of priest but also as King of Salem.[575] Jesus is King of kings (*Revelation* 17:14).

Once people repented of sin, made Jesus their Lord, and publicly formed oneness with the anointed (Christ) king in baptism, the kingdom became visible. In about 60 AD, Paul expressed great expectations of the Colossian church and prayed that:

> *you will walk in a manner worthy of the Lord, to please Him in all respects, bearing fruit in every good work and increasing in the knowledge of God; strengthened with all power, according to his glorious might, for the attaining of all steadfastness and patience; joyously giving thanks to the Father, who has qualified us to share in the inheritance of the saints in Light. For He rescued us from the domain of darkness, and transferred us to the kingdom of his beloved Son, in whom we have redemption, the forgiveness of sins.*576

---

572. Mark 9:1.

573. Matthew 16: 18 Peter acted as the chief spokesperson on Pentecost, but he didn't exclusively hold the keys. Current disciples who follow Jesus' conflict-resolution model can bind things in heaven (cf Matthew 18:15-20).

574. John 18:37 Williams Translation.

575. In Hebrew, *Melech* means king and the *zedek* part means righteousness. See Hebrews 5:1-10; 7:1-10. As Melchizedek was both high priest and King of Salem, Jesus is God's high priest, and King of kings and the New Jerusalem.

576. Colossians 1:10-14 NASB. In Luke 22: 28, 29, Jesus told the disciples: "You are those who stood by me in my trials. Just as my father has granted (aorist i.e. past tense) me a kingdom, I grant you ..." (present middle—literally, "I am granting you for myself").

The aorist (past) tense in the words translated *rescued* and *transferred* indicates that the kingdom then existed. The full numbers of persons in his kingdom will not be fully realized or complete until Jesus' second coming. Nonetheless, King Jesus established his rule by overcoming the world's ruler Satan and conquering death by his return from the grave.

On Pentecost, Christ began adding members to his kingdom, which grew rapidly among every tribe, and language, and people, and nation. When John received the *Revelation* and sent it to the Seven Churches, he stated: "I, John, your brother and fellow partaker in the tribulation and kingdom and perseverance *which are* in Jesus, was on the island called Patmos because of the word of God and the testimony of Jesus."[577] Note *the*, which precedes tribulation. As in English grammar so also in Greek: when a single definite article stands before words connected by *and*, that definite article links all the words. Tribulation, kingdom, and perseverance occur simultaneously-concurrently. This trio cannot be disengaged. We don't look forward to a one thousand year reign of Jesus. Godly people reign with him now.

Decades prior to *Revelation's* composition, the Ephesus saints received this consolation: "Because of his great love for us, God, who is rich in mercy, made us alive with Christ . . . And God raised us up with Christ and seated us with him in the heavenly realms in Christ Jesus . . ."[578] Philippians 3: 20 states: "Our citizenship is in heaven." Those who die to sin, join Christ in baptism (becoming one with him in his death and resurrection) already rule with him.

Are you unconvinced? Paul assured those submitted to Christ in Rome: "All who receive God's abundant grace and are freely put right with him will rule in life through Christ."[579] As we earlier established, "rule," "reign," and "kingdom" all come from the same Greek stem. Paul used the same word ($\beta\alpha\sigma\iota\lambda\epsilon\acute{\upsilon}\sigma o\upsilon\sigma\iota\nu$) in *Romans 5:17* as found in *Revelation* 5:10 and 20: 6.

In *Revelation's* dramatic fashion, King Jesus destroys the great deceiver and foe of righteousness. The Holy Spirit utilized *OT* imagery with classic style.[580] When the dragon assembles his fearsome, massive, evil force, the saints seem hopelessly overmatched. Yet the Lord suddenly, swiftly, and decisively acts to annihilate Satan.

20:7-10 NASB

When the thousand years are completed, Satan will be released from his prison, and will come out to deceive the nations which are in the four corners of

---

577. Revelation 1:9 NASB.

578. Ephesians 2: 4, 5, 6 NIV.

579. Romans 5:17 TEV.

580. *Ezekiel* 7:2; 38: 2-4, 9, 14-23; 39:1-8, and so on.

the earth, Gog and Magog, to gather them together for the war; the number of them is like the sand of the seashore. And they came up on the broad plain of the earth and surrounded the camp of the saints and the beloved city, and fire came down from heaven and devoured them. And the devil who deceived them was thrown into the lake of fire and brimstone, where the beast and the false prophet are also; and they will be tormented day and night forever and ever.

This passage both **cautions** and **comforts**. From the human perspective, wickedness always appears to overwhelmingly prevail. From heaven's view, however, earth's combined forces represent less than an anthill defending against a billion divinely aimed ICBMs. In his parables, Jesus repeatedly warned of the "landowner's" displeasure with those who resist his authority and fail to produce fruit. At great risk, we compromise our commitment and form alliances with those who resist God's complete rule.

20:11-15 NASB

*Then I saw a great white throne and him who sat upon it, from whose presence earth and heaven fled away, and no place was found for them. And I saw the dead, the great and the small, standing before the throne, and books were opened; and another book was opened, which is **the book** of life; and the dead were judged from the things which were written in the books, according to their deeds. And the sea gave up the dead which were in it, and death and Hades gave up the dead which were in them; and they were judged, every one **of them** according to their deeds. Then death and Hades were thrown into the lake of fire. This is the second death, the lake of fire. And if anyone's name was not found written in the book of life, he was thrown into the lake of fire.*

Though John saw the Judge, he made no attempt to describe him. The Creator's white throne likely represents absolute and unbiased justice. Our present existence will recede perhaps beyond memory. Jesus declared the eventual passing of heaven and earth. The *NT* tells of Creation's impermanence.[581] Not one past or future human earth inhabitant escapes judgment: "they will give account to him who is ready to judge the living and the dead."[582] The Lord allowed Daniel a fleeting glimpse of that sobering moment:

"I kept looking
Until thrones were set up,

---

581. Matthew 24:35; Hebrews 1:10-13; 2 Peter 3:10, 11, for example.

582. 1 Peter 4:5 NASB.

And the Ancient of Days took *his* seat;
His vesture *was* like white snow
And the hair of his head like pure wool.
His throne *was* ablaze with flames,
Its wheels *were* a burning fire.

"A river of fire was flowing
And coming out from before him;
Thousands upon thousands were attending him,
And myriads upon myriads were standing before him;
The court sat,
And the books were opened."[583]

Concerning the Judgment, the German scholar Friedrich Büchsel observed:

> *The concept of judgment cannot be taken out of the NT Gospel. It cannot even be removed from the center to the periphery. Proclamation of the love of God always presupposes that all men are moving towards God's judgment and are hopelessly exposed to it. For this reason mysticism and the Enlightenment, which either set aside or restrict the thought of divine judgment, are directly opposed to the NT Gospel.*[584]

Remove God's wrath from the Gospel and you corrupt it. The *Apocalypse* continues the same theme. God's authority and judgment overshadow all forces and actions. In *Revelation's* earlier chapters, the Lord cautioned the disobedient with partial punishment. This truth **comforts** the faithful. Judgment Day completes the Lord's plan for Creation. All evil ends. "It is finished."[585]

"We must all appear before the judgment seat of Christ, that each one may receive what is due him/her for the things done while in the body, whether good or bad."[586] How many of the billions on earth today awoke this morning thinking about their responsibilities to God and take into account that they must answer to him?

---

583. Daniel 7:8-10 NASB.

584. Friedrich Büchsel, *TDNT* Vol. III, p. 941.

585. The word translated "finished" that Jesus uttered from the cross (John 19:30) and the words translated "completed" in Revelation 20:5, 7 come from the same stem, telos, which we discussed in chap. 1. Jesus completed his earthly work on the cross. The church, his body, will complete her work on Resurrection-Judgment Day.

586. 2 Corinthians 5:10 NIV.

Most folks assume: "I am here to please me. It is my life; my body. I can do what I want." In addition most presume that when we die, our spirits bolt off to a better place. Each will receive a gold key to a mansion and enjoy full time golf, fishing, cycling, lounging, cards, or whatever one fancies. Those trendy notions lack factual bases. The Lord will not judge us by our intentions or what we urged our governments to do. We'll account for our actions during our waking hours and whether we produce the fruit God expects. "People are destined to die once, and after that to face judgment."[587]

Race, color, language, money, IQ, education, stature, and so on mean nothing. Jesus made God's kingdom available to all. Christ is the standard for judgment. The Judge accepts no finger-pointing, hateful speech, blame from news people, pundits, actors, preachers, tweeters, and politicians as happens on earth. No one will jive or bribe the Judge. "Everything is uncovered and laid bare before the eyes of him to whom we must account."[588] Jesus never referred to government policy or political platforms; only individual actions that glorify God: Each will receive what is due him/her for the things done while in the body, whether good or bad.[589]

Presuming we are savvy, knowledgeable, experienced, and above the ordinary, we proudly compare ourselves with others. Paul reminded us to think about who God is. Matched against him, all we puny creatures generate the punch of a corpse. We created beings should respectfully fear the living God, the source of all life.

Revelation 20:15
If anyone's name was not found written in the book of life,
he was thrown into the lake of fire.

The Book of Life reference spoke to both ancient biblical and contemporary first century usage. Moses asked the Lord to blot his name from his book if he (God) refused to forgive Israel's transgression.[590] The Lord kept a "registry" of Jerusalem's and Israel's deserving inhabitants.[591] David asked God to blot the names of evil persons from the book of life; "may they not be recorded with the righteous."[592] Jesus

---

587. Hebrews 9:27 NASB.

588. Hebrews 4:13b NIV.

589. See John 5:22, 29; Matthew 25:31-46; Acts 17:31; 2 Timothy 4:1, 2; Exodus 32:32; Hebrews 4:12; Psalm 96:11-13; 98:9.

590. Exodus 32:32.

591. Ezekiel 13:9; Daniel 12:1.

592. Psalm 69:28 NASB.

urged his disciples to rejoice that their names were written in heaven.[593] Paul referred to his coworkers "whose names are in the book of life."[594] *Hebrews* noted the "general assembly and church of the firstborn, who are enrolled in heaven."[595] These biblical citations seem to suggest that as from ancient times, local officials registered the names of qualified city residents for taxation and other legal reasons; the Lord knows his own.

References to the *Book of Life* appear in *Revelation* 3:5, 13:8, and 20:15. These citations make two points clear. First, though someone may be enrolled as a heaven-citizen, that person's name can also be removed for unbecoming behavior. Two, the Creator, who tracks hair numbers on each head doesn't need a scroll or huge, computerized, official registry. The Lord discerns and remembers all human thoughts and actions (*Hebrews* 4:12, 13).

---

593. Luke 10:20.

594. Philippians 4:3 NASB.

595. 12: 23 NASB.

Chapter 12, Part 1

A "Winning" View Of Revelation

For God's churches and his people facing intense trials and burgeoning antagonism, the Holy Spirit provided *Revelation — The Apocalypse* as a "Victory Manual."[596] From human perspectives, their opponents and obstacles seemed overwhelming **Chaos**. The Lord assured *triumph*, however, to those who persevered through faith in him. Though the Holy Spirit produced the manual for late first century believers, his cautions, comforts, promises, and path to *conquest* apply to every era until God concludes history. "Who is the one who *overcomes* the world, but he who believes that Jesus is the Son of God?"[597]

Our Creator rules the Cosmos. He began history and will finish it according to his divine plan. As the Apostle Paul reassured the Romans: "If God is for us, who can be against us? Certainly not God, who did not even keep back his own Son, but offered him for us all! He gave us his Son — will he not also freely give us all things?"[598] All spiritual and physical opposition remain under our Creator's control. Nothing finite can resist the only Infinite One.

By Divine design, we encounter testing as Israel did on their journey to the Promised Land. Faithfulness trials include doubt, the enticements of sex, gold, power, and pleasure complicated by government censure. The Romans took great pride in their legal system. In symbolic language necessitated by the need to confound authorities trying to press their case against Christians in courts of law, the manual explains the enemies' tricks, methods, and devices. The Lord devised imagery from the OT, the NT, and other recognizable sources, so the faithful could identify threats and temptations as well as successfully utilize his remedies.

Memorable scenes help believers perceive the necessary view point of world events and the salvation God made possible. *Revelation's* opening vistas enable us to see Jesus' identity and his accomplishments from many standpoints: powerful priest; conqueror; once

---

596. The terms *nike* (νίκη) and the verb form *nikao* (νικάω) are translated as victory, overcome, prevail, triumph, conquer, and win depending on the English version one uses.

597. 1 John 5:5 NASB.

598. Romans 8:31 TEV.

dead, but alive and one who intimately knows his churches and remains fully in charge of them.

Every one of the Seven Churches receives a different promise to the "one who *overcomes*," but all can be *victors* in Christ. Jesus *prevailed* over the great tempter, and also death, the penalty for sin. ***Revelation* 12: 11** assures: "They *overcame* him because of the blood of the Lamb and because of the word of their testimony, and they did not love their life even when faced with death."[599] Readers must not forget that God's messengers-angels repeatedly *showed* John past, present, and future significant events.

After the Lord's caution and comfort for his churches, John saw God's majesty unveiled. *Revelation's* early chapters are essential to grasping further events. The heavenly host praises God as Creator of all things (**Revelation 4**). If he created everything, Rome's emperors and all world leaders, the greatest minds, and the most powerful generals are subject to God's purposes and bidding.[600] The Lord destined even the dreadful enemy Satan to the fiery lake. The devil's disciples and adherents will join him.

The awesome scene in **Revelation 4** reminds folks in all eras that they should continually render thanks, honor, and glory to the ever-reigning eternal one. The Lord, the Almighty God created all things and gives them existence and life according to his will. Without faith in and faithfulness to the Creator, life persists hopelessly helpless.

In **Revelation 5**, John saw the sealed scroll (book) in the Creator's right hand containing information that will sustain and bring hope to the faithful. The Lamb unseals the book. He *overcame* the devil and made the way possible for people from every tribe and language and people and nation to *win*. The Lamb receives all praise given to the Father "for ever and ever." In loving grace, Father and Son accomplished all the heavy lifting.

Revelation's descriptive scenes do not appear chronologically. They often alternate between warnings to repent and encouragement for Jesus' witnesses (such as, Chapters 7-9). The prophecies foresee types of tests; wars, famine, and death always lurking. Though *The Apocalypse* predicts the fall of Rome and the world's end, it gives no timetables or tipoff signs. As Jesus continually warned in his parables, his servants must always be ready for his return. In the meantime, the Holy Spirit

---

599. NASB.

600. Revelation 14:7 NASB "Fear God, and give him glory, because the hour of his judgment has come; worship him who made the heaven and the earth and sea and springs of waters."

reminds: "Give praise to our God, all you his bond-servants, you who fear him, the small and the great."[601]

The joy and celebration of the Lamb's wedding, inheriting protected, enhanced Eden and its ever-bearing Tree of Life, where no evil ever encroaches, await martyrs and God's trustworthy servants. "He who *overcomes* will inherit these things, and I will be his God and he will be My son."[602]

The Music Key
The narrative in *Revelation's* songs including a condensation of heavenly and angelic announcements as translated in NASB.

In chapter 3, we posited that *Revelation's* "music" assists readers to follow the book's puzzling storyline. At times, declarations from the throne and angelic announcements help carry the "song" theme. To illustrate our thesis, this chapter includes the music, declarations, and announcements, which convey the narrative. Our brief commentary states our interpretation of *Revelation*. The **NASB** with cited locations appears in **bold print;** our observations in light type. Texts from two of *Revelation's* seven letters to the churches help grasp the storyline.

(1:1-8)
The revelation of Jesus Christ, which God gave him to show his bond-servants the things which must soon take place; and he sent and communicated it by his angel to his bond-servant John, who testified to the word of God and to the testimony of Jesus Christ, even to all that he saw.

Revelation discloses Jesus in numerous symbolic settings that emphasize his authority, his faithfulness to God, and the Good News he brought for all creation. The Lord communicated this news to John through his servant-messenger-angel. John faithfully witnessed God's Word in action from the time the Baptizer immersed Jesus in the Jordan River, through Christ's death on the cross, his resurrection, and his ascension. Add, too, all the visions John saw decades later on Patmos Island. Jesus' angel also divulged the future, which was immediately beginning to unfold. Purposes of this unveiling included:

---

601. 19:5 NASB.

602. 21:7 NASB Use of the word *Son* here reflects the longtime custom of giving the eldest son a double inheritance.

The imagery used here also fulfills the Ephesians promise of Christ's church, the bride being presented to Jesus, holy and blameless (Ephesians 5:25-33).

- help fellow believers prepare for tests they would face;
- assure them of Jesus' ultimate victory;
- relate God's promise to vindicate those faithfully witnessing to the Lamb.

Blessed is he who reads and those who hear
the words of the prophecy,
and heed the things that are written in it,
for the time is near.
John,
To the seven churches that are in Asia:
Grace to you and peace from him who is, and who was, and who is to come,
and from the seven Spirits who are before his throne,
and from Jesus Christ, the faithful witness, the firstborn of the dead,
and the ruler of the kings of the earth.
To him who loves us and released us from our sins by his blood—
and made us to be a kingdom, priests to his God and Father—
to him be glory and dominion for ever and ever! Amen.
BEHOLD, HE IS COMING WITH THE CLOUDS, and every eye will see him, even those who pierced him; and all the tribes of the earth will mourn over him. So it is to be! Amen.
"I am the Alpha and the Omega," says the Lord God,
"who is and who was and who is to come, the Almighty."

Those acquainted with the other Bible books recognize comforting and encouraging scenes of God's ultimate, powerful Judgment that results in the punishment of all evil and the eternal security of those who honor God and the Lamb. These same symbolic exhibitions confuse those unfamiliar with Scripture.

(1:9-20)

The Apostle John explained the what, when, why, and where of his visions and the instructions he received for communicating what he *saw* and *heard* to the seven churches. The trumpet-like voice drew John's attention to the seven golden lampstands and the priestly robed "son of man" walking in the midst of those ancient temple-lighting devices. The priestly figure held seven stars in his right hand. A sharp, double-edged sword extended from his mouth. His face shone as the sun in full strength.[603]

That same Jesus, whom John saw transfigured on the Mount, is Ancient of Days, royal High Priest, and King of heaven and earth. The scene terrified John, but the Magnificent One steadied and reassured him. To summarize: *Through my resurrection from the dead, I am finisher and ender of all Creation. I hold the keys of death and the grave, indeed all future events.* The resplendent Jesus ordered John to write what he had already seen, what he presently saw, and what will eventually take place. He explained to John that the stars in his right hand represent the seven churches' messenger-angels. The lampstands denote the seven churches tasked with sharing Jesus, the Splendid One's light.

(2:1-7)

The letter to the church in Ephesus, where some believers compromised with the world:

To the angel of the church in Ephesus write:
The One who holds the seven stars in his right hand,
the One who walks among the seven golden lampstands, says this:
"I know your deeds and your toil and perseverance, and that you
cannot tolerate evil men, and you put to the test those who call
themselves apostles,
and they are not, and you found them to be false;
and you have perseverance
and have endured for My name's sake,
and have not grown weary.
"But I have this against you,
that you have left your first love.
"Therefore remember from where you have fallen,
and repent and do the deeds
you did at first; or else I am coming to you and
will remove your lampstand out of its place—unless you repent.
Yet this you do have, that you hate the deeds of the Nicolaitans,
which I also hate.
"He who has an ear, let him hear what the Spirit says to the churches.
To him who overcomes, I will grant to eat of the tree of life,
which is in the Paradise of God."

---

603. Numerous *OT* and *NT* references contribute to these figurative visions, for example: *Exodus* 20:26; 25:31-40; 28:1-43; *Ezekiel* 8:2; 43:2; *Daniel* 7:9; 10:5, 14; *Matthew* 14:27; 17:2; *Luke* 24:5; *Hebrews* 4:12.

The term *Nicolaitans* appears also in the letter to Pergamum (2:14-16) which links Nicolaitans with those who follow Balaam's teaching. Moabite leaders offered the prophet Balaam a hefty reward to place a spell, hex, or curse on Israel (*Numbers* 22-25). Though Balaam tried multiple times, the Lord allowed him to only bless Israel. Still hoping to earn the offered sum, Balaam later devised a plan to harm God's people. He suggested that the Moabite women seduce the male Israelites. They succeeded in doing that. Moab conquered Israel by means of idolatrous immorality.

- Balaam is a compound Hebrew word: *Bela*-conquer, *ha'am*– the people.
- *Nicolaitan* is a Greek compound word: *Nikon*-conquer, laos- the people.

First-century Greek and Roman societies offered even greater enticements than Balaam did. Irenaeus wrote: "They (the Nicolaitans) lived lives of unrestrained indulgence." Clement of Alexander said of them: They "abandoned themselves to pleasure like goats." By means of pornography, child enslavement, alcohol, illegal drugs, government funding, and so on, groups, and individuals now greedily profit.

(2:8-11)

To Smyrna, a church dedicated at great cost to Jesus and his Good News:

And to the angel of the church in Smyrna write:
The first and the last, who was dead, and has come to life, says this:
"I know your tribulation and your poverty (but you are rich), and
the blasphemy by those who say they are Jews and are not, but are a
synagogue of Satan.
Do not fear what you are about to suffer.
Behold, the devil is about to cast some of you into prison, so that
you will be tested, and you will have tribulation for ten days.
Be faithful until death, and I will give you the crown of life.
He who has an ear, let him hear what the Spirit says to the churches.
He who overcomes will not be hurt by the second death."

The references to Jews are not anti-Semitic. "True Jews" would not act out of envy or stir mob violence. Neither would they convict a person without fair presentation of evidence. First century Jerusalem religious leaders violated many clear commandments in Moses' Law.[604] Jewish activists in Smyrna apparently operated similarly.

The mention of **"tribulations for ten days"** intimated that the local church's "great tribulation" would not ease; thus **"Be faithful until death."** *Ten* represents completeness. The Smyrnans already "died" with Christ; the second death will not "hurt" them.

(4:1-7)

That first trumpet-like voice, which John heard invited him to **"come up here"** to heaven so he could he see **"what must take place after these things."** John saw the one sitting on the throne. Though the Lord's magnificent glory awed John, he never attempted to describe God. Thunderous sounds, astonishing colors, remarkable bolts of light, the immense crystal sea, and extraordinary beings (the 24 worship leaders and the multiple eyed, four living beings) attested the Creator's majestic aura.

(4:8-11)

At the Maker's throne surrounded by the 24 elders, the four winged, living creatures with manifold eyes never stop praising the absolutely supreme God:

Day and night they do not cease to say, "HOLY, HOLY, HOLY is THE LORD GOD,
THE ALMIGHTY, WHO WAS AND WHO IS AND WHO IS TO COME."
And when the living creatures give glory and
honor and thanks to him
who sits on the throne, to him who lives forever and ever,
the twenty-four elders will fall down before
Him who sits on the throne,
and will worship him who lives forever and ever,
and will cast their crowns before the throne, saying,
"Worthy are You, our Lord and our God, to receive glory and honor
and power;[605]
for You created all things,
and because of Your will they existed, and were created."

---

604. Matthew 27:18; Exodus 20: 16, 17; Deuteronomy 19:15-21.

605. Daniel 2:37 uses this word order: "the kingdom, the power, the strength and the glory." In Revelation, threes often represent God, fours usually refer to earth and created things.

The four living beings seem to represent all creation; the 24 elders (*presbyters*) likely epitomize worship leaders. Under his extensive organization plans for worship arrangements, King David employed 24 courses of priests to provide full coverage of Temple duties (*1 Chronicles* 24). Present human centered, self-glorification, greed, pursuit of pleasure, sexual deviance, and violence advance societies away from praising our resplendent maker.

(5:1-5)

In the Creator's right hand, John saw a scroll with writing on both sides and sealed with seven seals. A strong angel asked:
Who is worthy to open the book and to break its seals?

John wept when he realized that no one qualified to open the scroll-book that contained divinely planned info about the future. One of the elders told John:

> *Stop weeping; behold, the Lion that is from the tribe of Judah, the Root of David,*
> *has overcome so as to open the book and its seven seals.*

(5:6-8)

John saw a Lamb, looking as if it had been slain standing in the middle of the throne[606] encircled by the four living creatures and the 24 elders. The Lamb with seven horns (absolute power) and seven eyes (fully endowed with God's Holy Spirit) took the scroll from God's right hand. The living creatures, and the elders (holding harps and golden bowls full of incense-i.e. believers' prayers) immediately knelt before (worshiped) the Lamb.

(5:9, 10)

They sang a new song:

> *Worthy are you to take the book and to break its seals;*
> *for you were slain, and purchased for God with your blood*
> *men from every tribe and tongue and people and nation.*
> *You have made them to be a kingdom and priests to our God;*
> *and they will reign upon the earth.*

God has chosen no particular race, language, nation, or people. We qualify by turning from pride, selfishness, greed, hate, and lust,

---

606. This phrase suggests John 1:18, which the KJV translates as well as any: "in the bosom of the Father."

to honor the slain Son for his sacrifice, and pay full, lasting tribute to God, our Creator.

(5:11, 12)

John heard the voices of countless angels.[607] Encircling the throne, the living creatures, and the elders loudly sang:

> *Worthy is the Lamb that was slain*
> *to receive <u>power</u> and <u>riches</u> and <u>wisdom</u> and <u>might</u> and <u>honor</u> and <u>glory</u> and <u>blessing</u>.*[608]

(5:13, 14)

Then John heard every creature in heaven and all physical creation say:

> *To him who sits on the throne, and to the Lamb,*
> *be <u>blessing</u> and <u>honor</u> and <u>glory</u> and <u>dominion</u> forever and ever.*
> *And the four living creatures kept saying, "Amen."*
> *And the elders fell down and worshiped.*[609]

Father and Son cannot be separated; to honor one, glorifies the other. The four living beings gave the **"Amen;"** the elders dropped and adored. **(6:1-17)**

Expecting to see a ferocious lion, John saw a Lamb open the first four of the seven seals.

- He heard one of the four living creatures thunderously shout: **"Come!"** he saw a white horse, with its rider holding a bow. After the mounted rider received a crown (*stephanos*-victor's laurel), he rode out as a conqueror intent on triumph.
- When the Lamb opened the second seal, the second living creature said: **"Come!"**

John saw a red horse, whose rider received a large sword and the power to take peace from the earth and cause people to kill one another.

- As the Lamb opened the third seal, the third living creature said: **"Come!"**

---

607. The μυριάδες μυριάδων και χιλιάδες χιλιάδων (NASB-"myriads of myriads, and thousands of thousands") in Revelation 5:11 compares to the χιλιάδες μυριάδας (NASB-"myriad thousands") of Israel in Numbers 10:36 (in the Septuagint).

608. The seven-fold (full) praise here tells us that to honor the Son is to honor the Father (the seven being underlined).

609. The four-fold reminds earthlings they must honor the Creator and the Lamb.

John saw a black horse. Its rider held a pair of scales. What seemed as a voice from one of the living creatures, said: **"A quart of wheat for a day's wages and three quarts of barley for a day's wages and do not damage the oil and wine."** Behavior of the rich and powerful during the Covid-19 pandemic with resultant inflation and suffering of common people illustrates the truth of this statement. Through the ages, "oil and wine" elites seem unaffected by the misery most others suffer.

- The Lamb opened seal four. John heard the fourth creature say: **"Come!"**

John saw a pale horse. Death rode that horse. Hades (the grave) followed close behind. Using sword, famine, and plague, they received power to kill a fourth of the earth's population. Wild beasts aided death and Hades.

The opening of the first four seals recalls the predictions Jesus made in Matthew 24 stating that wars, rumors of wars, famine, and so on will continue throughout history. In the meantime, God's people wonder when he will bring justice—"Lord, why don't you act?"

- When the Lamb opened the fifth seal, John saw those slain because of God's word and the testimony they maintained. They loudly called:

How long, O Lord, holy and true, will you refrain from judging and avenging our blood on those who dwell on the earth?

Each received a white robe with instructions to wait a little longer until the designated number of their fellow servants (brothers and sisters) to be killed is complete (fulfilled-πληρωθῶσιν-plarōthōsin). The fullness of God's plan remains beyond human comprehension.

- John watched as the Lamb opened the sixth seal. The earth quaked. The sun turned black like goat hair sackcloth. The moon turned blood red. As late figs drop from trees in strong winds, stars fell to the earth. The sky receded as a rolled up scroll. Every mountain and island moved from its place. Kings, princes, generals, rich, slaves, and all free people hid in caves, behind mountains and rocks. Calling to the mountains and rocks, they cried,

Fall on us and hide us from the presence of him who sits on the

> *throne and from the wrath of the Lamb; for the great day of their wrath has come, and who is able to stand?*

The opening of the sixth seal appears to indicate the fearsome final Judgment when proud, rebellious humans will find no hiding places. In the meantime, God seems to put limits on human evil. Though we earth-dwellers reluctantly see connections between our sin and various disasters, Jesus taught that God often punishes hateful actions straightaway. In the first century, Israel's leaders became increasingly spiteful, vengeful, and corrupt. They agitated hostility toward Rome and its representatives. As Jesus made his way to Golgotha, many women wept over his agony. He advised them not to shed tears for him: **"weep for yourselves and for your children."** Jesus foresaw the extreme misery they would suffer at the hands of the Romans beginning in the mid-sixties of the first century AD. "They will say to the mountains, **'Fall on us!'** and to the hills, **'Cover us,"** nearly verbatim what those who rebel against God will lament on the day of God's wrath.[610] Jesus' generation suffered because they did not follow his counsel to "go the second mile," "turn the other cheek," and bless one's enemies. Jesus' Sermon on the Mount ethics guide his servants until Judgment Day.

(7:1-17) Another vision.

Before the Lord destroyed Sodom and Gomorrah, he rescued Lot (*Genesis* 18, 19). Prior to Jerusalem's destruction by the Babylonians (*Ezekiel* 9), God's servant equipped with a writing kit marked those faithful to the Lord, who grieved and lamented the grossly detestable acts committed by idolaters. God intends devastation for those who reject his righteous rule. Four angels stood at the "earth's four corners" with power of the four winds (from any direction) to destroy earth, trees, and sea. As God earlier rescued the righteous, another angel arose from the east with God's seal loudly commanding the four destroying angels:

> *Do not harm the earth or the sea or the trees until we have sealed the bond-servants of our God on their foreheads.*

John <u>heard</u> the amount of those sealed—144,000; 12,000 from each of Israel's twelve tribes. After he heard the number, John <u>saw</u> countless white-robed multitudes holding palm branches from every nation, tribe, people, and tongue. The throng loudly cried:

---

610. See Luke 23:26-31 NIV.

Salvation to our God who sits on the throne, and to the Lamb.

The angels standing near the throne, the elders and the living creatures fell on their faces before the throne and worshiped God declaring:

Amen, blessing and glory and wisdom and thanksgiving and honor and power and might,[611] *be to our God forever and ever. Amen.*

As if to clarify whether John understood the scene, one of the elders asked him:

"These who are clothed in the white robes, who are they, and where have they come from?"

"My lord, you know," John replied.

The elder explained:

These are the ones who come out of the great tribulation, and they have washed their robes and made them white in the blood of the Lamb. For this reason, they are before the throne of God; and they serve him day and night in his temple; and he who sits on the throne will spread his tabernacle over them. They will hunger no longer, nor thirst anymore; nor will the sun beat down on them, nor any heat; for the Lamb in the center of the throne will be their shepherd, and will guide them to springs of the water of life...[612]

Unlike many in ancient Israel, who forsook the **"spring of living water"** and tried to dig their "own cisterns," which proved incapable of holding water,[613] the 144,000 faithfully followed the good shepherd. Jesus promised the woman at the well in Samaria a,

"spring of water welling up to eternal life."[614]
"and God will wipe every tear from their eyes." No salty tears in heaven.

A remarkable prophecy (*Isaiah* 12:3) foretells: **"you will joyously draw water from the springs of salvation."** The Hebrew word for "salvation" is *Yeshua*, the same as Jesus. When reading *Isaiah* 12, one

---

611. Note the seven types of praise here to the Creator.

612. Jesus is the living spring. See John 4: 4-15.

613. See Jeremiah 2:13.

614. John 4:14 NIV For this Scripture section, see also Ezekiel 36, 37.

can reasonably substitute Jesus' name for the word "salvation." No wonder the throng praises the Shepherd Lamb for his guidance to the living water.[615]

(8:1-13; 9:1-21)

The Lamb broke the seventh seal bringing one half hour of silence. Zephaniah the prophet foretold **(1:6, 7 NASB:**

"Those who have turned back from following the Lord, And those who have not sought the Lord. Be silent before the Lord God."

As at Joshua's conquest of Jericho (*Joshua* 6), seven trumpets startlingly broke the stillness. In this *Revelation* scene, seven trumpets in sequence announce **cautionary** punishment by thirds bringing death and plagues to those not sealed. *"Take heed"* these disasters warn.[616] All must be cleansed by the blood of the Lamb, then exclusively honor and serve the living God.

(9:20, 21) Sadly,
The rest of mankind, who were not killed by these plagues, did not repent of the works of their hands, so as not to worship demons, and the idols of gold and of silver and of brass and of stone and of wood, which can neither see nor hear nor walk; and they did not repent of their murders nor of their sorceries nor of their immorality nor of their thefts.[617]

From *Genesis* to *Revelation,* the Bible links widespread suffering from plagues, pestilence, disasters, and war with people neglecting God and ignoring his will. Unfortunately, few associate these occurrences with trends away from honoring God, as *Revelation* 6, 8, and 9, keenly caution.

Instead, people seek only medical, economic, and political solutions. Total calamity results. The next chapters of *Revelation* both **caution** and **console** believers, who thrash and struggle in the midst of the

---

615. The water theme will continue in Revelation 22.

616. For punishment by thirds, see Ezekiel 5:11, 12.

617. For the abomination of these idols, note Deuteronomy 29:17; Jeremiah 1:16; Daniel 5:4, 23.

world's nearly perpetual and proud defiance of God. Failure to repent and to follow the Lord always results catastrophically.

(10:1-11) John saw another mighty angel.

The symbols: rainbow, sun, pillar-like-feet, standing on sea and land, thunderous voice, and so on (vv.1-4) point to the Angel of the Lord. Though John intended to write what the strong angel proclaimed, a heavenly voice forbade him, ordering him to "seal up" what the seven thunders spoke. With his right hand raised to heaven, the angel swore by,

Him who lives forever and ever, WHO CREATED HEAVEN AND THINGS IN IT, AND THE EARTH AND THINGS IN IT, AND THE SEA AND THINGS IN IT, that there will be delay no longer, but in the days of the voice of the seventh angel, when he is about to sound,[618] *then the mystery of God is finished* (completed in the Judgment as in telos), *as he preached* **(declared Good News)** *to his servants the prophets.*

The above accords with history's completion as Paul described in
1 Corinthians 15:
Behold, I tell you a mystery; we will not all sleep, but we will all be changed, in a moment, in the twinkling of an eye, at the last trumpet; for the trumpet will sound, and the dead will be raised imperishable, and we will be changed. For this perishable must put on the imperishable, and this mortal must put on immortality. But when this perishable will have put on the imperishable, and this mortal will have put on immortality, then will come about the saying that is written, "DEATH IS SWALLOWED UP in victory."[619]

"Take the book from the mighty angel's right hand," the heavenly voice instructed John. After John asked for that special piece of writing, he received orders to eat it. The heavenly authority told John the tome would taste sweet, but upset his stomach.[620] One might feel honored when being let in on a great secret. If that mysterious message contained tragic news, however, the person might soon crave antacids.

---

618. Sound as of a trumpet.

619. 1 Corinthians 15:51-54 NASB.

620. OT readers will see the similarity between John's experience and the disturbing news about the destruction and overthrow of nations in existence in the seventh century B.C. (See Jeremiah 1).

> *And they*[621]*said to me, 'You must prophesy again concerning many peoples and nations and tongues and kings.'*

(10:11)

An undescribed being gave John a gauging rod telling him to measure the temple of God, the altar, and the worshipers. The voice instructed him not to measure the outer court (court of the Gentiles) because it had been given over to the nations so they could tread over the Holy City (God's church) 42 months=1,260 days.

The voice informed John that two witnesses wearing sack-cloth would prophesy during that specified period. The speaker identified the witnesses as the two olive trees and lampstands that stand before the **"Lord of the earth"** (v. 4). The combination of *OT* settings consists of:

- A) Lampstands[622] that perpetually lighted the Tabernacle-Temple Holy Place. In order to continue the supply of olive oil, the lamps needed constant tending. Thus in *Zechariah* **4**, the prophet reported his vision of a seven-lamp-stand. Seven supply channels led from a reservoir at the top.

- B) Olive trees to the right and left of the bowl directly supplied oil to the container.

According to the Lord's word for Zerubbabel (a Jewish leader after the Babylonian Captivity, who faced numerous challenges as he rebuilt the Temple), the vision (of the olive trees connected to the lampstands) meant:

"'Not by might nor by power, but by my Spirit,' says the Lord Almighty."[623]

God's people always depend on Him, not on earthly resources. Zechariah asked the meaning of the two olive trees with gold pipes which supplied gold oil.

---

621. Whether the plural *they* reflect the use of the plural in respect to God as in Genesis 3:22 or that it refers to the two separate angels in this Chapter 10 narrative, I cannot say. In the last phrase, note the four-connection with creation.

622. Exodus 25:6, 31-40; 27:20, 21; 31:1-8; 37:17-24; 40:24, 25; Numbers 8:1-4; 1 Kings 7:49; Hebrews 9:2.

623. Zechariah 4:6 NIV.

"These are the two who are anointed to serve the Lord of all the earth," (*Zech.*4:14 NIV).

Numerous *OT and NT* references help us identify the two as God's Word and Spirit, personified by Moses, the lawgiver (Word) and Elijah, the prophet (Spirit).[624] Elijah used fire against his enemies: (***Revelation* 11:5 and 2 *Kings* 1:1-14)**.

God employed Moses as his agent to bring the plagues on Egypt. Despite severe death threats, both men boldly spoke for God.[625] Similarly, God's church must fearlessly, by God's Spirit, proclaim his Word to every generation. Some viciously oppose Jesus' Good News and those who testify to it. Believers who persevere in Christ might face death. At times, sincere, truth-filled preaching torments the consciences of those doing evil. Perpetrators of wrong often celebrate when they silence the voices of those who speak God's Good News (***Revelation* 11:10)**.

Nothing can muzzle God's Word. Thus after 3 ½ days: **"the breath of life from God came into them and they stood on their feet."** This scene recalls Ezekiel's vision: the Valley of Dry Bones, when Israel seemed defeated and helpless:

This is what says the Sovereign Lord says to these bones:
"I will make breath **(Spirit)** *enter you will you come to life . . ."*
Then you will know that I am the Lord (Ezekiel 37:5, 6c NIV).

At times, but not always, God rescues those who boldly proclaim Jesus' resurrection and the coming Judgment.[626] In any case, the Lord consistently preserves his Word, which endures forever. The command, **"Come up here,"** given the two witnesses closely resembles the order given John when he saw the door standing open in heaven **(4:1-3)**. The pair's ascent to heaven in a cloud seems reminiscent of Elijah's whirlwind rise **(2 *Kings* 2:11)**. This persecution of God's witnesses brings a punishing response; the final (seventh trumpet) call warning that the third woe will soon take place.

(11: 15).[627]

---

624. Note the coordination of Word and Spirit in 1 Peter 1:12, 22-25. The Spirit confirms God's Word and vice versa (Acts 10: 34-48).

625. Moses barely survived at birth and a later manhunt (Exodus 1 and 2). Jezebel targeted Elijah (1 Kings 18, 19).

626. Why the Lord allowed James to die early and permitted his brother to survive remains a mystery, (Acts 12: 1, 2).

627. We should probably understand the aorist (past) tense of the verbs concerning the arrival of God's kingdom ("have begun to reign") in the sense that God's kingdom

In rejoinder, heaven's voices loudly proclaim:

The kingdom of the world has become the kingdom of our Lord and of his Christ;
and he will reign forever and ever.

The church must never forget Jesus' calming promise:
These things I have spoken to you so that in me you may have peace. In the world you will have tribulation (thlipsis), but take courage, I have overcome (nike) *the world (John 16:33* **NASB**). [628]

(11:16-18)

With faces down, the 24 elders knelt and worshiped God, voicing:

We give you thanks, O Lord God, the Almighty, who are and who were, because You have taken Your great power and have begun to reign. And the nations were enraged, and your wrath came, and the time came for the dead to be judged, and the time to reward your bond servants the prophets and the saints and those who fear your name, the small and the great, and to destroy those who destroy[629] *the earth.*

---

began with the establishment of the Church on Pentecost.
In Matthew 16:18, 19, Jesus seemed to equate the church and kingdom in the sense that true believers consist of those who allow the Lord to rule and fully control their lives. We can't always identify sincere believers because we are unable to read hearts as the Lord does. As the Lord reminded the discouraged Elijah, God always preserves a remnant; 1 Kings 19: 9-18. We also look through imperfect glasses. Neither can we overlook Daniel's prophecy (7:27) or Colossians 1:13 **NASB** "For he has rescued us from the dominion of darkness and brought us into the kingdom of the Son he loves..."

628. The "have" prior to tribulation here is present tense-active voice indicating that God's people will always face difficulty in the world. In Psalm 34:19 NASB, David declared "Many are the afflictions of the righteous." The Septuagint, which the Apostles often quoted, reads *Hai poloi thlipsis*. You will recognize that *poloi* translates as "many" or "much" and thlipsis can be translated as "affliction," "tribulation," "persecution," "trouble," and so on. Tribulation is not a single occurrence and not confined to a certain period. In every age, God's people face *trouble*.

629. The verb here (*diaphthiro*) sometimes conveys the idea of corrupt, which would indicate a warning to those who sabotage others' morality and ethics. *Diaphthiro* also appears however, in *Revelation* 8:9 in the sense of destroy.

(11:19)

Thunder and lightning emanating from the temple remind us of the ominous sounds that came from God's throne **(4:5)**. These signs strictly warn anyone who tries to defy the Creator.[630]

When God gave Moses the Ten Commandments, awesome rumblings at Mount Sinai sternly cautioned the Israelites not to approach the mountain.

Before attempting to interpret *Revelation* **12**, students should read: *Exodus 9:18-35; 19, 20, and 25; Psalm 77: 11-20; Ezekiel 13:1-15.* Of particular importance in this scene, the Ark of the Covenant powerfully conveys the idea of God's presence and our need to respectfully and reverently obey him:

You shall put the mercy seat on top of the ark, and in the ark you shall put the testimony which I will give to you. There I will meet with you; and from above the mercy seat, from between the two cherubim which are upon the ark of the testimony, I will speak to you about all that I will give you in commandment for the sons of Israel. [631]

(12:1-6)

Those who devised the *Bible's* chapter divisions often awkwardly placed them resulting in considerable confusion. The separation between Chapter 11 and 12 serves as a sad example. Chapter **12's** first two verses belong with **11:15-19**. This section recalls God's deliverance of Israel from Egypt, and his care for the former slaves as he preserved them in hostile wilderness conditions.

For essential reasons, God preserved the *OT* into the new era. Paul repeatedly reminded the Corinthians that the Lord made sure Israel kept a written record of his dealings with the oft complaining, oft ungrateful, oft unbelieving nation:

For I do not want you to be unaware, brethren, that our fathers were all under the cloud and all passed through the sea; and all were baptized into Moses in the cloud and in the sea; and all ate the same spiritual food; and all drank the same spiritual drink, for they were drinking from a spiritual rock which followed them; and the rock was Christ. . .

---

630. See also Exodus 9: 18-35; Psalm 77:18; Ezekiel 13:13.

631. The Lord's instructions to Moses at Sinai: Exodus 25: 21,22 NASB.

> *Now these things happened as examples for us, so that we would not crave evil things as they also craved. Do not be idolaters, as some of them were; as it is written, "THE PEOPLE SAT DOWN TO EAT AND DRINK, AND STOOD UP TO PLAY." Nor let us act immorally, as some of them did, and twenty-three thousand fell in one day. Nor let us try the Lord, as some of them did, and were destroyed by the serpents.*
>
> *Nor grumble, as some of them did, and were destroyed by the destroyer.*
>
> *Now these things happened to them as an example, and they were written for our instruction, upon whom the ends of the ages have come.*[632]

When attempting to decipher *Revelation* 12 signs, we look first to the OT. Scholars debate the meaning of the first heaven-based sign — the woman clothed with the sun, and so on. Joseph's dream of his parents and brothers in *Genesis* **37:9, 10** shows a clear connection. Joseph's dad, Jacob, quickly interpreted it:

> *Now he (Joseph) had still another dream, and related it to his brothers, and said, "Lo, I have had still another dream; and behold, the sun and the moon and eleven stars were bowing down to me." he related it to his father and to his brothers; and his father rebuked him and said to him, "What is this dream that you have had? Shall I and your mother and your brothers actually come to bow ourselves down before you to the ground?"* **(NASB)**

The nation Israel descended from Jacob and his twelve sons. Christ came as descendant of Jacob's son Judah, but not without many Israel birth pangs. In a remarkable passage **(Micah 4:1-5:5a)** the prophet foretold the pains of writhing, **(4:10; 5:3)** and he predicted Bethlehem as Jesus' birthplace. Isaiah twice spoke of Israel's labor pains **(26:18; 66:7-9)**. Jesus also mentioned them *(John 16:16-23)*.

John saw signs that **"appeared in heaven"** (12:1). That doesn't mean that the events the signs portended took place in heaven. Mary didn't give birth to Jesus there. Jesus constantly battled the devil and his agents on earth. The phrase **"rule all the nations with a rod**[633] **of iron"** points to the *Psalm* **2:9** prophecy of God's anointed. The Lord promised Christ's faithful who overcome in Thyatira that they would benefit from his rule with a **"rod of iron,"** *(Revelation* **2:27)**. After

---

632. 1 Corinthians 10: 1-11 NASB underline emphasis mine and in following pages as well.

633. Such as ruler's scepter.

evil representatives crucified him, God raised Jesus and caught him up to his throne. The woman which Satan relentlessly pursued represents the Church, the true Israel, now undergoing its own wilderness testing.[634]

(12:7-14)

In Hebrew, the name *Michael* means **"who is like God?"** Because no created being ever existed who qualifies to wear that title, evidence leads me to think that *Michael* is synonymous for Christ. M*essenger* is the primary meaning of *angel;* God appeared numerous times in angelic-messenger form.[635] Some take the 1,260 days (verse six) literally and try to match them with history's events. The *1,260 day — 42 months — 3½ years* likely represents a portion of history God predetermined for certain events to occur. As with all time, God completely controls this allotted period.

God cares for his people during the 1,260 days. We leave events in his hands and we resist becoming riled by Satan and the world's turmoil. The Lord knows what he is doing. Through the present "wilderness," believers trustfully follow his lead, while boldly testifying to Jesus' resurrection. The early church left us a faithful example **(see esp.** *Acts* **2-9).**

In accord with all parts of *Revelation,* this **Chapter 12** scene **cautions** and **consoles** us, **warns,** and also **reassures** us. Ponder the grounds for the popularly supposed "pre-history war in heaven." In verse 8, the Greek text word count is 11; English translations usually exceed 11.[636] For example, in the phrase referring to Satan and his angels, the NASB (verse 8) reads: *"and they were not strong enough."* Powerfully and briefly, the Greek text uses three words: **"and not strong;"** vernacular, **"bunch of weaklings."** The Holy Spirit writer followed that phrase using precise words from Daniel 2:35 in the Septuagint: (τόπος οὐχ εὑρέθη) *"no place was found"* for them.

Lyrics of the v. 10 music instruct us:[637] The loud song or statement John heard reads:

Now the salvation, and the power, and the kingdom of our God and the authority of his Christ have come, for the accuser of our brethren

---

634. In reviewing his nation's history, Stephen referred to Israel as the church (ecclesia) in the wilderness (Acts 7:38).

635. The Moses and the burning bush incident in Exodus 3 demonstrates the impossibility of distinguishing God from his Angel.

636. The TEV for example uses nineteen words.

637. The lyrics in the poetic sections I consider to be music.

has been thrown down, he who accuses them before our God day and night. And they overcame him because of the blood of the Lamb and because of the word of their testimony, and they did not love their life even when faced with death. For this reason, rejoice, O heavens and you who dwell in them. Woe to the earth and the sea, because the devil has come down to you, having great wrath, knowing that he has only a short time.

Folks spend valuable time arguing whether Satan ever inhabited heaven. The song lyrics indicate that this scene about the devil-dragon being cast out of heaven doesn't describe a pre-creation event. **"Hurling Satan down"** hardly refers to what happened before history began.

This scene tells what befell the devil when Jesus came to earth on his rescue mission. The passage reminds us of the Messiah's accomplishments in history. While he was here, Jesus overcame the devil in every respect. He withstood all Satan's temptations. He fulfilled each command and mission God assigned him. Jesus met every test that you and I face: **" Because he himself suffered when he was tempted, he is able to help those who are being tempted."**[638]

Jesus totally defeated the devil. He died on the cross and by his blood paid to save every person who has ever lived or will live.

In the original of *Revelation* **12**, the Greek word **eblāthā**[639] keeps appearing translated **"thrown down"** as underlined. This encouraging news likely seized the attention of first century readers and listeners:

And the great dragon was thrown down, the serpent of old who is called the devil and Satan, who deceives the whole world; he was thrown down to the earth, and his angels were thrown down with him (v. 9).

Each time those listeners heard "eblāthā" it would be as if we heard: **"He's out of here!"**

Eblāthā appears again in verse 13:

And when the dragon saw that he was thrown down to the earth, he persecuted the woman who gave birth to the male child.

What does **Chapter 12** teach? Satan threatens us, but Jesus mortally wounded the devil-dragon. He will finish him off when he returns in the Judgment. Though Satan repeatedly, furiously mugs the world, we can win. How?

---

638. Hebrews 2:18 NIV.

639. Accent is on the second syllable, ἐβλήθη.

The devil overwhelms the world because people do not know or remember Jesus' Good News and lack faith that Jesus mortally wounded the dragon and threw (hurled) him down.

(v. 11) *And they overcame [640] him because of the blood of the Lamb and because of the word of their testimony, and they did not love their life even when faced with death.*

We obey **"God's commandments and"** we hold **"to the testimony of Jesus."** Unless we do God's will and faithfully, lovingly state our Christ-commitment to those around us, we are not and will not be standing with the winners. With the fury of a wounded wild beast, Satan attempts to wreak havoc on the woman (the church).[641] The author returns again to OT imagery: the woman's two wings resemble the Lord's reminder to Israel that he bore them on eagle's wings.[642]

(15-17)
*And the serpent poured water like a river out of his mouth after the woman,
so that he might cause her to be swept away with the flood.
But the earth helped the woman, and the earth opened its mouth and drank up the river which the dragon poured out of his mouth.*

Rivers presented great obstacles to ancient people. The Euphrates (often referred to as the *Great River*) severely limited travel. Waterways divided families and nations (recall that half the tribe of Manasseh lived east of the Jordan River; the other half on the west side).[643] Rivers also brought devastating floods. Those who frequent deserts understand the dangers of camping in arroyos and dry river beds. Storms miles away fill ravines with sudden, unexpected torrents.

Numerous *wadis* (Arabic for riverbeds) can be found in and around Jerusalem. To counter Satan's assaults, Paul urged the Ephesian and Colossian churches to sing psalms hymns and spiritual songs. The subject matter of this section of *Revelation* resembles the attacks on David recounted in Psalm 124. At times God uses forces of nature to protect his people in their duress.

---

640. "Nike" in Greek.

641. Church (ecclesia) is a feminine term in Greek. Recall also how John addressed his second epistle to the *elect* or *chosen "lady and her children."*

642. Exodus 19:4, Isaiah 40:31, cf Psalm 61:4.

643. Cf Numbers 32; Joshua 1:12-18; 4:12; 22: 1-34.

The devil particularly targets those who obey God's commands, and who testify to Jesus and his resurrection (v. 17). We cautiously draw conclusions about *Revelation's* symbolic passages.

(Revelation 13)

You already know the serpent's identity. He continually stalks us. We easily identify Satan when he appears as vicious, malevolent, vindictive, and hateful. Too often he masquerades as innocent and agreeable. Yet his intentions never vary; he always lures, corrupts, and divides.

What or who is the beast coming out of the sea? Some people love oceans and seas. The Israelites never did. They liked water in wells and cisterns, but not in large bodies. In ancient times, warlike, conquering people often arrived by sea. For Israel's people, seeing foreign ships probably meant bad news. Unannounced watercraft often brought conquering armies. To first century Christians in the Eastern Mediterranean area, the beast clearly represented the Roman government. In that region, Rome's armies usually arrived by ship.

We know what it is like when governments grow increasingly hostile. Ungodly regimes invade homes, break up families, and devastate churches. They can be agile as leopards, fearsome as bears and ferocious as lions.[644] The beast's crowns, heads, and horns in sevens and tens signified new, far-reaching, intense methods and threats.

What does our text mean when it reads **(13:3a): "I saw one of his heads as if it had been slain and his fatal wound was healed."**?

On the 19th of July, 64 AD, a fire broke out in Rome. For six days and seven nights, the blaze raged. Thousands died. Of the city's fourteen regions, only four remained unaffected. Three suffered total destruction. Nero actually helped many of those affected. Still, rumors circulated that the Emperor not only caused the fire, but also played his lyre and sang during the conflagration. Suspicions of Nero's guilt persisted. In an attempt to end the rumors, Nero blamed the fire on Christians. Many believers suffered.

> *They were clothed in the skins of wild beasts, and torn to pieces by dogs; they were fastened to crosses, or set up to be burned, so as to serve the purpose of lamps when daylight failed.*[645]

Within five years, Nero became so unpopular with the Roman Senate, he committed suicide. Rumors circulated. Some thought that Nero

---

644. See Daniel 7 for background of this imagery.

645. Tacitus, *Annals*, 15. 38-44 – As quoted by E.M. Blaiklock, *The Christian in Pagan Society*, Inter-Varsity Fellowship, Oxford, 1956.

did not really die. Others alleged that he came back from the dead. The stories grew intensely a few decades later when Emperor Domitian insisted that he was god and renewed persecution of Christians. *"Nero has returned,"* many thought, *"His death-wound has been healed."* In the eastern part of the Roman Empire, persecution became especially extreme. **"Who can resist it?"** Christians asked. God permitted the beast to subject his people to severe persecution. Many chose to give in and renounce God rather than to suffer through the test.

Christians then faced the same questions we do today:

- Do we trust Jesus' promise to be with us in tough circumstances?
- Or is our faith in government, money, and politicians?
- Do you believe that your name is written in Jesus' Book of Life?

(13:10) NIV

This calls for patient endurance and faithfulness on the part of God's people.

(13:11-18)

John then saw another beast arise from the earth, a creature outfitted with two horns **"like a lamb."** The description possibly symbolizes Jesus' warning: **"Beware of the false prophets, who come to you in sheep's clothing, but inwardly are ravenous wolves,"**[646] This scene more likely represents the first-century trend toward Caesar worship and/or those in the church motivated by greed, power over others, and other ungodly passions.[647] For a full discussion of 666, "the mark of the beast," see chapter 10, **"Looking Anew at 666."**

(14:1-7)

Revelation's scenes often shift quickly from fearful to consoling. As if the Spirit nudged John wanting him not to dwell long on the dreadful beasts, he saw a contrasting picture, which evoked: "Look!" "Wow!" "Don't be dismayed. See all God's people (the 144,000)." God's Lamb stands right here with us, his church." John heard the divine, authoritative voice, (**"like the sound of many waters," "loud thunder"** and harmoniously played harps). Before the four living creatures and the elder worship leaders, the heavenly chorus sang a new song. Only

---

646. Matthew 7:15 NASB.

647. For example, Philippians 3:17-19; 1 Peter 5:1-3.

God's church, (the 144,000), the ones **"purchased"** from the earth could learn the tune. Their moral purity, truthfulness, and total commitment to God and the Lamb identify them as those purchased-redeemed.[648]

The Apostle Peter helped us understand the symbolism of these *Revelation* 14 scenes:

*Since you call on a Father who judges each man's work impartially, live your lives as strangers here in reverent fear. For you know that it was not with perishable things such as silver or gold that you were redeemed from the empty way of life
handed down to you from your forefathers,
but with the precious blood of Christ, a lamb without blemish or defect.
He was chosen before the creation of the world, but was revealed in these last times for your sake. Through him you believe in God, who raised him from the dead and glorified him, and so your faith and hope are in God.
Now that you have purified yourselves by obeying the truth so that you have sincere love for your brothers, love one another deeply, from the heart. For you have been born again, not of perishable seed, but of imperishable,
through the living and enduring word of God.*[649]

John beheld another flying messenger in mid-heaven, loudly declaring eternal good news to all earth-dwellers — every nation, tribe, tongue, and people:

*Fear God, and give him glory, because the hour of his judgment has come;
worship him who made the heaven and the earth and sea and springs of waters.*[650]

---

648. The word **agoradzo** (ἀγοράζω) described buying, redeeming, or ransoming objects as at the agora-marketplace.

649. 1 Peter 1:17-24 NIV Underlining used for emphasis in the above.

650. As the Lamb Jesus announced to the woman at the Samaritan well: "Whoever drinks of the water that I will give him shall never thirst; but the water that I will give him will become in him a well of water springing up to eternal life," (John 4:14 NASB). Note the earth-creation related four: *heaven, earth, sea, springs of water.*

(14:8)

An additional messenger announced Rome's (the contemporary Babylon) end:

> *Fallen, fallen is Babylon the great,*
> *she who has made all the nations drink of the wine of the passion of her immorality.*

(14:9-11)

Strongly cautioning the faithful not to give up, a third messenger continued:

> *If anyone worships the beast and his image,*
> *and receives a mark on his forehead or on his hand,*
> *he also will drink of the wine of the wrath of God, which is mixed in full strength in the cup of his anger; and he will be tormented with fire and brimstone in the presence of the holy angels and in the presence of the Lamb. And the smoke of their torment goes up forever and ever; they have no rest day and night,*
> *those who worship the beast and his image, and whoever receives the mark of his name.*

(14:9-12)

To avoid the punishment of God's righteous fury, one must persevere, keep God's commandments, and remain faithful to Jesus.

(14:13)

A powerful voice from heaven assured John and all the saints,

> *Blessed are the dead who die in the Lord from now on!*
> *"Yes," says the Spirit, "so that they may rest from their labors, for their deeds follow with them."*

(14:14, 15)

Recalling the initial announcement (Chapter 1:1) that God would *show* his servants what will soon begin taking place,[651] messengers arrive in swift succession. Imagine a play in which actors rapidly appear from right, left, and from above, to report on a decisive moment.

---

651. See Chapter 6, Sections: **From Book to Stage** and: **Show and tell**.

Yet another stunning exhibit seized John's attention. First he saw a white cloud and sitting on the cloud, a figure resembling the Son of Man (background *Daniel* 7 and *Revelation* 1), wearing a victor's crown (*stephanos*) and holding a sharp sickle for cutting grain stalks. From the temple sanctuary, an additional angel emerged loudly ordering:

Put in your sickle and reap, for the hour to reap has come, because the harvest of the earth is ripe.

(14: 16-19)

The one seated on the cloud swung his sickle and harvested the earth. Another messenger came out of heaven's temple with a sharp sickle. An added messenger in charge of fire came from the altar commanding the one with the sharp sickle:

Put in your sharp sickle and gather the clusters of grapes from the vine of the earth, because her grapes are ripe.

The reaper swung his sickle, gathered the earth's grapes, and threw them into God's great wrath winepress. Jesus clarified the meaning of this scene when he explained his Parable of the Tares in *Matthew* 13: "The harvest is the end of the age and the reapers are angels."[652]

(14:20)
And the winepress was trodden outside the city, and blood flowed from the wine press as high as a horse's bridle for a distance of about 200 miles.[653]

---

652. Matthew 13:39 NASB cf verses 40-43; Jeremiah 51:33; Hosea 6:11; Joel 3:13; Mark 4:29.

653. NRSV Zephaniah wrote prophetically of this time (1:14-18).

Chapter 12, Part 2

*The Narrative In Revelation's Songs Including
A Condensation Of Heavenly And Angelic
Announcements As Translated In NASB (Continued)*

(15:1-4)

John saw a further (great-marvelous) sign in heaven. Seven messengers brought the finishing, last seven plagues of God's wrath. John also observed the comforting scene similar to the Exodus victory God won for Israel when he destroyed Pharaoh's army in the sea. This new display featured those who endured the fiery testing of the beast, his image and the number of his name by testifying to the Lamb. They stood on what seemed like a fiery, glassy sea holding God's harps and sang the praise song of God's servant Moses and the song of the Lamb:

> *Great and marvelous are your works,*
> *O Lord God, the Almighty;*
> *Righteous and true are Your ways,*
> *King of the nations! Who will not fear, O Lord, and glorify your name?*
> *For you alone are holy;*
> *For ALL THE NATIONS WILL COME AND WORSHIP BEFORE YOU,*
> *FOR YOUR RIGHTEOUS ACTS HAVE BEEN REVEALED.*

(15:5-8)

As Egypt's Pharaoh, Assyria's Sennacherib, and Babylon's King Nebuchadnezzar learned (and Rome's emperors discovered), no power can delay, stymy, or overcome God's will and his actions. The Universe King always completes (telos) what he begins.[654] Once Israel arrived safely on the far side of the sea, the Lord punished the Egyptians. This *Revelation* 15 sight shows the believer's security and victory before the final bowls of God's just wrath pour. Indeed, the next scene visible to John centered on heaven's tabernacle.[655] The vista here probably relates to the subject matter in *Revelation* 16: *judgment coming on*

---

654. Exodus 3-14, 2 Kings 19:8-37, Isaiah 37, Daniel 4:37.

655. A moveable tent-*skana*-σκηνή- housed the Ark of the Covenant during Israel's wilderness wandering and for centuries afterward (Exodus 25-40).

earth's unrepentant inhabitants. This likely recalls the wilderness incident involving the unsuccessful rebellion Korah led against the Lord's anointed priest Aaron (*Numbers 16*). The linen garb worn by the seven angels appointed to pour out the vials of God's anger lends credence to this theory. God's harsh punishment of Korah led many Israelites to murmur resulting in a divinely produced plague.

Few contemporaries seem aware that God does not look kindly on constant complaining, immoral behavior, and the worship of any earthly being or object. That fact did not escape the Apostle Paul. His *1 Corinthians 10* warnings prove he understood.

(16:1-12)

From the temple came a loud command for the seven angels: pour your bowls of God's wrath on the earth. After the first *messenger* emptied the contents of his bowl, a loathsome, malignant sore developed on those marked by the beast and who worshiped his icon.[656] The contents of the second *messenger's* bowl emptied into the sea, resulting in it becoming like blood of a dead person; every creature in the water died.

All river and spring liquid became blood, too, when the third *messenger poured his* bowl's contents. These pictures resemble the Egyptian plagues described in *Exodus* 7:14-25 and 9:8-17. The *messenger-angel* of waters declared:

> **Righteous are you, who are and who were, O Holy One,**
> **because you judged these things;**
> **for they poured out the blood of saints and prophets,**
> **and you have given them blood to drink. They deserve it.**

(16:5, 6).

Lyrics in this song-poetic section indicate that these scenes describe God's final judgment.

> Clue # 1: The wording of the first phrase resembles Chapter 1:4 **"From him who is and who was,"** but lacks the verb change, **"is to come;"** no longer appropriate because God has *come* to Judge. Paul warned concerning: **"the day of wrath and revelation of the righteous judgment of God, who will RENDER TO EACH PERSON ACCORDING TO HIS DEEDS."**[657]

---

656. Compare the forewarnings of God's wrath in Deuteronomy 28:15 to 29:1, and Jeremiah 10: 23 to 11: 23. The Lord sharply alerted Israel and Jerusalem in Isaiah 51:17-23 and Jeremiah 25:15, 16.

657. Romans 2:5b, 6 NASB; see also Revelation 22: 12.

Clue # 2: In the phrase **"You judged these things,"** *judged* is in the aorist or past tense.

> Even though this is only about two thirds of the way through *Revelation*, the Lord gives assurance that in his final Judgment, he will make all things right, fulfilling his promise to the souls under the altar crying for justice.[658] Thus John heard the altar say,

> *Yes, O Lord God, the Almighty, true and righteous are your judgments.*

> In his parable of the vineyard owner, Jesus spoke of those who reject the Lord's ownership and refuse to pay him what is due him: **"When the owner of the vineyard** *comes,* **what will he do to those vine-growers?"**[659]

That these scenes present symbolic[660] pictures should be evident from the fourth *messenger's task*. He poured his bowl's fillings upon the sun, so it scorched[661] wrongdoers with ferocious fire and heat. Rather than repent and glorify their Creator, they stubbornly blasphemed his name. When the fifth *angel* tipped his bowl on the beast's throne, the creature's kingdom darkened.

People gnawed their tongues. Suffering painful sores, they too, refusing to express regret for their evil deeds, blasphemed God. The Lord didn't punish only the beast. He chastened all who followed the beast rather than listen to and obey the Creator. God's people must carefully submit to God's word. We judiciously avoid being wooed by society's trends.

The sixth *messenger* discharged his bowl's contents on the Euphrates River causing it to dry. For centuries, armies from the east intent on conquering the "Holy Land," needed to travel northwest hundreds of

---

658. Revelation 6:9-11.

659. Matthew 21:33-41; Verse 40 NASB quoted above.

660. This is not to say that God's Judgment will not be devastatingly real.

661. The curious parallel in Proverbs 6:20-35 with the scorching and darkness related to the 4th and 5th bowls (Revelation 16:8-11) deserves further study. Revelation's frequent warnings concerning immoral behavior (fornication and adultery, for example 2:14, 20, 21; 9:21; 14:8, 17:2, 4, and so on) make the subject vital. Contemporaries increasingly disregard God's word.

miles in order to cross the Euphrates at its shallower headwaters. [662]In league with the devil, a terribly unholy alliance of dragon, beast, and false prophet formed to speak evil, perform demonic signs, and enlist world powers to war against God.

As in most eras, few twenty-first-century world leaders acknowledge the Universe's Creator or show any interest in submitting to his will. Era after era, greedy power struggles continue. Selfish, dominance-driven human chiefs assemble to crusade against the Almighty God and his Great Judgment Day.

(16:15)

The Lord cautions:

> *Behold, I am coming like a thief.*
> *Blessed is the one who stays awake and keeps his clothes,*
> *so that he will not walk about naked and men will not see his*
> *shame.*

We clothe ourselves by trusting Jesus, putting on Christ, and wearing his righteousness — that fine linen (bussos).

(16:16)

Meanwhile, the *Unholy Leaders League* gathers at Har-Mageddon. Interpreters frequently misunderstand and misconstrue the term Armageddon. In Hebrew, *Har* means hill or mount. Archaeologists have unearthed evidence of settlements (some as early as 3,000 BC) at the site of Megiddo, a ridge about twenty miles SSE of Haifa, Israel.[663] The Egyptians later maintained a fortress at the location. Both King Solomon and Ahab possibly maintained large chariot and horse facilities at Megiddo. My wife and I toured the site in 1980 and saw remains of extensive stables as well as a model of a well-designed, secured city gate.

Three factors help us understand this Chapter 16 reference to Megiddo. First, Robert Young's concordance informs us that the term means "Place of God." Second, two ambitious biblical kings tragically died at Megiddo.[664] Josiah, the latter of the two, brought refreshing reform and renewed hope to the southern kingdom, Judah. He arrogantly tried to intervene, however, in a dispute between Pharaoh Neco

---

662. As the Mississippi River interfered with westbound US travel until well into the nineteenth century, the Euphrates seriously impeded the march of conquering armies as well as the movement of people in ancient times.

663. See article "Megiddo," by T.C. Mitchell of the British Museum in *The New Bible Dictionary*, pp. 804-806.

664. 1 Kings 9:15-18; 2 Kings 23: 29, 30; 2 Chronicles 35: 20-27.

and the king of Assyria.⁶⁶⁵ Josiah died of his wounds at Megiddo. The prophet Zechariah wrote of the national mourning as a result of that calamity.⁶⁶⁶ Har-Megiddo became synonymous with defeat. The *Revelation* 16 reference apparently signifies that Har-Megiddo is "God's place." Human effort, even by the world's greatest rulers, always results disastrously. As Waterloo means to the French, Har-Megiddo symbolizes absolute catastrophe for all human striving against God. To attach the term to a place seems folly.

(16:17-21)

The seventh *angel* poured his bowl's contents upon the air. Out of the temple, from the throne, a voice loudly uttered **"It is done;"** the Greek text tersely states these three English words with a single perfect tense verb pronounced, *Gegonen*.

God spoke and created colossal phenomena as he willed.⁶⁶⁷ In concert with lightning flashes and tremendous thunder, an earthquake of unequalled force shook the entire planet. The mighty tremor split the "city" into three parts; the nations' cities fell.⁶⁶⁸ Babylon the Great received the wine cup of God's fierce wrath. All islands fled away and mountains disappeared. One hundred pound hailstones indicate that no human structure can withstand God's wrath. Even on earth's ending day, some rebellious unbelievers will insolently curse the Creator, blaspheming him because of the hail plague's severity. Titus's Roman army used heavy hurl stones against the defenders of the Masada. Perhaps the Visigoths and Vandals used such "hailstones" when they sacked Rome in the fifth century.⁶⁶⁹

(17: 1-7)

---

665. For some reason, 2 Kings reads Assyria here; this was more likely Nabopolassar, King of Babylon.

666. See Zechariah 12, especially 10-12.

667. Regarding Genesis 1:3, notes in *The Pentateuch and Haftorahs* state: "One of the names for God in later Jewish literature is 'He who spake and the world came into existence (*Authorized Prayer Book*, p. 16). 'The phrase *God said* must be taken as a figurative equivalent of "God willed"' (Saadyah). *The PENTATEUCH and HAFTORAHS: Hebrew Text, English Translation and Commentaries*, Second Edition, p-2, Ed., Dr. J.H. Hertz, Soncino Press.
New York, 5742-1981.

668. The psalmist similarly lamented to God: "You have made the land quake, You have split it open . . ." (Psalm 60:2 NASB).

669. The Lord enabled Joshua to defeat the five Amorite kings by throwing large hailstones on them, (Joshua 10).

Now the focus returns to the present powers that be. One of the bowl-carrying messengers said to John:

Come, I will show you the punishment of the great prostitute, who sits by many waters. With her the kings of the earth committed adultery, and the inhabitants of the earth were intoxicated with the wine of her adulteries.[670]

The drama's spotlight centers on the current world player responsible for the prevalent immorality and the callous persecution of God's people.[671] **"In Spirit,"** the messenger took John into a "wilderness." That word translates the same Greek term found in the *Septuagint* that described the area and conditions Israel encountered on its way to the Promised Land. On their forty year journey, the Lord tested Israel (see *Exodus* 15:22-26; 16: 4). As the letters to the Seven Churches indicate, those trials resemble the tests God uses to maintain faithfulness in his church as well as in all earth dwellers:

- A) **To Ephesus (2:2)** -"test those who call themselves apostles;"

- B) **To Smyrna (2:10)** — The devil would cast some into prison so that **"you will be tested and you will have tribulation. . ."**;

- C) **To Philadelphia (3:10)** "Because you have kept the word of my perseverance; I will also keep you from the hour of testing, which is about to come upon the whole world to test those who dwell on earth."

In his *Luke* 8 sower parable, Jesus told about those who first accept the gospel joyfully, but in **"time of temptation (testing) fall away."**[672] On every step of the church's journey through history, God tests his people. To expect life to be otherwise, disregards the *Bible's* cover to cover teaching.

In the *wilderness*, John saw the astonishing seven-headed, ten-horned scarlet beast overlaid with anti-God profanity and sacrilegious names. On the beast, sat a woman dressed in purple, scarlet, glittering

---

670. Assyria (Nineveh) and Babylon had been formerly guilty of this "filth"; see for example Jeremiah 51:7 and Nahum 3:1-7.

671. This includes first-century Rome and subsequent nations opposing God's authority and persecuting his people.

672. See verse 13. In the above instances, the word for testing is either a form of the verb peiradzo (πειράζω) or noun peirasmos (πειρασμός).

gold, precious stones, and pearls.[673] The woman held a golden cup brimming with abomination and filth of her infidelities. A mysterious name was written on her forehead:

BABYLON THE GREAT, THE MOTHER OF HARLOTS AND OF THE ABOMINATIONS OF THE EARTH.[674]

The blood of God's people, those who witnessed for Jesus, intoxicated the woman. The sight of her utterly flabbergasted John. **"What astonishes you?"** asked God's messenger.

The angel-messenger promised to explain the mystery of the seven-headed, ten-horned beast and the woman riding it: **"The beast, which you saw, once was, now is not, and yet will come up out of the Abyss and go to its destruction."** Though the phrasing of this sentence, which identifies the beast, shares the same structure as that which describes God in 1:4, clues within indicate that the beast is under God's control. During his ministry, Jesus stated a truth that apparently amazed his students. Many believers seem not to grasp what he said:

> *Very truly I tell you, a time is coming and has now come when the dead will hear the voice of the Son of God and those who hear will live. For as the Father has life in himself, so he has granted the Son also to have life in himself. And he has given him authority to judge because he is the Son of Man. Do not be amazed (thaumadzete) at this, for a time is coming when all who are in their graves will hear his voice and come out—*
> *those who have done what is good will rise to live,*
> *and those who have done what is evil will rise to be condemned.*[675]

Jesus' *"amazing"* comment in *John* 5 enables us to understand the 17:8 three-part-phrase regarding the beast. On the last day, Jesus will descend to judge. All the dead will come forth.

As an evil-doer, the beast (probably Nero, already dead ("was") will be raised from his grave to be sent to Gehenna or hell (the "Abyss")). A new version of the beast, Domitian (recall his connection with wis-

---

673. H.B. Swete aptly described this as "ostentatious magnificence of the [Roman] Empire." p. 215 *The Apocalypse of John*.

674. Basis for much of this imagery can be found in the prophecy of the original Babylon's fall in Jeremiah 29 and 50, 51. OT and NT writers consistently deplored prostitution-adultery-fornication as abuses of marriage's oneness sanctity. God's word also uses adultery to symbolize unfaithfulness to him, which often leads to adultery and fornication as people rebel against God's commands.

675. John 5:25-29 NIV The same root word *thauma* for amazed or marvel is used as in Revelation 17, there translated by the NASB as *wonder* and *astonished* by the NIV. Translators bear some blame for laypeople's confusion in biblical matters.

dom), brought renewed, more intense persecution. The references to seven kings and the eighth probably foresaw the lengthy Roman hostility towards God's faithful. The seven heads clearly identify the woman as the authority centered in the seven-hilled city. Verse 12 appears to inform us that "the beast" also likely represents governments antagonistic to God's rule throughout history's remainder. The complete number "ten" confirms that evil "collaboration" will continue.

(17:13)
These have one purpose, and they give their power and authority to the beast.

(17:14)

They will battle against the Lamb, but the Lamb will win **(nike).**

He is Lord of lords and King of kings, and those who are with him are the called and chosen and faithful.

The angel further explained that the waters represented the various nations, languages, and people under Rome's control. Verse 16 tells and reminds of hate, spite, and envy prevalent among various tribal and national leaders. Power, animosity, greed, and unbridled lust eventually led to Rome's fall. Note the contrast between human purposes (gnoman-γνώμην, 17: 13) and God's purpose (same word, but opposite purposes, 17:17). Events work according to God's plan and will continue unfolding until his words are fulfilled (telos). The messenger clarified:

"The woman you saw is the great city, which reigns
(recall basileon)
over the kings of the earth."

(18:1-8)

John saw another authoritative angel descend from heaven, whose glory illumined the earth. The messenger mightily shouted:

Fallen, fallen is Babylon the great! She has become a dwelling place of demons and a prison of every unclean spirit, and a prison of every unclean and hateful bird. For all the nations have drunk of the wine of the passion of her immorality, and the kings of the earth have committed acts of immorality with her, and the merchants of the earth have become rich by the wealth of her sensuality.

Another voice said:

Come out of her, my people,[676] so that you will not participate in her sins and receive of her plagues; for her sins have piled up as high as heaven, and God has remembered her iniquities. Pay her back even as she has paid, and give back to her double according to her deeds; in the cup which she has mixed, mix twice as much for her.
To the degree that she glorified herself and lived sensuously, to the same degree give her torment and mourning; for she says in her heart, "I SIT as A QUEEN AND I AM NOT A WIDOW, and will never see mourning."
For this reason in one day her plagues will come, pestilence and mourning and famine, and she will be burned up with fire; for the Lord God who judges her is strong.

(18:9, 10)

And the kings of the earth, who committed acts of immorality and lived sensuously with her, will weep and lament over her when they see the smoke of her burning,
standing at a distance because of the fear of her torment, saying, "Woe, woe, the great city, Babylon, the strong city! For in one hour your judgment has come."

Human behavior changes little over history. Devious, greedy folks grow rich from child pornography, human trafficking, slavery, narcotics, smuggling, dishonesty, and illicit sex.

(18:11-19)
And the merchants of the earth weep and mourn over her, because no one buys their cargoes any more — cargoes of gold and silver and precious stones and pearls and fine linen (bussinou) and purple and silk and scarlet, and every kind of citron wood and every article of ivory and every article made from very costly wood and bronze and

---

676. This echoes the pleas of Isaiah 52:11, and 2 Corinthians 6:14-18 ff. God's people must separate themselves from evil societal influences. The Lord repays every type of wrongdoing: Psalm 137:7-9.

> *iron and marble, and cinnamon and spice and incense and perfume*
> *and frankincense and wine*
> *and olive oil and fine flour and wheat and cattle and sheep,*
> *and cargoes of horses and chariots and slaves and human lives.*[677]
> *The fruit you long for (epithumia) has gone from you, and all things*
> *that were luxurious and splendid have passed away from you and*
> *men will no longer find them.*
> *The merchants of these things, who became rich from her,*
> *will stand at a distance because of the fear of her torment, weeping*
> *and mourning, saying,*
> *"Woe, woe, the great city, she who was clothed in fine linen and*
> *purple and scarlet,*
> *and adorned with gold and precious stones and pearls;*
> *for in one hour such great wealth has been laid waste!"*
> *And every shipmaster and every passenger and sailor, and as many*
> *as make their living by the sea, stood at a distance, and were crying*
> *out as they saw the smoke of her burning, saying, "What city is like*
> *the great city?"*
> *And they threw dust on their heads and were crying out, weeping and*
> *mourning, saying,*
> *"Woe, woe, the great city, in which all who had ships at sea became*
> *rich by her wealth,*
> *for in one hour she has been laid waste!"*
> *(18:20)*
> *"Rejoice over her, O heaven, and you saints and apostles*
> *and prophets,*
> *because God has <u>pronounced judgment</u> for you against her."*

God punishes evil and all who take part in it. Peter gave three important warnings. After reviewing instances of the Lord's punishments in OT times, he asked and cautioned:

A) **"What sort of people ought you to be in holy conduct and godliness?"**

B) **"Be diligent to be found by him in peace, spotless and blameless."**

---

[677]. See the lament for Tyre in Ezekiel 27, 28. Even after 70 years of captivity, for various transgressions against their Law, many Israelite merchants and clients, too, wanted to violate the Sabbath (Nehemiah 13:15-22).

C) **"Be on your guard so that you will not be carried away by the error of unprincipled men and fall from your own steadfastness."**[678]

(18:21-23)

A powerful messenger threw a rock resembling a great millstone into the sea, stating,

So will Babylon, the great city, be thrown down with violence, and will not be found any longer. And the sound of harpists and musicians and flute-players and trumpeters will not be heard in you any longer; and no craftsman of any craft will be found in you any longer; and the sound of a mill will not be heard in you any longer; and the light of a lamp will not shine in you any longer; and the voice of the bridegroom and bride will not be heard in you any longer; for your merchants were the great men of the earth, because all the nations were deceived by your sorcery.[679]

Modern Rome remains, but historians, archaeologists, and so on penetratingly research the city's rise and ultimate fall to relative decaying impotence after God pronounced Judgment on the once proud, opulent superpower.

(18:24)
And in her was found the blood of prophets and of saints and of all who have been slain on the earth.[680]

Those who oppose God's people must account to him.

(19:1-4)

Out of heaven, John heard a loud voice similar to a vast multitude saying:

Hallelujah! [681] *Salvation and glory and power belong to our God;*

---

678. 2 Peter 3:11, 14, 17 NASB.

679. Many of the above themes restate and modify prophecies found in Jeremiah 25:10; 51:48, 64; Ezekiel 26:13, 14 and others passages.

680. Compare with Jesus' prophecy against Israel in Matthew 23:34-36.

681. In verses 19:1, 3, 4, 6, *Revelation* transliterates the Hebrew expression, "Hallelujah," meaning, "Praise the Lord." Interesting, that in verse 19:5, a voice from the throne orders: "Praise to our God" using the Greek verb **aineo**, second person plural

BECAUSE HIS JUDGMENTS ARE TRUE AND RIGHTEOUS;
for He has judged the great harlot who was corrupting the earth with her immorality, and **HE HAS AVENGED THE BLOOD OF HIS BOND-SERVANTS ON HER.**
"Hallelujah! **HER SMOKE RISES UP FOREVER AND EVER,**" the heavenly voices added.

Falling down, the twenty-four elders and the four living creatures worshiped God on the throne declaring their, "**Amen. Hallelujah!**"

(19:5)

From the throne, a voice enjoined,

Give praise to our God, all you his bond-servants,
you who fear him, the small and the great.

(19:6-8)

Like the **"sound of many waters"** *and* **"mighty peals of thunder,"** the volume of the great multitude's Hallelujah Chorus increased:

Hallelujah! For the Lord our God, the Almighty, reigns.[682] *Let us rejoice and be glad and give the glory to Him, for the marriage of the Lamb has come and his bride has made herself ready. It was given to her to clothe herself in fine linen,* **bright** *and clean;*
for the fine linen (bussinon) *is the righteous acts of the saints.*

In *Ephesians* 5, Paul encouraged church married couples to godly, selfless interactions. Advising wives to submit to their husbands, he charged husbands to love their wives as,

Christ also loved the church and gave himself up for her, so that he might sanctify her, having cleansed her by the washing of water with the word, that he might present to himself the church in all her glory, having no spot or wrinkle or any such thing;
but that she would be holy and blameless.[683]

---

imperative active (αἰνεῖτε). Similar phrasing can be found in the LXX, Psalm 135:1, 2. Without the benefit of word processing, The **Revelator** made phenomenal use of both OT and NT Scripture combining and rephrasing to tell *The Apocalypse's* vital message.

682. Many English versions unfortunately make a paragraph break at this point. The NASB for example, entitles the new section beginning in verse 7 as the **Marriage of the Lamb**.

683. Ephesians 5:25-27 NASB.

The Apostle spent two years teaching in Ephesus, the first church mentioned in *Revelation* As a result of Paul's work there, "all who lived in Asia heard the word of the Lord."[684] The seven churches of Asia likely knew the *Marriage of the Lamb* theme well because of Paul's teaching and evangelizing work. Isaiah the prophet used this symbolic subject matter.[685] Jesus delivered one of his great parables on the wedding feast of the king's son. He concluded by telling the story of the fellow who tried to attend without the proper attire (*Matthew* 22:1-14).

(19: 9, 10)

The messenger told John:

Write, "Blessed are those who are invited to the marriage supper of the Lamb."

The messenger added: **"These are true words of God."** John attempted to worship him, but the messenger rebuked him:

Do not do that; I am a fellow servant of yours and your brethren who hold the testimony of Jesus; worship God. For the testimony of Jesus is the spirit of prophecy.

(19:11-13)

Heaven opened and John saw a white horse and Jesus, the one deserving worship. Each phrase in the following paragraph not only identifies Jesus but also reveals his worthiness. In contrast with the rider on the white horse at the opening of the first seal (chapter six), Jesus doesn't attempt to conquer, he already conquered. Now he judges. God's Word crushes all foes. The Chapter 6 rider wore a victor's wreath (stephanos); this Chapter 19 rider wears a crown of royalty (diadems-many).

He who sat on it is called Faithful and True,[686] and in righteousness he judges and wages war. His eyes are a flame of fire,[687] and on his head are many diadems; and he has a name written on him which no one knows except himself. He is clothed with a robe dipped in blood,

---

684. Acts 19: 10 NASB.

685. Isaiah 62:1-5 *Beulah* means *married*.

686. See 1:5; 3:14 This fulfills Zechariah's prophecy to Israel that God would one day be their God in truth (faithful) and righteousness 8:8 (pantokrator) cf Isaiah 11:4, 5.

687. Compare Daniel's vision of a man "dressed in linen" with eyes like "flaming torches" (10:6).

and his name is called The Word of God.[688]

General Joshua evidently had a preview meeting with his namesake, Jesus (Yeshua), the night before the battle of Jericho. He suddenly encountered the **"captain of the Lord's host"** before whom he fell on his feet and worshiped. The *captain* ordered the commander of Israel's army, to remove his sandals, **"'for the place you are standing is holy.' And Joshua did so."** [689]

(19:14-16)

And the armies which are in heaven, clothed in fine linen,[690] *white and clean, were following him on white horses. From his mouth comes a sharp sword, so that with it he may strike down the nations, and He will rule them with a rod of iron;*[691] *and He treads the wine press of the fierce wrath of God, the Almighty.*[692] *And on His robe and on His thigh he has a name written, "KING OF KINGS, AND LORD OF LORDS."* [693]

Jesus' identity and person certify that all the fullness of God dwells in him, (*Colossians* 2:9). He deserves absolute respect and honor.

(19:17, 18)

John then saw a messenger standing in the sun, who cried out loudly to all the birds flying in mid-heaven:

Come, assemble for the great supper of God, so that you may eat the flesh of kings and the flesh of commanders and the flesh of mighty men and the flesh of horses and of those who sit on them and the flesh of all men, both free men and slaves, and small and great.

At his transfiguration, Jesus' face shone like the sun and his clothes became bright white. His presence here as Commander of heaven's "armies" creates "sunlight" for the battle scene, which will soon ensue. The Son is the Light. The messenger merely invites the birds to

---

688. John 1:1-14.

689. See Joshua 5: 13-15 NASB.

690. Bussinon.

691. Cf Psalm 2:9 ; Isaiah 11:4; Hebrews 4:12.

692. Cf Isaiah 63:1-3; Joel 3:13; Amos 4:12, 13.

693. Deuteronomy 10: 17; Daniel 2:47; 1Timothy 6:15.

supper.[694] Over the millennia, fowl have feasted at countless bloody battlefields.

(19:19-21)

The future of Christ's enemies comes into view — beast, the false prophet, and those influenced by the evil trio. John saw the beast and earth's kings assemble their armies (the ultimate unholy union) to war against the Son and his army. The Son arrested the beast, the deceitful, sign-performing prophet, and those who received the beast's mark and worshiped his image. The two deceivers were thrown alive into brimstone burning lake of fire. The sword, which came from the Son's mouth, killed all their followers. Because they denied the authority of true, faithful Jesus, their words and actions condemned them. During his ministry, Jesus warned: **"By your words you will be justified and by your words you will be condemned."**[695]

And all the birds were filled with their flesh.

Chapter 20

Satan and those persecuted and martyred for their faith come into view in *Revelation* 20. Giving assurance to those who have "died with Christ," this section contains symbolic narrative, mostly based on what John saw. No songs or announcements appear in this portion, which we discussed at length in our Chapter 11.

(21: 1, 2)

John saw the "new heaven" and "new earth," permanent replacements for the present heaven and earth. *Kainos* (καινός), the word translated "new" of heaven and earth denotes something entirely original and unknown before. Seas no longer separate and threaten. John also beheld the "holy city," the "new Jerusalem," descending from God. People vainly struggle for property, status, and rights during this present temporary "test time." Paul reminded the Philippian church that our "citizenship is in heaven."[696] He counseled the Galatian churches that the "Jerusalem that is above is free, and she is our mother."[697]

---

694. This fulfills the Ezekiel 39:4 prophecy that Gog will one day become bird and animal food. This also may warn disobedient servants of God as in Deuteronomy 28:26.

695. Matthew 12:37 NASB.

696. Philippians 3:20, 21.

697. Galatians 4:26 NIV.

In *Ephesians*, Paul advised the church to be prepared for "her" pure, blameless presentation to Jesus. The event, he wrote, compares to a bride readying herself to wed a selfless, loving husband (Jesus). The prophet Isaiah long ago uttered this expectation (61:10). Ezekiel the prophet foresaw this restored relationship which Adam and Eve lost and the nation of Israel also ruined by their disobedience.[698]

(21: 3, 4)

A loud voice from heaven declared: "Behold, the tabernacle of God is among men and
He will dwell among them and they shall be His people and God Himself will be among them,
and He will wipe away every tear from their eyes; and there will no longer be any death;
there will no longer be any mourning, or crying, or pain; the first things have passed away."

The Lamb's unselfish sacrifice revoked Eden's curse. God dwelling with his people relates to and fulfills the promise he made in *Ezekiel* that David "again" would rule. The root and offspring of David[699] perfectly accomplished his work.

(21: 5-8)

Comfort and Caution:

And He who sits on the throne said, "Behold, I am making <u>all things new</u>." And He said, "Write, for these words are faithful and true." Then He said to me, "It is done. I am the Alpha and the Omega, the beginning and the end. I will give to the one who thirsts from the spring of the water of life without cost. He who overcomes will inherit these things, and I will be his God and he will be My son. But for the cowardly and unbelieving and abominable and murderers and immoral persons and sorcerers and idolaters and all liars, their part will be in the lake that burns with fire and brimstone, which is the second death."

In the above list of those the Lord destines for the fiery lake, cowards come first. The expression **"It is done"** translates only one Greek

---

698. Genesis 3; Jeremiah 30:18-24, 31:1-14; Ezekiel 34: 20-31.

699. Ezekiel 37:24-28, v. 24 -"My servant David will be king over them ..." v. 27- "My dwelling place also will be with them, NASB; Revelation 5: 5 "The Root of David has overcome ..."

word, *gegonan* (γέγοναν). Instant action results from God's words. Humans emptily and endlessly opine, rant, and lecture. In Genesis Chapter 1, a three letter Hebrew word pronounced "tov," which means good, repeatedly describes various aspects of God's wondrous Creation.[700]

(21: 9-27)

An angel who had poured one of the last seven plague bowls approached John saying: **"Come here, I will show you the bride, the wife of the Lamb."**[701] Recently, while reviewing the Greek text of this section, I experienced my own "apocalypse." This revealing didn't occur because of extraordinary spiritual loftiness. Rather, noggin obtuseness hindered me from recognizing powerful symbolic likenesses decades ago.

The fact that for the past few years, I've done my daily Bible reading from the NASB partially hindered me from recognizing what I should have seen earlier. NASB editors interrupted the scene's flow by inserting the title *The New Jerusalem* between verses 9 and 10. John made no such break in his Greek text. His Holy Spirit guided pen wrote the word *deikso* (δείξω) the future tense of *deiknumi* (δείκνυμι) which means to show, point out, reveal, and so on. Thus, **"I will show you the bride, the wife of the Lamb."** *Want to see the Lamb's bride to be?"* The host angel-messenger carried John in Spirit to a prominent mountain. **"And he showed me"** (ἐδειξέν- third person aorist active of that same verb *deiknumi* [δείκνυμι] "to show or point out") **"the holy city, new Jerusalem"**[702] lowered from heaven brilliantly reflecting God's glory.

Considerable biblical evidence convinces me that the New Jerusalem is another figure or metaphor for God's people in Christ, the Church, the Lamb's betrothed. As we stated, the tenses of the verb "to show" give our first indication- **"I will show you,"** followed by **"he showed me. . ."**

Second, note Paul's wording regarding the Church in *Ephesians* 2:22 NIV:

<u>**Built on the foundation of the apostles**</u> *and prophets, with Christ*

---

700. Genesis 1: 4,10,12,18,21,25,31. Luke (24:12) used a form of *gegonen* when describing Peter's amazement with the evidence of Jesus resurrection ("marveling at what <u>had happened</u>"- [gegonos]).

701. Why the NASB publishers put a break between verse 9 and 10 with the heading *The New Jerusalem* puzzles me.

702. The prophet Joel predicted (3:17 NASB): "Then you will know that I am the Lord your God, dwelling in Zion, My holy mountain. So Jerusalem will be holy, and strangers will pass through it no more."

Jesus Himself as the chief cornerstone. In whom the whole building is joined together and rises to become a holy temple in the Lord. And in whom you also are being built together to become a dwelling in which God lives by his Spirit.

(21:12-14)

The city featured a great, high wall, *with twelve gates, and at the gates twelve angels; and names* were *written on them, which are* **the names** *of the twelve tribes of the sons of Israel. There were three gates on the east and three gates on the north and three gates on the south and three gates on the west.*
<u>*And the wall of the city had twelve foundation stones, and on them* **were** *the twelve names of the twelve apostles of the Lamb.*</u>

Third, when Jesus introduced himself as God's chosen in the Nazareth synagogue, he read Isaiah's prophecy: "The Spirit of the Lord is upon me. . ."[703] *Isaiah* brims with imagery to which the *Revelation* 21 scene refers. A few examples should suffice. Compare *Isaiah* 54:11, 12 (NASB), which describes the new relationship of the previously afflicted bride:

O afflicted one, storm-tossed, **and** *not comforted,*
Behold, I will set your stones in antimony,
And your foundations I will lay in sapphires.
Moreover, I will make your battlements of rubies,
And your gates of crystal,
<u>*And your entire wall of precious stones.*</u>

(19, 20)[704]

<u>*The foundation stones of the city wall were adorned with every kind of precious stone*</u>**.** **The** *first foundation stone was jasper; the second, sapphire; the third, chalcedony; the fourth, emerald; the fifth, sardonyx; the sixth, sardius; the seventh, chrysolite; the eighth, beryl; the ninth, topaz; the tenth, chrysoprase; the eleventh, jacinth; the twelfth, amethyst.*

---

703. Luke 4:16-30.

704. H.B. Swete envisioned the wall "broken into twelve sections by the twelve gates, and each section . . . seen to rest on a single" foundation stone.

Each of the twelve gates consisted of a single massive pearl. City streets were paved with pure gold that resembled transparent glass. In *Ephesians,* Paul described the similarity of God's plan for Christian marriages to his Church 5:25-27 (NIV).

Husbands, love your wives, just as Christ loved the church and gave himself up for her to make her holy, cleansing her by the washing with water through the word, and to present her to himself as a radiant church, without stain or wrinkle or any other blemish, but holy and blameless.

On the basis of our belief in the word, the waters of baptism cleanse us.[705] The New Jerusalem appears to be same as the bride, Jesus' glorified church:

Isaiah 60:14c: "They will call you the city of the Lord."[706]

During the Temptation, Satan took Jesus to a high mountain to show him the splendor of this planet's monarchs and their domains (*Matthew* 4:1-11). The grandeur of twenty-first-century's glitzy sights will join the devil and the remnants of sites past civilizations considered magnificent. All will be less than rubble when God's new handiwork appears. To measure the city, its gates, and wall, the host angel held a gold rod. The city's measurements showed it to be a perfect cube, 12,000 stadia in each length, width, and height. The city's wall measured 144 cubits in thickness (human and angel cubits equal each other).[707] In converting stadia to miles and cubits to feet, translators lose the symbolism of the twelves involved. The "jasper" wall of the city was pure gold as clear as glass.

{22, 23}

The New Jerusalem needs no temple. The city's inhabitants exclusively worship the Lord God Almighty and the Lamb. Their glory constantly illuminates the city making sun, moon and other light sources unnecessary.

{24- 27}

---

705. For "washing" see Acts 22:16. "For by one Spirit, we were all baptized into one body" 1 Corinthians 12:13 NAB.

706. Compare also Isaiah 60:19-21 with Revelation 21: 22-25.

707. In view of the symbolic importance of the number 12, the NASB decision to convert the 12 thousand stadia in verse 16, and the 144 cubits in verse 17 into current measurements (miles and yards) bewilders me, too.

> *The nations will walk by its light,*
> *and the kings of the earth will bring their glory into it.*[708]
> *In the daytime (for there will be no night there) its gates will never be closed;*
> *and they will bring the glory and the honor of the nations into it;*[709]
> *and nothing unclean, and*
> *no one who practices abomination and lying, shall ever come into it, but only those whose names are written in the Lamb's book of life.*

No locks, no alarms, no worries; God knows the hearts of people. No one of evil intent or motives eludes his security. Not the real estate; the purity of its inhabitants makes space holy.

(Special note about Revelation 22)

As a child might run and sample playthings in a toy store, Chapter 22's text jumps from one subject to another. Beginning with the warning of someone arriving soon, other topics follow.[710] They include:

- A blessing for the ones keeping the words of the letter's prophecy;
- An angel refusing to accept worship;
- Someone who is both first and last;
- Commendation of people with washed robes;
- Folks eat from a magnificent tree.

Why does *Revelation* close so disjointedly? With mostly empty conjectures, scholars endlessly speculate. The "rambling" can be easily explained. When a loved one visits, we speak at length about things dear to both of us. Then it comes time for our beloved to leave. In saying "goodbye", we remind each other of interests we share.

Parting conversations do not necessarily follow any particular order. Sendoff words often include: "I love you;" "I'll miss you;" "Text me when you get home." At "goodbye" time, last-minute concerns dominate. *Revelation* closes with a "farewell" type conversation. In some statements, it's difficult to ascertain exactly who is speaking. For these reasons, we include comments on the full text.

---

708. The reference to "kings" likely fulfills the promise concerning reigning as kings; also note Revelation 22:5.

709. Jesus keeps his word and rewards those who invest in heaven (Matthew 6:20).

710. In many ways, this section's (Revelation 21, 22) themes (thirsting, light, "river whose streams make glad the city of God," "God is in the midst of her," and so on) seem to parallel those found in Book 2 of the Psalms, which begins with Psalm 42. Note Psalm 46, for example.

(22:1)

Genesis 1-3, Joel 3, Ezekiel 47, Zechariah 4, and various parts of *Isaiah* provide extensive background for this scene's symbols. The guide angel[711] showed John the life-river emanating from the throne of God and the Lamb. The British Coronation Chair in Westminster Abbey appeared much smaller than I imagined it would be. That throne would look even less impressive standing over the Thames, the Euphrates, or even the Jordan River. The river Ezekiel viewed measured perhaps 5,000-6,000 cubits wide.[712] The mighty river John saw ran in the middle of heaven's great Broadway.[713] The scope, beauty and majesty of what John beheld staggered his imagination.

Folks pointlessly conjecture the size of heaven's throne and dimensions of the New Jerusalem. Even with twenty-first-century urban sprawl, the city's size seems colossal. These descriptions intentionally intimate elements, facets, and extents inconceivable to us. The fact that Jesus at his return will become instantaneously visible to everyone on this globe should prevent us from attempting to rationally explain divine and eternal aspects.

(22:2)

John glimpsed delights of reentering Eden. Attributing it to superstitions of unlearned, primitive beings, generations of people have scoffed at the Creation story. They fail to perceive timeless truths the story witnesses. Contemporary folks should take note of the garden incident's veracity. Two important plants stood in Eden's center. God permitted Adam and Eve to eat fruit from one select tree, the *Tree of Life,* but they never savored it. Instead, they ate of the forbidden *knowledge* tree. Francis Bacon recognized the potential of knowledge.[714]

Recall why the couple coveted that fruit: The devil claimed that eating from the knowledge of good and evil tree would make them god-like. That desire captivated the couple. Craving power, they disobeyed the one command God gave them. In order to taste whatever kind of fruit the tree produced, the two defied their Creator. Human

---

711. One of the seven, who poured out God's bowls of wrath.

712. A cubit measured roughly eighteen inches.

713. Re: Broadway: As Williams noted in his translation, this is the exact meaning of the Greek word *plateia*. In addition to comforting believers, does the immense watercourse with its healing tree on both sides somehow mock Babylon in Mesopotamia, which means "between the rivers" (meso=middle; potamos=river) and/or Rome, which the Tiber River divides?

714. He wrote "Knowledge itself is power," "Of Heresies" in *Religious Meditations*.

knowledge usually comes swathed in the question: "How will I use the capabilities gained from acquiring these facts?"

Though "Knowledge College" should help us live better, we utilize new info variously:

    A) Some use trivial learning to harmlessly solve crossword puzzles;

    B) Many elevate their egos by gossiping and strewing unconfirmed reports about others;

    C) In some instances, information (nuclear-energy details and hacking ability) comes loaded with immediate ultimate consequences.

Will we use this knowledge to harm or to help others? The potential for using knowledge should never exceed the ethics or the ability of the person(s) gaining or holding it. In what human hands can such intelligence be completely safe? The present generation faces grave dangers inherent when unethical people possess "ultimate" knowledge. The world repeatedly suffers from people corrupted by knowledge-power.

As you well know, evilly intended people have hacked into nearly every federal agency.

Even worse, unprincipled folks appear to work in all federal agencies of this country and apparently control other superpowers. Fortunately, they all eventually die. Evil people should not live forever.

Adam and Eve gained knowledge-power, but they could not be trusted. They also did not know the short-term or long-term effects of disobeying. God evicted them from Eden for those reasons. Though prospects might at times seem bleak to believers, current rulers, schemers, and controllers remain under God's ultra-ultimate authority.

After he drove the man out, he placed on the east side of the Garden of Eden cherubim and a flaming sword flashing back and forth to guard the way to the tree of life.[715]

---

715. Genesis 3:24 NIV.

The couple lost access to eternity. God made sure they could not reenter.[716]

The *Old Testament* chronicles the misery of those who followed Adam and Eve in rebellion.

The *New Testament* reveals how Jesus the Lamb helps us regain friendship with God:

For God so loved the world that he gave his one and only Son, that whoever believes in him shall not perish but have eternal life.[717]

Revelation 22 reveals the fullness of wonders the Lamb's sacrifice achieved for us—regaining access to the tree of life—to eternity. Consistently relating the story in symbolic form, *Revelation* tells how to find real, lasting life. Honor God, respect his laws, repent of wrongdoing, and believe in his Son. If we have not glorified God by obeying Him, we must repent-change, believe in the slain, yet risen Lamb, and boldly witness to his saving work. Regardless of persecution or trials, we faithfully serve God to the end. Without *The Apocalypse*, the Bible remains incomplete.

(22:2 continuation)

On either side of the river was the tree of life, bearing twelve **kinds** *of fruit, yielding its fruit every month; and the leaves of the tree were for the healing of the nations.*

This remarkable tree denotes full obedience to God but also the healing that serving him brings to his faithful subjects. Greek-reading believers had to notice the irony that God made the life-tree accessible through the Lamb's obedient suffering on the cross, the ugliest tree imaginable. Using the same Greek term *xulon* for the tree of life, the Apostles referred to the cross as a tree three times in the *Book of Acts*.[718] Adam and Eve did not foresee the short and long term lethal effects of disobedience: loneliness, loss of purpose, guilty feelings, and separation from God.

---

716. He also shut down (confused) the Shinar plains super-tower project. The confines and limitations our Creator puts on nations and peoples make an intriguing study. The remnants of numerous "lost" civilizations and various biblical references, for example Genesis 11:1-9; 12:1-3; 15:1-20; 19:1-29; Exodus 3:1-9; Leviticus 18:24-28; Deuteronomy 2:16-25; Jeremiah 47:1-7 large sections of Daniel; Amos 1:1-5; 9:5-15; Matthew 10:24-31; *et al* allude to and evidence God's complete control. The Creator set boundaries for human habitation: Acts 17: 22-31.

717. John 3:16 NIV.

718. Cf Acts 5:30; 10:39; 13:29, also 1 Peter 2:24. Compare to Revelation 2:7; 22: 2, 14.

- **Remember the last time you felt rejected by some individual or group of people?**
  You probably died a little.
- **Recall when you did something that you repeatedly vowed you'd never do again?**
  You probably died some then, too, didn't you?
- The last time you got angry, a part of you died didn't it?
- Disobeying our Creator gives rise to loneliness, hate, and divisiveness. Crippling guilt and adverse physical effects often result from wrongdoing.
- Only God's forgiveness and true, loving fellowship can cure us. Heaven incudes perfect *salvation* and *health*. In the *New Testament,* they are the same word.

We weren't made to sin. God made us for fellowship, pure love, and faithful godliness.

(22:3-5)
There will no longer be any curse; and the throne of God and of the Lamb will be in it, and his bond-servants will serve **(worship)** *Him; they will see His face, and His name* **will be** *on their foreheads. And there will no longer be* **any** *night; and they will not have need of the light of a lamp nor the light of the sun, because the Lord God will illumine them;*
and they will <u>reign</u> forever and ever.

God's curses on Adam's and Eve's progeny will be lifted (*Genesis* 3:16-19) including the scourge of death. Jesus promised (*Matthew* 5:8) that the "Pure in heart will see God;" his name written on their foreheads, not the beast's ugly mark. The Lord and the Lamb will not be distant, but close. Darkness will not frighten, separate, or provide opportunity for deceit or violence. God's people will reign—enjoy *kingly* circumstances (recall *basileusousin* from Chapter 20).

(22:6)
And he said to me, "These words are faithful and true"; and the Lord, the God of the spirits of the prophets, sent His angel to show to His bond-servants the things which must soon take place.

The events *The Apocalypse* drama prophetically reveals will immediately begin taking place on the world stage. Jesus, the faithful, true witness of God warned both in parable and plain speech that he will reappear at a time when no one expects (*Matthew* 24:42-44); "be on the alert . . . you do not know which day your Lord is coming . . . when you do not think He will." People vainly listen to false prophets who claim to know when that *soon* is.

(22:7)

Chapter 22:7-21 restate vital topics covered earlier as verse 7 shows. Recall *Revelation* 1:3:

Blessed is he who reads and those who hear the words of the prophecy, and heed the things which are written in it; for the time is near.

Now we see the pleasant results from obeying God:

And behold, I am coming quickly.[719]

Blessed is he who heeds the words of the prophecy of this book.

Jesus demands ready response from his disciples.

(22:8, 9)
I, John, am the one who heard and saw these things. And when I heard and saw, I fell down to worship at the feet of the angel who showed me these things. But he *said to me, "Do not do that. I am a fellow servant of yours and of your brethren the prophets and of those who heed the words of this book. Worship God."

Why God's servants wear titles, want reverence, and seek honor from other servants remains a mystery. Though Jesus absolutely forbade doing it (*Matthew* 23:5-12), many church representatives and leaders still strive for and crave titles of respect and honor. No angel or true Apostle ever accepted any form of worship, adulation, or veneration.

(22:10, 11)
And he said to me, "Do not seal up the words of the prophecy of

---

719. The dative form of the word *taxos* appears in verse 6 and the NASB translates it *soon*. The accusative form of the word appears in verse 7 rendered as quickly. The term emphasizes the suddenness and rapidity with which something will happen, not the when. When I was a child, my dad warned me and my siblings at night: "If I come up there, I'll settle that problem in a hurry." He didn't let us know when; he referred to how quickly he'd deal with our misbehavior once he came upstairs to our bedroom. The Living Bible includes this footnote to *soon* in Revelation 22:12, "suddenly" "unexpectedly".

this book, for the time is near. Let the one who does wrong, still do wrong; and the one who is filthy, still be filthy; and let the one who is righteous, still practice righteousness; and the one who is holy, still keep himself holy."

The Lord wanted Daniel not to talk about what he saw and heard. In contrast, John was to immediately declare what the angel showed and told him. Our master doesn't expect us to change society; only to declare his message. Christ conquered sin and death. In him, all can win.

(22:12, 13)
Behold, I am coming quickly, and My reward is with Me, to render to every man according to what he has done. I am the Alpha and the Omega, the first and the last, the beginning and the end.

Jesus gave notice of his sudden appearance and stressed: "I will bring my reward and I will allocate according to each one's faithful accomplishments." As the only genuine starter and finisher of life, Jesus warned:

Be on guard, so that your hearts will not be weighted down with dissipation and drunkenness and the worries of life, and that <u>day will not come on you suddenly like a trap</u>; for it will come upon all those who dwell on the face of all the earth.[720]

(22:14-16)
*Blessed are those who wash their robes, so that they may have the right to the tree of life, and may enter by the gates into the city. Outside are the dogs and the sorcerers and the immoral persons and the murderers and the idolaters, and everyone who loves and practices lying.
I, Jesus, have sent My angel to testify to you these things for the churches.
I am the root and the descendant of David, the bright morning star.*

The seventh and last of *Revelation's* beatitudes comforts and cautions. Those who enter by the narrow gate have washed their sins clean by the blood of the slain Lamb. Those who disdain God's truth and live as they please will not gain entrance. The bearer of this news is both root and descendant of David. Jesus created David and his lin-

---

720. Luke 21: 34, 35 NASB.

eage; when Jesus, the King of kings appeared in human flesh, he was born as a descendant of David, Israel's greatest king.

(22:17)
The Spirit and the bride say, "Come." And let the one who hears say, "Come." And let the one who is thirsty come; let the one who wishes take the water of life without cost.

Heaven and earth, the Spirit and the church (bride) unite to invite those inside to enjoy the fullness of life in God. Drink God's new life to the fill. Those who have hungered and thirsted for righteousness finally find satisfaction (*Matthew* 5:6). *Come* is the exact term found in Chapter 6 when the first four seals were opened. A resource many of us once took for granted now appears scarce. Finding naturally pure water is nearly impossible. Clean water currently comes at high prices. Jesus provides life-water free to all. After foretelling the Servant's suffering in amazing detail (*Isaiah* 52-54), the prophet Isaiah extended this invitation 700 years prior (*Isaiah* 55:1).[721]

(22:18, 19)
I testify to everyone who hears the words of the prophecy of this book: if anyone adds to them, God will add to him the plagues which are written in this book; and if anyone takes away from the words of the book of this prophecy, God will take away his part from the tree of life and from the holy city, which are written in this book.

This warning echoes those given to Israel in *Deuteronomy* 4:2. Some adhere strictly to Lectionary readings which neglect certain parts of Scripture. Many church leaders promote ethical decisions that thwart specific Bible teachings. A major group holds that the decisions of its leaders share equal authority with Scripture. We neglect any part of his Word to our peril.

(22: 20, 21)
He who testifies to these things says, "Yes, I am coming quickly." Amen. Come, Lord Jesus. The grace of the Lord Jesus be with all. Amen.

The faithful witness Jesus testifies. Perhaps John, or the guide angel, utters the **"Amen"** and the salute to Jesus. The final words ring similar to Paul's Thessalonians welcome and also compare with the famed *Marana Tha* closing to the Corinthians, an Aramaic plea—**"O Lord, come!"**[722] The request in Jesus' model prayer for his disciples will

---

721. See also Isaiah 12:3, John 4:7-15, and Revelation 7:17.

722. 2 Thessalonians 3:18, 1 Corinthians 16:22.

be fully answered: God's will accomplished on earth and continuing eternally in heaven. Though most credit John the Apostle for writing *Revelation*, beyond doubt I am convinced that John could have written this complex document only "in Spirit"—enabled by the Holy One. *From beginning to end,* **The Apocalypse** *emphasizes: Praise God and the Son.*

He has made us **to be** *a kingdom, priests to His God and Father—to Him* **be** *the glory and the dominion forever and ever. Amen (1:6).*

Holy, Holy, Holy **Is** *The Lord God, The Almighty, Who Was And Who Is And Who Is To Come* **(4:8).**

Worthy are You, our Lord and our God, to receive glory and honor and power; for You created all things, and because of Your will they existed, and were created (4:11).

Fear God, and give Him glory, because the hour of His judgment has come; worship Him who made the heaven and the earth and sea and springs of waters (14:7).

Give praise to our God, all you His bond-servants (19:5).

I saw no temple in it (the holy city), for the Lord God, the Almighty and the Lamb[723] **are its temple (21:22).**

---

723. Of the three terms for lamb in the NT, Revelation uses only *arnion* (ἀρνίον). J Jeremias reviewed their occurrences aptly concluding concerning Jesus the lamb in Revelation: "As victor he is the Lord of lords and King of kings (17:14; 19:16)..." TDNT, Volume 1, pp. 338-341.

Bibliography — Books

Bainton, Roland H. *Here I Stand: A Life of Martin Luther,* New York: A Mentor Book published by The New American Library, 1950.

Barclay, William *The Revelation of John,* Vol. I and II, The Westminster Press, Philadelphia, 1976.

Benson, Edward White and Margaret Benson THE APOCALYPSE, AN INTRODUCTORY STUDY OF THE REVELATION OF ST. JOHN THE DIVINE, MacMillan and Co. Limited, London 1900. A Nabu Public Domain Reprint.

Blaicklock, E.M. *Cities of the New Testament,* Fleming H. Revell Company, Westwood, NJ 1965.

Blaicklock, E.M., *The Christian in Pagan Society,* Second Edition, Inter-Varsity Fellowship, London, 1956.

Blaicklock, E.M., THE COMPACT HANDBOOK of NEW TESTAMENT LIFE, Bethany House Publishers, Minneapolis, MN, 1979.

Brenton, Sir Lancelot C.L., THE SEPTUAGINT WITH APOCRYPHA: GREEK AND ENGLISH, Hendrickson Publishers Marketing, Peabody MA, 2015- Originally published by Samuel Bagster and Sons, London, 1851.

Brown, Francis, Editor, Based on William Gesenius Lexicon, *A HEBREW AND ENGLISH LEXICON OF THE OLD TESTAMENT,* Clarendon Press, Oxford, 1978.

Bruce, F.F. Gen. Editor, *New International Bible Commentary,* Zondervan, Grand Rapids, 1979.

Cassell's Latin-English English-Latin Dictionary compiled by D.P. Simpson, Cassel and Company Limited, London, 1963.

Chamberlain, Gary Alan, THE GREEK of the SEPTUAGINT; **A SUPPLIMENTAL LEXICON,** Hendrickson Publishers Marketing, Peabody, MA, 2011.

Clarke, Adam *Clarke's Commentary,* Abingdon Press, 1966.

Cohen, Abraham, *EVERYMAN'S TALMUD: The Major Teachings of the Rabbinic Sages,* Schocken Books, New York, 1949.

Craigie, Peter C. *Ezekiel,* Daily Bible Study Series (Old Testament), The Westminster Press, Philadelphia, 1983.

Cunliffe, Barry, *Europe Between the Oceans: 9000 BC – AD 1000,* Yale University Press, New Haven and London, 2008.

Dana, H.E., *The New Testament World,* Broadman Press, Nashville, 1937.

Davidson, Lance, *The Ultimate Reference Book: The Wits Thesaurus*, Avon Books, New York, 1994.

Davidson, Professor F., Editor, *The New BIBLE Commentary*, Wm. B. Eerdmans Publishing Company, Grand Rapids, 1954.

Dickinson, G. Lowes, *The Greek View of Life*, University of Michigan Press, 1958.

Douglas, J. D., Organizing Editor, *The New Bible Dictionary*, Intervarsity Press, London, 1965.

Echols, Eldred, *Haven't You Heard? There's a WAR GOING On!: Unlocking the Code to Revelation*, Sweet Publishing, Ft Worth, TX, 1992.

Gillis, Carroll, *REVELATION: An Exposition*, Sunburst Press, Pacoima, CA, 1989.

Glasson T.F., *Cambridge Bible Commentary*, "Revelation of John," Guy, H.A. *THE NEW TESTAMENT DOCTRINE of 'THE LAST THINGS': A study of Eschatology*, Oxford University Press, London, 1948.

Halliday, W.R., *Pagan Background of Early Christianity*, originally pub by Tinling and C. Liverpool, republished by Kessinger Publishing.

Hamilton, Edith, *THREE GREEK PLAYS* translated with introduction, W.W. Norton Co. New York, Bethany House Publishers, Minneapolis, MN, 1979.

Hanegraaff, Hank, *THE APOCALYPSE CODE*, Thomas Nelson, Nashville, 2007.

Hengstenberg, Ernst Wilhelm, *The Revelation of St. John: Expounded for Those Who Search the Scriptures*, Vol. 2.

Hitchcock, Mark, *IS AMERICA IN BIBLE PROPHECY?*, Multnomah Publishers, Sisters, OR, 2002.

Josephus, *Life and Works of Flavius Josephus*, trans. William Whiston, The John C. Winston Co. Philadelphia.

Kittel Gerhard, editor, *THEOLOGICAL DICTIONARY OF THE NEW TESTAMENT*, ten volumes, Wm. B. Eerdmans Publishing Co. Grand Rapids, 1964.

LaHaye, Tim and Jenkins, Jerry, *Left Behind* series, novels, published 1995-2007.

Lenski, R.C.H., *THE INTERPRETATION OF ST. JOHN'S REVELATION*, Lutheran Book Concern, Columbus, Ohio, 1935.

Lindsey, Hal, *The Late, Great Planet Earth*.

Malherbe, Abraham J., *Social Aspects of Early Christianity*, Second Edition,

Fortress Press, Philadelphia, 1983.

Morris, S.L. *The Drama of Christianity*, paperback edition, issued 1982 by Baker Book House from the 1928 edition of the Presbyterian Committee of Publication.

Newman, Barclay M. Jr., *A Concise GREEK-ENGLISH DICTIONARY of the NEW TESTAMENT*, United Bible Societies, London, 1971.

North, Stafford, *Unlocking Revelation: Seven Simple Keys*, Twenty-First Century Christian, Nashville, 2003.

NOVUM TESTAMENTUM GRAECE et LATINE, Eb. Nestle, Stuttgart, 1909.

Ramsay, W.M., *The Church in the Roman Empire Before A.D. 170*, G.P. Putnam's Sons, New York, 1912.

Pfeiffer, Charles, and Harrison, and Everett F., eds., *The Wycliffe Bible Commentary*, Moody Press, Chicago, 1962.

Shelly, Rubel, *The Lamb and his Enemies*, Twenty-First Century Christian, Nashville, 1983.

Stuart, Moses, *Future Punishment: Essays*

Swete, Henry Barclay, *THE APOCALYPSE OF ST JOHN*, third edition, MacMillan and Co. London, 1909.

The HOLY SCRIPTURES according to the Masoretic (Hebrew) *Text*, The Jewish Publication Society of America, Philadelphia, 5707-1947.

THE TORAH, THE PROPHETS, AND THE WRITINGS IN HEBREW, The Hebrew Publishing Co. New York.

Taylor, Bernard A., *ANALYTICAL LEXICON to the SEPTUAGINT*: Expanded Edition, Hendrickson Publishers Marketing, Peabody MA, 2009.

The Epistles of Pliny (Three Volumes) as Translated by William Melmoth, edited by Clifford H. Moore, The Bibliophile Society, Boston, 1925.

Westcott, Brooke Foss and Hort, Fenton John Anthony, *THE NEW TESTAMENT IN THE ORIGINAL GREEK*, The Macmillan Co, New York, 1940.

Whiston, William, trans., *Life and Works of Flavius Josephus*, The John C. Winston Co. Philadelphia.

Wishart, Charles Frederick, *THE BOOK OF DAY: A study in the Revelation of St. John*, Oxford University Press, New York-London, 1935.

Young, Robert *Analytical Concordance to the Bible*, Wm. B. Eerdmans Publishing Co. Grand Rapids, 1979.

Bible Versions

The Good News Bible: the Bible in Today's English Version, American Bible Society, NY, 1976.

The Holy Bible Authorized King James Version, 1611, by Zondervan, Grand Rapids, MI, 1972.

The Holy Bible Containing the Old and New Testaments, New Revised Standard Version, Thomas Nelson Publishers, Nashville, 1989.

The Holy Bible, Revised Standard Version, Catholic Edition, Thomas Nelson and Sons, Camden, N. J., 1966.

The Living Bible, Paraphrased, Tyndale House, Wheaton, IL, 1971.

The NIV Study Bible (2011 Edition) Zondervan, Grand Rapids, MI, *General Editor*: Kenneth L. Barker.

The New Testament, A Translation in the Language of the People, by Charles B. Williams, Moody Press, Chicago, 1950.

The New American Standard Version -- Accessed through sermoncentral.com/bible

New International Version, 1978 – Some accessed through sermoncentral.com/bible

The New Living Translation – Accessed through sermoncentral.com/bible

Periodicals

"Archaeology Magazine," March/ April 2015, Urbanus, Jason, **Rome's Imperial Port** (Portus).

USA Today, Tuesday, May 5, 2015, Section 4B by Charisse Jones.

Other

Ancient Greek Manuscripts, The Collection of in the British Museum, Part III, PRIENE, IASOS and EPHESOS Newton, C.T. Editor, by E. L Hicks, Clarendon Press, Oxford, 1890.

www.biblicalarchaeology.org Alternative Facts: Domitian's Persecution of Christians, "**Was Roman emperor Domitian really the great persecutor of Christians?**" Wilson, Mark, May 31, 2020

biblearchaeology.org/research/new-testament-era/3080-the-king-and-i-the...

britannica.com/editor/the-editors-of-encyclopedia-britannica, 4419, updated by J.G. Leubering, Executive Editorial Director www.britannica.com *Domitian: Roman emperor,* By Guy Edward Farquhar Chilver, Professor of Classical Studies, University of Kent at Canterbury, England, 1964–76.

The Apocrypha of the Old Testament, Revised 1957, Thomas Nelson and Sons, New York.

Index

Winning in Christ: Seeing through Revelation
by Robert Blair

Numbers

1,000, 6, 21, 62, 82, 185, 207, 276

1,260 days, 61, 227, 232, 275

12, 3, 5, 12–13, 26–29, 32, 45, 49, 51–52, 54, 56, 58, 60–63, 65–66, 68, 75, 80–82, 84–85, 97, 104–105, 109, 111, 116, 123, 128–131, 139–140, 143–144, 147, 152, 155, 160, 163–166, 168, 171–172, 190, 195–196, 200–201, 203–204, 211–214, 217, 221, 223, 225, 228, 230–234, 238, 240–241, 244, 247, 253–254, 256–258, 262, 264–266, 275–276

12,000, 5, 62, 140, 223, 258, 276

144,000, 5–6, 48, 63, 130–131, 140, 185, 223–224, 236–237, 276

24, 3, 18, 31, 45, 49, 52, 55, 62, 64–65, 71–81, 83–85, 95–96, 101, 104, 110–111, 126, 128–129, 143–144, 147, 168, 171–172, 184, 189, 202, 205, 209, 217, 219–220, 222, 227, 229, 237, 250, 255–256, 258, 261–263, 275

3, 3, 7, 10–11, 13, 18, 21, 28–29, 31–34, 36–37, 40, 45, 48–50, 52, 54–59, 61, 63–65, 68–69, 72, 74–75, 77–78, 84, 97, 103–104, 109–110, 115–116, 120, 123, 128, 130–131, 133–134, 143–145, 147, 149–150, 159, 166, 168–171, 183–184, 186, 189–194, 196, 199–202, 208–209, 212, 215, 225, 227–228, 231–232, 236, 239–240, 243–245, 250–256, 260–264, 266, 275

3 ½, 61, 228, 275

4, 3, 5, 7, 11, 13, 22, 25, 28–29, 33–34, 36, 40, 43, 45, 48, 50–52, 55–59, 62–67, 69, 71–73, 78, 81–82, 84–85, 87, 93, 97, 100, 103–105, 109, 112, 114, 116, 120, 123–124, 126, 129–132, 134–136, 138, 145, 148, 151, 158–161, 164, 166, 169, 172, 177, 179, 181, 184–185, 190–191, 193–195, 198, 200, 202–204, 206, 208, 210–212, 214, 217, 219, 224–228, 230–231, 234, 237, 239–242, 245–246, 250–258, 260, 266–267, 275

666, 60–61, 155, 157, 167, 171, 179, 236, 244, 275

7, 3, 5, 7, 10, 13, 30, 33, 35, 40, 48–49, 51–52, 55–56, 58–59, 61–62, 64, 70, 80–81, 84–85, 93–94, 98, 103, 111–114, 117, 120–121, 123, 126, 129–135, 139–140, 144, 152, 162, 164, 169, 184–185, 188, 190, 192, 194, 202–203, 207–210, 214–215, 217, 219, 223, 225, 227, 229, 231–232, 235–236, 239, 241, 244–245, 248, 251, 262, 264, 266–267, 275

A

Abigail, 89–90, 127, 273

Abominations, 184–185, 246, 273

Abraham, 32, 49, 52, 61, 104, 106–107, 112, 127, 129–131, 140, 145, 182–183, 193, 195, 201, 268–269, 273

Abyss, 30, 172, 182–183, 186–188, 190–195, 246, 273

Allegiance, 41, 119, 122, 157, 196, 199, 273

Alpha and Omega, 33, 62, 97, 194, 273

Amen, 117, 120–121, 138, 140–141, 172, 216, 221, 224, 251, 266–267, 273

Ancient of days, 210, 217, 273

Angel, 28, 49–53, 58–59, 61, 96, 114–115, 125, 127, 142, 162–163, 170, 182–184, 186, 192–193, 215, 217–218,

220, 223, 226, 232, 239, 241–242, 244, 246–247, 256, 258–259, 263–266, 273

Angel of the Lord, 52, 127, 226, 273

Anointed, 17, 74, 116, 196, 198, 207, 228, 231, 241, 273

Apocalypse, 6, 9–10, 12, 14–17, 20–24, 26, 28–30, 33, 40–41, 43, 48, 55, 57, 59, 64–66, 68, 88, 90, 92, 96, 112, 115, 117, 119, 124–126, 136, 147, 164–165, 181, 187, 190–191, 210, 213–214, 246, 251, 256, 262–263, 267–270, 273

Apocalyptic Literature, 10

Apostles' Teaching, 64, 273

Ark of the Covenant, 50, 104, 190, 230, 240, 273

Armageddon., 243, 273

Assyrians, 34, 273

Augustus, 24, 65, 156, 273

B

Babylonian captivity, 34, 71, 103, 227, 273

Baptism, 65, 82, 125, 149, 151, 199–203, 207–208, 258, 273

Believe, 9–10, 14, 29, 34, 112, 135, 145–146, 160, 178, 198–199, 201–202, 236–237, 262, 273

Beside, 103, 134, 148, 273

Bind, of Satan, 273

Birds, 89–90, 203, 253–254, 273

Blood, 13, 48, 58–60, 63, 78, 84–85, 120, 128–131, 151, 163, 174, 184, 189, 214, 216, 220, 222, 224–225, 233–234, 237, 239, 241, 246, 250–251, 253, 265, 273

Bond-servants, 125, 215, 223, 251, 263, 267, 273

Book of Life, 172, 209, 211–212, 236, 259, 273

Bowls of wrath, 260, 273

Breath, 152, 155, 189, 203, 228, 273

Bride, 190, 202, 215, 250–251, 255–258, 266, 273

C

Caution, 40, 72, 128, 187, 214, 225, 255, 273

Chain, 181–183, 273

Chaos, 12, 14–15, 39–41, 66, 77, 79, 112, 130, 182, 213, 273

Cherubim, 50–51, 134, 189, 230, 261, 273

Choke, 127, 191, 273

Christ, 1, 5–6, 9–10, 12–14, 17–18, 24–28, 30, 33–34, 38–42, 57–58, 60–65, 67–70, 77, 82–83, 86, 91, 94, 96–99, 102, 104, 106, 108–109, 112, 116–126, 130–131, 133, 135, 138, 140, 142, 145–147, 151, 153–154, 159–160, 165, 171, 173–174, 177–178, 180, 182, 186–187, 189, 194, 196–197, 199–208, 211, 214–216, 219, 228–232, 234, 237, 243, 251, 254, 256–258, 265, 273, 279

Church, 12, 16, 18, 22, 24–25, 27–28, 30–31, 39, 49, 51, 54–56, 64, 67–69, 71, 80, 84–88, 92, 95–96, 99–100, 102–104, 107, 109, 113, 116, 122–124, 127–128, 133, 136–137, 140, 149, 158, 165, 168–169, 171, 177, 186, 190, 196–197, 201, 203, 205, 207, 210, 212, 215, 217–219, 227–229, 232, 234, 236–237, 245, 251–252, 254–256, 258, 264, 266, 270, 273–274, 279

Claudius, 16, 113, 167, 273

Code, 16, 19, 23, 26–27, 29, 42–43, 54, 69, 88, 117, 269, 273

Coin, 152, 168

Comedy, 11, 94, 273

Comfort, 13, 39–40, 48, 66, 69, 182, 187, 199, 202, 214, 255, 273

Coming, 17, 23, 28, 33, 38, 48, 72,

76–78, 89, 99, 106, 109, 114, 116–122, 134, 144, 154, 156, 182–183, 190, 202–203, 207–208, 210, 216–217, 228, 235, 240, 243, 246, 264–266, 273, 276

Compromise, 41, 68, 165, 209, 273

Conflict, 11–12, 18, 29, 40–41, 66, 87, 112, 130, 140, 207, 273

Confound, 24, 27, 40, 72, 213, 273

Conquest, 9, 213, 225, 273

Consolation, 91, 93, 208, 273

Continuous-Historical, 21–22, 62, 181, 273

Convict, 40, 178, 218, 273

Covid19, 273, 279

Creator, 9, 17, 29, 39–40, 43, 51, 53, 66, 71, 86, 115, 119–121, 125, 130, 137, 141, 159, 182–183, 188, 198, 203, 205, 209, 212–214, 219–221, 224, 230, 242–244, 260, 262–263, 273

Crown of life, 218, 273

Crucified, 13, 17, 76, 147, 199, 207, 232, 273

D

Daniel, 28, 32–33, 51, 55–57, 61, 74–75, 81, 83, 85, 104–105, 117–118, 123, 129, 149, 152, 169–170, 201, 203–204, 210, 212, 217, 219, 224–225, 229, 232, 235, 239–240, 252–253, 262, 265, 273

David, 54, 61, 63, 71, 89–90, 104, 127, 164, 170, 190, 212, 220, 229, 234, 255, 265, 273, 276

Death, 9, 35–36, 64–65, 68, 82, 92, 97, 111, 121–123, 125, 133, 135–137, 139, 143–144, 156, 161, 165, 168, 173, 179, 182–183, 185, 188–190, 192, 194, 197–201, 203–204, 207–209, 214–215, 217–219, 222, 225–226, 228, 233–234, 236, 255, 263, 265, 273, 276

Decapolis, 93–94, 131, 273

Deeds, 31, 36–37, 138, 149, 198, 209, 217, 238, 241–242, 248

Deep, 165, 184, 187–188, 191–192, 194–195

Demons, 94, 146, 183, 186, 188, 191, 194, 225, 247, 274

Devil-Satan, 274

Dominus et deus, 65, 179, 274

Domitian, 16, 65, 138–139, 156, 170–173, 177, 179, 236, 247, 272, 274

Dragon, 11, 27, 51, 147–148, 154–155, 163, 166, 181, 183, 208, 233–234, 243, 274

Drama, 91–92, 94, 97, 125–126, 245, 263, 270, 274

Dramatic view, 274

E

Ears, 64, 128, 133, 274

Earthquake, 59, 162, 244, 274

Ecclessia-church, 274

Egypt, 35, 51, 57, 59, 61, 69–70, 100, 104, 113, 134, 158, 163, 167, 169, 182, 204, 228, 230, 240, 274

Eikon, 152, 154, 168, 274

Elders, 48, 58, 62, 84, 93, 123, 131, 140, 151, 172, 176, 178, 219–221, 224, 229, 251, 274

Elijah, 45, 80, 104, 132, 145, 228–229, 274

Emperor, 12, 16, 18–19, 24, 30, 65–66, 87–88, 96, 101, 113, 138–139, 153, 156–157, 167–168, 170, 172–173, 175, 177, 179, 199, 235–236, 272, 274

Encouragement, 5, 20, 25–26, 30, 115, 165, 214, 274

Ephesus, 25, 49, 67, 92, 102, 113, 116, 121, 123–124, 133, 181, 190, 200, 202, 208, 217, 245, 252, 274

Epi, 148, 274

Euphrates River, 242, 274

European Common Market, 62, 111

Eyes, 10, 17, 24, 28, 31, 44, 51, 75, 86–87, 93, 121, 132, 168, 170, 182, 191, 193, 211, 219–220, 224, 252, 255, 274

Ezekiel, 28, 50–51, 56–57, 104, 123, 129, 133–134, 159–160, 169, 192–193, 203, 208, 212, 217, 223–225, 228, 230, 249–250, 254–255, 260, 268, 274

F

Faith, 7, 13, 18, 23, 26, 33–34, 41–42, 63, 67–70, 73, 86–88, 101, 112, 126–127, 131, 149, 173, 175–177, 181–182, 195, 197–198, 200–201, 213–214, 234, 236–237, 254, 274

Faithful and true witness, 86, 147

Fallen, 36, 82, 170, 172, 202–203, 217, 238, 247, 274

Figurative, 6, 22, 42, 45, 54, 74, 88, 115, 155, 182, 184, 187, 217, 244, 274

First resurrection, 197, 203, 274

Forehead, 134, 158, 160, 184, 196, 238, 246, 274

Foundation, 43, 72, 257, 274

Fountains, 194, 274

Fulfillment, 32–34, 75, 78, 95, 111, 118, 125, 274

Futurist, 21, 62, 274

G

Gematria, 274

Glory, 30, 44, 51, 53, 58, 60, 66, 120, 131, 134–135, 138, 140, 151, 154, 160–161, 172, 199, 205, 214, 216, 219, 221, 224, 237, 247, 251, 256, 258–259, 267, 274

Goal, 6–7, 27, 33, 115, 274

God, 5–6, 9–13, 15–20, 22–34, 36, 39–45, 48–53, 55–71, 73, 75–76, 82–84, 86–88, 90–94, 96–101, 103–104, 106, 108, 111–112, 114–135, 137–141, 143, 145–152, 154–155, 158–163, 165–166, 168, 170, 172, 174, 176–177, 179–183, 185–189, 191–267, 274, 276, 279

Gold, 50, 103, 152, 160, 168, 170–171, 184, 191, 198, 211, 213, 225, 227, 237, 246, 248–249, 258, 274

Gospel, 31, 48, 58, 64, 73–74, 77, 79, 83, 91, 93, 98, 100, 105, 125, 128, 133, 138, 143–144, 148, 150–151, 160, 168, 171, 183, 194, 197, 210, 245, 274

Gospels, 17, 28, 43, 47, 52, 64, 72, 79, 91, 93–95, 98, 119, 124, 127, 142, 171, 204, 274

Government, 5, 12, 15, 18–19, 24–25, 27, 41–42, 49–50, 66, 75, 85–87, 112–113, 130, 138, 153–155, 167–168, 178–179, 199, 211, 213, 218, 235–236, 274

Great Commission, 17, 30–31, 96, 274

Greed, 8, 12, 15, 18, 26, 40–41, 68–69, 88, 93, 112–113, 122, 126–127, 147, 159, 168–169, 182, 198, 205, 220, 236, 247, 274

Greek Culture, 91, 274

Guilds, 24–25, 112, 274

H

Habakkuk, 162–163, 274

Hades, 122–123, 183, 192, 204, 209, 222, 274

Hagar, 52, 182, 274

Half-hour of silence, 162, 274

Harlot, 192, 251, 274

Harps, 148, 220, 236, 240, 274

Harvest, 37, 99, 115, 193, 239, 274

Hear, 15, 28, 34, 36–37, 43, 48, 54, 59, 63–64, 73, 96, 124, 127–128, 130, 135, 158, 171, 201, 204, 216–218, 225, 246, 264, 274

Heaven, 33, 39, 43–44, 48, 60, 63, 71, 81–82, 97, 99, 103, 114–115, 117, 129, 133, 138–139, 146–148, 152, 154, 162, 164–166, 170, 172, 182–183, 192, 194–195, 197–198, 200, 202, 204, 207–209, 212, 214, 217, 219, 221, 224, 226, 228–229, 231–233, 237–240, 247–250, 252–256, 259–260, 263, 266–267, 274

Hebrew Alphabet, 66, 97, 134, 274

Hierophant, 49–50, 274

Holy City, 36, 227, 254, 256, 266–267, 274

Holy Spirit, 5, 7, 10, 12, 14, 19, 23–24, 29, 31, 39–40, 57, 59–60, 71, 88, 108, 112, 120, 125, 135, 140, 147, 151, 159–160, 166, 169, 202, 208, 213–214, 220, 232, 256, 274

Honor, 13, 18, 30, 34, 39–40, 53, 58, 60, 66, 76, 122, 131, 138–140, 152, 155–157, 163, 172, 198, 214, 216, 219, 221, 224–225, 253, 259, 262, 264, 267, 274

Hope, 5, 7, 26–27, 29–30, 33–34, 64, 112, 129, 131, 136, 165, 202, 214, 237, 243, 274

Hour, 21, 32, 36, 62, 77, 110–111, 129, 162, 165, 199, 201, 214, 225, 237, 239, 245, 248–249, 267, 274

Husbands, 251, 258, 274

I

Idolatry, 32, 70, 168, 177, 182, 195, 274

Image, 44–45, 58, 148–149, 152–155, 157, 160, 168, 177, 196–197, 238, 240, 254, 274

Immersion, 149, 201–202, 274

Immortality, 30, 203–204, 226, 274

In Spirit, 19, 102, 184, 192, 245, 256, 267, 274

Incense, 162, 168, 170, 173, 199, 220, 249, 274

Interpretation, 6, 22, 45, 47–48, 75, 78, 117, 130, 142, 157, 181, 215, 269, 274

Interpretive, 5, 19, 23, 38, 46–47, 74, 89, 111, 122, 124–125, 142, 181, 274

Ishmael, 182, 275

Israel, 5, 12, 17–18, 25, 34, 45, 51, 55–56, 61–62, 65, 69–71, 79, 89, 94, 96, 98, 104, 112–113, 118, 130–135, 140, 149, 158–159, 165–166, 168–171, 177, 193–194, 196, 204–205, 211–213, 218, 221, 223–224, 228, 230–232, 234–235, 240–241, 243, 245, 250, 252–253, 255, 257, 265–266, 275

J

Jacob, 59, 104, 129–130, 132, 163–166, 182–183, 188, 195, 201, 231, 275

Jehovah's Witnesses, 6, 275

Jesus, 5–6, 9–10, 12–13, 15–17, 19, 23–25, 27–35, 37, 39–43, 47–49, 52, 54–56, 58–61, 63–88, 91, 93–105, 108–133, 136–140, 143–151, 154, 156, 161, 164–166, 168, 171–172, 175–178, 180–183, 185–218, 222–225, 228–229, 231–239, 242–243, 245–246, 250, 252–260, 262–267, 275

Jezebel, 26, 37, 40, 84, 88, 113, 164, 169, 228, 275

Joseph, 9, 104, 148, 164–166, 182–183, 188, 190, 231, 275

Joshua, 49, 104, 165, 193, 202, 225, 234, 244, 253, 275

Josiah, 61, 71, 243–244, 275

Journey, 12, 23, 69–70, 123, 129, 133, 164–165, 213, 245, 275

Judah, 164–165, 193, 220, 231, 243, 275

Judgment, 20–21, 45, 48, 59, 61, 68–69, 77–78, 80, 82, 85, 95, 97, 108–109,

111, 114–115, 129, 133–134, 139–140, 143, 168, 182, 194–196, 198, 204, 207, 209–211, 214, 216, 223, 226, 228, 233, 237, 240–243, 248–250, 267, 275

Julius Caesar, 156, 275

K

Keys, 13, 16, 23, 39, 41, 54, 56, 104, 122–123, 125, 147, 149, 183, 207, 217, 270, 275

King of kings, 39, 182, 207, 247, 253, 265, 267, 275

Kingdom, 34, 37, 62, 78, 83–86, 96, 99, 111, 118–122, 127–128, 131–133, 146, 151, 170–171, 181, 186, 188, 195, 199–201, 204–208, 211, 216, 219–220, 228–229, 232, 242–243, 267, 275, 279

KJV, 51, 59, 82, 102, 115, 142–144, 150, 187–188, 190, 203, 220, 277

Knowledge, 6, 23, 35, 42, 44, 54, 105, 118, 133, 142, 177, 184, 190, 207, 260–261, 275

L

Labor, 37, 73, 231, 275

Lake of fire, 149, 190, 209, 211, 254, 275

Lamb, 13, 17, 39–40, 48–49, 59–60, 63, 71, 84, 86, 93–94, 116, 126, 130–132, 140, 149, 151, 154–155, 166, 172, 182, 190, 206, 214–216, 220–225, 233–234, 236–238, 240, 247, 251–252, 255–260, 262–263, 265, 267, 270, 275

Lament, 117, 134, 159, 223, 248–249, 275

Lampstand, 36, 56, 102–104, 217, 275

Language, 5, 9, 26–27, 31, 40, 42, 45, 47–48, 54, 58–59, 69, 74, 84, 87–88, 94–95, 98, 101, 115, 118–121, 131–133, 135–136, 140, 142, 146, 151, 157, 184, 187, 194–195, 203–204, 208, 211, 213–214, 220, 271, 275

Last Day, 21, 48, 69, 84, 106–107, 109–111, 204, 246, 275

Last Days, 21, 24, 78, 82, 105–110, 117, 146, 275

Life, 5, 7, 9, 11, 15, 20, 27, 36–37, 48, 50, 55, 62, 64, 72–73, 86–87, 92, 98, 105, 109, 118–119, 121, 125, 128, 130, 133, 136–138, 145–146, 150, 161, 172, 177, 182–183, 189, 191, 193–194, 196–200, 202–203, 208–209, 211–212, 214–215, 217–218, 224, 228, 233–234, 236–237, 245–246, 255, 259–262, 265–266, 268–270, 273, 275, 277

Linen, 134, 190, 192, 241, 243, 248–249, 251–253, 275

Living Beings, 172, 219–221, 275

Living water, 93, 193, 224–225, 275

Lord's Day, 102, 121, 275

Luther, 14, 22, 202, 268, 275

M

Mark of the beast, 152, 157, 160, 167, 236, 275

Mark-karagma, 275

Marriage of the Lamb, 251–252

Martyrs-witnesses, 275

Matthew 24, 31, 64–65, 71–75, 77–79, 81, 83, 85, 95–96, 101, 110–111, 126, 128, 144, 209, 222, 263, 275

Mega, 35, 44, 80, 83–84, 99, 148, 163–164, 166, 192, 275

Melchizedek, 55, 207, 275

Merchants, 159, 170–171, 248–250, 275

Message, 5, 9, 12, 15, 19–20, 23–24, 26–27, 29–30, 42, 46, 50, 53, 58, 64, 66, 78, 96, 101, 123, 126, 143, 150–151, 160, 200–201, 226, 251, 265, 275

Messenger, 49, 51, 53, 159, 162, 183, 185, 215, 217, 232, 237–239, 241–242,

245–247, 250, 252–254, 256, 275

Messiah, 13, 17, 31, 34, 54, 73, 78, 86, 96, 106–108, 116, 121–123, 139, 145, 147, 165–166, 171, 183, 233, 275

Michael, 49, 232, 275

Millennium, 85, 98, 275

Minerva, 177, 179, 275

Miracles, 94, 138, 144, 147, 275

Miriam, 148, 275

Monuments, 70–71, 275

Mosaic Law, 55, 158, 176, 275

Multitude, 58, 84, 86, 130–131, 135, 190, 250–251, 275

Music, 35, 58, 63–64, 89, 109, 125, 151, 159, 215, 232, 275

Myth, 122, 275

N

NASB, 33–34, 48, 125–126, 142, 144–145, 151, 169, 171–172, 177, 182–184, 186, 189, 191–195, 197, 199–200, 202–204, 206–215, 221, 225–226, 229–232, 236–237, 239–242, 244, 246, 250–258, 264–265, 277

Nation, 12, 58–59, 62, 67, 84, 104, 111, 131–133, 140, 151, 159, 165, 182, 204–206, 208, 214, 220, 223, 230–232, 237, 255, 275

Nero, 16, 45, 65, 113, 156–157, 167, 178, 235–236, 246, 275

New, 5–6, 9, 14, 16–19, 23–25, 28, 30–35, 38–39, 47, 49–50, 52, 55, 62, 64, 69, 71, 73–75, 81–83, 93–96, 98–99, 101–105, 108, 111–112, 115, 117–118, 122–123, 125, 130, 134, 142–143, 148, 151, 164, 167–169, 175, 185, 188–192, 194, 196, 201–202, 207, 220, 230, 235–236, 240, 243–244, 247, 251, 254–258, 260–263, 266, 268–272, 275–276, 279

New Testament, 6, 9, 16–18, 31–32, 35, 50, 55, 64, 69, 75, 81–83, 95, 99, 102, 105, 108, 117–118, 125, 134, 142–143, 148, 164, 167, 169, 185, 190–192, 196, 201, 262–263, 268–271, 275–276, 279

Nicolaitans, 168, 217–218, 275

NIV, 6–7, 10, 17, 28, 30–31, 33–37, 43, 45, 48, 50–51, 53, 55, 58–60, 62–64, 66, 71–72, 74–81, 83–85, 92–94, 96, 100, 103, 105, 108–117, 119–123, 129, 131–135, 138–140, 142–152, 154–156, 158–164, 170, 176–178, 182, 185, 187–188, 190–191, 196, 198, 200–201, 203, 205, 208, 211, 223–224, 227–228, 233, 236–237, 246, 255–256, 258, 261–262, 271, 277

NRSV, 34, 52, 63–64, 76, 108, 115, 138, 142, 148, 191, 239, 277

Numbers, 6, 8, 21, 26–27, 32, 42–45, 48, 57, 62, 68, 74, 123, 125, 155, 157, 168–169, 175, 185, 208, 212, 218, 221, 227, 234, 241, 275

O

Old Testament, 5–6, 17, 20, 23, 25, 28, 34–35, 40, 45, 52, 54, 57, 88, 96, 104–105, 116–117, 122, 125, 148, 164, 262, 268, 272, 276

Overcome, 5, 63, 83, 93, 190, 194, 213, 220, 229, 231, 240, 255, 276

P

Pale horse, 222, 276

Palm Branches, 131, 135–136, 140, 223, 276

Para, 148, 276

Parable, 67, 79, 83, 91, 99, 119, 127–128, 163, 168, 190–191, 195, 239, 242, 245, 263, 276–277

Paradise, 115, 164, 217, 276

Passover, 76, 133–134, 158, 276

Patmos, 16, 101, 121–122, 208, 215, 276

People, 5–6, 9–13, 17–19, 21, 25–27, 29, 33–36, 39–41, 46–48, 51, 54, 58–60, 62–64, 72–73, 78–79, 82, 84, 86–87, 91, 93, 95–96, 98–102, 105–106, 108–109, 112–114, 116, 118–119, 122, 127, 130–134, 137–140, 143, 145–147, 149–152, 154–155, 157–160, 162–163, 165–166, 168–169, 176, 179, 181–182, 184, 186–188, 190–191, 193, 195–196, 198–200, 204–205, 207–208, 211, 213–214, 218, 220–223, 225, 227, 229, 231–232, 234–237, 242–243, 245–250, 254–256, 259–261, 263–264, 271, 276

Perfection, 33, 161, 276

Persecution, 5, 12–13, 16, 18, 24–26, 30, 35–36, 67–69, 73, 75, 83, 85, 88, 91–92, 99, 101, 126–127, 139, 165–166, 173, 182, 228–229, 236, 245, 247, 262, 272, 276

Persevere, 7, 40, 77, 112, 115, 228, 238, 276

Pharaoh, 59, 148, 169, 190, 240, 243, 276

Plagues, 36, 45, 56–57, 59, 61, 92, 99, 114, 148, 225, 228, 240–241, 248, 266, 276

Pleroma, 31–32, 276

Pliny, 20, 93, 153, 169, 173, 175, 177–179, 270, 276

Portus, 167, 271, 276

Post-resurrection, 143, 145, 276

Power, 9, 12–13, 18, 44, 50, 52, 57–58, 60–61, 66, 78, 86–88, 103, 111, 120, 122, 128–131, 138, 140, 145, 151–152, 154–157, 161–163, 165–170, 172, 183–185, 188–189, 197–199, 203–204, 207, 213, 219–224, 227, 229, 232, 240, 243, 247, 251, 260–261, 267, 276, 279

Praise, 13, 30, 35, 49, 51, 58, 60, 131, 135, 137–138, 140, 151, 160, 172, 179, 181, 188, 190, 214–215, 221, 224, 240, 251, 267, 276

Precious stones, 168, 184, 246, 248–249, 257, 276

Preterist, 20, 112, 276

Priests of God, 62, 197, 204, 206, 276

Promise, 33, 124, 131, 133, 136, 151, 196, 214–216, 229, 236, 242, 255, 259, 276

Promised Land, 69–70, 129, 165, 213, 245, 276

Prophecy, 28, 36, 59, 105, 108, 111, 132–133, 149, 170, 183, 192, 216, 225, 229, 231, 246, 250, 252, 254, 257, 259, 264, 266, 269, 276

Prophesy, 108, 227, 276

Prophet, 26, 37, 51, 57, 67, 73–74, 78, 83, 97, 103–105, 108, 114, 117, 132–133, 143, 146, 149, 154, 159, 162, 171, 209, 218, 225, 227–228, 231, 243–244, 252, 254–256, 266, 276

Purchase, 25, 41, 276

Purple, 184, 190, 245, 248–249, 276

R

Rapture, The, 80–81, 276

Reign, 6, 16, 41, 47–48, 62–63, 65, 74, 81–82, 104, 151, 156, 179, 189, 197, 204–206, 208, 220, 228–229, 263, 276

Remnant, 130, 134, 229, 276

Resurrection, 13, 25, 30, 52, 64–65, 80, 102, 108, 121, 125, 129–131, 137, 143, 145–146, 156, 165, 182, 189–190, 197–204, 208, 210, 215, 217, 228, 232, 235, 256, 274, 276

Reveal, 9, 23, 59, 63, 116, 137, 256, 276

Right hand, 13, 28, 45, 49, 114, 122–124, 172, 214, 216–217, 220, 226, 276

Roman Empire, 5, 24–25, 65–67, 96, 113, 157, 199, 236, 270, 276

Rome, 12, 16, 24, 57, 65, 67–69,

75–76, 85, 88, 92, 100, 103, 111, 113, 156, 167–175, 179, 184, 197, 208, 214, 223, 235, 238, 240, 244–245, 247, 250, 260, 271, 276

Root of David, 220, 255, 276

Rule, 10, 20, 44, 65, 67, 94, 97, 107–108, 119, 142, 151, 166, 168, 182, 188, 205, 208–209, 223, 229, 231, 247, 253, 255, 276

S

Saints, 61, 163, 196, 207–209, 229, 238, 241, 249–251, 276

Salvation, 10, 30, 33, 58, 130–132, 135, 140, 151, 160, 172, 201, 213, 224–225, 232, 251, 263, 276

Scarlet, 111, 184, 192, 245, 249, 276

Scenes, 9, 21–22, 35–36, 45, 49, 64, 89–92, 94, 98–105, 111, 115, 126–132, 135–136, 140, 156, 165, 181–182, 184, 213–214, 216, 236–237, 241–242, 276

Scroll, 36, 45, 53, 59, 102, 105, 121, 151, 162, 172, 212, 214, 220, 222, 276

Sea, 12, 16, 57–58, 60–61, 94, 101, 107, 114–115, 148–149, 155, 157, 163, 167, 184, 192, 194, 209, 214, 219, 223, 226, 230, 233, 235, 237, 240–241, 249–250, 267, 276

Sea of glass, 149, 276

Seal, 5, 45, 105, 128–130, 134–135, 137, 140, 146, 150–151, 160, 162, 193, 221–223, 225–226, 252, 264, 276

Second Coming, 38, 78, 99, 109, 117, 182, 190, 203, 207–208, 276

Second death, 197, 199, 203, 209, 218–219, 255, 276

Septuagint, 23, 28, 31–32, 35, 56, 117–118, 134, 142, 144, 150, 152, 162, 182–183, 187–188, 190, 192–193, 204, 206, 229, 232, 245, 268, 270, 276

Seraphim, 50–51, 276

Serpent, 27, 166, 181, 183, 233–235, 276

Sheol, 192, 204, 276

Sign-sameion, 276

Simultaneous scenes, 90, 94, 126, 276

Smoke, 162, 193, 238, 248–249, 251, 276

Sodom, 52, 112, 127, 193, 223, 276

Solomon, 43, 61, 71, 102, 169–171, 177, 179, 243, 276

Son, 13, 28, 31, 34, 48–49, 54, 56, 60, 64, 67, 77–78, 88, 91, 94, 98, 100, 103, 108, 110–111, 120–123, 126, 128, 134–135, 145, 147, 150, 154, 158, 164–165, 168–169, 171, 179, 182–183, 189, 195, 198–199, 207, 213–216, 221, 229, 231, 239, 246, 252, 254–255, 262, 267, 276

Song, New, 276

Sophia-wisdom, 276

Sower, Parable of, 277

Strategy, 16, 27, 31, 33, 166, 277

Strength, 38, 60, 131–132, 135, 138, 140, 158, 172, 186, 217, 219, 238, 277

Sword, 28, 122–123, 152, 155–156, 189, 217, 221–222, 253–254, 261, 277

Symbolic, 6, 22, 24, 42, 47–48, 51, 57 58, 62, 64, 80, 88, 101, 111, 122, 126, 136, 155, 182, 184–185, 187, 195, 201, 213, 215–216, 235, 252, 254, 256, 258, 262, 277

Symbolism, 10–11, 23, 26, 47–48, 54, 57, 69, 105, 115, 167, 181, 185, 193, 202, 204, 237, 258, 277

Synagogue, 25, 34–35, 132, 185, 206, 218, 257, 277

T

Tares, parable, 277

Teaching, 31, 34–35, 37, 40, 64, 67, 71, 77, 79, 82, 88, 116, 134–135, 144, 149, 181, 187, 196, 203–204, 218, 245, 252, 273, 277, 279

Telos, 32–34, 114–115, 118, 125, 194, 210, 226, 240, 247, 277

Temple (Jerusalem), 277

Testimony, 28, 34, 63–64, 96, 121, 128, 131, 150, 196, 204, 208, 214–215, 222, 230, 233–234, 252, 277

Testing, 12, 35–37, 61, 73, 84, 116, 153, 165, 187, 213, 232, 240, 245, 277

TEV, 142, 148, 208, 213, 232, 277

Thanks, 58, 131, 140, 172, 207, 214, 219, 229, 277

Theater, 25, 92, 101, 277

Thief, 33, 36, 201, 243, 277

Thlipsis, 35, 80, 84–86, 122, 229, 277

Thousand years, 6, 47, 62, 81, 183, 186, 196–197, 204, 206–207, 209, 277

Throne, 9, 13, 44, 58–60, 62, 64, 84, 93, 120, 125, 131, 135, 140, 151, 162, 170–172, 209–210, 215–216, 219, 221, 223–224, 230, 232, 242, 244, 251, 255, 260, 263, 277

Thrown down, 232–233, 250, 277

Thunder, 39, 59, 66, 162, 230, 236, 244, 251, 277

Titus, Roman general, 277

Tragedy, 11–12, 94, 277

Trajan, 153, 167, 173, 177–179, 277

Transfiguration, 28, 64, 183, 253, 277

Tree of Life, 36, 62, 98, 189, 193, 215, 217, 260–262, 265–266, 277

Trials, 30, 88, 126, 129, 173, 175, 177, 207, 213, 245, 262, 277

Tribe, 58–59, 62, 84, 131–133, 140, 151, 208, 214, 220, 223, 234, 237, 275, 277

Triumph, 9, 12, 91, 190, 213, 221, 277

Trumpets, 58–59, 129, 162–163, 193, 225, 277

Tyre, 57, 94, 131, 169, 192, 249, 277

V

Versions, Bible, 277

Victor's crown, 36, 133, 239, 277

Victory, 9–10, 12–13, 26, 29, 93, 124, 126, 140, 165–166, 168, 186, 190, 196, 207, 213, 216, 226, 240, 277

W

War, 15, 20, 26–27, 29–30, 71, 155, 163, 209, 225, 232, 243, 252, 254, 269, 277

Water of life, 125, 194, 224, 255, 266, 277

Wealth, 60, 168–170, 172, 191, 248–249, 277

Well, 19, 21, 23, 26, 28–29, 35, 44, 49, 54, 59, 63, 67, 69, 73, 86–87, 90, 92–93, 99–100, 105, 114, 119, 122, 135, 143–144, 147, 162, 164, 168–169, 177–179, 181–182, 193, 196, 201, 213, 220, 224, 231, 237, 243, 245, 252, 261, 277

White horse, rider on, 277

White robes, 48, 84, 130–131, 133, 135–136, 140, 224, 277

Wilderness, 7, 12, 18, 45, 51, 69–70, 89–90, 146, 164–165, 192, 194, 230, 232, 240–241, 245, 277

Williams, 118, 207, 260, 271, 277

Winning, 1, 9, 12, 30, 41, 166, 213, 273, 277

Wisdom, 35, 38, 60, 100, 131, 140, 155, 157, 170–172, 177, 179, 221, 224, 247, 276–277

Witnesses-martyrs, 277

Wives, 65, 170, 251, 258, 277

Woe, 58, 83, 163, 192–193, 228, 233,

248–249, 277

Woman, 37, 51, 87, 111, 138, 147–148, 164, 166, 172, 184–185, 202, 224, 231–234, 237, 245–247, 277

Wonders-terata, 277

Word, 5–6, 9–10, 12, 15, 17–18, 23, 26–33, 35, 40, 42–43, 45–46, 49–50, 52–55, 58–59, 63–64, 66, 73, 78, 80–85, 92, 96–97, 99–102, 104–106, 109, 115, 117, 119–124, 127–128, 131, 133–134, 142, 144–148, 150–152, 155, 160, 162, 166, 168, 172, 174–175, 183–191, 194, 196–198, 201–203, 205, 208, 210, 214–215, 218–219, 222, 225, 227–228, 232–234, 237, 242, 245–247, 251–254, 256, 258–260, 263–264, 266, 277

Worship, 12, 18, 35, 41, 53, 55, 58, 65–66, 70–71, 96, 101–102, 151–152, 154–157, 161, 176, 178, 180, 197–198, 214, 219–220, 225, 236–238, 240–241, 252, 258–259, 263–264, 267, 277

Worthy, 58–60, 66, 151, 172, 207, 219–221, 267, 277

Wound, 45, 152, 154–156, 235–236, 277

Z

Zechariah, 45, 51, 56–57, 71, 103–104, 149, 193, 227, 244, 252, 260, 277

Zephaniah, 162–163, 169, 225, 239

Acknowledgements

The vaudeville actor W.C. Fields remarked: "It was a woman who drove me to drink, and I never had the courtesy to thank her for it." Of the numerous temptations that have beset me, by God's grace, drink can't be counted.[724] Yet I have lacked the decency to thank legions of friends, relatives, teachers, acquaintances, and enemies for assisting me at crucial junctures during my decades of life. I especially wish I could recall and adequately express appreciation to all who helped with this *Revelation* effort.

Writers traditionally express gratitude to those who aided in various stages of a manuscript's preparation for publication. Acknowledging indebtedness to my parents is long overdue. They were hardworking folks of modest means who honored God in ways that took me years to understand and appreciate. Neither one graduated from high school. Still my mother taught me to love music and my dad, poetry: features of *Revelation* that deserve far more attention. Above all, Frank and Jessie Teghtmeyer Blair conscientiously tried to serve our Creator.

L.D. Webb, founder of Columbia Christian School in Portland, Oregon, encouraged me to learn Scripture. Among the first *Bible* texts he assigned me was *Revelation* 3:14 -16, part of the Lord's scathing criticism of ancient Laodicea's lukewarm believers. Other former godly educators who greatly assisted include: Hugo McCord, Vice President of Central Christian College and his enthusiastic affection for *New Testament* Greek; Wade Ruby, Head of the English Department at George Pepperdine College, who introduced me to *Old Testament* symbolism and who encouraged me in English studies; Pepperdine's Michio Nagai, from whom I learned Hebrew and gained insights into *Old Testament* theology; Frank Pack, who led and supervised graduate level seminars that broadened and enriched my biblical perspectives through independent research. Prominent among those who led rigorous seminars at Pepperdine was Dr. William M. Green, *Professor* of Latin, Emeritus, at the University of California, Berkeley.

Old adages stress what children learn from their parents. Yet Steve, Rob, Steph, Janice, and their mates, have all as individuals and collectively taught me and are still teaching me profound lessons too numerous to itemize.

---

724. Though Fields garnered many laughs with this comment, "drink" led to his early demise (age 66) on Christmas Day, 1946 in in a Pasadena, California sanitarium. Fields's attending physician listed his "immediate cause of death" as "Cirrhosis of the Liver" Due to "Chronic alcoholism." Many tend to focus on alcoholism, but greed, fear, guilt, hate, and a poor self-image often lead folks to "drink." Jesus' example of forgiveness and love for enemies helps us renew our hearts and minds. Thank God for the encouragement His Holy Spirit and Living Word bring us.

Insofar as assisting with the manuscript, Pat Blair read much of the manuscript in its early stages of development and offered strong reassurance. Janice read much of the MS sharing her infectious enthusiasm; Steve and Steph helped me brainstorm many concepts. Our friend and sister in the Lord, Kathy Wankum offered straightforward advice, not only in her specialty of math, but also gave me invaluable writing tips. I'm deeply grateful to my treasured brothers in Christ, Merle Muller and Eno Otoyo for their endorsements and to another Christian brother, Larry Walker for his valuable assessments. CSS President David Runk and his staff at CSS-Fairway Press deserve abundant thanks for their efficient help and cooperation. Flaws will no doubt appear in this publication, for which none of the above named persons bears responsibility; that belongs to me alone and the Lord will hold me accountable.

Last and foremost; the Greek philosopher Socrates advised: "By all means marry; if you get a good wife you'll become happy; if you get a bad one, you'll become a philosopher." I never pursued much philosophy, yet the Lord has exponentially increased my joy through Norma's loving, honest, patient support. For decades, as I researched, and repeatedly re-wrote, Norma endured what must have seemed to her an *Apocalypse* obsession. She heard and read scores of my sermons on *Revelation* and attended countless classes I conducted.

We two unworthy servants thank our magnificent Creator for allowing us to parent for a while four extraordinary offspring. Most of all we, praise Him for His mercy in Christ, the Living Word and the daily encouragement His Spirit brings. May God's vibrant love and peace further enhance your life until He completes His plan that exceeds all human comprehension.

About Robert and Norma Blair

Born in Hoisington, Kansas. Parents moved to Oregon, when he was ten years old. Graduated from Milwaukie, Oregon, Union High School. Began college at Portland State; transferred to Central Christian College in Bartlesville for one year. BA (Religion and English) and MA (Religion) from George Pepperdine College, where he also studied Greek, Hebrew, and German. Taught *Revelation* to numerous types of groups, church and unchurched.

Preached for the Church of Christ in Hollywood nearly 29 years and spent the last few decades teaching Bible studies and preaching New Testament Christianity in Northwest Iowa. On *www.robertblairbooks.com*, he posts sermons weekly. Baker published first book, *The Minister's Funeral Handbook*. College Press published the second, *The Funeral and Wedding Handbook*. CSS has published subsequent books, *The Great Omission* and *Luke Alive, Volumes 1 and 2;* also publishes *The Funeral and Wedding Handbook,* Second Edition, one of their best sellers. Written for **Leadership Magazine, Our Iowa Magazine,** and **Power for Today**. Wrote the section: "Planning Funeral Services" for the *Leadership Handbooks of Practical Theology,* Vol. 1, co-published by Baker Book House and Christianity Today.

Norma graduated from Tigard, Oregon, High School. They now live on an acreage southwest of Cleghorn, Iowa. They are near the most remote place in the state—and also the coldest. Their loving four children, grandkids, and great-grandchildren make them very thankful. Bob still preaches every Sunday. Until Covid19, the Blairs hosted a popular weekly neighborhood Bible study at their home. Accompanied by Josie, their frisky farm Lab, Bob and Norma enjoy gardening and taking walks together near their rural home. Corpulent cat Smash usually tags far behind.

God bless you for your interest in God's Kingdom.

Robert Blair
phone 712-445-2455
email: nwb1937@yahoo.com
PO Box 176
Cleghorn, IA 51014
www.robertblairbooks.com

www.ingramcontent.com/pod-product-compliance
Lightning Source LLC
Chambersburg PA
CBHW022107150426
43195CB00008B/308

Racialized Visions
HAITI AND THE HISPANIC CARIBBEAN

EDITED BY
VANESSA K. VALDÉS

Cover art: "Liberation Will Not Come Through Compromise & Fear" (2018–2019) by Rivka Louissaint. Photo transfer, oil, gold leaf on a 3' × 4' wood panel. Used with permission from the artist.

Published by State University of New York Press, Albany

© 2020 State University of New York

All rights reserved

No part of this book may be used or reproduced in any manner whatsoever without written permission. No part of this book may be stored in a retrieval system or transmitted in any form or by any means including electronic, electrostatic, magnetic tape, mechanical, photocopying, recording, or otherwise without the prior permission in writing of the publisher.

For information, contact State University of New York Press, Albany, NY
www.sunypress.edu

Library of Congress Cataloging-in-Publication Data

Name: Valdés, Vanessa Kimberly, editor.
Title: Racialized visions : Haiti and the Hispanic Caribbean / Vanessa K. Valdés.
Description: Albany : State University of New York, [2020] | Series: SUNY
   series, Afro-Latinx futures | Includes bibliographical references and index.
Identifiers: LCCN 2020023212 (print) | LCCN 2020023213 (ebook) | ISBN
   9781438481036 (hardcover : alk. paper) | ISBN 9781438481043 (pbk. : alk.
   paper) | ISBN 9781438481050 (ebook)
Subjects: LCSH: Caribbean literature (Spanish)—History and criticism. |
   Caribbean literature (Spanish)—Haitian influences. | Race in literature. | Blacks in
   literature. | Blacks—West Indies—Social conditions. | Racism—West Indies—
   History. | Haiti—Relations—West Indies. | West Indies—Relations—Haiti.
Classification: LCC PQ7361 .R33 2020 (print) | LCC PQ7361 (ebook) | DDC
   860.9/9729—dc23
LC record available at https://lccn.loc.gov/2020023212
LC ebook record available at https://lccn.loc.gov/2020023213

10 9 8 7 6 5 4 3 2 1

To the peoples of the Caribbean and her children

Contents

List of Illustrations — ix

Acknowledgments — xi

Foreword — xiii
    Myriam J. A. Chancy

Introduction: Centering Haiti in Hispanic Caribbean Studies — 1
    Vanessa K. Valdés

1 The Border of Hispaniola in Historical and Fictional Imaginations since 1791: Redemption and Betrayals — 27
    Claudy Delné

2 "The Road of Social Progress": Revolutions and Resistance in the 1936 Lectures of Dantès Bellegarde — 55
    Vanessa K. Valdés

3 The Dictator's Scapegoat: Emilio Rodríguez Demorizi's *Invasiones haitianas de 1801, 1805 y 1822* — 73
    Carrie Gibson

4 Mucho Woulo: Black Freedom and *The Kingdom of This World* — 89
    Natalie Marie Léger

5 The Haitian Revolution and Tomás Gutiérrez Alea's *La última cena* (*The Last Supper*, 1976) — 113
    Philip Kaisary

Contents

6 Haiti: Jesús Cos Causse's Prelude to the Caribbean 135
   Erika V. Serrato

7 "But the Captain Is Haitian": Issues of Recognition within
   Ana Lydia Vega's "Encancaranublado" 159
   Mariana Past

8 Haitian and Dominican Resistance: A Study of the Symptom
   in Edwidge Danticat's *The Farming of Bones* 177
   Ángela Castro

9 "The Black Plague from the West": Haiti in
   Roberto Marcallé Abreu's Dystopia 191
   Ramón Antonio Victoriano-Martínez

10 "And Then the Canes Shrieked": Haitianism and Memory in
   Junot Díaz's *The Brief Wondrous Life of Oscar Wao* 209
   Mohwanah Fetus

11 Haiti and the Dominican Republic: Teaching about the
   Un/Friendly Neighbors of Hispaniola 227
   Cécile Accilien

Concluding Thoughts: Afro-Latinx Futures 247
   Vanessa K. Valdés

Timeline: Pertinent Events in the Greater Antilles Cuba, Haiti,
the Dominican Republic, and Puerto Rico 259

Contributors 265

Index 271

Illustrations

5.1 "Don Manuel in the slave hut," still from *La última cena*   117

5.2 "Portrait of Sebastián," still from *La última cena*   121

5.3 "The Count kisses his slaves' feet," still from *La última cena*   121

5.4 "The Count's Last Supper," still from *La última cena*   123

5.5 "The Count and Sebastián at the supper table," still from *La última cena*   125

Acknowledgments

I thank God, my ancestors and guiding spirits, and my orishas for this, my fifth book. Thank you, Iris Delia Valdés, Robert Valdés Jr., Gina Bonilla, Iya Dawn Amma McKen, Leroy Martin Bess, Mercedes Robles, and Vicky Martinez, for your love, guidance, and support. My students at the City College of New York continue to provide immeasurable inspiration to me: each semester, I get to meet human beings of all ages and races and ethnicities who come to that school to better their lives, and without knowing it they guide me and my scholarship. I thank President Vincent Boudreau; Dee Dee Mozeleski, Senior Advisor to the President and Executive Director of Combined Foundations at City College; and Erec Koch, Dean of the Division of the Humanities and the Arts, for your support and mentorship over the years.

The compilation of this book has required that I study even further the cultural and intellectual production of the Dominican Republic in particular, a nation that itself continues to inspire more and more students every day. I teach at the university that houses the CUNY Dominican Studies Institute, the only academic center outside of the nation that focuses on Dominican studies, and this has been a blessing for me, both personally and professionally: I thank Sarah Aponte, Anthony Acevedo-Stephens, Jessy Pérez, Jhensen Ortiz, and Ramona Hernández for their love and support over the years.

I thank Edwidge Danticat, who was an inspiration for this study; for many here in the United States, Ms. Danticat has singlehandedly represented her country in the public sphere for more than two decades now. For me personally, her anthology *The Butterfly's Way: Voices from the Haitian Dyaspora* (2001), and her book of essays, *Create Dangerously: The Immigrant Artist at Work* (2010), remain touchstones to reflect on the necessity of breathing life into our experiences and putting words on the page.

In the last several years, in my capacities as scholar and educator, as writer of the most recent biography on Mr. Schomburg, and as book review editor of *sx salon*, the publication that saw the first renderings of this project, I have met and become friends with Caribbeanists who continue to push the field forward: my thanks to Myriam J. A. Chancy, without whom this book would not be in existence, and to Kelly Baker Josephs and the larger *Small Axe Project* collective, chief among them David Scott, Kaiama Glover, and Alex Gil. Thank you to Anne Eller, April Mayes, Dixa Ramírez, Raj Chetty, Nathan Dize, and Philip Kaisary for your friendship over the years. Thank you, Philip, Natalie Marie Léger, Mariana Past, Ramón Antonio Victoriano-Martínez, Carrie Gibson, Erika Serrato, Cécile Accilien, Mohwanah Fetus, Ángela Castro, and Claudy Delné for your contributions to this project, and thank you for your patience with me as the editor. Thank you for trusting me with your work.

At State University of New York Press, I thank Rebecca Colesworthy, acquisitions editor extraordinaire, who traveled from Albany to Harlem one cold winter's night in January of 2018 to celebrate the paperback publication of *Diasporic Blackness* as part of the annual Schomburg celebration at the Schomburg Center, and whose tangible support from that moment on has been unparalleled. Thank you for hearing me when I pitched the Afro-Latinx Futures series; thank you for your support and encouragement of writers and scholars. Thank you to the anonymous readers who offered substantial commentary and for whose effort I am ever grateful. Thank you to everyone at the press who was instrumental in the publication of this book: Dana Foote, who painstakingly copyedited this manuscript; Ryan Morris, who has overseen production of every one of my publications at the press; and Kate Seburyamo, who is overseeing the marketing. I thank Rivka Louissaint for granting permission to use her beautiful work, "Liberation," as the cover image.

And finally, thank you, dear reader, for your time and your interest.

An earlier version of Erika Serrato's essay was published as "Lamentos haitianos: Jacques Roumain, Haiti, and the Familiar in Jesús Cos Causse's Poetry," in *sx salon* 22 (June 2016), smallaxe.net/sxsalon/discussions/lamentos-haitianos.

An earlier version of Mariana Past's essay, originally entitled "Missing the Boat? Signaling Haiti's Role in Vega's 'Encancaranublado,' " was published in *sx salon* 22 (June 2016), smallaxe.net/sxsalon/discussions/missing-boat.

Foreword

MYRIAM J. A. CHANCY

I first became aware that my work, *From Sugar to Revolution: Women's Visions of Haiti, Cuba, and the Dominican Republic* (2012), was making an impact in the field of Haitian and Latin American studies in three distinct moments. The first was when I attended a Haitian Studies Association meeting in Port-au-Prince a year or two after the publication of the book. Most of the scholars who approached me about the book were based in Canada, where it had been published. The fact that the text was supported by a Canadian university press reveals something of the resistance to its themes, making Haiti central to a conversation of the *Latin* Caribbean that did not only involve geopolitics or totalitarian regimes, and which also connected issues of gender and sexuality nonconformity to a legacy of imperialism and its implicit penchant for patriarchal orders buttressed through racism. For, traditionally, if Haiti is discussed at all in Latin American studies, it has been in the sector of political science and rarely in the arts or literary imagination, where differences of "race" or "ethnicity" and "language" are invoked in order to exclude Haiti. This despite the fact that, in Caribbean studies, by and large, at least in literary studies, the region can only be studied via translation because of the variety of languages, dialects, and colonial heritages that compete for precedence in and among the nations that inhabit the Caribbean basin. That Haiti has a long literary lineage, once fully recognized in French and Francophone studies, has by and large been forgotten as Haitian studies in the United States has come to be grounded in an Anglophone world that knows little of this heritage for reasons as knotty as the colonial heritage from which such literature springs, even if the themes of much of Haiti's literature have been pronouncedly anticolonial if not anti-French.

The second moment I realized that the text was having an impact was a combination of the publisher quickly moving to sell out the hardcover edition within the first year of publication—something they had not expected to happen—and the publication of the paperback in 2013 due to high demand. Simultaneously, I received reviews lauding the book for its theoretical and cross-cultural reaches both in Canada and in the United States, while those (in the minority) that critiqued the book would not discuss its main purpose: to "deracialize" Haiti from its current position as an outlier community. I realized with the latter that I had hit a nerve. The third moment was when I saw a call for papers for a special discussion section of *sx salon*, *Small Axe*'s online journal, by the editor of this volume, asking contributors to chime in on a discussion that would destigmatize and include Haiti in the larger conversation of the "Hispanic Caribbean." And, now, here, is this collection.

Changes in fields are always slow, and sometimes painful: it is difficult for scholars who have long worked in a field and cherish it for various reasons, personal, political, cultural to open it up to a critique that might also devastate their understanding of its contours. At the same time as I have had, in the last few years, conversations that suggest that the work has been useful to scholars in the field grappling with Haiti's place in their field of vision, teaching, and scholarship, I have also had conversations with well-meaning and earnest scholars of the Spanish Caribbean who insist that a field of Afro-Latin Caribbean studies does not exist, despite the works of scholars in Black Atlantic studies, inaugurated by that of Paul Gilroy, despite the presence of constituencies and communities of people of African descent throughout the Latin Caribbean. It is not new to have suggested that Haiti be included in Latin Caribbean studies in the sense that Haiti's historical/political disavowal has been noted for some time, especially by scholars Sibylle Fischer and Michel-Rolph Trouillot. What is new is to suggest that the barriers that have long held Haiti outside of a comparative field with Latin Caribbean subjects could be overcome were we to redirect our notion of the continuities and shared histories among and between nations of the Caribbean that may have linguistic differences but whose makeup and realities have overlapped and cannot truly be understood fully without one another. In this case, I argued that Cuba, the Dominican Republic, and Haiti share overlapping histories that make the reality of Haiti central to the realities of Cuba and the Dominican Republic in ways that the reverse is often not true. The post-earthquake civic violence between the Dominican Republic's government and its citizens of Haitian descent in 2013 is symptomatic of a relationship that has been distorted over time to benefit the Dominican Republic's economic advancement; however, it is a violence that the Dominican Republic does to itself (since the disenfranchised, in this case, are Dominican not Haitian citizens) and to its history, since all Dominicans were once Haitians, and Haiti has no reason to define itself in contradistinction to the Dominican Republic. That myths of Haitian inferiority due to culture or "race" persist post-earthquake is only a testament to what little has been learned from history, that there is no connection between poverty, devastation, and worthiness. We know very well that the impoverishment of developing countries worldwide is the aftereffect of long-standing colonialism; the present state of Haiti, as I explain in *From Sugar to Revolution*, is simply causal to the persistence of a neocolonialism that has extended itself from times of slavery.

If I am encouraged by anything, it is the extent to which a post-earthquake literature by Haitians writing out of Haiti and elsewhere, writing in French, Kreyòl, and English, has sprung up (authors like Lyonel Trouillot and Yanick Lahens have published recent works that have gone on to be nominated for and win prestigious literary awards), making a continuity with the past and a need for translation more evident. I am encouraged by the willingness of scholars to engage with the proposition that Haiti, past and present, matters, in the Caribbean basin, and that though some of our discussions regarding Haiti's exclusion will be difficult—bringing up issues of nationalism, colorism, ethnocentrism, *blanqueamiento*, frankly, of *racism*—these are discussions that must be had to push our fields of inquiry further, to make them more true, to having more integrity.

I am encouraged by the scholars in this collection who, in following this perspective, offer thought-provoking essays linking Haiti to Cuban film and letters and the importance of the Haitian Revolution to the Cuban imaginary, political exchanges that impacted Puerto Rican sensibilities in terms of thinking through the impact of US gunboat diplomacy and military occupation of Caribbean territories; those who rethink the root causes for the anti-Haitian discourse in the Dominican Republic in terms of border studies and examinations of the effects of dictatorship; and those who examine movements of migrants in and among the islands, and the ways in which post-earthquake migration tapped into long-forgotten histories of "anti-abolition history" signaled by the Haitian Revolution and that provided much of Latin America with a template for actualizing their own freedom movements.

My hope is that such efforts will not only recover buried and maligned histories but realign the region as a whole rather than as splinters of our colonial "fathers." My hope is also that we will begin to understand our contemporary moment as one filled with the potential for a better understanding, a better realization of who we are as people of the Caribbean, as scholars of a region, where, despite our differences, a common allegiance to a syncretic history and pluralism that is neither simplistic nor easy, defines us, and is worth investigating, enriching, and cultivating for future generations and future scholarly endeavors.

Introduction

Centering Haiti in Hispanic Caribbean Studies

VANESSA K. VALDÉS

> En dépit de ces limites-là, en dépit de sa pauvreté, de ses vicissitudes politiques, de son exiguïté, Haïti n'est pas une périphérie. Son histoire fait d'elle un centre.
>
> In spite of these limits, in spite of its poverty, of its political vicissitudes, of its narrow existence, Haiti is not a periphery. Its history makes of her a center.
>
> —Yanick Lahens, translated by Myriam J. A. Chancy

In the aftermath of the 2010 earthquake, Haitian writers and intellectuals throughout the hemisphere were forced to once again defend their country in the onslaught of media coverage that emphasized the economic condition of the country and the devastation that the disaster had caused. Countering a predominant narrative that solely emphasizes poverty and suffering, these commentators had to remind an international audience about the humanity of their compatriots. Writer Yanick Lahens's succinct statement challenges

---

My usage of the adjective "Hispanic" as a modifier of "Caribbean" references the languages of these nations as predominantly Spanish and harkens back to Hispania as the Roman name for the Iberian Peninsula; this stands in contradistinction to "Spanish Caribbean," which would recall a colonial relationship with Spain.

us to reconsider how we define centers and peripheries; she alludes to a lauded history, one that prompts us to review what we think we know about this nation and its relationship to the countries that surround it. It serves as a challenge, particularly for those of us who have not studied the first independent Caribbean nation: What would it mean to put Haiti at the center of our understanding of this region? For those of us who study the Spanish-speaking countries in this hemisphere, how does studying Haiti, its history, and for the purposes of this study its culture, influence how we conceive of the Americas? And for those of us who study the histories and cultures of the peoples of African descent in Latin America, what role has Haiti historically played in the region and what is the relationship between this Kreyòl-speaking country and its Spanish-speaking brethren now?

Lahens's quote appears in the midst of Myriam J. A. Chancy's stunning introduction to her critically important study *From Sugar to Revolution: Women's Visions of Haiti, Cuba, and the Dominican Republic* (2012). Chancy directly addresses the anti-Blackness that in a great many ways has historically defined the region as well as the discipline of Latin American studies itself within the US academy. In a discussion about the history of the Spanish-speaking Americas, Chancy writes: "it was often necessary for African-descended individuals in the colonies to find a way to negate, obliterate, or have excused their African ancestry in order to be given a pass into political and social society. This process is very much in keeping with models of *blanqueamiento* established throughout the region in colonial times that continue to the present day" (14).[1] The epistemology that justifies whitening is one grounded in white supremacist thought, and is one that underscores that whiteness is better and therefore everything in relation to its Manichean opposite, that is, Blackness, must be worse.[2] Chancy goes on to highlight how this history of denying Blackness, particularly within Latin America, collides with the foundation upon which an independent Haiti was built: in the country's first constitution, "slavery was abolished; Africans and mulattoes were afforded rights of citizenship; [and] all citizens of the nation were re-categorized as 'Black,' whatever their racial or ethnic antecedents" (22).

At a time when citizenship was categorically being denied peoples of African descent in the rest of the hemisphere, where "African" would come to be conflated with "slave," here, in the land where formerly enslaved men and women successfully defeated not only landowners but also the military of Napoleon Bonaparte to establish Haiti as independent of the French colonizer, here to be Black was, is, to be a citizen, is to be human. In this second decade of the twenty-first century, when throughout the hemisphere Black people continue to declare their humanity and insist that our lives matter, this legacy of the Haitian Revolution is one that goes unknown for a significant portion of the population. Yet for those who do know, as several essays in this collection attest, Haiti remains a beacon of freedom for Black peoples across the hemisphere, an inspiration particularly against the neocolonialist impulses of its neighbor, the United States.

Racialized Visions: Haiti and the Hispanic Caribbean explores the cultural impact that Haiti and its writers and artists have had on their counterparts in the surrounding Spanish-speaking nations of Cuba, the Dominican Republic, and Puerto Rico. This collection challenges the notion that linguistic difference has kept the populations of these countries apart, instead highlighting the exchange that has been ongoing in the region since the Haitian Revolution. *Racialized Visions* also contests the rampant anti-Blackness of the region made perhaps most evident in the problematic representation of Haiti within curricula in the Dominican Republic and its erasure in the curricula of Puerto Rico as well as in the disciplines of Latin American and Caribbean studies in the US academy.[3] In the aftermath of the 1804 revolution, Haiti as a nation became conflated with Blackness, and Spanish colonial powers used these racist representations to threaten their holdings in the Atlantic Ocean. Throughout the nineteenth and into the twentieth century, white elites of the three countries utilized Haiti as a symbol of barbarism and savagery, successfully suppressing demands for increased civic participation on the part of populations of African descent in the name of not being like Haiti. This collection refutes this symbolism by highlighting how cultural producers in the region have long resignified Haiti to mean liberation; it also investigates the processes by which such resignification became possible in the first place.

In his 1995 critical study *Silencing the Past: Power and the Production of History*, anthropologist Michel-Rolph Trouillot issued a clarion call about the silence that had marked the scholarly treatment of Haiti, most notably in works assessing the great revolutions of the Western world. While the American and French revolutions have come to be considered the manifestation of the writings of Enlightenment intellectuals and philosophes, the Haitian Revolution had been treated as an anomaly. Trouillot argues that the revolution itself was "unthinkable" (72, 82) given that it was fought by a group that had been deemed less than human:

> In the early 1700s, the ideological rationalization of Afro-American slavery relied increasingly on explicit formulations of the ontological order inherited from the Renaissance. But in so doing, it also transformed the Renaissance worldview by bringing its purported inequalities much closer to the very practices that confirmed them. Blacks were inferior and therefore enslaved; Black slaves behaved badly and were therefore inferior. In short, the practice of slavery in the Americas secured the Blacks' position at the bottom of the human world. With the place of Blacks now guaranteed at the bottom of the Western nomenclature, anti-Black racism soon became the central element of planter ideology in the Caribbean. (77)

Trouillot's study serves as a meditation on how whole systems of thought and knowledge are produced when we go without questioning what we think we know. As Chancy writes: "In the history books, Haiti's revolution was deemed a violence emanating from the depravity of subaltern bodies and minds, rather than as a *reasoned response* to an unjust and dehumanizing system of enslavement and exploitation" (34–35, italics in the original).

We learn to celebrate the insurrections that took place in eighteenth-century France and in the thirteen English colonies of North America as justifiable struggles that took place in the name of liberty and emancipation; Haitians are often not accorded the same veneration. Erased is the fact that Haiti became a destination for ships transporting Africans across the Atlantic; revolts happened in the midst of transoceanic journeys, as those men and women on board had heard that they would be free if they got to Haiti.[4] Erased also was the fact that, as Dixa Ramírez points out, "anxieties about Haiti often applied equally to the entire island, Hispaniola, which in the early nineteenth century encompassed both Haiti and the eastern colony of Santo Domingo" (2).[5] Within the Spanish-speaking world of the Americas, the Haitian Revolution was instead viewed as a threat and utilized by the white upper classes of the region as such to quell incipient insurrections and discipline peoples of African descent well into the twentieth century.

It is accurate to write that those in power of the Viceroyalty of New Spain, the capital of which was Mexico City, and the Viceroyalty of New Granada, the capital of which was Bogotá, as well as the elites of the Spanish colonies of Santo Domingo, Cuba, and Puerto Rico, were all threatened by the series of revolts that took place in the French colony of Saint-Domingue beginning in 1791.[6] In 1797, the *audiencia* (the governing body in the region and high appeals court) that had been established in Santo Domingo in 1526 was transferred to Puerto Príncipe (present-day Camagüey), Cuba, due to the fighting.[7] In perhaps the most well-known study of the influence of Haiti on the cultural production of the Hispanic Caribbean, *Modernity Disavowed: Haiti and the Cultures of Slavery in the Age of Revolution* (2004), Sibylle Fischer writes:

> In the letters and reports of white settlers, the revolution is not a political and diplomatic issue; it is a matter of body counts, rape, material destruction, and infinite bloodshed. It is barbarism and unspeakable violence, outside the realm of civilization and beyond human language. It is an excessive event, and as such, it remained for the most part confined to the margins of history: to rumors, oral histories, confidential letters, and secret trials. There was a consensus in the region among settlers of European descent that Haiti was not a commendable model of emancipation. In response to the revolution, a cordon sanitaire was drawn around the island to interrupt the flow of information and people. (4)

While the narratives of the American and French revolutions have successfully managed to underplay the role of peoples of African descent in both insurrections (including incipient discussions about abolition and the extension of citizenship to men of African descent), there was simply no way to avoid the realities of the revolts in Saint-Domingue.[8] Settlers were attacked and killed; plantations were destroyed. Human beings once enslaved claimed their own freedom. All of this was characterized, as Fischer reflects, as "barbarous" and "excessive" by those who were literate and who could compose this history. Myriam Chancy writes: "Haiti's violation of the codes of structural subalternity—obedient subjugation—was labelled a *violence* not because the revolutionaries took up arms within the militarized colonial context but because their acts undercut the systematic ideology of Enlightenment philosophy which, at that time, simultaneously advocated for an end to slavery while asserting there were differing classes of man, and thus, of humanity (legitimizing the arrested rights of and violence against those deemed inferior by racialist thought, namely, enslaved Africans)" (35). These were Black people, who challenged a worldview that held to be true that they were incapable of reason much less the capacity to successfully organize, revolt, and succeed. The maintenance of that worldview, and the material realities of settler colonialism in the Americas, demanded that the revolution and its successes be overlooked, ignored, or used to signify a nightmare.

The metaphor most often used in relation to Haiti, and more specifically its revolution, within Latin American historiography, particularly that of the Hispanic Caribbean, is that of a spectral presence that haunted the region. Writing about the participation of Afro-Cubans in the fight for Cuban independence at the end of the nineteenth century, a full century after the insurrection in Saint-Domingue began, Aline Helg writes: "On the eve of Cuba's last war against Spain . . . Afro-Cuban overrepresentation in the liberation forces revived the specter of a Haitian-style Black dictatorship among Autonomists, partisans of Spanish rule, and some Cuban separatists. In particular, certain white separatists used that image to impose their leadership in the war, to the detriment of Black leaders, and to deflect Afro-Cuban demands for equality" (*Rightful* 54). The fear of a rebellion by the enslaved was a real one: women and men of Haiti had aptly demonstrated that revolt was no idle threat. David Geggus notes: "News of the Haitian Revolution spread wide and fast; nothing remotely like it had happened before, and nobody could think about slavery in quite the same way again. Whites in many parts of the Americas began complaining of a new 'insolence' on the part of their slaves, which they attributed to awareness of the successful Black revolution" (20). Carrie Gibson notes that in 1795 alone rebellions broke out throughout the Caribbean region:

> Rebellions started in Grenada and St. Vincent, while the maroons in Trelawny Parish, Jamaica, once again took up arms against the British. Even in Curaçao, which did not have a large slave population, a revolt began in August after slaves there heard about the Netherlands' defeat at the hands of French forces and the subsequent establishment of the Batavian Republic that had taken place in January. . . . The Dutch colony of Demerara, in South America, also experienced a revolt by slaves allied with maroons living in the jungle, though this, too, was suppressed. (163)

This is not to say that uprisings had not occurred prior to the events in Saint-Domingue; it is to counter, again, the perception for those who do know about the Haitian Revolution that it was the only insurrection in the region. It was not.[9]

Within Cuba and Puerto Rico, Spanish colonies until 1898, Haiti signified not only insurrection led and won by the enslaved, it also meant freedom and equality under the eyes of the law for Black populations. This was true throughout the Caribbean, particularly in the port cities and growing urban centers in the region. Julius S. Scott writes how maroons, *cimarrones*, as well as free Black peoples traveled freely to the colonies of all of the European powers. He notes:

> If ships and boats sailing among the island colonies of the Caribbean brought the region together commercially, their movement also aided those seeking to escape the rigorous social control of these slave societies. The prospect of attaining a masterless existence at sea or abroad lured every description of mobile fugitive in the region, from runaway slaves to military deserters to deep-sea sailors in the merchant marines of the European empires. . . . For all the colonial powers, the mobility of these unauthorized seaborne travelers presented social dilemmas at home as well as diplomatic problems abroad. (59)

News of the insurrections in Saint-Domingue and the new nation of Haiti spread quickly. For white elites in the area, the threat of the creation of Black nations, in which whites and those who shared the legal privileges of whiteness in the form of freedom, citizenship, the ability to own land, and the vote, would be subservient to those occupying the lowest rungs of society, posed the greatest danger.[10] This apprehension was not confined to the Hispanic Caribbean; indeed, it was shared by Creole revolutionaries in the lands of the Circum-Caribbean, who by the first decade of the nineteenth century were eager to declare their independence from Spain. Perhaps the most eminent of the region is Simón Bolívar; the "Libertador," he dreamed not only of regional independence but also the unification of these lands. In order to fund his dreams of regional sovereignty, Bolívar went to Haiti in 1816; there he found a president, Alexandre Pétion, who provided funds on the condition that slavery be abolished in Venezuela. Haitian soldiers would, in fact, go on to fight for Venezuelan independence (Geggus 24). Five years later, the first constitution of Gran Colombia was enacted; the emancipation of enslaved peoples of African descent was not included in the document.[11] Pétion's offer to Bolívar was not the first time the Haitian government supported area revolutionaries in their efforts for independence: Carrie Gibson details how Francisco de Miranda of Venezuela (1806), Ignacio López Rayón of Mexico (1813), and later Francisco Xavier Mina of Mexico (1815) all physically visited Haiti or sent representatives to Haiti so as to receive support from the Republic (Gibson 185–87). These actions gave credence to rumors at the time that Haiti sponsored "revolutionary antislavery," rather than simply an end to enslavement that could endure under a colonial framework.[12] The concerted efforts on the part of elites in the region, including the United States, to withhold diplomatic recognition of Haiti (in the case of the United States, until 1862) meant that it could not enact economic relations with potential markets in the area. Combined with the indemnity that France enacted in 1825, forcing the government of Jean-Pierre Boyer to pay 150,000,000 francs in reparations for property lost during the revolution in exchange for diplomatic recognition, as well as the indemnities of 225,000 pesos fuertes paid to Spain by President Fabre Geffrard when Spain recolonized Santo Domingo in 1861, it is easier to understand the groundwork for Haiti's current economic positioning in the hemisphere.[13]

Despite economic and political isolation, Haiti remained an inspiration for peoples of African descent throughout the region for decades following its establishment as an independent nation.[14] In 1812 José Antonio Aponte, a free Black man in Havana, was charged with leading a conspiracy to revolt; found in his possessions was a sketchbook with drawings of the leaders of a free Haiti: Toussaint Louverture, Jean-Jacques Dessalines, and Henri Christophe.[15] While this is the most prominent of the thwarted rebellions to have taken place that year, there were accompanying uprisings in Puerto Rico (the Day of Kings slave rebellion) and Santo Domingo (the Rebelión de Mendoza y Mojarra and a slave rebellion in Santiago de los Caballeros).[16] Antonio J. Pinto writes that these insurrections were "echoes of the same wave of uneasiness that shook the Spanish Antilles" in the aftermath of the coronation of Henri Christophe in Northern Haiti and of debates about abolition in the Cortes de Cádiz in Spain (121). Anticolonialism and fights for independence surrounded the islands, as the incipient nations of South America were all in the midst of battling Spain for self-rule.

The ensuing decades did not mean peace in the two remaining Spanish colonies, of Cuba and Puerto Rico, where slavery remained a way of life, or in the greater Caribbean. In 1844, another large-scale conspiracy was discovered in Cuba, that of the Escalera. While ten men were initially held responsible and killed by the state, there were widespread repercussions, as thousands of Afro-Cubans were tortured, killed, or banished from the island.[17] Perhaps the most well-known victims of this repression were Gabriel de la Concepción Valdés, known as Plácido, and Juan Francisco Manzano, the author of, to this point, the sole-extant slave narrative of Latin America.[18]

The disparity in the response of Spanish colonial authorities is striking; as Aisha K. Finch notes:

> But the two decades leading up to La Escalera also witnessed some of the largest and most organized slave rebellions and conspiracies in the Atlantic world. This resistance, largely inspired by the Haitian Revolution, included the 1822 Denmark Vesey conspiracy in South Carolina, the 1823 rebellion in Demerara (now Guyana), the Antigua slave rebellion of 1831, the Nat Turner rebellion of 1831 in Virginia, the "Christmas rebellions" of 1831–32 in Jamaica, the 1835 Malê rebellion in Brazil, and the 1843 slave rebellions in Venezuela and Colombia, among others. As other scholars have argued, the regional wave of antislavery protest and liberatory struggle that Cuban slaves joined in 1844 helped to usher in such events as general emancipation in the British Caribbean. (226)

While these rebellions may have failed, they reveal Haiti's scope of influence throughout the hemisphere; we must also take into account that the governments of all of these nations were better prepared militarily to squash revolt in the aftermath of the revolution.

This was particularly true in Cuba and Puerto Rico; in Cuba, the years after La Escalera saw increased calls for independence by both white and Black populations in the region. Michele Reid-Vazquez details how the advances that free people of color (*libres de color*) in Cuba had made in prior decades collapsed during the Escalera era, so that everyone was deemed race of color (*raza de color*). No distinction was made between free and enslaved peoples during this repressive time, which fomented subsequent calls for independence. She writes: "These critical developments in resistance, slavery, labor, and colonialism forged the conditions and alliances that would spark the Ten Years' War and its dual struggle for the abolition of slavery and national independence" (8). Joseph Dorsey specifies how during the decades after the end of the British slave trade in 1807 Spanish slaveholders continued to allow a coastal slave trade between Cuba and Puerto Rico, thereby incentivizing abolitionists from the islands to call for independence as well.

The revolutionary armies that fought in the Ten Years' War (1868–1878), the Little War (1879–1880), and the Spanish-Cuban-American War (1895–1898) were all racially mixed, as men and women of African and European descent fought together against a collapsing Spanish Empire. Nevertheless,

Spanish officials continued to utilize Haiti as a threat, Ada Ferrer observes. As usual, the references to Haiti became ubiquitous. But they were almost always brief and nebulous—as if merely to speak the name sufficed to call up concrete images of Black supremacy. "The movement's detractors utilized the same images and arguments again—to even better effect—during the second separatist uprising known as the 'Little War' of 1879–80. . . . Race, and its manipulation by colonial authorities, are therefore absolutely central to understanding the limits of multiracial insurgency in the first half of the nationalist period" (Ferrer, *Insurgent* 8).

Ferrer highlights how Spanish authorities maintained their greatest holding in the Caribbean, Cuba, by feeding the fears about Blackness and the creation of a Black state. In Puerto Rico, the call for independence was launched by the uprising known as the Grito de Lares, which occurred September 23, 1868; following this moment, many of the leaders of independence were banished from the island, as were their Cuban compatriots. Puerto Ricans such as Ramón Emeterio Betances and Eugenio María de Hostos met with Cuban leaders José Martí and Rafael Serra, among others, and traveled throughout the hemisphere, soliciting support from amenable leaders. For Betances, Caribbean independence would be complete with the creation of an Antillean Confederation, a political unit that would include Cuba, Puerto Rico, the Dominican Republic, and Haiti.[19]

The relationship between the Dominican Republic and Haiti is more complex than those of the other two nations. Fischer notes: "Nowhere in the Greater Caribbean did the Haitian Revolution have a more immediate impact than in Santo Domingo" (*Modernity* 131). If Haiti has been silenced from Western historiography, it must be noted that so too has the history of the Dominican Republic. While specialists both on the island and in the United States are contributing to a field that continues to grow, particularly in the last five decades or so, on the whole the study of the Dominican Republic remains outside the purview of traditional Hispanic Caribbean scholarship. This is to the detriment of those of us who claim to be scholars of the field; Dominican history, literature, and culture provides nuanced and complicated renderings of such themes as independence, citizenship, colonialism, and racial formations that are separate and distinct from those of the other nations of the Greater Antilles. For those of us who are scholars and students of the African diaspora, the study of the Dominican Republic presents us with great opportunities to go beyond facile and yet seemingly pervasive conclusions about Blackness, anti-Blackness, and anti-Haitianism so that we may instead delve into the particular and specific histories of this culture and its peoples.

The summer 2015 issue of *The Black Scholar* (vol. 45, no. 2) is dedicated to "Dominican Black Studies"; there, building on the work of such scholars as Silvio Torres-Saillant, guest editors Raj Chetty and Amaury Rodríguez write: "By moving beyond the narrow focus on Dominicans' alleged Black denial, [the essays in the issue] advance the multidisciplinary conversations about Dominican Blackness in relation to identity, to be sure, but also struggles against patriarchy, heteronormativity, and imperialism" (7).[20] For some, the notion that there is such a lived subjectivity as Dominican Blackness might be a novel one, and yet it has existed for centuries. The CUNY Dominican Studies Institute at the City College of New York has launched a bilingual website, *First Blacks in the Americas: The African Presence in the Dominican Republic*, that details arrivals of peoples of African descent in the fifteenth and sixteenth centuries.[21] Ana-Maurine Lara poses two simple questions regarding the Dominican Republic and its relationship to Haiti: "Why have we naturalized anti-Blackness as an element of the modern nation-state?," and "What does Blackness look like in the Dominican Republic?" (471) Rather than utilize a metric about Blackness formulated from sources external to Dominican culture—that is, this is what US/Cuban/Brazilian Blackness looks like, does it match—it is incumbent for us as students and scholars of the region to learn from the country itself.

Nations, products of the human imagination, define themselves in contradistinction to each other. The anti-Haitian sentiment that is today a feature of Dominican conservative voices did not always exist; on the contrary, even elites of the Spanish colony at one time viewed Haiti as a harbinger of progress. Edward Paulino notes: "Throughout the seventeenth and eighteenth centuries authorities in Santo Domingo considered their neighbor Saint Domingue's reliance on slavery as a model for progress and economic development, even espousing the importation of African slaves" (19). In 1801, Toussaint Louverture, leading forces against French troops who had retreated to the eastern part of the island, ended slavery in Santo Domingo; among those who signed the document declaring this abolition were four Dominicans (Eller 4). Fischer writes: "Slavery was reintroduced the following year, when Napoleon seized the eastern part of the island of Hispaniola in his attempt to recapture the former French colony in the West. In 1805 the slaves were freed again when Dessalines invaded, but slavery was eventually reintroduced once more and continued first under

French and then, after 1809, under Spanish rule" (*Modernity* 131). Andrew J. Walker notes that in the capital of the neighboring Spanish colony of Santo Domingo, the enslaved were buoyed by news of emancipation. While students of history may be more comfortable with the notion that an event as substantial as one marking the end of the sale of human beings be accomplished in one fell swoop, students of slavery in the Atlantic world know that this back and forth negotiation is more in keeping with how the emancipation of enslaved Africans and their descendants occurred in the Americas. The Haitian Revolution was the exception to the standing order, not the rule.

In the introduction to *We Dream Together*, Anne Eller writes that after 1809, "for more than a decade, as Spanish authorities practically ignored the territory, colonial sovereignty eroded. Dominican conspirators regularly appealed to Haitian rulers for arms and support for the many revolts and conspiracies that ensued, and pro-unification plans emerged. Dominican residents of center-island towns held ceremonies that celebrated Haitian independence" (5). Eller makes the important distinction between those who were in power in the capital of Santo Domingo and those who lived away from this urban center. Particularly notable is her highlighting of those who lived near the center of the island, near the tenuous border dividing the two nations that would, in the twentieth and twenty-first centuries be politicized and militarized, interrupting the flow of peoples that have characterized life on that island.

On December 1, 1821, José Núñez de Cáceres, the colonial governor for the previous twelve years, declared Santo Domingo to be the "Estado independiente de la parte Española de Haití."[22] Núñez de Cáceres was a Spanish criollo whose plan was to have his country be a part, ironically enough, of Bolívar's Haitian-funded Gran Colombia. This incarnation of an independent Dominican Republic, under the title of "Spanish Haiti," lasted for a few months, until Jean-Pierre Boyer unified the island in 1822. Eugenio Matibag notes that Dominicans of the Cibao (the northern part of the country) rejected Núñez de Cáceres's plan; they instead "raised the Haitian flag above the cities of Montecristi and Santiago de los Caballeros" (95), which eased Boyer's arrival. In her book *The Dominican Racial Imaginary*, Milagros Ricourt makes the point that, despite its later characterization as an invasion, this move was supported by many on the eastern side: whereas the elite had desired being a part of Gran Colombia, "the Black and mulatto masses, however, inspired by the Haitian Revolution, favored unification with Haiti" (28–29). Again we see the distinction drawn by class and race, calling our attention to the narrators of history. Paulino notes that this period is known by different names across the island: 1822–1844 marks the "unification" for Haitians, "invasion" for Dominicans" (8).[23]

The year 1844 marks the date from which Dominicans currently celebrate their independence; two decades later, from 1861 to 1865, the Dominican Republic was annexed once again to Spain, an effort that was led by elites but that was almost immediately rejected by the people of the nation, who fought the War of Restoration from 1863 to 1865. Dominicans, therefore, can rightly speak of three dates of independence: 1821, 1844, and 1865. April Mayes notes that from the perspective of recent Dominican historiography, a national sensibility emerged "after 1865, not in the wake of separation from Haiti in 1844 and certainly not during the colonial period" (4). For each of these dates, the country's neighbor to the west remained as an important, to use Eugenio Matibag's terminology, counterpoint for the Dominican Republic. As Dió-genes Abréu states quite clearly in the title of his 2014 prize-winning study: "Sin haitianidad no hay dominicanidad."

In the first decades of the twentieth century, Haitian migrant laborers would move to, work, and live in all three of the countries of the Hispanic Caribbean, providing inexpensive labor for US-owned sugar plantations.[24] In the midst of a racial climate throughout the Western hemisphere steeped in scientific racism and social Darwinism, elites of Latin America countries, as well as those in North America, found themselves having to reconcile their histories of indigenous and African enslavement and their resulting racially mixed populations. Each of the nations of the Hispanic Caribbean were engaged in efforts to whiten their populations, and so with Haitian immigration came the recycled tropes about the "specter" of the Revolution and the threat posed by supposed "Africanization" (Andrews 117–51). At the same time, after decades of considering whether to annex the Dominican Republic or not, the United States invaded the island, beginning an occupation that would last eight years in the Dominican Republic, from 1916 to 1924, and nineteen years in Haiti, from 1915 to 1934.[25] Concomitantly, these years saw the flourishing of the embrace of African heritage on the part of writers and artists in the *negrismo* movement in both Puerto Rico and Cuba, as well as the *indigenisme* movement in Haiti itself. In the Dominican Republic Rafael Trujillo rose in the ranks of a Dominican military trained by those invading US forces, becoming the dictator of the nation until his assassination in 1961. In addition to the propagation of anti-Haitian rhetoric, the whitening campaigns of the previous decades culminated in the massacre of Haitian migrant workers in 1937, a tragedy that is commemorated in Jacques Stephen Alexis's *Compère Général Soleil* (1955), Freddy Prestol Castillo's *El Masacre se pasa a pie* (1973), and Edwidge Danticat's *The Farming of the Bones* (1998). This slaughter had largely gone unnoticed by the world arguably until Danticat's novel, published in English in the United States. Literature and, more broadly, culture itself can therefore be a site of remembrance and commemoration, as that which has escaped the notice of historians can make its way into the hands of artists such as novelists, dramatists, poets, dancers, filmmakers—all who remind us to access and who themselves create alternative archives from which we can draw understanding of our identities, be it on the level of the individual, the national, or a region itself.

There are few books on the market that examine the representation of Haiti in the cultural production of its Spanish-speaking neighbors. Published jointly in San Juan by Puerto Rican publisher Isla Negra and in Santo Domingo by Dominican publisher La Trinitaria, Pedro L. San Miguel's *La isla imaginada: historia, identidad y utopía en La Española* appears in 1997; consisting of four essays in total and interested primarily in the narratives of Dominican nationhood, San Miguel focuses on the relationship between the Dominican Republic and Haiti in two essays, "Discurso racial e identidad national: Haití en el imaginario dominicano" and "La isla de senderos que se bifurcan: Jean Price-Mars y la historia de La Española." Perhaps the most widely recognized in English is Sibylle Fischer's *Modernity Disavowed: Haiti and the Cultures of Slavery in the Age of Revolution* (2004). Taking literally Trouillot's charge about the silence surrounding the revolution, Fischer examines the literary, print, and visual cultures of the nineteenth century, focusing on Cuba, the Dominican Republic, and Haiti. Ifeoma Kiddoe Nwankwo's *Black Cosmopolitanism: Racial Consciousness and Transnational Identity in the Nineteenth Century Americas* (2005) examines the construction of identity within populations of African descent in the United States, Cuba, and the British West Indies in the aftermath of the Haitian Revolution. Lucía M. Suárez's *The Tears of Hispaniola: Haitian and Dominican Diaspora Memory* (2006) analyzes the works of Jean-Robert Cadet, Junot Díaz, Loida Maritza Pérez, and Edwidge Danticat; she highlights how these writers, all of whom reside outside of the island of their birth, incorporate the island's histories of violence, trauma, and silenced memories in their art. Two that have been published outside the US academic market are Elzbieta Sklodowska's *Espectros y espejismos: Haití en el imaginario cubano* (2009) in Madrid by Iberoamericana-Vervuert and Emilio Jorge Rodríguez's bilingual collection of essays, *Haiti and Trans-Caribbean Literary Identity / Haití y la transcaribeñidad literaria* (2011), published in Saint Martin by House of Nehesi. As made explicit in their titles, both works solely analyze the literature of the region, without taking into account other modes of cultural production.

In the years following the publication of Myriam Chancy's study (2012), we see the emergence of Maria C. Fumagalli's impressive *On the Edge: Writing the Border between Haiti and the Dominican Republic* (2015) focusing on the representation of the border on the island of Hispaniola through analysis of both fictional and nonfictional texts, as well as other cultural artifacts such as songs, films, paintings, sculptures, photographs, and visual performance. We also see the release of Sara Johnson's *The Fear of French Negroes: Transcolonial Collaboration in the Revolutionary Americas* (2012), Philip Kaisary's *The Haitian Revolution in the Literary Imagination: Radical Horizons, Conservative Constraints* (2014), Marlene L. Daut's *Tropics of Haiti: Race and the Literary History of the Haitian Revolution in the Atlantic World, 1789–1965* (2015), Víctor Figueroa's *Prophetic Visions of the Past: Pan-Caribbean Representations of the Haitian Revolution* (2015), Marlene L. Daut's *Baron de Vastey and the Origins of Black Atlantic Humanism* (2019), and Grégory Pierrot's *The Black Avenger in Atlantic Culture* (2019). These do not focus solely on the relationship between artists of Haiti and the Hispanic Caribbean; rather, the majority of these studies emphasize representations of Haiti within the artistic productions of writers and artists from the Anglophone Caribbean. Both Daut's and Pierrot's studies examine literary histories and cultures that arose in Europe, the United States, and Haiti itself during the continuous insurrections by enslaved peoples in the seventeenth, eighteenth, and nineteenth centuries.

Of all of these studies, none incorporate works from Cuba, Puerto Rico, and the Dominican Republic in one text: *Racialized Visions: Haiti and the Hispanic Caribbean* is, to my knowledge, the first to include the work of Puerto Rican writers and thinkers in conversation with not only Haitian artists and intellectuals but also their Cuban and Dominican peers. There are twelve essays in this collection, with a foreword, introduction, and conclusion; of the essays, three center on Cuba, two on Puerto Rico, and six on the Dominican Republic. While this editor would have liked to have seen more essays about Cuba and Puerto Rico, this range accurately reflects the work submitted in response to the call for abstracts. It also unintentionally reflects the populations of Haitian descent within these three nations.

The volume begins with Claudy Delné's analysis of the representation of crossing the border in Haitian and Haitian American fiction in his essay,

"The Border of Hispaniola in Historical and Fictional Imaginations since 1791: Redemption and Betrayals." He argues that while the border has been tenuous since the eighteenth century, the crossing of that territorial marker to the Dominican Republic by Haitian migrants has been represented by Haitian writers Jacques Stephen Alexis, René Philoctète, and Edwidge Danticat as both an act of deliverance and disloyalty. In "'The Road of Social Progress': Revolutions and Resistance in the 1936 Lectures of Dantès Bellegarde," Vanessa K. Valdés examines the four lectures that the former Haitian ambassador to Washington delivered at the University of Puerto Rico in April of 1936. Bellegarde's visit to the US colony took place two years after the end of the US occupation of Haiti and only two months after police opened fire and killed members of the Puerto Rican Nationalist Party on the university campus, in what is known as the Río Piedras Massacre. Billed as an event meant to "inaugurate cultural relationships between Haiti and Puerto Rico," Bellegarde's visit provides a striking though implicit critique of the US imperialist enterprise.

Next, Carrie Gibson offers a reflection of the composition of historical texts in "The Dictator's Scapegoat: Emilio Rodríguez Demorizi's *Invasiones haitianas de 1801, 1805 y 1822*." She analyzes this canonical text of Emilio Rodríguez Demorizi, a prolific Dominican historian whose works, produced during the Trujillo dictatorship, continue to influence conservative Dominican historiography. In "Mucho Woulo: Black Freedom and *The Kingdom of This World*," Natalie Marie Léger takes on the most famous representation of the revolt in Latin American letters, Alejo Carpentier's *El reino de este mundo* (1949). Much has been made about Carpentier's prologue to this novel in which he establishes the tenets of *lo real maravilloso* (the marvelous real), later interpreted to be a precursor of magical realism. Carpentier writes about how a visit to Haiti in 1943 inspired him: "Despues de sentir el nada mentido sortilegio de las tierras de Haití, de haber hallado advertencias mágicas en los caminos rojos de la Meseta Central, de haber oído los tambores del Petro y del Rada, me vi llevado a acercar la maravillosa realidad recién vivida a la agotante pretensión de suscitar lo maravilloso que caraterizó ciertas literaturas europeas de estos últimos treinta años" (5). Léger reminds us that Carpentier composes his novel following the decades in which tens of thousands of Haitian migrants arrived in Cuba to work on US-owned sugar plantations. She posits the Haitian revolutionaries of the novel as well as their Cuban descendants as *cimarrones*, maroons still in search of their own space.

With "The Haitian Revolution and Tomás Gutiérrez Alea's *La última cena* (*The Last Supper*, 1976), Philip Kaisary examines this cinematic representation of slavery in nineteenth-century Cuba. With numerous allusions to the Haitian Revolution, Kaisary argues that the film, made seventeen years after the Cuban Revolution of 1959, is a call for the necessity of revolution to destroy social hierarchies of race and class.

In "Haiti: Jesús Cos Causse's Prelude to the Caribbean," Erika V. Serrato analyzes the Haitian references in the work of contemporary Afro-Cuban poet Jesús Cos Causse. For the poet, Haiti is not only a metaphor of liberation but also a homeland, as it is the land of his grandfather's birth. Juxtaposing his words with those of one of Haiti's greatest writers and poets, Jacques Roumain (1907–1944), Serrato reveals how Haiti is both "encapsulation and crossroads of Caribbean history."

Almost fifty years after Dantès Bellegarde's lectures in Río Piedras, Ana Lydia Vega publishes her short story "Encancaranublado" (translated in English as "Three Men and a Boat"). A tale of three migrant workers in a raft, a Haitian, a Dominican, and a Cuban, this is one of Vega's most famous works from her collection *Encancaranublado y otros cuentos de naufragio* (1982); in her essay "But the Captain Is Haitian: Issues of Recognition within Ana Lydia Vega's 'Encancaranublado,'" Mariana Past argues that Vega's work reinforces the perception of Haiti as emblematic of disaster, and she examines the seeming intransigence of nationalist paradigms within Latin American and Caribbean studies.

The execution of Haitian and Afro-Dominican women and men is the subject of Edwidge Danticat's second novel; in her essay "Haitian and Dominican Resistance: A Study of the Symptom in Edwidge Danticat's *The Farming of Bones*," Ángela Castro utilizes Slavoj Žižek's theory of the symptom through which to analyze representations of trauma and violence on the island of Hispaniola.

Ramón Antonio Victoriano-Martínez analyzes the continued discursive aggression against Haitians in his essay "'The Black Plague from the West': Haiti in Roberto Marcallé Abreu's Dystopia." Winner of the 2015 Premio Nacional de Literatura for decades-long contributions to Dominican letters, Marcallé Abreu is a journalist and prolific writer. He is the author of a trilogy of novels published between 2006 and 2012 that contribute to lingering anti-Haitian sentiment by perpetuating stereotypes of the past; Victoriano-Martínez demonstrates how these works reflect a conservative political agenda that continues to construct a Dominican nationalism in contradistinction to the nation to its west.

This theme of brutality continues in the essay that follows, Mohwanah Fetus's "'And Then the Canes Shrieked': Haitianism and Memory in Junot Díaz's *The Brief Wondrous Life of Oscar Wao*." There, she argues that the cane fields of Díaz's novel are a spectral space, one that serves as an archive that links slavery, colonialism, and dictatorship. For her, the text suggests that these lands are animated by the violations of the past committed against Black women, men, and children.

Finally, understanding the tangled histories of Haiti and the Dominican Republic is the subject of Cécile Accilien's "Haiti and the Dominican Republic: Teaching about the Un/Friendly Neighbors of Hispaniola." Accilien provides for scholars a full syllabus along with pedagogical suggestions regarding the teaching of this subject matter; for her, an examination of the tensions of these two nations is particularly critical in the aftermath of the 2013 Constitutional Court decision that denationalized hundreds of thousands of Dominicans of Haitian descent.

The collection's conclusion is a meditation by the editor on the ways in which we learn, unlearn, and produce new ways of thinking as students and scholars alike. It is followed by a timeline that offers a model of learning about events in the region in a more integrated fashion. In the case of Haiti in relation to the rest of the Caribbean and indeed to the Americas as a whole, for those of us in the position to do so, who have access to means of production—to newspapers, academic presses, podcasts, and the like—it is incumbent upon us to follow Gina Ulysse's 2015 exhortation: Haiti needs new narratives, ones that challenge the well-worn adage focusing on its material conditions. We must create the spaces and the opportunities for these new modes of thinking to flourish.

Notes

1. *Blanqueamiento*, or whitening, would become the official policy of countries throughout Latin America in the aftermath of their independence from Spain and Brazil in the nineteenth and twentieth centuries. For an introduction to this history, see Andrews, particularly his fourth chapter, "'A Transfusion of Blood': Whitening, 1880–1930."

2. A complete historical rendering of this worldview is outside of the scope of this study; however, Nell Painter has provided this history in her 2010 study, *The History of White People*. For a recent history that examines these ideas in the United States, see Kendi.

3. In their study *Unmastering the Script: Education, Critical Race Theory, and the Struggle to Reconcile the Haitian Other in Dominican Identity* (2019), Sheridan Wigginton and Richard T. Middleton IV highlight how textbook authors are slowly

recovering a Dominican Black identity and yet continue to struggle to disassociate that position from an entrenched discursive conflation of Blackness with Haiti.

4. Gerald Horne records one such incident: "For as Christmas was about to be celebrated in Cap-Haïtien in 1825, France's delegate reported to Paris a typical event: a ship had run aground on Haitian soil with scores of enslaved Africans aboard—fresh from the 'Ivory Coast'—presumably destined for Cuba, then experiencing a customary spate of imports of human cargo" (22).

5. In *An Islandwide Struggle for Freedom: Revolution, Emancipation, and Reenslavement in Hispaniola* (2016), Graham T. Nessler writes up the "forgotten Dominican chapters of the Haitian Revolution" (4), a striking intervention in the historiography about this pivotal event that underscores that the fighting "did not simply 'spill over' from French Saint-Domingue into Spanish Santo Domingo by virtue of geographical proximity" (3). Anne Eller provides an indispensable revision of our understanding of the period of unification of the two nations from 1822 to 1844 and the subsequent Dominican War of Restoration of 1865 in her study, *We Dream Together: Dominican Independence, Haiti, and the Fight for Caribbean Freedom* (2016). She too emphasizes that the island as a whole signified freedom of peoples of African descent in the face of continued threats of imperialistic encroachment by the slaveholding powers that were Spain, France, and the United States.

6. The Viceroyalty of New Spain in 1791 included the US states of Florida and the coastline of the Gulf coast states of Mississippi and Alabama, as well as the continental states west of the Mississippi River: Louisiana, Texas, Arkansas, Missouri, Iowa, Minnesota, Oklahoma, Kansas, Nebraska, North and South Dakota, New Mexico, Colorado, Wyoming, Montana, Arizona, Utah, Nevada, Idaho, California, Oregon, and Washington. It also included present-day Mexico, Guatemala, Honduras, El Salvador, Nicaragua, and Costa Rica. The Viceroyalty of New Granada included what is known today as Panama, Colombia, Ecuador, and Venezuela; by 1791, both Cuba and Venezuela had gained more autonomy as both were formally recognized as captaincy generals, that is, districts within the viceroyalties. For an introduction in English to the history and politics of colonial Latin America, see Burkholder and Johnson.

7. About this C. H. Cunningham writes: "The unqualified success of the Audiencia of Santo Domingo, both as a tribunal of justice and as an administrative organ, led to the general establishment of the institution throughout the Spanish colonial empire" (16).

8. For an introduction to the critical role that men and women of African descent played in both revolutions, see *The Abolition of the Slave Trade*, a permanent virtual exhibit by the Schomburg Center for Research in Black Culture of the New York Public Library, abolition.nypl.org/essays/african_resistance/7/.

9. Dominican historian Frank Moya Pons makes the point that the first insurrection by enslaved Africans to occur in this hemisphere happened on the island

of La Española: "Muy poca gente sabe que el primer grupo de esclavos africanos que llegó a la isla de Santo Domingo en 1503 no aceptó su condición servil y escape hacia los montes tan pronto tuvo la oportunidad desapareciendo para siempre del contacto con los españoles" (65). Insurrection is therefore foundational in the fabric of the two nations that remain on that island.

10. It is not insignificant that the greatest number of settlers from Saint-Domingue fled to Cuba; Gibson writes: "Some 15,000 to 20,000 refugees landed there [in Cuba], while around 1,000 made their way through Santo Domingo and on to Mayaguez and San Juan in Puerto Rico" (163). Whereas Saint-Domingue had been the richest colony in the Caribbean prior to the revolt, these settlers helped to transform Cuban society into the wealthiest of the region. Ada Ferrer examines this history in her most recent book-length study, *Freedom's Mirror: Cuba and Haiti in the Age of Revolution* (2014). In his 1986 dissertation, "The Hispaniola Diaspora, 1791–1850: Puerto Rico, Cuba, Louisiana, and Other Host Societies," José Morales details this migration, highlighting not only the territories already mentioned but also Jamaica and Venezuela. It is important to note that the majority of these lands, including Louisiana, were Spanish colonies at the beginning of the insurrection in 1791; Jamaica was the sole English possession, having been ceded to England from Spain in 1670.

11. For more on Simón Bolívar's concerns about uprisings led by peoples of African descent in Gran Colombia, see Helg, *Liberty*, and Fischer, "Bolívar."

12. For more on how these efforts were in conflict with the constitution of 1807 under Henri Christophe and the 1816 constitution of Pétion, see Fischer, *Modernity* 238–39.

13. Eller writes how the Spanish government, then newly reestablished in Santo Domingo, faced Haitian opposition to its recolonization; Spain remained a slaveholding imperial power at the time, with its remaining colonies of Puerto Rico and Cuba on either side of the island, and therefore a real threat to descendants of those who had fought for and won emancipation decades before. She details how Spanish warships arrived in the waters outside Port-au-Prince in the summer of 1861: after first declaring martial law, Geffrard quickly succumbed to Spanish demands so as to prevent an invasion (122). For more on this moment, see chapter 4, "The Haitians or the Whites? Colonization and Resistance, 1861–1863," of *We Dream Together*. The Haitian government finished paying this indemnity to France in 1947; by then it had mortgaged its own future by taking out loans from other governments, including the United States. In the twenty-first century, Jean-Bertrand Aristide campaigned for France to return the money that Haiti had paid for its own freedom. For more on the history of the role of multinational banks in ensuring Haiti's debt, see Hudson.

14. For more on the relationship between peoples of African descent throughout the hemisphere and Haiti, see Nwankwo; Polyné; Johnson; Fanning; Gaffield; and Mills.

15. Fischer focuses on the Aponte Conspiracy in the first chapter of *Modernity Disavowed*; Ferrer does so in the last chapter of *Freedom's Mirror*. It is the subject of Matt D. Childs's 2006 study, *The 1812 Aponte Rebellion in Cuba and the Struggle against Atlantic Slavery*. It is also the focus of the website *Digital Aponte*, aponte. hosting.nyu.edu/, and the subject of a digital-only article, "Collaborating with Aponte: Digital Humanities, Art, and the Archive," smallaxe.net/sxarchipelagos/issue03/ferrer-rodriguez.html, which offers a succinct history of the conspiracy itself. The article is written by the curators of the website, Linda M. Rodriguez and Ada Ferrer.

16. For more on slave rebellions in Puerto Rico, see works by Baralt; for more on slave insurrections in Santo Domingo prior to abolition, see Lora Hugi.

17. For more on La Escalera, see Paquette; Reid-Vazquez; and Finch.

18. For more on Plácido, see the second chapter of Fischer's *Modernity* and the third chapter of Nwankwo; for more on Manzano, see Manzano; Azougarh; and Luis. Arturo Schomburg wrote about both of these men in his *crónicas*; see Valdés, *Diasporic Blackness*.

19. For an overview of Cuban and Puerto Rican independence efforts, see the first chapter of Valdés, *Diasporic Blackness*.

20. For a classic article in English on Dominican racial identity widely available in PDF, including on the website of the CUNY Dominican Studies Institute, see Torres-Saillant.

21. firstblacks.org/en/ and http://firstblacks.org/spn/.

22. See "The Dominican Bolívar: José Núñez de Cáceres."

23. Among the Dominican historians who have pushed back against simplistic narratives of Dominican nationalism that rely heavily on anti-Haitianism and instead draw nuanced portraits of the nation, we must name Frank Moya Pons, Franklin Franco Pichardo, Raymundo González, and María Filomena González.

24. The most recent study to examine this moment is Matthew Casey's *Empire's Guest Workers: Haitian Migrants in Cuba during the Age of US Occupation* (2017).

25. The US occupation of Haiti has been the subject of only a handful of historical studies, and it has borne two important cultural studies: the first, Mary A. Renda's *Taking Haiti: Military Occupation and the Culture of U.S. Imperialism, 1915–1940* (2001), examines the work of writers at the time such as Eugene O'Neill, Zora Neale Hurston, James Weldon Johnson, and Langston Hughes, as well as songs of the time and the diaries and journals of the military personnel stationed on the island. She argues that the seeds of the impressions many here in the United States have about Haiti to this day—the fascination with Vodou and the figure of the zombie that we see in shows like *The Walking Dead*—can be traced to this occupation. The second important work is the most recent study of Raphael Dalleo, *American Imperialism's Undead: The Occupation of Haiti and the Rise of Caribbean Anticolonialism* (2016). There, Dalleo aptly demonstrates how the occupation of Haiti by US Marines influenced Caribbean and African American writers in the 1920s and 1930s. These artists—C. L. R. James, Eric Walrond, Claude

McKay, Marcus and Amy Jacques Garvey, George Padmore, Eulalie Spence, and Alejo Carpentier—all engage in the task of decolonization in their work while the presence of the United States military actively called into question the sovereignty of the hemisphere's first free Caribbean nation.

Works Cited

Abréu, Dió-genes. *Sin haitianidad no hay dominicanidad: cartografía de una identidad que se bifurca*. Editora Nacional, 2014.

Andrews, George Reid. *Afro-Latin America, 1800–2000*. Oxford UP, 2004.

Azougarh, Abdeslam. *Juan Francisco Manzano: esclavo poeta en la isla de Cuba*. Episteme, 2000.

Baralt, Guillermo A. *El Machete de Ogún: las luchas de los esclavos en Puerto Rico (siglo 19)*. Río Piedras, PR: CEREP, 1989.

———. *Esclavos rebeldes: conspiraciones y sublevaciones de esclavos en Puerto Rico (1795–1873)*. Río Piedras PR: Ediciones Huracán, 1985.

———. *Slave Revolts in Puerto Rico*. Translated by Christine Ayorinde, Markus Wiener, 2014.

Burkholder, Mark A., and Lyman L. Johnson. *Colonial Latin America*. 9th ed. Oxford UP, 2014.

Carpentier, Alejo. "Prólogo." *El reino de este mundo*. 1949. Seix Barral, 2004, pp. 5–12.

Casey, Matthew. *Empire's Guest Workers: Haitian Migrants in Cuba during the Age of US Occupation*. Cambridge UP, 2017.

Chancy, Myriam J. A. *From Sugar to Revolution: Women's Visions of Haiti, Cuba, and the Dominican Republic*. Wilfred Laurier UP, 2012.

Chetty, Raj, and Amaury Rodríguez. "The Challenge and Promise of Dominican Black Studies." *Dominican Black Studies*, edited by Raj Chetty and Amaury Rodríguez. Special issue of *The Black Scholar*, vol. 45, no. 2, 2015, pp. 1–9.

Childs, Matt D. *The 1812 Aponte Rebellion in Cuba and the Struggle against Atlantic Slavery*. U of North Carolina P, 2006.

Cunningham, C. H. *The Audiencia in the Spanish Colonies as Illustrated by the Audiencia of Manila (1583–1800)*. U of California P, 1919.

Dalleo, Raphael. *American Imperialism's Undead: The Occupation of Haiti and the Rise of Caribbean Anticolonialism*. U of Virginia P, 2016.

Digital Aponte. aponte.hosting.nyu.edu/.

"Dominican Bolívar: José Núñez de Cáceres." *The Dominican Republic Reader: History, Culture, Politics*, edited by Eric Paul Roorda, Lauren H. Derby, and Raymundo González. Duke UP, 2014, pp. 128–29.

Dorsey, Joseph. "Seamy Sides of Abolition: Puerto Rico and the Cabotage Slave Trade to Cuba 1848–73." *Slavery and Abolition*, vol. 19, no. 1, 1998, pp. 106–28.

Eller, Anne. *We Dream Together: Dominican Independence, Haiti, and the Fight for Caribbean Freedom*. Duke UP, 2016.

Fanning, Sara. *Caribbean Crossing: African Americans and the Haitian Emigration Movement.* New York UP, 2015.

Ferrer, Ada. *Freedom's Mirror: Cuba and Haiti in the Age of Revolution.* Cambridge UP, 2014.

———. *Insurgent Cuba: Race, Nation, and Revolution, 1868–1898.* U of North Carolina P, 1999.

Finch, Aisha K. *Rethinking Slave Rebellion in Cuba: La Escalera and the Insurgencies of 1841–1844.* U of North Carolina P, 2015.

Fischer, Sibylle. "Bolívar in Haiti: Republicanism in the Revolutionary Atlantic." *Haiti and the Americas*, edited by Carla Calargé, Raphael Dalleo, Luis Duno-Gottberg, and Clevis Headley. UP of Mississippi, 2013. pp. 25–53.

———. *Modernity Disavowed: Haiti and the Cultures of Slavery in the Age of Revolution.* Duke UP, 2004.

Gaffield, Julia. *Haitian Connections in the Atlantic World: Recognition after Revolution.* U of North Carolina P, 2015.

Geggus, David. "The Sounds and Echoes of Freedom: The Impact of the Haitian Revolution on Latin America." *Beyond Slavery: The Multilayered Legacy of Africans in Latin America and the Caribbean*, edited by Darién J. Davis. Rowman & Littlefield, 2007, pp. 19–36.

Gibson, Carrie. *Empire's Crossroads: A History of the Caribbean from Columbus to the Present Day.* Atlantic Monthly, 2014.

Helg, Aline. *Liberty and Equality in Caribbean Colombia, 1770–1835.* U of North Carolina P, 2004.

———. *Our Rightful Share: The Afro-Cuban Struggle for Equality, 1886–1912.* U of North Carolina P, 1995.

Horne, Gerald. *Confronting Black Jacobins: The United States, the Haitian Revolution, and the Origins of the Dominican Republic.* Monthly Review, 2015.

Hudson, Peter James. *Bankers and Empire: How Wall Street Colonized the Caribbean.* U of Chicago P, 2017.

Johnson, Sara E. *The Fear of French Negroes: Transcolonial Collaboration in the Revolutionary Americas.* U of California P, 2012.

Kendi, Ibram. *Stamped from the Beginning: The Definitive History of Racist Ideas in America.* Bold Type, 2016.

Lara, Ana-Maurine. "A Smarting Wound: Afro-Dominicanidad and the Fight against Ultranationalism in the Dominican Republic." *Feminist Studies*, vol. 43, no. 2, 2017, pp. 468–84.

Lora Hugi, Quisqueya. "El sonido de la libertad: 30 años de agitaciones y conspiraciones en Santo Domingo (1791–1821)." *CLÍO*, vol. 182, 2011, pp. 109–40.

Luis, William, editor. *Autobiografía del esclavo poeta y otros escritos.* Iberoamericana Vervuert, 2007.

Manzano, Juan Francisco. *Autobiography of a Slave / Autobiografía de un esclavo.* Translated by Evelyn Picon Garfield, bilingual edition, Wayne State UP, 1996.

Matibag, Eugenio. *Haitian-Dominican Counterpoint: Nation, Race, and State on Hispaniola*. Palgrave Macmillan, 2003.
Mayes, April J. *The Mulatto Republic: Class, Race, and Dominican National Identity*. UP of Florida, 2014.
Mills, Sean. *A Place in the Sun: Haiti, Haitians, and the Remaking of Quebec*. McGill-Queen's UP, 2016.
Morales, José. *The Hispaniola Diaspora, 1791–1850: Puerto Rico, Cuba, Louisiana, and Other Host Societies*. PhD dissertation, University of Connecticut, 1986.
Moya Pons, Frank. *La otra historia dominicana*. Librería La Trinitaria, 2008.
Nessler, Graham T. *An Islandwide Struggle for Freedom: Revolution, Emancipation, and Reenslavement in Hispaniola*. U of North Carolina P, 2016.
Nwankwo, Ifeoma Kiddoe. *Black Cosmopolitanism: Racial Consciousness and Transnational Identity in the Nineteenth-Century Americas*. U of Pennsylvania P, 2005.
Painter, Nell Irvin. *The History of White People*. Norton, 2010.
Paquette, Robert. *Sugar Is Made with Blood: The Conspiracy of La Escalera and the Conflict between Empires over Slavery in Cuba*. Wesleyan UP, 1988.
Paulino, Edward. *Dividing Hispaniola: The Dominican Republic's Border Campaign against Haiti, 1930–1961*. U of Pittsburgh P, 2016.
Pinto, Antonio J. "Negro sobre blanco: la conspiración esclava de 1812 en Puerto Rico." *Caribbean Studies*, vol. 40, no. 1, 2012, pp. 121–49.
Polyné, Millery. *From Douglass to Duvalier: U.S. African Americans, Haiti, and Pan Americanism, 1870–1964*. UP of Florida, 2010.
Ramírez, Dixa. *Colonial Phantoms: Belonging and Refusal in the Dominican Americas, from the 19th Century to the Present*. New York UP, 2018.
Reid-Vazquez, Michele. *The Year of the Lash: Free People of Color in Cuba and the Nineteenth-Century Atlantic World*. U of Georgia P, 2011.
Renda, Mary A. *Taking Haiti: Military Occupation and the Culture of U.S. Imperialism, 1915–1940*. U of North Carolina P, 2001.
Ricourt, Milagros. *The Dominican Racial Imaginary: Surveying the Landscape of Race and Nation in Hispaniola*. Rutgers UP, 2016.
Rodriguez, Linda M., and Ada Ferrer. "Collaborating with Aponte: Digital Humanities, Art, and the Archive." *Slavery in the Machine*. Special issue of *sx archipelagos* 3, edited by Jessica Marie Johnson, 2019, smallaxe.net/sxarchipelagos/issue03/ferrer-rodriguez.html. Accessed 10 Aug. 2019.
Roorda, Eric Paul, Lauren H. Derby, and Raymundo González, editors. *The Dominican Republic Reader: History, Culture, Politics*. Duke UP, 2014.
Scott, Julius S. *The Common Wind: Afro-American Currents in the Age of the Haitian Revolution*. Verso, 2018.
Torres-Saillant, Silvio. "The Tribulations of Blackness: Stages in Dominican Racial Identity." *Latin American Perspectives*, vol. 25, no. 3, 1998, pp. 126–46.
Trouillot, Michel-Rolph. *Silencing the Past: Power and the Production of History*. 1995. Beacon, 2015.

Ulysse, Gina Athena. *Why Haiti Needs New Narratives: A Post-Quake Chronicle.* Wesleyan UP, 2015.

Valdés, Vanessa K. *Diasporic Blackness: The Life and Times of Arturo Alfonso Schomburg.* State U of New York P, 2017.

Walker, Andrew J. *Strains of Unity: Emancipation, Property, and the Post-Revolutionary State in Haitian Santo Domingo, 1822–1844.* PhD dissertation, University of Michigan, 2018.

Wigginton, Sheridan, and Richard T. Middleton IV. *Unmastering the Script: Education, Critical Race Theory, and the Struggle to Reconcile the Haitian Other in Dominican Identity.* U of Alabama P, 2019.

1

The Border of Hispaniola in Historical and Fictional Imaginations since 1791

Redemption and Betrayals

CLAUDY DELNÉ

Ayiti was the name of the entire island inhabited by the natives before the arrival of the conquistadors who exterminated them thereafter through genocide on a scale with no historical precedent in human history. The chronic unrest, the episodic battles for monopoly between European settlers, led to the division of the island into two parts, the Hispanic or eastern side known as Santo Domingo and the western part under the French rule as Saint-Domingue (now Haiti). This geographical situation that compels the two nations to share the same island, far from being an anomaly, is not a rare case. Jean-Marie Théodat, an expert on Haitian-Dominican relations, has explained: "This border, as enigmatic as it is, is not more absurd than that which separates Venezuela from Colombia or the United States from Canada. But the smallness of the space creates a feeling of confinement that makes it appear paradoxical" (13, my translation). In both peoples' imagination, there is no sentiment of oneness or *une dimension insulaire commune* (Théodat). Each side expresses a different collective posture toward the past and displays respectively an uncompromised sense of belonging. The border has become a topic on its own and gives rise to an ongoing field of study, under the label border studies that encompasses history, geography, sociology, literature, and so forth.

In this essay, I consider the physical border as the potential sources of tensions between the two sides of the island, and offer a reassessment of the literary representation of crossing in and out of the border of Hispaniola by Haitian immigrants in order to show how the border has historically been imagined. This essay aims to show the portrayal of border crossing by Haitians in binary terms, in that it has always been both a redemptive act as well as one of betrayal. The border can signify a locus of freedom and nightmare. I will offer a short analysis of *General Sun, My Brother* by Jacques Stephen Alexis, *Massacre River* (*Le peuple des terres mêlées*) by René Philoctète, and *The Farming of Bones* by Edwidge Danticat to show how the border of Hispaniola has been envisioned in the collective imaginary since colonial times.

Haiti and the Dominican Republic are destined to historically share a common destiny given their geographical determinism. As in the past, whether in times of peace or conflict, in time of tears or prolonged conviviality, the borders that have divided the island have always played a redemptive or treacherous role for both slaves and masters before the revolution. Ever since, the Haitian-Dominican border has also been, as Edward Paulino describes it, a site of contestation between central and local authorities or different interest groups (8). The current legal imbroglio between the two states does not and will not stop the economic elites of both sides from trading with one another as was occurring during colonial times. Frank Moya Pons put it bluntly: "commerce with the French was a natural response to the Spanish monopoly" (67). This characterization is still relevant today when one looks at the disproportionate outcomes of the bilateral economic cooperation between the two nations.

Historical Background

The history of the relations between Haiti and the Dominican Republic is marked by a series of contentious issues that date back before their independence from European powers. The oldest and still most important cause of frontier instability in Hispaniola, as offered by Nathalie Bragadir, upends the geography and history of the island.[1]

The contrasts between the two nations are vivid: they form two distinct countries, and the frontier divides two cultures, two geographical systems. Most of the cultural and economic differences that started between the French and Spanish settlers on both sides since the early seventeenth century have survived until today. The western part of Hispaniola is more agrarian and mountainous with one third of the island. As a legacy of the slave mode of production, its economy is more directed toward *multifundias*, where peasants still farm small plots for subsistence, in contrast to Santo Domingo, where *latifundia* culture is more prevalent in that the peasants work on large landed estates. Théodat summarizes the contrast as follows:

> At first glance, everything separates the two countries; on one side, Quisqueya: the eldest daughter of the Church in the West Indies, the land where was created the first University of the Americas, where the first convent, the first cathedral were built, the first city was erected. That is, in 2003, a country with middle income, whose economy relies increasingly on revenues from tourism and the export processing zones, two areas in which it occupies a prominent position in the Caribbean. On the other, Haiti, the first Black Republic (1804), which struck the first blow to the slave system and was the seat of the first creative experience of a free state by slaves after the victory over their former masters . . . it is the poorest of all America, where the life expectancy is the lowest per capita. (9, my translation)

Bragadir's text finds many echoes in Théodat's by underlining the fact that "every border has a different history, and Hispaniola's particular history of slavery greatly influenced the groups who became most associated with the border region and the ways border figures—maroon slaves, free people of color, military officials, and contrabandists—identified one side or the other" (27). Incontestably, Saint-Domingue or the French side of Hispaniola was the most prosperous, a flourishing and powerful slave colony of the Americas by the end of the eighteenth century due to an economic system based on slavery and sugar production. Just before the Haitian Revolution, the total population was around five hundred thousand people comprising forty thousand whites, twenty-eight thousand free people of color, and the remaining 450,000, almost 90 percent of the population, were enslaved. In contrast, the Spanish side of Santo Domingo, made up mainly of cattle ranchers, or *hateros*, to borrow Bragadir's expression, was poorer and had a population about half the size of its neighbor, 15 percent of whom were enslaved (27). On the role of the border as a space of redemption for both sides and for many regardless of racial makeup or economic status, Bragadir reminds us:

> Maroon communities of escaped slaves from both sides of the island occupied the still relatively unknown territory of the border region, which was also inhabited by free people of color who made their living by buying and selling contraband goods that included cattle from the Spanish side and agricultural and manufactured items from the French side. (27)

Besides this succinct presentation of the economic and geographic differences, no one can deny the weight of religion and race in the makeup of the two nations. As John P. Augelli writes, the reminiscences of racial and cultural hatred "gave rise to *repeated, savage* bloodletting" (22).[2] Among the factors that encouraged Haitians to gradually encroach and settle at the border regions are:

> The ill-defined boundary, the enormous difference in population pressure between the two countries, the inability and weakness of the Dominican government that rendered it helpless to control the border regions and to integrate them with the rest of the country, all these factors contributed to the eastward march of Haitian people and culture and to the creation of a political "shatter belt" on Hispaniola. (23)

The preceding statement has some validity in that it is somehow corroborated by Turits, who links historically the Haitian immigration at the northern frontier areas, in particular, with the stimulation of land surplus and sparse population on the Dominican side of the border amid increasing land and sparse population pressures in Haiti (594). This border issue is also known in historiography as the Haitian question (Moya Pons). Inherited from the past, Trujillo attempted to solve the seemingly permanent repopulation of Haitians in the borderlands of the Dominican side, despite the fact that Haitians had been residing and working on fertile lands left by their Dominican counterparts since the mid-nineteenth century as a result of wars between the two nations. Citing the poetic work of Manuel Rueda and Ruben Silié's analytical essay, Lorgia García-Peña characterizes this protracted border dispute as the result of the violence of coloniality by which metropolitan interests used the island as a backdrop (136). This characterization is similarly apprehended by Turits as the story of the horrific explosion of state violence (593). The same goes for Lauren Derby, who alleges that anti-Haitianism must be understood as more than racism as such by providing some layers of meaning that arose from the mimesis of colonial powers of France and Spain (495).

Furthermore, Derby has shown that from the mid-eighteenth century there was a reliance of the Dominican Republic upon the Haitian economy, the primary market for its products. She then declares if, for the Dominican Republic, the border during that time was the locus of a struggle to secure the benefits of a speedy, mainly illegal cattle trade, for Haiti the porous border was a funnel for escaped slaves, a continual thorn in the side of the French colonial planter class that mourned the constant drain of capital in labor (497). She then alleges:

> The Spanish side of the border was a desirable refuge for runaway slaves, as they were rarely repatriated, manumission was more liberally practiced under Spanish colonial policy, and a life of semi-autonomous cattle herding was far less arduous than the backbreaking travail of cutting cane. By the mid-1700s, Lundahl reports, 3,000 slaves from the French colony were resident in the Spanish border areas; by the 1770s, Haitian maroons constituted the majority in the Dominican border towns. (497)

Derby also provides an explanation for the Haitian wave of emigration from the border regions. The first half of the nineteenth century, due to a period of political chaos in Hispaniola, witnessed a halt in the frontier regional economy, as she puts it, and caused extensive emigration from these zones. The Haitian Revolution, she asserts, brought the eastern side of the island into the widening civil war, a series of Haitian military incursions culminated in a twenty-two-year occupation of the Spanish colony (1822–1844), along with the war against the Spanish from which the Dominican Republic become independent in 1865. Espousing Lundahl's beliefs, Derby states that the territory freed by emigration from the frontier was quickly taken over by Haitian immigrants, particularly in the central region of the frontier. By the end of the nineteenth century, she indicates that the depression in the Dominican frontier was compounded when US-owned sugar plantations developed in the southeast, causing yet another wave of emigration from the border (498). However, this problem has never apparently been solved until Trujillo made it a priority in his state policy toward the Dominicanization of the borders.[3] This long excerpt from Moya Pons is worth noting:

> The Haitians living near the border were completely marginal to Dominican society and the territory they occupied functioned as an extension of Haiti. Haitian currency circulated freely in Cibao, the main agricultural region of the country, and in the south it circulated as far as Azua, only 120 kilometers from Santo Domingo. Trujillo did not want to accept that fact. He traveled to the frontier at the beginning of October 1937, and there gave a speech announcing that the occupation by Haitians of the frontier territories must not continue. Afterwards, he ordered that all Haitians remaining in the country be exterminated. In the days following October 4, 1937, the army assassinated all Haitians on sight. Eighteen thousand Haitians were killed. The only ones able to save their lives were those who managed to cross the border and those protected by the sugar mills, which did not want to lose their Haitian labor force. (368)

This passage highlights, through the state-sponsored violence, the island's colonial history around territorial claims, as Bragadir puts it in *Transnational Hispaniola* (24). She convincingly demonstrates, like a number of other scholars on the issue (Turits, Lauren Derby, García-Peña, Edward Paulino, et al.), despite the violence, how the official mapping practices about the border display a volatile reality creating swirl and anxiety for both sides since colonial times. Bragadir's analysis of the mapping and spatial practices during the creation of the artificial border shows the ultimate linkage between status and racialized subjecthood and territorial possession and sovereignty. Her glimpse into the history of the border in Hispaniola demonstrates:

> They were actively crossing the border themselves or having the limits redrawn around them, people have been crossing this border since its inception. Some had the power to transform their status through adopting a new allegiance, but others who were not fortunate found themselves constrained by the border and without access to their freedom or their property. (24)

This assertion is important to get a better understanding of the status and life conditions of the border people before and after Trujillo's era as illustrated in the novels considered in this essay. On another note, it is believed from the archives that the frontier dispute had never been a serious issue per se between the two nations before Trujillo's era given the volatile reality of the border. The imperial authority, as Bragadir states it, whether on the island or in Europe, had hardly been recognized on the ground. That's why an analysis of the contested regions that became borders enlightens our understanding of the imperial authority and power in daily life (25). Whether porous or rigid, state and imperial power have rarely been able to completely prevent people from interacting at the border. Citing border studies scholars Michiel Baud and Willem van Schendel on the paradox of the border, Bragadir says: "From the perspective of national centers of authority, the border between countries is a sharp line, an impenetrable barrier. But from the perspective of the border, borderlands are broad scenes of interactions in which people from both sides work out everyday accommodations based on face-to-face relationships" (25). In the case of the Haitian-Dominican border disputes, these dichotomous viewpoints put forward the official and elite historiography in the Dominican Republic as antithetical to or exclusive of Haitians and Haitian culture, as Turits puts it. He further observes that prior to 1937, Dominicans in the frontier were not struggling against a perceived cultural and demographic onslaught by Haitians (593). However, with the systematic decline in reinforcing or maintaining an efficient policy of nationalization or Dominicanization at the frontier zones since Trujillo, other legal fictions are to be created by the state apparatus aiming at preventing or stopping further Haitian penetration in the Dominican borderlands. It is at this juncture that we witness from time to time the invention of a legal artifice from Dominican central government to decide the fate of Haitians who had either already settled there for a long period of time or were potential border crossers.

In the historical records, there is a plethora of instances where the eastern borderland as site of encounter had been both attractive and repulsive to every group in French Saint-Domingue regardless of its racial grouping or social status. Apart from various episodic incursions of mulattoes and whites seeking asylum by crossing the Dominican borders, we can say with certainty that the issue of border crossing by slaves had always been a recurrent one since the establishment of the French colony.[4] It was a systematic issue that gave rise to negotiations between French and Spanish authorities for the compulsory return of runaway slaves. Rubén Silié, former Dominican ambassador in Haiti, in his recent book on the topic, provides some rational for the redemptive flight of slaves at the Santo Domingo border:

> Most of the documents and works of contemporary authors coincided that the causes of the border crossing should be sought in the gentle manners of the Spaniards toward Blacks, that's what we found for example in Américo Lugo's reasoning,

which speaks of the sweetness. This suggests that the Spaniards had against Blacks a special attitude that helped obscure the racist character of the slave system that prevailed in the country. (61, my translation)

The quote itself indicates that Silié does not endorse Lugo's reasoning, since he further explains that the benevolent treatment found by slaves after crossing the border was imposed by the necessity of the system itself—given the paucity of slave labor and the issue of access to the slave trade—that forced the colonists to keep the slaves or free Blacks by any means and to willingly want to extend the life of a slave as long as possible (62, my translation). But, in contrast to Lugo's suggestion, as Silié[5] reported it, knowing the long history of Spanish settlers toward slavery and its ramifications, the rhetoric of sweetness tends to exonerate them from past cruelties. Moya Pons offers a counterargument to Lugo's assertion:

> The colony's poverty and the presence of the French also involved the slaves and former slaves. In 1677, 12 slaves fled from the French possessions and sought refuge in Santo Domingo where the authorities accepted them and granted them freedom. This policy was based on the belief that by liberating the Blacks who had run away from the French, the Spanish authorities could encourage more slaves to desert, thus harming the enemy. (65)

Moya Pons's approach is also in line with David P. Geggus in his *Haitian Revolutionary Studies*, who underlines many factors that shed light on the Spanish reaction via its colonies toward French colonists, the French, and the slave revolution. According to Geggus, there is enough evidence in the historical record that suggests some sort of sympathy or leniency on the part of the Spanish in Santo Domingo toward Black insurgents who may have been used as scapegoats to avenge their French rivals. Governor García of Santo Domingo at that time hated the French so much that he ignored Madrid's recommendations in preventing French refugees from crossing the border of Hispaniola while expressing some sympathy with the Blacks. Geggus says of the governor:

> He contrasted their martial spirit with that of the once arrogant, now barefoot French colonists. He described slavery in Saint Domingue as "horrifying," and apparently found reasonable the

rebels' pursuit of freedom, albeit believing they were secretly led by white liberals. His letters, however, also expressed hopes for peace; disappointment when negotiations failed; contempt for the "ferocious brigands," "that barbarous people"; and orders that none be allowed to cross the frontier. Spanish officers on the frontier, unlike García, formally corresponded with, and occasionally met, the rebel leaders, but that they encouraged them remains unproven. (173–74)

Two elements in particular need to be considered here. The Haitian Revolution from the start had been thought as unthinkable, as one can infer from the governor's correspondence. The underlying idea associated with the *unthinkable* was the issue of a white conspiracy, a belief that suggests slaves were ontologically unfit to break their chains, think, and plan a revolution. That said, the governor, torn apart between Madrid's suggestions and his own beliefs, chose to be neutral. But this neutrality, as Geggus explained, rather denotes a fear of massive invasion to the borderland of Hispaniola (174).

Fictional Narratives

Historical narratives on the tensions, frictions, and even wars over the border of Hispaniola even before the two nations came into existence are legion. Jacques Stephen Alexis, far from putting a heavy emphasis on the border, places it in his novel's diegesis as incidental. *General Sun, My Brother*, an avant-garde text, is the first fictional story of Haiti to offer a counterdiscourse to the Hispanocentric element of Trujillo discourse that presents Haiti, to use Strongman's term, as an old intrusion in the Americas (27). Alexis disputes this premise by incorporating the Dominican Republic in his narrative as an accessory, or transient incursion, but not as the main plot since the universe of the novel takes place in Port-au-Prince, Haiti, as the grand narrative. Alexis shows the crossing of the Dominican border by the couple Hilarion and Claire-Heureuse as a temporary incident, a secondary place in the geography of the novel (27). The ideology conveyed by the Trujillo regime, perpetrated and illustrated later as shown in many Dominican fictional stories about Haitians, was based on an old conception of history that saw the French settlement in Santo Domingo as a historic theft. The extension of this vision, which is fueled by the question of color due to the presence of Haitians in the border regions, has become a serious problem of national security for the Dominican regime. The nationalist policy of Trujillo, Balaguer, and their successors aims to erase or limit the presence or traces of Haitians by promoting migration strategies favoring the whitening of the Dominican nation.[6]

Alexis, as a keen observer of social inequalities of his time, made a digression from his Marxist worldview then to highlight the skin color of his protagonists, and at the same time show the correlation between poverty and dark skin in the society of the time, which hardly gave any social mobility for the suffering Black majority. But the relative illegal crossing of the couple Hilarion and Claire-Heureuse and the tragic outcome of their fate can only be explained in terms of class, and not as a race report or counterdiscourse against the racist ideology of Dominican literary discourse opposing these two nations. Alexis rids the Dominican people of any involvement in the massacre of Haitians. He blames the army, and instead calls for solidarity of both peoples who are the victims of their corrupt governments' greed.

General Sun, My Brother is an ode to the life of ordinary people beaten down by daily misery and also to the solidarity of peoples of both sides of the border that are linked by common destiny. The border, far from being an antagonistic space, bearer of violence and protracted conflict, is posited by Alexis as a place of sharing, mutual aid, and cooperation between two sister nations that ignore one another. He therefore takes into account this dynamic of hybrid cultures that marks the borderland of Hispaniola. In this sense, Alexis is right to stress the unusual side of this region in these terms:

> The Haitians remained quite Haitian and they kept thinking about their distant homeland, but they were no longer the same. Like François Crispin, they had their own way of thinking, their own gestures, and their special way of doing things. The other inhabitants of the region were not like other Dominicans either. They spoke a language in which Haitian Kreyòl and Dominican Spanish mingled. Certain songs and dances were virtually the same as in Haiti. The two national cultures mingled here. Who knew what the future held in store? These two nations were sisters. What had been impossible to accomplish through war in earlier times and could never be brought about by constraint and violence, everyday life might perhaps achieve. Through work, song, common joy, and suffering, something was being woven here that would eventually create one heart and one soul for

two peoples chained in the same servitude. The workers were seated. One of the Haitians took out a little reed flute. The guitarist was picking out a new melody in the low notes as the flute produced its clear, piercing high notes. All the voices came together. It was a song of hard cane, lacerating leaves, torrid sun, burned legs, and sweating torsos. They were all children with similar hopes. (218)

This excerpt helps to understand in a practical way what Maria-Sabina Draga-Alexandru called, in *Crossing Boundaries*, psychological displacement of migrants transferring their mores and customs to a new territory (Scanlon and Waste 123). Nowhere in *General Sun, My Brother* is Alexis seeking to understand the Haitian genocide by a frame of *Trujillismo* or Dominican racism in general.[7] Instead, he focuses on the concrete conditions of existence that subject peoples of the two countries to totalitarian regimes. His conflict analysis grid is that of historical materialism, which sees class struggles as the motor of history. As a product of his time when Marxism was becoming more popular, Alexis called on the union and solidarity of the international proletariat as a united front against the abuses of capitalism to transform the lives of both peoples. As Elissa L. Lister puts it: "Conflicts between Dominicans and Haitians are the result of historical processes between the two nations that, in addition to living on the same island, share traditions, beliefs and elements of history" (75, my translation). Here the issue of hybrid cultures as displayed at the border in Alexis's depiction is in line with what Fumagalli refers to as the revolutionary potential of the border. It is a sort of mingling of thoughts, ideas, peoples of both nationalities, beliefs, and a way of life that is supposed to be discredited by the vertical forces, the national power in place. This kind of reconfiguration of life at the borderland of Hispaniola constitutes, in her own words, "the insurrection of a discredited transcultural and multilingual borderland culture which brings to the fore a different linguistic and cultural landscape, and a literary geography that goes well beyond national languages and colonial mappings" (192).

What resulted from this supposedly transcultural transgression was the policy implemented by Trujillo in the Dominican borderland with Haiti:

Beginning in the mid-1930s and continuing until the dictator's assassination in 1960, the policy proposed to stabilize the boundary and presumably to lessen the tensions of what had been the most volatile frontier in the Americas, to block further occupation of Dominican territory by Haitians, and to foster a strong sense of national identity among the people of the Dominican border provinces. (Augelli 20)

Alexis situates Haitian daily life and experiences at the center of his narrative. In doing so, he speaks out, as do Philoctète and Danticat, against racist discourse by restoring Haitians' humanity. He puts the emphasis on the subjectivity of his characters that the Dominican hegemonic ideology has long denied. What is, however, particular to Alexis is, unlike the other two authors discussed here, he completely erases the question of color or race in the treatment that he makes of the incursion of the Dominican Republic in his account. The storyline is vividly compelling in the way he brings his readers to the insights of Hilarion, the main protagonist of the novel, and his wife Claire-Heureuse. All his life, Hilarion has been driven by odd struggles to survive, from his first appearance as a restavec and robber of a bourgeois family, to prison, multiple collapsing jobs, and finally to his crossing of the border with all its trials and tribulations till his crossing back and his death. The hero dies near the border after having expressed to Claire his sort of epiphany in understanding the necessity of struggles, the mechanism of oppression, and the deep meaning of liberation principles. His last exchange carries a messianic mission he wants to pass on to Claire and to those who enlightened his conscience:

> Tell Jean-Michel that I saw the light when a great red sun lit the chest of a worker named Paco Torres. Tell him to keep following the road he tried to show me. He has to follow the sun! . . . He raised up and yelled. General Sun! See him! He's right on the border, at the doors of our native land! Don't ever forget, Claire, never, never! (290)

But why is the border so attractive and what does it symbolize here for Alexis? Despite all resentment they may have, from real-life experiences, stories, or anecdotal narratives, heard from a *viejo* about Haitians' lives in sugarcane plantations in Santo Domingo, Haitian peasants and unemployed urban workers wanted to cross the border to experience on their own the seasonal work there.[8] As Hilarion internalizes Gabriel's frustration about leaving the country, he makes the border crossing appear to be the solution if nobody wants to starve in a country that is so screwed up (169).

Hilarion's socioeconomic circumstances forced him to leave his land, but Trujillo's repressive regime precipitated his return. But near the border and while dying, he sums up for his surviving wife the lessons of the future with an indispensable erasure of the past:

> At first, I hardly dared believe it because those marvels were so new to me. Now, you will have to forget that and live as if it never happened. The morning of our first meeting is dead, the evenings on Rue Saint-Honoré, the Feast of Saint John when I first took you away is dead, our nights together, Désiré, my life—they're all gone. In a little while, you will have to go away alone and find your way without turning back. You must give birth to another Hilarion, other Désirés, and only you can create them. You have to go forward to other mornings of love, other Saint John Days, begin a new life. (289)

The forced return to native land through the perilous escape of Hilarion, his wife, and their newborn Désiré produces a "border gnosis" by which Hilarion became fully aware of contingences of history and has reached at this time a complete metamorphosis that is subsumed in the aforementioned passage.[9] The nightmares endured in joining the border from the city of San Macoris are incumbent on Claire-Heureuse to create a new future, to find another Hilarion, to give birth to other Désirés, and so forth.

The fictional representation of social inequalities in Haitian society, border crossing by Haitian workers to Santo Domingo, and the call for international solidarity among working classes as depicted in *General Sun, My Brother* has inspired the works of other Haitian writers like Philoctète and Danticat. René Philoctète's *Massacre River* draws largely from Alexis while being original in his own way.[10] Although *Massacre River* is the subject of the novel, the name of the river where multiple massacres had been committed, especially the Trujillo October 1937 massacre of thousands of Haitians, the English title does not translate what the original French poetically convey. *Le peuple des terres mêlées* is a beautiful and powerful allegory that refers to the very same people of mixed lands. It helps to break up the concept of double insularity that has long poisoned the promise of a friendly relationship between two brotherly peoples (Wattara 95). The poetic of Philoctète carries a new vision that transcends the mutual suspicions and animosities amid racial prejudice that fuel the concept of double insularity. Two nations, one island, and one people, that's the poetic story of *Massacre River*. It is told through the love story of a Haitian peasant, Adele, and Pedro, a Dominican worker in Elías Piñas, a borderland town where Haitians were targeted during the massacre. Philoctète shows how history was rewritten and manipulated by a dictator who in his debilitating madness breaks dreams and hearts. It invites us to a poetic hope that goes beyond the sufferings of the massacre, the madness of Adele and Pedro's trials. But Philoctète's poetic is far from being complacent even though it speaks the language of the dignity of the Haitian people (Lyonel Trouillot in the introduction to the French text). Philoctète, frankly and bluntly, plunges us into a tale of horror of the massacre by proposing, among existing assumptions, that Trujillo maintained a visceral hatred for Haiti since childhood by popular stories. Then fascinated by the Henri Citadel, he wanted to take possession of it.[11] The narrator says:

> The Citadel became ever more deeply rooted in his memory. The thing is, before Rafaelito was even ten years old he was already gorging himself on the stories told on the street corners of Santo Domingo by grannies in their Black mantillas. The pace and vividness of their narration usually determined the child's judgment of the characters and events depicted. (39)

Philoctète's narrative theory is built around this hypothesis to explain the genocide of Haitians planned and executed by the pogroms of Trujillo. "Haiti had become, for the young Trujillo, *a priori*, a dogmatic opponent. And the citadel, his phantasm" (41). The fraternity that the author dreams about and promotes seems almost impossible insofar as it flirts from all sides with the genocidal apparatus of power. Philoctète deplores and condemns the general silence and complicity of all sectors of the country on genocide:

> Everything is there for the glory of Trujillo. Adèle is right. No! It's a savage transmutation: everyone is in the village square: workers, professionals, civil authorities, soldiers, nuns, executives, children, parents, servants. Massive, total, direct participation. Unconditional acceptance of an agenda of ideas, a state of affairs. Of mind. The mikes crackle. Everyone huddles under the same carapace. Concurs with the sharp-fanged words. Abundance becomes scarcity. Liberty buys itself chains. Brotherhood strikes a deal with genocide. Mutual congratulations. General

embarrassing. Pats on the back for everyone. We're all in the same boat. And we'll run like rats, if the ship sinks. There's no difference among us. You lie down with a wolf as with a lamb. The lamb howls? The wolf bleats? We huddle together under either skin. Indifferently! Perfectly at ease! One's no better than the other. We become a mass. We gorge ourselves on platitudes. From speeches to applause, we complete and perfect ourselves. Shedding our skin. Collectively! Me, Pedro Brito, I refuse to join in. everything must become normal, human. We must put an end to the nightmare. No one attacks Monsieur le Président with impunity, I know. Miel Roca perished at San Pedro de Macorís. Orlando Díaz was shot in Samaná. Maybe I'll wind up in a hole in La Romana. But we must stop the machine in its tracks. (45)

In this worthwhile passage, Philoctète tries to grasp the collective involvement of Dominican society in the genocide, described as massive and total either by silence or direct participation. The massacre is then the result of a program implemented by all spheres of power, whose official agents of the regime even take great pleasure to do the counts on the radio as the narrator reports it. The accumulation of Haitian heads on Dominican radio waves is an understatement, a euphemism in which much is said by saying less (Wattara 97). It is a mise en abyme par excellence of the writing of the novel. So, the passive and indifferent attitude of the Dominican people will contrast with the singular voice of Pedro that rises to denounce the fury of the beast, this monster bird that flies over and ravages everything in its path in the sky over Elías Piñas, a small Dominican border town. Pedro symbolizes the rarity of which Philoctète speaks.

The psychoanalytic portrait of the dictator that Philoctète draws for us in his obsession to take possession of Henri Citadel is part of nationalist ambitions to reclaim Haitian territories on the border, since the Treaty of Aranjuez concluded in 1777 between France and Spain extended to various eastern campaigns conducted by the heads of State of Haiti (Toussaint, Dessalines, Boyer, Faustin Soulouque). It appears to be, indeed, a spirit of vengeance among the Dominican leaders who mobilize all the ideological apparatus of the state to galvanize nationalist spirit and maintain awareness. This mind-set, illustrated by Philoctète, causes a chronic or episodic border dispute between the two republics (40). Moreover, if the dream possession of Trujillo's citadel receded more and more, he managed to maintain and to perpetuate the myth of the *blanco de la tierra* against what Philoctète calls the mirror syndrome, this collective madness:

> Every day, fourteen out of fifteen Dominicans spent hours consulting mirrors. Studying and taking stock of themselves. Anyone who saw himself as light brown, a betwixt-and-between brown, could breathe easy; he fit the anthropologico-Trujillonian criterion: he was a *blanco de la tierra*. Or pretty close to it. Suitable for social advancement. But anyone who found he was one-quarter, or one-third, or one-half, or completely Black . . . got really worried. He was destined to suffer. (110)

However, Dominicans have lost faith in this mirror-identity because they concluded that the mirrors were having nervous breakdowns (110). Morning, noon, and night people looked at themselves in mirrors, but deep down, they didn't trust them. Someone who had seen himself as snow-white fifteen minutes earlier would detect a café-au-lait tint an hour afterward (111). The identity machine of the power of Trujillo's racism turns joyous Dominicans, for a long time, into ghosts (112).

Philoctète draws upon his *Spiraliste* literary movement to project or reiterate what has always been the communal life of both people living side by side in the borderland of Hispaniola. They came to public markets held on Haitian territory. Adèle and Pedro had their first love encounter during one of those visits before the massacre. Pesos and Haitian gourdes are used interchangeably at the border zones. This powerful imagery is captured from the scene that highlights the friendship between two Black children. They were born in Bahoruco, he to the Haitian François family, and she to the Dominican Cortez family. They met at the foot of a lemon tree growing on the border itself (145). The narrator explains that they are having fun by casually hopping on one foot from this side of the border to the other, and back: now on Haitian territory, now on Dominican soil. As they are growing into that friendship:

> The little girl asks the little boy to please say "perejil." Nathan—that's the boy's name—opens his mouth. The word has seized up. Nathan, all smiles, tells Juanita—that's the girl's name—that he just can't say "perejil." Juanita ceremoniously takes Nathan's hand. The two children go off to sit under the lemon tree. The little Dominican girl has the little Haitian boy rehearse the word. The

day is waning, and the children are still sing-songing "¡perejil! ¡perejil!" . . . Then Nathan and Juanita fall asleep side by side. They'll be found the next morning, at first light, holding hands around a bouquet of parsley. The border guards won't have the courage to cut off either head. (146)

The reality is that people of both sides from border towns (Dajabón, Ouanaminthe, Banica, Mont Organisé, Cerca, Cabajal, Hinche, Thomassique, Lascahobas, Belladère, Elías Piñas, Jimani, Pedernales, Malpasse, and Malpaso) have lived harmoniously, intermingled, collaborated, traded peacefully for generations. As Philoctète poetically puts it: "A bell rings. No one can tell whether it's from here or the next hamlet over. The people in both villages simply wind up their watches at the same time" (146). "From now on, the vendors will have to take the smugglers' routes to get to the rural markets. Because it has been decided that the Dominican border will be opened only when the Haitian population can properly pronounce the word 'perejil'" (147).

Furthermore, if there is a thread that connects Alexis, Philoctète, and Danticat's texts both in their ideological orientation and in the narrative content, *The Farming of Bones* offers a feminine vision of the literary representation of these two aspects of the conflict through Amabelle, whose view orients the narrative perspective (Genette 203). The aesthetic choice is conscious because Amabelle as a homodiegetic narrator tells and participates in the action of the story. Danticat's novel is another tour de force. *The Farming of Bones* is a narrative aesthetic that invites us to rethink the issue of memory. Danticat puts us at the border of literary and historical memory. In doing so, she invites us to a process of forgetting and remembering. The massacre of 1937 and the conditions of the crossing in and out of the border are treated to preserve the memory of these events against the deadly power of forgetting. Amabelle reports:

> It is perhaps the great discomfort of those trying to silence the world to discover that we have voices sealed in our heads, voices that with each passing day, grow even louder than the clamor of the world outside. The slaughter is the only thing that is mine enough to pass on. All I want to do is find a place to lay it down now and again, a safe nest where it will neither be scattered by the winds, nor remain forever buried beneath the sod. I just need to lay it down sometimes. Even in the rare silence of the night, with no faces around. (266)

The themes of forgetting and the duty to remember are recurring in Danticat's story. She assigns to Father Romain, the priest who works with Haitians in the border regions, the role of the custodian of memory. The narrator reports: "In his sermon to the Haitian congregants of the valley he often reminded everyone of common ties: language, foods, history, how remembering—though sometimes painful—can make you strong" (73). In her novel, Danticat shows an admitted desire to stress the obligation to remember and to fight against wholesale erasure. She puts a watermark on the thousands of anonymous deaths of the massacre of those whose only inexcusable weakness is their absence and silence (279).

The Farming of Bones must be seen as a guardrail, a bulwark against the evanescence of collective memory, and of this tragic event experienced by Haitians under the government of Trujillo. Danticat places her story beyond 1937 to show the inscription of the drama and its most disastrous repercussions in the long term in historical memory. It is in that sense that we must understand this tale of the genocide as a function of memorialization and mythologizing of what happened. The life stories of those who survived the massacre are even more harmful or dramatic insofar as these Haitians who have managed to escape the Dominican Vespers do not find support, help, or supervision required upon their return home. This is what the peregrinations of Amabelle and Yves inspire in us, a desire to honor those whose lives become meaningless after crossing the Dominican border to the Haitian side. The post-genocide narrative posture dramatizes the silence of the Haitian government in its neglect of the victims, the abandonment of and indifference that it shows them. Danticat does not absolve Sténio Vincent's government of its implicit involvement in the massacre by the illicit trade agreements on cane cutters with Trujillo, and the explicit relegation of the genocide into oblivion. As one character notes:

> When Dessalines, Toussaint, Henry, when those men walked the earth, we were a strong nation. Those men would go to war to defend our blood. In all this, our so-called president says nothing, our papa Vincent—our poet—he says nothing at all to this affront to the children of Dessalines, the children of Toussaint, the children of Henry; he shouts nothing across this river of our blood. (212)

This open criticism of the Haitian state is characteristic of Alexis, Philoctète, and Danticat's novels that highlight the double tragedy that genocide survivors had to face. Amabelle notes in her dream with Sebastien, the lover who did not survive Trujillo's carnage: "The slaughter showed me that life can be a strange gift, I say. Breath, like glass is always in danger. I chose a living because I am not brave. It takes patience, you used to say, to raise a setting sun. Two mountains can never meet, but perhaps you and I can meet again. I am coming to your waterfall" (283). But this caution against forgetting as beautifully narrated by Danticat as well as by Alexis and Philoctète is a powerful challenge to the denial of Haitian subjectivity. Roberto Strongman summarizes this poignantly:

> Through their writing of the Haitian experience during the massacre of 1937, the fictions of Jacques Stephen Alexis and Edwidge Danticat challenge the denial of subjectivity which the Trujillista discourse has projected onto Haitian bodies, both male and female, through the representation of those bodies as negative spaces perpetually stealing to fill their emptiness, as voids of uncleanness, hyper-sexuality, exaggerated reproduction, incest, and disease. (34)

This quote must also be put in the context of a global racism. It is not limited to Trujillo's borderland racism with Haiti. Mark Q. Sawyer and Tianna S. Paschel, in their scholarly work "We Didn't Cross the Color Line, the Color Line Crossed Us," state that the cases of the Dominican Republic and Puerto Rico expose the layers of racialization for Blacks and demonstrate the ways in which race, nation, and identity interact through migration: "Blackness produces, therefore, what we identify as a *global anti-Black racism*, which stems from the logics of the transatlantic slave trade and continues into our contemporary moment in almost every nation of the world" (304). This worldwide anti-Black racism dates back after independence and the abolition of slavery during which many Latin American countries sought, as Sawyer and Paschel put it, to "whiten" their populations by limiting the number of Black migrants. Consequently, immigration policies in Latin America in the early twentieth century were a key source of racialization (304). For this purpose, the Trujillo phantasm depicted in the identity mirror in *Massacre River* and the color-line issue problematized in the birth of Señora Valencia and Señor Pico's twins in *The Farming of Bones* are a micro-phenomenon of a global attack on Blackness.

Danticat has produced an original work that is fully contemporary because it echoes the current realities of the peoples of the border areas who are facing acts of mass deportation and denationalization plans by the government of the Dominican Republic. Despite the fictional nature of *The Farming of Bones*, Danticat's emplotment seems to be less utopian than those of Alexis and Philoctète. Those two, as Fumagalli observes, foreground a high level of integration and transnational solidarity in the mixed communities they depict, but Danticat's novel stresses on the tensions and real-life struggles (189). Amabelle's ambivalent situation informs readers of the current issue of deterritorialization, crises of birth, birthright, and the linguistic and cultural hybridity that define the Haitian-Dominican borderland (James 6). Life in Alegría, the fictional border town where most of the action of Danticat's novel takes place, is rendered angrily through the voice of Amabelle, "a border woman," to use James's expression. She feels both at home and homeless, deterritorialized in the borderland of her birth (6). Amabelle has a traumatizing memory concerning the massacre river. Both her parents were drowned there when she was an infant. She was found there and adopted as an orphan by Señora Valencia's parents. Her life at Don Carlos and Doña Eva's house, an elite family of Alegría, typifies the status of those who fall in the legal category of people "in transit" as evidenced by the amendment of the Dominican Constitution in 2010, and the recent 2013 decision of the Constitutional Court defining undocumented residents as "in transit." The narrator reports testimonies of parents expressing concerns about their exclusion, alienation, rejection from Alegría's elite establishment, the social, class, and race makeup of which is very diverse:

> "I pushed my son out of my body here, in this country," one woman said in a mix of Alegrían Kreyòl and Spanish, the tangled language of those who always stuttered as they spoke, caught as they were on the narrow ridge between two nearly native tongues. "My mother too pushed me out of her body here. Not me, not my son, not one of us has ever seen the other side of the border. Still they won't put our birth papers in our palms so my son can have knowledge placed into his head by a proper educator in a proper school."
>
> "To them we are always foreigners, even if our granmèmès' granmèmès were born in this country," a man responded in Kreyòl, which we most often spoke—instead of Spanish—among ourselves. "This makes it easier for them to push us out when they want to." (69)

The novel was published more than twenty years ago, but its relevancy today in regard to the legal status of Dominicans born Haitian in the Dominican Republic is compelling. The antagonisms as well as instances of mutual cooperation and exchanges must be rendered equally so that centuries of bilateral continuities and discontinuities that represent the history of the two nations can be ascertained.

This brief analysis of the three novels analyzed here shows a particular emphasis on the border of Hispaniola as an unavoidable topic in the island's narrative. With the exception of Alegría in Danticat's novel, the towns or settings where the action of the stories occurred are historical. The border plays a pivotal role in alleviating characters' burdens or sealing their fate. *General Sun, My Brother* and *Massacre River* are critical texts since they advocate for cooperation between the two peoples of the border, for solidarity, friendliness of the two sister nations bound by a common destiny that would promote a hybrid culture and language. This call for cooperation between the two peoples has always existed, whether in intermarriage, folklore, religion, work practices, and so on, Martínez reminds us, through a recent survey: "the more Dominicans interact with Haitians as neighbors and co-workers the less they develop anti-Haitian sentiments" (89). Amabelle, the frustrated narrator's voice in Danticat's novel, reports the concerns of a woman who while both she and her son were born on the Spanish side of the border have never seen its other side (69). She claims a birthright for herself and her son as she has been "rooted yet de-territorialized in the borderland of her birth" (James 6). James notes that danger and fear permeate the border and a discourse of separation of us/them frustrates any possibility of communication or solidarity. However, the border paradoxically produces its own discourse or knowledge that transgresses "the official ideals of separation and the maintenance of a pure, Hispanophile Dominican race" (6). There seems to be a consensus that stresses the cordial relations, friendliness between the two peoples as highlighted in the fictional narratives of Alexis, Philoctète, and Danticat, respectively. Martínez echoes those powerful stories by inviting us to rethink the cultural, religious, and linguistic practices common to both peoples toward a real integration policy. A powerful aphorism, *Massacre River* testifies to this argument for a possible unity or willingness for the two border peoples to live together. In that regard, most of the authors cited here all recognize that the seemingly ethnic conflict is a mere theater of appearance, beyond which we need to look at the real issue of the power of coloniality and of the economic monopoly of the elites of both sides of the island. In the same vein, García-Peña invites us to rethink and transcend the political and conceptual limits of the Haitian-Dominican border by embracing what she terms a "*rayano* consciousness" and defines as encompassing the multiplicity of borders (transnational, interethnic, and multilinguistic) that characterize the Dominican experience on and beyond the island.[12] She relates *rayano* consciousness to the historical and present awareness of Dominican borders (symbolic, political, and geographical) and sees it as a process that includes marginalized subjectivities in the imagining and narrations of Dominicanidad (18). Thus devised, the 1937 massacre must be revisited, as she convincingly argues, not "as an anti-immigrant state-sponsored crime against Haitians living on the Dominican side of border rather than as the genocide of the intraethnic border population of rayanos who lived and worked in the northwestern border towns of the Artibonite Valley" (14).

Beyond the power of fiction by authors trying on their own merits to instill hope in the midst of government policies or lack thereof, one will be amazed by the cooperation by people on both sides, whether in the Dominican Republic, Haiti, and in the diaspora. The works of compassion, solidarity, and of humanity that they display remind us as *prisoners of hope* that we are bound to live together, and that unity and peace are still possible. Alexis, Philoctète, and Danticat's novels can be characterized as what David W. Orr calls a literature of redemption. How can we make good, atone for, offset the bad effect of, or make worthwhile the lives of the borderlands of Hispaniola and the prolonged hatred of Haitians? Inspired by Orr's analogy between literature of redemption and slavery or racism, the border literature to this effect is growing and must be sprouted from the deep within the lives of people of the border regions. If there is hope for ending the divisions, antipathy, hatred toward Haitians or Dominicans of Haitian descent at the frontier's zones or the Dominican mainland as motivated by the Dominican state's racist policies, it must be through our moral imagination and progress (Orr 305) to apprehend what it means to be sugarcane cutters, Dominicans of Haitian ancestry despised for the false pretense of color, to be invisible in the country in which you were born, a country that strips your citizenship and turns you into a dangerous *other*.

Notes

1. Bragadir gives an interesting account of the story of Pierre Ravel, a French freeman of color, who was arrested in 1768 by Spanish authorities for crossing

the Spanish territory near the border town of San Rafael. His arrest involved the purchase of a piece of property acquired from another person of French nationality. Ravel was indignant for being imprisoned for two years in the custody of Spanish authorities. Bragadir reports that he testified before the *audiencia* in Santo Domingo, the Crown's appellate court in the colonies, as follows: "When a Frenchman wishes to acquire a certain property from a master or lord, he will only do so on French domain, not Spanish, whose limits should be known by the respective lords of both nations, and in the case that some error should occur, he who bought the property in good faith, acquiring the title from its legitimate sovereign, should not be the victim." Bragadir asks two very important questions regarding the matter as follows: Why was he held responsible for a boundary issue that should have been settled between French and Spanish sovereigns? And why should he, as a Frenchman, have to ask permission of the Spanish side to acquire land sold to him by another Frenchman? Ravel's testimony before the court stressed the inability of the states to define and police firm boundaries between their territories, which created, as Bragadir puts it, unpredictable and dangerous consequences for those who lived in this contested space. Bragadir concludes her report of Ravel's ordeal to show that in his attempt to settle in highly contested territory away from Spanish authority, he realized too late that contact with both sides was indispensable for his survival. See Mayes and Jayaram 23–43.

2. Although Augelli's text is relatively old and controversial for its racist tone and its emphasis on conflict theory, it has some historical value that can be confirmed or corroborated by most recent works. For example, Richard Lee Turits does underscore that the Haitian massacre was a result of ethnic conflict and racism, but he refrains from essentializing it by stating that the story of the massacre is also one of Dominicans versus Dominicans, of Dominican elites versus Dominican peasants, of the national state against Dominicans in the frontier, of centralizing forces in opposition to local interests, and the like (593).

3. García-Peña also gives a brief history of the Haitian-Dominican border by first stating that it was defined as a result of a colonial transaction. Following the Treaty of Ryswick in 1697 that ended the Nine Years' War between several European nations, Spain conceded some part of its colony to France with a borderline along the Dajabón River in the northwest of the Dominican Republic. After several protracted territorial conflicts, in 1777, the Treaty of Aranjuez was signed between the two colonial powers as a first attempt to clearly define a border to divide the two colonies. With the independence of the Dominican Republic from Haiti, the frontier had been redrawn several times through multiple official and unofficial treaties between the two governments of the island. Most importantly, García-Peña reiterates the well-known fact that Haitians had been living on the borderland of Hispaniola for at least a century after the signature of the Treaty of Aranjuez, knowingly ignoring colonial laws (136).

4. The other official case (besides Ravel that readers may think of) is the horrible fate of Ogé and Chavannes, the leaders of the free colored people's

movement fighting for equal rights with the whites in Saint-Domingue. Vincent Ogé, the mulatto, aided by Jean-Baptiste Chavannes and more than three hundred mulattoes, launched an armed attack on whites and pillaged a few plantations in the north to force the full implementation of a decree passed by the French National Assembly granting civil and political rights to free people of color with income qualifications. Ogé's rebellion was defeated, and as a result he and his accomplice Chavannes crossed the border of Hispaniola for asylum. The Spanish turned them over to the French authorities and they were summarily executed, tortured on the wheel. At the onset of and during the slave uprising, many whites were able to seek refuge at the Dominican border despite the fact that few of them were returned to the Black revolutionaries. Another category of people, beyond the political spectrum, was the free colored smugglers who often crossed the border in their dealing with Spanish soldiers (see Geggus 173).

    5. Silié further offers a clear explanation of the absence of a plantation economy in Santo Domingo in contrast to the French side of Hispaniola. He postulates that "from the most general point of view, the unlimited supply of land and the abundance of wild cattle were the determining factors in the establishment of the farming economy. The limited manpower required by the *Hato* was also linked to the establishment of the farming economy. These were the factors which allowed the interrupted reproduction of the latter until other internal and external factors came to slow down this reproduction. . . . The masters had few slaves. Since it was not the intensive work of the plantation, the masters were obliged, in order to preserve their slaves, to grant them a share in the profits of the production. Similarly, the reduction in Black slave trade resulted from the absence of a plantation economy requiring abundant labor. This reduction also made it possible that special means were used to obtain certain slaves and in particular, the continual flight of French slaves towards the Spanish colony of the island of Santo Domingo. The slaves who arrived in this way did not change the economic structure or the structure of the labor force. They only strengthened the farming economy and especially the owner of the *Hato* who ensured in this way a great availability of manpower" (my translation, 249–50).

    6. See Augelli 29; Yadira Perez; and Hazel Y. Perez.

    7. According to Ernesto Sagás, in the concluding chapter, "The Political Manipulation of Race," of his book *Race and Politics in the Dominican Republic*: "In the nineteenth and twentieth centuries, antihaitianismo went through a series of stages, and its intensity varied, depending on historical circumstances. From a high in the years after Dominican independence, anti-Haitian sentiment declined toward the end of the nineteenth century but did not disappear. After the U.S. occupation of Haiti and the Dominican Republic, relations between the latter two countries were described as 'correct.' It was not until the years after the 1937 massacre that antihaitianismo ideology reached its zenith" (117–18). He goes on to say that "probably the only moment in Dominican history when antihaitianismo could be

classified as a state-sponsored ideology was during the Trujillo era" (118). Addressing the long history of antihaitianismo as equated with other racist ideologies in more developed nations such as Nazism in Germany and Apartheid in South Africa, Sagás states that "from its origins as Hispanic racism, to its transformation into anti-Haiti nationalism, to its culmination as Trujillo's state ideology, antihaitianismo has had one main objective: the protection of powerful personal and elite interests through the subjugation of the lower (and darker) sectors of the Dominican population" (119).

  8. *Viejo* is a familiar name for Haitian migrant sugarcane workers who have long been either in Cuba or the Dominican Republic.

  9. Border gnosis, as defined by Walter Mignolo and cited by Fumagalli, "is a knowledge from a subaltern perspective conceived from the exterior borders of the modern/colonial world system" (90).

  10. *Massacre River* is the English title for his original novel in French, *Le peuple des terres mêlées* in 1989; it was translated by Linda Coverdale and published in 2005.

  11. Henri Citadel, otherwise known as the Citadel Laferrière, bears the name of the Emperor or King Henri Christophe of the Northern kingdom. The citadel is a mountaintop fortress located on the northern coast of Haiti.

  12. The Spanish word *rayano* is translated in English as a borderer, someone or a group of people living at the border or the borderland, border town.

Works Cited

Alexis, Jacques S. *Compère Général Soleil*. Paris: Gallimard, 2011.

———. *General Sun, My Brother*. Translated by Carrol F. Coates, UP of Virginia, 1999.

Augelli, John P. "Nationalization of Dominican Borderlands." *Geographical Review*, vol. 70, no. 1, 1980, pp. 19–35.

Bell, Madison Smartt. *All Soul's Rising*. Penguin Books, 1995.

Bragadir, Nathalie. "Shifting Territories: The Production of Space on Eighteenth-Century Hispaniola." *Transnational Hispaniola: New Directions in Haitian and Dominican Studies*. UP of Florida, 2018, pp. 23–43.

Danticat, Edwidge. *The Farming of Bones: A Novel*. Penguin Books, 1998.

Delné, Claudy. *La Révolution haïtienne dans l'imaginaire occidental: occultation, banalisation, trivialisation*. Éditions de l'Université d'État d'Haïti, 2017.

Derby, Lauren. "Haitians, Magic and Money: Raza and Society in the Haitian-Dominican Borderlands, 1900 to 1937." *Comparative Studies in Society and History: An International Quarterly*, vol. 36, 1994, pp. 488–526.

Fumagalli, Maria C. *On the Edge: Writing the Border between Haiti and the Dominican Republic*, Liverpool UP, 2015.

García-Peña, Lorgia. *The Borders of Dominicanidad: Race, Nation, and Archives of Contradiction*. Duke UP, 2016.

Geggus, David P. *Haitian Revolutionary Studies*. Indiana UP, 2002.
Geggus, David P., and Norman Fiering. *The World of the Haitian Revolution*. Indiana UP, 2009.
Genette, Gérard. *Figures III*. Seuil, 1972.
Hugo, Victor. *Bug Jargal*. Translated and edited by Chris Bongie, Broadview Edition, 2004.
James, Conrad M. "Fictions of Sex, Fear and Loathing in the Caribbean: Revisiting the Haitian/Dominican Borderland." *Culture & History Digital Journal*, vol. 2, no. 1, 2013, doi.org/10.3989/chdj.2013.012.
Lister, Elissa L. *Le conflit Haitiano-Dominicain dans la littérature Caribéenne*. C3 Éditions, 2013.
Martínez, Samuel. "Not a Cockfight: Rethinking Haitian-Dominican Relations." *Latin American Perspectives*, vol. 30, no. 3, 2003, pp. 80–101.
Mayes, April J., and Kiran Jayaram. "Shifting Territories: The Production of Space on Eighteenth-Century Hispaniola." *Transnational Hispaniola: New Directions in Haitian and Dominican Studies*. UP of Florida, 2018, pp. 23–43.
Moya, Pons F. *The Dominican Republic: A National History*. Markus Wiener, 1998.
Orr, David W. "A Literature of Redemption." *Conservation Biology*, vol. 15, no. 2, 2001, pp. 305–07.
Paulino, Edward. *Dividing Hispaniola: The Dominican Republic's Border Campaign against Haiti, 1930–1961*. U of Pittsburgh P, 2016.
Perez, Hazel Y. "Sensing Difference: Whiteness, National Identity, and Belonging in the Dominican Republic." *Transforming Anthropology*, vol. 22, no. 2, 2014, pp. 78–91.
Perez, Yadira. *Blanqueamiento in Paradise: Nation-Building, Immigration and Whiteness in the Dominican Republic*, PhD dissertation, University of Virginia, 2009.
Philoctète, René. *Massacre River*. Translated by Linda Coverdale, New Directions, 2005.
———. *Le peuple des terres mêlées: Roman*. H. Deschamps, 1989.
Popkin, Jeremy D. "Facing Racial Revolution: Captivity Narratives and Identity in the Saint-Domingue Insurrection." *Eighteenth-Century Studies*, vol. 36, no. 4, 2003, pp. 511–33.
Price-Mars, Jean. *La république d'Haiti et la république dominicaine: les aspects divers d'un problème d'histoire, de géographie et d'ethnologie*. Tome 1 et 2. Éditions Henri Deschamps, 2007.
Sagás, Ernesto. *Race and Politics in the Dominican Republic*. UP of Florida, 2000.
Sawyer, Mark Q., and Tianna S. Paschel. "We Didn't Cross the Color Line, the Color Line Crossed Us: Blackness and Immigration in the Dominican Republic, Puerto Rico, and the United States." *Du Bois Review*, vol. 4, no. 2, 2007, pp. 303–15.
Scanlon, Julie, and Amy Waste, editors. *Crossing Boundaries: Thinking Through Literature*. Sheffield Academic Press, 2001.

Silié Valdez, Rubén. *Population, économique et esclavage.* C3 Éditions, 2013.
Strongman, Roberto. "Reading through the Bloody Borderlands of Hispaniola: Fictionalizing the 1937 Massacre of Haitian Sugarcane Workers in the Dominican Republic." *Journal of Haitian Studies*, vol. 12, no. 2, 2006, pp. 21–46.
Théodat, Jean-Marie. *Haïti, République Dominicaine: Une Île Pour Deux, 1804–1916.* Karthala, 2003.
Turits, Richard L. "A World Destroyed, a Nation Imposed: The 1937 Haitian Massacre in the Dominican Republic." *The Hispanic American Historical Review*, vol. 83, no. 3, 2002, pp. 589–635.
Wattara, Mamadou. "Le peuple des terres mêlées de René Philoctète: Dire L'histoire Par 'la Parole Baroque.'" *Journal of Haitian Studies*, vol. 17, no. 2, 2011, pp. 94–112.

2

"The Road of Social Progress"

Revolutions and Resistance in
the 1936 Lectures of Dantès Bellegarde

VANESSA K. VALDÉS

In April of 1936, Dantès Bellegarde, Haitian ambassador to Washington from 1930 to 1933, delivered a series of four lectures at the University of Puerto Rico. Arranged by Richard Pattee, professor of Latin American history and director of the recently inaugurated Ibero American Institute at the university, Bellegarde's visit was meant to "inaugurate cultural relationships between Haiti and Puerto Rico" (5). He does so in a moment when the insular government was facing a growing anticolonial movement led by the Puerto Rican Nationalist Party, headed by Pedro Albizu Campos. This essay examines Bellegarde's references in his lectures to the Haitian Revolution as well as to the nineteen-year US occupation of Haiti, from 1915 to 1934, during which he served as a diplomat representing his nation. During this period, Bellegarde had been an outspoken critic of the United States' military presence on the island of his birth; in contrast, in these lectures he provides an implicit critique of the United States' colonizing presence in its Spanish-speaking colonial possession. Though perhaps understandable, given the growing violence on the island, Bellegarde's decision to not name mounting resistance to the United States is striking. On their face and lacking historical context, the lectures appear relatively innocuous; Bellegarde's comments take on additional sting with an awareness of the environment in which he delivered them.

> We now know that narratives are made of silences . . .
>
> —Michel-Rolph Trouillot, *Silencing the Past: Power and the Production of History*

The 1930s was a turbulent decade in Puerto Rico; a devastating hurricane, San Felipe, struck the island in September of 1928, destroying hundreds of thousands of homes, leaving half a million people homeless and over $85 million in losses (Morales Carrión 212). The economic collapse of the Great Depression, beginning with the stock market crash of October 1929, exacerbated an already precarious living situation for an impoverished populace. Meanwhile the profits of US sugar companies soared: as José Trías Monge notes, "In 1899 the sugar cane industry used 15 percent of the land available for cultivation. In 1930 that percentage had increased to 44 percent. Taxes on these corporations were kept low, while the dividends distributed to the foreign shareholders often exceeded their investment" (83). US capital had saturated the Puerto Rican market, thereby creating a complete dependence on its colonizing power.

Deteriorating economic conditions and unrelenting poverty emboldened calls for independence from the United States. These demands were led by the Partido Nacionalista de Puerto Rico, the Puerto Rican Nationalist Party. Founded in 1922, the party elected a new leader, Pedro Albizu Campos, in 1930. Born in 1891 in Ponce to a Black Puerto Rican domestic worker and a white Basque merchant who refused to recognize him until later in life, Albizu Campos would leave the island to attend first the University of Vermont and later Harvard University, from which he would graduate with an undergraduate degree and, after being drafted into military service for the First World War, later one in law. Upon his graduation in 1921, he returned to Puerto Rico, working as a lawyer and, beginning in 1923, writing for local publications *El Nacionalista de Ponce* (later, *El Nacionalista de Puerto Rico*) and *El Mundo*. He joined the Nationalist Party in 1924, and within a week was elected vice president of the party as well as the director of *El Nacionalista de Ponce* (Rodríguez León xi–xiii). Three years later, beginning in 1927, he toured Latin America, connecting with local politicians and activists, to garner support for Puerto Rican independence.

He was familiar to many on the ground, given the distribution of his articles, where he was frank in his criticism of US imperialism and his support of the sovereignty of the nations of Latin America. He denounced US involvement in the Mexican Revolution, its invasions of both Haiti (which had begun in 1915) and the Dominican Republic (which had begun in 1916), as well as its continued incursions in Cuba, and he condemned plans to annex the islands of Cuba and Hispaniola.[1] For many, this sojourn solidifies his connection with past leaders of the Puerto Rican independence movement, namely, nineteenth-century heroes Ramón Emeterio Betances and Eugenio María de Hostos, both of whom had been exiled from Puerto Rico when it had been a Spanish colony and who had organized insurrections while abroad.[2] Albizu Campos's travels included a stay in Haiti, where he met with nationalists Pierre Paulie and Joseph Jolibois fils (Go 87).[3]

Albizu Campos returned to Puerto Rico at the beginning of 1930 and shortly thereafter was elected president of the Nationalist Party. Two years later, in 1932, the Nationalist Party won less than 1 percent of the votes cast in the island's elections for seats in the legislature, and thereafter, Albizu Campos rejected electoral politics as a legitimate process that would result in national liberation.[4] Thereafter his rhetoric became increasingly strident, as he justified armed insurrection in the struggle for independence. At the same time, workers lobbied for Albizu Campos to lend his support in their efforts for fair wages, at times requesting that he lead their strikes; he did so in 1934, when sugarcane workers asked him to intervene in negotiations that had begun the previous year.[5] As James Dietz observes, during the 1930s, labor strikes took place in a number of industries in addition to sugar, including needlework, dockyard workers, and transportation, with more than sixty thousand workers fighting for fair labor conditions (164).

Another such strike occurred in October 1935 at the flagship campus of the University of Puerto Rico at Río Piedras in San Juan; a clash between protesters and the police on the 24th of that month resulted in the deaths of one policeman and four Nationalists, including Ramón S. Pagán, who had served as treasurer of the Nationalist Party. Four days after what would come to be known as the Río Piedras Massacre, *La Democracia*, the newspaper of the Liberal Party, the majority party in the legislature, published an account in which the US-appointed chief of police, Francis Riggs, declared war on the Nationalist Party.[6] Four months later almost to the day, on February 23, 1936, Hiram Rosado and Elías Beauchamp, two members of the Nationalist Party's Cadetes de la República, the party's youth brigade, killed Riggs;[7] apprehended quickly, both were killed upon entering the police station by arresting officers.[8] Within two weeks, on March 5, 1936, Albizu Campos and six other Nationalist Party leaders were arrested and charged with conspiracy to overthrow the government; at a March 18th cabinet meeting, US president Franklin D. Roosevelt asked Secretary of the Interior Harold Ickes as to the advisability of holding a plebiscite regarding independence (Gattell 31.) A month later, Senator Millard Tydings introduced a bill calling for Puerto Rico's independence on April 23, 1936; it was almost immediately denounced both on the island and in Washington. The Tydings Bill called for a referendum in which islanders would answer the following: "Shall the people of Puerto Rico be sovereign and independent?" A "yes" vote would prompt a constitutional convention, which would then have to be voted upon again by the Puerto Rican populace, and if the majority again voted in the affirmative, the island would transition to independence within a four-year period.

The bill was roundly criticized by prominent members of almost all of the more prominent insular political parties, with the exception of the Nationalists; as César J. Ayala and Rafael Bernabe note, "Albizu Campos had called for the organization of a constituent assembly. Puerto Ricans, he argued, had to organize themselves as a sovereign body" (112). Others viewed as putative the economic terms of a transition to sovereignty: Roland Perusse writes, "U.S. tariffs on Puerto Rican goods entering the United States would be levied at the rate of 25 percent each year until full independence was achieved. In the same way, U.S. economic assistance would be eliminated" (26). On an island in which the majority of the population already lived in poverty, such terms would have been disastrous. While Tydings maintained that the terms of independence mirrored the bill he had cosponsored leading to the independence of the Philippines, Perusse notes that the Tydings-McDuffie Act of 1934 had been more generous, allowing for a ten-year transition period, for example (26).[9] Another historian, Frank Gattell, characterized the bill as the "act of an angry man," going on to write:

> The virulence and audacity of the Nationalist attacks on the American administration caused Tydings and the administration to draw hasty conclusions about the strength and nature of Puerto Rican independence sentiment. If Puerto Rico rejected independence, she would have to eat crow and thus appreciate the "great blessing" of the American market; if she accepted independence, the "erring step-sister" could depart in peace and poverty. Tydings had written off the island as incapable of

achieving American democracy or an indigenous counterpart derived from it. (44)

It was into this juncture of socioeconomic and political instability, of strikes and police violence, that Dantès Bellegarde entered with his visit to the site of the Río Piedras Massacre, the University of Puerto Rico, in April 1936.

> Like countless other Americans and Europeans, through Bellegarde the man, they have seen Haiti, the magnificent!
>
> —Mercer Cook, "Dantes Bellegarde"

So ends the 1940 profile of retired diplomat Dantès Bellegarde in *Phylon*, the scholarly journal founded by W. E. B. Du Bois in that year at Atlanta University. At the time of publication, Bellegarde was a visiting professor of French; in this detailed biographical sketch, Cook, himself a prominent professor of French who would go on to serve as ambassador to Senegal and Gambia under the administration of Lyndon Johnson, highlights for his audience the distinguished career of his Haitian colleague. For Cook, and seemingly, for many in his acquaintance, during the course of his life, Dantès Bellegarde would become emblematic of the nation he loved. Born in 1877 in Port-au-Prince to Marie Boisson, a seamstress, and Jean-Louis Bellegarde, director of the botanical gardens at the Faculté de Médecine, Louis-Dantès Bellegarde would go on to excel academically and became a teacher of French, Latin, and philosophy. He also wrote for newspapers and journals, including *La Ronde*, for which he served as secretary.[10] The writers of this periodical, the Generation de La Ronde, aimed for the "rejuvenation of society through literature" and dominated the early twentieth-century literary scene in the capital (Bellegarde-Smith 59). In 1901, after earning his degree, Bellegarde was admitted to the bar; three years later he began his life in public service, first by being named to a commission within the Ministry of Foreign Affairs and Public Instruction and shortly thereafter named Chef de division, charged with the entirety of educational affairs in the nation (Bellegarde-Smith 61–62).

Education would be a key focus for Bellegarde; in 1918, after working at the Banque Nationale in accounting services, he was named minister of public instruction and agriculture in the Dartiguenave administration, which had been established by the US government in 1915 with its military occupation of Haiti. Patrick Bellegarde-Smith recounts the opposition Bellegarde faced in this position: whereas he took seriously the charge of implementing free education on primary, secondary, and university levels (as established in the constitutions of 1816 and 1879), US politicians were content with an emphasis on vocational training. "American policy for Haiti was similar to that [which] it adopted for Blacks in the United States. Ready acceptance of Booker T. Washington's practical ideas on Negro development through the acquisition of manual skills was within the broad framework of 'scientific' progress as perceived in the United States in the late nineteenth century"(-Bellegarde-Smith 65). Bellegarde, who understood agriculture and education as fields that needed to work in tandem, wished to overhaul school districts in rural areas so that they would be accountable to local populations rather than to the capital. His proposals were summarily ignored by occupation authorities (Bellegarde-Smith 66; Cook, "Dantes Bellegarde" 127–28.)

In 1920 he began to serve as a diplomat on behalf of his nation, when he was appointed to the Permanent Court of Arbitration at the Hague and the Haitian minister to France and the Vatican; he also represented Haiti in 1921 in the second assembly of the League of Nations and participated in W. E. B. Du Bois's Pan-African Congress session in Paris (Bellegarde-Smith 69–73; Cook, "Dantes Bellegarde" 129–30).[11] Recalled by the Borno administration, Bellegarde would continue to represent Haiti abroad as representative of the Haitian Chamber of Congress in both the Congress of the International Union of Associations for the League of Nations in 1924 and the Universal Congress for Peace in 1925, both of which, under his leadership, passed resolutions calling for the reestablishment of Haitian sovereignty and the end of the US military occupation in Haiti (Bellegarde-Smith 75). He continued his criticism of the United States in 1927, at the fourth Pan-African Congress in New York, and in a speech for which he received much attention in 1930 at the eleventh assembly of the League of Nations. There, he said: "So long as there is military and civil occupation of the Haitian Republic—unjustified by law and resting upon a treaty imposed by force on the Haitian people—fear and suspicion will continue to exist among the American nations" (Cook, "Dantes Bellegarde" 132).[12]

In centering Haiti and the US overthrow of its democratic structures in support of financial interests, Bellegarde made the persuasive argument that the United States was a threat to the hemisphere itself; the United States, in response, demanded his recall. He would go on to serve as the Haitian ambassador to the US and as its representative in the Pan-American Union from 1931 to 1933, when he resigned.[13] The United States withdrew its military apparatus from Haiti in 1934, after nineteen years and the deaths of tens of thousands of Haitian men, women, and children.[14] Matthew J. Smith notes, "after 1934, the United States became Haiti's leading trading partner, importing more than half of its annual coffee yield and carefully maintained influence of Haitian finance" (13).

Bellegarde himself represented Haiti on an economic trip to Canada in 1934, before a return to teaching (Cook, "Dantes Bellegarde" 135). He also continued writing, having published several books, including *Morceaux choisis d'auteurs haïtiens* (1904); *L'écolier haïtien* (1913) and *L'année enfantine d'histoire et de géographie d'Haïti* (1913), textbooks that he cowrote with Sténio Vincent, who would go on to serve as president of Haiti from 1930 to 1941;[15] *Haïti et les Etats-Unis devant la justice international* (1924); *Pages d'histoire* (1925); the two volumes of *Pour une Haïti heureuse* (1928, 1929). In 1929 he published the pamphlet *L' occupation américaine d'Haïti*, and in 1934, *Un haïtien parle*. The publication of his lectures at the University of Puerto Rico in the *University of Puerto Rico Bulletin* in September 1936 were his first to appear in English (Cook, "Writings" 233).

> Haiti claims proudly her place among the sovereign nations of the world.
>
> —Dantès Bellegarde, *Haiti and Her Problems: Four Lectures*

Presented as *Haiti and Her Problems*, Bellegarde's lectures serve as an introduction to the nation of his birth. In his four talks, "Haiti and Its People," "The Population and Economic Life of Haiti," "The Economic Life of the Republic of Haiti," and "Haiti and International Cooperation," he presents informative truths about its population, its history, the challenges it has faced, as well as possible solutions and his wishes for his compatriots. The title of the publication is in keeping with a narrative already well developed in 1936 about Haiti and its difficulties, one circulated with greater frequency in the US press as a justification for the occupation.[16] Yet while Bellegarde himself acknowledges the challenges that his country faces, at no point does he present the country as problematic. Outside the scope of this essay is a detailed summary of each talk; instead, this section focuses on his criticism of the United States, as well as his comments that are directly applicable to a Puerto Rican context.

Within his first talk, Bellegarde directly challenges the notion that his country is perhaps more challenging than others; instead, he "insist[s] on the conditions under which the young State came into existence" (10). His emphasis on the age of the nation is instructive, as he prompts his audience to recall that its origin as an independent state dates to 1804, until the occupation in 1915. In the same talk, he calls into question expectations for Haiti: "Perhaps because Haiti is of African descent, the world expected her to be immediately perfect—although in seasoned Europe and immemorial Asia, peoples with long centuries of civilization, even to this very hour, present the sad and shameful spectacle of illiteracy, poverty, civil strife, and revolution" (17). Bellegarde turns on its head contemporary racist stereotypes of peoples of African descent, directing attention instead to a supposedly civilized Europe that had, by 1936, already seen the destruction caused by the Great War and the rise of the dictators of that continent, as well as in Asia. He also rejects outright the notion that Communism would thrive in Haiti, again, in contradistinction to Stalin's Soviet Union and an early rejoinder to such suspicions about Latin America as a region held by some within the US government (39).

The United States is but one of the "innumerable difficulties" the Haitian people faced as they attempted to "organize themselves into a civilized society" (10). Nevertheless, Bellegarde highlights the advantages his country holds over its imperialistic neighbor: "What no traveler has ever denied in regard to the people of Haiti is their great gentleness and the simplicity of their customs. . . . Haiti has no venomous reptiles, nor gangsters, racketeers, nor kidnappers, and . . . Lindbergh could live in Haiti without fear for his baby" (13). Referencing the crime and corruption that beset the United States, including a mention of the abduction and murder of the Lindbergh baby in 1932, Bellegarde again rejects myths about his own nation by instead holding up a mirror to the United States, suggesting that the monstrous nation of the hemisphere is the one that had presented itself as the protector of her neighbors, beginning with the Monroe Doctrine and most vividly in his historical moment with the Roosevelt administration's Good Neighbor Policy, cited as a reason for the withdrawal of troops from the nation.

Violence is at the heart of Bellegarde's comments about the United States; the title of this essay comes from a section in which he addresses directly the perception about Haiti's political instability:

> Unfortunately, the excess brought about by our too-frequent revolutions and so greatly exaggerated by many malicious writers have [sic] created in the world outside a most regrettable reputation for our people, whereas their sociable habits and manners and their undeserved misfortunes should on the contrary arouse

universal sympathy. No one deplores more deeply than I do the "revolutions" that have all too frequently upset the economic life of the Haitian nation and given many a set-back to its social evolution. Nevertheless, the history of Haiti clearly shows that those disturbances were more often the outcome of governmental despotism or dictatorship. Most of these so-called revolutions may be regarded as so many painful stages on the road of social progress. Many of them, it should be noted, were merely mutinous or insurrectionary activities that did not attain to the gravity of many strikes in Chicago nor of certain lynchings in Alabama. This is so true that some of these "revolutions" began and ended without the shedding of a drop of blood. (13–14)

While he recognizes the interruptions to the democratic process, he again lends perspective, first, by highlighting the role of writers in the creation of a perception of constant political turmoil. While he bemoans the effects of these disturbances on economic development, principally for a populace that lives, for the most part, off the land, he again calls attention to events in the United States, demonstrations in the name of economic equity in the Midwest ("strikes"), indiscriminate murders of men and women in the US South ("lynchings"). While Bellegarde's mention of lynchings immediately identifies the victims as Black men and women, his inclusion of strikes also speaks to economic inequities based on race within the largest economy in the hemisphere. He therefore ties political and economic violence, as both are destructive forces, particularly for peoples of African descent. An alternative goal, and one that he posits for his country, is a commitment to a peace; he emphasizes: "but a real peace, fruitful and founded on the consent of all and on liberty under the law; not the precarious and artificial peace which rests on the brute force of machine guns in the service of private interests" (17–18).[17] Here, Bellegarde most specifically recalls the occupation of his nation and the protection of Wall Street interests; in *Bankers and Empires: How Wall Street Colonized the Caribbean* (2017), Peter James Hudson provides an incisive historical overview of the role of US finance in the destabilization of various Caribbean nations, including both Haiti and Puerto Rico. Hudson focuses primarily on the National City Bank of New York, which had branches in both nations and which played a critical role in the economies of both.[18]

This is also a moment where his audience may have more viscerally understood Bellegarde's references; certainly, his interpretation of revolutions as impermanent, transitory, and even necessary episodes at a moment when physical conflict between members of the Nationalist Party and the insular police may have provided some consolation. Throughout his talks, in fact, much of his content is directly applicable to a Puerto Rican context. Primary among these is his description of agriculture as the foundation of the Haitian economy, as well as its dependence on a single crop, in Haiti's case, coffee (Bellegarde 26–30, 33–36). Puerto Rico, in comparison, was fully dependent on sugarcane as a crop, and much of the land was owned by US-based companies. Haiti being a mostly rural country, Bellegarde explains the division of land under the French colonial system as well as in the aftermath of the establishment of its independence; after his description of the *faire-valoir* direct, rent, and metayage systems, he offers: "Practically the entire rural population of Haiti, that is to say, over two million persons, thus live from their own labor and consume the greater part of the produce of the soil. By their labor, this rural population also provides the food supply of the cities. Providing for their sustenance by the produce of their fields, the Haitian peasants supply also—through their industry—many of the needs of their living quarters" (29–30). Similar to Puerto Rico at the time, peasant-laborers in Haiti provided for a great deal of the economy, and yet there had been little done to improve their livelihoods:[19]

> Among possible solutions is mechanization of the agricultural sector, as he himself admits: it is clear that the industrialization of agriculture, implying the use of machinery and of hired labor, would develop Haitian production considerably. But it would bring with it the destruction of the small property class. And Haiti would run the risk of becoming a richer country with a population more poverty-stricken than it is today. The American Occupation attempted to apply this solution, but it ran into the energetic opposition of the Haitians, who believe in the progress of their rural democracy by the application of surer and more simple methods. (39)

Seemingly, Bellegarde is offering a warning about the possible implementations of the supposed progress offered through US investment, particularly given how this particular solution would affect how people have traditionally lived. He also gives these speeches during the execution of the Roosevelt administration's New Deal, locally realized as the Puerto Rico Reconstruction Administration.[20] It would be a decade before the United States applied a policy of a large-scale industrialization; Operación Manos a la Obra (Operation Bootstrap) would result in the displacement of hundreds of thousands of Puerto Ricans who would thereafter migrate to the US mainland in search for employment.

The pursuit for social, political, and economic well-being is the heart of Bellegarde's last lecture. He concedes the volatility of his moment: "A wind of pessimism is blowing all over the earth. Internal discords, economic crises, commercial unrest, paralyzation of industry, signs of war, cries for vengeance: all these create a heavy atmosphere which seems scarcely favorable to universal peace. But these anxieties make the necessity for 'peace organizations' more evident and must make their existence more desirable to us" (46). While these words certainly reference instabilities on an international scale, they also are directly applicable to a Puerto Rican reality in which labor strikes were occurring across industries, calls for independence at all costs by the Nationalist Party were met with an insular police force empowered by the federal government to maim, and rampant inequality meant a great part of the populace lived in poverty. Bellegarde's solution is an insistence on peace, and on a calm brought about by a real investment in the inhabitants of Latin America. He says: "We also, in the Latin countries of America, have need of renewing confidence in ourselves and inspiring confidence in others. Nature has endowed us with too much in the way of resources, our peoples are too eager to work, too anxious for progress, too devoted to their ideals, for us to have any reason to doubt ourselves and to abandon ourselves to despair" (53). Offering hope to his audience, then, he advises against isolation, instead bringing attention to the riches that the peoples themselves represent. While he earlier makes mention of needing the "benevolent support of the richer and more enlightened nations" (11), here he suggests that the solutions will come not from those countries that are more easily recognized as prosperous but instead from Latin American nations themselves. In this way, Bellegarde's message resonates with that of Pedro Albizu Campos, in that they both insisted on the riches that the peoples of their respective nations themselves offer.

> For silencing here is an erasure more effective than the absence or failure of memory, whether faked or genuine.
>
> —Michel-Rolph Trouillot, *Silencing the Past: Power and the Production of History*

While Dantès Bellegarde's audience at the University of Puerto Rico would have understood the subtext for his lectures, readers of those pronouncements in subsequent decades may have lost the implications of his comments on freedom, sovereignty, and a government's responsibilities to his citizens. Bellegarde's contributions to Haitian intellectual history have been woefully understudied; his grandson, prominent scholar Patrick Bellegarde-Smith, has written the sole book-length study on him in English, *In the Shadow of Powers: Dantès Bellegarde in Haitian Social Thought* (1985).[21] Most of his books, published originally in French, remain untranslated.

This essay underscores the historical context in which Dantès Bellegarde delivered these lectures. In the five months between these talks, in April of 1936, and their publication in September of that year, Pedro Albizu Campos and other Nationalist leaders would be tried twice on charges of sedition and conspiracy to overthrow the government of the United States. After a deadlocked jury in the first trial, they were found guilty on July 31, 1936, and were sentenced to serve fifteen years in an Atlanta federal prison.[22] His conviction spurred demonstrations throughout the Puerto Rican nation; in New York, for example, Congressman Vito Marcantonio led a protest of ten thousand in Harlem, denouncing the "political lynching" of Albizu Campos as well as the imperialism of the United States.[23] He was freed in 1947, after eleven years; 1950 saw Nationalist revolts on both the island and the US mainland, and he was charged, tried, and convicted of attempted murder, illegal use of arms, and subversion in three trials, and received separate sentences of thirty to eighty years. After being subject to radiation while in prison, Albizu Campos was pardoned in 1953; within months, after an attack on the House of Representatives in March 1954, his pardon was revoked and he was returned to prison, where he would remain until he was pardoned again in 1964. He died on April 21, 1965.

Into these first decades of the twenty-first century, Pedro Albizu Campos continues to be a beacon for those in support of the independence of Puerto Rico. Nineteenth-century figures such as Ramón Emeterio Betances and Eugenio María de Hostos continue to provide a foundation for these calls; Albizu Campos remains its emotional center. In the aftermath of his death in 1965, activists, scholars, and students alike have used his words and most strikingly his image to evoke a patriot's love for his homeland. In 1973, on what would have been his eighty-second birthday, the Instituto de Cultura Puertorriqueña in San Juan opened an exhibition, *Exposición Imagen de Pedro Albizu Campos*, honoring the image of Albizu Campos;

given the institute's standing as the official arbiter of culture on the island, this honoring of Albizu Campos within a decade of his passing speaks to the magnitude of his influence. Ricardo E. Alegría, head of the institute at the time, wrote the following in his introduction to the exhibition catalog: "Las divergencias de criterios no han tenido suficiente fuerza para impedir que la figura de Albizu Campos se haya ido agrandando con el tiempo, convirtiéndose en el símbolo de la lucha por la soberanía nacional, lucha en la cual, aunque bajo diferentes modalidades, participa hoy un número considerable de nuestros compatriotas" (9).[24] Irrespective of their voting habits, then, men, women, and children across the island and its diaspora recognize Albizu Campos as the heart of the nation's quest for freedom. César J. Ayala and Rafael Bernabe make clear his critical importance: "It was Albizu Campos who first insisted that independence was something for Puerto Rico not to receive but to make through its own activity. It is this notion of self-determination and self-activation underlying his vision of independence that made his intervention such a radical departure in the Puerto Rican political landscape of the 1930s" (109).

Bellegarde's lectures at the University of Puerto Rico had previously been, for the most part, lost to the annals of history. Yet this moment illuminates one man's interpretation and discernment of the political situation with which he was confronted. Within his own country, and as a government official representing his country both in the League of Nations and later in the United States itself, Bellegarde could be more forcefully critical of the imperialistic overreach of the neighboring superpower. As a retired diplomat and a guest in this nonincorporated territory of the United States, he would offer a more discreet critique.

Notes

1. See Albizu-Campos Meneses and Rodríguez León 39–52 for his articles, "Protesta a un plan para la anexión de Cuba, Haití, Santo Domingo y Puerto Rico a Estados Unidos," "La Convención Dominicana-Angloamericana," "La retirada de Santo Domingo," and "Ecce Homo Dominicanos!"

2. For more on these men, see Ojeda Reyes, *Peregrinos de la libertad* (1992).

3. Go details that during this tour Albizu Campos also met with Federico Enríquez Carvajal in the Dominican Republic, leaders of the opposition against Venezuela's Juan Vicente Gómez, and those against Cuba's Gerardo Machado, as well as visited Mexico, Panama, and Peru (86–87). For more on Joseph Jolibois fils, see Casey; McPherson; and Schmidt.

4. Morales Carrión writes: "At the 1932 elections, he received slightly over 11,000 votes and the party 5,257 votes out of the 383,722 votes cast" (226).

5. See Taller de Formación Política and Santiago-Valles " 'Our Race Today.' "

6. Albizu Campos, "La massacre de Río Piedras: declaración de la Junta Nacional," in Albizu-Campos Meneses and Rodríguez León 127.

7. Go observes that this brigade was modeled after the Irish Citizen Army, as beginning at least during his years at Harvard, Albizu Campos had been inspired by the Irish fight for independence (86–87).

8. For more on this decade of violence, see Rosado.

9. Ronald Fernandez highlights that in addition, the "Philippine bill mandated a twenty-year introduction of tariffs" (125).

10. In addition to Mercer Cook's sketch, see the third chapter of Bellegarde-Smith's study, "Milieu and Moment: The Career and Life of Dantès Bellegarde," 54–88.

11. For more on his collaboration with Du Bois, his speeches at these Pan-African Congresses, and later speeches in front of African American audiences and their coverage in the US Black press, see Jean-Louis.

12. Earlier that year, in March of 1930, Bellegarde had offered testimony to the Forbes Commission criticizing the United States' unwillingness to implement Haitian proposals for bettering the economic standing of his nation. This group was a board appointed by then-president Herbert Hoover and charged with facilitating communications between John H. Russell, the US high commissioner in Haiti; the Haitian president Louis Borno; and Haitian forces. For more on the ineffectiveness of this commission, see Polyné.

13. For a detailed analysis of Bellegarde's years in the United States, see Jean-Louis.

14. For more on the occupation, see Castor; Hudson, "National City Bank"; Schmidt. To understand its cultural impact throughout the hemisphere, see Baptiste; Dalleo; Dash; Karem; and Renda. For more on African-American involvement in efforts to end the occupation, see Logan and Jean-Louis.

15. Smith notes that Vincent had "position[ed] himself as an anti-occupationist . . . a liberal nationalist whose challenge to U.S. control was a sharp contrast to the accommodation of the previous two regimes" (9). Soon after the *désoccupation*, the withdrawal of the United States in January 1934, his administration became more repressive: he "place[ed] the country in a state of siege shortly after taking office and instituting martial law at various points throughout his rule" (17). Repression of radical groups was widespread: activists Joseph Jolibois fils, Georges Petit, and famed writer Jacques Roumain were jailed several times, accused, and found guilty of communist activities. Vincent's most critical moment would be his slow acknowledgment of the 1937 massacre of over fifteen thousand Haitians and Dominicans along the border (31); while he would accept an indemnity of $750,000 from the Dominican government, he faced attempted coups and by the following

year would openly declare his government a dictatorship (36). He would go on to declare no plans to run for reelection, allowing for a smooth transition of power at the end of his term in 1941 (37).

16. See Renda.

17. He offers references to the occupation throughout his talks; describing Port-au-Prince, he says, "It offers a secure roadstead, where the largest warships of the United States have entered without difficulty" (23).

18. Bellegarde name checks this bank in his second lecture (25); the National City Bank of New York is now known as Citibank.

19. For more on the Puerto Rican economy of the early twentieth century, see Santiago-Valles, *"Subject People."*

20. For more, see Rodríguez; and Santiago-Valles, *"Subject People."*

21. This book was reissued in February 2019 as part of Vanderbilt University Press's Black Lives and Liberation series.

22. Peter James Hudson writes: "[Albizu Campos] was convicted by a jury that included Frederick J. Todd, the head of the City Bank's collection department, and Henry Shoemaker, an officer of the Chase National Bank, the latter institution having arrived on the island in 1933. Puerto Ricans working under Todd in the City Bank gave sworn statements alleging that Todd had made negative, biased comments about Albizu Campos and the other nationalists before the trial. Albizu Campos, Todd had declared, should be 'burned alive.' Todd denied the accusations. . . . Years later, Todd took charge of the City Bank's Cuban branches and was appointed a vice president. The City Bank fired the Puerto Rican employees. Albizu Campos spent the better part of the next eleven years in an Atlanta penitentiary" (*Bankers and Empires* 266).

23. "10,000 Parade Here for Puerto Ricans," *New York Times*, 30 August 1936, p. 24.

24. "Different opinions have not had enough strength to interrupt the process by which the idea of Albizu Campos has expanded with time, becoming the symbol of the fight for national sovereignty, a fight in which a considerable number of our compatriots participate today, although through different means" (translation by the author).

Works Cited

Albizu-Campos Meneses, Laura, and Mario A. Rodríguez León, editors. *Albizu Campos: Escritos*. Publicaciones Puertorriqueñas, 2007.

Alegría, Ricardo. "Introducción." *Imagen de Pedro Albizu Campos*, edited by Benjamín Torres, Marisa Rosado, and José Manuel Torres Santiago, Instituto de Cultura Puertorriqueña, 1973, pp. 9–11.

Ayala, César J., and Rafael Bernabe. *Puerto Rico in the American Century: A History since 1898.* U of North Carolina P, 2007.
Baptiste, Stephanie Leigh. *Darkening Mirrors: Imperial Representation in Depression-Era African American Performance.* Duke UP, 2012.
Bellegarde, Dantès. *Haiti and Her Problems: Four Lectures.* U of Puerto Rico, 1936.
Bellegarde-Smith, Patrick. *In the Shadow of Powers: Dantès Bellegarde in Haitian Social Thought.* Humanities, 1985.
Casey, Matthew. *Empire's Guestworkers: Haitian Migrants in Cuba during the Age of US Occupation.* Cambridge UP, 2017.
Castor, Suzy. *L'occupation américaine d'Haïti.* Imprimerie Henri Deschamps, 1988.
Cook, Mercer. "Dantes Bellegarde." *Phylon*, vol. 1, no. 2, 1940, pp. 125–35.
———. "The Writings of Dantès Bellegarde." *Books Abroad*, vol. 23, no. 3, 1949, pp. 233–35.
Dalleo, Raphael. *American Imperialism's Undead: The Occupation of Haiti and the Rise of Caribbean Anticolonialism.* U of Virginia P, 2016.
Dash, J. Michael. *Haiti and the United States: National Stereotypes and the Literary Imagination.* 2nd ed. St. Martin's, 1997.
Dietz, James. *Economic History of Puerto Rico.* Princeton UP, 1986.
Fernandez, Ronald. *The Disenchanted Island: Puerto Rico and the United States in the Twentieth Century.* 2nd ed. Praeger, 1996.
Gattell, Frank Otto. "Independence Rejected: Puerto Rico and the Tydings Bill of 1936." *Hispanic American Historical Review*, vol. 38, no. 1, 1958, pp. 25–44.
Go, Julian. "Anti-Imperialism in U.S. Territories after 1898." *Empire's Twin: U.S. Anti-Imperialism from the Founding Era to the Age of Terrorism*, edited by Ian Tyrrell and Jay Sexton, Cornell UP, 2015, pp. 79–96.
Hudson, Peter James. *Bankers and Empires: How Wall Street Colonized the Caribbean.* U of Chicago P, 2017.
———. "The National City Bank of New York and Haiti, 1909–1922." *Radical History Review*, vol. 115, Winter 2013, pp. 91–114.
Jean-Louis, Felix, III. "Harlemites, Haitians and the Black International: 1915–1934." 2014. *FIU Electronic Theses and Dissertations*, digitalcommons.fiu.edu/etd/1154.
Karem, Jeff. *The Purloined Islands: Caribbean-U.S. Crosscurrents in Literature and Culture, 1880–1959.* U of Virginia P, 2011.
Logan, Rayford W. "James Weldon Johnson and Haiti." *Phylon*, vol. 32, no. 4, 1971, pp. 396–402.
McPherson, Alan. "Joseph Jolibois Fils and the Flaws of Haitian Resistance to U.S. Occupation." *Journal of Haitian Studies* 16:2 (2010) 120–147.
Morales Carrión, Arturo. *Puerto Rico: A Political and Cultural History.* Norton, 1983.
Ojeda Reyes, Félix. *Peregrinos de la libertad.* Editorial de la Universidad de Puerto Rico, 1992.
Pattee, Richard. Foreword. *Haiti and Her Problems: Four Lectures*, by Dantès Bellegarde, University of Puerto Rico, 1936, pp. 5–7.

Perusse, Roland I. *The United States and Puerto Rico: The Struggle for Equality.* Krieger, 1990.

Polyné, Millery. "'To Combine the Training of the Head and the Hands': The 1930 Robert R. Moton Education Commission in Haiti." *From Douglass to Duvalier: U.S. African Americans, Haiti, and Pan-Americanism, 1870–1964.* UP of Florida, 2010, pp. 56–88.

Renda, Mary. *Taking Haiti: Military Occupation and the Culture of U.S. Imperialism, 1915–1940.* U of North Carolina P, 2001.

Ribes Tovar, Federico. *Albizu Campos: Puerto Rican Revolutionary.* Plus Ultra, 1971.

Rodríguez, Manuel R. *A New Deal for the Tropics: Puerto Rico during the Depression Era, 1932–1935.* Markus Weiner, 2011.

Rodríguez León, Mario A. "El periodismo nacionalista de Pedro Albizo Campos." *Albizu Campos: Escritos*, edited by Laura Albizu-Campos Meneses and Mario A. Rodríguez León, Publicaciones Puertorriqueñas, 2007, pp. xi–xvi.

Rosado, Marisa. *El Nacionalismo y la violencia en la década de 1930.* Ediciones Puerto, 2007.

Santiago-Valles, Kelvin. "'Our Race Today [Is] the Only Hope for the World': An African Spaniard as Chieftain of the Struggle against 'Sugar Slavery' in Puerto Rico, 1926–1934." *Caribbean Studies*, vol. 35, no. 1, 2007, pp. 107–40.

———. *"Subject People" and Colonial Discourses: Economic Transformation and Social Disorder in Puerto Rico, 1898–1947.* State U of New York P, 1994.

Schmidt, Hans. *The United States Occupation of Haiti, 1915–1934.* 1985. Rutgers UP, 1995.

Smith, Matthew J. *Red and Black in Haiti: Radicalism, Conflict, and Political Change, 1934–1957.* U of North Carolina P, 2009.

Taller de Formación Política. *¡Huelga en la caña! 1933–34.* Ediciones Huracán, 1982.

Trías Monge, José. *Puerto Rico: The Trials of the Oldest Colony in the World.* Yale UP, 1997.

Trouillot, Michel-Rolph. *Silencing the Past: Power and the Production of History.* 1995. Beacon, 2015.

3

The Dictator's Scapegoat

Emilio Rodríguez Demorizi's *Invasiones haitianas de 1801, 1805 y 1822*

CARRIE GIBSON

In a disturbing scene in Edwidge Danticat's *The Farming of Bones*, a priest who had been beaten and imprisoned for helping Haitians cross the border in order to save their lives during the 1937 massacre loses his mind and parrots the official propaganda of the 1930s Dominican Republic:

> "On this island, walk too far in either direction and people speak a different language," continued Father Romain with aimless determination. "Our motherland is Spain; theirs is darkest Africa, you understand? They once came here only to cut sugarcane, but now there are more of them than there will ever be cane to cut, you understand?"

He continues for some time this manner, going on to say, "we, as Dominicans, must have our separate traditions and our own ways of living. If not, in less than three generations, we will all be Haitians" (260–61).

Danticat's novel is a well-known and haunting imagining of the 1937 massacre, the bloody nadir of the thirty-one-year dictatorship of Rafael Trujillo in which an estimated twenty-five thousand people—Haitians, Black

Dominicans, and Dominicans of Haitian descent—were brutally murdered. This was part of Trujillo's attempt to "Dominicanize" a borderland area that had long been a zone of overlapping lives, lived across a fluid space. This act was the violent culmination of a particular anti-Haitian worldview and the product of a discourse whose shape was given form not only by politicians but also by some of the historians of the era.

Trujillo, like many dictators, was aware of the need to craft and refine his message and reinforce it with violence. To Trujillo, who wore makeup to make his mulatto features appear whiter, the "Africans" next door were an existential threat to the "Spanish" culture of the Dominican Republic. Such a manipulation was possible in part because of the long and entangled history of the two sides of Hispaniola and the complex way the relationship between Haiti and the Dominican Republic had been depicted, especially since Dominican independence in 1844. Trujillo, who was in power from 1930 until 1961, took a particularly active interest in the production of history. Under his regime, the Academia Dominicana de la Historia (Dominican Academy of History) was founded in 1931, as was the Archivo General de la Nación (National Archive) in 1935. Sympathetic historians often found themselves in roles of national prominence, not least Joaquín Balaguer, who was one of Trujillo's ministers and would go on to be his successor, and Manuel A. Peña Batlle, another ideologue rewarded with high office.

Among these historians was also the prolific Emilio Rodríguez Demorizi. The work that will be discussed in this essay, *Invasiones haitianas de 1801, 1805 y 1822*, was but one of more than 120 of books and numerous articles he produced over a long career.[1] Rodríguez Demorizi was born in Sánchez, Samaná, in 1906 and during his decades in public life, he also held a number of political posts. He was named president of the Academy of History in 1955—a role he kept until his death in 1986—and earlier had been appointed to diplomatic jobs, including ambassador to Nicaragua in 1952 and Costa Rica in 1953.

Out of his many works, it is his 1955 *Invasiones haitianas* that lodged most firmly in my mind. Like a large number of Rodríguez Demorizi's books, it is mostly a collection of documents and essays. My initial encounter with it was to consult some of the documents inside, as part of my master's research. Volumes such as these are, for the most part, an everyday resource for the historian of the Dominican Republic. Yet something about this book leapt out, not least the title: *Haitian Invasions*. At a time when I was taking my initial steps into Dominican history, it signaled to me that I was about to embark on a journey into a complex and charged historiography. One of the uncomfortable aspects of *Invasiones haitianas* was the fact of its dual role. It occupies a worrisome place, as both a historical artifact and source. This is not entirely unusual—there are plenty of document collections from times when ideas about race, class, or other aspects of society differ significantly from the present day. Yet such volumes have a special resonance in Hispaniola. As Michel-Rolph Trouillot has explained, there are four moments that silences can enter in the production of history: at fact creation (sources), at fact assembly (archives), at fact retrieval (narratives), and finally, the making of history with retrospective on the fact (26). Work such as that produced by Rodríguez Demorizi, during the Trujillo regime, is full of such silences and suppressions.

In thinking about the purpose of this volume—the representation of Haiti in Hispanic Caribbean cultural expression—works like those of Rodríguez Demorizi's must not be ignored. If anything, such books have underpinned a version of society to which other forms of cultural production have long been compelled to respond. For Andrés Mateo, the perniciousness of the Trujillo regime touched all aspects of cultural life: "La filosofía, la educación, la visón de la historia, la poesía, el arte, la novela, todo se transfirió al circuito del mito." This, to Mateo, allowed a "usando el pasado como ideología" (15).[2] Rodríguez Demorizi's work also represents a certain idea of Haiti as expressed through a generation of historical writing. Ernesto Sagás has noted that many of Rodríguez Demorizi's compilations "are still basic reference sources for the study of Dominican history and are even used by leftist and revisionist historians" (54). For that reason, Rodríguez Demorizi must, then, be used with caution. As Anne Eller has observed, reading his collections "requires a peeling back of two narrative layers that mystify, diminish, or deny individual or collective discourses generated in response to dominant voices" ("Race Records" 92).

In many ways many books from this period could have substituted for *Invasiones haitianas*; it is a synecdoche of the Trujillo era historiography. In that sense, it is also an artifact by its very nature. As Sibylle Fischer has observed: "Postcoloniality in the Dominican Republic is unlike postcoloniality anywhere else in Spanish America" (132). Given that this volume is examining the representation of Haiti through a number of outlets of cultural production—plays, short stories, poetry, speeches—it seems only fitting to include at least one remnant of Trujillo's historians.

After the death of Trujillo, a new generation of historians burst this historiographical bubble. Scholars such as Franklin Franco Pichardo, Raymundo González, Roberto Cassá, Emilio Cordero Michel, and Frank Moya Pons revisited all aspects of Dominican history, including nineteenth-century indigenism and the long-running discourse that Pedro San Miguel has called a "tragic narration," which presents the island's history as one of decades of decline, of which its unification with Haiti was also considered a part (9, 22). More recent and crucial interventions have pushed back against these ideas and also considered connection, not confrontation, with historians taking pains to point out that anti-Haitian discourses were not rooted among the general population; rather, they had been produced by elites.[3] This turn came as the Anglosphere scholarship of the Haitian Revolution was placing the Haitian Revolution in its rightful place in the history of the revolutionary Americas, and revising Haiti's role in wider Atlantic history.[4] Yet the idea of inter-island opposition did not simply disappear, nor did the racialized discourse that grew up alongside it. In more recent times, criticism has been directed at engaging with these older binaries, the "fatal-conflict model," as Samuel Martínez has described it (80).[5] This mode fails for many reasons, according to Martínez, not least because "few in Haiti, elite or working-class, perceive their country to be engaged in a struggle for supremacy with the Dominican Republic" (83). Indeed, Silvio Torres-Saillant has suggested the focus on Dominican "negrophobia" and its relation to Haiti causes historians to overlook "alternative narratives that would place Dominicans at the forefront of the struggle for Black liberation in the modern world" ("Blackness and Meaning" 181). Certainly, recent historiography has begun to move in new directions, away from the capital and its elites and to questions such as Dominican fear of reenslavement in the nineteenth century and people who supported Haitian unification.[6] However, there is no denying that under Trujillo, a discourse developed, and while historians have gone beyond it in terms of research, for sections of the public and the structures of power, such as the courts, it has not been completely left behind. As Pedro San Miguel has pointed out, in historiography "discourses on what is 'real' are joined to the practices of fiction in a hidden and surreptitious way," and it becomes "an attempt to transform particular, partial, limited, contingent, and biased knowledge into *the* truth" (32). This essay will use *Invasiones haitianas* as a way to connect the question of Haiti and the production of history—and the attempts to forge historical "truths"—during the dictatorship of Trujillo, with the wider implications of this particular intellectual legacy.

Sources and Silences

Invasiones haitianas sets out its stall straight away, with an epigraph by Rodríguez Demorizi claiming the creation of the Dominican Republic "fue, principalmente, la culminación de la heroica y persistente empresa defensiva de una cultura y de un espíritu, de la cultural y del espíritu hispánicos en el primer establecimiento español del Nuevo Mundo."[7] His purported aim is to tell the story of these three nineteenth-century periods of "invasion" "a través de sus desdichadas víctimas" (11).[8] He lists in the introduction a timeline of the "desmanes" (outrages) committed against the Spanish, starting with the arrival of French buccaneers on the Isle of Tortuga in 1630, taking it all the way up to the 1940s. For Rodríguez Demorizi, the history of Haiti starts in the seventeenth century, with the French, not with the arrival of Columbus, nor with the indigenous past: "Su historia comienza aquí hacia 1650, y su preshistoria hay que estudiarla en el Africa tenebrosa" (50).[9]

He spends some of the introduction on more contemporary times, discussing immigration and the "desafricanización" of the border. In the 1940s, the Dominican Republic had around 1.7 million people to Haiti's three million; by 1955 it was around two to four million. Rodríguez Demorizi describes the Haitian immigrants as "la peor especie"—the worst sort—because they were "casi desnudos, analfabetos, casi siempre famélicos y enfermos, tribus nómadas desprovistas de todo, oscuras caravanas que traían consigo la miseria, las supersticiones, la amoralidad, el voudou, la africanización . . ." (46).[10] At the same time Trujillo had been placing agricultural settlements in the west of the Dominican Republic, and by 1952 there were seventeen of these "colonies," with just under twenty thousand people living in them, thousands of them laborers brought over in a deal brokered with the Haitian government (Sagás 57–58). In the introduction, Rodríguez Demorizi touches on this through bringing up what he considers "la tradición de la amenaza haitiana" and invokes the 1937 massacre by claiming that "angustioso riesgo de perder los atributos que nos son más caros: nuestra libertad y nuestra fisonomía hispánica, hoy a salvo gracias a la magna empresa de dominicanización de las regiones fronterizas realizada por Trujillo" (9).[11]

The final and longest section of the introduction falls under the heading "Al margen de la obra del Dr. Price-Mars." In this part, Rodríguez Demorizi turns to the work of scholar Jean Price-Mars, who presented a Haitian perspective of the island's history in his 1953 book *La République d'Haïti et la République dominicaine*. With Blackness and the question of liberty central to his inquiry, Price-Mars's concerns and conclusions are quite distinct from his contemporaries in the Dominican Republic. Rodríguez Demorizi discusses what he calls a "libro amargo y triste" (48), and expresses his exasperation that Price-Mars does not unreservedly accept Dominican whiteness and that "somos descendientes de españoles; de que en nosotros predomina lo hispánico, la invencible hispanidad que nos ha salvado de la *haitianización*". (62).[12] This work attracted no small amount of criticism from the Dominican academy as well, with a number of prominent historians quick to attack all aspects of Price-Mars's scholarship, from his methodology to his interpretation of certain sources.[13] Despite this sixty-page introduction, Rodríguez Demorizi claims his vision of the *Invasiones haitianas* "es una simple compilación . . . de documentos, de observaciones e informaciones, que constituyen un necesario cuerpo de antecedentes—cuyo conocimiento es imperativo para las presentes generaciones—de la obra de dominicanización de las regions fronterizas . . ." (49).[14]

Moving into the main text, in the first section he turns to the unification of the island under Toussaint Louverture in 1801. At this juncture, the general was acting on behalf of France, seeking to bring the island together under French administration, knowing that Santo Domingo had been ceded to the French under the Treaty of Basle in 1795. Louverture managed to issue a constitution and attempted to make land reforms on the Spanish side of the island, before he was stripped of his role and imprisoned in France, where he died in 1803. There are a couple of Dominican eyewitness accounts in this section, and it is worth noting—though it is not entirely surprising—that most of the primary documents come from other collections, some from the nineteenth century, or from the Academy of History's journal *Clío*. Although not an uncommon historical practice, in this particular work it lends itself to a sense of a historiographical genealogy and institutional buttressing. The real source is not stated—instead another official history must be consulted.

Many of the selected primary texts are also from Dominicans who left the island and were writing from places such as Cuba. This, coupled with the fact of their literacy, implies that they were elites. Far harder to know—and this has long been a complaint from today's scholars—are the other, nonelite, voices at the time. Not only are the questions over what sorts of records they left, if any and in what form, but how likely their inclusion would have been.

Toward the back of the book, there is an essay by Alejandro Llenas, which first appeared in 1874, giving a narrative version of the arrival of Louverture in the capital, before foreshadowing "las crueldades de Dessalines y a las pérfidas vejaciones de Boyer" (188) still to come.[15] Indeed, the 1805 section on Jean-Jacques Dessalines's attempt at unification includes a copy of an 1804 "Proclama a los habitantes de la parte Español" from him. It may seem a straightforward document, but in a footnote Rodríguez Demorizi cannot resist adding that "esta es una falaz alocución del bárbaro invasor, cuyas depredaciones causaron tanta ruina, sangre y espanto en la parte española de la Isla" (97).[16]

Finally, although promising documents regarding 1822 in the title, there is little included in this volume. The events of 1822, which led to unification with Haiti for twenty-two years, was one of the most sensitive points for Dominican historians. At issue was whether Haiti was invited to unite the country, or whether it was invaded. Many Dominican historians, such as Rodríguez Demorizi, favored this latter view, while Price-Mars, for instance, considered the former, and so came under much criticism from his Dominican counterparts. Such was the extent of this question, as Quisqueya Lora Hugi has explained, that the Instituto e Investigaciones Históricos decided to discuss it at length—an event that even garnered press coverage. Its timing was auspicious, with much of the debate taking place in 1937, the same year as the killings. Indeed, Price-Mars contributed a paper to the debate, but could not attend. It was read aloud on October 2, only days before the massacre of Haitians would begin.[17]

In his book, Price-Mars had published documents illustrative of support for unification in 1821–1822; many were sources known to Dominican historians, but they now had a potentially wider audience. Rodríguez Demorizi, in responding to Price-Mars in *Invasiones haitianas*, does not address that particular issue. As Lora Hugi has noted, Rodríguez Demorizi "no mencionó los llamamientos a pesar de que esta eras una de las razones funadmentales de contradicción y debate" (104–08).[18] Within *Invasiones haitianas*, the only essay for that period is built around Guy-Joseph Bonnet's 1822 *Recuerdos históricos*; Bonnet, a Haitian general, advised Jean-Pierre Boyer that it would not be worth the effort to control both parts of the island, suggesting it was better to come together through agreement, rather than by force, saying: "Pero si es preciso obtener todas estas ventajas [de Santo Domingo] por la fuerza de las armas, aunque la empresa sea fácil y el éxito seguro, yo pienso que el resultado sería perjudicial y tal vez funesto a los verdaderos intereses y la seguridad futura de la República de Haití" (276).[19] In that way, the source neatly fits with the idea of Boyer as an invader who was not interested in the advice of his generals. The book then finishes with three documents relating to 1843, on the eve of Dominican independence, before finishing with a list of some of the acts of the Haitian government, "dictados por el despótico gobierno de Boyer" from 1822–1843 (305), and a list of key public officials in this period.[20]

Rodríguez Demorizi's response to Price-Mars ends up being delivered in a number of ways beyond the introduction of *Invasiones haitianas*, including the subsequent volumes *Antecedentes de la anexión a España* (1955), *Guerra*

Dominicano-Haitiana (1957), and *Santo Domingo y la Gran Colombia: Bolívar y Núñez de Cáceres* (1971), all of which examine this contentious period in more detail. As a work in itself, *Invasiones haitianas* moves in a jagged fashion over this rocky historical terrain; today, its holes are all too evident.

A Question of Whiteness

In addition to the Dominican historians taking issue with Price-Mars's interpretation on the level of documents and sources, it is worth considering the larger backdrop against which they were all working: the recent military occupations by the United States. Both sides of the island were caught up in the imperial machinations of the United States in the early twentieth century, with the US Marines stationed in the Dominican Republic from 1916 to 1924 and in Haiti from 1915 to 1934. Their responses, as reflected in the types of history produced in the aftermath, would be quite distinct. Price-Mars would lead the scholarly turn toward examining the African roots of Haitian society, while Dominican discourses focused on whiteness.[21]

Throughout the preceding century whiteness had been bound with ideas of progress, and those beliefs seeped into the twentieth century. As Matthew Guterl explains, the "racialized world economy rested upon a deep and fervent belief that economic, intellectual, technological, and cultural capital all resided in the West—and in 'white America' more particularly." In the case of Haiti, he notes that the occupation "was marked by a drive to improve its infrastructure" in part to "demonstrate the technological, cultural, and intellectual superiority of white Nordic America" (345). Such positivist imperial behavior was not limited to the western side of Hispaniola.

The US Marines' legacy in the Dominican Republic was also profound, resulting in the question of Blackness taking on existential dimensions in scope—after this nothing was more seemingly threatening to the progress of the nation than the Blackness of Haitians. They are portrayed in the Trujillo era as an impediment to the modernity and "civilization" of the Dominican Republic, which was striving to put on whiteface for the outside world. As April Mayes has observed, Trujillo saw firsthand during the US occupation that race mattered and "the closer the Dominicans were to whiteness, the more positively they would be received in the international arena" (112). The elites, therefore, doubled down on *hispanidad*. For Teresita Martínez-Vergne this claim of superiority allowed Trujillo "to more closely approximate Western notions of political order, economic organization, and social balance" (18). This also extended into cultural arenas and the wider body politic, and for Lauren Derby this means that "the era of Trujillo thus promised to make whiteness available to all Dominicans by incorporating them into the modern nation" (24).

However, this embrace of *hispanidad* was not entirely unprecedented. As Lorgia García-Peña has pointed out, the roots of this whiteness are much longer, with anti-Haitianism being a "colonial ideology that traverses Hispaniola's historical struggle with European colonialism and US imperial expansion" (10). Rodríguez Demorizi and his fellow historians ascribed "Blackness" to Haitians, and they attempted to place Haitians in a space outside of their shared history. At the same time this sort of historicizing also attempts to put the Dominican Republic outside of the larger West Indian historical processes, not merely those unleashed by the Haitian Revolution but also later ones, such as the rise of US power. Such a view underscored Rodríguez Demorizi's claim: "La lucha contra el haitiano fue lucha nacional: de todos contra el invasor. La lucha contra España fué propiamente una lucha civil y por tanto de más defícil término . . ." (24).[22]

Trujillo was assassinated in 1961, and while the dictatorship itself came to an end, the politics he had forged on the island continued in the form of the presidency of Joaquín Balaguer, who ended up holding the office a number of times (1960–1962, 1966–1978, 1986–1996). Trujillo's ideas lived on in the work of Balaguer, who was also a historian and had long served in various ministerial capacities in the dictator's regime. One of his best-known works is *La isla al revés: Haití y el destino dominicano*. First published in 1983, it has run into multiple editions, sitting at odds alongside the work produced by the successive waves of revisionist historians.

Balaguer's intentions are clear from the very outset, as he pits Jean-Jacques Dessalines against Dominican father of independence Juan Pablo Duarte in the epigraphs. Dessalines says, "No existiréis sino mientras mi clemencia se digne preservaros," while Duarte extols, " 'Nuestra patria ha de ser libre e independiente de toda potencia extranjera, o se hundirá la isla" (1).[23]

Balaguer does later admit that "sería infantil negar que una parte de la población de nuestro país es negro" (189).[24] However, the overall work is underscored by this civilized-barbarian dichotomy—putting Dominicans on the side of civilization—and references are peppered throughout. For instance, he describes modern Haitians as having "costumbres bárbaras" (barbaric customs) and "las unions incestuosas" (incestuous sexual unions) (40). Balaguer continues to insist on the supremacy of Hispanicness, arguing:

"Nuestro origen racial y nuestra tradición de pueblo hispánico, no nos deben impedir reconocer que la nacionalidad se halla en peligro de desintegrarse si no se emplean remedios drásticos contra la amenaza que se deriva para ella de la vecindad del pueblo haitiano" (45).[25] He also takes aim at Price-Mars, but before he doing so, he writes a *dedicatoria* to him, saying, "Por lo que representa su obra de investigador como un noble esfuerzo para situar, en un plano rigurosamente científico, los estudios históricos relacionados con Haití y la República Dominicana" (x). As with the epigraph, he also puts a corresponding dedication, this one to José Antonio Caro Álvarez, "primer director del museo del hombre dominicano, por cuanto hizo a su vez para definir y enaltecer los valores autóctonos de la raza dominicana" (x).[26]

The work of Balaguer kept the ideas of the Trujillo era alive for decades, and the issue of whiteness remains charged. David Howard's work on race and color found that many Dominicans try to disassociate with Blackness by using terms such as *indio* (Indian) to describe themselves. He also noted that this idea of whiteness corresponding to civilization remains alive in the present day, "a sentiment that is regularly expressed in everyday language, in the newspapers and in contemporary literature" (Howard 17).

Conclusion

While most historians have turned away from lines of inquiry found in the work of Rodríguez Demorizi or Balaguer, the imprint across public institutions remains. There exists today La Fundación Rodríguez Demorizi Inc., which is involved in historic preservation. And in 1986, the Instituto Tecnológico de Santo Domingo (Intec) named its library after Rodríguez Demorizi, claiming, "La versatilidad de su producción intelectual constituye una fehaciente prueba de su respeto por las diversas manifestaciones del arte y la cultura, como invaluables recursos para interpretar la historia y contextualizar las ideologías."[27] The contradictions of the present and past persist in uncomfortable proximity.

Such incongruities can be seen in more recent times, such as the 1994 elections in the Dominican Republic. The frontrunner was the opposition leader José Francisco Peña Gómez. He was a hugely popular dark-skinned politician who narrowly lost the race for the presidency to an aging Balaguer, who was aiming for a seventh term. There were claims of electoral fraud, as the final count led to a victory by only around twenty thousand votes for Balaguer. Worse than that, however, were the racial slurs made against Peña Gómez during the campaigning. Peña Gómez had been born in the Dominican Republic to Haitian parents who had abandoned him during the 1937 massacre and he was adopted by a Dominican family. During the campaign there was a slew of racist ads taken out against him, highlighting or caricaturing his Blackness. Though, as Samuel Martínez noted, few people reflected on the obvious fact that "a near majority of Dominican voters chose *el haitiano*" (a nickname given to Peña at the time) (88). Rumors also circulated that he planned to unite the two sides of the island again.[28] His adversaries attempted during this period to link him to Haiti and to try to prove he was not a real Dominican; in doing so, they continued to promote the idea of the savage, invading Haitian.

The perception of the Dominican Republic having problematic notions about race and Haiti have, in the past few years, attracted international attention. In 2013 there were controversial and heavily criticized moves by the island's government and court to deport any "undocumented" migrants through the overturning of long-standing legal citizenship norms. What the court decision meant was that any person born in the Dominican Republic between 1929 and 2007 to foreign, undocumented parents was no longer eligible for citizenship, with some people being stripped of their birth certificates because their parents were "in transit" as laborers, at once making hundreds of thousands of people undocumented and stateless. Deportations began of some of these "undocumented" people, while others went to Haiti as a preemptive measure, many finding themselves in a place where they did not know the language and had few remaining familial connections. The echoes of the events of 1937 were very clear to many, and there was an international outcry. Many Dominican and Haitians in the diaspora, including Danticat, spoke out against the measures. There has been some bowing to international pressure, and the government has put forward plans for pathways to residency in order to solve the crisis brought on by the court's decision, but tens of thousands of people remain in legal limbo. As Michel-Rolph Trouillot has astutely observed: "We are never as steeped in history as when we pretend not to be" (xix).

Power relies on its own narrative. Although historians have moved beyond the fatal-conflict model, it continues to serve in some quarters. Controlling the production of history and forging a racialized national mythology in the Trujillo era created a discourse underpinned by an institutional structure whose dismantling has been the work of historians for decades. Rodríguez Demorizi was, of course, not the only historian to take part in this ideological project. His work, and that of his contemporaries, cannot be summarily rejected. Instead, they leave vital and critical lessons about the production of history—both its power and its potential.

Notes

1. For a full list, see Inoa; and Eller, "Race Records."
2. All translations, unless noted otherwise, and errors are my own: "Philosophy, education, the vision of history, poetry, art, the novel, everything was transferred to the circuit of myth . . . using the past as an ideology."
3. For an overview of these historiographical changes, see Mayes's introduction. On the uses of indigenism, see Candelario.
4. On revolutionary Haiti, see for instance—among many others—Dubois; Geggus and Fiering; Buck-Morss; Garraway; and of course the earlier classic James.
5. For more, see Eller, "'Awful Pirates.'"
6. See, for instance, Eller, *We Dream Together*, or Nessler.
7. "was, principally, the culmination of the heroic and persistent defensive enterprise of a culture and spirit, of a Hispanic culture and spirit in the first Spanish establishment of the New World."
8. "through their ill-fated victims."
9. "Its history started here about 1650, and its prehistory one must study in dark Africa."
10. "almost naked, illiterate, almost always starving and ill, nomadic tribes devoid of everything, dark caravans that brought with them misery, superstitions, immorality, voodoo, Africanization . . ."
11. "the tradition of the Haitian threat . . . the anguished risk of losing the attributes that are the most dear to us: our liberty and our Hispanic physiognomy, today is out of danger thanks to the great enterprise of the Dominicanization of our of border regions carried out by Trujillo."
12. "bitter and sad book"; "we are descendants of Spaniards; that in us the Hispanic dominates, the invincible Hispanicness that has saved us from Haitianization."
13. For a discussion about the response to Price-Mars, see San Miguel 67–97; Sagás 55–57; and Lora Hugi.
14. "a simple compilation . . . of documents, of observations and information, that constitute a necessary body of antecedents—whose knowledge is imperative for the present generations—of the work of the Dominicanization of the border regions . . ."
15. "the cruelties of Dessalines and the perfidious vexations of Boyer . . ."
16. "this is a fallacious statement by the invading barbarian, whose depredations caused so much ruin, blood, and terror in the Spanish part of the island."

17. Lora Hugi 99–102.

18. "he did not mention the calls [for unification] even though this was one of the fundamental reasons for contradiction and debate. See Lora Hugi 137–45 for an examination of how post-Trujillo historians responded to this question.

19. "But if it is necessary to obtain all these advantages [of Santo Domingo] by force of arms, even if the enterprise is easy and the success is certain, I think that the result would be detrimental and perhaps fatal to the true interests and the future security of the Republic of Haiti."

20. "dictates by the despotic government of Boyer."

21. See San Miguel 68–69.

22. "The struggle against Haiti was a national struggle: everyone against the invader. The fight against Spain [in 1861] was properly a civil war and therefore more difficult to end . . ."

23. "You would not exist but for my clemency that deigns to preserve you"; "Our country must be free and independent of all foreign powers, or the island will sink."

24. "it would be childish to deny that a part of the population of our nation is Black."

25. "Our racial origin and our traditional Hispanicness, should not prevent us from recognizing the danger of disintegrating if drastic measures are not used against the threat stemming from the neighboring Haitian people."

26. "For what his work as a researcher represents as a noble effort to place, on a rigorously scientific level, the historical studies related to Haiti and the Dominican Republic"; "first director of the Museum of Dominican Man, for what he did in his time to define and enhance the autochthonous values of the Dominican race."

27. "The versatility of his intellectual production constitutes reliable proof of the diverse manifestations of art and culture, as invaluable resources for interpreting history and contextualizing ideologies." www.intec.edu.do/biblioteca/emilio-rodriguez-demorizi/.

28. See Martínez 87–89; Sagás 105–06.

Works Cited

Balaguer, Joaquín. *La isla al revés: Haití y el destino dominicano*. 6th ed. Fundación José Antonio Caro, 1990.

Buck-Morss, Susan. *Hegel, Haiti, and Universal History*. U of Pittsburgh P, 2009.

Candelario, Ginetta E. B. "La Ciguapa y El Ciguapeo : Dominican Myth, Metaphor, and Method." *Small Axe*, vol. 20, no. 51, 2016, pp. 100–12.

Danticat, Edwidge. *The Farming of the Bones*. Abacus, 2013.

Derby, Lauren. *The Dictator's Seduction: Politics and Popular Imagination in the Era of Trujillo*. Duke UP, 2009.

Dubois, Laurent. *Haiti: The Aftershocks of History*. Picador, 2013.
Eller, Anne. "'Awful Pirates' and 'Hordes of Jackals': Santo Domingo/The Dominican Republic in Nineteenth-Century Historiography." *Small Axe*, vol. 18, 2014, pp. 80–94.
———. "Race Records." *NACLA Report on the Americas*, vol. 49, 2017, pp. 90–94.
———. *We Dream Together: Dominican Independence, Haiti, and the Fight for Caribbean Freedom*. Duke UP, 2016.
Fischer, Sibylle. *Modernity Disavowed: Haiti and the Cultures of Slavery in the Age of Revolution*. Duke UP, 2004.
Fumagalli, Maria Cristina. *On the Edge: Writing the Border between Haiti and the Dominican Republic*. Liverpool UP, 2015.
García-Peña, Lorgia. *The Borders of Dominicanidad: Race, Nation, and the Archives of Contradiction*. Duke UP, 2016.
Garraway, Doris L., editor. *Tree of Liberty: Cultural Legacies of the Haitian Revolution in the Atlantic World*. U of Virginia P, 2008.
Geggus, David Patrick, and Norman Fiering, editors. *The World of the Haitian Revolution*. Indiana UP, 2009.
Guterl, Matthew Pratt. "The New Race Consciousness: Race, Nation, and Empire in American Culture, 1910–1925." *Journal of World History*, vol. 10, no. 2, 1999, pp. 307–52.
Howard, David John. *Coloring the Nation: Race and Ethnicity in the Dominican Republic*. Signal Books, Lynne Rienner, 2001.
Inoa, Orlando. *Bibliografía e Iconografía de Emilio Rodríguez Demorizi*. Letra grafica, Fundación Rodríguez Demorizi, 2003.
James, C. L. R. *The Black Jacobins: Toussaint L'Ouverture and the San Domingo Revolution*. 1938. Penguin, 2001.
Lora Hugi, Quisqueya. "¿Llamamientos o invasión? El debate en torno a los llamamientos de 1821 y 1822." *Clío*, vol. 85, no. 192, 2016, pp. 98–151.
Martínez, Samuel. "Not a Cockfight: Rethinking Haitian-Dominican Relations." *Latin American Perspectives*, vol. 30, no. 3, 2003, pp. 80–101.
Martínez-Vergne, Teresita. *Nation and Citizen in the Dominican Republic, 1880–1916*. U of North Carolina P, 2005.
Mateo, Andrés L. *Mito y Cultura en la era de Trujillo*. Librería la Trinitaria e Instituto del Libro, 1993.
Mayes, April J. *The Mulatto Republic: Class, Race, and Dominican National Identity*. UP of Florida, 2014.
Nessler, Graham T. *An Islandwide Struggle for Freedom: Revolution, Emancipation, and Reenslavement in Hispaniola, 1789–1809*. U of North Carolina P, 2016.
Price-Mars, Jean. *La République d'Haïti et la République dominicaine*. N.p., 1953.
Rodríguez Demorizi, Emilio. *Invasiones Haitianas de 1801, 1805 y 1822*. Editora del Caribe, 1955.

Sagás, Ernesto. *Race and Politics in the Dominican Republic.* UP of Florida, 2000.
San Miguel, Pedro L. *The Imagined Island: History, Identity, and Utopia in Hispaniola.* U of North Carolina P, 2005.
Torres-Saillant, Silvio. "Blackness and Meaning in Studying Hispaniola: A Review Essay." *Small Axe,* vol. 10, 2006, pp. 180–88.
———. "The Tribulations of Blackness: Stages in Dominican Racial Identity." *Race and National Identity in the Americas Latin American Perspectives,* vol. 25, no. 3, 1998, pp. 126–46.
Trouillot, Michel-Rolph. *Silencing the Past: Power and the Production of History.* Beacon Press, 1995.

4

Mucho Woulo

Black Freedom and *The Kingdom of This World*

NATALIE MARIE LÉGER

Eeeeeeeeeeee	
Gen lontan n'ap chèche	We've searched a long time
Yon kote pou n viv	A place for us to live
Yon kote pou nou tou ka viv anpè vre	A place where we can all truly live in peace
W'a ede m chante sa	Help me sing this song
Monkonpè mwen	My comrade
Ah woulo, woulo, woulo	Ah woulo, woulo, woulo
. . .	. . .
Monkonpè mwen	My comrade
W'a ede m chante sa	Help me sing this song
. . .	. . .
Mucho woulo	Mucho woulo
Frè mwen	My brother
Mucho woulo . . .	Mucho woulo . . .

—Boukan Ginen, "Ede m Chante"

Boukan Ginen's song "Ede m Chante (Help Me to Sing)" offers a poignant delineation of Black life in a world still resistant to Black freedom and, as such, affords a provocative means by which to bridge newly independent

Cuba to post-revolutionary Haiti.[1] Lead vocalist Eddy François's masterfully drawn out cry ("eeeeeeeeeee") opens the song, capturing the immense pain and frustration born from a generational pursuit of the elusive: a place to live *and* be at peace ("Gen lontan n'ap chèche / Yon kote pou n viv / Yon kote pou nou tou ka viv anpè vre"). The song's 1995 release date weds this pursuit to the nation's recent experience of unrest, "Twòp pwoblèm nan peyi mwen / Fè nou paka jwenn / Yon kote pou nou tou ka viv anpè vre."[2] The "twòp pwoblèm" specifically refers to the 1991 military coup that overthrew Jean Bertrand Aristide's first presidency and destabilized the nation. While this precise national experience has made life fundamentally unbearable ("Nou wè se tout bon lavi n menase vre"), the lived reality of a menaced existence is not particular to this moment alone.[3] The recurring phrase "mucho woulo"—many revolving turns—imbues the reality of a harassed existence with a temporal and spatial scope that extends well beyond the song's particular context.[4] The song's anchoring in a communal "we" ("*n'*ap, "*n* viv," and "*nou* tou") indicates this; as this "we" extends well into the past, drawing, on the one hand, from the deferred hopes and aspirations of the enslaved in Saint-Domingue who chose maroonage, revolution, or suicide (among other options) in their quest for a safe haven. This "we" concurrently draws, on the other hand, from their liberated descendants: contemporary Haitians whose poverty and Blackness have left them free to flee the continued injustice of a nation and larger world deeply committed to colonialism's continuation. The linguistic fusion of Spanish and Kreyòl in the recurring phrase "mucho woulo" intimates then the song's commitment to conveying a broader experience of unfreedom, where movement across linguistic geopolitical spaces offers no respite from a menaced existence.[5]

The persistent reality of a hemispheric harried Haitian existence becomes more pronounced when "Ede m Chante" is experienced through the cover offered by Grupo Vocal Desandann. Known in the US as the Creole Choir of Cuba, Desandann is a musical ensemble of Haitian-descended Cubans who reside in Cuba and sing in Kreyòl.[6] Desandann's riveting rendering of "Ede m Chante" is lyrically indistinguishable from Boukan Ginen's, however; the Spanish-inflected Kreyòl through which it is sung is nonetheless tonally distinctive. Cuba is heard even as Haiti and the particularities of the Haitian national experience are sung. The hearing of Cuba charges this song with an interesting ambiguity as when one hears "Twòp pwoblèm nan peyi mwen,"[7] one cannot help but to ask which "peyi," Cuba or Haiti? More than that, if Cuba was the place to which Haitians in the past migrated to in search of "Yon kote pou nou tou ka viv anpè vre,"[8] what does it say then that this longing for a place of peace remains despite having established oneself in Cuba and recognizing oneself as proudly Cuban *and* Haitian? The ambiguities of belonging and not belonging that are key to the song's affective poignancy are heightened when one begins to realize that the trajectory of movement uniting Haiti and Cuba in the covered rendering of "Ede m Chante" is rooted in a geopolitics of anti-anticolonialism.[9] This geopolitics has made it so that places of peace are few and far between for impoverished Haitians in particular, individuals whose lived existence attests to a global hostility toward successful anticolonial defiance and whose steady search for a place to be free abrogates the lie that is slavery and colonialism's definitive termination.

"Ede m Chante," in both its Haitian and Cuban iterations, is consequentially unwavering regarding one point: for the enslaved peoples who defiantly made themselves into liberated Haitians in 1804, and for their contemporary descendants, there has yet to exist a place to build and grow beyond anti-Black coloniality, that is to say, beyond colonial power and its racist influence in the present. Indeed, "mucho woulo" is intentionally interchanged with "moun chowoulo" in the song to lend historical veracity to this reality.[10] I preface this reading of Alejo Carpentier's efforts to think revolution, on the one hand, and to continue to be revolutionary, on the other, in his Haitian revolutionary novel, *The Kingdom of This World*, with this song because Carpentier's narrative underscores how radical Caribbean nations, like Cuba and Haiti, can remain in the hold of colonial enchainment despite successful revolutionary movements. Carpentier's 1949 novel was written well before the Cuban Revolution of 1959; it nonetheless anticipates the possibility of this happening via its concerted effort to tie the Haitian Revolution to colonial Cuba. In this regard, it is written with the real sense that anticolonial revolutions can happen in the most unlikely of places, like the wealthy slaveholding colony of Saint-Domingue and the modern pro-colonial Cuba of the twentieth century. That revolutions happened in both Cuba and Haiti has not safeguarded each nation from colonialism's ideological hold. Both efforts for independence were fought against a colonial order that racialized existence and yet both nations have equally acted to sustain this racialized order throughout their independent existences. Despite Cuba having abolished racism in 1959 and despite Haiti's political and symbolic existence as the place "where négritude stood up for the first time" (Césaire 47), inherited forms of colonial conduct remain influential to communal relations in postrevolutionary Cuban and Haitian society, giving anti-Blackness fertile ground.[11] Cuba and Haiti therefore serve as harbingers of a new decolonial order to come *and* as beacons of an old colonial order's impenetrable entrenchment. Why this is the case becomes clearer with attention to Carpentier's project and the obscured subject through whom it is actualized—the *cimarrón*, the first enslaved person to have experienced existence as *mucho woulo* post 1492. I understood *mucho woulo* as an enduring form of marronage that is predicated on the flight away from the trials and tribulations of the unfreedom sanctioned by slavery, colonialism, and their respective afterlives in the present; *mucho woulo* is equally predicated on the determined flight toward total freedom undertaken by the most debased subjects of slavery, colonialism, and coloniality: enslaved and liberated Blacks and natives.[12] The phrase *mucho woulo* is used then as a conceptual means through which to name Carpentier's attempt to read Cuban prerevolutionary independence with attention to the Haitian experience of itinerant unfreedom.

I read Carpentier's efforts to write the Haitian Revolution from below (that is, with a focus on unnoted revolutionaries) as a direct consequence of reading the revolution with attention to Haitian migration to Cuba in both the revolutionary period and in his own moment. The continuous presence of Haitians in Cuba, as marginalized laborers subjected to legislative and social discrimination, coupled with the reality of a Haitian state unable to support a substantial portion of its population, as key to understanding Carpentier's ambivalent treatment of the Haitian Revolution as failed (at worst) or ongoing (at best). I argue that this ambivalence occurs because the Haitians residing in Cuba as he writes *The Kingdom of This World* are as marginalized and disenfranchised as the Haitian revolutionary subjects that most interest Carpentier in the novel, namely, unknown revolutionaries. Indeed, each indicts the colonial system—in its slaveholding and its anti-Black postcolonial variations—*and* the anticolonialism that gave rise to the nations founded by revolutionary leadership (be it Haitian or Cuban). Carpentier's reading of the Haitian Revolution necessitates then careful engagement with one crucial question: Where is there a place and space for the small-time Haitian revolutionary and his or her descendant who finds herself or himself ever on the move for safer pastures? I read Carpentier's unnoted Haitian revolutionary subjects as *cimarrones* because there has yet to exist a place where displaced Haitians can concretize their ancestors' revolutionary endeavors and build a life beyond the colony and the legacy of anti-Black slavery that built it. I conclude this piece with attention to contemporary Haitian-descended Cubans, who self-designate in 2015 as *cimarrones*, to firmly underscore how the migratory flows of *mucho woulo* connecting Haiti and Cuba in Carpentier's project reveal more than the ongoing abjection of Haitians and Haitian-descended peoples. More significantly, they draw attention to an enduring cimarronian effort to strive otherwise: that is, to envision and enact an existence beyond the inherited colonial order of life as it is in postrevolutionary Cuba, postrevolutionary Haiti, and in the Americas, on the whole.

Blackness and the Marvelous Real

Cuba had experienced forty-seven years of independence and 457 years of colonial subjugation when Carpentier published *The Kingdom of This World* in 1949. This prolonged experience of colonial subjection did not end with independence from Spain in 1902. Immediately after securing independence, Cuba became the neocolonial subject of the United States.[13] The colonial order flourished in independent Cuba, and it did so not simply because Cuba was nominally self-governing but because Carpentier's Cuba was rabidly anti-Black. Roberto González Echevarría writes that "when Carpentier began to write [in the 1920s] . . . intellectuals were preoccupied with [the nation's political status, the European avant-garde, and the Afro-Cuban movement, three issues that had] at least one common denominator: the problem of assimilating a large and impoverished Black population, the backbone of the labor in sugar industry, into the mainstream of political, social, and cultural life" (42). Black Cubans were a "problem" population for Cuba's white and white-identifying governing elite because they were Black *and* other. The virulent anti-Black racism that constrained their economic, political, and social prospects, from the colonial period to independence, created the context where a distinct West African cultural identity could be maintained (43). This identity threatened the modern, US-approximate, republic that elite Cubans strove to create as it too closely associated the entire nation with Blackness;[14] US intervention, however, had already cemented this association with Blackness. The racial anxiety that gripped Cuba concerning its Black populace at the start of Carpentier's literary career is not simply an outcome of the nation's slaveholding past, but it attests to how very much the governing elite class desperately tried to retain a cultural whiteness that the US called into question. The overwhelming concern with "assimilating a large and impoverished Black population" (Echevarría 42) cannot be divested from the realization that Cuba was being treated, on the whole, as if each and every person were Black and thus fit for tyrannical oversight. Carpentier began writing in the 1920s when assimilating Blacks was a key concern because of Cuba's neocolonial condition, and he composed *The Kingdom of This World* in the 1940s when conformity prevailed over assimilation and foreign Black immigrants were eagerly cast off because they did not fit the Cuba the ruling bourgeoisie had in mind.

From 1898 until 1933 "two hundred thousand to as many as six hundred thousand" Haitian laborers (Hume 42) had migrated to Cuba to supply US sugar companies with cheap labor (Hume 42; Serviat 80).[15] Of the Haitian migrants that chose to remain in Cuba, "approximately thirty-eight thousand" were deported in a repatriation process that began in 1933 and ended in 1939 (Hume 42). The deportation occurred in part because influential members of the Cuban elite "fear[ed] . . . a 'disproportionate' increase in the Black population" would forestall Cuban modernization (Serviat 80). Yanique Hume writes, "even with the rise of the revolutionary government, the Haitian cane-cutter remained synonymous with an image of the savage slave past, . . . thwarting Cuba's vision of a modern republic" (42). Haitian migrants, like Black Cubans, were an othered, marginalized population because they also possessed a distinct cultural identity that was regarded as "primitive" in orientation and innately rebellious because of its revolutionary history.[16] The number of Haitian migrants would add to an already culturally distinct Black population and was imagined as sufficient to further regress a purportedly backward demographic toward barbarity and worse yet radicalize them against whites. The addition of Haitian migrants to the natal Black population accordingly rekindled white Cuban fear of "Black rebellion similar to that of 1912 in Cuba and 1790 in Haiti," instances in which Blacks rose to counter white supremacy (Serviat 80).[17] The increasing angst concerning Black peoples in neocolonial Cuba emphasizes the way in which the nation's colonial condition was intricately bound to the relative absence of Black autonomy in the nation and in colonial as well as postcolonial spaces in Carpentier's moment. Haitian migrants were marginalized in Cuba because they were Black within a nation-state clinging to a self-determination it could only exercise through anti-Blackness. Furthermore, Haitians were subjugated because they were symbolically representative of Black power and Black defiance, which threatened both the US imperial project and the Cuban nationalist project, as the latter not only agreed to neocolonial subjugation under the United States but did so to revive a sugar industry predicated on Black exploitation.[18] The space to be Black and free did not exist in Cuba, nor did it exist in Haiti for impoverished Haitians who migrated for a more secure existence. Carpentier's decision to narrativize the Haitian Revolution in this particular time period strongly suggests a willingness to critically grapple with coloniality and race so as to assess how Black freedom could prove to be so elusive notwithstanding revolutionary action and success. The precarious lived existence of Haitian migrants in Cuba serves as the necessary context to recognize Carpentier's project as foregrounding how the colonial order's deep commitment to racialization gave rise to and sustained coloniality in independent Caribbean and Latin American nation-states, effectively undermining efforts to imagine and achieve beyond the world created by colonialism and slavery.

The Kingdom of This World is composed with this latter effort in mind since the narrative champions the effort put forth by enslaved and free Black Saint-Dominguans to exist otherwise and, as such, it is largely faithful to Haiti's revolutionary history. The novel narrates the day-to-day exploits of a nondescript enslaved creole (Ti-Noël) and his lascivious French enslaver (M. Lenormand de Mézy). It begins in the mid-1700s, before the maroon, rebel, and oungan (Vodou priest) François Macandal's siege of poison, his death, and simultaneous resurrection in 1758. Macandal's rebellion is treated at length in the novel and sets the stage for Carpentier's portrayal of the Haitian Revolution, which is largely rendered through the Vodou ceremony at Bois Kaïyman that provided the logistical groundwork for the 1791 revolution. The novel ends in the early 1800s with the fall of King Henri Christophe's reign and the unification of Haiti under President Jean Pierre Boyer. Although *The Kingdom of This World* is framed by revolts that precede and follow the Haitian Revolution (Macandal's rebellion and the uprising against King Christophe, respectively), the 1791–1804 revolution is its principle subject. Carpentier's recounting of this historic mass insurgency is largely divested of the famed leaders through which the revolution is often told; Toussaint Louverture, Jean-Jacques Dessalines, André Rigaud, and Alexandre Pétion are dealt with minimally, if at all. Carpentier does provide extensive attention to the former revolutionary general turned king, Christophe. Christophe's heroic revolutionary personage is not of significance; his reign and the cycle of tyranny it unleashed are, however. With the intent to write the revolution exclusive of its most heralded figures, the novel is centered on Ti-Noël, through whom Carpentier presents the enslaved's experience of revolutionary events.

Notwithstanding the historicist care with which Carpentier attends to this experience, the prologue framing the narrative strongly suggests that the intricacies of Haiti's revolutionary history are immaterial to Carpentier's project of writing the revolution from the unlauded enslaved revolutionary's social positioning. The 1949 prologue delineates Carpentier's theory of "the marvelous real" (*lo real maravilloso*), which intimates that comprehensive knowledge of Haiti's revolutionary history is consequential if only for this history's inspirational salience: in effect, if only for what it can inspire in decolonial thought and being for Caribbean and Latin American peoples.[19] The theory is a faith-based expression of lived wonder and unprecedented potentiality principally concerned with hemispheric American existence. Specifically, it is an anticolonial articulation of a real and, at times, historically verifiable Caribbean and Latin American occurrence that appears so fantastic and inconceivable by Western ontological standards for existence that it defies reason and, as such, is perceivable only because of a culturally derived spiritual conviction. Haiti's long revolutionary history is key to Carpentier's formulation of the marvelous since it provides the dissident (anti-anti-Black) source material through which to note and understand it; indeed, the theory was occasioned by Carpentier's 1943 visit to Haiti.

When Carpentier details this visit in the prologue, he deliberately highlights this dissidence with his description of Haiti's famed La Citadelle Laferrière, a fortress that he professes is "without architectonic antecedents [and] portended only in Piranesi's *Imaginary Prisons*" (30; "On the Marvelous Real in America" 87); that is to say, it is conceivable only through the imaginative unreality of Western Europe's fantastical arts, be they unusual engravings or surrealist fiction.[20] In this respect, the Citadel underscored how Caribbean and Latin American realities were ripe with wondrous actualities that Western European artists and thinkers could only realize as real via fictive art. The specific uniqueness of the Americas becomes readily identifiable with attention to the Citadel (for instance) because it exists wholly in the real; more than that, it is grounded in the history and culture of a new kind of people (Haitians), who have forged their own distinct cultural realities. Therein lies the political impetus of Carpentier's artistic theory, the defiant power of one's own modalities for being. Accordingly, the turn to Haiti's most potent cultural realism (Vodou) in the prologue establishes how distinct cultural invention promotes politically effective alternative realities: "I tread[ed] earth where thousands of men eager for liberty believed in Macandal's lycanthropic powers, to the point that their collective faith produced a miracle the day of his execution" ("Prologue" 30). With this remark, Carpentier reveals that Haiti's revolutionary success has as much to do with the military genius of its famed creole generals as it does with the inspired genius that existed among the enslaved; it was the latter's self-fashioned ontology that steadfastly engendered a "collective faith" in rebellion no matter the violent reprisals (e.g., Macandal's execution).

The Citadel's physical existence, and the story of resistance that necessitated its advent (the revolution), and which precipitated its incompletion (rebellion against King Christophe), is a testament then to how this conviction in self-determined resistance would embolden the enslaved of Saint-Domingue (and their descendants) to continually strive for an existence beyond hierarchical tyranny, whether in the colony or the postcolonial state; accordingly, should hemispheric Americans recognize their region and particular homeland's own novel cultural realities as valuable, they too can engender the same kind of conviction and revolutionary strivings that inspired the enslaved in Saint-Domingue. In Carpentier's estimation, the collective inability to ascribe value to one's own culture is profoundly telling of the controlling and corrosive influence of white colonial domination, which makes it so that all thinking and all imagining must conform to the epistemological and ontological standards of the West. If, however, Western Europeans were ill equipped to imagine a structure like the Citadel because their own cultural realities normalized the racial enslavement that the Citadel was built to stand against, then, for Carpentier, their modes of thought in art and politics would be equally unable to contend with a hemisphere whose entire topography and peoples were shaped by enslavement and resistance to enslavement.[21] The marvelous as a theoretical construct is purposely anticolonial in orientation precisely because it is intended to inculcate within Caribbean and Latin American thinkers, artists, and laymen a firm sense of cultural self-worth and distinction from Western Europe. With a clear sense of cultural exception they, as Haitians before them, can resist the world as is (as it has been rendered by Western Europeans) and strive to depict it as they experience it. They can resolve then to imagine otherwise and, in so doing, work like Haitians, to pursue a new existence committed to realizing the anticolonial aims and decolonial needs of their respective homelands.

Imagining otherwise, however, requires more than a conviction in one's cultural worth; it necessitates reckoning with one's racial categorization. To that end, if Haiti provides the dissident source material to express the marvelous because of its revolution, it further denotes the marvelous because of its racial classification as a Black nation. Indeed, the vision needed to engage the Americas marvelously hedges on one key point of signification—Blackness. Black peoples, Black cultural innovation, and Black resistance are the points through which Carpentier denotes the singularity of the region in the prologue. In addition to a Haitian revolutionary edifice (the Citadel) and a prerevolutionary rebellion (Macandal's campaign), the prologue situates the region's cultural distinction in novel domestic cultural practices derived from Africans and African descended peoples; these practices include the "drums of the Petro and the Rada" from Haitian Vodou, "the dances of Cuban Santeria," and "the prodigious African version of the Corpus festival" found in "San Francisco de Yare, Venezuela" ("On the Marvelous Real" 83, 87).[22] The move to positively distinguish Black cultural invention strongly suggests that the demand to own and laud cultural distinction cannot be dissociated from why this distinction remains unnoted to begin with: namely, the ingrained regional bias against Black peoples and Black cultural production. The marvelous real is an anticolonial theory of cultural modalities that tacitly calls for serious engagement with race and, to that end, with Black peoples. In this respect, *The Kingdom of This World* is not simply a narrative concerned with the Haitian Revolution but, because of the theoretical intentions of its prologue, it is a story concerned with the maligned people whose collective genius made the revolution. It is written from below precisely to address an enduring anti-Black colonial order that continually tries and fails to diminish Black efforts to strive for another kind of existence. As such, a key concern of Carpentier's Haitian revolutionary project is to interrogate the price of Black freedom within a larger world for which this pairing (Blackness and freedom) has yet to exist in secure relation. Furthermore, the project attempts this interrogation by presenting the Haitian Revolution as an ontological conflict carried out in Saint-Domingue and wherever the effort is made to imagine otherwise.

Santiago de Cuba, I

> Santiago, I am the son of war:
> Santiago,
> Can't you see I am the son of war?

Santiago de Cuba is one such place and serves as the only Cuban setting in *The Kingdom of This World*. Ti-Noël chants the above prayer to the *lwa* (Vodou spirit) Ogoun Faï while in Santiago at the end of a chapter titled for the Cuban city. He is still enslaved in the chapter and made to routinely accompany an aged M. Lenormand de Mézy to a Catholic Cathedral in

Santiago following their departure from Le Cap. While de Mézy beseeches God for Christian salvation and admission into the kingdom of heaven, Ti-Noël turns to his own belief system to secure fortitude for the liberation struggle happening now in the kingdom of this world. This struggle, however, is not the chapter's outward focus; de Mézy's émigré experience ostensibly is. The chapter therefore centers the white flight from Saint-Domingue to colonial Cuba that occurred throughout the Haitian revolutionary moment and minimizes the accompanying (compelled and voluntary) movement of black peoples. This latter movement is far more consequential because it gave rise to the black majority (white identified) nation that Cuba was in Carpentier's moment and that Cuba remains today. The Haitian Revolution hastened this demographic change because it occasioned Cuba's sugar revolution (Ferrer 10, 17). The collapse of Saint-Domingue's sugar industry gave Cuban creoles the opportunity to "emulate the magnificent wealth and power of the Saint-Domingue planter class" (Ferrer 4). Ada Ferrer writes that ambitious Cuban creoles "ramped up [sugar] production, purchasing more and more land and mills and enslaved laborers to fill the world demand for sugar" that Saint-Domingue previously satiated (17). As a result of this fervent activity, a "society with slaves [became in a short span] a slave society" (17). The city of Santiago de Cuba, and much of eastern Cuba where sugar and coffee cultivation dominated industry, was soon governed by the political and economic desires of Cuba's planter class and, consequentially, was increasingly peopled with enslaved black laborers.[23] Émigrés, like de Mézy, who chose this city as their port of entry did so because it was the closest to Saint-Domingue; while Cuban planters remained apprehensive of their steady arrival, fearing the free and enslaved blacks who disembarked with them, the revolution did not arrive. Ferrer writes, "curiously, the place closest to Haiti, with the largest concentration of French people of color, slave and free, appears to have produced no slave conspiracy or rebellion, even though it, too, was witnessing a boom in slavery as a result of the Haitian Revolution" (224). Still, even as Cuban planters, colonial officials, and enterprising white émigrés managed "to contain Haiti" as they replicated Saint-Domingue (Ferrer 38), Ti-Noël's prayer suggests that a revolution was produced, one that Carpentier believed the city could not bring itself to see: recall Ti-Noël's prayer, "Santiago, / Can't you see I am the son of war?" (*The Kingdom* 87).

Ti-Noël's direct address to the city of Santiago intimates that this new metropolis is like the city of Le Cap he has left: it cannot see the men and women whose work toward a new life calls the city's existence into question. The prayer's positioning at the end of a chapter focused exclusively on de Mézy's émigré experience in Santiago reveals how Carpentier viewed the Haitian Revolution as uncontainable even with Cuban colonial efforts, as the chapter's last word is unyielding black resistance. This defiant final word points both to the black resistance that innately existed in Cuba among the enslaved population due to the colony's ever increasing commitment to slavery and plantation industry; it equally establishes how black Saint-Dominguan *and* black Cuban participation in the Haitian revolutionary struggle required little more than the attempt to think toward freedom. For Carpentier, a break with colonial ontology had to happen for the revolution to occur and it had to continue for the revolution to spread to Cuba. Ti-Noël's prayer serves the purpose of showing how this break was thought into existence; originally, "an old song that [Ti-Noël] learned from Macandal" (*The Kingdom* 87), the chant is offered as a prayer because the Cathedral's "Voodoo warmth" (86) led Ti-Noël to reason, "St. James is Ogoun Faï," the *lwa* "under whose spell Bouckman's followers had risen" (87). A delegate at the famed Bois Kaïyman assembly that laid the strategic ground for the revolution's opening sieges (65–69), Ti-Noël is an early member of Bouckman Dutty's army.[24] Ti-Noël participates in the attack on de Mézy's plantation when the rebellion commences (74) and is forcibly removed from the struggle once captured by colonial authorities; he is sentenced to death soon after and subsequently "saved" by de Mézy for reenslavement in Cuba (77). He remains a devout "follower" of Bouckman without ever inciting an antislavery rebellion or conspiracy while enslaved in Santiago because he consciously chooses to envision otherwise. He reasons that "St. James is Ogoun Faï" and attempts to conceive beyond the pale of an antiblack colonial world in which his captivity is normalized through Judeo-Christian teachings. Accordingly, if the Catholic saint, "St. James," is too complicit with a colonial order deeply committed to slavery and white supremacy, then the estimation that "St. James is Ogoun Faï" divests the saint from this collusion; it repurposes him as an Afro-Saint-Dominguan deity who can readily see (and help embolden others to see) that a colonial order, predicated on black enchainment, is unjust and should be resisted. In this respect, "St. James is Ogoun Faï" is an affirmation of a way of being fundamentally opposed to the Eurocentric and white supremacist worldview that bore chattel slavery and made antiblackness an acceptable norm within the Americas. Carpentier's decision to depict Ti-Noël's conscious alteration of Christian iconography with Vodou cosmology demonstrates a concerted effort to read *and* represent Haitian revolutionary resistance as momentous precisely because ordinary people thought and acted their liberation into existence. Their epistemological practices—their myths and spiritual beliefs—made the possibility of a new kind of existence real; they were, in other words, conceptually marvelous, providing the cognitive ground for the armed component of the revolutionary war.

As an ontological struggle, Carpentier's Haitian Revolution is fought with the mind and body. The dissident West African folktales that open the novel, the mythic heroics of Macandal that follow, and the Vodouian spirituality that runs throughout the narrative emblematize how Carpentier read common enslaved Saint-Dominguans as nurturing cultural practices that generated and sustained an ontological break with a mode for existence that upheld and promoted their subjugation. De Mézy's journey to Santiago is consequently prefaced with a telltale reminder of the ideological divide between the enslaved and planters that would continue in Cuba. Prior to his departure, de Mézy learns from the governor that the enslaved "had a secret religion that upheld them in their revolts" (*The Kingdom* 78–79); upon hearing this he asks, "But could a civilized person have been expected to concern himself with the savage beliefs of people who worshipped a snake" (79)? This question mirrors a rhetorical query offered by the enslaved years prior during Macandal's public execution. They ask, "What did whites know of Negro matters?" (50), in reaction to the colonists' close scrutiny of their unmoved response to Macandal's death. The stylistic similarity of both questions lends clarity to Carpentier's efforts to present the enslaved as immensely cognizant of the cultural vanity and intellectual imprudence needed to self-identify as civilized and as white. The enslaved in *The Kingdom of This World* recognized that their enslavers had a distinct epistemology that read every aspect of their humanity as "savage" so as to sustain the world their greed and conceit created. Their resistance required thinking beyond the world, as is, an intellectual effort evident in Ti-Noël's prayer. Movement from one colonial space of slavery to another cannot then mean that this ontological break ceased to exist because armed conflict was absent. A revolution in thought had occurred and it would, for Carpentier, be preserved even in the increasingly brutal plantation colony of Cuba.

Santiago de Cuba, II

This silent revolution, however, does not change conditions for the enslaved in Cuba, nor does the success of the Haitian Revolution appear to have substantively change the lived existence of the formerly enslaved in Haiti. Carpentier's postrevolutionary Haiti is a space where colonial rule survives in blackface. The chapters in parts 3 and 4 of the novel depict the newly emancipated as nominally free. King Henri Christophe's reintroduction of forced labor to construct the Citadel and palace Sans Souci is accordingly treated at length (*The Kingdom* 119–25). The institution of obligatory farming that follows the collapse of Christophe's northern kingdom and that prompts the country's reunification into a republic is noted as well (176).[25] The entire postrevolutionary Haitian experience is reduced to an "endless return of chains, [a] rebirth of shackles, [and] proliferation of suffering" (178). This reduction has provoked criticism of Carpentier's work, causing Philip Kaisary to argue that Carpentier's pessimistic portrayal of the revolution's hereafter "undermines the unprecedented historic actuality of the transformational actions taken by enslaved blacks in Saint Domingue" (175). Carpentier merits the criticism he has received as his presentation of postrevolutionary Haiti fits too cleanly within white supremacist narratives of black incompetence in governance, a racist fabrication that has always been deployed against Haiti, however. He does not write *The Kingdom of This World* to "undermine[]" the Haitian Revolution: he writes this novel to understand how a revolution that inspired a radical transformation in thought and that engendered a free black space because it facilitated the decolonization of the mind could prove unable to sustain freedom for all its people. Carpentier's gauche rendering of free Haiti must be read with attention to the stateless Haitian migrants suffering in Cuba as he composes *The Kingdom of This World*. His trips to Santiago de Cuba during the novel's composition likely occasioned visual contact with Haitians and Haitian-descended Cubans; Santiago was (and remains) a city with a large Haitian population due to its location in eastern Cuba where modern Haitian migration replicated the past migratory movement of Saint-Domingue's planter class, free blacks, and enslaved subjects in the revolutionary moment.[26] It is worth stressing that Haitian immigrants resided in Cuba as a marginalized population not only because Carpentier's Cuba clung to antiblackness to preserve a semblance of autonomy denied by US intervention; but just as Cuba's revolutionary party in 1898 produced a state-building project that remained faithful to the colonial order with its racist labor practices (practices that bore Haitian repatriation in the 1930s), in Carpentier's estimation, newly independent Haiti remained just as devout to the colonial order because of its own exclusionary labor policies. The extensive consideration afforded Christophe's kingdom in the novel is intended to exemplify this; the kingdom's black "white-hosed ministers," black "footmen," and a black "Immaculate Conception" (115) attest to the realm's free political status (115). Yet the realm is also black and subsisting through a state-sanctioned campaign of forced labor, with "many people . . . working . . . fields under the vigilance of soldiers carrying whips" (113). Christophe's court and the republican government that followed were the product of an antislavery and anticolonial nationalism (or, with respect to Christophe, monarchism), which recognized that the plantocracy's colonial order was oppressive and inherently racist. This realization did not prevent the implantation of structurally racist institutions (like corvée labor), which encouraged the resedimentation of racist practices in politics and everyday existence. Carpentier's grim portrayal of postrevolutionary Haiti is directly tied to what he saw in the Haitian presence in Cuba, which was not the failure of the Haitian Revolution but its negation by prominent political figures who fought in the revolution.

When Ti-Noël returns to Haiti as an elderly, slightly senile, freeman, he survives a tenure as Christophe's forced laborer and witnesses, years later, the rise of "Republican mulattoes" (*The Kingdom* 176) to which he offers the following reflection: "Macandal had not foreseen this matter of forced labor. Nor had Bouckman, the Jamaican. The ascendancy of the mulattoes was something new that had not occurred to José Antonio Aponte . . . whose record of rebellion Ti-Noël had learned of during his slave days in Cuba" (176–77). Of the three figures of resistance Ti-Noël references, only Bouckman fought in the Haitian Revolution and he did so only for a brief duration, as he was killed a few months into the initial uprising in 1791. Macandal's rebellion preceded the Haitian Revolution by thirty-nine years and Aponte's rebellion took place in Cuba in 1812, eight years after the revolution.[27] That Macandal, Bouckman, and Aponte are associable, in Ti-Noël's opinion, with the revolution is directly tied to Carpentier's effort to divorce the revolution from its famous creole (island born) vanguard. Toussaint Louverture, Jean-Jacques Dessalines, and Alexandre Pétion (among other creole generals) are accordingly absent from the novel save for the tyrannical Christophe. Carpentier's Christophe is emblematic of a pattern of creole revolutionary leadership that remains the same in postrevolutionary Haiti whether it serves monarchial rule or republican. This leadership fails to create a new, fundamentally free, existence for all of Haiti's citizens because it refuses to draw from the inspired genius of the people who served in the revolution's armies and chooses instead to pursue the cultural vanity of those who enslaved humans for profit.[28] A failure of vision in the eighteenth century helped sow the seeds then of nineteenth- and twentieth-century Haitian displacement, as the state was set against the nation, creating a fissure that would be fully exploited by imperial powers in the years to come.[29] Inasmuch as Haiti can be deemed a "weak" state, this weakness is prompted, in Carpentier's view, by the very same desire to continue to exploit black labor that cemented Cuba's neocolonial standing and made a farce of Cuban independence in his moment. The fissure between Haiti's governing class and its people that compromised the revolution lies at the heart of *The Kingdom of This World*'s most pressing query: namely, where is there a space to freely exist within a state still beholden to colonial rule for the unnoted, small-time, Haitian revolutionary subject turned indentured peasant, who is without the standing to remain free in postrevolutionary Haiti as all whites were free in Saint-Domingue? More urgently: if not in Haiti, where then is there a space to be black, ordinary, and free?

A space to be black, ordinary, and free does not exist in Carpentier's narrative; in fact, Ti-Noël dies championing the struggle to continue fighting for just such a space. He realizes:

> [Man] suffers and hopes and toils for people he will never know, and who, in turn, will suffer and hope and toil for others who will not be happy either, for man always seeks happiness far beyond that which is meted out to him. But man's greatness consists in the very fact of wanting to be better than he is. (*The Kingdom* 184–85)

This broad sentiment could relate to any human struggle, but Ti-Noël knows one struggle intimately well: antiblack servitude and postcolonial black indentureship. His reflection can be taken out of this context, but doing so facilitates facile consideration of how this sentiment pivots on the relative absence of a space to be black, ordinary, and free within Carpentier's moment in Haiti and Cuba.[30] The novel's Cuban chapter, "Santiago de Cuba," is instructive in this regard as Carpentier's decision to displace Ti-Noël, a revolutionary combatant, from an ongoing struggle to hostile (proslavery) territory strongly suggests that the novel's implicit interest in black freedom is tied to a lived reality common to Saint-Domingue, colonial Cuba, postrevolutionary Haiti, and Carpentier's "independent" Cuba. Indeed, the disregard for black revolutionary action and the decision to focus instead on Ti-Noël's captivity in Cuba suggests that the narrative's core interest concerns the continued negation of black freedom across space and in related but distinct places. This negation occurs because the attempt to achieve another kind of existence in the here and now that Carpentier reads into the Haitian Revolution could only subsist liminally, at the threshold of the world as is and of the world to come.

This world to come is present throughout the narrative and associated with resistance figures like "Macandal . . . Bouckman . . . [and] Aponte" (*The Kingdom* 176–77), who are linked together in Ti-Noël's aforementioned reflection on slavery's return to his homeland under republican leadership. Unlike the creole generals who became postrevolutionary leaders, these resistance leaders are figures of antislavery and anticolonial resistance who can denote a free decolonized existence that does not depend on Western European models. They are not associated with Western European culture or ideology in the narrative and, in this respect, could not "foresee" the continuation of "forced labor," a lasting characteristic of the West and Western-identifying enclaves (176–77). The maroon Macandal, in particular, is the figure of the Haitian Revolution in the novel because his resistance melded cerebral and corporeal modes of resistant violence that lent credence to the enslaved's ontological perspective.[31] In death, Macandal became "a transcendent register to slavery [in the novel], forever reappearing throughout space and time like a specter, heralding freedom to come" (Roberts 101). He returned to aid in the Haitian revolutionary struggle as the "buzzing mosquito" the enslaved at his execution believed he would metamorphose into when defying death (*The Kingdom* 51) and reappears later in the narrative as the "buzzing" "killjoy" that infected Napoleon's army with yellow fever (96). The privileged transcendence of space and place that is granted to Macandal alone in the novel purposely reorients the revolution from the creole leader to place the marooning rebel at the helm so as to draw attention to the overshadowed individuals in the revolutionary struggle who never sought acceptance in the "kingdom of this world," particularly if such a world remained antiblack and colonized. More compelling, the perennial existence of Macandal in the novel shows how Carpentier reads the anticolonial and antislavery freedom that Macandal names as tied to "a state of being" as opposed to a specific "place" (Roberts 11). If it can be said that there is no secure place for the unnoted Haitian revolutionary to exist freely in when now living as a common Haitian peasant in liberated Haiti, then freedom cannot be attached to the place that is Haiti but to the furtive flight toward the possibility of freedom elsewhere. "Freedom is marronage," to paraphrase Neil Roberts, and marronage in the wake of the

Haitian Revolution remains a freedom project in the twentieth and twenty-first centuries because of the untenability of black freedom in postcolonial places and in hemispheric American spaces, on the whole.

At the foreground of Carpentier's work is how the inability to concretize the Haitian revolutionary vision tied to resistance figures like Macandal has shaped the migratory flows connecting Haiti to Cuba so decisively that iterant Haitian movement is inevitable, necessitating a subaltern engagement with Haiti's revolution. Without a place to nurture a life beyond the colony, Carpentier writes as if modest Haitians will necessarily experience life as *mucho woulo*. That is to say, they will experience life as the flight toward the possibility (and only the possibility) of freedom in Cuba; that this life remains simply a possibility results from how Cuba proves to be just as inhospitable (in fact, more hostile) to Haitian efforts to construct a life removed from the economic and political disenfranchisement that centuries of slavery and colonialism bore and years of coloniality made rote in Haiti. The absence of freedom does not mean, however, that a life of *mucho woulo* is a passive existence where Haitians in movement survive as "bod[ies] of flesh to which this happened" (*The Kingdom* 184). Their movement approximates the flight of the *cimarrones* of yesteryear whose quest for unrestricted freedom ignited the unprecedented revolution that occurred in mind in Macandal's moment (1750 Saint-Domingue) and came into praxis during Bouckman's time period (1791 Saint-Domingue). In this respect, Haitian migrants who journey to Cuba are implicitly figured as the direct descendants of small-time Haitian revolutionaries because, like them, they do not "leave[] [behind] the same inheritance [they] have received" (Ibid. 184); they choose instead to further the cimarronian effort they inherited by endeavoring to construct realities beyond the colonial order of life as it is in pos revolutionary Cuba, postrevolutionary Haiti, and in the Americas, on the whole.

In the summer of 2015, I presented at the cultural festival Festival de Caribe, in Santiago de Cuba, and met a Cuban *cimarrón* of Haitian descent. He self-identified as a *cimarrón* precisely for the reasons outlined by Carpentier in *The Kingdom of This World*: the space did not exist to be free, black, and radically Haitian. This *cimarrón* was an artist in a Haitian-descended commune that petitioned, and was subsequently denied, funds from the Cuban government to support their efforts to secure agricultural independence and, in doing so, sustain the commune's holistic Vodou-inspired vision of existence. The commune was denied support because of the lingering bias against Haitian culture that still exists in Cuba, notwithstanding the inroads against anti-Haitianism in the nation.[32] Living with residual anti-Haitianism, he (and his community) understood full well that the project of building a distinct existence, predicated on Vodou's nonracist egalitarian ethics, was not one that a postrevolutionary anticolonial or colonial state would support. His sense of Haitianness, accordingly, pointed otherwise, beyond the lived reality these states supported. Indeed, he was a *cimarrón* because his Haitian sensibility was not tethered to a patriotic identification with Haiti, the nation, but to the revolution that engendered the nation. Such is the power of a revolution in the mind; it prompts the desire to fly toward freedom in the intellect, spurring the need for this freedom's actualization in a space within which the body can exist without impediment. *The Kingdom of This World* is written with this power in mind, reminding readers that black migratory flight is not errancy but a freedom-building project intended to secure a place to be peaceably black *and* unconditionally free. *Mucho woulo, monkonpè* (comrade), Carpentier therefore advises, for the life of freedom to come.

Notes

1. See Boukan Ginen for lyrics and Anton Channel for video, my translation.
2. "Too many problems in the country / Makes it so that we cannot find / A place where we can all truly live in peace."
3. "We recognize that our lives are utterly and completely imperiled."
4. The word *woulo* literally denotes wheels, rollers, or rolls. The translation I have offered is intended to express the movement implied in *woulo* in the context of the song's treatment of compelled and self-initiated migration.
5. I understand unfreedom as referring to a particular predicament of blackness, where individuals raced as black are ostensibly free but so politically and economically disenfranchised, because of the continuation of racist practice, that this freedom subsists through new forms of enchainment (i.e., corvée labor and criminalization).
6. The group began in Camagüey, a city in eastern Cuba with a large Haitian population. The eastern portion of Cuba is peopled with large numbers of Haitian-descended individuals (Cuba's largest immigrant population) because of the Haitian Revolution and the US imperial presence in Cuba, two influential happenings that will be treated in greater detail later in the essay.
7. "Too many problems in the country."
8. "A place where we can all truly live in peace."
9. I borrow the phrase "ambiguities of belonging" from Laurie Lambert and the American Studies Association conference panel she spearheaded in 2015.
10. "Moun chowoulo" could either be a Kreyòl neologism referring to people ("moun") in commotion, denoted by the indefinable "cho" prefacing "woulo." Or

it is a particular idiom that, as the wikimizik user Didier provocatively suggests, refers to an "[e]kspresyon Afrikèn ki vle di 'Nou tout nan menm bato a'" ("An African expression that means we are all in the same boat," my translation). Many revolving turns ("mucho woulo") emerges then from the colonial life that the slave ship made foundational to modern existence; see Boukan Ginen.

11. Fidel Castro announced the Proclamation against Discrimination on March 22, 1959, seeking to definitively "dismantle institutionalized racism" (Pérez Sarduy and Stubbs 6). He essentially stated that "racial discrimination and racial prejudice [were] 'anti-nation,'" asserting: "What the eternal enemies of Cuba and enemies of this Revolution want is for us to be divided into a thousand pieces, thereby to be able to destroy us" (Pérez Sarduy and Stubbs 6).

12. I will not discuss native peoples in this piece, but for a reading of twentieth-century Caribbean writers' efforts to think the Haitian Revolution and hemispheric American modernity with equal attention to black and native lives, see my manuscript in progress *Envision Otherwise: Haiti and the Decolonial Imaginary*.

13. Following the Spanish-American War in 1898, the Platt Amendment was issued by the United States stipulating how American troops would vacate Cuba. The amendment also delineated the neocolonial conditions that would ensure US dominance in Cuba up until 1959.

14. Yanick Hume's "Performing Haiti" situates Cuba's prerevolutionary desire to be a modern republic as a push to embody "an idea of modernity" (41) tied to the United States, which stood in sharp contradistinction to the idea of modernity Cuba's ruling elite imagined Haiti exemplified; see 41–43.

15. The planter class of colonial Cuba had long turned to the slave trade to derive the manpower needed for the colony's full commitment to plantation industries (like sugar and coffee) following the collapse of Saint-Domingue. The abolition of the slave trade and the rising interference of the United States in Cuban colonial and later national affairs, after independence in 1902, necessitated a new pool of labor that was both cost efficient and could act as "army reserve of labor" against a Cuban workforce seeking greater economic equity (Serviat 80). This reserve was predominantly derived from Haiti and Jamaica, with the largest migrants arriving from Haiti.

16. See Serviat for the "propaganda campaign" that depicted Haitian and Jamaican migrants as "inferior" 80.

17. The year 1790 refers to Haiti's revolution, 1912 to Cuba's one and only "race war" (Pérez Sarduy and Stubbs 8). Rafael Duharte Jiménez writes that black Cubans who had participated in the war for independence discovered soon thereafter that "the republic they helped create turned its back on them" (45). The Independent Colored Movement (Independientes de Color), organized by Evaristo Estenoz and Pedro Ivonnet, sought a political intervention, which would result in full and equal inclusion in the republic. However, a political intervention was not possible because their movement was deemed a "race war" against whites and condemned

by the new national government. Consequently, when the movement turned to limited military engagement, the government deployed its armed forces and "over 3,000 black [Cubans, movement soldiers and unaffiliated peasants, were] brutally massacred in the Oriente countryside by the republican army" (45).

18. A pro-US Cuban government accepted the neocolonial conditions outlined in the Platt Amendment and the ratification that followed, which gave Cuban sugar preferential treatment within the US market, in order to strengthen its economy. Little thought was given to the predominately black laborers who would be exploited within the sugar industry for the national economy's growth.

19. While the "marvelous real" was first articulated in the prologue, it was later augmented in "On the Marvelous Real in America" (1967) and later "The Baroque and the Marvelous Real" (1975).

20. Giovanni Batista Piranesi was an eighteenth-century Italian engraver whose peculiar artistry inspired the surrealists. These European artists were contemporaries of Carpentier and extensively critiqued in his explication of the marvelous real for their inability to truthfully describe the sterility of their own lived realities. In *The Kingdom of This World*, Carpentier is more explicit in detailing the originality of the Citadel with reference to Piranesi, writing, "Hundreds of men worked in the bowels of that vast edifice, always under the vigilance of whip and gun, accomplishing feats seen only in the imagined architecture of Piranesi" (120).

21. Carpentier therefore argues that in much the same way that the Spanish archetype of imperial politics, Hernán Cortez, could not describe the Americas—"As I do not know what to call these things, I cannot express them" ("The Baroque" 104)—the French surrealist and heir to Cortez's imperial project, André Breton, would prove equally unable to depict the region's vegetation. He remarks, "observe that when André Masson tried to draw the jungle of Martinique . . . the marvelous truth of the matter devoured the painter, leaving him just short of impotent when faced with the blank paper. It had to be an American painter—Wifredo Lam—who taught us the magic of tropical vegetation" ("On the Marvelous Real" 85).

22. The other cultural aspects that Carpentier highlights in the prologue include Europeans who searched for El Dorado well into the French Revolution ("On the Marvelous Real" 87); these are activities that are not invented by regional peoples but are adopted behaviors add to the region's marvelousness because they accentuate the irreality shaping how the region is thought and lived by Americans and others.

23. For the changing demographics in colonial Cuba, see Ferrer 37.

24. The Jamaican-born Boukman convened the meeting at Bois Kaïyman and served as the first of the Revolution's many leaders. I defer to Carpentier's spelling, Bouckman, in this essay.

25. Following independence in 1804 and the assassination of then-emperor Jean-Jacques Dessalines, in 1806, Haiti was divided into a kingdom in the north and a republic in the southwest. In 1820, it was unified as a liberal democratic republic by former revolutionary general Jean-Pierre Boyer.

26. For Haitian migration to eastern Cuba, see Hume, 42 and 45 (specifically, figure 2). Regarding Carpentier and Santiago, see Echevarría, who writes: "In the forties, Carpentier's places of residence—Havana, Caracas—would not leave as much of an imprint on his works as did his travels. Of these, four should be emphasized: the two already mentioned [Haiti in 1943 and Mexico in 1944] and the trips to the Venezuelan jungle in the summers of 1947 and 1948. (There were other trips within Cuba, mainly to Santiago)" (97). While Carpentier's trips in Cuba are parenthetical to Echevarría interests, I find that the temporal convergence of these inland trips with Carpentier's sojourn to Haiti strongly influenced how Carpentier approached his Haitian revolutionary novel.

27. Aponte was a free black man who was convicted for conspiring to incite a slave rebellion in Havana. He was inspired by the Haitian Revolution and he motivated his followers with a book of drawings and paintings, several of which were of Haitian revolutionary generals.

28. See my article "Faithless Sight: Haiti in *The Kingdom of This World*," particularly 98–101, for an extended discussion on how the erasure of Toussaint and Dessalines in *The Kingdom of This World* obscures the failure of their revolutionary endeavors and in doing so perseveres in the necessity of revolution for colonized peoples.

29. Michel-Rolph Trouillot's *Haiti: State against Nation* persuasively demonstrates how disparate visions for the nation set a postrevolutionary governing elite, committed to the plantation economy, apart from the masses, fundamentally opposed to plantation industry. He argues that this division gives rise to Duvalierism in the twentieth century and to Haiti's protracted experience of neocolonial destabilization and exploitation in the nineteenth, twentieth, and twenty-first centuries.

30. I am stressing ordinariness because Ti-Noël's nondescript characterization is a purposeful means through which to write him as an everyman character and in so doing address the lived existence of common individuals in the revolutionary struggle as opposed to the creole generals typically rendered as exceptional revolutionary personages.

31. His stories motivated Ti-Noël's inquisitive engagement with his surroundings and his ongoing effort to secure his freedom; when the novel begins, Macandal's tales of "the great kingdoms of Popo, of Arada, of the Nagos, or the Fulah" led Ti-Noël to "boldly" ask a white bookseller about an engraved coin depicting black royalty notwithstanding the violence that could result from his temerity (*The Kingdom* 13, 12). Moreover, the prayer he recites in Santiago is a song he learned from Macandal (87), which now serves to embolden his commitment to a revolutionary struggle he has been forcibly removed from.

32. Hume's incisive essay "Performing Haiti" argues that the Haitian-Cubano's move in the 1980s "from the disparaged image of cultural other to that of the immigrant national" resulted from the "cultural policy and the systematic cultural agenda of Casa del Caribe," the publishing house that organizes the Festival de Caribe

(59). The house provided the space for a celebratory engagement with *haitianidad*, which helped (and still helps) to assuage the lingering anti-Haitianism that exists in revolutionary Cuba (59).

Works Cited

Anton Channel. "Boukan Ginen—Ede m Chante (PAWOL)." Online video. *YouTube*, 30 Aug. 2014, youtube/11MyCF_k06c. Accessed 18 Apr. 2016.
Boukan Ginen. "Ede m Chante (Help Me to Sing)." *Jou A Rive*. Green Linnet, 2006. *Tidal*. tidal.com/track/11555473.
———. "Ede m Chante (Help Me to Sing)." pawolmizik.com/lyrics/paroles-ede-m-chante-boukan-ginen/. Accessed 22 Apr. 2016.
———. "Ede m Chante (Help Me to Sing)." wikimizik.com/lyrics?song=638&title=Ede'm%20Chante&artist=Boukan%20Ginen. Accessed 22 Apr. 2016.
Carpentier, Alejo. "The Baroque and the Marvelous Real," translated by Tanya Huntington and Lois Parkinson Zamora. *Magical Realism: Theory, History, Community*, edited by Lois Parkinson Zamora and Wendy B. Faris, Duke UP, 1995, pp. 89–108.
———. *The Kingdom of This World*. Translated by Harriet De Onis, Farrar, Straus, and Giroux, 1957.
———. "On the Marvelous Real in America," translated by Tanya Huntington and Lois Parkinson Zamora. *Magical Realism: Theory, History, Community*, edited by Lois Parkinson Zamora and Wendy B. Faris, Duke UP, 1995, pp. 75–88.
———. "Prologue. The Kingdom of This World," translated by Alfred Mac Adam. *Review: Literature and Arts of the Americas*, vol. 26, no. 47, 1993, 47, pp. 28–32.
Césaire, Aimé. "Notebook of a Return to the Native Land," translated by Clayton Eshleman and Annette Smith. *Aime Césaire: The Collected Poetry*. U of California P, 1983, pp. 33–85.
The Creole Choir of Cuba. "Edem Chanté." *Tande-La*. Real World Records, 2012. *Tidal*. tidal.com/track/54929494.
Echevarría, Roberto González. *The Pilgrim at Home: Alejo Carpentier*. U of Texas P, 1990.
Ferrer, Ada. *Freedom's Mirror: Cuba and Haiti in the Age of Revolution*. Cambridge UP, 2014.
Hume, Yanick. "Performing Haiti: Casa del Caribe and the Popularisation of Haitian Heritage Communities in Cuba." *Caribbean Quarterly: A Journal of Caribbean Culture*, vol. 62, no. 1, 2016, pp. 39–68.
Jiménez, Rafael Duharte. "The 19th Century Black Fear." *Afro-Cuba: An Anthology of Cuban Writing on Race, Politics, and Culture*, edited by Pedro Perez Sarduy and Jean Stubbs, Ocean Press, 1993, pp. 37–46.

Kaisary, Philip K. *The Haitian Revolution in the Literary Imagination: Radical Horizons, Conservative Constraints*. U of Virginia P, 2014.

Léger, Natalie M. "Faithless Sight: Haiti in *The Kingdom of This World*." *Research in African Literatures*, vol. 45, no. 1, Spring 2014, pp. 85–106.

Pérez Sarduy, Pedro, and Jean Stubbs. "Introduction: The Rite of Social Communion." *Afro-Cuba: An Anthology of Cuban Writing on Race, Politics, and Culture*, edited by Pedro Pérez Sarduy and Jean Stubbs, Ocean Press, 1993, pp. 3–26.

Robaina, Tomás Fernández. "The 20th Century Black Question." *Afro-Cuba: An Anthology of Cuban Writing on Race, Politics, and Culture*, edited by Pedro Pérez Sarduy and Jean Stubbs, Ocean Press, 1993, pp. 92–103.

Roberts, Neil. *Freedom as Marronage*. U of Chicago P, 2015.

Serviat, Pedro. "Solutions to the Black Problem." *Afro-Cuba: An Anthology of Cuban Writing on Race, Politics, and Culture*, edited by Pedro Pérez Sarduy and Jean Stubbs, Ocean Press, 1993, pp. 77–90.

Trouillot, Michel-Rolph. *Haiti: State against Nation: Origins and Legacy of Duvalierism*. Monthly Review Press, 1990.

5

The Haitian Revolution and Tomás Gutiérrez Alea's *La última cena* (*The Last Supper*, 1976)

PHILIP KAISARY

Le Blanc est un maître qui a permis à ses esclaves de manger à sa table. (The white man is a master who has allowed his slaves to eat at his table.)

—Frantz Fanon, *Peau noire, masques blancs*

Count de Casa Bayona: "¡Esto no es Santo Domingo!" (This is not Santo Domingo!)

—Tomás Gutiérrez Alea, *La última cena* screenplay

Introduction

This essay considers the ideological resonance of the Haitian Revolution in *La última cena* (*The Last Supper*), a masterpiece of Cuban cinema from 1976 written and directed by Tomás Gutiérrez Alea (1928–1996). Critically applauded as one of Gutiérrez Alea's most fully realized films, *La última cena* has generated considerable critical commentary and discussion in academic and mainstream circles, but the film's Haitian dimension has gone largely unnoted.¹ This essay will argue that in narrating a historically documented episode of slave resistance in late nineteenth-century Cuba in relation to the Haitian Revolution, *La última cena* is attentive to a transnational, pan-Caribbean history of resistance in which freedom and liberation necessarily entails freedom from economic domination. In the context of this argument, the film's identification of slavery as a regime of labor exploitation intricately related to capitalism is of primary concern.

Gutiérrez Alea is widely regarded as the preeminent filmmaker of Cuba's postrevolutionary period. He undertook formal training as a filmmaker between 1951 and 1953 in Rome's Centro Sperimentale di Cinematografia, a film school closely associated with Italian neorealism. The politics and aesthetics of his films reveal this influence and his work has been praised for its nondoctrinaire political commitment as well as for its aesthetic and narratological innovation. He is best known for his award-winning 1968 film, *Memorias del subdesarrollo (Memories of Underdevelopment)*, which tracks Sergio, an alienated bourgeois, who elects to remain in Cuba after Castro's revolution of 1953–1959 while his wife, family, and friends choose to relocate to Miami. However, his considerable corpus of work includes both documentary and fiction films that are often marked by comic social satire and ironic political critique. These span such diverse subjects as political corruption, homophobia, sexism, the sociology of race and class, and the nature of radical social transformation.²

La última cena however stands out for a number of reasons. While all of Gutiérrez Alea's other films are set in the twentieth century, *La última cena* is set on a Havana sugar plantation in the final decade of the eighteenth century. As such, the film foregrounds the history of plantation slavery in Cuba—which was booming in the wake of the revolution in neighboring Saint-Domingue—while also recuperating Cuba's African heritage.³ In addition, *La última cena* is remarkable for its strategic invocation of the Haitian Revolution, which looms large throughout the film even while it is only rarely mentioned explicitly. By this means, Alea places Cuban history in the context of a wider Caribbean history. In the spirit of C. L. R. James's underanalyzed appendix essay to the second edition of his classic study of the Haitian Revolution, *The Black Jacobins*, "From Toussaint L'Ouverture to Fidel Castro," Alea invites the viewer to think comparatively and transhistorically and to juxtapose Haitian and Cuban revolutionary history.⁴

Alea's invocation of the Haitian Revolution in *La última cena* should be situated in relation to other cinematic reflections on the Haitian Revolution and the desire for freedom. It should be noted at the outset that Hollywood films on slavery have generally avoided discussing Haiti. Indeed, until the recent boom of slavery on film, which includes works of such diverse ideological and aesthetic orientation as Quentin Tarantino's *Django Unchained* (2012), Amma Asante's *Belle* (2013), Steve McQueen's *12 Years a Slave* (2013), and Nate Parker's *Birth of a Nation* (2016), Hollywood has produced lamentably few films focused on Atlantic slavery and even fewer worthy of note.[5] However, with a handful of exceptions, Haiti's filmic representational history bears witness to its excessive imperialist denigration. Colorful takes on Haitian Vodou, zombies, and a derogatory general emphasis on black magic and witchcraft have for long predominated in films impinging on Haiti's revolutionary history. Consider, for example, Victor Halperin's 1932 film, *White Zombie*, the first feature-length zombie movie, which was based on William Seabrook's 1929 novel, *The Magic Island*, as well as more recent productions such as *The Serpent and the Rainbow*, Wes Craven's sensationalist adaptation of Wade Davis's anthropological work.[6] However, outside Hollywood—an engine of cultural production created by and for capitalism—there exists a tradition of serious attempts to represent both Atlantic slavery and Haitian history on film. Prime among these is Gillo Pontecorvo's 1969 feature, *Quemada* (Burn!), which is set on the fictional Caribbean island of Quemada and tells the story of a slave uprising loosely based on the Haitian Revolution. Further, from the 1970s onward, the Cuban Institute of Cinematographic Art and Industry has been responsible for the production of a corpus of powerful and provocative films about slavery in which slave resistance is a central motif.[7] Within this corpus Haiti is often explicitly figured as a nation of comrades and an ongoing inspiration to Cuba's revolutionary project. For example, in Sergio Giral's 1975 *El otro Francisco* (The other Francisco), which serves as a corrective to *Francisco*, a romantic antislavery sensationalist novel of 1839 by the renowned Cuban author Anselmo Suárez y Romero, Giral thanks in the opening credits "The Haiti Group"—Haitians resident in Cuba. In this manner, the structural bonds connecting Cuba and Haiti's national histories are evoked. However, within this corpus of radical Cuban films, it is Alea's *La última cena* that most clearly demonstrates the impact of the Haitian Revolution on the mind-set of Cuba's plantocracy.

The plot of *La última cena* is based on a single paragraph taken from *El Ingenio* (*The Sugarmill*), a groundbreaking work of scholarship by the Cuban historian Manuel Moreno Fraginals. In Fraginals's telling of the historical events, one Holy Week in the late 1780s (*sic*), an aristocratic Havana plantation owner, Count de Casa Bayona, "decided in an act of deep Christian fervor to humble himself before [his] slaves" and "[o]ne Holy Thursday he washed twelve Negroes' feet, sat them at his table, and served them food in imitation of Christ" (53). However, far from "behaving like the Apostles" (53), the slaves' response to their master's antics was to organize an uprising and burn down the sugar mill, demonstrating their selfhood and asserting their agency. The Count's reaction to the mutiny was as brutal as it was predictable, ordering his *rancheadores* (slave-catchers) to hunt down and slay the rebels. Thus, the events of this particular Holy Week, which began with the Count washing the feet of twelve of his slaves, end with the Count ordering that the same slaves be caught and executed, and that their severed heads be stuck on spikes mounted on a hilltop. These historical events, which Alea transposes from the 1780s to the 1790s, and hence into the shadow of the Haitian Revolution, culminate in a scene that evokes Aimé Césaire's withering critique of the monstrous hypocrisy of Christian colonialism and its "reddened waters": the Count pronounces his intention to build a church, on the very same hilltop, in honor of the slaves' overseer who was killed in the uprising.[8] Provocatively, Alea has the Count make this pronouncement from the hilltop that is now testament to the barbarity of colonial slavery: the Count is encircled by his gruesome trophies—eleven severed human heads. Only one rebel remains—Sebástian—and he serves as a poignant symbol of the inevitability of resistance and of its eventual triumph.

The film opens with the camera panning slowly over medieval frescoes: we see close-ups of an infant bearing a crucifix, Christ and the Virgin Mary, a rosary, and thorny pink roses that recall prelapsarian paradise and man's fallen nature. The camerawork is accompanied by polyphonic, Renaissance choral music—a motet—that together with the splendid visuals establishes an aesthetic of faux decorum. The use of European aesthetic modes—aural and visual—to establish a false tranquility (that will be shattered abruptly by the violence of the first scene) recalls Aimé Césaire and Frantz Fanon's denunciations of the faux humanism of European so-called civilization.[9] Later in the film, the strategy of juxtaposing European and African musical traditions will also enable Alea to evoke Haiti as, in Césaire's words, "the most African of the Antilles" and also refute the figuration of Cuba as a site in which the "African influence" has been tempered.[10] Then, a subtitle informs the viewer that it is Ash Wednesday, and the camera looks in on a dark and oppressive slave barrack, little more than a cell; it is notable that the slaves' claustrophobic living quarters represented in *La última cena* are a far cry from the pristinely prettified slave huts of more recent Hollywood movies addressing slavery.[11] The plantation overseer, Don Manuel, a robustly built, muscular, and olive-skinned man of early middle age, bursts into the barrack holding a riding crop. A slave, Sebastián, has escaped and Don Manuel accuses a slave resting in the barrack of aiding him in his escape attempt. Don Manuel seizes the slave by his clothing, the slave protests his innocence, and Don Manuel throws him to the ground (fig. 5.1). The runaway's meager bedclothes are identified and presented to the wildly barking sniffer dogs so the runaway can be tracked, captured, and punished. Thus, from the very first scene *La última cena* makes clear that the institution of slavery was founded on systemically orchestrated violence and terror. Within such a system, as the film will also make clear, the notion of a paternalistic, benevolent master is a ridiculous paradox, at best an impotent charade, or, at worst, an ideological falsehood that blinds the planter class and the Atlantic world's privileged consumers to the irredeemable monstrosity on which their consumption is based.

Figure 5.1. "Don Manuel in the slave hut," still from *La última cena*.

Then, the film communicates with great economy and clarity how the hierarchical structure of the plantation system, and its concomitant forms of labor specialization, which includes the Count's delegation of brutality and torture to the overseer, results in a fractured community of radically unequal individuals with incommensurable worldviews. For example, the overseer, Don Manuel, charged with maintaining discipline on the plantation and the recapture of runaways, begins to tell the Count, who has just returned on horseback from Havana, about the fact of Sebastián's running away. The Count, however, is uninterested and he cuts Manuel off: he has neither the desire nor the capacity to recognize that one of the day-to-day dirty realities of plantation life is dealing with incessant slave resistance. Such recognition would necessarily require at least an implicit admission of the slaves' capacity for a political practice of dissent. In turn, this would of course destabilize the Count's conviction that Blacks were ideal slaves. The Count's worldview thus remains coherent only to the extent to which it is unsullied by certain realities to which his overseer, and others, are routinely exposed. Hence, when Don Manuel in a subsequent scene attempts to explain to the Count that the only way to counterbalance the fall in production caused by affording the slaves time off for religious holidays is more frequent whippings, the Count does not dwell on the matter long enough to recognize any contradiction. Instead, the essence of his curt response is to tell the overseer that matters of torture are his business and his business alone. The maintenance of such a strictly compartmentalized perspective ensures that the Count remains blind to the fact that the logic of the plantation system is that all social relations are rendered subordinate to its demands. Further, in closing his mind to the reality under his nose of slave resistance and of the dependence of productivity on practices of torture, the Count was, by extension, also closing his mind to the revolutionary events occurring just seven hundred miles away across the Windward Passage in the French colony of Saint-Domingue. For the Count, the facts of slave resistance and of the Haitian Revolution were "unthinkable" and to be actively disavowed in order that he might continue to deceive himself as to the fundamental barbarism of slaveholding, capitalist, colonial modernity.[12] Such perspicuity identifies the sugar plantation and slavery as central to pan-Caribbean history.[13]

Having introduced at the outset the subject of the Manichean struggle of the slaves for their freedom and the efforts of the overseer to deny them such freedom, Alea situates this dichotomy alongside another: the contradictions between the Count's religious faith and his economic interests as the owner of the mill and plantation. In this regard, Alea makes great use of dramatic irony in revealing to the viewer the tragic shortcomings of the Count's sincerely held religious humanism while sardonically depicting the Count's anguish and his murky moral consciousness and bizarre behavior. Hence, in the following scene, the plantation's priest conveys to the Count his concerns about what he regards as a creeping moral lassitude on the plantation: the overseer is not God-fearing and the slaves are not receiving the necessary religious instruction due to overwork. Moreover, while the Count is bathed, pampered, and massaged by one of his slaves, the priest gently rebukes him for his drinking and, euphemistically, for spending so much time with his slave women. In response, the Count admits that he is uneasy, unable to find peace, and that "aunque sea de día, ando como perdido en un laberinto lleno de tinieblas" (even by day, I walk lost in a maze of darkness). The Count is materially rich, but spiritually impoverished. Slave societies everywhere it is implied—Cuba, Saint-Domingue, and throughout the Americas—are debased, rotten, and no individual can escape the taint of slavery, the Count included. Shortly after his admission of aimlessness, the Count, together with his overseer, and priest, is taken on a tour of the mill by the engineer, Monsieur Duclé, a mulatto refugee from the revolution in Saint-Domingue. The Count and the engineer discuss the purchase of a new, technologically advanced sugarcane press—a state-of-the-art, three-beamed English model—the origin of which serves to evoke the multinational aspect of the Atlantic slave system. Far from being an outmoded relic of a feudal order, slave labor, Alea shows us, both fed on and drove capitalist technological advancement. Monsieur Duclé approves of the more advanced technology—"no hay duda que el trapiche horizontal terminará por imponer" (there is no doubt that the horizontal press is the future)—but he notes, in a foreboding tone, that the new press "necesitará de seguro más caña" (will definitely need more cane) and that more cane will require a greater numbers of slaves. This, Duclé muses, will tip the demographic power on the island in the favor of the Black slave population. While the Count is unfazed by this prospect, remarking, "No se preocupe, señor Duclé. Nosotros aquí sabemos tratar a los negros" (Don't worry Mr. Duclé. We know how to treat the Blacks here), Duclé's silence in response suggests that his experience in Saint-Domingue weighs heavily on his mind. The opening of the subsequent scene resonates ambivalently with the Count's blithe words: Sebastián, the runaway, has been caught by the *rancheadores* on horseback and he is thrown to the ground at the Count's feet. Punishment from Don Manuel is swift and brutal: addressing Sebastián he states, "A ver si ahora te quedan ganas de escaparte otra vez" (Now, let's see if you feel like running away again), before he cuts off his left ear and tosses it to the dogs who quickly devour it. The Count is nauseated by the scene but does not object to Don Manuel's brutality. The scene serves to reiterate that systemic terror and barbarity underpinned plantation slavery, and it serves as one of a number of dramatic counterpoints in the film to the attempted civility and formality of the lengthy supper sequence that is the film's centerpiece.

The following day, Maundy Thursday, the Count instructs the overseer to pick out twelve slaves who will be his "disciples" and dinner guests in his reenactment of Christ's last supper. Among the Count's chosen ones is Sebastián, and the Count insists on his release from the stocks where he is presently held. The twelve slave-disciples are then brought to the chapel where, while they wait for the Count to wash their feet, the priest offers instruction on the glory and generosity of God who permits His followers to dine at His table. This scene is punctuated by stunning cinematographic portraits that are, in the words of the critic Penelope Gilliat, "startlingly beautiful" and evocative of "Rembrandt's portraits" (124, 120). The portrait of Sebastián (fig. 5.2) is worthy of close analysis. With his eyes swollen nearly shut, a bloodied bandage wrapped around his head and over the wound caused by his amputation, Sebastián remains strikingly beautiful, dignified, and defiant. Moreover, up to this point, Sebastián has not uttered a word, so all that he can be judged on to this point are his actions (which we know to be justly rebellious), his physical composure, and his countenance. By these measures, his character recalls not Toussaint Louverture nor even Jean-Jacques Dessalines, those two most celebrated heroes of the Haitian Revolution, but rather the sentiments of universalist négritude and the grassroots radicalism of the Haitian Revolution: an affirmation of dignity and a potent symbol of the possibility of the negation of subjugation via resistance.

The series of cinematographic portraits of the twelve slaves waiting in the chapel also has the effect of dramatically individualizing each of the slaves. Each portrait is powerful testimony to slave suffering, but Alea's genius is to capture suffering while carefully preserving agency as in the portrait of Sebastián. When the Count washes the twelve slaves' feet at the front of the church, the tension is palpable and Alea does not overlook the comic potential of this bizarre ritual. The first slave to have his feet washed cannot help himself from bursting into a fit of uncontrollable laughter. Finding the whole affair comic-absurd, and perhaps ticklish to boot, the slave's inconvenient reaction to the Count's highly choreographed, hubristic imitation of Christ threatens to derail the Count's best-laid plans. Then, after the Count kisses his bathed foot (fig. 5.3), the first slave shakes

Figure 5.2. "Portrait of Sebastián," still from *La última cena*.

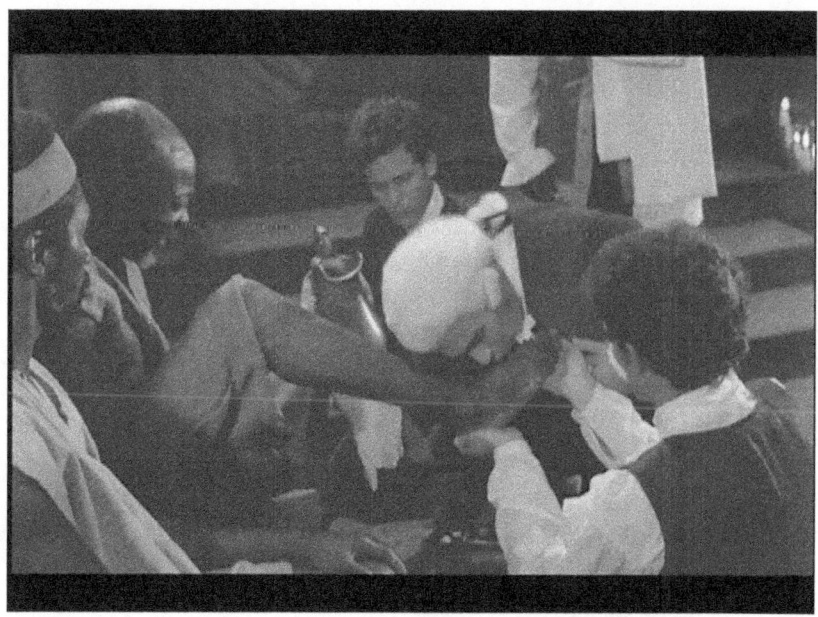

Figure 5.3. "The Count kisses his slaves' feet," still from *La última cena*.

his head in bewilderment and it is clear that these slaves will not meekly play their assigned roles in the Count's show. To the overseer's discomfort, Sebastián is next to have his feet washed by the Count, and as the Count prepares to kiss Sebastián's bathed foot, the overseer walks out of the church in disgust. He proceeds straight to the engineer's quarters, where he quite accurately states, "Yo no entiendo nada pero aquí está pasando algo muy raro" (I don't understand it, but something very strange is going on here), before he rhetorically asks Monsieur Duclé, "¿Adónde vamos a parar?" (Where will this take us?). Don Manuel then reveals his astonishment that the Count kissed Sebastián's feet before marveling at Sebastián's recuperative healing powers and his indefatigable nature. This prompts Duclé to make the film's first explicit reference to the Haitian Revolution, which is a red rag to the overseer:

> M. Duclé: "Beba, beba. Beba mientras pueda hacerlo. No sabe lo que pasa cuando los negros se alborotan. En Santo Domingo . . ." (Drink, drink. Drink while you can. You don't know what it's like when the Blacks rise up. In Santo Domingo . . .]
>
> Don Manuel: "Ah ¡siempre por el mismo camino! Santo Domingo." (Ah! Always on about the same thing! Santo Domingo.)
>
> M. Duclé: "Porque lo conozco. Ahí habían más negros que blancos y mulatos. Ahora solamente hay negros. A mí tampoco me gustaría ver mi cabeza sirviéndole de pelota a un juego de negritos." (Because I know it. There were more Blacks than Whites and Mulattos there. Now there are only Blacks. I wouldn't want to see my head used as a ball for little Blacks to kick around either.)

And with Duclé's words and grim laughter, the camera pans to Don Manuel, foreshadowing his killing by the slaves in the forthcoming uprising. Once again, the Haitian Revolution is an event that must be silenced and disavowed: Don Manuel does not want to hear any talk of it.[14] And with those words, the scene ends and the film's extraordinary centerpiece, the fifty-five-minute supper scene, begins.

From Supper to Revolution

The film's focal point, the supper sequence, is a theatrical set piece that is structured so as to underscore *La última cena*'s ideological thrust: that freedom and liberation cannot be passively received, the egoism of the Count's charity, the richness of Cuba's African heritage, and the political agency of the enslaved. As such, the legacy of the Haitian Revolution simmers away throughout (fig. 5.4). The enslaved men who sit at the Count's table display their humanity with every gesture, word, and expression: among them there are tellers of stories and fables, musical performers, and dancers. Without ever descending into sentimentality, Alea's orchestration of this scene powerfully conveys the sickness of a world system that wantonly wastes such an abundance of human talent and experience. Throughout the supper scene the slaves are individualized: they are no anonymous mass and they are given carefully constructed individual voices and histories, which serves to communicate the diversity of slave experience while also conveying the challenge of constructing a politics of solidarity among the enslaved given the hierarchical and stratified structures enforced upon slave populations.

Figure 5.4. "The Count's Last Supper," still from *La última cena*.

For example, there is a house slave who cannot bear the prospect of being sent back to the field "con todos los negros sucios, éstos" (with all these dirty Blacks).[15] Social divisions caused by the prior status of the enslaved are also communicated: among the Count's supper guests there is African royalty—Bangoché, a Yoruban king, who was captured in war and sold into slavery in Guinea.

The film's meditation on the nature and politics of freedom and bondage is elaborated with great clarity in the supper scene when an elderly slave named Pascual approaches the Count to ask for his freedom. Pascual explains that he is old and worn out and of little use now as a field slave. Indeed, Pascual personifies the human capacity to endure not only the inflictions of cruelty but also its debilitating consequences. To his surprise, the Count grants Pascual his freedom, though Pascual's initial joy quickly sours: he breaks down for not knowing what to do with his newfound liberty. The Count quizzes him: Where will he go and what will he do? These are questions to which Pascual has no answer. The Count's cruel taunts—"¡Vean ustedes, acaba de obtener su libertad y no sabe qué va a hacer con ella!" (Look everyone! He's just got his freedom and he doesn't know what to do with it!)—compound Pascual's existential grief. Pascual's realization that he may not be able to redeem or salvage what remains of his life serves to demonstrate that the scale and depths of slavery's monstrosity will forever be a stain on human history: it is a crime for which all measures of compensation are inadequate and for which there can be no true justice. However, Pascual's experience suggests the political imperative for the enslaved is not to achieve a negotiated emancipation, but rather the total destruction of a social order premised on human domination. The example of the Haitian Revolution thus lingers, ever present in the film's presentation of self-emancipation by means of revolution, as the only possible route to political and psychological regeneration for the enslaved. The exchange between the Count and Pascual thus recalls the thesis articulated by Frantz Fanon, recently recapitulated and elaborated by Marcus Wood, that freedom granted by permission constitutes a "horrible gift." Wood argues that Fanon searched "deeply into the appalling aporia lying within the myth that freedom can ever be given by any master to any slave" since freedom is "beyond the power of any human . . . to endow another human with."[16]

The counterpoint to Pascual's story is Sebastián. Throughout the supper scene, Sebastián remains a picture of quiet defiance as he allows his peers and the garrulous (and increasingly drunken) Count to dominate the conversation. Seated directly on the Count's right-hand side, and with the bloodstains still fresh on his bandaged head, his mere physical presence sustains a simmering dramatic tension. When the Count asks Sebastián the question "¿Quién soy?" (Who am I?), he refuses to call his master by his name, title, or anything at all (fig. 5.5). Instead, Sebastián spits on the Count's face from point-blank range, an act that constitutes a rejection of the Count's faux civility and a refusal of their relationship in its entirety. The Count's response is to raise his arm in readiness to strike him with the nearest thing that he can lay his hands on—ridiculously, this is a spoon, and this deepens the Count's humiliation. However, the Count recovers his composure, lowers the silver spoon in his right hand, and does not strike Sebastián. Still consciously modeling his behavior on Christ, the Count exclaims that he can forgive Sebastián for his actions. The Count utters: "Un día como hoy, Cristo se humilló ante los hombres. No tiene nada de grandioso que un amo se humille ante sus esclavos. Ven, beba. ¡Beba! (On a day like today, Christ humbled himself before men. There is nothing remarkable about a master humbling himself before his slaves. Come, drink. Drink!), before he likens Sebastián to Judas, who spat in Christ's face just as Sebastián spat in his master's face. The limits of the Count's professed capacity for forgiveness, however, are soon to be exposed.

Figure 5.5. "The Count and Sebastián at the supper table," still from *La última cena*.

The tension between the Count and Sebastián is defused somewhat by the appearance of a house slave bringing bread to the supper table, and it becomes clear that the Count intends to lead his slave disciples in a version of the Holy Communion. This set piece serves as a further opportunity for Alea to reveal the dishonesty of any equations of paganism and savagery, Christianity and civility. In the midst of explaining the Eucharist, the Count is interrupted by a bewildered slave who asks in disbelief, "A lo Cristo ¿se lo comieron?" (What happened to that Christ? They ate him?), a subversive-comic exchange that recalls a similar episode in Peter Shaffer's 1964 play, *The Royal Hunt of the Sun*.[17] The religious instruction of the enslaved in Latin America was indeed a responsibility of slave masters, and the fact that a number of enslaved men on the Count's estate did not know of the Eucharist is itself an indication that he has been lax in his instruction of them. The Count then tells the story of Saint Francis, the moral of which, according to the Count, is: "de todas las cosas buenas del Espíritu Santo que Cristo considera sus amigos la mejor es avergonzarse uno mismo y soportar penas e injurias por amor a Cristo. . . . Solo el dolor es lo único verdaderamente nuestro y eso es lo único que nosotros podemos darle a Dios con alegría" (of all of the good things about the Holy Spirit that Christ loves, the best is humbling oneself and suffering hardships and insults for His love. . . . Sorrow is the only thing that is truly ours to give to God with joy). Then the Count proceeds to expound upon a hodgepodge of stock racist justifications for slavery: "El negro está mejor preparado por la naturaleza para resistir el dolor con resignación" (The Black man is by nature better able to put up with pain), "¿Cuándo han visto ustedes a un blanco cantando mientras corta caña? El negro, en cambio, siempre canta. Y eso es bueno porque con el canto uno se olvida de lo que está haciendo. Se alegra el espíritu" (Have you ever seen a White man singing when he cuts cane? The Black man, in contrast, is always singing. And that's good because when you sing you forget what you're doing. It gladdens the heart). And more specifically: "Dios hizo las cosas de tal modo que el negro tiene como una disposición innata para el corte de caña (God gave the Black man an innate ability for cutting cane), and, "Puede decirse que el negro ha nacido en medio de la caña" (You could say that the Black man was born in the cane field). Then, having dominated the conversation for so long, the Count passes out at the table and Sebastián speaks for the first time in the film. He tells a creation myth in which the central characters are "Truth" and "Lie": Lie beheads Truth with a machete and places his own head on the body of Truth. Sebastián then explains that ever since then, the body of "Truth" has been deceiving people. Sebastián's creation myth serves as a rebuttal of the entirety of the Count's discourse and of all justifications for his enslaved status. Sebastián finishes his speech by declaring his commitment to the pursuit of his freedom, and his words—which are testimony to the power of the "marvelous" to sustain political will—foreshadow his eventual escape:

> SEBASTIÁN: "Sebastián se hace palo en los montes, se hace pescado en los ríos, se hace piedra, se hace *susundamba*. ¡Vuela! Nadie me puede agarrar. A mí nadie me puede matar." (Sebastián will turn himself into a tree in the woods, a fish in the rivers, he will change into a stone, he will become a *susundamba* [an owl]. Fly away! Nobody can catch me. Nobody can kill me.)

The inspiration behind these words of Sebastián would appear to belong to the character of the Vodou priest turned slave rebel Makandal in Alejo Carpentier's classic novel of marvelous realism and the Haitian Revolution, *El reino de este mundo* (*The Kingdom of This World*). Working in different mediums, both Alea and Carpentier appear to have gazed from Cuba across the Windward Passage to Haiti to seek aesthetic and historical inspiration for their representations of resistance and the possibility of social transformation. Then, with Sebastián's words of marvelous dissent still hanging in air, the Count, drunk and barely conscious, is carried away by his house slave Edmundo.

The following day, Good Friday, Don Manuel awakens the slaves to work. Pascual attempts to tell Don Manuel that he is now a free man, having been granted his liberty by the Count at the previous night's supper. Don Manuel dismisses Pascual's claim as nonsense and he insists that the slaves, Pascual included, must get to their work in the fields. It is the final catalyst for the uprising: as Don Manuel prepares to strike Bangoché, the slaves resist their overseer. Bangoché fights back and Sebastián quickly joins in the struggle. Within seconds they have restrained and captured Don Manuel as a hostage. Initially, the uprising is a demand not for freedom but for a modicum of justice and it takes the form of a workers' rebellion: having been promised Good Friday off as a religious holiday, the slaves refuse to work. These initial demands recall the attempts of the ex-slaves of Saint-Domingue under the leadership of Toussaint Louverture to negotiate better treatment rather than the immediate end of slavery in the early stages of the Haitian Revolution. And just as in the case of Haiti, a negotiated peace is beyond the vision of the planter class. News of the uprising rapidly reaches the Count, who assembles an armed band of slave-catchers to begin hunting down and killing the slaves immediately. Reasonably sensing the necessity of a ruthless, preemptive violence of self-defense, Sebastián kills Don Manuel. The Count's discovery of his overseer's body prompts one of his most remarkable analogical contortions as he likens this cruel and vicious man to Christ. Whereas at the previous evening's supper the Count had admitted to his slaves that Don Manuel "jamás podrá parecerse a Jesús Cristo" (could never be like Jesus Christ), now, on finding his corpse, the Count inquires of the priest, "Padre ¿a qué hora murió Cristo?" (Father, at what time did Christ die?), to which the Priest responds: "A esta misma hora, señor" (At this very hour, sir). Further, Don Manuel's death brings thoughts of the Haitian Revolution rushing to the Count's mind. Hours later, in the plantation church with Don Manuel's dead body on display, the Count angrily insists "¡Esto no es Santo Domingo!" (This is not Santo Domingo!). However, the merciless hunting down and slaying of the slave rebels certainly recalls the atrocities of the Haitian Revolution. Cuba may not be Saint-Domingue, but Alea communicates the parallels for all to see: grotesquely uneven slave societies beholden to the Atlantic world economy and a racial conflict, the logical end point of which is genocidal war.

One by one, the Count's *rancheadores* succeed in their murderous enterprise: the defenseless Pascual is brutally murdered by two members of the Count's band, another dies in attempted escape leaping to his death into a gorge believing that he will sprout feathers and wings and fly to his freedom. Soon the heads of eleven of the Count's twelve slave disciples are mounted on spikes on a hilltop—only Sebastián has evaded capture. The film's dramatic final scenes are of Sebastián on the run—the defiant runaway—and now the organ music and baroque Christian music is replaced by African drumming and nonlexical singing. The musical substitution is an indication of Sebastián's rejection of a faux civilization and an embrace of his African origins. Though we do not know whether Sebastián is an African-born *bozal*, the shift in music also indicates Cuba's musical-cultural bond with Africa—Haiti may be "the most African of the Antilles," but Alea affirms that Cuba too is African. Alea's film thus poses the question, at what point does the incorporation of the African element into the Cuban national imaginary take place?

As Sebastián continues to run—with the drumming and singing becoming ever more intense—Alea intersperses highly emotive images of freedom in nature. There is a bird in flight, water running over rocks in a riverbed, rocks tumbling into a gorge, a herd of wild horses, and then, finally, there is Sebastián, in profile, still running. Such imagery must be regarded as a filmic language of magical realism that communicates not a human right to freedom but the immanence of freedom in nature and mankind, a freedom entirely antithetical to the bondage of labor under capitalist modernity. Further, in connecting slave resistance to an aesthetics of magical realism and an ontology of the marvelous, *La última cena* again invokes the origins of the Haitian Revolution, the character of Makandal whose magical "escape" is vividly narrated in Carpentier's *El reino de este mundo*, and the Bois Caiman Vodou ceremony that preceded the uprising on the northern plains, the initial catalyst to the revolution in August 1791. Like Carpentier's *El reino de este mundo* before it, Alea's *La última cena* thus suggests that slave resistance could be informed by "magical" beliefs as well as rational thought. Thus, the achievement of *La última cena* is not only its affirmation of the agency of enslaved Blacks and maroon populations, but its evocation, via an aesthetics of the marvelous and the magical, of a radical conception of anticapitalist freedom in the abstract *and* in its material reality in the Haitian Revolution.

Conclusion

In conclusion, I wish to suggest that engaging with the radical aesthetics and representational politics that we find in *La última cena* enables us to construct a narrative of slavery and abolition in which slave resistance—and the impact of the Haitian Revolution—assumes a role center stage. This makes for a powerful contrast with the recent upsurge in popular cinematic works ostensibly focused on slavery and Black experience. Unlike *La última cena*, these recent Hollywood productions conspicuously avoid reference to the Haitian Revolution and fail to register the larger meaning of slavery, while also implicitly presenting racism as anachronistic under today's neoliberal order rather than as a vector of continuing systematized oppression.

The larger meaning of slavery concerns its systemic function in the evolution of modern capitalism as well as its widespread and pernicious legacies. In this respect, it is also striking that revisiting Alea's *La última cena* serves as a corrective to a new wave of widely celebrated historical scholarship that has sought to reassess slavery's relationship to capitalism.[18] The chief claims and arguments of these contemporary histories of capitalism are rigorously made, convincing, and include emphases on commodities as explanatory categories, capitalism's coercive violence, slavery as a system of capital accumulation, and the reifying core impulses of slavery and capitalism. However, Peter James Hudson has perspicaciously observed that this new history of capitalism has "selectively cited, completely ignored, or borrowed without acknowledgment" a radical intellectual tradition that took slavery and capitalism for its subject, even while it repeats many of the claims of these earlier scholars, who include C. L. R. James, Eric Williams, W. E. B. Du Bois, and Walter Rodney (n.p.). The unwavering emphasis on capitalism in Alea's *La última cena* clearly marks it as ideologically belonging to this radical tradition, and, as such, constitutes further evidence that in some circles a conception of slavery's intricate relationship with and fundamental importance to capitalism has a long history. As such, this body of work reminds us that situating Haiti's and Cuba's revolutionary traditions in comparative critical context—as Alea's *La última cena* challenges us to do—holds the promise of revealing deep causal explanations. Further, in Alea's hands, the subject of slavery becomes the basis for an elaborate meditation on revolutionary politics and the possibility of true liberation. Alea's *La última cena* links the brutalities of slavery to capitalist economic forces and thereby exposes the impossibility of social justice under capitalism. Also stunningly revealed is the inevitable failure of Christian humanism as a means of forging social bonds that might transcend the divisions of race and class in slave society given its complicity with the interests of the plantocracy and its insufficiency as consolation for systemically induced suffering. Instead, invoking the Haitian Revolution, not as a horrifying example, but as a crucial landmark on the way to the realization of a free and dignified postcolonial future, *La última cena* insists on the necessity of revolutionary social transformation and the dissolution by the oppressed of race- and class-based social hierarchies if the universal human desire for freedom is to be realized.

The author would like to thank Gabrielle Etcheverry for her transcriptions of the original Spanish and for her assistance with translation.

Notes

1. Recent English-language scholarship addressing *La última cena* includes Blasini; Davis; and Schroeder.
2. See Schroeder for a discussion of all twelve of Alea's feature films. For a complete filmography, see "Tomás Gutiérrez Alea" at the Internet Movie Database.
3. For an analysis of the retrenchment and intensification of slavery in Cuba as a consequence of the Haitian Revolution, see Ferrer.

4. See James.

5. The absence of a serious and major film about the Haitian Revolution is a source of comic satire in Chris Rock's *Top Five* (2014). For an elaboration of this argument, see Kaisary, "Slave Narrative."

6. However, Jean Negulesco's *Lydia Bailey* (1952) constitutes an important exception to this tradition of denigration. For analysis, see Kaisary, *Haitian Revolution* 7–8.

7. In addition to Alea's *La última cena*, Cuban films from this period representing slavery include Sergio Giral's trilogy *El otro Francisco* (1975), *Rancheador* (1976), and *Maluala* (1979), all produced by the Instituto Cubano del Arte e Industria Cinematográficos.

8. Césaire 36.

9. See Césaire; and Fanon, *Wretched*.

10. Césaire 90.

11. Consider, for example, Steve McQueen's 2013 adaptation of Solomon Northup's narrative, *Twelve Years a Slave*; for analysis, see Kaisary, "Slave Narrative."

12. Michel-Rolph Trouillot famously argued that the Haitian Revolution was "unthinkable" in the late eighteenth and early nineteenth centuries. Going further, Sibylle Fischer has argued that the entire edifice of Western modernity was constructed on the disavowal of the Haitian Revolution and its political and philosophical ramifications.

13. Here too the analysis evokes C. L. R. James and his argument for linking Toussaint Louverture to Fidel Castro, Haiti to Cuba: "The history of the West Indies is governed by two factors, the sugar plantation and negro slavery" (391).

14. On the Haitian Revolution, silencing, and disavowal, see Trouillot 70–107; and Fischer.

15. The existence of comparable factions, which could cross lines of race, color, and class, it should be recalled, are central to an understanding of the course of the Haitian Revolution.

16. Wood 22.

17. Shaffer's play, a masterpiece of total theater, tells the story of Pizarro's conquest of Peru in the sixteenth century.

18. Three of the most celebrated works in this burgeoning subfield are Edward Baptist's *The Half Has Never Been Told: Slavery and the Making of American Capitalism* (2014); Sven Beckert's *Empire of Cotton: A Global History* (2014); and Walter Johnson's *River of Dark Dreams: Slavery and Empire in the Cotton Kingdom* (2013).

Works Cited

Baptist, Edward E. *The Half Has Never Been Told: Slavery and the Making of American Capitalism*. Basic Books, 2014.

Beckert, Sven. *Empire of Cotton: A Global History*. Alfred A. Knopf, 2014.
Belle. Directed by Amma Asante, Fox Searchlight, 2013.
Birth of a Nation. Directed by Nate Parker, Fox Searchlight, 2016.
Blasini, Gilberto M. "*The Last Supper* (1976): Cinema, History, and Decolonization." *Film Analysis: A Norton Reader*, edited by Jeffrey Geiger and R. L. Rutsky, Norton, 2005, pp. 678–94.
Carpentier, Alejo. *El reino de este mundo*. 1949. Seix Barral, 2008.
Césaire, Aimé. *Discourse on Colonialism*. 1955. Translated by Joan Pinkham, Monthly Review Press, 2000.
Davis, Natalie Zemon. "Ceremony and Revolt: *Burn!* and *The Last Supper*." *Slaves on Screen*, Harvard UP, 2000, pp. 41–68.
Davis, Wade. *The Serpent and the Rainbow: A Harvard Scientist's Astonishing Journey into the Secret Societies of Haitian Voodoo, Zombis, and Magic*. 1985. Simon & Schuster, rpt. 2010.
Django Unchained. Directed by Quentin Tarantino, Columbia Pictures, 2012.
Fanon, Frantz. *The Wretched of the Earth*. 1961. Translated by Richard Philcox, Grove Press, 2004.
———. *Peau noire, masques blancs*. Éditions du Seuil, 1952.
Ferrer, Ada. *Freedom's Mirror: Cuba and Haiti in the Age of Revolution*. Cambridge UP, 2014.
Fischer, Sibylle. *Modernity Disavowed: Haiti and the Cultures of Slavery in the Age of Revolution*, Duke UP, 2004.
Gilliat, Penelope. "The Current Cinema: Last Supper in Havana." *New Yorker*, 15 May 1978, pp. 120–24.
Hudson, Peter James. "The Racist Dawn of Capitalism: Unearthing the Economy of Bondage." *Boston Review*, 14 Mar. 2016, bostonreview.net/books-ideas/peter-james-hudson-slavery-capitalism. Accessed 19 June 2016.
James, C. L. R. *The Black Jacobins*. 2nd ed. 1963. Vintage, 1989.
Johnson, Walter. *River of Dark Dreams: Slavery and Empire in the Cotton Kingdom*. Harvard UP, 2013.
Kaisary, Philip. *The Haitian Revolution in the Literary Imagination: Radical Horizons, Conservative Constraints*. U of Virginia P, 2014.
———. "The Slave Narrative and Filmic Aesthetics: Steve McQueen, Solomon Northup, and Colonial Violence." *MELUS*, vol. 42, no. 2, 2017, pp. 94–114.
Lydia Bailey. Directed by Jean Negulesco, 20th Century Fox, 1952.
Maluala. Directed by Sergio Giral, Instituto Cubano del Arte e Industria Cinematográficos, 1979.
Memorias del subdesarrollo (*Memories of Underdevelopment*). Directed by Tomás Gutiérrez Alea, Instituto Cubano del Arte e Industria Cinematográficos, 1968.
Moreno Fraginals, Manuel. *The Sugarmill: The Socioeconomic Complex of Sugar in Cuba, 1760–1860*. Translated by Cedric Belfrage, Monthly Review Press, 1976.

El otro Francisco. Directed by Sergio Giral, Instituto Cubano del Arte e Industria Cinematográficos, 1975.
Rancheador. Directed by Sergio Giral, Instituto Cubano del Arte e Industria Cinematográficos, 1976.
The Serpent and the Rainbow. Directed by Wes Craven, MCA/Universal Pictures, 1987.
Schroeder, Paul A. "*The Last Supper*: Marxism Meets Christianity." *Tomás Gutiérrez Alea: The Dialectics of a Filmmaker.* Routledge, 2002, pp. 78–91.
Seabrook, William. *The Magic Island.* 1929. George G. Harrap, 1931.
Shaffer, Peter. *The Royal Hunt of the Sun.* 1964. Penguin, 2007.
Suárez y Romero, Anselmo. *Francisco.* 1839. Instituto Cubano del Libro, 1974.
"Tomás Gutiérrez Alea." Internet Movie Database, www.imdb.com/name/nm0349425/. Accessed 19 June 2016.
Top Five. Directed by Chris Rock, Paramount Pictures, 2014.
Trouillot, Michel-Rolph. *Silencing the Past: Power and the Production of History.* Boston: Beacon Press, 1995.
12 Years a Slave. Directed by Steve McQueen, Fox Searchlight, 2013.
White Zombie. Directed by Victor Halperin, United Artists, 1932.
Wood, Marcus. *The Horrible Gift of Freedom: Atlantic Slavery and the Representation of Emancipation.* U of Georgia P, 2010.

6

Haiti

Jesús Cos Causse's Prelude to the Caribbean

ERIKA V. SERRATO

Cuban poetry holds an important place in the study of not only the Caribbean but also in Latin American literature. Yet much-studied giants such as Nicolás Guillén overshadow the literary landscape. Jesús Cos Causse, a poet whose craft renders him arguably more Caribbean than uniquely Cuban, branches out in all directions. His verses reach other shores, calling out to leading figures of the greater Caribbean, the continental Americas, and Europe. Though Cos Causse's literary influence reveals a complex, rhizomatic network, the ultimate axis reveals itself to be none other than the lost Africa that haunts the diaspora he urgently entreats. The impossibility of Africa, however, is mediated by Haiti. Haiti, for Cos Causse, is the door to the Caribbean. It is the threshold that announces the bloodlines that were lost, the battles fought for emancipation, the miscarried history that never was, and the political struggles it birthed. Haiti rests at the intersection of imperial violence, Amerindian genocide, and the bondage of African peoples. Haiti, for Cos Causse, encapsulates the history of the world.

While Cos Causse upholds Haiti's sui generis place in the history of the world, his poetry reveals a much more intimate attachment. Haiti, those who write about her, and the ideals she represents call Cos Causse, claiming the dispersed bloodlines. Jacques Roumain, one of Haiti's foremost children, who thought, wrote, and argued for the social and political sovereignty of the country and its people, leaves indelible traces on the Cuban poet's work. Roumain, as part of the *indigéniste* movement, meditated on what it meant to be Haitian, to be Caribbean, and to relate to countries of the African diaspora and Latin America. Roumain labored to highlight the Haitian subject's relationship to the land and the *paysan*'s place within the larger context of Caribbean struggles (i.e., *huelgas* in Cuba) in his well-known *Gouverneurs de la rosée* (1944). The poetic voice of Afro-Cuban Cos Causse indissolubly links Roumain to Haiti. Haiti, in turn, occupies the enviably privileged connection with Africa. Cos Causse's native Santiago de Cuba allows him to both explore distant parts of the Caribbean and delve into the figurative and literal currents that flow through him. Santiago de Cuba's history of receiving people from neighboring islands—namely, the 1800–1804 influx of white slave owners and those they had enslaved following Haiti's fight for independence from France—nourishes Cos Causse's coalescence of familial and geographic history.[1] I contend that a concentrated examination of Cos Causse, as a reader of Roumain's poetry, gives insight into the Cuban's conceptualization of Haiti and its implications for the African diaspora. Given that the academy has largely neglected Cos Causse (receiving virtually no critical attention outside of Cuba), I lay the foundation for the critical analysis of his writings.

Prelude to a "Prélude"

Jesús Cos Causse (1945–2007) gained fame as one of the more prominent voices of the second generation of writers after the Cuban Revolution of 1959. His first collection of poetry, *Con el mismo violín* (1970), won the Premio 26 de julio for best poetry collection of the year; there he offered his vision of the revolution as a fulfillment of past promises. As Ángela Castellanos notes, "El triunfo de la Revolución significó el triunfo del pensamiento del 95 y el de la revolución frustrada del 33. El año 59 no desveló la continuidad del *ser* revolucionario. Cos Causse recoge esta continuidad en su libro dándole una amplitude poética. Su poesía revela el triunfo del *ser*, que es el *ser* humano, el *ser* poeta, el *ser* Cubano, el *ser* revolucionario."[2] Cos Causse would go on to publish more than twenty books of poetry, as well as become an accomplished playwright and journalist; he would also serve as assistant director of international relations for Casa del Caribe, a prominent cultural institution in Santiago de Cuba, and as vice president of the Unión de Escritores y Artistas de Cuba (UNEAC), the Union of Writers and Artists of Cuba.³

Jacques Roumain (1907–1944) is one of the most important writer-activists of twentieth-century Haiti: born to a prominent family, he was a member of the indigenist movement as a founder of the journal *La Revue Indigène* in 1927. As a group, these intellectuals called for the rejection of French cultural values and instead the embrace of Haiti's African heritage and the development of an authentic Haitian literature, one true to the values of its populace.⁴ By the 1930s, Roumain was a staunch communist, founding the Haitian Communist Party and working toward the mobilization of his country's workers; jailed for a month in 1933, he was arrested in 1934 and sentenced to three years, a verdict that galvanized Black communities throughout the hemisphere, including Latin America and the United States.⁵ Released in 1936, he fled to Europe, where he would remain for five years, before leaving for Cuba in 1940 at the invitation of Nicolás Guillén, whom he had met in Spain and France in 1937.⁶ He returned to Haiti the following year, and soon thereafter accepted a diplomatic position that saw him stationed in Mexico in 1942. There he completed work on his masterpiece, *Gouverneurs de la rosée*, in late 1943, after which he returned to Haiti and died unexpectedly in late 1944 at thirty-seven years of age.⁷

I would like to frame this analysis as Cos Causse frames "Las Islas y las luciérnagas," the poem that christens the collection of poetry *Las Islas y las luciérnagas* (1981). Cos Causse introduces the heading section of the collection with an epigraph where he cites Roumain directly.

> ¿reconoceré la rebelión en tus manos?
> y que yo escuchaba en las Antillas
> porque este canto negra
> quien te enseñó negra este canto de inmensa pena
> negra de las Islas negra de las plantaciones
> esta desolada queja. (*Las Islas* 54)⁸

> reconnaitrai-je la révolte de tes mains?
> et que j'écoutai aux Antilles
> car ce chant négresse
> qui t'enseigna négresse ce chant d'immense
> peine
> négresse des Iles négresse des plantations
> cette plainte désolée. (Roumain, *Bois-d'ébène* 3–4)

Cos Causse inserts a Spanish rendering of Roumain's poem "Prélude" from the collection of poems *Bois-d'ébène* (1945). Let us focus on the myriad of significations offered by the title of Roumain's poem "Prélude." In addition to the figurative meaning of the word, the shared origin of music and poetry calls to mind the musical aspect of a prelude. A prelude calls for improvisation and the coming together of various apparatuses that could include both voice and instruments. Another meaning of the word indicates a sort of overture and a call for liturgical action or official acts. I argue that a general, all-encompassing meaning of the word *prélude* is intended in Roumain's poem. The prelude, in the "proper sense" of the word, prompts an action. Or better, in Roumain's case, a prelude calls for action. By including the epigraph, Cos Causse undertakes a similar venture. The section cited by Cos Causse communicates a summoning. The poetic voice asks itself whether it will be able to recognize revolt once it presents itself ("reconnaitrai-je la révolte de tes mains?"). The poem alludes to the great sorrow of the islands and the need for action. In particular, the poetic voice mentions a chant ("ce chant"). It is through this chant that revolt, sorrow, and grievance have been transmitted. More importantly, it is through the chant that the sorrow will be recognized and entreat those who hear it to take the necessary steps to aid in a time of trouble.

In a 1944 article for the short-lived journal *Gaceta del Caribe*[9] entitled "La Poesía como arma," Roumain voices his conviction that, as the title suggests, poetry is a weapon. Poetry is not, writes Roumain, "pure idealist distillation" ("pura destilación idealista" [15]). Rather, poetry is grounded on the language and concrete reality of each historical period. Poetry serves as society's "testimony and element of analysis" ("testimonio y elemento de análisis de esta sociedad" [15]). As such, it is the poet's responsibility to not only assume but also to exercise the full role of his vocation:

> El arte del poeta de hoy debe ser un arma semejante a un volante, un panfleto o un cartel. Si logramos aliar al contenido de clase del poema la belleza de la forma, si sabemos aprender la lección de Mayakovsky, podremos crear una gran poesía humana y revolucionaria, digna de los valores del espíritu que tenemos la voluntad de defender. (15)[10]

Roumain underscores that the poet's art should be similar to a pamphlet, that is, become a channel or a weapon of subversive might. As I will show, this revolutionary élan resounds in Cos Causse's poetry. Although I argue in favor of historical, cultural, and literary heritage from Roumain, I would be remiss not to acknowledge the political circumstances of the Cuban poet:

> Es a partir de la Revolución—de la cual el poeta es hijo—que se ha hecho un enorme esfuerzo moral y objetivo por la historicidad del cubano, recuperando su raíz, indagando su fondo, su más allá del tiempo, estableciendo puentes y lazos espirituales que logran una continuidad, una totalidad cubana . . . que crean una unidad del pensamiento cubano a todo lo largo de su lucha histórica por la liberación. (Castellanos 80)[11]

The Cuban Revolution's aim to look within and around one's environment nourished Cos Causse's interest in the historical and sociopolitical points of confluence in the Caribbean. Cos Causse's oeuvre—and certainly *Las Islas y las luciérnagas*—articulates the impulse to attempt to traverse the long washed over paths that trace how the Cuban subject came to be. As Angela Castellanos suggests, Cos Causse's regard for the political is elevated to an ontological imperative (80).

Ontological imperatives, however, are problematic in the Caribbean context. Questions of historical amnesia, blurredness, deterritorialization, the Middle Passage, and slavery make for a problematic delineation of the self. There can be neither finitude nor plenitude of being without origins. It is perhaps for this reason that both Roumain and Cos Causse address the ever-pending question of Africa and the fact that none of the roads will ever lead there. Instead, Roumain envisages the multiplicity of ways to get to the ancestral land and the opposition from within that very multiplicity.

> Nègre colporteur de révolte
> tu connais tous les chemins du monde
> depuis que tu fus vendu en Guinée
> une lumière chavirée t'appelle
> une pirogue livide
> échouée dans la suie d'un ciel de faubourg. (*Bois d'ébène* 2)[12]

The "nègre colporteur de révolte," the enslaved African, as a result of the violent deterritorialization of slavery, has been dispersed throughout the world, rendering him familiar with the routes of the trade. The "lumière chavirée" projects both the capsizing of innumerable boats carrying priceless human cargo as well as the alternation of the light that could signal home.

The certitude of the reader comes in the conviction that the image conveys the inevitability of catastrophe.

A Familiar Myth

Roumain's "Prélude" calls on the Caribbean subject to recognize the call to arms. For him, writing as a vocation is lost if not used in the capacity that would allow man to exist fully. I argue that Cos Causse's poetics not only recognizes the need for action but also advances the cause by actualizing the general call before relaying the message. Cos Causse's genealogical ties to Haiti via his grandfather amplify his political convictions. The song of sorrow and call for action evoke not an ancestral archetype but the immediate reality of parental lineage. The poem "Leyenda familiar" in *Las Islas y las luciérnagas* exemplifies the coalescence of personal and regional history. The poem communicates an experiential essence—a by-product derived from slavery. Cos Causse transforms elements of Cuban folklore into historical reminders and agents of subversion. The poet endows the "güije," a mischievous Black, a dwarflike otherworldly creature exclusive to Cuban folklore, with historical import:

> Abuela me llevó una vez a ver los güijes del río Cauto
> pero los güijes se asoman a la superficie de noche
> cuando la luna está muy llena y se derrama sobre la tierra
> o cuando tiembla porque salen a observar si todavía existe
> y por eso no pudimos verlos. El güije es la infancia perseguida
>   del esclavo
> que se le escapa del cuerpo después del latigazo.
>   Y los güijes viven
>   en los ríos de África y del Caribe, me decía,
>   vigilando el universo
> si los sorprendes dormidos se transforman en una mancha de
>   sangre. (*Las Islas* 28)[13]

Cos Causse presents the "güije" as equaling the "chased childhood of a slave that escapes the body after a whiplash." I propose that the "güije" represents both hardship and revolt. Cos Causse associates the character with slavery, warning against passivity and advocating for marronage. For, when asleep, that is, when dormant and passive, the "güije" transforms into a bloodstain.

Cos Causse implies the need for active participation in revolutionary struggle. Through the use of folklore, Cos Causse inculcates the Spanish-language reader (Cuban or otherwise) to resist becoming passive and to resist hardship.

The poetic voice now turns to the grandfather, who sings "Haitian laments" and becomes nostalgic about Haiti.

> Todas las tardes abuelo cantaba lamentos haitianos y las manos
> le temblaban de tocar la guitarra de ébano, de notas y de trinos
> y se iba a llorar debajo de la guásima que estaba en el fondo
>   del patio,
> mirando al mar, solo el viejo, cerca de los cafetales y de los
>   cañaverales.
>   Cuando se marchaba de viaje entonces era feliz.
>   Luego regresaba
>   con canastas llenas de pájaros, de campánulas
>   y de luciérnagas de otra isla
>   diciéndome que conversó con las sirenas y que
>   tenía miles de corales escondidos. (*Las Islas* 28)[14]

The grandfather's happiness is contingent upon travel: "Cuando se marchaba de viaje entonces era feliz." The word "entonces" (at that moment, then) sets up the condition of travel. Traveling or, rather, displacement, becomes a source of happiness. The poem focuses the reader's attention to distance. But this distance is requisite nay essential to happiness and plenitude. This need for transit, an implicit allusion to the Middle Passage, is supplanted and remembered with Haiti as a starting point, or indeed a guiding star.

A mother ("mi madre"), an obvious reference to she who bore the poet/poetic voice, evokes the more encompassing concept of origins. After all, Cos Causse writes that his mother is an island.

> Mi madre es una isla tan lejana, que a su costa
>   llegan los caracoles muertos.
> Mi madre es gris como Guadalupe y triste como Martinica.
> Por sus caminos cruza cabalgando Toussaint Louverture.
> Entre sus aguas navega la tripulación errante de Marcus Garvey.
>   (*Las Islas* 29)[15]

This island that binds him intimately remains distant—so distant, in fact, that snails and seashells ("caracoles") arrive at her shores only after perishing. Reminiscent of Martinican writer and philosopher Édouard Glissant's "gouffre-matrice," which simultaneously serves as womb and tomb, Cos Causse's mother, the island/place of birth cannot be reached in life.[16] One is inextricably linked yet destined to be forever apart. The space of birth effectively becomes a nullified dead space: empty of his presence and out of reach. Additionally, Santiago de Cuba's relative proximity to Haiti renders the two islands ever in pulling, attracting positions and suspended in distance.

The poetic voice informs the reader that his mother is gray like Martinique and Guadeloupe. This kinship signals to the shared experience of French colonialism. Despite the understandable historical link, the syntax of the following verse disturbs the signification. There are two consecutive verses referencing the mother—yet the poetic voice switches gears and tells us, "Por sus caminos cruza cabalgando Toussaint Louverture." It is not clear whether "sus" (hers, his, its?) continues to refer to the mother. If the poetic voice refers to a physical or biological mother, then the meaning is not clear and the reader is left to his or her interpretative devices. I argue that Haiti is the mother whose paths ("sus caminos") are traversed. This is further evidenced by the end of the verse, where one of Haiti's favorite sons, Toussaint Louverture, is explicitly mentioned. The sudden presence of Toussaint Louverture announces the arrival of other important figures in Caribbean history. Among its waters ("[e]ntre sus aguas") navigates the nomadic crew of Marcus Garvey. Though not Haitian, the Jamaican leader of the Pan-African movement became involved in political matters related to Haiti. In a letter to Haitian president Louis Borno in 1924, for example, Garvey praises Haiti as "the pride of the Black race of the Western world" (6). Cos Causse echoes Garvey's praise of the Haitian nation and its inimitable place in the world.

An approaching Jacques Roumain suddenly appears in the poem. As he looks for a door, a woman, an image of foam, distances herself.

> Con sus pasos se acerca Jacques Roumain buscando una puerta
> y se aleja una mujer que es una imagen de espuma y que amo.
> Alguien me llama y es cierto que mi sangre y mi isla fluyen,
>   que nací
> con los puños cerrados y mi nombre musical es una lágrima
>   antigua. (*Las Islas* 29)[17]

Although it is not clear whether the poetic voice refers to the woman herself or to the image, the reader is alerted as to the intimacy between the poetic voice and said undeclared woman. If this woman is the one previously mentioned in the poem—mother Haiti—then we can safely assume that Cos Causse privileges Haiti. Haiti, that loved woman who is akin to foam, materializes only to disintegrate just as fast. The last stanza further communicates ambiguity and impotence. An unknown voice calls out to the poetic voice.

> ¿Qué güije ronda mi infancia? ¿Quién levanta el látigo?
> ¿Quién canta este lamento y espanta esta paloma?
> ¿Cuál isla se hunde mientras una mujer me
>   espera entre héroes y poetas? (*Las Islas* 28–29)[18]

Blood and island flow in the same manner, as if mirroring each other. The poetic subject has been born with closed fists and his musical name is an ancient tear.[19] Through a series of questions, Cos Causse finalizes the poem by emphasizing the ambiguity that pervades over the it. The poetic subject asks what "güije" haunts his childhood, who picks up the whip, who sings this lament. Finally, and, ultimately more important for our purposes, Cos Causse ends the poem with the suggestive question of *which island* drowns while a woman awaits him among heroes and poets. Cos Causse dissolves the specificity of each island. The title "Leyenda familiar," then, alludes to not only a family legend but also to a familiar legend—one that, echoing Benítez-Rojo, would repeat in each island. Cuba, Haiti, and the entire Caribbean are muddled and complicit in history, myth, pain, and song.

Braulio Causse: Grandfather, Haitian, Troubadour, Cane Cutter, Maroon by Birth

The poem "Braulio Causse" evidences Cos Causse's ambiguity between the universal and the particular. Braulio Causse, the poet's grandfather, is presented in the epigraph to the collection of poetry *Las Luces y las luciérnagas* in the following manner:

> A la memoria
> de mi abuelo
> Braulio Causse:
> haitiano,
> trovador,

> cortador de caña,
> cimarrón de nacimiento,
> que va y a lo mejor anda
> escondido todavía por ahí.[20]

The fact that the book of poems *Las Islas y las luciérnagas* corresponds to a poem by the same title that treats the very concept of what it is to exist as a Caribbean subject is very telling. Indeed, the dedication to the personal bond to the Haitian grandfather heads a poem that attempts to encompass the entire Caribbean experience. Cos Causse exemplifies the Caribbean experience by highlighting the plight of a Haitian man who, himself, is constituted by major markers in the Caribbean context (family, cane cutter, maroon, et al.). The poem that bears his grandfather's name includes an epigraph taken from a statement made by Fidel Castro. The statement addresses the arrival of dozens and dozens of boats of Haitian immigrants who may have another destination in mind yet arrive to Cuban shores in broken boats in the years of the Duvalier dictatorship.[21] Cos Causse entreats the reader to approach the poem keeping in mind displacement and drifting, this time in the specific context of inter-Caribbean wanderings.

"Braulio Causse" is divided into two thematically different sections. The first section charts Braulio Causse's epic adventures throughout the Caribbean, while the second focuses on his intimate experiences. It is important to note that the first section is framed with references to Haiti, acting as bookends to a saga.

> Contaba
> que vino solo en el viaje
> y contra el viento desde Haití,
> emigrante hasta de sus propios sueños,
> polizonte sin ruta y sin Puerto. (*Las Islas* 30)[22]

The first stanza communicates deterritorialization and being lost at sea. Braulio Causse traveled alone and against the elements. He is doomed to be a migrant even in his dreams. He was a vagrant without route or port. In other words, he has been stripped of his identity as a person. In the second stanza, the poetic voice informs the reader that he has undertaken the voyage in an immense pumpkin, using cane as main mast and a yagruma leaf as flag. All without oars, candles, a map, or a compass. Nature itself—and a violent nature at that, in the form of cyclones—allowed itself to be read and, in turn, orient. Though the narrative of the poem focuses on the story of the eponymous figure of Braulio Causse, it can also be read as the universal experience of the Middle Passage. He who has been taken from his land of origin has suffered an ontological change. He has been estranged from himself. His very dreams—the most obscure part of his psyche—has been altered.

The third stanza takes the reader through a Caribbean excursion that includes, among others, Saint Lucia, Curaçao, and the Cayman Islands. The poetic voice recounts how Braulio Causse "had various dangerous shipwrecks" and how each island required or inspired a new lie.

The fourth stanza provides the reader with an enumeration of the items found in Braulio Causse's "barco de calabaza." It is important to note that the items mentioned (drums, flutes, guitars, maracas, codes, coconuts, and seashells) are of two, relatable natures. The most obvious of the categories is that of music:

Contaba
que en su barco de calabaza
traía tambores, flautas, guitarras,
maracas, claves, cocos y caracoles. (*Las Islas* 31–32)[23]

The remaining items, however, can be traced back to Vodou ceremonies. In addition to the religious and cultural import of said articles, I am reminded of Glissant's meditation on the relationship of Africans to instruments. Glissant explains that the status of a slave being equal to that of an "outil animé," he cannot cultivate the most typical relationship to instruments (*Le Discours antillais* 175–78). Nevertheless, Cos Causse's choice of instruments would seem to present an interesting opposition to Glissant's assertion, for they empower and guide he who possesses them.

The fifth and sixth stanzas undergo a rhythmic change. Whereas the stanzas leading up to the end began the same way, the last two change the structure, mirroring the content adjustment. Indeed, the first four stanzas began with the single-word verse: "Contaba," which would translate as "he used to relate/tell." The anaphoric repetition emphasizes the frequency and import of storytelling. Additionally, the reiteration serves as echo of the ubiquitous story of slavery. Cos Causse passes through the prism of the universal and arrives to the singularity of the familial. Braulio Causse's tipping pumpkin boat arrives in Santiago and sees the fish devour his ship. He makes a sea-neighboring life with the poet's grandmother.

The sixth stanza reveals how one day Braulio Causse began to cough and to feel "a thorn in the chest, a cramp in the head, a rumor in the head":

> Un día comenzó a toser,
> a sentirse una espina en el pecho,
> un calambre en la cabeza,
> un rumor en la memoria,
> fiebres y escalofríos
> y me regaló, tembloroso, dos centavos
> que llevaba envueltos en un pañuelo.
> En su delirio
> decía ver sombras y visiones
> inventó nuevos cuentos increíbles
> hasta que la muerte le cerró los ojos
> sin volver a pisar su Haití natal. (*Las Islas* 32)[24]

Mid-delirium, Braulio Causse begins to relate amazing stories yet again. Not having returned to his "native Haiti," he departs one final time. The second section of "Braulio Causse" contrasts with the juxtaposition of historical fact and mythical insinuations that extend to both widespread and individual experience. The poetic voice now attempts to fill in the gaps of the departed ancestor. Not rendered explicit until the middle point of the poem, Cos Causse writes about the experience of a runaway slave. Braulio Causse carries the indelible marks of a maroon. The external signs include chain demarcations on the wrists. The invisible effects of slavery are much more pervasive. Cos Causse describes a character suspect of his surroundings. Time catches up with Braulio Causse, finally feeling the weight of the "antigua agonía de la jornada de trabajo junto / al trapiche, de sol a sol, bajo la lluvia y un latigazo / y otro y otro si se cansaba, como si hubiera sido un buey" (33).[25] There is an omnipresence of fear and malaise that extends beyond individual marronage. Cos Causse discusses the details of his grandfather, fully aware of the parallel stories.

Jacques Roumain: Cos Causse's Quijote Negro

Although Cos Causse never consecrates an entire poem to Jacques Roumain, many of his poems address directly, allude to, or cite the Haitian author.[26] Indeed, Roumain has a pervading, silent presence in Cos Causse's writing.

The closing poem of the collection of poetry *Concierto de jazz* (1994), entitled "El Quijote Negro," discloses Cos Causse's high regard and response to Roumain's ruminations on Africa, included in the form of an epigraph: "África, he guardado tu memoria, África. / Tu estás en mí como la espina está en la herida . . ."[27] Cos Causse echoes and amplifies this sentiment in the poem that ensues. The poet imparts the anonymous and consequently universal tale of an African man who is forced to leave his land and the deterritorializing experience he will never forget:

> Desde un lugar del África
> cuyo nombre nunca olvidaría
> partió en un barco de la trata
> este Quijote Negro encadenado. (*Concierto de jazz* 73)[28]

Cos Causse exploits the semantic value of the first stanza. The verses are the mirror image of Miguel de Cervantes's *chef d'oeuvre*: "En un lugar de la Mancha, de cuyo nombre no quiero acordarme . . ." (27). Cos Causse's use of Cervantes's Don Quixote, the most emblematic figure of Hispanic letters, disrupts the cultural wavelength and concretizes the lived experience of the Caribbean for the larger Spanish-speaking world. Whereas the eponymous hero of the Spanish author would rather not remember his provenance, the Quijote Negro of Cos Causse's poem would never choose to forget. The irony implied by the image Cos Causse offers the reader is quite striking. While the memory of the Middle Passage and slavery percolates in Cos Causse's writing, it remains a vague reality for the text's poetic voice ("un lugar del África"). The Quijote Negro, he who was chased as an animal, however, would never forget. The poet attempts to imagine the great, indescribable loss of family ("sin despedirse," "reino de su infancia" [73]), landscape, and culture ("No tuvo más fortuna que el tesoro / de la floresta, sus fetiches y sus ofrendas" [74]). This erosion of self precipitates the Quijote Negro's call for rain and the need to take root elsewhere ("Danzaba con sus hermanos para llamar la lluvia / y para mirar como estallaba la semilla sembrada" [74]). Cos Causse grazes a scar whose origin was never known. The lone item that would remain within the Quijote Negro's grasp, however, would allow him to attain a vestige of freedom and a glimpse of the past:

> Nuestro Quijote Negro viajó con su tambor,
> un tambor ancestral y más fiel que Sancho Panza.
> Un tambor telúrico y místico, hijo legítimo de los dioses.

> Un tambor custodiado por Obbatalá, Oggún, Shangó,
> Oshún, Eshu y Erinle. Un tambor que conversaba en el barco
> con los esclavos y que solo Quijote Negro podía tocar y mandar.
> (76)[29]

Cos Causse renders the realm of signification equally ample in the preceding stanza. The poet introduces the pantheon of the Regla de Lucumí or Ocha.[30] In religious ceremony, these gods are accessed through the beating of a drum. The Quijote Negro's ancestral, mystical, and faithful drum, as the legitimate son of (read: vessel to) the gods, communicates with and listens to him. Though this explanation by itself would be faithful to the cultural context of the poet, I suggest that it is nonetheless incomplete. Given that one of the main preoccupations of Cos Causse is the very figure and the various roles played by the poet,[31] I propose that this stanza veils the latent power of poetry. Indeed, the drum, a musical instrument sanctioned by the gods, cannot but recall the "batá de fundamento" (consecrated *batá* drums), whose physical makeup is joined by a spiritual component only accessed by those initiated into the religious belief system (Schweitzer 4). Cos Causse presents a Quijote Negro fully initiated and able to access the wealth of divine poetics. It is poetry that allows the Quijote Negro to ponder and commune with those outside of his temporal and spatial reach. Thanks to the drum's power to connect, the Quijote Negro is able to never forget. In this sense, Cos Causse emphasizes the role of poetry in the formation of Caribbean identity via religious and cultural elements. To write, to sing, and to play the drum is to reify the self.

Las Islas y las luciérnagas

Having addressed Cos Causse's intertextual references to Roumain, I would now like to focus on the most solid of spectral traces, namely, on motifs and on their execution through imagery. I will show that Roumain's thought pervades Cos Causse's poetics even in absentia. Indeed, even when Roumain's concrete, textual presence vanishes, his intertextual traces remain. The poem "Las Islas y las luciérnagas" presents the reader with what can only be described as a revolt of the landscape. Since I am interested in accentuating Roumain's poetic traces, I shall give the most succinct excerpt of the phenomenon rather than include the epic-like poem in its entirety:

Los culpables de este mapa de islas que naufragan pagarán sus
   deudas
y las luciérnagas serán testigos y el cielo será sorprendido
por un eclipse que tendrá la dimensión de un sismo misterioso
   o de una catástrofe cósmica
y despertarán los volcanes viejos y sus hijos y todas las naves
que se hundieron durante la trata se asomarán a la superficie
con los esqueletos a bordo y con las banderas de las
   transnacionales
en los mástiles y los elementos de las tormentas y las aguas
   angustiadas
vigilarán los barcos cargados de azúcar y los reptiles clavarán
   sus garras en los ojos de los burgueses
y la cáscara de cacao será un cuchillo y el humo del tabaco
   un gas tóxico
y el algodón tendrá espinas inesperadas y el plátano pólvora
y por la herida de la madera saldrá un enjambre de abejas
   enfurecidas con aguijones envenenados
y el ron saltará de la botella convertido en llamas y las redes
   estarán
llenas de grandes agujeros y la bauxita se convertirá en ceniza
y tendremos un fósforo listo para cuando brote el petroleo
   desesperado
y botaremos la miel en la tierra y cortaremos los troncos de la
   yagruma
y el tambor que llama al combate sonará como si el animal
   regresara a su piel aullando eternamente. (*Las Islas* 52)[32]

Those responsible for the shipwreck of Caribbean colonialism, interventionism, and exploitation will pay their figurative debt. The fireflies will witness and the heavens will be surprised by natural disasters that have devastated the Caribbean. More importantly, the natural resources and commodities will become hostile: the cacao shell will turn into a knife, tobacco smoke into toxic gas, plantains into gunpowder, and the rum will set itself aflame. The struggle for independence and sovereignty will become a struggle fought from the very fruits of the land. I advance that Roumain's poem "Sales nègres" provides Cos Causse with the imagery and force of a vengeful nature. Indeed, "Sales nègres" revolves around those who exploit not only the Caribbean island but also the African diaspora throughout the Americas. Roumain's poem confounds man and product:

> nous n'acceptons plus
> ça vous étonne
> de dire: oui missié
> en cirant vos bottes
> oui mon pé
> aux missionaires blancs
> oui maître
> en récoltant pour vous
> la canne à sucre
> le café
> le coton
> l'arachide
> en Afrique
> en Amérique
> en bons nègres
> en pauvres nègres
> en sales nègres.(*Bois-d'ébène* 26–27)[33]

Plantation stock and men are indexed the same way—seemingly equaling each other. But just like Cos Causse illustrates in his epic poem, the abuse will prove too much.

> trop tard il sera trop tard
> pour empêcher dans les cotonneries de Louisiane
> dans les Centrales sucrières des Antilles
> la récolte de vengeance
> des nègres
> des niggers
> des sales nègres
> il sera trop tard je vous dis (*Bois-d'ébène* 33)[34]

Plantations and factories are directly involved in the "vengeance harvest," as instruments, stock, and the landscape itself will retaliate and join the vengeful ire of the Caribbean man.

cette plainte désolée ... tiene un rostro ...

I started this analysis by invoking Roumain's "Prélude" and Cos Causse's epigraphical inclusion into his book of poems *Las Islas y las luciérnagas*. I would now like to return our attention to the "Prélude." As already established, revolutionary ideals, Haiti, and Africa comprise Cos Causse's conceptualization of Jacques Roumain. The third section of *Las Islas y las Luciérnagas*, entitled "La tierra canta y tiene un rostro," includes two epigraphs. One is by Puerto Rican poet Luis Palés Matos and evokes the chant of liberty in the Caribbean.[35] The main epigraph, however, is the excerpt mentioned at the beginning of this study regarding the recognition of the need to rebel.[36] The poetic voice in Roumain's poem asks whether he will be able to recognize rebellion when it will be before him. The verses are grounded in the Antilles—taking a reprieve from island hopping or the focus on Africa that reigns over the rest of the poem. Furthermore, Roumain's poem alludes to a chant, a chant of immense sorrow and a devastated complaint.[37] As we have already seen, Cos Causse echoes this chant in his poems. His chant, however, does not lose force in the ether. On the contrary, Cos Causse's chant becomes concretized. After all, "the land chants and it has a *face*." Cos Causse's poetic voice no longer questions whether he will recognize rebellion. The chant before us has origins. The chant now belongs to a particular experience. This concretization becomes more visible in the poem that bears the very title of the section:

> Por el mar llegaron desde África nuestros
>   hermanos, no sólo
> a cortar cañas como esclavos ni a morirse como
>   cimarrones,
> sino a levantarse y a luchar y a entender juntos
>   la llamarada revolucionaria (*Las Islas* 66)[38]

"La tierra canta y tiene un rostro" crystallizes Roumain's revolutionary ideals for poetics. In "La tierra canta y tiene un rostro," Cos Causse strives to give a global overview of the Caribbean experience. Cos Causse acknowledges departure from the ancestral land of Africa. The complicity of the sea in dissolving ties all while maintaining confluence is also highlighted. Cos Causse paints a picture of the spectrum of the deterritorialized, enslaved African—from the subdued slave to the rebellious maroon. Above all, the poem zeroes in on rising together in the name of rebellious struggle. The legend of that Haitian musician ("la leyenda de aquel músico haitiano" [66]) connects with nostalgic souvenirs of the Caribbean waters. Cos Causse's interest in the universal reappears under the light of different dimensions and possibilities of being, prompting the reader to imagine an alternate course of history. Though all of the aforementioned elements are present in the poem, Cos Causse centers the poem on not only revolution but also on the force behind any one revolution:

> Ahora quiero hablarte de la tierra que nos pertenece, nos une,
> nos sostiene, nos alimenta y nos anuncia que la vida existe,
> que están cayendo las flores del flamboyán, que los obreros
> están construyendo piedra a piedra nuevamente el mundo,
> que los campesinos están abriendo un surco
>   desde el presente hasta el porvenir,
> porque estamos de prisa, nos esperan los asuntos urgentes,
> los documentos, los testimonios, los estandartes, las conquistas,
> quiero decir, la sangre y la canción de los héroes y de los hombres
> de esta isla donde la tierra canta y tiene un rostro de esperanza
>   (*Las Islas* 67)[39]

Cos Causse gives prominence to the binding force behind working together: the land itself. The land for Cos Causse, as is for Roumain, fights back. It provides sustenance for the future yet holds the key to the past. The chant, that same chant, is repeated. It is the island itself that sings and cries. This island—all islands—that no longer hides has the face of hope.

Cos Causse associates Haiti and her sons with Africa. It is, in his writings, a lineage that refuses dissolution, for Cos Causse mentions them in the same poetic breath: "África, Cuba y Haití / aguas y más aguas y aguas" (*Confesiones del poeta* 27). This sentiment goes beyond the poetic and metaphorical. Indeed, the preceding verse belongs to the poem "Autobiografía" and, as we have seen, the poem "Braulio Causse" intimates the poet's Haitian origins. Jacques Roumain, for Cos Causse, embodies the poet, the Haitian, the African within the Cuban family. Cos Causse hears Roumain's call for action and echoes the enmeshed history of the Caribbean archipelago. Cos Causse infuses the poetic with the political. His poetry explores entwining origins: intellectual formation, familial history, and ancestral inheritance. He garners and maps out Roumain's refracted capsized light ("lumière chavirée") throughout the Caribbean. By focusing on Haitian grandfather Braulio

Causse's modern-day retelling of violent displacement, Cos Causse makes Caribbean history an ardent, urgent, painful family affair. In so doing, the family scar becomes a permanent aperture to the past.

Notes

1. For more information concerning Haitian and French migrations to Cuba, see Jean Lamore's edited volume *Les Français dans l'orient cubain* and Agnès Renault's *D'une île rebelle à une île fidèle*. For a concentrated examination of Francophone groups in Santiago de Cuba in particular, see Aisnara Perera Díaz and María de los Ángeles Meriño Fuentes's *El Cabildo carabalí viví de Santiago de Cuba: familia, cultura y sociedad (1797–1909)* and Sandra Estévez Rivero and colleagues' edited *Por la identidad del negro cubano*.

2. "The triumph of the Revolution meant the triumph of the thought of 1895 and of the thwarted revolution of 1933. The year 1959 revealed to us the continuity of the revolutionary *being*. Cos Causse harvests that continuity in his book, giving it poetic breadth. His poetry reveals the triumph of the *being*, which is the human *being*, the poet *being*, the Cuban *being*, the revolutionary *being*" (81).

3. For more on the critical reception of Cos Causse among Cuban writers and artists, see Ruiz Miyares.

4. For more on the importance of this journal, see Perry.

5. See Smith 21.

6. Smith 51.

7. Smith 55–56.

8. "will I recognize the revolt in your hands? / and which I used to hear in the Antilles / because this chant, negra / who taught you, negra, this song of immense sorrow / negra of the islands, negra of the plantations / this desolate cry." Unless otherwise noted, all translations are mine. In this case, my translation leaves the ambiguity of "negra" as both a "Black woman" and a term of endearment. I also change "canto" (Roumain's "chant") to a chant, a song, and a cry.

9. *Gaceta del Caribe* was founded by Cuban writers Nicolás Guillén, Mirta Aguirre, Ángel Augier, and José Antonio Portuondo with the goal of treating literary and cultural issues related to Cuba and the rest the Caribbean. The journal only produced half a dozen issues, dying out before the year was over. Guillén and Roumain's well-known friendship as well as literary and political collaborations and exchanges are detailed in the former's memoirs, *Paginas vueltas* (1982).

10. "The art of the poet today should be a weapon similar to a flyer, a pamphlet, or a poster. If we achieve combining the beauty of form to the class content of the poem, if we know to learn Mayakovsky's lesson, we will be able to create a great human and revolutionary poetry, worthy of the values of spirit that we have the will to defend" (translation by the editor of this volume).

11. "It is beginning with the Revolution—the poet being its child—that a great moral and objective effort has been made for the historicity of the Cuban, recovering his origin, investigating his depth, his beyond time, establishing bridges and spiritual ties that achieve a Cuban continuity, a totality . . . that create a unity of Cuban thought throughout its historical struggle for freedom" (translation by the editor of this volume).

12. "Negro peddler or rebellion / you know all the routes of the world / since you were sold in Guinea / a capsized light calls on you / a ghostly canoe / run aground on the soot of a suburban sky" (Roumain, *Tom-Tom* 75).

13. "Grandma took me to see the güijes at the Cauto river / but the güijes only come to the surface at night / when the moon is very full and spills over the earth / or when it trembles when they come to see if it still exists / that is why we cannot see them. The güije is the hounded childhood of the slave. / It escapes his body after he was whipped. / And the güijes live / in the rivers of / Africa and the Caribbean, she told me, surveilling the universe / and if you catch them asleep they become a bloodstain."

14. "Every afternoon grandfather sang Haitian laments and his hands / trembled each time he played the ebony guitar of notes and trills, / and he went to weep under the guásima in the far side of the patio, / contemplating the sea, alone, the old man, near the coffee plantations and reedbed. / When he was only happy when he went on trips. / He would later be back / with baskets filled with birds, bluebells, / and fireflies from another island / and tell me that he spoke / with sirens and that / he had thousands of corals hidden."

15. "My mother is such a faraway island, that to her shores / dead seashells arrive. / My mother is gray like Guadeloupe and melancholic like Martinique. / Her trails are traversed by Toussaint Louverture on horseback. / Amid her/his/its waters navigates Marcus Garvey's wandering crew."

16. "Le ventre de cette barque-ci te dissout, te précipite dans un non-monde où tu cries. Cette barque est une matrice, le gouffre-matrice. Génératrice de ta clameur. Productrice aussi de toute unanimité à venir. Car si tu es seul dans cette souffrance, tu partages l'inconnu avec quelques-uns, que tu ne connais pas encore. Cette barque est ta matrice, un moule, qui t'expulse pourtant. Enceinte d'autant de morts que de vivants en sursis" (*Poétique de la relation* 18).

17. "Step by step Jacques Roumain looks for a door / and a woman that is an image of foam, whom I love, moves farther away. / Someone calls me and it is true that my blood and my island flow, that I was born / with closed fists and my musical name is an ancient tear."

18. "What güije stalks my childhood? Who raised the whip? / Who sings this lament and scares away this dove? / Which of the islands will sink while a woman / awaits me among heroes and poets?"

19. I would like to point out that Cos Causse uses the trope of a tear when speaking of Haiti throughout his oeuvre. Haiti's association with a tear is especially clear in "Las Islas y las luciérnagas."

20. "To the memory / of my grandfather / Braulio Causse: / Haitian, / troubadour, / cane cutter, / maroon by birth, / what if he is / hidden still around here."

21. ". . . un fenómeno que se ha ido produciendo de modo creciente en los últimos años, que es la llegada de decenas y decenas de barcos, de inmigrantes haitianos que pretenden ir para Bahamas, para Estados Unidos, para otras partes, y llegan en sus barcos, muchas veces descompuestos, a veces sin combustible. En ocasiones se han dado casos también de naufragios. Pero llegan por la costa norte, por la costa sur. —Fidel Castro Ruz, 8 de Marzo de 1980" (*Las Islas* 30).

22. "He would tell / that he came on the voyage alone / and against the wind all the way from Haiti, / migrating even from his own dreams, / stowaway without route or port."

23. "He would tell / that in his pumpkin ship / he brought drums, flutes, guitars, / maracas, keys, coconuts, and snails."

24. "One day he started to cough, / to feel a thorn in his chest, / a cramp in his head, / a rumor in his memory, / fevers and shivers, / and he gave me, while shaking, two cents / he had covered in a handkerchief. / In his delirium / he said he saw shadows and visions / he came up with incredible tales / until death closed his eyes / without ever setting foot again in his native Haiti."

25. "ancient agony of a day's work next to the sugar mill, from sun to sun, under the rain and a whiplash / and another and another if he became tired, as if he were an ox."

26. In addition to the preceding poem ("Leyenda y una espada para Toussaint Louverture") and his epigraphs, Roumain appears in "Leyenda familiar" and "Leyenda y tributo a Marcos Garvey" in *Las Islas y las luciérnagas* alone.

27. "Africa, I kept your memory, Africa / you are in me / Like a splinter in the wound" ("El Quijote negro," ll. 77–79).

28. "From a place in Africa / whose name he would never forget / he left in a slave ship / this chained Black Quijote."

29. "Our Black Quijote traveled with his drum, / an ancestral drum and more faithful than Sancho Panza. / A telluric and mystical drum, legitimate son of the gods. / A drum guarded by Obbatalá, Oggún, Shangó, / Oshún, Eshu, and Erinle. A drum that chatted with the ship / slaves and that only the Black Quijote could play and command."

30. For more detailed information regarding the complex ceremonies, divinities, and musicality of the Regla de Lucumí, see Katherine J. Hagedorn's *Divine Utterances: The Performance of Afro-Cuban Santería*, Kenneth Schweitzer's *The Artistry of Afro-Cuban Batá Drumming: Aesthetics, Transmission, Bonding, and Creativity*, Natalia Bolívar Aróstegui's *Los orishas en Cuba*, and Joel James Figarola's *Los sistemas mágico-religiosos cubanos: principios rectores*.

31. This is evidenced by Cos Causse's *Confesiones del poeta* as well as his compulsion to evoke and cite poets, writers, and a myriad of artists throughout his works.

32. "Those guilty of this map of shipwrecked islands will pay their debts / and fireflies will be witnesses and the sky will be caught by surprise / by an eclipse

with the dimension of a mysterious earthquake or that of a cosmic catastrophe / and old volcanoes will wake up and their children and all the ships / that sank during the Middle Passage will appear on the surface / with the skeletons aboard and with multinational corporations' flags / on the masts and the storms' elements and anxious waters / will watch ships heavy with sugar and reptiles will nail their claws on bourgeois eyes / and cacao shell will be a knife and tobacco smoke a toxic gas / and cotton will have unexpected thorns and plantain gunpowder / and through the woods' wound will come out a swarm of furious bees with poisoned stings / and rum will jump from the bottle transformed in flames and nets will be / full of great holes and bauxite will turn into ash / and we will have a match ready for oil's frenzied spring / and we will throw honey on the earth and we will cut the trunks of the yagruma / and the drum that calls for combat will sound as if the animal came back to its skin / ever howling."

33. "we won't take anymore / that surprises you / to say: *yessuh* / while polishing your boots / *oui mon pé* / to the white missionaries / yes, master / while harvesting your / sugarcane / coffee / cotton / peanuts / in Africa / in America / like good boys / poor negroes / filthy niggers." My translation is a variation of Roumain, *Tom-Tom* (84–87). I have edited the translation in order to more accurately convey the ambiguity of "nègre" in French and the contextualized intensification in Roumain's original from the paternalistic ("good boys") to the purposefully degrading ("filthy niggers").

34. "too late it will be too late / on the cotton plantations of Louisiana / in the sugarcane fields of the Antilles / to halt the harvest of vengeance / of the negroes / the niggers / the filthy negroes / it will be too late I tell you" (Roumain, *Tom-Tom* 95).

35. "Porque eres tú, mulata de los trópicos, / la libertad cantando en mis Antillas" (Because it is you, *mulata* of the tropics / liberty singing in my Antilles [54]).

36. "reconoceré la rebelión en tus manos? / y que yo escuchaba en las Antillas / porque este canto negra / quien te enseñó negra este canto de inmensa pena / negra de las Islas negra de las plantaciones / esta desolada queja" (will I recognize the revolt in your hands? / and which I used to hear in the Antilles / because this chant, negra / who taught you, negra, this song of immense sorrow / negra of the islands, negra of the plantations / this desolate cry [54]).

37. "reconnaîtrai-je la révolte de tes mains? / et que j'écoutai aux Antilles / car ce chant négresse / qui t'enseigna négresse ce chant d'immense / peine / négresse des îles négresse des plantations / cette plainte désolée" (*Bois-d'ébène* 19–20).

38. "By the sea arrived from Africa our brothers, not only / to cut sugarcane as slaves nor to die as maroons, / but also to get up and to fight and to understand together the revolutionary flare."

39. "Now I want to talk to you about the land that belongs to us, unites us, / supports us, feeds us and announces to us that life exists, / that flowers are falling from the flamboyán, that the workers / are building the world anew stone by stone, / that the farmers are opening a furrow from the present to the future, / because we are in a hurry, urgent matters await us, / documents, testimonies,

banners, conquests, / I mean to say, blood and the heroes' song and that of men / from this island where the land sings and has the face of hope."

Works Cited

Bastien, A. Remy. "Jacques Roumain." *Boletín bibliográfico de antropología americana (1937–1948)*, vol. 8, no. 1, 1945, pp. 73–57.
Bolívar Aróstegui, Natalia. *Los orishas en Cuba*. Editorial José Martí, 2014.
Bruner, Charlotte H. "An Audio-Visual Presentation of Black Francophone Poetry." *The French Review*, vol. 55, no. 6, 1982, pp. 862–68.
Castellanos, Ángela. "Las armas de Cos Causse." *Cos Causse: Tiempo y poesía*, edited by Oscar Ruiz Miyares, Editorial Oriente, 1988, pp. 78–86.
Cos Causse, Jesús. *Confesiones de un poeta*. Editorial Oriente, 2006.
―――. *Balada de un tambor y otros poemas*. Editorial Unión de Escritores y Artistas de Cuba, 1987.
―――. *Concierto de jazz*. Editorial Oriente, 1994.
―――. *Las Islas y las luciérnagas*. Editorial Letras Cubanas, 1981.
De Cervantes, Miguel. *Don Quijote de la Mancha, I*, edited by John Jay Allen. Cátedra, 2005.
Estévez Rivero, Sandra, Pedro Manuel Castro Monterrey, and Olga Portuondo Zúñiga, editors. *Por la identidad del negro Cubano*. Ediciones Caserón, 2011.
Figarola, Joel James. *Los sistemas mágico-religiosos cubanos: principios rectores*. Ediciones Unión de Escritores y Artistas de Cuba, 2001.
Garvey, Marcus. "Letter to Honorable Louis Borno, President of Haiti, Port-au-Prince, Haiti." *Negro World*, 9 August 1924, p. 6.
Glissant, Édouard. *Le Discours antillais*. Gallimard, 1997.
―――. *Poétique de la relation*. Gallimard, 1990.
Guillén, Nicolás. "Présentation." *Bois-d'ébène suivi de Madrid*. Mémoire d'encrier, 2003, pp. 9–13.
―――. *Páginas vueltas: memorias*. Ediciones Unión de Escritores y Artistas de Cuba, 1982.
Hagedorn, Katherine J. *Divine Utterances: The Performance of Afro-Cuban Santeria*. Smithsonian Institute Press, 2001.
Lafontant, Julien T. "De l'Imitation à l'authenticité dans la poésie haïtienne." *The French Review*, vol. 54, no. 4, 1981, pp. 551–57.
Lamore, Jean, editor. *Les Français dans l'orient cubain: actes du colloque international de Santiago de Cuba, 16–18 avril 1991*. Maison des pays ibériques, 1993.
Perera Díaz, Aisnara, and María de los Ángeles Meriño Fuentes. *El Cabildo carabalí viví de Santiago de Cuba: familia, cultura y sociedad (1797–1909)*. Editorial de Oriente, 2013.
Perry, Amanda T. "Becoming Indigenous in Haiti, from Dessalines to *La Revue Indigène*." *Small Axe*, vol. 21, 2017, pp. 45–61.

Renault, Agnès. *D'une île rebelle à une île fidèle: les Français de Santiago de Cuba, 1791–1825*. Publications des Universités de Rouen et du Havre, 2012.
Reyes, Susana. "Un Poemario del Caribe." *Cos Causse: Tiempo y poesía*, edited by Oscar Ruiz Miyares, Editorial Oriente, 1988, pp. 116–18.
Roumain, Jacques. *Bois-d'ébène*. Imprimerie Henri Deschamps, 1945.
———. *Bois-d'ébène suivi de Madrid*. Mémoire d'encrier, 2003.
———. "La Poesia como arma." *Gaceta del Caribe*, vol. 1, 1944, p. 15.
———. *When the Tom-Tom Beats*. Translated by Joanne Fungaroli and Ronald Sauer, Azul Editions, 1995.
Ruiz Miyares, Oscar, editor. *Cos Causse: Tiempo y poesía*. Editorial Oriente, 1988.
Schweitzer, Kenneth. *The Artistry of Afro-Cuban Batá Drumming: Aesthetics, Transmission, Bonding, and Creativity*. UP of Mississippi, 2013.
Smith, Matthew J. *Red and Black in Haiti: Radicalism, Conflict, and Political Change, 1934–1957*. U of North Carolina P, 2009.

7

"But the Captain Is Haitian"

Issues of Recognition within Ana Lydia Vega's "Encancaranublado"

MARIANA PAST

When asked about my employment status some years ago, I said that I taught Caribbean literature, and my interlocutor responded dubiously, "*They* have literature?" The ignorant remark epitomizing a racialized, consumerist mind-set—and bringing to mind boorish cruise ship passengers—never left me. Later on, while reading "Encancaranublado" (Three men in a boat) (1982), a short story by Puerto Rican writer Ana Lydia Vega, it struck me that the text affords readers an enlightening anti-cruise ship experience while leveling a verbal cannon at Northern agents who command, protect, and populate such vessels (among other spaces). That Vega's narrative also speaks volumes about perceptions of Haiti's role within the Spanish-speaking Caribbean and the larger Americas is the reason I offer the following reflections to the collection at hand. Perverse racial and political discourses about the Caribbean bear critical examination precisely because they know no national or geographic bounds.

The vexing ignorance exhibited earlier illustrates but one aspect of an enduring and problematic cultural dynamic, anchored in the Americas' history of colonization. The assumption underlying my interlocutor's skepticism that "they" could have literature was unquestionably bound up in entrenched, externally imposed North-South discourses of race. For an earlier example that also exposes the gendered dynamics of these power relations, one might glance at late nineteenth-century US newspaper illustrations depicting Cuba as a voluptuous *mulata* tempting the honorable Uncle Sam—a luscious fruit ripe for the picking.[1] In the contemporary moment, educated readers are more apt to recognize the ways in which Caribbean islands have been considered racialized, sexualized commodities by Europeans and North Americans alike. Despite the political and cultural morass into which the United States has recently slid, intensifying and validating long-existing bigotries and hate that were formerly less acceptable, institutions of higher learning teach how Caribbean citizens have been exploited, enslaved, and denied both agency and historical density by forces outside the region. What remains much less transparent, inside and outside the archipelago, are processes by which such patterns of oppression and discrimination are perpetuated within the region itself (to be sure, diasporic communities bear their own hallmarks). As we will see shortly, Vega's "Encancaranublado" tale, featuring the literal and metaphorical shipwreck of a trio of Caribbean immigrants, evinces many of these issues. But the story simultaneously gestures to nineteenth-century Spanish Caribbean discourses of *antillanismo*, which—in the face of growing US interventionism—sought to advance what Sara Johnson describes as "transcolonial collaborations" (18) across the region. These efforts, inspired and informed by the "big bang" of the (1791–1804) Haitian Revolution, were connected to other emancipatory struggles in Jamaica and Louisiana alongside independence movements in Latin America (20). In *Our Caribbean Kin: Race and Nation in the Neoliberal Antilles* (2015), Alaí Reyes-Santos posits this Antillean activism as a kind of Black politics (62). Can it be coincidence that one of the protagonists in "Encancaranublado" shares a first name with a nineteenth-century *antillanista*?

Prior to addressing the primary text at hand, I will broadly sketch some contours of the Spanish-speaking and Francophone Caribbean cultural landscape. Concepts of center and periphery diverge significantly across the Caribbean—whose islands have conventionally been associated in terms of nationalistic, linguistic blocks—and ideas of culture, race, and citizenship continue to be negotiated in dissimilar, contestatory ways despite common experiences of slavery and resistance that remain subjacent. "Hispanic" and Francophone Caribbean islands maintain vastly different cultural reference frames: the latter traditionally regard France as foil, so to speak, while Cuba and Puerto Rico engage more directly with the United States and Latin America. On the other hand, the prevailing identity narrative of the

Dominican Republic is rooted in nostalgic ties to Spain, alongside indigenous origins. In *Mulatto Republic: Class, Race, and Dominican National Identity* (2014), April Mayes uncovers how the neighboring presence of Haiti, an independent Black republic since 1804, was embraced by some nineteenth-century Dominican intellectuals seeking cultural solidarity facing US economic encroachment in Latin America and the Caribbean. Mayes emphasizes that "anti-Black Hispanophilia" was not a central aspect of Dominican national identity, particularly among the rural majority (4); to the contrary, racist ideologies have been imposed and manipulated by elite factions within the population at specific instances across the nineteenth and twentieth centuries—most notoriously during the (1931–1961) regime of Rafael Leónidas Trujillo, directly referenced in Vega's narrative.

Accordingly, Haitian-Dominican relations have varied considerably over time. My own 2012 *PALARA* essay notes, "Early Haitian efforts towards unification were viewed by many, but not all, Dominicans as unjust aggressions. In 1844, fearing continued colonization by their western neighbor, the Dominican elite faction negotiated annexation to Spain, who they felt had abandoned them; this group suppressed a pro-independence movement supported by Dominican peasants, who saw Spain as a white supremacist power" (52). At other times—especially during the twentieth century—elite Dominicans considered Haiti a threat to national sovereignty and propagated anti-Black prejudices where they did not exist before. Silvio Torres-Saillant's *Introduction to Dominican Blackness* addresses this paradox of race:

> Dominican society is the cradle of Blackness in the Americas. The island of Hispaniola or Santo Domingo . . . served as port of entry to the first African slaves who stepped on Spain's newly conquered territories [in 1492]. . . . Blacks and mulattoes make up nearly 90% of the contemporary Dominican population. Yet no other country in the hemisphere exhibits greater indeterminacy regarding the population's sense of racial identity. (1)

Haiti, independent since 1804—and whose original constitutions abolished slavery and guaranteed universal liberty to all citizens of Hispaniola, who were defined as free, equal, and Black—remains a perpetual outlier in the Caribbean context. Unsurprisingly, perhaps, the devastating January 2010 earthquake in Haiti, which scholars agree was an entirely man-made tragedy, afforded other Caribbean and Latin American nations the chance to show their standing in the region by the measure of assistance they gave to their neighbor in need, reinforcing stubborn notions of Haiti as "disaster." This image has played out in Spanish Caribbean cultural production since long before the earthquake, of course, and I argue that "Encancaranublado," published in the 1980s by Cuban and Puerto Rican presses, essentially follows suit.

A last point of emphasis seems appropriate here. Haitian anthropologist Michel-Rolph Trouillot famously argues in *Silencing the Past* (1995) that Haiti's history and its revolution have been systematically erased within the official records generated by the West (a category that his later work subsequently problematizes). Along with other Haitianist scholars, I have respectfully endeavored to further nuance this assertion, signaling the repeated deployment of the Haitian Revolution in twentieth-century literature (and beyond), which acts as a historical and cultural *poto-mitan*, or pillar. While the unprecedented, yet exemplary slave revolution—rooted in a well-established tradition of resistance in the Caribbean—may have been disavowed by Western historical accounts (borrowing Sibylle Fischer's term), its traces and memories have remained alive among Caribbean intellectuals, including Alejo Carpentier, Aimé Césaire, Jean-Michel Cusset, Jean-Claude Fignolé, Édouard Glissant, Nicolás Guillén, Jean Métellus, Luis Palés Matos, René Philoctète, and Vincent Placoly. Across many works of theater in particular, Haiti's Revolution has held center stage, literally and figuratively; the country's nineteenth century, on the other hand, gets short shrift. For the purposes of this volume, it is worth noting that the majority of these writers are French- or Creole-speaking. Spanish-speaking Caribbean writers may tend to engage Haiti less because they recognize to a different degree, or in different ways, what Martha Cobb's *Harlem, Haiti and Havana* describes as "the concept of a shared Black experience" that during the Harlem Renaissance period "emerges conjointly in the islands of the Caribbean and in North and South America" (4). But the aforementioned recent work of Johnson, Mayes, and Reyes-Santos sheds light on important "alternative community formations" emerging within the nineteenth-century Spanish Caribbean that "contested the racialized violence endemic to European imperialism and creole nation-building projects" (Johnson 22). The shared aspirations of these early *antillanista* collaborators—who included Ramón Betances and Eugenio de Hostos of Puerto Rico, and the Dominican Gregorio Luperón—were certainly less explicit than those articulated by the French Caribbean authors of the well-known *Éloge de la créolité* (1989, *In Praise of Creoleness*), with its celebrated and collective statement of pride in complex, creolized origins, and its deliberate distancing from outside cultural models.² Notwithstanding this relative lack of visibility—especially as Mayes and Reyes-Santos argue—*antillanismo* should be better recognized as a developing form of Black political consciousness.

The complexities of Caribbean and American cultural reference frames and particular histories are present throughout Vega's literary corpus, and her personal and professional experiences transcend linguistic and hemispheric boundaries. Having begun writing stories and poems during her childhood, Vega completed graduate studies in France, at the University of Paris, then returned to Puerto Rico and worked as a professor of French and Caribbean literature at the University of Puerto Rico, Río Piedras. Her publications span various genres—fiction, essays, poetry, literary criticism, and film—and explore numerous social and political issues, including Puerto Rico's history and its ambiguous status; one of the author's clear priorities is that of giving voice to the marginalized. Vega's best-known publications include a story collection, *Vírgenes y mártires* (1981, written with Carmen Lugo Filippi), *Pasión de historia y otras historias de pasión* (1987), and *Ciertas crónicas del norte* (1992); among other awards, such as the Juan Rulfo prize, Vega garnered a Guggenheim Fellowship for the Creative Arts in 1989. According to Jorge J. E. Gracia, she has "infused Puerto Rican literature with a self-conscious dose of humor, irony, and popular culture, and in so doing has deconstructed traditional narrative models. Her writing certainly contributes to the growing body of a Puerto Rican 'literature of [its] own,' and is 'new' narrative in every sense of the word" (121). Although some have considered Vega's work to exemplify "feminist doctrine," Gracia observes, the writer has vigorously resisted this categorization and any notions of "difference" associated with the output of women writers (121–22). Her story "Encancaranublado" sidesteps such concerns, raising provocative questions about Caribbean history, geopolitics, and constructions of citizenship.

Critics of Vega's story have repeatedly wrestled with the matter of the boat at the center of the tale. Often, discussions contemplate whether the Caribbean protagonists—male migrants fleeing adverse economic and political conditions in Haiti, the Dominican Republic, and Cuba—can most aptly be sited in "the same boat," geopolitically speaking; not in the same boat; or in an indeterminate imagined space somewhere in between. Critical interpretations situate the story in comparative political, consumerist, and literary-cultural terms: for example, Johanna Emmanuelli-Huertas links "Encancaranublado" with the broad hemispheric vision expressed in José Martí's *Nuestra América*, while Magda Graniela underlines the semiotic difference between the boat people featured in the story and the omnipresent pleasure cruise boats that became popular in the 1980s. Others address the burlesque aspects of Vega's text, along with chaos and cultural flows in the narrative. Pointing to the story's conclusion, wherein the imperiled protagonists are debatably "rescued" by a racist US Coast Guard official and his Puerto Rican helper, Josefa Lago-Graña submits that "Encancaranublado" primarily deals with Puerto Rico's ambiguous status vis-à-vis the United States. Indeed, most scholars emphasize the story's ironic ending and the issue of Pan-Caribbean identity. The narrative's beginning, anchored in a Haitian frame, is less explicitly discussed.

Previous interrogations of Vega's text, however compelling, literally and figuratively miss the boat. My rereading of "Encancaranublado" underscores the pivotal placement of the Haitian-made boat—a credible synecdoche for the nation and its revolutionary past—within the Caribbean space, lived and imagined. Fresh evidence thus surfaces apropos the problem Myriam Chancy charts in *From Sugar to Revolution*: the disciplinary exclusion of Haiti within the fields of American, Latin American, and Caribbean studies lends evidence that "racist essentialism has demarcated Haitians and other groups of African descent within the Caribbean as subalterns without agency" (xv). Tellingly, although "Encancaranublado" references a wide variety of figures, places, and emblems of Caribbean culture and history, the Haitian Revolution (1791–1804) goes unmentioned, almost (for reasons to be explained). In this sense, Vega's writing is not atypical of Puerto Rican literature: other than the poet Luís Palés Matos, relatively few Puerto Rican writers directly address the Western hemisphere's first Black republic.

Through the following exploration of Vega's text and related criticism, I argue that understandings of "Encancaranublado," and of Haiti itself, in the broader frame, have been limited to traditional, exclusive notions of nationalism. As happens within literary works by other Hispanophone Caribbean writers, such as Freddy Prestol Castillo and Aída Cartagena Portalatín, Haiti's role within the region is fundamental, yet often goes fundamentally unrecognized. Because Vega's writing has arguably entered the canon of Caribbean letters, the treatment of Haiti and Haitians in "Encancaranublado" and relevant scholarship begs examination all the more. Vega's story resonates with present-day debates over borders, citizenship, and sovereignty, but critical treatment of the text tends to emphasize national identity, postcoloniality, migration patterns, and issues of language and power.

The short narrative under consideration appears in *Encancaranublado y otros cuentos de naufragio*, Vega's second book, which received the prestigious Casa de las Américas award in 1982. With a title presaging linguistic and cultural contestations ahead, Vega's sardonic, carnivalesque text highlights deep-seated tensions among a trio of prototypical emigrants setting forth for Miami from their respective home countries at an unspecified moment in the twentieth century. The title of the book and the story at hand is a tongue-twister, simultaneously playing on the Spanish words *encantado* (enchanted) and *nublado* (cloudy). "Encancaranublado" offhandedly alludes to the bleak economic and political conditions faced by many during the dictatorships of François and Jean-Claude Duvalier (1957–1986), the Cuban Revolutionary period (1959–), and the Trujillo regime. Unsurprisingly, the protagonists' tumultuous encounters end in literal and metaphorical shipwreck, nearly killing them all. Throughout the story, what anchors the migrants to life is the Haitian-made craft, signifying present-day economic desperation layered upon subjacent, if neglected, rupture and revolution. But before the boat is further considered, a snapshot of the story is warranted.

Anténor, a Haitian man, travels north under calm skies in a self-fashioned boat whose sail consists of a mere *guayabera*, a shirt typically associated with Cuba.[3] He decides to rescue Diógenes, a Dominican man emerging from the waters, who expresses great distrust toward the Haitian; differences are temporarily overcome through the pair's recognition of their analogous colonial pasts and contemporary difficulties. When Carmelo, a Cuban—initially spewing insults at everyone—is likewise allowed aboard by Anténor, the Dominican sides with the Cuban against the Haitian; together, the two Hispanophone subjects attack the Creole speaker. A fierce storm suddenly brews, imperiling all, and the trio is intercepted by an obviously bigoted white Coast Guard officer and his dark-skinned Puerto Rican assistant. The latter offers the men dry clothing down in the hold and forewarns them of hardships in the United States; he also bridges the distance between his Caribbean neighbors and the precarious circumstances awaiting them in their collective destination.

These exaggerated representations provide ample fodder for analysis on many levels. To begin with, the obvious linguistic barriers among the characters harbor larger implications, as Diana Vélez proposes in her *Callaloo* article "We Are (Not) in This Together": "Indexing the problem of language, of speech—How do we talk to each other? Which way to a unified Caribbean, given the colonial heritage that divides us linguistically?—one is reminded that this is not some reified History, but an everyday impediment, as common as rain during the rainy season. It is as hard to find a language for Pan-Caribbeanism as it is to speak this tongue-twister" (829). The general argument that Vélez makes, using "Encancaranublado" as departure point, is that the possibility of a shared Caribbean imaginary appears to be foreclosed by linguistic variations, among other obstacles. The critic notes: "Each character is actually a caricature or stereotype of 'national traits.' . . . Though the three are not, strictly speaking, stock characters, they do have their particularities based on the histories of each nation, figured as these are in the memories of each character. For Anténor, we're given the determining traits of Haiti: the French Creole language, poverty, illiteracy and vodun religion. Anténor's Creole allows the other two to exclude him. They speak excitedly in Spanish while he marks his presence occasionally with a *Mais oui* or a *C'est ça*" (830). Anténor's brief utterances, curiously, appear in standard French instead of the Haitian Creole language, which is more plausible for a migratory subject (since French, the language of power in Haiti, is spoken by only 5–8 percent of the population). In any case, he is unquestionably displaced in the context of what Vega depicts as a "monopolio cervantino" (15), wherein the language of Cervantes, imposed by Spain, prevails. While "Encancaranublado" only indirectly addresses Caribbean colonial history, it is worth remembering that the fledgling Dominican nation elected reannexation to Spain from 1861 to 1865 to avoid being recolonized by its Western neighbor, perceived then—and too often now—as Black "Other." And contemporary legal disputes over Dominican citizenship, which have resulted in the forcible repatriation of thousands of Haitians since June 2015, gloss over the reality that many present-day Dominicans continue to identify themselves as white descendants of Spanish ancestry.[4]

A closer look at Vega's protagonists reveals a profound distanciation from most things Haitian. Though all the migrants suffer "la jodienda de ser antillano, negro y pobre" (the bullshit of being Antillean, Black and poor[5] [14]), and for a brief moment enjoy "el internacionalismo del hambre y la solidaridad del sueño" (the internationalism of hunger and the solidarity of dreams [14]), Anténor maintains the lowest status in the boat. Earlier, the Dominican Diógenes calls Anténor "herman*ito*" (little brother, emphasis mine) to establish his own superiority (14), although the vessel "navegaba después de todo bajo bandera haitiana" (sailed in any case under a Haitian flag [15]); this is the only direct reference to the boat's Haitian origins. Later, as the quarrel intensifies, the Cuban Carmelo helps Diógenes assault Anténor and appropriate his carefully prepared supply of provisions (rum, water, cassava, and tobacco), which the Haitian ultimately throws into the ocean to prevent his newly declared enemies from consuming them. What Vega appears to imply is that Anténor's agency resides in self-denial. But the Haitian's sabotaging of his precious stores effectively returns the three

Caribbean citizens to an equal footing: all will now suffer the same hungry plight in the shark-infested waters.

Another minor but significant aspect of "Encancaranublado" that has gone unremarked is that the Cuban character hails from Santiago, or the Oriente province. This descriptor is revealing in that the economically ambitious migrant embodies the shared history of Haiti and eastern Cuba, where numerous revolutionary movements have begun; indeed, the 1959 Cuban Revolution has been deemed an "echo" of Haiti's revolution. So while "Encancaranublado" makes no explicit reference to the unprecedented triumph of a formerly enslaved population, textual implications surrounding Cuba's Oriente region do point toward it, albeit faintly. If, as J. Michael Dash proposes, the Haitian Revolution is a "floating signifier" that twentieth-century Caribbean writers seek to pin down to their own ends, within Vega's story Haiti and its history remain a submerged signifier, suppressed and disavowed (to borrow Sibylle Fischer's words).[6]

Margaret Carson's exploration of the "postcolonial Caribbean" presence in "Encancaranublado" examines the linguistic violence committed against Anténor as a metaphor for Dominican political discourse toward Haiti. In the story, when insults fly, Diógenes calls Anténor "madamo," a highly pejorative racial epithet transcending the more general—and sometimes even affectionately intended "prieto" (dark-skinned) hurled by Carmelo; this reflects the historically fraught relationship between Haiti and the Dominican Republic. Anténor states defensively, while removing water from the boat: "Pa que se acuerde que los invadimos tres veces" (so [Diógenes] remembers that we invaded them three times[7] [Vega 16]). In response, Diógenes declares, "Trujillo tenía razón" (Trujillo was right), implying that the notorious dictator was justified in ordering the execution of over fifteen thousand Haitian laborers in the northern border region in October 1937 (Carson n.p.). In his well-respected study "A World Destroyed. A Nation Imposed," Richard Turits maintains that these racial tensions were hardly a cause; rather, they were created and reinforced by the genocide. In any case, Carson may be the sole critic of "Encancaranublado" to acknowledge that although each migrant man took to the ocean independently, only Anténor's boat has "survived the ocean's vicissitudes" (Carson n.p.). In this sense, Haiti is thus recentered within Hispanic Caribbean discourse.

Haitian-Dominican relations aside, it is striking that scholars addressing Vega's text have failed to remark that the vessel in question was made by the Haitian, literally and figuratively. If one accepts that Vega's three protagonists are in the same metaphorical boat at the story's end, thanks to the ignorant, racist attitudes of the Coast Guard captain who instantly lumps them together into the category of undesirable, dark-skinned foreigner/Other, one cannot deny that they begin their travels in the same boat—which is Haitian-made—and that they owe their lives to its construction. It should not be neglected that Anténor constructed the boat under duress, at great sacrifice, and subsequently saved his Caribbean compatriots from near-certain death. It should also not be neglected that he has the same first name as Anténor Firmin, a nineteenth-century Haitian political activist who collaborated with *antillanistas* Luperón and Hostos[8] on forming a Pan-Antillean "transnational collectivity" to counter a "U.S. proposed Pan-American economic system directed by Washington" (Mayes 28–29). Vega herself, whom Reyes-Santos includes on a list of *antillanista* writers (60), was certainly familiar with this history of Black Caribbean activism. Summoning an even earlier example: might Vega also have composed "Encancaranublado" as a contemporary, more cautionary telling of the Cuban legend of the Virgen de la Caridad del Cobre? That famous story—portraying the Virgin Mary appearing to a pair of Amerindian brothers and an enslaved African boy as they navigated a boat in search of salt—has been widely interpreted as a pivotal moment in the development of a Cuban national consciousness embracing both African and indigenous heritages. Vega's narrative echoes of these historical examples showing Caribbean racial solidarity cannot be coincidental. Regardless, the fact that Anténor's fragile craft subsequently shipwrecks as a result of the trio's fierce dispute (combined with bad weather) evokes the position of Haiti itself within the Caribbean.

This question is certainly simplistic, but can we pause for a moment to imagine a different sort of ending for "Encancaranublado"? What might it have looked like for Vega's three protagonists to have reached some kind of mutual, cross-cultural understanding in the boat, based upon their shared experiences of oppression, and to have joined their efforts during the journey north, akin to a *koumbit* (community effort)? One could imply from the story that, had the trio collaborated from the beginning, the storm clouds might have remained at bay, and Anténor, Diógenes, and Carmelo could well have reached their shared destination, where they would have certainly encountered difficulties, but where solidarity would have served them well while negotiating the US cultural and racial context. That even in fiction this rosier outcome resists being imagined suggests how firmly established are patterns of South-South power relationships in the Caribbean space, wherein Haiti all too often occupies the bottom rung.

Indeed, in the place of solidarity among Vega's protagonists, Vélez argues that a kind of negative unity is possibly achieved in the narrative's conclusion:

> The story's closure is effected by having the three men "in the same boat," both figuratively and literally. Speaking extra-textually, does the racism they will face in the U.S. operate as a unifying factor as it does in the story? If we read beyond the ending, are all three men going to face the same kind of prejudice once on land? Won't the Haitian be the most likely to be sent back given his "economic refugee" status and the definition of him as "Black" rather than as "Hispanic" or better still, as Cuban? Although they are all "Black" in the eyes of the captain, will that be the case in the United States? Those differences are collapsed in some settings and not in others. (I am thinking of the very different treatment given to Cubans and Haitians by the U.S. Immigration and Naturalization Service.) (832)

To a similar end, Fernando Valerio-Holguín suggests more firmly in "Postcolonial Encounters" that the three immigrants' experience with US racism in "Encancaranublado" serves as an important unifying factor: "Being considered as the Other from the North American perspective forces the characters and the reader alike to 'discover' their Caribbeanness from the outside and in opposition to Anglo Saxon subjectivity" (n.p.). Citing Angel Rama's theory of the process of cultural differentiation, or "macroregionalism," Valerio-Holguín emphasizes Caribbean concepts of exteriority and opposition to the Other: "While Latin America defines itself in relationship to its Anglo Saxon neighbors, the Caribbean exists as a cultural space that defines itself in relation to both Latin American [sic] and the United States. According to some anthropologists, the unity of the Caribbean as a differentiated cultural space is undeniable, given its historical, racial and economic development" (n.p.). These reflections are in concert with the previously discussed problem of South-South tensions, representing competing reference frames in the Spanish and French-speaking Caribbean.

I do not dispute that the ending of Vega's story illustrates the (negative) process of Caribbean citizens being unified through having their individual identities "negated" (as Carson says) within a binary system of racial exclusion in the United States; this evokes my initial interlocutor's question about whether "they" can have literature. Vélez contends that "the punchline ending has some of the markings of a moral: 'Despite our differences, as far as THEY are concerned, we are all the same.' The Puerto Rican is 'someone in the know.' From within the belly of the beast he warns the other three that this is going to be no 'free ride.' Essentially, nothing changes" (832). But what is equally, if not more important to underline—precisely because this other sense of unity is "submarine," borrowing from Édouard Glissant[9]—is that the beginning and middle of "Encancaranublado" amply reveal how Spanish-speaking Caribbean subjects find common ground in their opposition to Haiti.

In the broad historical framework, given the catalyzing effects of the Haitian Revolution within the Latin American region, Caribbean citizens at home and abroad are similarly indebted to Haiti. As David Geggus observes in *The Impact of the Haitian Revolution in the Atlantic World*, "The slave uprising that began in August 1791 and transformed the immensely wealthy colony [of Saint-Domingue] was probably the largest and most dramatically successful one there has ever been. . . . Haiti became Latin America's first independent country, the first modern state in the Tropics" (vii). The new Haitian republic immediately came to symbolize Black freedom, and the triumph of Saint-Domingue's formerly enslaved population served as an important example for subsequent independence movements in Latin America: South American liberator Simón Bolívar, for example, was reluctant to acknowledge the new republic of Haiti, along with the fact that President Alexandre Pétion provided him substantial military and financial backing for his own efforts to achieve independence (Past, *Reclaiming* 55). So while the notion of *naufragio* (shipwreck) applies in literal terms to the fate of Anténor's boat in Vega's story, the metaphor easily extends to the Haitian Revolution, both in the narrative and in the broader frame: a shared revolutionary past, looming large, that is frequently repressed in the Latin American imaginary, where Creolophone Haiti is rarely imagined as being in the same, colonially oppressed boat.

Although Graniela's reading of "Encancaranublado" does not specifically discuss Haiti, its revolution, or the fact of its repression in the story, the critic convincingly articulates the underlying impasse of the men in the boat, which is a negation of shared Blackness: "Ni el fortuito encuentro en ese selectivo exilio del saberse 'a la deriva,' permite a los actantes superar su imposibilidad de reconocerse parte integral de una comunidad étnica esencialmente mulata. 'Encancaranublado' . . . , más que plantear, creemos, en términos generales el problema de la identidad caribeña, apunta a la ausencia de ese sema definidor que es el ser producto de la raza negra" (43).[10] Given sustained disputes regarding notions of citizenship within the island of Hispaniola in the contemporary moment, alongside a Dominican tendency to base national identity upon indigenous origins and "Hispanidad" (Spain-based cultural origins)—despite some important nineteenth-century examples of alternative, transcolonial collaborations transcending racial and economic divisions—the most direct acknowledgment of shared African origins appears on the surface more characteristic of Cuba and Puerto Rico.

Better understandings of Haiti and its revolution, along with complex processes of nineteenth-century nation-building and twentieth-century dictatorships, can only help bolster this sense of collective Caribbean identity, as the Cuban poet Nicolás Guillén suggests in his poignant "Elegía a Jacques Roumain" (Elegy to Jacques Roumain) that depicts Haiti's history as a giant page of stone that for three hundred years "everyone reads, reads, reads" but "no one gets beyond" because the bloody page of stone is never turned (Past, *Reclaiming* 3). The elegy is not among Guillén's most celebrated works, but it aptly articulates the conundrum of Haiti within the Latin American context during the mid-twentieth century, underlining both the relevance of the Haitian example and the nation's seemingly irreversible history of struggle. What is especially compelling about Guillén's six-page-long poem—of similar length to "Encancaranublado"—is his treatment of the Haitian Revolution. One witnesses the repetition of many words in later lines—especially "sangre," which appears fourteen times, echoing what the poet perceives to be recurring cycles of violence in Haitian history. For Guillén, Roumain personifies this bloody past that lingers in the memory of "todos" but remains repressed. While it is unclear whether Guillén refers here to the memory of people in the Caribbean, Latin America, both, or the world, his intention appears to be that of uncovering, with an eye to reactivating, this piece of history. Particularly significant within the elegy is the act of renaming. Roumain first incarnates the revolutionary heroes of his country's past (who are all mentioned at some point): "Él, Monsieur Jacques Roumain, / que hablaba en nombre / del negro Emperador [Dessalines], del negro Rey [Henri Christophe], / del negro Presidente [Pétion] . . ." The poet then acknowledges everyone else who fought in the struggle: "todos los negros que nunca fueron más que / Jean / Pierre / Víctor / Candide / Jules / Charles / Stephen / Raymond / André."[11] Guillén thus fills in historical blanks by acknowledging the role of the Haitian masses—heretofore largely unidentified—in the Revolution. The "Elegía a Jacques Roumain" can arguably be read as a microcosm of the Haitian Revolution in poetic form. Above all, the image of Haiti as a "tremendo libro abierto" (tremendous open book) stands out, evoking a collective, even universalized Caribbean past that is available to all, and thus bears remembering and rereading. And Guillén posits the poignant question, "¿Quién va a exprimir la esponja, la insaciable / esponja?" (Who will wring out the blood-spattered / sponge?). In other words, how do we get beyond this very difficult history? I find it striking that Vega, whose doctoral research focused upon Haitian revolutionary leader Henri Christophe,[12] suppresses Haiti in the story that anchors her collection.

Despite these shortcomings, "Encancaranublado" exhibits and eviscerates global and local discourses surrounding its three Caribbean subjects' stereotyped backgrounds, effectively interrogating notions of "difference" and "otherness" in South-South and North-South relationships. Succinctly but powerfully, Vega explicitly calls on "nuestros bilingües lectores" (our bilingual readers) to continue the struggle against racism and human rights abuses worldwide. This signals practical, compelling questions: How might Vega's literary admonishment be productively translated into action, within the sphere of Caribbean, Latin American, and American studies and elsewhere? Can these fields be further expanded linguistically and geographically to incorporate important perspectives that have long existed, but tend to stay submerged? Despite considerable attention brought to the 2004 bicentennial of the Haitian Revolution and the January 2010 earthquake, Haiti too often remains a floating signifier, adrift and at risk.

On the one hand, Haiti appears trapped within neocolonial conditions, plagued by poverty and state instability spurring continued migratory patterns. On the other hand, as Suzanne Oboler writes in an editorial after the 2010 earthquake in Haiti:

> Like the history of Latino/as in the United States, the history of the Haitian people embodies the hopes and ongoing resistance of the hemisphere's populations to the inequities imposed by U.S. domination throughout the Americas. . . . It also embodies Latin America's history of struggle and resistance against U.S. intervention and the imposition of U.S.-backed dictatorships and policies on that continent. . . . Like the millions of people of Latin American descent now in the United States, the ongoing ideological and practical repercussions of the U.S. imperial reach have long ensured the continued and largely forced displacement and migration of hundreds of thousands of Haitians from their homeland to the United States. (2)

Haiti's example helps shed light on Latinos in the United States: "Consciousness about Haiti's history and its ongoing centrality to the experience of the Americas will undoubtedly enhance our appreciation of the import of race both within and among Latino/a populations, and in the U.S. context" (3). Haiti remains central as a bellwether for the future of the Caribbean and Latin America. "Unnatural" disasters are an increasingly grave risk throughout the Caribbean, as the destruction wrought by Hurricane Maria in Puerto Rico in 2017 amply showed. New migration patterns will be generated, and new, intraregional collaborations and alliances will be required (Cuban climate researchers, proud of their country's strong record of hurricane preparedness, are currently spearheading these efforts). Unless the harmful effects of global extractive capitalism are rapidly reversed, the planet itself may be destined for shipwreck. But in a more immediate framework, contemporary readers and scholars must continue defying conventional attempts to apprehend Caribbean nations and their histories through myopic approaches, because all Americans are coterminous travelers and should all be in the same boat.

Notes

1. For further analysis of this and many related examples, see Pérez.

2. The authors of the *Éloge* proudly assert: "Neither Europeans, nor Africans, nor Asians, we proclaim ourselves to be Creoles. For us this will be a state of mind, or, rather, a state of vigilance, or, better still, a sort of mental envelope within which we will build our world, in full awareness of the world" (886).

3. It is tempting to presume that this shirt came literally off Anténor's back, but there are insufficient textual details to support that reading.

4. On September 23, 2013, the Dominican Republic Constitutional Tribunal ruled to strip citizenship from over two hundred thousand of its citizens. This law, which was internationally condemned, prompted the organization of a widespread protest group, "¡Eso no se hace!" (You can't do that!) migranteshoy.celam.org/derechos-republica-dominicana/172-republica-dominicana-eso-no-se-hace.html.

5. Translation mine.

6. See Dash; and Fischer.

7. Juan Bosch notes that Haiti thrice invaded the Dominican Republic (1844, 1849, and 1855) in an ostensible effort to unify the island and abolish slavery throughout.

8. Mayes writes that the three "advocated [for] the creation of an Antillean federation based on the geographic and historical unity of Cuba, Puerto Rico, the Dominican Republic, and Jamaica. As the struggle for independence in Cuba and Puerto Rico unfolded and U.S. commercial imperialism expanded, they expressed a

Pan-Antillean politics that, transcending race, would nurture freedom movements in Cuba and Puerto Rico, sustain democracy in the Dominican Republic, and secure Antillean political agency and sovereignty to counter U.S. influence" (28). Mayes continues, "Until 1898, Antilleanism provided an alternative to U.S.-sponsored Pan-Americanism" (29).

9. The Glissantian concept of "subterranean convergence" is produced by the "diverse histories in the Caribbean." As the Martinican famously muses in *Caribbean Discourse*, "The depths are not only the abyss of neurosis but primarily the site of multiple converging paths" (66). For Glissant, this "submarine unity" (borrowing Brathwaite's term) "can only evoke all those Africans weighed down with ball and chain and thrown overboard whenever a slave ship was pursued by enemy vessels and felt too weak to put up a fight" (66–67). The experience of having collectively suffered the Middle Passage underlies life on the Caribbean islands, in decidedly nonhierarchical form, with what Glissant calls "submarine roots": "that is floating free, not fixed in one position in some primordial spot, but extending in all directions in our world through its network of branches" (67).

10. "Not even the fortuitous encounter in this selective exile of knowing oneself while adrift allows the actors to overcome the impossibility of recognizing themselves as an integral part of an essentially mulata ethnic community. 'Encancaranublado' . . . more than poses, we believe, the problem of Caribbean identity in general terms, points to the absence of that defining seme that is being a product of the Black race" (translation by editor of the volume).

11. "He, Monsieur Jacques Roumain, / who spoke in the name / of the Black Emperor [Dessalines], of the Black King [Henri Christophe], / of the Black President [Pétion] . . . [. . .] All of the Black people who were never more than / Jean / Pierre / Víctor / Candide / Jules / Charles / Stephen / Raymond / André." Translation mine.

12. See Vega, *Le mythe*.

Works Cited

Bernabé, Jean, Patrick Chamoiseau, and Raphaël Confiant. *Éloge de la créolité*. Gallimard/Presses universitaires créoles, 1989; English translation by M. B. Taleb-Khyar, *In praise of Creoleness*. *Callaloo*, vol. 13, 1990, pp. 886–909.

Bosch, Juan. *Composición social dominicana: historia e interpretación*. Alfa y Omega, 1986.

Carson, Margaret. "El Caribe postcolonial en 'Encancaranublado' de Ana Lydia Vega." *LL Journal*, vol. 4, no. 2, 2009, n.p.

Chancy, Myriam J. A. *From Sugar to Revolution: Women's Visions of Haiti, Cuba, and the Dominican Republic*. Wilfrid Laurier UP, 2012.

Cobb, Martha. *Harlem, Haiti and Havana: A Comparative Critical Study of Langston Hughes, Jacques Roumain, Nicolás Guillén.* Three Continents Press, 1979.
Dash, J. Michael. "Postcolonialism and the French Caribbean." Lecture, Duke University, Durham, NC, 27 Sept. 2002.
Emmanuelli-Huertas, Johanna. "Antillanos, náufragos, míseros y trashumantes: A un siglo del toque de queda de Martí." *Confluencia*, vol. 3, no. 1, 1987, pp. 101–04.
Fischer, Sibylle. *Modernity Disavowed: Haiti and the Cultures of Slavery in the Age of Revolution.* Duke UP, 2004.
Geggus, David Patrick. *The Impact of the Haitian Revolution in the Atlantic World.* U of South Carolina P, 2001.
Glissant, Édouard. *Caribbean Discourse: Selected Essays.* UP of Virginia, 1989.
Gracia, Jorge J. E. *Philosophy and Literature in Latin America: A Critical Assessment of the Current Situation.* State U of New York P, 1989.
Graniela, Magda. "Semiótica del espacio en 'Encancaranublado' de Ana Lydia Vega." *PALARA: Publication of the Afro-Latin/Romance Association*, vol. 9, 2005, pp. 42–46.
Guillén, Nicolás. "Elegía a Jacques Roumain." *Sóngoro cosongo y otros poemas.* 1981. Alianza Editorial, 1998, pp. 188–93.
Johnson, Sara. *The Fear of French Negroes: Transcolonial Collaboration in the Revolutionary Americas.* U of California P, 2012.
Lago-Graña, Josefa. "El Caribe, identidad y nación en 'Encancaranublado' de Ana Lydia Vega." *Diáspora*, vol. 11, 2001, pp. 52–58.
Mayes, April J. *Mulatto Republic: Class, Race, and Dominican National Identity.* UP of Florida, 2014.
Oboler, Suzanne. "In Its Darkest Times, Haiti Is Still the World's Hope, and a Mirror of the Latino/a Experience." *Latino studies*, vol. 8, no. 1, 2010, pp. 1–3.
Past, Mariana. *Reclaiming the Haitian Revolution: Race, Politics and History in Twentieth Century Caribbean Literature.* PhD dissertation, Duke University, 2006.
———. "Unification through Zombification? Re-imagining Hispaniola's History from the 'Periphery of the Margins.'" *PALARA*, vol. 16, 2012, pp. 49–63.
Pérez, Louis, Jr. *Cuba in the American Imagination: Metaphor and the Imperial Ethos.* U of North Carolina P, 2008.
Reyes-Santos, Alaí. *Our Caribbean Kin: Race and Nation in the Neoliberal Antilles.* Rutgers UP, 2015.
Rosell, Sara. "El embarque y el desborde: Navegando el Caribe junto a Mayra Montero y Ana Lydia Vega." *South Eastern Latin Americanist*, vol. 44, no. 1, 2000, pp. 47–59.
Torres-Saillant, Silvio. *Introduction to Dominican Blackness.* CUNY Dominican Studies Institute, *Dominican Studies Working Paper Series* 1, 1999.

Turits, Richard Lee. "A World Destroyed. A Nation Imposed: The 1937 Haitian Massacre in the Dominican Republic." *Hispanic American Historical Review*, vol. 82, no. 3, 2002, pp. 589–636.

Valerio-Holguín, Fernando. "Postcolonial Encounters and the Caribbean Diaspora: 'Encancaranublado' by Ana Lydia Vega," translated by Shanna Lorenz. 5 Dec. 2009, lamar.colostate.edu/~fvalerio/PostcolonialEncounters2.html.

Vega, Ana Lydia. "Encancaranublado." *Encancaranublado y otros cuentos de naufragio*. Ediciones Antillana, 1990, pp. 13–20; first publication, Ediciones Casa de las Américas, 1982, pp. 11–20.

———. *Le mythe D'Henry Christophe dans le théâtre des Antilles et des États-Unis*. PhD dissertation, Université de Provence, Aix-Marseille 1, 1978.

Vélez, Diana. "We Are (Not) in This Together: The Caribbean Imaginary in 'Encancaranublado' by Ana Lydia Vega." *Callaloo*, vol. 17, no. 3, 1994, pp. 826–33.

8

The Haitian and Dominican Resistance

A Study of the Symptom in Edwidge Danticat's *The Farming of Bones*

ÁNGELA CASTRO

> They once came here only to cut sugarcane.... Our problem is one of domination... we as Dominicans, must have our separate traditions.... If not, in less than three generations we will all be Haitians.
>
> —Edwidge Danticat, *The Farming of Bones*

In her 2012 study *From Sugar to Revolution: Women's Visions of Haiti, Cuba, and the Dominican Republic*, Myriam J. A. Chancy asks Edwidge Danticat about the epigraph from Judges that opens her novel *The Farming of Bones* (1998). The passage describes how forty thousand Ephraimites (a tribe from Israel) were killed by the Israelites from Gilead under the leadership of Jephthah because they did not pronounce the word "Shibboleth" correctly. Chancy compares the story with that of the Haitians under Rafael Trujillo's dictatorship (1930–1961), who in 1937 could not pronounce the word "perejil" with a Spanish accent and who were subsequently also killed. Emphasizing the repetition of history, Danticat responds that we collectively have not learned from "all the killings" and that we have not done anything with our knowledge of the past, which is why the terror is repeated (113). This reiteration of history and our failure to understand our own misrecognition of reality is particularly salient in her novel, and serves as the primary focus of this essay.

The Slovenian psychoanalytic philosopher and Hegelian-Marxist scholar Slavoj Žižek is fundamental in the reading of this novel because he uses a method to comprehend how history can be studied emerging from its own *symptoms*. Alluding to Jacques Lacan in *The Sublime Object of Ideology*, Žižek writes that the truth is constituted through the illusion of transference that arises from recognition, insisting on the idea that replicas of the past are held in the future. These replicas can be studied in *The Farming of Bones*, where different notions of recognition and allusions to memories depict the violence exercised upon Haitians in the Dominican Republic in 1937. In this essay I propose that *The Farming of Bones* portrays Dominican-Haitian history through a symptomatic trauma imprinted through bodily and mental traces that can also be seen in recent interactions between the two nations, in particular the denationalization of an estimated 210,000 Dominicans born to Haitian sugarcane workers and left stateless in 2013 by the Dominican Republic's Constitutional Court. The representation of such historical events in this literary text illustrates how traumatic events can be understood through the study of the symptom.

The Farming of Bones, Danticat's second novel, tells the story of Amabelle Désir, a Haitian woman who lives in Alegría, a small sugarcane town in the Dominican Republic. She is the servant and companion of Señora Valencia, the wife of Señor Pico Duarte, an affluent colonel who serves under the dictator Rafael Trujillo. Danticat begins the novel by introducing Sebastien Onius, a cane worker and the lover Amabelle plans to marry, allowing the reader to see two narrations. This narrative separation creates an illusion of the existence of two parallel histories. The first narrative voice focuses on Amabelle's consciousness as she tells the story of genocidal violence driven by Generalissimo Rafael Trujillo in 1937, which leads to the slaughter of Haitian workers and those deemed unable to pronounce the word "parsley." The second narration centers on Amabelle's personal accounts of her past in Haiti, which at times resembles a shared memoir that tells the story of a community. At the end, the narratives connect, uniting the voices of individual corporeal domination, and ending with Amabelle submerging her body into the Massacre River, the symbolic and historic site of the Parsley Massacre and of her own parents' death.

Given the storyline, there is a deceptive first impression that the traumatic event is understood based on the racial prejudice of the Dominican Republic; nevertheless, there are certain fissures and ruptures that are formed in future events and not in the event itself. There is something repressed and hidden that the novel intentionally conveys, symptoms that are not elucidated but merely enunciated, and this is Danticat's major aim in the construction of the novel. Why are symptoms uttered but not fully revealed? What is necessary to evaluate assemblages of the present/future to reexamine the long history of discrimination against Haitians?

Danticat's work has been honored as a remarkable memorial to the victims of the Parsley Massacre and has also been considered a testimony to the memory of the past.[1] Multiple scholars have read Danticat's novel through the lens of trauma.[2] However, if we perceive trauma and memory as Danticat's ultimate focus, we fail to recognize the enigmatic paradox of the repetition of history that her work evokes. She reflects on the way trauma and memory are initiated in the body within the state: this evocation, I argue, describes an alternate vision of the subject, one that is not sealed in the past but emerges symptomatically through her narrative. The major symptoms of Haitian-Dominican relations are described mostly in the first part of the novel, which is concerned with the roots of the massacre, but also with exploring different methods of truth-seeking about historical resistance. It is through the depiction of the symptom and the future and through the repetition of history that Danticat creates an illusion of transference, thus reconstructing a recurrent legacy between the two sides of Hispaniola.

Primary Symptoms and the Future

The symptom for Žižek cannot be rationalized without revising the future. He suggests that for Lacan the symptom is a *return of the repressed*, and this creates the dialectic between the future and the past. Using Norbert Wiener's metaphor, Lacan says, "[t]he symptom initially appears to us as a trace, which will only ever be a trace, one which will continue not to be understood until the analysis has got quite a long way, and until we have realized its meaning" (55). The repressed thus comes from the future and it is from the future that events can be understood. For Žižek, our only reality is created through misrecognition, because there is no real recognition. We see the reality of the symbolic order and our place in it, so there is no point in revealing the truth of our deception. Our deception is our reality, and we have no other. The symptom is a way to conceive a coded message, or to decipher a kind of formation. This code is deciphered through verbalization, which is how the symptom is "automatically dissolved" (73), and that is why the events that occur in the second half of the novel demonstrate that what happens are the repetitions of already-established symptoms.

Žižek's discussions of the notion of the symptom help to resolve the fragmented core in Danticat's work, since the repressed can be studied as an essential component of the novel, in which she constantly demonstrates that traces are part of the symptom. The traces are seen in the traumatic incidents that are visible through depictions of the bodily scars, the skin, and through internal dialogues that take place at Señora Valencia's house. These events are initially shown in the consciousness of Amabelle, and subsequently, are manifested in the massacre—a space that functions to revive but also to misrecognize different voices that intend to tell their truth. The development of the truth of what is happening begins with the use of rumor, a murmur that cannot be spoken aloud, but which drives the major developments of the storyline: an accident that ends the life of Joël, a Haitian bracero who works with Sebastien in the cane field; the displacement of Haitians across the border, along with the killing of thousands of Haitians; and finally the return of Amabelle to the Dominican Republic and her encounter with the river. The core of the second half of the novel has to be studied through the signs that are embodied in these examples. Danticat begins her chronicle with these illustrations, perhaps to elucidate what I call mental symptomatic trauma.

As mentioned earlier, the first symptom is expressed through bodily traces, which are transformed according to the unfolding of the mental symptomatic trauma in Amabelle, who on some occasions appears to be absent from the tangible happenings around her. As Lacan says, these symptoms are not understood until time has passed and a meaning is offered. To that end, Danticat, at the very beginning, describes Sebastien's bodily traces: "the cane stalks have ripped apart most of the skin on his shiny Black face, leaving him with crisscrossed trails of furrowed scars," and how he touches her using a space within his hands, where the "palms have lost their lifelines to the machetes that cut the cane" (1). His body is ripped, but she still finds beauty in Sebastien's corporality without a real understanding of the marks, the scars, and what could result from these wounds. This initial bodily-trace description is essential to comprehend Žižek's suggestion of how, in the symptom, "the repressed content is returning from the future and not from the past" (56). In the development of these scars, a more responsive attitude is formed in the characters, especially in Amabelle, who perceives how what seems to be mentally harmonized is disturbed by the recurrence of the episodes that she desires to silence as she searches for or accepts the truth. Amabelle crosses the cane field to find Sebastien and feels how the cane spears cut her legs (160), thus experiencing what the cane workers do. This enables Amabelle, as the receptacle of everyone's story, to perceive the scale of their suffering.

The second symptom is the way the skin is depicted, which begins to be visible in the first part of the story, and to a certain extent it conveys how the Dominican and Haitian ideology of race is mediated, because skin does not in itself reveal whether one is Haitian or Dominican. Dominicans are symptomatically conditioned to differentiate themselves, but there is no material basis for that distinction. This symptom is first depicted in the interactions between Señora Valencia and Amabelle. Descriptions of skin color give prominence to the dark and clear colors. The skin of Señora Valencia's baby daughter, for example, is compared with a deep bronze shade, "between the colors of tan Brazil nut shell and black salsify" (11). Señora Valencia's consciousness about the hierarchy of skin color is expressed when she says that her daughter could be mistaken for a Haitian person because of her skin (12). Following this scene, in response to Doctor Javier (Señora Valencia's personal physician), who says that the daughter of Señora Valencia has a little charcoal behind the ears, Papi (Señora Valencia's father, named Don Ignacio) produces a long discourse that pretends to validate his grandchild's skin superiority:

> "My daughter was born in the capital of this country. Her mother was of pure Spanish blood. She can trace her family to the Conquistadores, the line of El Almirante, Cristobal Colon. And I, myself, was born near a seaport in Valencia, Spain. . . . You make a very impolite assertion," Papi scolded Doctor Javier in a low voice when he thought his daughter wasn't listening. "We don't want to hear anything more of the kind." (17)

As alluded to in the previous example, this depiction of darker skin as a sign of Haitian identification illustrates how some Dominicans perceive Haitians, and this is partially the reason for the massacre. However, it is with the validation of the skin that Amabelle stops being absent-minded and begins to perceive the dynamics inside the house—and how she and others were being evaluated there—as a representation of social hierarchy. On one occasion Señora Valencia holds Amabelle's hands, but she drops them when Pico comes into the bedroom (41), suggesting the possibility of

Pico's disgust, and how her Haitian identity prevents her from being treated as equal, even though no words are spoken. As well as the portrayal of the skin in the interior of the house, Danticat makes another categorization of the skin in the outside, where the distinction is more pronounced, visible, and verbalized. The skin is described, combined with the bodily scars, as burned and destroyed. For example, when Amabelle goes to visit Kongo, who was at a stream where cane workers bathed before heading out to the fields, she emphasizes the women's bodies, showing them as diminished by their injuries, some with missing ears, some with lost fingers as a result of a runaway machete (61). At the same time, the damage, paradoxically, is what allows the recognition of those who have been wounded and are subject to this suffering.

The third and the most repeated symptom is seen through the dialogues that occur within closed spaces. They play an important role in Danticat's novel since they appear on different occasions along with movement, thus creating events that should not be analyzed without taking into account the prior verbal exchange. There are several interactions between the characters in the novel that are significant but I will focus on those that build major changes. The initial conversation takes place in the house, the space where the conflict is created. This conflict is perceived, as mentioned before, through conversations and exchanges between the main characters in the story. In the conversation, Beatriz (Señora Valencia's friend and sister of Doctor Javier) asks Don Ignacio whether he enjoys his life in the Dominican Republic. This question comes after she has asked him about being an officer in the Spanish army forty years ago, when he fought for the colonies with the United States, perhaps looking for a parallel with Trujillo's war of the 1930s. His response is significant for comprehending the symptom that is created inside their exchange. He responds,

> "Do I like the way things are conducted here now, everything run by military men? Do I like the worship of uniforms, the medals like stars on people's chests? Do I like this?" . . .
>
> "Do you like it?" Beatriz persisted.
>
> "No," Papi says. "I don't like any part of it." (77–78)

His words represent the symptom of the distinction made through the physical spaces depicted in the novel: the intimate space of the house where this conversation takes places is represented as a community, a collective, made of Haitians as well as Dominicans, servants and masters, but one household. The army, on the other hand, is a group but not a collective, since this interior space allows a kind of resistance where the truth is told, whereas in the outside, Trujillo and his supporters fight for a cause that apparently unifies a patriotic sentiment but that ultimately divides the population by creating different reactions to his destructive acts.

Rumors become the last narrative apparatus for Danticat to show the initial symptoms in the novel and the ones that recreate what is hidden and enigmatic. If one looks at the accident that takes place in the beginning of the story, one can see that the calamity is not seen as an event in the house; the house is a different space, qualitatively, from the society outside. There are two kinds of rumors, one that creates misrecognition and one that denies the truth. The former can be appreciated when Pico and Papi, rushing home to see Señora Valencia's newborn babies, run over and kill a person they do not know. The significance of the killing of Joël (the bracero who is murdered) varies depending on the viewer and, more specifically, whether he or she is Dominican or Haitian. This episode is a major symptom that builds the beginning and the transition of the mental story. When Luis tells the housemaid Juana what happened to Joël, he does not say who he is, only describing him as "a bracero, maybe one who works at Don Carlos' mill" (39). This line is meaningful because the absence of the name of the bracero is a sign of confusion. Don Ignacio is the one who tells Amabelle, but he does not know who was killed, thus erasing Joël and the Haitians as a whole.

The second kind of rumor is the one that foments denial. For example, Doctor Javier tells Amabelle that, following the Generalissimo's order, "soldiers and civilians are killing Haitians" and she needs to leave the house. Amabelle says, "It couldn't be real. Rumors, I thought. There were always rumors, rumors of war, of land disputes, of one side of the island planning to invade the other. These were the grand fantasies of presidents wanting the whole island to themselves" (139). Apparently Amabelle is constantly imagining and then denying reality in her mind; she even develops and cultivates her inner subjectivity when she goes outside and gets involved in that same reality. In view of this one can say that the inner space or the house becomes a primary source of truth for what is happening outside; it becomes a systematized space where racial ideology can be seen but it is also a space of preservation. Danticat also includes exchanges between the inside and the outside, but the interaction among those spaces creates both collision and a deliverance of future events. On one occasion Señora Valencia invites the cane workers inside for coffee, but their response includes a reaction of uncertainty:

> What did she want with them anyway? . . . Many had heard rumors of groups of Haitians being killed in the night because they could not manage to trill their "r" and utter a throaty "j" to ask for parsley, to say perejil. Rumors don't start for nothing, someone insisted. . . . A week before, a pantry maid who had worked in the house of a colonel for thirty years was stabbed by him at the dinner table. (114)

Violating the sacrosanct space of the interior, violence, as announced or anticipated by rumors like these, blurs the ideological boundaries between inside and outside, past and future. This scene suggests that the interior itself is no longer safe, obligating the Haitians and Dominicans to mobilize, thus disturbing the separation between the interior and exterior spaces. There is a correlation between the past/future and the interior/exterior; if the house is the space of the past, one can say that the interior contains the fundamental signals that determine the future. Moreover, without an analysis of the symptoms experienced in the corporeal traces and the internal/domestic dialogues that take place in the indoors in Danticat's novel, the future events exposed on the outside cannot be recognized. The future is contained within the past, as has been mentioned before, but the past also is already occupied with the future. What is it, then, that repeats in history?

Repetition of History

The Farming of Bones functions as a remembrance of how history is repeated, but also how the past is written. As we see in the aforementioned symptoms in Danticat's novel, the events are undoubtedly retroactive because the major event, which is the massacre, happened sixty years before publication of the novel. Even without contemplating Danticat's work profoundly, it can be concluded that what is happening between the Dominican Republic and Haiti now evokes violence like that of 1937 but of course with other nuances. The origin and the symptoms of the conflict indicate that there are still stories that are not heard and that the invisibility of Black bodies is still at play in the Dominican Republic. In 2013, for example, the Dominican

Republic's Supreme Court ruled that people born between 1929 and 2010 in the country to noncitizen parents were not to be granted citizenship. This has brought major problems as people have been left nationless by the Dominican naturalization law, also named Law 169-14, passed in 2014.[3]

In contrast to the damaging effect of some kinds of replication, Žižek implies that there is a need for it, because "repetition is the way historical necessity asserts itself in the eyes of opinion" (61). When an event occurs for the first time, it is experienced as a contingent trauma; it is through repetition that the "symbolic necessity" of the event is recognized. When an event first occurs, it cannot be predicted, but when it is repeated several times one can say that its symbolism can be interpreted and can also be predictive. As Žižek explains, it is almost impossible for people to grasp the real meaning of a traumatic event based on its concrete form. The compulsion to repeat is the awareness of the way the present is charged with the past. This notion appears in the novel through several examples, but I will focus on the repetition of Haitian invisibility and the state of hunger. To illustrate this notion, Danticat, in the second half of *The Farming of Bones*, explains how events are repeated due to hidden problems that are not fundamentally solved. When people have crossed the river, they provide testimonies that allow them to be heard and speak their own "truths." One woman testifies:

> "I pushed my son out of my body here, in this country," . . . in a mix of Alegrían Kreyòl and Spanish, the tangled language of those who always stuttered as they spoke. . . . "My mother too pushed me out of her body here. Not me, not my son, not one of us has ever seen the other side of the border. Still they won't put our birth papers in our palms so my son can have knowledge placed into his head by a proper educator in a proper school. (69)

The aforementioned case recreated in Danticat's novel is reminiscent of the 1920s—as Hintzen points out—when Haitian immigrants were found in the country without documents, and "they were usually arrested and then deported. In the 1930s . . . soldiers and immigration inspectors . . . started frequently apprehending Haitian immigrants found outside of plantations and forcing them to return" (37). This episode has its origins in the constitution of 1929, which explicitly supported birthright citizenship for children of foreigners born in the Dominican Republic but "excluded people in transit . . . the children born to Haitian sugar cane workers whose labor migration had been organized by the US military government for nearly two decades" (Candelario 108). So this continuous denial of personhood also obliterates people's identity, social mobility, and progression within their nation if they are of Haitian descent, still causing resentment and thus creating mental and physical traces.[4]

Danticat also illustrates the repetition of history through the depiction of hunger. In the story, there is a recurrence of deprivation that is manifested through the state of hunger. The first reference to hunger in the novel occurs during the description of the first years of the North American occupation in Haiti (1915), which produced ruptures among Haitians, in which stealing from each other becomes the only way to survive within the same physical space. There is also a conversation held between Amabelle and Mimi (Sebastien's sister, who works for Beatriz as a servant), in which Mimi explains why she does not call Beatriz by her name: " 'What does it matter if Beatriz and your lady become angry with us?' she said. 'If they let us go, at least we'd have a few days of freedom before dying from hunger' " (63). Even though the notion of hunger here has a less negative connotation since it is associated with liberation, it also refers to the termination of life. The valley peasants in the novel, on the other hand, are depicted as those "who gathered outside in curiosity and hunger" (119). The aforementioned examples illustrate how the state of hunger or deprivation becomes a symptom of historical reiteration for those who are oppressed.

Another example offered by Danticat occurs when Amabelle crosses the river and stays with Man Rapadou, Yves's mom, in the Cap, who tells a story about Yves's father, who came out of prison after nothing but bread and water for thirty days. The first thing she cooked for him was " 'all the rich food he had dreams about in prison. He ate until he fell over on his plate in the middle of eating. He died eating,' she told the relations with a deep long laugh. 'Please, don't kill my son. A man can die of hunger, but a man can also die over a plate of food' " (224). Hunger makes the body vulnerable and acts as a synonym of forgetfulness where memory, on occasion, is just a mirror of what happens outside. At the same time the mental pain remains and repeats continually even when the event itself is not manifested. The reiteration of this notion is charged with similar occurrences that happen in the past and the future in the novel, but these events can only be elucidated when they occur again. This exemplifies Žižek's idea of the impossibility of comprehending the meaning of a traumatic event based on its initial appearance.

The Symptomatic Resistance

The appropriation of space becomes the final manifestation of the symptom. The symptom is perceived through the portrayal of the river that appears in Danticat's novel as the empty place around which the symbolic order is inscribed. The river that runs between Haiti and the Dominican Republic in the novel is fluid, and so shallow one can cross it by foot, so the boundaries of national sovereignty that the Dominican Republic aims to maintain are always undermined.

The liminal space of the river is featured early in the novel and is part of discussions, delusions, dreams, mobility, and the actions of the characters. The first mention of the river denotes birth, constructing a parallel of belonging. Amabelle says that Señora Valencia's child belongs to her as "watercress belongs to water and river lilies belong to the river" (9). This sense of belonging is shown to be an illusion, because just as water flows and changes constantly, so the meanings of the river vary. The river is described as a space of encounter and separation. When Amabelle loses her parents in the river, the space is depicted as a compound place that embodies histories. She indicates that in the river there is a combination of Haitians and Dominicans, who carry merchandise across the river to exchange it for food, but she also describes river rats, creating an atmosphere of obscurity and hope at the same time: "My father reaches into the current . . . as if to salute the spirit of the river and request her permission to enter. My mother crosses herself three times and . . . climbs on my father's back . . . once he is in the river, he flinches, realizing that he has made a grave mistake" (51). This initial depiction also indicates how the river has the power to generate life and death. It is through it that individuals produce new stories and beginnings but most importantly: social fragmentation.

In Amabelle's fantasies and deliberations, she constantly dreams of her parents in the river, even though she wants to silence her dreams (55). The river becomes the symbolic representation of Amabelle's trauma. In her sleep, she sees her mother rising, like the "mother spirit of the rivers, above the current that drowned her" (207) and this image confronts the group with whom she is reaching Haiti. For them, the river is charged with a false illusion of escape because it is the border: an apparent space of safety, but for Amabelle, it is the space of reiteration of her individual trauma. Both water and the river appear as intertwined and opposed symptomatic notions in the novel, and they tell simultaneous stories of separation and confrontation.

The river then is a symptom that indicates displacement, which both Amabelle and the "invisible-visible" Haitians undergo. Amabelle knows that the river is one of the symptoms that need to be interpreted to silence her thoughts. Water is a symbol of escape, encounter, and suffering, and it is also an element of freedom, and this is why freedom is another element of the fantasy. In the midst of the difficult journey to Haiti, one man without a name asserts that freedom "is a passing thing . . . someone can always come and snatch it away" (212), and the flesh becomes a synonym of nothingness that could lose its magic, as another man says (213). The last remembrance indicates how those who are crossing the border/river are unable to act according to their desire, which is the right to choose where to live.

The Generalissimo gives a speech on the radio, about repeated events and retaliations committed at the border in the river. The river for Trujillo is a liminal space for "enemies" to ambush, and the fear and menace of instability this space represents in his speech keep the Dominicans in a state of resistance against Haitians. It is the word "tradition" that makes his whole speech haunting because it embodies ruptures that are formed from historical dissociation. The alarmism of Trujillo's speech itself stems from another historical remembrance: the presence of Haiti in the Dominican Republic for twenty-two years in the nineteenth century, from whence comes the official national neurosis about being grouped together with Haiti.[5] This sheds light on Trujillo's proclamations about how the liberators of the nation "did their part" but the leaders of today "must play their part also" (97), emphasizing a long history of resistance between the two sides of Hispaniola.

Up to this point, we have emphasized the power of the river to connect human, natural, and physical spaces to interpret symptomatic individual and collective trauma[6] in the novel. Likewise, in order to comprehend the opposition of the river, we must appreciate Amabelle's final union with the river as an act of liberation and retaliation. When Amabelle decides to "slip into the current," describing the warm, shallow water, searching for the dawn (310), undeniably, she is fomenting resistance. The river is finally confronted when Amabelle chooses to remove her dress, folding it piece by piece and throwing her unclothed body into the river.

Conclusion

Danticat forms a parallel with the present moment that seems to build toward a future that continues from the scars of the past. The singularity of *The Farming of Bones* can be appreciated through Walter Benjamin's consideration of history as a text: "We can say about it what some modern author said about a literary text: the past has deposed in it images which could be compared to those retained by a photographic plate. Only the future disposes of developers strong enough to make appear the picture with all its details" (141).[7] The symptomatic symbolic idea of the *massacre* today is reiterated through what the current Dominican government calls "Operation Shield," which is intended to stop Haitian migration by placing two thousand troops along the border. Removing the protection from a physical space builds recognition of the symptom and struggle of the Haitian-Dominican conflict but it will not resolve the mental symptomatic trauma in the recurrent immigrant deportations. Analysis of the symptoms enables individual and collective subjects to see the indications of what is going to continue, but also what cannot be changed. Subjects only have the present moment in which to resist the symptoms of the past and contribute to human progress.

Notes

1. According to Lorgia Garcia-Peña: "the Haitian Massacre took place from October 2 to October 8, 1937. . . . Using machetes and knives to simulate a fight among peasants, Dominican military and civilian allies murdered an estimated fifteen thousand to twenty thousand people, converting a once peaceful, multiethnic border community into a site of horror" (93).

2. See Amy Novak's "A Marred Testament: Cultural Trauma and Narrative in Danticat's *The Farming of Bones*"; Heather Hewett's "At the Crossroads: Disability and Trauma in *The Farming of Bones*"; and Martin Munro's "Writing Disaster: Trauma, Memory, and History in Edwidge Danticat's *The Farming of Bones*."

3. A process that, according to Amelia Hintzen in her article "A Veil of Legality: The Contested History of Anti-Haitian Ideology under the Trujillo Dictatorship," aroused concern in 1920 when "the governor of the Dominican province of Monte Cristi wrote to the national Department of Interior and Police to complain about the deportation of Haitian residents living in his province" (28).

4. According to Jonathan M. Katz, in February 2015, "A Haitian man named Henry Claude Jean was found hanging from a tree across the street from the hospital in Santiago de los Caballeros, the country's second-largest city. A Dominican news channel aired footage showing his swollen body still dangling the following day, his hands and feet bound with black cord. The Santiago police blamed two undocumented Haitian immigrants who were supposed to have killed Jean over a lottery ticket. On the night of the killing, three miles from the park where Jean was hanged, a crowd burned a Haitian flag and chanted: 'Haitians, out!' "

5. See Edward Paulino's "Erasing the Kreyol from the Margins of the Dominican Republic: The Pre- and Post-Nationalization Project of the Border, 1930–1945."

6. Maria Rice Bellamy recently explored individual and collective trauma in *Bridges to Memory: Postmemory in Contemporary Ethnic American Women's Fiction*. She studies how trauma's ghost is reflected by the "haunting resonance left by trauma" (2) but also the space that is created and inherited by the "narrators and auditors, survivors and descendants, in which temporal and subjective boundaries are blurred" (4).

7. Quoted in Žižek 141.

Works Cited

Bellamy, Maria Rice. *Bridges to Memory: Postmemory in Contemporary Ethnic American Women's Fiction*. U of Virginia, 2015.

Candelario, Ginetta E. B. "La Ciguapa y El Ciguapeo: Dominican Myth, Metaphor, and Method." *Small Axe*, vol. 20, no. 3 51, 2016, pp. 100–12.

Danticat, Edwidge. *The Farming of Bones: A Novel*. Soho, 1998.

García-Peña, Lorgia. *The Borders of Dominicanidad: Race, Nation, and Archives of Contradiction*. Duke UP, 2016.

Hewett, Heather. "At the Crossroads: Disability and Trauma in *The Farming of Bones*." *MELUS: Multi-Ethnic Literature of the United States*, vol. 31, no. 3, 2006, pp. 123–45.

Hintzen, Amelia. "A Veil of Legality: The Contested History of Anti-Haitian Ideology under the Trujillo Dictatorship." *New West Indian Guide / Nieuwe West-Indische Gids*, vol. 90, no. 1–2, 2016, pp. 28–54.

Katz, Jonathan M. "In Exile." *New York Times Magazine*. 13 Jan. 2016, pp. 46–54.

Munro, Martin. "Writing Disaster: Trauma, Memory, and History in Edwidge Danticat's *The Farming of Bones*." *Ethnologies*, vol. 28, no. 1, 2006, pp. 81–98.

Novak, Amy. "A Marred Testament: Cultural Trauma and Narrative in Danticat's *The Farming of Bones*." *Arizona Quarterly: A Journal of American Literature, Culture, and Theory*, vol. 62, no. 4, 2006, pp. 93–120.

Paulino, Edward. "Erasing the Kreyol from the Margins of the Dominican Republic: The Pre- and Post-Nationalization Project of the Border, 1930–1945." *Wadabagei: A Journal of the Caribbean and Its Diaspora*, vol. 8, no. 2, 2005, pp. 35–71.

Žižek, Slavoj. *The Sublime Object of Ideology*. Verso, 1989.

9

"The Black Plague from the West"
Haiti in Roberto Marcallé Abreu's Dystopia

RAMÓN ANTONIO VICTORIANO-MARTÍNEZ

> De ambos lados el mismo dictador, un diseño americano
> —Luis Días, "La Yipeta"

The Dominican Republic is, for obvious reasons, the country in the Hispanic Caribbean region with the most sustained and deep concerns about Haiti. Not only is this involvement fueled by the geographical fact of sharing an island but also by the politico-historical reality that the creation of a Dominican nation-state starts with separation from the Republic of Haiti. Contrary to other separation stories, India and Pakistan, for example, the Dominican-Haitian one has the trauma at the moment of unification (1822) and not at the moment of partition (1844), at least from the point of view of Dominicans. Some of the images used to describe the relationship between the countries are telling: a counterpoint (Matibag), and tears (Suárez). The border between the countries also has been described as: "a world destroyed" (Turits), a veil (Danticat), a closed door to paradise (Mieses), and a bacá[1] (Díaz). As we can see, this uneasy relationship has been one characterized by instances of conflict, cooperation, and oftentimes avoidance and mistrust. The border is at the same time a site of destruction and trade, of intermingling and separation.

History has enormous weight on the formation of such ways of thinking about the relationship between the two countries. The Haitian Revolution is, in the mind of conservative Dominican historians, a catastrophic event. For Manuel Arturo Peña Batlle, the most prominent intellectual of the Trujillo era:

> La colectividad española de Santo Domingo, por determinación ineludible de la geografía y por incomprensible determinación política de la corte de Madrid, fue la más inmediata víctima de la Revolución Negra, es decir, del movimiento armado de manumisión dirigido por los esclavos negros y mulatos de la colonia francesa de Santo Domingo contra el patronato de su Metrópoli. todo el siglo xix lo vivimos bajo los efectos del horrible impacto. Los resultados sociales de aquello son de muy penosa y difícil descripción. (548)[2]

Peña Batlle would be an inspiration for the ideas later espoused in more haphazard writing by historian Manuel Núñez.

Seeing Haiti as an uncanny presence on the island, Sibylle Fischer makes a powerful case, supported by the work of Dominican scholar Franklin Franco, of its role as a modernizing force on the eastern side of the border, representing modern legislation (Napoleonic penal and civil codes) and laicization, a role that prompted the Dominican elites to maintain, as we have seen with Peña Batlle, a "strategy that appears to take hold is one of demonization and racist denigration" (134).

In the twenty-first century, Haiti continues to be portrayed in Dominican literature as a place of disease, plague, or as a potential invader. This is perhaps the most enduring trope in Dominican literature and the latest iteration of it is presented in Roberto Marcallé Abreu's dystopian trilogy published between 2006 and 2012: *Contrariedades y tribulaciones en la mezquina y desdichada existencia del señor Manfredo Pemberton* (2006), *No verán mis ojos esta horrible ciudad* (2009), and *La manipulación de los espejos* (2012). Marcallé's trilogy, totaling 1,730 pages, constitutes a somewhat failed attempt at a political roman à clef; in the following I will present in detail why this is so.

In other works by Dominican writers such as *La mucama de Ominculé* (Rita Indiana Hernández, 2015, translated as *Tentacle*, 2018), *El día de todos* (Juan Carlos Mieses, 2009), and "Monstro" (Junot Díaz, 2012) we can see these portrayals of Haiti in place. Hernández opens her novel, a time-bending story that takes place, at the same time, in a postapocalyptic

Santo Domingo, in the sixteenth-century colony of Saint-Domingue and in the late twentieth-century Dominican Republic, with an image of diseased Haitians being scooped from the street by Chinese robots:

> Bringing her thumb and index finger together, Acilde positions her eye and activates the security camera that faces the street, where she sees one of the many Haitians who've crossed the border, fleeing from the quarantine declared on the other half of the island. *Recognizing the virus in the Black man*, the security mechanism in the tower releases a lethal gas and simultaneously informs the neighbors, who will now avoid the building's entrance until the automatic collectors patrolling the streets and avenues pick up the body and disintegrate it. . . . As she smears the windows with Windex, she sees a collector across the street hunt down another illegal, a woman who tries to hide behind a dumpster, unsuccessfully. . . . China's communist government donated the collectors "to help with the terrible circumstances affecting the islands of the Caribbean after the March 19 disaster." (9–10, emphasis added)[3]

Mieses, for his part, opens his novel with a lengthy epigraph from Paul Valery's book *Crisis of the Mind* (1919), the first words of which are: "We later civilizations . . . we too know that we are mortal," signaling the tone of what is to come. One of the main characters is Jean Pierre, a figure modeled after Jean-Bertrand Aristide: "Brothers, said, in kreyòl . . . that's how he addressed himself to the parishioners in the small church in Jeremie when he was not yet Papá Yoyó but the good Father Jean Pierre, a simple Catholic priest . . ." (79, my translation). Papá Yoyó / Jean Pierre will become a charismatic shaman for the Haitian masses and will signal the final destination in a passage with ecological bend:

> Then I asked myself where have the voices of Haiti gone, the song of the birds, the sound of the wind on the chachás in the month of March, the cries of the parrot. . . . Jean Pierre raised, solemnly, the right arm and pointed it to the East, towards the border. . . . He knew that in their minds the border was figured as a closed door that leads to a forbidden paradise, like a wall that kept them trapped in misery, hunger, thirst and desperation. (135–36, my translation)

The novel ends with the character Tit'karine, a seven-year-old Haitian girl, residing in the borderlands as witness of the Haitian takeover: "Her grandmother called her but Tit'karine ignored her. All her attention was concentrated on the stain that blocked the road. A human avalanche was running down the hill through the old creek. It was as if every person in the world starting walking, Tit'karine felt a strange pang of joy" (167).

Junot Díaz masterfully combines all three views:

> At first Negroes thought it was funny. A disease that could make a Haitian blacker? It was the joke of the year. Everybody in our sector accusing everybody else of having it. You couldn't display a blemish or catch some sun on the streets without the jokes starting. Someone would point to a spot on your arm and say, Diablo, haitiano, que te pasó? La Negrura they called it. The Darkness. (107)

In the short story Díaz masterfully plays with the Haiti as diseased place trope in order to highlight the plight of Haitians in the aftermath of the January 2010 earthquake. But in opposition to other works of fiction and the traditional Dominican discourse, there is an empathetic undertone in Díaz's work:

> Reports arriving over the failing fatlines claimed that Port-au-Prince had been destroyed, that Haiti had been destroyed, that thirteen million screaming Haitian refugees were threatening the borders, that Dominican military units had been authorized to meet the invaders—the term the gov was now using—with ultimate force. (118)

The invasion to come is not a product of a political design to take over the island, as it is portrayed in Mieses's novel, but of an apocalypse of unknown origin.

Roberto Marcallé Abreu (b. Santo Domingo, 1948) is one of the most prolific and recognized writers in Dominican literature. Since his debut in 1972 with *Las dos muertes de José Inirio*, Marcallé has not stopped writing and publishing novels and short stories collections. He has been awarded the Premio Nacional de Novela (National Novel Prize) three times: in 1979 for *Cinco bailadores sobre la tumba caliente del licenciado*, 1999 for *Las siempre insólitas cartas del destino*, and 2013 for *La manipulación de los espejos*, the latter the culmination of a trilogy that will be the subject of analysis in this chapter. Marcallé's career and lifetime achievements were recognized when he was awarded the highest literary honor that the country confers: the Premio Nacional de Literatura (National Literature Award) in 2015 for his "outstanding contribution to Dominican narrative, in short stories and novels, in which he has reflected the palpitations on urban life; as well for his important contributions to the essay form."[4]

Marcallé's trilogy comes to represent another chapter in the long tradition of Dominican cultural production's engagement with Haiti and Haitian themes. In 1996 historian Orlando Inoa documented the Dominican textual output referring to Haiti, compiling a list of 796 works in different fields: history, sociology, migration, and border relations. This vast production seems to confirm Samuel Martínez's assessment that "the Dominican obsession with Haiti is an unrequited passion: Haitians do not regard Dominicans with anything like the same feeling as that of Dominicans looking upon Haitians" (83). One of the most important manifestations of this "unrequited passion" is the 1977 essay "Tipología del tema haitiano en la literatura dominicana," in which Marcio Veloz Maggiolo classifies the approaches to Haiti and Haitians in Dominican literature as follows: "a) Literatura del haitiano adulado; b) literatura del haitiano agredido o contra el haitiano; c) literatura del haitiano adulterado; d) literatura del haitiano compadecido; y e) literatura del haitiano integrado" (94).[5] The essay has been one of the main tools in the analysis of the representation of Haitians in Dominican literature and serves as a map of sorts to situate the ideological position of Dominican writers when writing about Haiti.[6] Marcallé's novels are squarely in the "literature of the attacked Haitian or literature against Haitians" category.

The critical reception of the trilogy has been very scattered, and this could be attributed to the state of literary criticism in the Dominican Republic: a lack of specialized publications and specialists in Dominican literature working on the island. It will be outside the purview of this chapter to address why this has come to pass, but I must point out that the most consistent effort to engage with the fiction produced in the Dominican Republic has come from scholars established outside the country in universities across the United States, Canada, and Europe. Nevertheless, two of the few critics that have engaged with the trilogy in question have been Giovanni Di Pietro and Doris Melo. The Italian-Canadian Di Pietro, who has dedicated a monograph to Marcallé's work, lauded the second installment: "*No verán mis ojos* as . . . una novela que le funciona a cabalidad a Marcallé. Le funciona, porque no está solamente bien escrita; también es más que apreciable su contenido. Hemos sostenido desde hace tiempo que Marcallé es de los pocos novelistas dominicanos, si no el único, que se enfrenta seriamente al descalabro social y moral de su país" (n.p.).[7] As I will show, these novels are not well written, and Marcallé is not the only novelist addressing the setbacks suffered by the country and its people. A short list of authors and their work will suffice: Juan Bosch with *La mañosa*, Pedro Mir with *Cuando amaban las tierras comuneras*, and Rita Indiana Hernández with *La mucama de Ominculé*. Scholar Doris Melo, from the Caribbean University of Puerto Rico, Bayamón, published on Research Gate a largely impressionistic article: "La manipulación de lo espejos de Roberto Marcallé Abreu: Una visión crítica a partir de la teoría literaria," in which she explains that the novel "está colmada de ideas e imágenes entrelazadas, que intentan explicar el mundo en forma de símbolos y metáforas" (n.p.)[8] and, in her view "[l]a prosa fraccionada es cruda, hiere, maltrata, es grotesca, transgresora. Diriamos [*sic*], que está construida a propósito de esta forma, presenta el deterioro de una ciudad y su presente actual" (n.p.).[9] I show that this is not the case, that Marcallé's lackadaisical writing is not intentional and it does not serve any aesthetic purpose.

The first novel of the trilogy, *Contrariedades y tribulaciones en la mezquina y desdichada existencia del señor Manfredo Pemberton* (2006), is dedicated to Manuel Núñez, Rafael Ramírez Ferreira, and Pelegrín Castillo: "Porque su espada es la palabra."[10] Manuel Núñez is the most prominent anti-Haitian intellectual in the Dominican Republic; he is the winner of two national essay prizes for *El ocaso de la nación dominicana*[11] and another Premio Nacional de Ensayo for *Peña Batlle en la era de Trujillo* (2008). Pelegrín Castillo is one of the founders of the far-right Fuerza Nacional Progresista (FNP), a party with a strong anti-Haitian rhetoric.[12] For a Dominican audience this dedication immediately sets the tone for what to expect in the book.

The novels take place in an unspecified near future in the city of Santo Domingo. At the beginning of *Contrariedades* the title character, Manfredo Pemberton, suffers a series of misfortunes (*contrariedades*) stemming from the deficiencies and venality of various officials at different level of government and from private companies. At the same time a paramilitary group called "La Causa" starts to execute criminals in a series of vigilante attacks. The novels move back and forth in time, narrating the beginnings of the "La Causa" reign and the tactics used to eliminate adversaries and all the measures against Haitians, "undesirable foreigners," and meddlesome Catholic priests. Chapter after chapter, Marcallé loosely connects his main ideas about what is wrong with Dominican society (corruption, lax customs agents, etc.) and who is to blame (the Jesuits, the so called "dominicanyorks," the NGOs, and Haiti and its "friends": the United States, Canada, and France) to portray a society in decadence that can only be rescued by the use of force, persecution, and a police state. *Contrariedades* ends with a chapter in which the future president and leader of "La Causa," Ulises María González, is described in the process of writing his book *Conceptos sobre el nuevo hombre* (Concepts on the new man), which brings to the mind of the reader the same concept as presented by Ernesto "Ché" Guevara in 1965, "El socialismo y el hombre en Cuba." González is presented as a "una persona refinada y culta. Siente una profunda admiración por Mozart y por Verdi" (501).[13] These images of the light-skinned *letrado* with the European education remind us of the admonition of José Martí against those youth who "salen . . . al mundo, con antiparras yanquis o francesas, y aspiran a dirigir un pueblo que no conocen" (33).[14] Ulises María González and his group will go on a string of vigilante justice attacks and will impose an authoritarian government that in some instances will resemble the Trujillo dictatorship.

Contrariedades begins in present-day Santo Domingo where Manfredo Pemberton in a "perverted and ill-fated day" has an encounter with a drag queen, which elicits a sensation of revulsion and rejection in him.[15] The image of the city is one of decadence, abandonment, dirtiness, and danger, the meeting of the two characters takes place "[m]inutos previos a sumergirse en las horrendas tinieblas, el calor, los insectos, y el hedor generalizado" (*Contrariedades* 20);[16] all Mr. Pemberton sees is "[b]asura desparramada sobre aceras destrozadas y bordillos, aireando una pestilencia insoportable" (24).[17] In this sense the way the city is presented could be compared to the one that greets the character Yolanda in Pedro Vergés's *Sólo cenizas hallarás* (1980) when she returns to Santo Domingo in 1961 after Trujillo's death:

> A principios de diciembre llegó a Santo Domingo y se encontró con la ciudad más limpia de América, la ciudad más tranquila de todo el continente, convertida en una especie de suburbio apartado por donde nunca pasaran los camiones de basura del Ayuntamiento . . . Una semana entera se pasó ella caminando de arriba para abajo y no consiguió otra cosa que no fuera miseria, desorden, relajo y suciedad. (27–28)[18]

There is in Marcallé too a nostalgic undertone that pines not only for the city under the dictatorship but also for a return to an authoritarian and patriarchal rule: the project that will take over the nation politically in the novel and that will "clean" the city, the so-called "La Causa" under the leadership of "El Hombre," is announced in the first pages of the novel when Mr. Pemberton, after his encounter with the transvestite, sees the poster that tells him, "Organize yourself!" (¡Organízate!) (*Contrariedades* 15–17). Haiti is introduced using the medical language of contamination:[19]

> El doctor Robles [Juan Pablo Robles, asistente del presidente] pensó con amargura que el dejar hacer y el dejar pasar habían ahondado hasta un punto el problema, que mucha gente creía desesperanzada que la presencia de *la peste negra del oeste* [italics in the original] ya no podía controlarse . . . es necesario implementar, desde ya, medidas encaminadas a liquidar *este virus* que perturba el espíritu de la patria y que amenaza de forma grave nuestra existencia. . . . Usted sabe lo que la gente *sana* de este país espera de nosotros.[20] (49, emphasis added)

Later on, Ulises María González (El Hombre), in a monologue that runs for ten pages, expresses his views on the relationship between the two countries thus:

> Hay indicios crecientes de la existencia de planes para refundir la Patria dominicana con el seudoestado colapsado del oeste para que nosotros, los dominicanos, nos veamos en la obligación de asumir la vida y obra, los desafueros y perversidades de la gente *dañada* y *dañina* que proviene de esos ámbitos de enfermedades contagiosas e incurables, de vudú y magia negra.[21] (256)

Here we can see at work all the clichés that for almost two hundred years have shaped how Dominicans view Haiti: fear of a "fusion," land of diseases, and black magic.

Fusion is the greatest fear that elite Dominicans feel toward Haiti. It is not a coincidence that the apocalyptic disease depicted in "Monstro" manifests itself through Blackness and the togetherness of bodies:

> Doctors began reporting a curious change in the behavior of the infected patients: they wanted to get together, in close proximity, all the time. They no longer tolerated being separated from other

infected, started coming together in main quarantine zone, just outside Champs de Mars, the largest of relocation camps. (108)

The fusion, in the conspiracy theory espoused by Marcallé (and a sizeable portion of the mainstream Dominican intelligentsia), is promoted by the so-called "Friends of Haiti": the United States, France, and Canada. In *Contrariedades* President González's chief of staff, Dr. Robles, gives voice to this theory in a conversation with Cardinal Alberto Castillo Tejada:

> Quieren obligarnos a coexistir con individuos con los que tenemos diferencias esenciales de toda naturaleza, individuos que, en términos históricos, han hecho graves daños a este país . . . gente primitiva, violenta y dañada. . . . Se pretende que acojamos sin protestas una "invasión pacífica" que persigue desnaturalizarnos como nación y como pueblo . . . Estados Unidos, Canadá, Francia. . . . Conspiran para que se produzca una gran confrontación interna que motive la intervención exterior.[22] (459–60)

In the second novel of the trilogy, *No verán mis ojos esta horrible ciudad*, this fear of fusion and of the diseases that Haitians supposedly carry drives the Dominican government, finally conquered by González and his group "La Causa," to issue a series of eugenic measures under a program called "Preservation." This program will start with a "census of people residing at the border," and at the end of the census form there are two questions: "1 ¿Aspira usted a residir de manera legal en el territorio dominicano? 2 ¿Aceptaría ser sometido voluntariamente a una operación de esterilización, requisito previo para calificar como residente legal?" (*No verán mis ojos* 199).[23] Later on, the director of migration, Lic. del Orbe, declares: "Su eficiencia se probará con esta primera partida de indeseables extranjeros como paso previo al *Programa Preservación* que supone la esterilización de cerca de dos millones de haitianos que residen en el país y que serán deportados en su casi totalidad" (199).[24]

Defending the program, Dr. del Orbe states: "No vamos a exterminar *la peste negra del Oeste*. Vamos a contribuir, de manera humanitaria, con un decaimiento que se está produciendo de manera dolorosa, llena de sufrimientos. . . . Pienso en una descendencia marcada, como si hubiera sido maldecida por la divinidad" (*No verán mis ojos* 200).[25] The Governing Council of President González relies on the existence of "Programas de

Planificación Familiar promovidos por países desarrollados"[26] to argue that "[e]s necesario acudir a razones científicas reale El hecho objetivo es que la población haitiana se encuentra maleada en términos de salud y maldita en términos de herencia" (202).[27] The metaphor of contagion and disease to describe Haiti has reached its logical conclusion: extermination of the whole Haitian community on the island.

Haiti will appear once again in the third and final installment of the trilogy, *La manipulación de los espejos* (2012), this time explicitly as a nightmare. The novel opens with Manfredo Pemberton having a dream in which he walks through an abandoned and dirty city and is being chased by a mob led by a figure that resembles Baron Samedi[28] of Haitian Vodou: a Black man in a black frock coat. This figure also evokes the Haitian dictator François Duvalier who use to dress as Baron Samedi.[29] Mr. Pemberton, in his nightmare, sees "paredes torcidas de bloques sin empañetar, en los que habían pintarrajeado leyendas diabólicas en creole. Se sintió mareado y débil" (*Manipulación* 35).[30] In contrast to this when Mr. Pemberton wakes up he sees: "Cuadros. Cortinas. Estantes con libros. Ventanas panorámicas que seducían la vista hacia un mundo sin fantasmas, de tranquila claridad" (37).[31] Haiti once again signifies ignorance, darkness, and savagery ("diabolical" phrases in walls) while the Dominican Republic is presented as the place of light and civilization (books, paintings). *La manipulación de los espejos* reiterates the themes of the previous two novels regarding the new road that the Dominican Republic needs to take. It depicts a near future in which the Dominican government, after a massacre of "undesirables" (59), establishes the ideal society: a Dominican society in which all traces of Haiti have been eliminated, there is an almost general militarization of society, with the death penalty as punishment "for certain crimes and misdemeanors," the internet is thoroughly controlled, and there is censorship imposed on "composers of popular music" (62). This society came about through a pact between "The Cause" commanded by President González, "El Hombre," and "The Dark City" (the name of both a secret place and the group of people that commands it), a place where all kind of depravity and debauchery is permitted and which Marcallé describes at length in various chapters.

The pact is an allegory of the Frente Patriótico Pact of 1996 between the Partido de la Liberación Dominicana (PLD) and then-president Joaquín Balaguer. This pact made possible the PLD's attainment of power for the first time and paved the way for twenty years of political supremacy by this party.[32] One of the main architects of the pact between The Dark City and The Cause was "El licenciado Vinicio del Orbe, jefe de Migración, calificado como uno de los personajes más enérgicos de La Causa y ejecutor de la deportación de miles de extranjeros calificados como indeseables" (*Manipulación* 470).[33] Vinicio del Orbe is a character most likely based on real-life lawyer Marino Vinicio Castillo (Vincho), father of Pelegrín Castillo, to whom *Contrariedades* is dedicated. Vincho Castillo has been for the last fifty years a staunch defender of the status quo, a rabid anti-Haitian, and lightning rod against progressive forces in the Dominican Republic, while holding very prestigious and powerful offices, especially in the PLD's governments.

The elements of continuity of plot, characters, and themes would validate the unity of the trilogy and its characterization as one big novel. The haphazard and careless writing, the long digressions that attempt to address what could be perceived as personal and political grievances of the author, the scarcity of moments of artistry, and the clumsiness in the presentation of political ideas and characters, some of them real-life ones, make this work difficult to engage with.[34] Strangely enough, it has been lauded by part of the official intelligentsia and recognized with the highest honors, all of which leads one to think that it is in the political ideas espoused and defended by Marcallé in his novels that we could find the reason for such accolades.

Roberto Marcallé Abreu with this work inscribes himself within that current of Dominican thinking that Pedro L. San Miguel calls the "homeland under siege" (45–49). The main representatives of the "homeland under siege" thought are Peña Batlle and Joaquín Balaguer during the Trujillo era. In contemporary Dominican cultural production, Manuel Núñez would be the most conspicuous intellectual espousing this view. Under this vision, the Dominican Republic is under a constant, permanent, and relentless threat from across the border, therefore Dominicans must be always on the lookout for danger coming from the west. This danger could manifest itself in diseases, undesirable aliens, nightmarish visions, invasion of dark bodies, and in the "threat" of fusion and mixing. Marcallé combines all of these myths to present a dystopian future for Hispaniola, ironically aligning himself with the famous Haitian intellectual Jean Price-Mars, who ends his essay on Haiti and the Dominican Republic, *La République d'Haïti et la République dominicaine* (1953), with a vision of ominous clouds on the horizon: "No querría ser profeta de desgracia. Pero, tal y como le sucedió a Casandra, veo el horizonte ensombrecido por nubes grávidas de tormenta" (813).[35] The "conflict model," as Samuel Martínez calls it, is the one most depicted across the cultural production on both sides of the border, more so than instances of cooperation.[36] This should be attributed to the adversarial nature of the origins of the national states that share the island and to the intervention of colonial powers that made a concerted effort to pit an "almost white" Dominican Republic against a "Blacker, and Blacker Haiti."[37]

The fact that these works, Marcallé's and Núñez's, have been awarded the highest prizes in Dominican letters helps explain the climate that would produce a groundswell of support for Ruling 168/13 of the Constitutional Tribunal of the Dominican Republic. On September 23, 2013, the Constitutional Tribunal of the Dominican Republic rendered its decision on the matter of Juliana Dequis Pierre, a Dominican citizen of Haitian descent, who had been denied her birth certificate by the Central Electoral Office (Junta Central Electoral). The tribunal ruled that Ms. Dequis Pierre was, in fact, not entitled to Dominican citizenship despite having been born in Dominican territory on April 1, 1984. The ruling also ordered an audit of all registries from 1929 to identify "irregularly registered aliens" and, once identified, to proceed with the "regularization" of such "aliens." This decision deprived at least two hundred thousand Dominicans of Haitian descent of their nationality. Although subsequent, and insufficient, remedies have been put in place by the government to alleviate the effects of Ruling 168-13, remedies that were a result of intense national and international pressure, the attitudes and ideas that gave birth to Marcallé's trilogy are still in place and keep making life very difficult for those who are perceived as Haitian or Dominican-Haitians in the Dominican Republic.

Notes

1. Bacá: shapeshifter.

2. "The Spanish collectivity of Santo Domingo, by unavoidable determination of geography and incomprehensible political determination of the Court of Madrid, was the most immediate victim of the Black Revolution, meaning, the armed manumission movement spearheaded by Black slaves and mulattoes of the French colony of Santo Domingo against the rule of their Metropolis. We lived all the nineteenth century under the effects of the horrible impact. The social results of those events are of a very painful and difficult description." All translations, unless otherwise noted, are by the author of this chapter.

3. The date of March 19 is a significant one in Dominican history as it marked the March 19th, 1844, battle in Azua, the first battle between Haitian and Dominicans after the separation; this battle ended with a Dominican victory and the date is marked by celebrations including a military parade attended by the president of the republic.

4. www.diariolibre.com/revista/otorgan-premio-nacional-de-literatura-a-novelista-roberto-marcall-abreu-AJDL984721.

5. "Literature of the praised Haitian; literature of the attacked Haitian or literature against Haitians; literature of the adulterated Haitian; literature of the pitied Haitian; and literature of the integrated Haitian."

6. See the articles by Fernanda Bustamante, Fernando Valerio-Holguín, and Ramón A. Figueroa as examples.

7. "It is a novel that works well for Marcallé. It works not only because it is well written; also it is more appreciable in its content. We have maintained for a long time now that Marcallé is one of the few Dominican novelists, if not the only one, who tackles seriously the moral and social setbacks of his country."

8. "it is full of ideas and interlaced images, which attempt to explain the world as symbols and metaphors."

9. "the fractured prose is raw, it hurts, it mistreats, is grotesque, transgressive. We would say, that is built like this on purpose to present the deterioration of a city and its actual present."

10. "Because their sword is the word."

11. The book was awarded the Premio Nacional de Ensayo in 1990 and the Premio Nacional Feria del Libro Eduardo León Jimenes in 2002. In both instances there was a lot of controversy for the content and form of the book, and in 2002 there was the added situation that that year's edition was not a different book in scope, it just had more pages added to it.

12. In the 2016 elections Núñez ran as a Diputado (representative) candidate for the FNP in Santo Domingo. The FNP only got 0.02 percent of the total vote, nationally. Núñez only got 793 votes in his district. See /transparencia.jce.gob.do/ Repositorio/EntryId/5395.

13. "a refined and cultured person. He has great admiration for Mozart and Verdi."

14. "go out into the world wearing Yankee or French spectacles, hoping to govern a people they do not know."

15. Manfredo Pemberton is the unifying character of the trilogy. Other recurring characters are: Ulises González "El Hombre," Lic. Del Orbe, and most importantly, Buenaventura Guerrero, the protagonist of "Las siempre insólitas cartas del destino" (1999).

16. "in the minutes before plunging into the horrible darkness, the heat, the bugs and the all-around stench."

17. "Garbage strewn over broken sidewalks and curbs, airing an unbearable pestilence."

18. "At the beginning of December she arrived to Santo Domingo and found the cleanest city in the Americas, the quietest city in the continent, transformed into a sort of faraway suburb where garbage trucks never go . . . a whole week she spent walking everywhere and all that she saw was poverty, disorder, dirtiness and laxity in customs" (27–28).

19. In this Marcallé follows a long line of conservative Dominican writers, especially Joaquín Balaguer with *La isla al revés* (1983). Balaguer sees Haitians as

physically strong and resistant to diseases themselves but able to bring diseases with them to Dominican soil. At the same time, Haitians constitute a danger to the Dominican soul due to the inferiority of their morals and intellect. Balaguer, in a phrase that was also used by Julio Ortega Frier, another prominent Trujillo intellectual, writes that Haitians "multiply like vegetables" ("aumento vegetativo de la raza africana" (*Isla* 35). For a comprehensive analysis of the tropes of disease, weakness, and contagion, see *Subjects of Crisis: Race and Gender as Disease in Latin America*, especially chapter 3, "Anemia, Witches and Vampires: Figures to Govern the Colony," where Trigo analyzes the ways in which Puerto Rican *letradas* constructed the Black body as a diseased and dangerous body that threatened the "jíbaro" (white) essence of the colony.

20. "Dr. Robles [Juan Pablo Robles, assistant to the president] thought bitterly that the laissez faire attitude had let the problem deepen up to the point that a lot of people believed, hopelessly, that the presence of the *Black plague from the West* [emphasis in the original] was out of control . . . It is necessary to implement, immediately, measures aimed to liquidate this virus that disturbs the spirit of the homeland and that is a grave menace to our existence . . . you know what healthy people of this country expect from us."

21. "There is growing evidence of the existence of plans to fuse the Dominican homeland with the collapsed pseudo-state west of us, so we Dominicans, end up with the obligation to take on the life and work, the excesses and perversities of damaged and damaging people that come from those areas plagued by contagious and incurable diseases, voodoo and black magic."

22. "They want to force us to coexist with individuals with whom we have fundamental differences of all kinds, individuals who, historically, have done serious damage to this country . . . primitive, violent and corrupt people . . . they pretend that we should accept without protest a 'peaceful invasion' that is trying to denaturalized us as a nation and as a people . . . the United States, Canada, France . . . conspire in order to provoke a massive internal confrontation that encourages a foreign intervention."

23. "1. Do you aspire to reside legally on Dominican territory?; 2. Would you accept to be subject to a sterilization operation, a previous requisite to qualify as a legal resident?"

24. "Its efficiency will be tested with this first batch of undesirable aliens as a first step toward the 'Preservation Program' that entails the sterilization of nearly two million Haitians living in the country, the majority of whom will be deported."

25. "We will not exterminate the Black plague of the West. We will contribute, humanely, with a decay that is occurring painfully and with a lot of suffering. . . . I think in a people marked, as if it were damned by the gods."

26. "Family Planning Programs promoted by developed countries."

27. "it is necessary to use real scientific reasons. The objective fact is that the Haitian population is damaged in terms of health and damned in terms of legacy."

28. Baron Samedi is the "Chief Lwa" of the Guédé family of *lwas* in Haitian Vodou. The Guédés are the *lwas* of death and fertility. Baron Samedi is depicted with a top hat, dark glasses, and a frock coat, sometimes with his nose plugged to indicate death. See Deren for an in depth analysis of the Haitian religion and its rituals.

29. "When the occasion demands, he [Papa Doc Duvalier] is able to enswathe himself in an air of virtual preternaturalism. Dresses in his favorite color, black, his smooth, round face assumes a special sheen. He moves hyperslowly, speaks in a whisper. His eyelids droop. Wearing a slightly bemused, unshakable half-smile, he does nothing for disconcertingly long periods of time and Haitians, receptive to the unusual, are awed. The man appears to be calm as death. When they first beheld this somber little figure they immediately made the connection—he was *like* Papa Guédé Nimbo of the powerful Guédé loa family, masters of the cemetery. In time the likeness gave way to kinship" (Diederich and Burt 354).

30. "crooked walls without finishing, in which there were diabolical phrases in Kreyol. He felt dizzy and weak."

31. "Paintings. Draperies. Bookshelves with books. Panoramic windows that seduced the sight toward a world without ghosts, of a clear tranquility."

32. In 2016 the PLD celebrated the twentieth anniversary of the pact while still holding onto the presidency, this time under Danilo Medina. The PLD has governed sixteen of the twenty years since the Frente Patriótico Pact.

33. "Vinicio del Orbe, Chief of Migration, namely one of the most decisive members of The Cause and executor of the deportation of thousands of foreigners described as undesirables."

34. The novels are marred by numerous instances of malapropisms, anachronism, and an utter lack of editorship, there are simply too many examples to recount, but a couple should suffice. For example, in chapter 41 of *No verán mis ojos*, a President Moronta appears without any indication whatsoever as to how or why he is president. In another instance, Marcallé has one character referring to the easiness of getting a "Canadian, American or European [*stc*] visa for problematic political people like us. New York? Miami? Madrid?" ("He oído que están concediendo visas estadounidenses, canadienses y europeas con una facilidad extrema, especialmente a gente contestaria como nosotros. ¿Nueva York, Miami, Madrid?" (*No verán mis ojos* 414). This, for an average Dominican reader, jumps out of the page. Yes, the American government issued visas for thousands of Dominicans with relative ease during the sixties in order to diffuse a tense political situation and remove left-inclined youth from the island (see Hoffnung-Garskof for an in-depth analysis of this particular time), but that was never the case for "Europe" and Canada.

35. The book was translated into Spanish under the title *La República de Haití y la República Dominicana: diversos aspectos de un problema histórico, geográfico y etnológico* and it generated immediate response from the intelligentsia of the Trujillo regime.

36. For a good example of cooperation between Haiti and the Dominican Republic, see "Las ramas del árbol de la libertad: la Guerra de Restauración en la República Dominicana y Haití," by Anne Eller.

37. See chapter 1 of Candelario for an explanation of how this process developed.

Works Cited

Balaguer, Joaquín. *La isla al revés: Haití y el destino dominicano*. 1983. Fundación Joaquín Balaguer, 2017.

Bosch, Juan. *La mañosa: novela*. La Verónica, 1939.

Bustamante, Fernanda. "Representar el 'problema de lo haitiano' o el problema de representar lo haitiano: una lectura de textos literarios dominicanos del 2000." *452ºF: revista de teoría de la literatura y literatura comparada*, vol. 11, 2014, pp. 125–41.

Candelario, Ginetta E. B. *Black Behind the Ears: Dominican Racial Identity from Museums to Beauty Shops*. Duke UP, 2007.

Danticat, Edwidge. *The Farming of the Bones*. 1998. Soho, 2013.

Deren, Maya. *Divine Horsemen: The Living Gods of Haiti*. McPherson, 1983.

Di Pietro, Giovanni. *La narrativa de Roberto Marcallé Abreu*. Créditos Editoriales, 2006.

———. "No verán mis ojos esta horrible ciudad, de Roberto Marcallé Abréu." 27 Feb. 2010, mediaisla.net/revista/2010/02/no-veran-mis-ojos-esta-horrible-ciudad-de-roberto-marcalle-abreu/. Accessed 1 Aug. 2016.

Díaz, Junot. "Monstro." *The New Yorker*. 4 June 2012, pp. 106–118.

———. *The Brief Wondrous Life of Oscar Wao*. Riverhead, 2008.

Diederich, Bernard, and Al Burt. *Papa Doc: Haiti and Its Dictator*. Bodley Head, 1970.

Eller, Anne. "Las ramas del árbol de la libertad: la Guerra de la Restauración en la República Dominicana y Haití." *Caribbean Studies*, vol. 43, no. 1, 2015, pp. 113–44. Project MUSE, muse.jhu.edu/. Accessed 1 Aug. 2016.

Figueroa, Ramón. "Fantasmas ultramarinos: la dominicanidad en Julia Alvarez y Junot Díaz." *Revista Iberoamericana*, vol. 71, no. 212, 2005, pp. 731–44.

Fischer, Sibylle. *Modernity Disavowed: Haiti and the Cultures of Slavery in the Age of Revolution*. Duke UP, 2004.

Hernández, Rita Indiana. *Tentacle*. Translated by Achy Obejas, And Other Stories, 2018.

Hoffnung-Garskof, Jesse. *A Tale of Two Cities: Santo Domingo and New York after 1950*. Princeton UP, 2008.

Inoa, Orlando. *Bibliografía haitiana en la República Dominicana*. 2 Vol. Centro de Investigaciones Históricas, Facultad de Humanidades, Universidad de Puerto Rico, Recinto de Río Piedras, 1994.

Marcallé Abreu, Roberto. *Contrariedades y tribulaciones en la mezquina y desdichada existencia del señor Manfredo Pemberton*. MC Editorial, 2006.

———. *La manipulación de los espejos*. Editorial Santuario, 2012.
———. *No verán mis ojos esta horrible ciudad*. MC Editores, 2009.
Martí, José, Juan Marinello, Hugo Achúgar, and Cintio Vitier. *Nuestra América*. Biblioteca Ayacucho, 1977.
Martínez, Samuel. "Not a Cockfight: Rethinking Haitian-Dominican Relations." *Latin American Perspectives*, vol. 30, no. 3, 2003, pp. 80–101.
Matibag, Eugenio. *Haitian-Dominican Counterpoint: Nation, State, and Race on Hispaniola*. Palgrave Macmillan, 2003.
Melo Mendoza, Doris. "Sobre la manipulación de lo espejos de Roberto Marcallé Abreu: Una visión crítica a partir de la teoría literaria." ResearchGate, 2015. www.researchgate.net/publication/281100630_Sobre_la_manipulacion_de_los_espejos_de_Roberto_Marcalle_Abre_Una_vision_critica_a_partir_de_l?channel=doi&linkId=55d4c49908aef1574e975a3e&showFulltext=true. Accessed 1 Aug. 2016.
Mieses, Juan Carlos. *El día de todos*. Alfaguara, 2009.
Mir, Pedro. *Cuando amaban las tierras comuneras*. 1st ed. Siglo XXI Editores, 1978.
Peña Batlle, Manuel A. "El tratado de Basilea y la desnacionalización del Santo Domingo español." *Colección pensamiento dominicano: historia*, edited by Luis O. Brea Franco and Mariano Mella, Sociedad Dominicana de Bibliófilos; Banco de Reservas de la República Dominicana, 2009, pp. 545–68.
Price-Mars, Jean. *La República de Haití y la República Dominicana: diversos aspectos de un problema histórico, geográfico y etnológico*. 3rd ed. Translated by Martín Aldao and José Luis Muñoz Azpiri, Sociedad Dominicana de Bibliófilos, 1995.
San Miguel, Pedro L. *La Isla imaginada: historia, identidad y utopía en La Española*. Isla Negra, 1997.
Suárez, Lucía. *The Tears of Hispaniola: Haitian and Dominican Diaspora Memory*. UP of Florida, 2006.
Trigo, Benigno. *Subjects of Crisis: Race and Gender as Disease in Latin America*. Wesleyan UP, 2000.
Turits, Richard Lee. "A World Destroyed, A Nation Imposed: The 1937 Haitian Massacre in the Dominican Republic." *Hispanic American Historical Review*, vol. 82, no. 3, 2002, pp. 589–635.
Valerio-Holguín, Fernando. "Nuestros vecinos los primitivos: identidad cultural dominicana." Prepared for the Latin American Studies Association Conference, Washington, DC, Sept. 2000.
Veloz Maggiolo, Marcio. "Tipología del tema haitiano en la literatura dominicana." *Sobre cultura dominicana . . . y otras culturas*. Editora Alfa y Omega, 1977, pp. 93–121.
Vergés, Pedro. *Solo cenizas hallarás*. Editorial Prometeo, 1980.

10

"And Then the Canes Shrieked"

Haitianism and Memory in Junot Díaz's *The Brief Wondrous Life of Oscar Wao*

MOHWANAH FETUS

In May 2018, Junot Díaz was accused of sexual misconduct and harassment by women writers such as Zinzi Clemmons, Monica Byrne, Alisa Valdes, and Carmen Maria Machado. While my chapter explores his Pulitzer Prize–winning novel *The Brief Wondrous Life of Oscar Wao* (2008), I do want to reiterate my support and admiration for these brave women for speaking up about their experiences. I do not condone any form of harassment or violence toward anyone.

"Pale Kreyòl?" my friend Elizabeth asked the two clerks in the smoke shop at our Punta Cana resort. It was July 2013—the year the highest court in the Dominican Republic ruled that if Dominican citizens were born to parents who entered the country illegally, then those citizens did not have a proper—"regular"—immigration status.[1] We were just two Haitian American girls in a resort catering to predominately white American and European tourists with a staff that was overwhelmingly Black. Elizabeth and I were considered an oddity the minute we entered the resort by the staff; we were constantly greeted warmly as "morenas" by staff, constantly codified as either "African" or "Martiniquais," and teased about not knowing Spanish (or having husbands). But we were the only Black folks who were able to "relax" on the grounds—our citizenship and American dollars allowing us the leisure to do so.[2]

Yet Elizabeth and I caught the heavy Haitian accents and the French names on tags for many staff members, especially when it came to the most menial jobs, such as janitorial or tourist guides who sold experiences at the gate of the resort. It was "Marie" who fixed our room daily with warm eyes yet spoke with the most monotone voice. It was "Jacques" who always chatted with us every morning, trying to get us to ride horseback in the countryside. It was "Anais" who worked the morning shift at the inclusive dining area, who had the sweetest laugh yet always warned us to stay away from the flirtations of the men of the resort. All of them reminded me of home.

We decided to break our vow of uttering our mothers' tongue and urged the cigar clerks to talk to us. The men stared at us but then their eyes gleaned the windows for passersby—*were they looking out for their manager?*—until they caught wind of our heavy American accents and begin to poke fun: "Ou pa Ayisyen!" Despite being the only tourists in the shop, Elizabeth and I noticed that whenever someone passed by or casually peeked in, their voices fell and reverted back to Spanish as if Kreyòl was not uttered a few minutes ago. The way their bodies stiffened and forced smiles when other tourists came into the store, we knew the switch of language was for the comfort of the other tourists but also for the fear of upper management being around.[3] We did not urge them to speak to us any further and returned to our rooms.

The cigar clerks, the hotel maids, and the groundskeepers. All of whom were of Haitian and Haitian-Dominican descent, moved throughout the resort in the background—unnoticed and unseen. Perhaps the moment when Haitians became hypervisible throughout the resort was when they snuck onto the private beach to sell peanuts, mango, or guinep to people lounging there on the beach. From Haitian old ladies to young kids, they would yell out their product, walk shyly over to anyone interested, speaking in fluent or hesitant Spanish to anyone willing to buy. If caught, they were either chased or escorted off the beach.

My experience of seeing this dichotomy—the silence of Haitians and Haitian-Dominicans in the background and the hypervisibility of their Blackness—mirrors Junot Díaz's treatment of Haitian characters and *Haitianism* in his text *The Brief Wondrous Life of Oscar Wao*.[4] I use Haitianism to point to Haitian identity, culture, and language in *Oscar Wao*. Additionally, I want to interrogate how Haitianism appears to haunt Oscar, Beli, and Yunior while also being a silent tertiary character in the novel. This juxtaposition of Haitianism and Dominican culture speaks to the history of the island's tense relationship, especially when it comes to race. Haitianism constantly poses as a haunting/threatening figure while dominant Dominican society wishes to marginalize its own Afro identity.

The Brief Wondrous Life of Oscar Wao intertwines Dominican history, science fiction, and magical realism to narrate the history of the Cabral family from the Dominican Republic to Paterson, New Jersey (with a return back to the Dominican Republic as well). Through the street-smart narrator Yunior, we learn of Oscar's mishaps in romance and not fitting into rigid Dominican masculinity. Additionally, we follow Oscar's mother Hypatia Beli Cabral in 1950s Dominican Republic as a dark skin Black woman during the height of Rafael Trujillo's dictatorship.[5] I argue that Haitianism (and extensively Haitians) serves as the haunting tertiary character of the novel. From the subtle Vodun imagery to the racialization of the cane fields as a "Haitian space" in Trujillo's nation-state, Haitianism remains in the background in *Oscar Wao*.

Haitianism and magical realism explode in the violent archival space of the cane fields. Birthed by slavery, the fields become a space where dictatorial violence and anti-Blackness converge. Through Beli, we discover the horrors of Trujillo's regime and the sentient nature of the cane fields in the Dominican Republic; the canes become alive through "shrieking," "cutting flesh," and "clogging the air" while shrouding the act of violence through their tall stalks. All these violences converge and swallow Beli, a victim of physical and unspoken sexual assault by Trujillo's soldiers. I posit that the cane fields become physical sites of memories where intergenerational memory is relived through violence without the necessity of language. In other words, Oscar relives his mother's violence without her sharing the details of her beating with Oscar. Beli's trauma is a secret to her son, yet Oscar experiences "nostalgia" when being dragged into the cane fields for the first time. I assert that *The Brief Wondrous Life of Oscar Wao*'s treatment of intersecting histories of colonialism, slavery's brutal dictatorship, and manual labor explodes in the racialized space of the cane fields.

Mapping Haitian Tropes in *The Brief Wondrous Life of Oscar Wao*

To discuss anti-Blackness, anti-Haitianism, and legacy of colonialism in the Dominican Republic and her diaspora Díaz blends myth, memory, and history to introduce us to the fukú curse. Fukú plays as a major character in *Oscar Wao*. I argue that while the fukú is illustrated as a curse that was birthed by anti-Black violence, such as colonialism and enslavement, it molds Dominican society in the novel through its violent treatment of Black Dominicans like Beli and the ruin of lives such as Dr. Abelard, who refused to offer his daughter to Trujillo. While the Dominican Republic is "ground zero" for the fukú, there is no way to escape the curse, as we will see with Beli and Oscar toward the latter half of the novel. The fukú ensnares the family for generations. Yunior states that the fukú's origins were through Christopher Columbus, his discovery of Hispaniola, and the transatlantic slave trade:

> They say it came first from Africa, carried in the screams of enslaved; that it was the death bane of the Tainos, uttered just as one world perished and another began: that it was a demon drawn into Creation through the nightmare door that was cracked open in the Antilles. *Fukú americanus*, or more colloquial, fukú—generally a curse or a doom of some kind; specifically the Curse and the Doom of the New World. . . . No matter what its name or provenance, *it is believed that the arrival of Europeans on Hispaniola unleashed the fukú on the world, and we've all been in the shit ever since. Santo Domingo might be fukú's Kilometer Zero, its port of entry, but we are all of us its children, whether we know it or not.* (1–2, emphasis mine)

Fukú is anti-Black violence—brought in by the Europeans thanks to the transatlantic slave trade—that birthed the New World. According to Yunior, Hispaniola is the locus of the fukú. Hispaniola becomes the space where colonialism takes place in the New World through the importation of enslaved Africans and the genocide of Tainos. This narrative move also establishes Hispaniola (and the greater Caribbean world) as being birthed through the extermination of indigenous communities and the importation of Black bodies for colonial capital. While Santo Domingo is the port of entry, the fukú's reach spans throughout her diaspora, as we will see with the Cabral downfall.

The bloody birth of Hispaniola appears otherworldly through the lens of magical realism, science fiction, and fantasy. While the three aforementioned genres are under the same literary tradition of fantastic fiction, scholar Emily Maguire posits that science fiction and fantasy depict "what could happen" while magical realism illustrates "what has happened." Yunior bridges "what could happen" through his usage of *Star Wars* and *Lord of the Rings* references with "what has happened" by revealing the horrors of Trujillo's negrophobic regime: "At the end of *The Return of the King*, Sauron's evil was taken by 'a great wind' and neatly 'blown away,' with no lasting consequences to our heroes; but [Rafael] Trujillo was too powerful, too toxic a radiation to be dispelled so easily. Even after death his evil lingered" (211). The blending of these two genres illustrates two points. First, it highlights Yunior's and Oscar's subjectivity as Black nerd children of Black immigrant parents living in the United States. In other words, Dominican folklore and US science fiction and fantasy coexist in their world in Paterson, New Jersey. Second, the text highlights the fantastical and otherworldly violence of colonialism and despotic violence. The bloody birth of the New World, which creates the fukú, and Rafael Trujillo carrying out the curse with his despotic anti-Black regime, appears like a plot straight out of a science fiction / fantasy novel. Yunior compares Trujillo to every notable literary and pop culture villain such as Lord Sauron from J. R. R. Tolkien's *Lord of the Rings* series. Colonial violence—through the extermination of indigenous communities, the forced enslavement of Africans, and years of anti-Black dictatorship—appears *too otherworldly* to take place in the Caribbean. As if this high level of violence is from a fantasy novel.[6] But this fantasy is real and affects Beli, Yunior, and Oscar throughout *Oscar Wao*.

In some ways, *Oscar Wao* counters the fukú and Trujillo's dictatorship by placing Haitian Vodun tropes throughout the text. I read this as a way to explain how close yet fraught the two countries are. In *The Tears of Hispaniola: Haitian and Dominican Diaspora Memory*, Lucía Suárez positions Haiti and the Dominican Republic as *marassa*: "Marassa is defined as spirit twins, or child spirits, they are inseparable, conflicted, and in solidarity" (6).[7] By positioning the two countries as marassa, Suárez reveals the fraught dualities of the two countries but also their shared experience with violence and Blackness. The two countries may have "seemingly contradictory concepts"—just like the marassa twins—but are complementary.

With the island of Hispaniola depicted as marassa, *Oscar Wao* takes liberties to show how Vodun is scattered throughout the text. Maritza, one of Oscar's first Dominican loves, embodies the fury of the Vodun god Ogún: "Maritza, with her chocolate skin and narrow eyes, already expressing the *Ogún* energy that she would chop at everybody with for the rest of her life" (14). With dark skin and the fury of the *loa* of war and metal work, Maritza represents *what the Dominican imaginary refuses to believe*. Yunior conflates dark skin and Vodun spirituality—two components on which the anti-Black

Dominican mestizaje pins as *solely* Haitian—to a Dominican body.[8] Another example of Vodun imagery in *Oscar Wao* is in the form of dreams. When La Inca worries about Beli's safety in the Dominican Republic after her assault in the cane fields, she is visited by her late husband, who instructs La Inca to send Beli to New York: "and then he strutted proudly into the water; she tried to call him back, Please, come back, but he did not listen" (158). Within Haitian Vodun, being visited by a loved one through dreams can be seen as good luck and as an omen. For La Inca, her husband's instructions prove to be vital for Beli's survival. Additionally, dreaming is the medium for dead loved ones and spirits to contact the living world. Finally, water is the pathway to Guinea, the spirit world.[9] Haitian spiritual traces serve to help the Cabrals survive.[10]

Along with Vodun imagery and dark skin, Yunior plays on the "fears" of intra-ethnic relationships between Haitians and Dominicans We see this through Lola's high school friend Leticia: "Leticia, just off the boat, half Haitian half Dominican, that special blend the Dominican government swears *no existe* . . ." (26). Just as the border towns of Hispaniola are full of intra-ethnic relationships, Leticia reminds the readers that these relationships do exist to *spite* Trujillo.

While *Oscar Wao* highlights Haitian-Dominicans as real and utilizes Haitian Vodun as a magical realist maneuver, the text also reiterates dominant negative narratives of Haitians and Haitianism in the Dominican Republic. Although Yunior calls out Dominican hypocrisy, which is denial of African roots in the Dominican Republic, Yunior and Oscar's families fall into the trap of anti-Haitianism. When a young Oscar returns from the Dominican Republic with darker skin, he is met with disgust: "Great, his tio said, looking askance at his complexion, now you look Haitian" (11). Colorism and anti-Blackness riddle the text, especially when it comes to Beli, a dark-skinned Dominican woman: "Watch out, Mom, Lola said, they probably think you're Haitian—La única haitiana aquí eres tú, mi amor [The only Haitian here is you my love], she [Beli] retorted" (219, translation mine). Here, dark skin is a label of Africanness and of Haitianism (that "other Black" on the western side of the shared island), both stains in Dominican society. Beli's and Tio's vehement disgust reveals the push and pull of anti-Blackness and anti-Haitianism.

While Haiti is an African, Vodunesque, Black nation, the Dominican Republic was a Hispanic, fair-skinned, and Christian nation-state. This logic also spearheaded Dominican fears of a Haitian takeover as Elizabeth Abbott argues in *Sugar: A Bittersweet History*: "[Trujillo] fed Dominicans' fears that armies of Haitians would Haitianize the republic" (388). The illustration of Haiti as the dark opposite plotting to take over the Dominican Republic is echoed through *Oscar Wao*. La Inca's loyal servant cries out "HAITIANS" in a state of delirium before passing away (270). The haunting illustration of Haitians as dark invaders riddles *Oscar Wao*: in its attempt to portray Haitianism, it continues to illustrate Haiti, her diasporas, and cultural production as "haunting" or dark.

Haitianism remains in the background of *Oscar Wao*. It is portrayed by Vodun tropes, Dominican-Haitian relations that Trujillo swears "no existe," and by the negative portrayals of Haitians as "dark conquerors" as well. While I do believe that the text does not mean to regurgitate anti-Haitianism, it is worth noting how *The Brief Wondrous Life of Oscar Wao* highlights and vilifies Haitianism at the same time.[11]

Beli and the Disruption of Mestizaje

The audience is introduced to Hypatia Belicia Cabral as Oscar's mother during the first two sections of the novel. However, Yunior begins to narrate her early years in Baní, "a city famed for its resistance to Blackness, and it was here, alas, that the darkest character in our story resided":

> The family claims that the first sign was that Abelard's third and final daughter, given the light early on in her father's capuslization, was born black. And not just any kind of black. But *black* black—kongoblack, shangoblack, kaliblack, zapotecblack, rekhablack—and no amount of fancy Dominican racial legerdemain was going to obscure the fact. That's the kind of culture I belong to: *people took their child's black complexion as an ill omen*. (248, emphasis mine)

Yunior evokes dark tropes throughout Global South communities—Shango, Kongo, Kali, Zapotec, and Rekha—coating Beli's dark skin. Her dark skin harkens not just to Hispaniola's notions of Blackness but also within other non-Western communities. Family oral history claims that Beli's dark skin was the beginning of decline for the Cabrals, when in actuality it was the violence of colonialism and anti-Blackness that marked the end of the Cabrals and de Leons. In this scene, Yunior acknowledges and mocks Dominican society's obsession and marginalization of dark skin. While mestizaje valorizes racial and cultural mixture, it also marginalizes Afro-Latinos and indigenous Latinos who do not fit the "racially ambiguous" quota. I argue that identifying as Black or having dark skin in *Oscar Wao* to being Haitian, a nation that is constantly positioned as a "very Black" nation. When a young Oscar returns from the Dominican Republic with darker skin, he is met with disgust: "Great, his tio said, looking askance at his complexion, now you look Haitian" (32). I assert that fukú, through family gossip and mestizaje, is inscribed on Beli's dark skin and is also aligned to anti-Haitianism.

While Beli's dark skin challenges Trujillo's mestizaje project in the Dominican Republic, Beli replicates anti-Haitianism sentiments throughout the text. She refuses to align herself with those "maldito haitianos" (273). Beli inflicts anti-Haitianism and anti-Black psychic violence when she shouts, "I'm not morena, I'm india" when her lover, The Gangster, comments on her dark skin. I argue that while Beli acknowledges her dark skin, she also vehemently refuses to be read as Haitian, a marker of "bad" or "other" Blackness. While she cannot escape her dark black skin, Beli believes her dark skin is *only* rooted in indigeneity. This is the same logic that Trujillo pushes in his Indio campaign according to Silvio Torres-Saillant:

> They recognized the historical identification of the Dominican population with the indigenous Taino inhabitants of Hispaniola, who had endured oppression and extermination at the hands of Spanish conquerors at the outset of the colonial experience. Ethnically, the Indians represented a category typified by nonwhiteness as well as non-Blackness, which could easily accommodate the racial in-betweenness of the Dominican mulatto. Thus, the regime gave currency to the term *indio* (Indian) to describe the complexion of people of mixed ancestry. (139)

Beli is cognizant of her dark skin but it is not because of Haitianism (the "other" in the Dominican racial imaginary) or due to the import of enslaved Africans that arrived in the Dominican Republic. Beli believes she is dark, but as long as she's not "that other Black," she can exist as a Dominican subject. But thanks to sheer irony, Beli is constantly racialized as Haitian or marked as a Latino of another nation. During her young years before meeting La Inca, Beli is a restavec (Díaz 253).[12] While at a bar with Oscar and Lola, and the latter warning her mother that the patrons may view her as Haitian, Beli retorts back, with Caribbean curt sarcasm, "La única haitiana aquí eres tú, mi amor [The only Haitian here is you, my love]"

(276, translation mine). Beli refuses to be seen as "maldito haitiano" while also denying any possibility of being Afro-Dominican.

While Beli grapples with anti-Haitianism and anti-Blackness, residents of Baní also struggle with seeing Beli as Dominican due to her black skin. Beli becomes the "dark other" in Baní that cannot be placed: "Everybody mistook her for a bailarina cubana [Cuban dancer] from one of the shows and couldn't believe she was dominicana like them. It can't be, no lo pareces [do not look], etc., etc." (114). Beli's Dominican identity is constantly in contention because of her dark skin tone; Dominican mestizaje nullifies and marginalizes Afro-Dominicans and Afro-Haitians. While she is read as Haitian, Beli is also viewed as hailing from Cuba, another former Spanish colony with an abundance of peoples of African descent. I posit that *Oscar Wao* critiques this racial hypocrisy; while the nation celebrates mestizaje and Indio lineage, this "celebratory" racial move also debunks and vilifies Afro-Latinidad. By marking Beli as Haitian or Cuban, Dominican mestizaje posits that Blackness exists in other Latin American and Caribbean countries but not the Dominican Republic. Blackness exists elsewhere rather than as inherent in Dominican society.

Because of her illegibility as a Dominican, Beli's affair with the husband of La Fea—Trujillo's sister—appears impossible. While visited by La Fea, Trujillo's sister, Beli faces Trujillo's negrophobe legacy in the face. Calling her racial epithets such as "mi monita" (my monkey) and "Black cara de culo" (Black ass face), La Fea refuses to acknowledge Beli as her husband's lover or her child as his due to Beli's Blackness. Why would her husband, a Trujillo supporter, be with Beli? Because Beli's Blackness threatens Trujillo's mestizaje and La Fea's marriage, Beli is beaten and dragged to the cane fields, a common site of Trujillo's murders and the heart of the sugar industry. I argue that the cane fields are a Haitianized space within the Dominican nation-state. While its roots are in African slaves, Dominican sugar industries' current use of Haitian manual laborers transforms the cane fields and bateyes as Haitian.[13] Driving out east to the cane fields, while also simultaneously being beaten by the goons, temporalities shift while heading to the cane fields: "one second you were deep in the twentieth century (well the twentieth century of the Third World) and the next you'd find yourself plunged 180 years into rolling fields of cane" (148). This "leaking of pasts and futures" occurs in the cane fields; by placing slavery and postslavery/dictatorship in conversation with each other, *Oscar Wao* reveals the maddening nature of the fukú curse and its effect on Beli and Oscar.[14] The intersecting histories of colonialism, the transatlantic slave trade, and intra-ethnic conflict create what I call maddening geographies within the cane fields. By "maddening geographies," I refer to vexed spatial formations that are rooted in anti-Black violence because of colonialism. In other words, spaces like the plantation become traumatic spaces for Black people because of the legacy of the transatlantic slave trade and colonialism. The maddening space of the cane fields will subsume Beli.

While the madness of the cane fields shifts temporalities while heading to and being there, the canes also become sentient. The canes shriek and rustle as the goons drag Beli to the heart of the cane fields: "They walked until the cane was roaring so loud around them it sounded as if they were in the middle of a storm" (147). In addition to the sonic potentiality of the fields, the canes "didn't want her to leave, of course; it slash at her palms, jabbed into her flank and clawed her thighs, and its sweet stench clogged her throat" (150). The cane field is personified in *Oscar Wao*, roaring, rustling, and swallowing Beli whole in its mazelike construct. I argue that the canes' shrieking voice Beli's trauma in this maddening space of the cane fields. This reading is influenced by Fred Moten's argument on the shrieking object, the slave. He argues that the shrieking object, the slave, asserts his or her own value in the act of shrieking.[15] Shrieking is phonic not linguistic so it resists the codification that language requires but, nevertheless, expresses value and meaning. I argue that the canes shriek Beli's suffering when she cannot. With the canes becoming alive, the site becomes *Black and horrific*. The canes are animated through the violence of the fukú curse.

The cane fields also shroud the truth as to what Trujillo's goons *really* did to Beli. "Was there time for a rape or two? I suspect there was, but we shall never know because it's not something she talked about. *All that can be said is that it was the end of language, end of hope*. It was the sort of beating that breaks people, breaks them utterly" (147, emphasis mine). The absence of the truth—the rape of Beli—in the narrative by Yunior leads us back to the shifting of temporalities between colonial slavery and Trujillo's legacy of the cane fields. With the canes shrieking, it reveals the mental, physical, and sexual violence inflicted upon the Black female body. The cane fields mark the enslavement and sexual domination of Black bodies. I argue that the cane fields are an archival sentient space with the haunting of slavery, despotic violence, and Haitian manual labor converging to create a maddening space. *Oscar Wao* excavates the horrors of Trujillo's regime, which regurgitates coloniality through anti-Blackness and anti-Haitianism, and the multitude of silenced Black female narratives through Beli's ordeal in the cane fields.[16]

Although various histories of colonialism converge and create a sentient space, notions of magic and resistance also occur. "So as Beli was flitting in and out of life, there appeared at her side a creature that would have been an amiable mongoose if not for its golden lion eyes and absolute black of its pelt . . ." (149). The mongoose's presence guides Beli out of the monstrous cane fields. During the eighteenth century, mongooses were imported to the Caribbean to control rat infestations in the sugarcane fields. By importing the mongoose from India for the purpose of slavery, the animal becomes a retroactive colonial subject. So, of course Beli, a descendant of slaves, would be greeted by the mongoose in the cane fields. Their encounter is not unusual in the Dominican Republic.

With the help of the mongoose and also tapping into her Cabral magic, Beli emerges out of the cane fields alive: "She came to in the ferocious moonlight. A broken girl, atop broken stalks of cane. Pain everywhere but alive. Alive" (148). When Beli is brought back home to La Inca with the help of a traveling wedding band, who also feared Beli was Haitian, La Inca swears that Beli met God in the cane field, not the fukú (152). La Inca sees the mongoose as zafa or good magic. Through the mongoose and La Inca's husband visiting La Inca, magic and Haitian traces help Beli leave the Dominican Republic and her brutal regime.

Beli's dark skin tone, her relationship to anti-Blackness/anti-Haitianism, and her survival of Trujillo's regime intersect within the cane fields. She escapes with the help of a mongoose, a colonial subject and symbol of zafa. Beli was also able to have two children, each with their episode of magic and clairvoyance. However, while the canes roared with Beli, the canes will shriek and subsume Oscar as he returns to the cane fields where his mother escapes.

"The Canes Shrieked": Haunting of Violence of Oscar

While his mother survives the assault in the cane fields, her son Oscar would soon find himself there too, for his true love Ybón. After years of being the fat nerd who could not woo a girl, Oscar finally finds a woman who loves him back. However, Ybón's boyfriend Capitán, a former Trujillo officer, wants to end Oscar's life. Ordering his goons—which Yunior names Grundy and Grod—to kidnap Oscar, Yunior remarks: "Where did they take him? *Where else?* The cane fields. How's that for eternal return?" (296). Due to cane fields being a constant site of terror and trauma in *Oscar Wao* and Dominican history, Oscar's "first time" to the cane fields is more of a return.

As Grundy and Grod walk Oscar through the canes, the titular character feels as if he has been to the canes before despite walking through an "alien" space:

> Their flashlight newly activated, they walked him into the cane—never had he heard anything so loud and alien, the susurration, the crackling, the flashes of motion underfoot (snake? mongoose?), overheard even the stars, all of them gathered in vainglorious congress. *And yet this world seemed strangely familiar to him, he had the overwhelming feeling that he'd been in this very place, a long time ago.* (298, emphasis mine)

Without sharing her experiences with her son, Beli's episode in the cane fields becomes familiar to Oscar. While this is his first time being in the fields, Oscar's out-of-body experience is a normalized "Caribbean phenomena": the otherworldly that Western societies mark as indecipherable or irrational. From spirit possessions, zombies walking in the light of day, to tales of sorcery, the "otherworldly" is considered the everyday in the Caribbean, while in the West it is deemed unfathomable. So it may be "strange" for the fukú to lead Oscar back to the site of Beli's assault. While Beli experiences the violence of the negrophobe regime of Trujillo, so does Oscar twenty years later. This generational inheritance allows Oscar to feel remnants of his mother's trauma.[17] The inheritance of earlier generations gives way to inheriting collective memory that is the ability for future generations to remember certain events from the past. Oscar, unwittingly, inherits his mother's memories of the cane fields although she does not share her memories with him.

How Oscar remembers his mother's experience in the cane fields is through embodied memory. As Barbara Misztal posits in her study *Theories of Social Remembering* (2003), "*Embodiedness* alerts us to the ways in which feelings and bodily sensations, generated in the past, help to interpret the past" (77). The overwhelmingly familiar feeling that Oscar experiences when he walks into the cane fields is his mother's embodied memory during the 1950s. While he does not fully understand the memories he is experiencing during his first trip to the cane fields, Oscar's second and final trip there allow him to fully understand the terrifying legacy of Trujillo's regime.

What makes collective memory and embodied memory unique in Oscar's episode in the cane fields is the fact that his mother Beli never tells Oscar about her experience in there. Oscar's strange familiarity in the cane fields is rooted in the otherworldly. Magic and cyclical time allow Oscar to experience collective memory without his mother sharing her experiences with him. The cane fields are archival spaces, or memory spaces, that house the two characters' experiences in the tall stalks of cane. This memory space also recreates bodily sensations that allow Oscar to feel exactly what Beli experienced during the 1950s. Additionally, the two characters also share the magical encounters within the fields. Unlike his mother, Oscar is not visited by the mongoose, however, he is saved from the jaws of death. The zafa saves Oscar in the fields, which allows him to leave the Dominican Republic. However, after dreaming and listening to the canes while he is in Paterson, New Jersey, Oscar decides to return to the Dominican Republic (307).

In contrast to his first violent encounter in the cane fields, during the second and final time in the cane fields, Oscar no longer fears for his life. Additionally, Oscar is greeted by Haitian voices in the fields, bringing his narrative in conversation with the Perejil Massacre and current Haitian manual labor: "This time Oscar didn't cry when they drove him back to the cane fields. Zafra would be here soon, and the cane had grown well and thick and in places you could hear the stalks clack-clack-clacking against each other like triffids and you hear krïyol voices lost in the night. The smell of the ripening cane was unforgettable . . ." (320). Just like Beli's experience, the cane fields become animated just before Oscar's death. The intermingling of the otherworldly, science fiction, and Haitianism highlights Yunior's hybrid storytelling of syncretizing the fantastical nature of science fiction to the fantastical nature of Blackness in the Dominican Republic. The otherworldly—triffids, mongooses, clairvoyant dreams—becomes the norm within the Dominican Republic while also creating a stark contrast to the horrors of slavery and Trujillo's regime. Additionally, embodied memory allows for Oscar to embrace and understand the horrifying legacy of the cane fields; he still does not know of his mother's experiences; however, the rustling of Haitian voices and the magical nature of the fields allows him to fully understand the haunting of the Perejil Massacre and Trujillo's regime. Generational memory passes down to Oscar without his mother sharing her story with him, yet Oscar understands the legacy of Trujillo's reign in the Dominican Republic. As Michaeline Crichlow states in her text *Globalization and the Post-Creole Imagination: Notes on Fleeing the Plantation*, "Caribbean histories and cultural processes are multidirectional, making for complex postcolonial creolization processes" (2). There is a "creolization" that occurs in the cane fields in Oscar's second episode of *Oscar Wao*. The merging of slavery, manual labor (by Haitians and Dominicans alike), and despotic violence creates a cyclical postcolonial creolized space.

Oscar's episodes in the cane fields highlights the importance of sentient archival spaces and collective embodied memory. The inheritance of generational trauma and memory creates nostalgia yet it also claims Oscar's life. Beli could not escape the fukú and neither could Oscar. While the fukú has roots in colonial violence, it also recapitulates intergenerational pain. How do we heal from intergenerational pain? How can we break free from the fukú's grasp? While the maddening archival space of the cane fields claims Black lives, it also houses forms of magic and resistance against the fukú. Oscar's first time is more of a return and is greeted by lost Kreyòl voices. Beli's guide to surviving the cane fields is a mongoose. The relationship between violence, resistance, and the otherworldly illustrate the complexity of Blackness in the Dominican Republic and her diaspora.

The Brief Wondrous Life of Oscar Wao begins with the fukú and ends with the zafa. Yunior ponders, "Even now as I write these words I wonder if this book ain't a zafa of sorts. My very own counterspell" (7). Yunior's detailing of Dominican history through science fiction and magical realism positions the Dominican Republic as a surreal nation. *The Brief Wondrous Life of Oscar Wao* also illustrates how Haitianism and Afro-Dominican identity haunt and reveal the anti-Blackness of mestizaje in Dominican society. Finally, Yunior's depiction of the cane fields as a sentient archival space where intergenerational memory, trauma, magic, and cyclical time blend emphasizes the legacy of colonialism throughout time. While violent colonial legacies haunt various diasporas, *The Brief Wondrous Life of Oscar Wao* offers zafa through unearthing familial history and cultural memory, and embracing Blackness in all forms.

Notes

1. Jones n.p.

2. By our fifth day at the resort, we were amicably joined by a group of Howard alumni girls from DC who were struck by the color and class differences as well.

3. In linguistics, many would call this code-switching: the practice of alternating between two or more languages or varieties of language in conversation. However, this act of code-switching between the two Haitian clerks was a means of survival. Many Black American writers, scholars, and artists dedicate time to explain code-switching between African American Vernacular and Standard English in Black communities as 1) survival 2) steeped in colorism, classism, and educational bias. To read more about code-switching, please read Lewis.

4. I use the term Haitianism to point to Haitian identity, culture, language, and Blackness rooted in Haiti. The text establishes Santo Domingo as the "point of entry" of the New World created by the genocide of Tainos and the birth of slavery. However, Díaz's usage of distinct Haitian aspects throughout this Dominican-American epic establishes that the two nations share an inherent Blackness due to proximity and shared violent histories.

5. Rafael Leónidas Trujillo Molina (October 24, 1891–May 30, 1961), was a Dominican politician and soldier who ruled the Dominican Republic from February 1930 until his assassination in May 1961. He served as president from 1930 to 1938 and again from 1942 to 1952. His thirty-one years in power, to Dominicans known as the Trujillo era (*El Trujillato*), are considered one of the bloodiest eras ever in the Americas. It has been estimated that Trujillo was responsible for the deaths of more than fifty thousand people, including possibly as many as ten thousand in the Parsley Massacre—the genocide of Haitian and Afro-Dominicans—in 1931.

6. But as we know, the Caribbean is a strange space: where magic realism heightens everyday life and violence. We see this in tales about zombies that lurk the streets, where ghosts speak through dreams, children who relive the traumas of their parents in unspoken silences, where spiritual possessions take hold of people, and where dictators execute orders to turn the border into sites of bloodshed and leave bodies washed ashore.

7. Marassa are the sacred twins within Vodun cosmology. They represent the result of a union of higher forces, bringing into reality a third potentiality. They are often called Marassa Dosu Dosa—a reflection of the two-is-three idea. They represent love, truth, justice, faith, hope, and charity. The sacred twins are invoked at the beginning of every service along with Papa Legba, for without the marassa, nothing can come into existence. Like all sacred twins, they are identical, yet sexless—they are the potential, therefore, they contain everything—male and female, light and dark, positive and negative. For more, read Deren; and Brown.

8. Racial and cultural mixture within Latin American and Caribbean nations. Although mestizaje romanticizes racial ambiguity and harmony, it upholds notions of upward mobility, identity, and solidifies the marginalization of Afro-Latinos and indigenous Latinos. For more, please read Jiménez Román and Flores.

9. For more, see Perry.

10. For more on the importance of dreams within Haitian spirituality, see Bourguignon.

11. I do believe that *Oscar Wao* seeks to critique the anti-Blackness of the Dominican Republic and her diasporas. Yunior's tone as a satirical narrator illustrates the idiocy of Afro-Dominicans and Dominican society denying that Blackness does not exist in the country. However, I am concerned with how the text critiques the dismissal of African roots while also labeling Africanness as just "Haitian." Enslaved Africans were brought to both sides rather than just the western side of Hispaniola. My reading of Trujillo's Indio/mestizaje campaign was influenced by Torres-Saillant.

12. A restavec, from the French *reste avec,* "one who stays with," is a child in who is sent by his or her parents to work for a host household as a domestic servant because the parents lack the resources required to support the child. This system is used throughout Haiti and I was taken by Yunior's use of the term restavec to talk about Beli's upbringing before La Inca.

13. Sugar history scholarship such as those studies by Abbott; Murphy; McKenzie; and Bott historicizes the rise of the sugar industry throughout the Caribbean, specifically in the Dominican Republic. Prior to 1870, the Dominican Republic did not base its economy on sugar but rather on subsistence agriculture. Around 1870, though, when a series of wars affected world sugar production and when Dominican land and capital were available, the Dominican Republic suddenly entered the world sugar trade with the labor force predominately being Dominican peasants (Murphy 15). However, an 1884 slump in sugar prices resulted in a wage freeze, causing a critical labor shortage. "Consequently, two trends emerged that have characterized the sugar industry since: first, immigrants replaced Dominican workers; second, the economic exploitation of the migrant labour force was essential for the success of the industry. The first immigrants were mainly Cocolos (citizens of West Indies British colonies), preferred because they demanded less in working, housing and sanitary conditions than Dominicans" (McKenzie 1). By the beginning of the twentieth century, the deterioration of Haitian agricultural land and the availability of Dominican land had lured Haitians across the border for employment. The Americans, who also occupied Haiti from 1914 to 1934, saw that Haitians would be manual laborers rather than Cocolos in Dominican sugar plantations, because at the time, "The use of Haitian laborers was not only easier—they were close at hand and already under United States control—but also gave the Americans a way to diffuse some of the tensions in the Haitian countryside which fed the campesino guerrilla efforts against the North American occupation" (National Coalition for Haitian Rights, "Beyond the Bateyes," quoted by McKenzie 1). Soon after, Haitian peasants were forced to the Dominican sugar plantations for employment.

14. My theoretical concept of the "leaking of pasts and futures" in Black geographies was greatly inspired by my reading of Katherine McKittrick's phenomenal 2013 article "Plantation Futures." I also delve deeper into this exploration of different temporalities existing in one geography in my dissertation "This Land Screams in Pleasure and Ecstasy: Geographies of Memory and Pleasure in African American and Caribbean American Literatures," which is in progress at the time of this writing.

15. Fred Moten's theorization of the shriek and the Black body is crucial in my reading of the shrieking canes; for more, please read *In the Break: The Aesthetics of the Black Radical Tradition.*

16. Katherine McKittrick's *Demonic Grounds: Black Women and the Cartographies of Struggle* articulates the unearthing of female histories and knowledges in relation to land (x); this mirrors Yunior's project of unearthing Beli's trauma in the cane fields.

17. Reulecke explores "generational baggage" or generativity in his essay; generativity "refers primarily to the—unconscious or conscious—examination, especially within particularly distinctive generationalities, of their ties to the diachronic sequence of 'generations' in the genealogical sense of the word" (122).

Works Cited

Abbott, Elizabeth. *Sugar: A Bittersweet History*. Duckworth Overlook, 2009.
Bott, Uwe. "Sugar in the Dominican Republic: How Sweet Is It?" *The Politics of the Caribbean Basin Sugar Trade*, Praeger, 1991.
Bourguignon, Erika E. "Dreams and Dream Interpretation in Haiti." *American Anthropologist* vol. 56, no. 2, 1954, 262–68.
Brown, Karen McCarthy. *Mama Lola: A Vodou Priestess in Brooklyn*. U of California P, 2011.
Crichlow, Michaeline. *Globalization and the Post-Creole Imagination: Notes on Fleeing the Plantation*. Duke UP, 2009.
Deren, Maya. *Divine Horsemen: The Living Gods of Haiti*. 1953. McPherson, 1983.
Díaz, Junot. *The Brief Wondrous Life of Oscar Wao*. Riverhead Books, 2007.
Jiménez Román, Miriam, and Juan Flores, editors. *The Afro-Latin@ Reader: History and Culture in the United States*. Duke UP, 2010.
Jones, Brittany. "Stripped of Citizenship: The Dominican Republic's Deportation of Haitian Descendants." *Michigan State University College of Law International Law Review*, www.msuilr.org/msuilr-legalforum-blogs/2018/4/30/stripped-of-citizenship-the-dominican-republics-deportation-of-haitian-descendants. Accessed 12 Mar. 2019.
Lewis, Maya. "As a Black Woman, I Wish I Could Stop Code-Switching. Here's Why." *Everyday Feminism*, everydayfeminism.com/2018/04/stop-code-switching/. Accessed 12 Mar. 2019.
Maguire, Emily. "Zombies, Vampires, and Planets for Rent: The Science Fictional Turn in Caribbean Literature." Northwestern University, Latin American and Caribbean Studies, Evanston, IL, 6 Feb. 2016.
McKenzie, Ryan. "The Plight of Haitian Workers in the Dominican Sugar Industry." *Windows on Haiti*, Spring 1999, windowsonhaiti.com/windowsonhaiti/hdr-rmk2.shtml. Accessed 1 Aug. 2016.
McKittrick, Katherine. *Demonic Grounds: Black Women and the Cartographies of Struggle*. U of Minnesota P, 2006.
———. "Plantation Futures." *Small Axe*, vol. 17, 2013, pp. 1–15.
Mintz, Sidney W. *Sweetness and Power: The Place of Sugar in Modern History*. Viking, 1985.
Misztal, Barbara A. *Theories of Social Remembering*. McGraw Hill, 2003.

Moten, Fred. *In the Break: The Aesthetics of the Black Radical Tradition*. University of Minnesota P, 2003.
Murphy, Martin. *Dominican Sugar Plantations*. Praeger, 1991.
Perry, Yvonne. "Haitian Vodoun Perspectives on Death and Dying." ezinearticles.com/?Haitian-Vodoun-Perspectives-on-Death-and-Dying&id=3172822. Accessed 12 Mar. 2019.
Reulecke, Jürgen. "Generation/Generationality, Generativity, and Memory." *A Companion to Cultural Memory Studies*, edited by A. Erll and Ansgar Nünning, De Gruyter, 2010.
Suárez, Lucía M. *The Tears of Hispaniola: Haitian and Dominican Diaspora Memory*. UP of Florida, 2000.
Torres-Saillant, Silvio. "The Tribulations of Blackness: Stages in Dominican Racial Identity." *Latin American Perspectives*, vol. 25, no. 3, 1998, pp. 126–46.
Trouillot, Michel-Rolph. *Silencing the Past: Power and the Production of History*. Beacon Press, 1997.
Wucker, Michele. *Why the Cocks Fight: Dominicans, Haitians, and the Struggle for Hispaniola*. Hill and Wang, 1999.

11

Haiti and the Dominican Republic

Teaching about the Un/Friendly Neighbors of Hispaniola

CÉCILE ACCILIEN

> . . . it is remarkable that Dominicans have been able to, by and large, emerge from the Caribbean space as being typified not by phenotype (though this is increasingly not the case) but by language. That is, they are regarded as Latinos whose heritage is contiguous with that of other nation-states in the region, but ultimately understood as having nothing to do with the population and nation with which they share a physical land mass as well as ties of mixed and spilled blood. . . . Within the Americas, perhaps no transnational relationship is more vexed than that of Haiti and the Dominican Republic.
>
> —Myriam Chancy, *From Sugar to Revolution: Women's Visions of Haiti, Cuba, and the Dominican Republic*

In her teaching trilogy, *Teaching to Transgress, Teaching Critical Thinking,* and *Teaching Community,* cultural critic and teacher bell hooks emphasizes that it is important for teachers and scholars to assist students in developing critical thinking skills, to understand that being a critical thinker is an ongoing process, and to recognize and appreciate the power of critical thinking. Furthermore, she prescribes the necessity for students to have a harmonious space that will allow them to learn more effectively in the classroom environment.[1] Hooks's ideas inspired me in designing and teaching a course on Haiti and the Dominican Republic. I wanted to "teach to transgress"[2] and build an inclusive classroom community by "recogniz[ing] the value of each individual voice" (*Transgress* 40). The course that fulfills the non-Western requirement was taught from the African and African American Studies Department and cross-listed with Latin American and Caribbean studies at a large public university. The students were a mix of male and female; African Americans, Latino, and white; first generation as well as traditional students. In order for my students to develop their own voice and critical thinking skills, they needed to understand the complexities of borders in geopolitical, economic, political, linguistic, and cultural terms. Likewise, it was essential for them to have a grasp on the interconnectedness of American economic and political interests, and how the United States creates and supports socioeconomic situations in which these borders can exist.

This essay provides practical tips and best practices to help scholars like myself teach the history and culture of the two unfriendly neighbors of Hispaniola. I also propose some ways to teach the course in order to transgress the stereotypical ideas generally associated with borders. Moreover, I offer several approaches through assignments that aid students to challenge these borders while creating a rewarding experience for both teachers and students.

The Historical Complexities of Borders

In preparing to teach the course, I thought it was central for students to be aware of the intricate rapport of the borders between Haiti and the Dominican Republic, and how the borders affect the identity of both countries. It was also crucial for students to comprehend the stereotypes that are associated with both countries: Haiti primarily with disaster and poverty, and the Dominican Republic with tourism—both travel and sexual—and baseball. It was equally important for students to recognize the density of borders and their relations to larger themes such as citizenship, migration, colonization, history, and culture. Such themes can be taught in a way that challenges students to understand their complex nature and avoid a binary good/bad or victim/oppressor mind-set in regard to Haiti and the Dominican Republic.

The Latin American studies curriculum in US universities often obliterates the historical importance of Haiti. Anthropologist Michel-Rolph

Trouillot, in his seminal work *Silencing of the Past*, highlights the "many ways in which the production of historical narratives involves the uneven contribution of competing groups and individuals who have unequal access to the means of such production" (xix). In the hierarchy of countries in Latin America, Haiti is positioned at the very bottom, so it is not surprising that, despite being the first Black republic in the Western hemisphere, there is a complete erasure of its history. There is a long and complex history of invasion between Haiti and the Dominican Republic. Haiti invaded the neighboring Dominican Republic a number of times during the nineteenth century when it felt it was under threat. To understand the rapport between these two island countries, it is critical to return to the colonial era. Through the course's content and pedagogy, my aim was to transgress the stereotypical beliefs associated with the borders of Haiti and the Dominican Republic in order to discuss the current political tensions between the two nations. I also aspired for students to recognize how borders are historically created, since histories create identities.

Both Haiti and the Dominican Republic have been in the news over the last few years regarding the issue of citizenship. In 2013, the Supreme Court of the Dominican Republic ruled that anyone born between 1929 and 2010 to noncitizen parents did not qualify as a Dominican citizen and was therefore subject to deportation. Many intellectuals, including Haitian American writer Edwidge Danticat and Dominican American writer Junot Díaz, have publicly declared their outrage regarding the injustice and prejudice behind this ruling. Living in the US where they migrated as children, Danticat and Díaz are writers of color who often denounce the injustices of capitalism and colonialism. They are thus in a diasporic geographical space that facilitates a conversation about the Haitian migrant crisis in the Dominican Republic, as well as the multifaceted history between the two countries. For many Haitians, the 2013 ruling has brought to the forefront the ongoing *antihaitianismo* (anti-Haitian) sentiments in the Dominican Republic that have exacerbated Haitian and Dominican imaginations since the 1937 massacre.[3]

Hispaniola is one of only two islands in the Caribbean that comprises two countries (the other is Saint Martin, shared by France and the Netherlands). Haiti is located in the western third of Hispaniola, and the Dominican Republic is in the eastern two-thirds. Both countries exist as a result of European colonialism (French and Spanish, respectively). When Christopher Columbus landed in Hispaniola in 1492, his aim was to use the island as a safe port to further explore the continent in the hopes of discovering gold and thus enriching the Spanish crown. Already in the sixteenth century, the Spanish were importing a large number of African slaves to replace the Native Americans killed through harsh labor and diseases brought to the island by Europeans. The Spanish used the mercantilist system to ensure that all the nation's wealth went back to the state. Through the Treaty of Ryswick in 1697, the French gained control of the western part of the island—which they named Saint-Domingue—while the Spanish retained the eastern part. The French economy was based exclusively on slavery and produced sugar, cocoa, indigo, and coffee; this trade was so productive that in the eighteenth century, Saint-Domingue (present-day Haiti) was France's most economically important colony with more than half a million slaves. Due to the large number of slaves living there, Saint-Domingue was home to a mixed population.[4] Despite the racial anxiety associated with whiteness, pigmentocracy, and colorism, most people of African descent in Haiti took pride in their African heritage and embraced their Blackness. Unlike Haiti, the Dominican Republic during and after the Spanish rule embraced Spanish culture and tried to deny its African heritage. In 1791, two years after the French Revolution, Haiti started a twelve-year revolt that would culminate in obtaining its independence in 1804, and establishing itself as the first Black republic, and the second independent country in the Western hemisphere. Fearful that the French would reestablish slavery and recolonize them, Haitian leaders made a strategic political move and occupied the Dominican Republic from 1822 to 1844.[5]

The Dominican Republic is interesting in that it is the only former colony in Latin America that voluntarily returned to Spanish rule. In fact, when the Dominican Republic celebrates its independence today, there is a historical amnesia about its Spanish colonization; the focus is only on Haiti as the occupier and not Spain, even though Spanish colonization was for a longer period. The United States occupied Haiti from 1915 to 1934 and the Dominican Republic from 1916 to 1924. In the Dominican Republic, the United States imposed what they deemed appropriate cultural norms based on their own beliefs and ideologies. This was accepted by the Dominican middle class, but the elite idolized Spain as the motherland and considered it culturally superior to the Yankees. During this time, the United States had a number of work programs that attracted Haitians to the Dominican Republic. Thus, the notion that white equals success and Black equals poverty, misery, and barbaric culture was further supported by the United States. Trujillo used these ideas and started promoting a propaganda of nationalism that posited a binary description of Haitians as "the primitive other" and the invader. However, the antihaitianismo sentiments propagated by the

US influence and the Trujillo regime has a long history. It is important to note that both Haitian and Dominican elites reimagined their respective nations in a way that benefited them and disenfranchised the majority of the people who were dark-skinned and mostly peasants. As a result, dark-skinned Haitians and Dominicans were victims of the neocolonizers and their respective country's elite class.

In his article "Primitive Borders: Cultural Identity and Ethnic Cleansing in the Dominican Republic," Fernando Valerio-Holguín notes that since the nineteenth century, Dominicans have constructed their identity in opposition to the Haitian Other:

> Of the binary oppositions good/bad, rational/irrational, civilized/savage, cultural/natural, many Dominicans expel from themselves the second term and project it upon the Haitians as a defense mechanism. A great majority of Dominicans have based their cultural and national identities upon the negation of Haitian culture. In this manner they also construct themselves in the imaginary as that-which-they-are-not. For many Dominicans, Haitians not only constitute a Primitive-Other but also a Neighbor-Other and an Other-Within. (76)

It is this binary thinking and Trujillo's ironic dislike of Blackness (his maternal grandmother was a mulatto), that led to one of the worst massacres in Haitian-Dominican history—the 1937 massacre that aimed to cleanse the Dominican Republic of Haitians. However, the two countries are intrinsically linked geographically, historically, and culturally.

Despite their struggle against colonial rule (in the case of Haiti) and dictatorship, both Haiti and the Dominican Republic are victims of history, treaties, colonialism, neocolonialism, revolutions, corruption, economic hardships, repression, and sheer human greed. As a result of these unfortunate circumstances, many people from both islands have suffered greatly at the hands of greedy dictators and neocolonizers and have been forced to migrate in search of a better life. Haitians suffered great hardship under the hands of the father and son Duvalier regimes (1957–1986), and the Duvaliers' secret police force, the Tonton Macoute. Likewise, Dominicans lived under a repressive regime from the *generalissimo* Rafael Leónidas Trujillo (1930–1961). Trujillo, following the racist ideologies that dominated the 1920s and 1930s whereby the white race was thought to be superior, started a crusade in which he aimed to erase the African tradition from the

Dominican Republic and create (both ideologically and physically) a country that highlighted its Spanish and Native American heritage. Although the majority of the Native Americans were decimated less than a century after Columbus's landing in Hispaniola, a large number of Dominicans today consider themselves *Indio* and believe that they are a mix of Spanish and Native American and do not have any African blood.

For many Dominicans, it is when they migrate to the United States that they are forced to face their Blackness and are assigned minority status, given racial politics in the United States.[6] Oftentimes they are categorized as Blacks by mainstream America and not even necessarily Latino when a linguistic issue is not involved. Although both nations are considered developing countries, the Dominican Republic—in part due to its relative stability compared to Haiti, as well as its tourist industry—seems to propose greener pastures, and many Haitians flock there in search of a better life. This economic superiority further reinforces or enlarges different types of borders already existing between the two countries: physical, floating, historical, linguistic, and cultural. It is important to think of these borders as constantly changing based upon many factors including class, access, and mobility. Many Haitians from the upper class have property in the Dominican Republic, frequently travel there, and are able to easily negotiate these borders.

A border is generally defined as a line separating two countries politically or geographically. However, in the case of Haiti and the Dominican Republic, the borders of the two islands are much more complex because some are tangible and some are intangible; some are real and others are imaginary. Furthermore, the physical and cultural borders are constantly shifting and there are not clear demarcations. In *The Tears of Hispaniola: Haitian and Dominican Diaspora Memory*, Lucía M. Suárez emphasizes that both Haiti and the Dominican Republic have similar histories of dictatorship, poverty, and violence. However, she notes: "In contrast to a Haitian tradition of disclosure of misery and violence, the politics of silence—or rather denial—have been dominant in Dominican memory" (7). There is ongoing racial and cultural tensions reflected in popular discourse and represented in popular culture wherein Haiti is seen as poor and Black and the Dominican Republic as economically better off, and some Dominicans view themselves primarily as mulatto or mestizo, rejecting their African roots. However, recent studies such as Milagros Ricourt's *The Dominican Racial Imaginary: Surveying the Landscape of Race and Nation in Hispaniola* challenge this thinking and present a much more complex picture of racial imaginings, cultural heritage, the legacy of slavery, and colonialism as well as nationalism. Teaching a course on the two island nations requires that students think critically about history, representation, culture, and the various tensions between the two. It was essential for students to also deconstruct simplistic nations of race, border, culture, identity, nationality, and nationhood.

Teaching Critical Thinking in Order to Teach to Transgress

I aspired for my students to have a better understanding of the complex relations between Haiti and the Dominican Republic, as well as the various types of borders. In order to achieve this goal, I carefully chose texts and films as well as assignments reflective of this complexity. I was limited to texts that were in English since the class was for students who were not expected to be fluent in Spanish, French, or Haitian Creole.

This was a 300-level course, and the majority of students were juniors and seniors. From the very beginning of class, I stressed to students that this was their class and not mine, and as bell hooks says, it was of utmost importance that we have a "shared learning experience" (*Community* 21). To make this more evident, I invited everyone to sit in a circle during each class to facilitate exchanges about the texts or films in a physical space where everyone felt that his or her voice mattered. At each class meeting, one or two students were responsible for bringing two or three open-ended questions that served as the core of our discussion. Our role in class was to work together to analyze the questions and come up with possible answers. This was a challenging assignment for many students because they were not sure how to ask questions that would foster discussion and critical thinking.

An interesting aspect was the variety of majors represented. The class was taught as an African and African American studies course and crosslisted with Latin American studies. About half of the students came to class with a Latin American studies background and were easily able to make comparisons between the issues of im/migration and borders between the United States and Mexico, and Haiti and the Dominican Republic. This was very helpful and allowed them a comfortable space to discuss sensitive issues such as race, class, culture, history, and prejudice in a global context and from transdisciplinary perspectives.

My desire was to teach my students about Haiti and the Dominican Republic in a manner that was not black and white but showed them the shades of gray that color this complicated topic. This is the reality of history;

this is also how the borders between the two countries are. With this goal in mind, my focus was to create a space in my classroom for students to think critically as defined by Daniel Willingham: "Critical thinking consists of seeing both sides of an issue, being open to new evidence that disconfirms young ideas, reasoning dispassionately, demanding that claims be backed by evidence, deducing and inferring conclusions from available facts, solving problems, and so forth" (21). As a teacher-facilitator, my primary role was to help students engage in critical reflection regarding these complex issues.

Structure of the Course and Examples of Assignments

The course was titled "Hispaniola, an Island Divided: Haiti and the Dominican Republic."[7] The course was largely discussion-based, and participation was an important percentage of each student's grade. At times, we had small group discussions, but the majority of the time we remained in the larger group in a circle. In choosing texts and films for the class, I had to be conscious of materials that would elicit discussion and were accessible to the students. The class was divided into four sections: Haiti and the Dominican Republic: A Complex History; Im/migration and Citizenship; Re/presentation of the Dominican Republic from the US; and Gender and Sexuality. The first section introduced students to the history of both island nations. The second section highlighted the ongoing migrant crisis on the Haiti–Dominican Republic border from different sources. The third section comprised the novels *The Farming of Bones* by Edwidge Danticat and *Geographies of Home* by Loida Maritza Pérez, and the film *Sugar* by Anna Boden and Ryan Fleck. These works allowed our class to have insightful discussions on the pressure of being an athlete and negotiating identity in a new space. In the last section, students viewed the films *Heading South* by Laurent Cantet and *Sand Dollars* by Israel Cárdenas and Laura Amelia Guzmán, and read excerpts from Miriam J. A. Chancy's *From Sugar to Revolution: Women's Visions of Haiti, Cuba, and the Dominican Republic*.

In structuring the class, it was necessary for students to be able to connect the issues we were discussing with real life. In order to facilitate this, I invited two Dominicans to share their experiences with the class. Scholar Rita Tejada, who teaches Dominican culture at a Midwest university, met with the students via Skype. Betsaida Reyes is an area librarian who specializes in Spanish and Portuguese, and Latin American and Caribbean studies; she came to the class to interact with the students. I also invited law professor Lua Yuille, who lived and worked in the Dominican Republic, to help students understand the complexity of statelessness and citizenship through the concept of *jus soli* (the law of the land) and *jus sanguinis* (blood citizenship). She explained how the current immigration crisis of Haitians living in the Dominican Republic started in 2013. She further analyzed from a legal perspective what it means for people to retroactively lose their citizenship, their vulnerability in becoming stateless, and the racism of the Dominican government in its actions to once again "cleanse" the Dominican Republic of Haitians. Having a law expert interpret for students how citizenship could be obtained via either *jus soli* or *jus sanguinis* helped them to concretely grasp the complexity of migration and identity politics; it also allowed them to make cross-cultural comparisons with the United States where these issues have come up, especially during election seasons.

Betsaida Reyes discussed her life as an immigrant from the Dominican Republic and her feeling of exile and alienation while living in the United States. Likewise, Rita Tejada recounted her experience as a Dominican in the Midwest and the perception of her Latino identity when she moved to the United States and became a minority. She also emphasized how she and her students experienced firsthand the realities of the issues of borders, race, and class during a recent service learning trip to Haiti and the Dominican Republic in January 2016. Unlike the Haitians who had traveled with them on the same bus and who were held for hours at the border, she and her students easily negotiated their entry into the Dominican Republic because of the cultural and economic weight their American passports carried. Through their exchange with the guest professor, students in the class were able to ask a multitude of questions about both Haiti and the Dominican Republic, how people from the two islands interacted with each other, and how the borders are constructed.

It was important for students to think about the various themes from several perspectives and to hear different voices. It was also impactful for them to ponder and appreciate that personal testimony and experience are as valid as published texts as a way to understand multiple perspectives.

Finally, I invited scholar Anne François, who is doing research on Haitian immigrants in the Dominican Republic, and she emphasized how the Haitian government profited monetarily when they sent Haitians to work in the Dominican Republic in the early part of the twentieth century. This further problematizes the binary victim/oppressor roles that people often posit when talking about Haitians and Dominicans. By accentuating the Haitian government's participation in this neo-slavery enterprise, the scholar helped the students understand that the Haiti-Dominican Republic relationship is a complicated one that cannot be reduced to easy explanations.

The two novels we read in class—*The Farming of Bones* by Edwidge Danticat and *Geographies of Home* by Loida Maritza Pérez—are both complex texts that allowed students to explore issues of borders, im/migration, identity, class, and religion. As students read the novels, they were able to make comparisons between the common plights that Haitian immigrants face in the Dominican Republic and prejudice that Dominicans face in the United States. They also compared and contrasted themes in both novels, including trauma, violence, exile, displacement, gender, and the importance of maintaining identity. Students had to draw parallels between the experiences of characters from both novels who are trying to find a space to exist. For instance, we analyzed the character of Amabelle from Danticat's novel and her connection to parsley. In the novel, "perejil" is intrinsically linked to the massacre of thousands of Haitians because it is the Spanish word for "parsley" that Haitians had to pronounce to prove their citizenship. In fact, when reflecting upon this superficial linguistic test, Amabelle notes: "We used our parsley for food, our teas, to cleanse our insides as well as our outsides. Perhaps, the *Generalissimo* in some larger order was trying to do the same for his country. To devil with your word, your grass, your wind, your water, your air, your words. You ask for perejil, I give you more" (203). In our analysis of the massacre and its link to the language test, students became aware of the power of language.

Like Amabelle, Aurelia—the main character in *Geographies of Home*—is trying to find a place of belonging in the United States. In her search she reflects: "In the presence of strangers like those she had sheltered herself from since her arrival in the United States and in a hospital worlds removed from the New York depicted on postcards her eldest daughter had mailed to the Dominican Republic, Aurelia for the first time granted herself permission to sprout roots past concrete into soil" (137). Students were able to critically analyze the difficulty of being an immigrant through Amabelle and Aurelia's lenses. By comparing the lives of these two female characters, my goal was to help students create borders but also transgress them. Through these two complex characters created by Haitian American and Dominican American writers living in the United States, students were able to interpret the challenges of immigrants in general and problematize the too often binary media and literary representations of Haiti (victim) and Dominican Republic (oppressor). They were pushed to think about the intersectionality of class, economy, and location in regard to these issues.

Students were assigned an essay on *Geographies of Home* in order to help them think critically about what home means to an immigrant, displaced or exiled, in another country. Students' answers reflected the complexity of what home means, including the roles that gender, religion, abuse, mental illness, racism, migration, immigration, and economic and political status play in the search for home.

This assignment was valuable because it helped students problematize the notion of home for immigrants and assisted students in being able to compare that experience for both Dominicans and Haitians. It also underscored how home is intrinsically linked to im/migration, citizenship, belonging, and prejudice, whether based on race, class, language, or culture. Students were able to compare the prejudice Iliana, Aurelia, Papito, and Rebecca face as Spanish speakers to that faced by the Haitian migrants, Creole speakers in the novel *The Farming of Bones*. Using language as a strategic divider and forcing Haitians to enunciate the word "perejil" was a way to make a specific distinction since phenotypically, the majority of Dominicans look similar to Haitians. Likewise, students made the connection to Miguel, the main character in the film *Sugar* and his linguistic struggles and the cultural barriers he faced when he arrived in Iowa from the Dominican Republic. Thus, language is a vital aspect in defining one's home. As one student noted: "A home is not just where you were born, it is a place that assists you in the creation and development of your identity. . . . In this novel, each character found their geography of home." Students were able to connect home to the larger themes of history and borders.

Thinking Critically about History and Borders

As we started discussing a particular text or film, we sometimes approached it from a historical perspective. This was especially useful as we analyzed the history of the 1937 massacre of Haitians, Haitian Dominicans, and Dominicans. Students had to carefully reflect on the paratext (author, date of publication, preface, etc.). A historical novel is different from a historical text in depicting the event of the massacre. In fact, we had a lot of discussion on Danticat's historical novel *The Farming of Bones* and the various possible readings. Danticat was criticized by historian Bernardo Vega over the veracity of one of her descriptions of a scene during the massacre (Suárez 12–13). Our long discussion centered around the themes of history, memory, retelling, and their intricacies. In *Poetics of Relation*, Martinican critic Édouard Glissant observes that only the writer can truly delve into the depth of people to be able to tell history. For Glissant, writers serve as guardians of history and have the duty to tell the stories of the people in a way that historians cannot. Our class spent some time deconstructing and decolonizing history, and challenging ourselves to think about history from various perspectives, including: Who is writing the history? What is the context? Who is the audience?

We arrived at the conclusion that ultimately neither the controversy over the actual number of people killed during the 1937 massacre nor whether the victims who supposedly "looked" Haitian were forced to take the linguistic test that Danticat refers to in her novel matter. Rather, what is important is the fact that she gives her characters, both female and male, agency to tell their story. Another crucial point was the fact that the massacre of 1937 in many ways sealed the border issue between Haiti and the Dominican Republic by distancing and disconnecting the two nations.

When we initially discussed the event, students were randomly assigned to a group that was either for or against the massacre. This allowed for constructive and complex discussions of this horrible historical event, as well as problematizing it. They had to come up with very concrete reasons why they believed the massacre was necessary or unnecessary. We also examined some of the reasons why the massacre is so important in Haiti-Dominican relations. The fact that so many Dominicans deny the historical importance of the massacre while Haitians continuously mourn it shows the lack of recognition in Dominican narratives.

Understanding Multiple Borders

Discussions of borders allow students to bring forth other issues that are connected to identity and immigration. Students were given the following essay question: "Describe the complex nature of the borders between Haiti and the Dominican Republic (linguistic, historical, post/colonial, cultural, social, geographical/physical). Choose three of the different types of borders mentioned. How do these borders create conflict between the two countries? In your opinion (and based upon the readings), what are some possible solutions to resolve some of these conflicts?" In order to help students understand the complexity of borders, we discussed examples of other countries that have borders, such as Israel and Palestine, North Korea and South Korea, and the United States and Mexico. For Dominicans, Haitians are not neighbors. As Valerio-Holguín states: "Dominicans do not think of borders as 'something we share,' rather they think it as 'something that separates us' from the Haitians. . . . Borders then become not the space of cultural negotiation but the limits of threatening 'Africanization' and 'corruption of the good customs inherited from Spain'" (78).

This assignment pushed students to think critically about the notion of borders from various perspectives, how it creates conflicts, how it manifests itself, and how it helps construct identity and create division between two neighboring countries. It also challenged students to comprehend the intertwined relations between agency and power. Students answered the questions in a variety of ways. Some focused on how the borders manifested themselves, stating, for instance, that the borders exist because of colonial and postcolonial history and geography. Others viewed the borders as contested sites where issues of race, class, gender, economy, and politics are confronted. For instance, the marketplace on the border is largely a female space where negotiations take place. However, solidarity can also exist on the border because it allows both countries to benefit. The physical border can be a dynamic that allows an opportunity for cooperation between Haiti and the Dominican Republic through the markets that exist. Out of economic necessity, the two nations have a space of necessary exchange. Overall, the majority of the students explored the cultural, geographical, economic, and linguistic borders. Exploration of borders allowed students to concretely understand the rift between the two countries.

There is a social divide between Dominicans and Haitians as evidenced by the fact that the Dominican Republic—despite its label as a developing country—is more advanced and seems to offer more opportunities for Haitians to have some economic stability. In reality, many Haitians find themselves living in slave-like conditions in the bateyes (sugar plantations) once they arrive in the Dominican Republic. Yet, they cannot escape because they have no identity and no agency. The economic freedom they had dreamed of turned into a nightmare and another border is created—one even more complex and problematic than the actual physical border. It results from the common rejection of the history that exists between the two nations. The fact that the Dominican Republic considers Haiti the "primitive other" and that it defines its identity by the denial of being Haitian (i.e., being "Black") further cements the border between the two countries.

In addition to discussing border issues, students had to come up with the reasons why the borders exist. They had to draw on readings to support their argument of problematic borders. Some mentioned the fact that Dominicans appropriated European discourse when talking about Haiti and Haitians as the primitive "Other" in order to justify their superiority vis-à-vis Haitians. The borders originate from a complicated past as well as the negative perceptions of the two nations with unresolved tension, also the fact that the majority of Haitians are living in plantations in situations akin to slavery does not help. Moreover, because the Dominican Republic is economically independent, it is natural to deem Haiti as inferior. Additionally, the historical/racial discourse and identity construction of the Dominican Republic is one whereby it sees itself as *mestizo* and *indio*, and not Black, as opposed to Haiti. So, the binary of black/white and superior/inferior is at play yet again.

Students pointed to the fact that borders work when they are convenient, because markets on the borders where Haitians and Dominicans exchange goods are not problematic. As students came up with possible sustainable solutions to the border issue, they noted that first there is a necessity for the recognition of a common history and cultural bond between the two countries; second, there also needs to be an acceptance of each other as neighbor. A student quoting Lucía Suárez suggested that literature can be a great starting point to cross these borders. "Through fiction, different versions of life in Haiti and the Dominican Republic are shaped from the darkness of silence. . . . memory functions as a memorial that permits the recognition of trauma, creates a space for mourning losses . . . and moving on" (60).

Interactive Learning:
Creative Space for Everyone to Teach and Learn

I believe the most important assignment in the class was an interactive learning assignment—students had to research, present, and teach the class on a topic that they wanted to investigate further. Students had to choose their topic about three weeks before their presentations were due. The whole class also met with the area librarian for Latin American and Caribbean studies in order to get help researching their topic. This assignment provided a space for students to be self-directed learners and engaged with a subject that they were curious about. It also provided an opportunity for them to teach their peers as well as their professors. Topics ranged from human trafficking to a comparison of the education systems in Haiti and the Dominican Republic to the agricultural systems in the two countries. One student's presentation, titled "Vulnerability, Citizenship and the Potential of Human Trafficking," highlighted what human trafficking is, the current policies in the Dominican Republic, and the global risk factors for human trafficking, such as poverty, lack of education, and chronic mobility. The student also discussed how Haitians living on the Dominican Republic border are more subject to human trafficking. Another presentation, "Trujillo and Duvalier: Birds of a Feather," analyzed the similarities between the two dictators, including their cult of personality, and the way they manipulated people into thinking they were the champion of the masses. The student also emphasized the notion of the intrusive state that aimed at creating the illusion that the dictators were everywhere in order to maintain a reign of terror, and their use of religion—Catholicism for Trujillo; Catholicism and Vodou for Duvalier, who personified Baron Samedi, the Vodou *lwa* or spirits of the dead. There was a student who explored the trajectory of baseball players who leave the Dominican Republic in search of the American dream. The student was able to critically explore issues such as migration and immigration in the context of baseball players migrating to the United States and the economic aspect of that migration.

This assignment was an occasion for students to practice their critical thinking skills. They had to take initiative by choosing their topic and think about an issue from various perspectives. As the teacher-facilitator, it was also an opportunity for me to affirm their contribution by letting them know that I was learning from them and that the learning process is interactive. This was an opportunity for "everyone in the classroom, teacher and students [to] recognize that they are responsible for creating a learning community together. . . . Everyone [was] participating and sharing . . . resource[s]" (hooks, *Critical Thinking* 11).

Conclusion

The island of Hispaniola is home to the countries of Haiti and the Dominican Republic, two nations that have more commonalities than differences. Despite different colonizers, different languages, and different dictators, both countries are struggling to maintain their identity and survive in the face of challenges such as natural disasters, a shared history of colonialism and transatlantic slave trade, corruption, human right abuses, political and economic instability, and gender and class inequality, to name a few. If the countries could visualize working together as neighbors instead of seeing each other as enemies, one wonders about the benefits and friendship both could enjoy. However, in order to do so, there has to be a common desire to acknowledge the past, to communicate and move forward as neighbors. In teaching this class entitled "An Island Divided: Haiti and the Dominican Republic," it was indispensable for students to understand the complexity of borders as well as how they relate to larger themes such as im/migration, class, gender, economy, politics, and religion. Students also needed to ponder the effects and results of colonization centuries after the Europeans arrived in the New World under the guise of civilizing first the Native Americans and later the African slaves to benefit their own greed and endeavors. As global citizens, migration is part of the current human condition, and one cannot discuss migration without borders nor study borders without reflecting upon the complexity of inequalities. We must constantly reflect on the old Rousseauist beliefs:

> The first man who, having fenced in a piece of land, said "This is mine," and found people naïve enough to believe him, that man was the true founder of civil society. From how many crimes, wars, and murders, from how many horrors and misfortunes might not any one have saved mankind, by pulling up the stakes, or filling up the ditch, and crying to his fellows: Beware of listening to this impostor; you are undone if you once forget that the fruits of the earth belong to us all, and the earth itself to nobody.[8]

It was fundamental for me to challenge my students—who view themselves as global citizens—to think critically about borders and be ready to transgress them. In so doing, we were able to collectively create a space of "fierce engagement and intense learning" (hooks, *Critical Thinking* 5).

Notes

1. See especially *Teaching Critical Thinking: Practical Wisdom*. In chapter 1, "Critical Thinking," hooks describes the process of critical thinking, why it is important, and some of the required steps for all participants to make it an interactive process in the classroom.

2. The idea of "teaching to transgress" is the notion of engaging in radical pedagogy, meaning a pedagogy that challenges the white male privilege gaze. For hooks, it is essential to have critical perspectives with the intersectionality of class, race, sexual practice and orientation, nationality, among other issues. The pedagogy

must also intertwine anticolonial and feminist pedagogies. For more information, see the introduction of *Teaching to Transgress: Education as the Practice of Freedom*.

3. Trujillo ruled the Dominican Republic for thirty-one years in a period known as *El Trujillato* or the Trujillo era from 1930 until 1961 when he was assassinated. For more information about Trujillo and his rule, see Derby.

4. There is a large body of work on Haitian and Dominican history. For more information please see the following: Franco; Wucker; and San Miguel. For more detailed information on Haitian history, please see Dubois; and Trouillot.

5. For more information about this as well as the complex relation between the two islands, please see Price-Mars; see also Théus.

6. For an in-depth analysis of Dominicans racial identity in the United States, please see Duany.

7. The title was inspired by Henry Louis Gates Jr.'s four-part documentary series entitled *Black in Latin America*. The first episode—"Haiti and the Dominican Republic: An Island Divided"—analyzes race and identity in Haiti and the Dominican Republic.

8. See Rousseau.

Works Cited

André, Richard. "The Dominican Republic and Haiti: A Shared View from the Diaspora." *Americas Quarterly*, Summer 2014, www.americasquarterly.org/content/dominican-republic-and-haiti-shared-view-diaspora. Accessed 22 Apr. 2016.

Chancy, Myriam J. A. *From Sugar to Revolution: Women's Visions of Haiti, Cuba, and the Dominican Republic*. Wilfrid Laurier UP, 2012.

Charles, Jacqueline. "Haitian Migrants Living Life on the Border." Online video clip. *Miami Herald*, 21 Aug. 2015, https://www.miamiherald.com/news/nation-world/world/americas/haiti/article31840869.html. Accessed 3 May 2016.

Danticat, Edwidge. *The Farming of Bones*. Soho Press, 1998.

Derby, Lauren. *The Dictator's Seduction: Politics and the Popular Imagination in the Era of Trujillo*. Duke UP, 2009.

Duany, Jorge. "Reconstructing Racial Identity: Ethnicity, Color and Class among Dominicans in the United States in Puerto Rico." *Latin American Perspective*, vol. 25, no. 3, 1998, 147–72.

Dubois, Laurent. *A Colony of Citizens: Revolution and Slave Emancipation in the French Caribbean, 1787–1804*. UP of North Carolina, 2004.

Franco, Franklin J. *Blacks, Mulattos, and the Dominican Nation*. Routledge, 2015.

Glissant, Édouard. *Poetics of Relation*. Translated by Betsy Wing, U of Michigan P, 1997.

"Haiti and the Dominican Republic: An Island Divided." *Black in Latin America*. Written by Henry Louis Gates Jr., *PBS*, 2011. Accessed 3 May 2016.

Heading South. Directed by Laurent Cantet. Studio Canal, 2006.
hooks, bell. *Teaching Community: A Pedagogy of Hope.* Routledge, 2003.
———. *Teaching Critical Thinking: Practical Wisdom.* Routledge, 2010.
———. *Teaching to Transgress: Education as the Practice of Freedom.* Routledge, 1994.
Jean, Martine. "Haiti and the Dominican Republic: A Conflict Captured on Film." *Indiewire: Shadow and Act. Indiewire,* 26 June 2015, leflambeau-foundation.org/2015/06/haiti-and-the-dominican-republic-a-conflict-captured-on-film. Accessed 3 May 2016.
Minn, Paul. "Medical Humanitarianism and Health as a Human Right on the Haitian Dominican Border." *Haiti and the Haitian Diaspora in the Wider Caribbean,* edited by Philippe Zacaïr, UP of Florida, 2010, pp. 103–20.
Pérez, Loida Maritza. *Geographies of Home.* Viking Penguin Books, 1999.
Price-Mars, Jean. *La République d'Haïti et la République Dominicaine, Tome I et II.* Collection du Tricinquantenaire de l'Indépendance d'Haïti, 1953.
The Price of Sugar. Directed by Bill Haney. Uncommon Productions, 2007.
Ricourt, Milagros. *The Dominican Racial Imaginary: Surveying the Landscape of Race and Nation in Hispaniola.* Rutgers UP, 2016.
Roorda, Eric Paul. *The Dictator Next Door: The Good Neighbor Policy and the Trujillo Regime in the Dominican Republic, 1930–1945.* Duke UP, 1998.
Rousseau, Jean-Jacques. *On the Origin of the Inequality of Mankind and Is It Authorised by Natural Law?* Translated by G. D. H. Cole, *Marxist Org References,* n.d., https://www.marxists.org/reference/subject/economics/rousseau/inequality/index.htm. Accessed 17 July 2016.
Sagás, Ernesto. "A Case of Mistaken Identity: Antihaitianismo in Dominican Culture." Webster University, n.d. http://faculty.webster.edu/corbetre/haiti/misctopic/dominican/antihaiti.htm. Accessed 3 May 2016.
Sand Dollars. Directed by Israel Cárdenas and Laura Amelia Guzmán. Aurora Dominicana, Canana, Rei Cine, 2014.
San Miguel, Pedro L. *The Imagined Island: History, Identity, and Utopia in Hispaniola.* U of North Carolina P, 2006.
Suárez, Lucía M. *The Tears of Hispaniola: Haitian and Dominican Diaspora Memory.* UP of Florida, 2006.
Sugar. Written by Anna Boden and Ryan Fleck. Sony, 2008.
Théus, Beguens. *Conflit haïtiano-dominicain au-delà de l'arrêt 168–13: le massacre physique de 1937 et le massacre civil de 2013.* Les Éditions Mémoire, 2016.
Trouillot, Michel-Rolph. *Silencing the Past: Power and the Production of History.* Beacon, 1995.
Valerio-Holguín, Fernando. "Primitive Borders: Cultural Identity and Ethnic Cleansing in the Dominican Republic." *Primitivism and Identity in Latin America: Essays on Art, Literature, and Culture,* edited by Erik Camayd-Freixas. U of Arizona P, 2000, pp. 75–88.

Willingham, Daniel T. "Critical Thinking: Why Is It So Hard to Teach?" *Arts Education Policy Review*, vol. 109, no. 4, 2008, pp. 21–29.

Wucker, Michele. *Why the Cocks Fight: Dominicans, Haitians, and the Struggle for Hispaniola*. Hill and Wang, 1999.

Concluding Thoughts
Afro-Latinx Futures

VANESSA K. VALDÉS

> To contribute to new knowledge and to add new significance, the narrator must both acknowledge and contradict the power embedded in previous understandings.
>
> —Michel-Rolph Trouillot, *Silencing the Past: Power and the Production of History*

This collection was born of a confluence of events that include both the development of my own interests as well as changes in the broadly conceived field of African Diaspora studies. I organized a three-day conference, "Let Spirit Speak! Cultural Journeys through the African Diaspora," which took place April 22–24, 2010. We began the gathering with an invocation by Gina Ulysse, who performed excerpts from her piece, *When God Is Too Busy: Haiti, Me and THE WORLD*. Three months earlier, on January 12th, a 7.0 earthquake had devastated the nation, and Ulysse plaintively called out to the lwas, to Erzulie, for her salvation. While the conference was open to scholars who worked broadly on the African diaspora in the Americas, those who presented did so focusing on the Circum-Caribbean and the communities of migrants from those nations in the United States. This became more clear as I organized the proceedings of the conference, published in 2012 under the same name.

Three years later, in 2013, I wrote a review of Myriam Chancy's *From Sugar to Revolution: Women's Visions of Haiti, Cuba, and the Dominican Republic* (2012) for *Anthurium*, the University of Miami's digital Caribbean literary studies journal.[1] Chancy's indictment of the discipline of Latin American studies in terms of its anxiety about race in general, and about Blackness in particular, inspired me to reflect on my place in the academy. As a self-described scholar of African diasporic literature in the Americas, I knew her words to be true: after decades, Afro-Hispanic and Afro-Brazilian literary studies remain small subfields within the larger field of Latin American literary studies. Though there is growing awareness and movement toward change, students often continue to learn about Caribbean literature as per the language spoken on the island: students of English may learn about the Anglophone Caribbean, of Spanish of the Hispanophone, of French the Francophone. If you learn about the Dutch Caribbean within the US academy, you are in rarefied company, as the peoples, cultures, and histories of these islands are very often overlooked, even among Caribbeanists. One almost never learns about movement between the islands as a student of literature, or about shared histories and cultures that defy the categoric simplification imposed by the academy. There is ease in the flattening of histories; knowledge is more easily acquired when there is a smaller amount of information to know.

Problems may, and normally do, arise when one begins to notice gaps in knowledge, begins to question perspective and the subject position of the narrators writing the narratives. As an undergraduate English major, I learned about the Caribbean in the context of migration to the United States in a US Latinx literature class; as a graduate student of Spanish and Portuguese, in the context of the Caribbean I learned about Cuba. As a woman of African descent, I was struck by articulations of race (read: Blackness) in my undergraduate Afro-Hispanic literature course. As a graduate student I would write papers examining intersections of race and gender. My personal interest in Puerto Rico meant that I read outside of the classroom the books and articles I needed to satisfy my curiosity; despite family and friends of Dominican heritage, I did not begin to study that country in depth until early in my career as a professor, teaching students about the Hispanic Caribbean. I write this observation to underscore that learning is a continuous process and also to offer insight into knowledge acquisition and production. Intellectual genealogies are important, not only when they recount the scholars with whom we as academics study but also when they recount how we come to decide on our research interests. For many of us who study marginalized countries, in this case, Puerto Rico and the Dominican Republic, there are personal incentives that fuel the desire to learn and to write against damaging scholarship that often casts aspersions on whole peoples and their histories without a thought.

In graduate school, I noticed the absence of Haiti in my learning; almost twenty years have gone by, then, since I desired to read a book that took into account *all* of the islands of the region and how they interacted. I became interested in the larger Circum-Caribbean and began to think of the region within that frame. As I pursued advanced degrees, I was attuned to representations of gender, with an eye toward constructions of masculinity and femininity, and race, meaning Blackness: how it was thought of, constructed, deployed in literary texts. I was trained as a comparatist and so I began to take note of similar themes, metaphors, and tropes that I found across literatures across the Americas. I have organized a conference and conference panels, have written and edited books that center on how Black men and women throughout the Americas understand their own worlds and histories. There have been several occasions, particularly when I was writing *Oshun's Daughters: The Search for Womanhood in the Americas* (2014), when interlocutors asked about my decision to not include Vodou in the book. My focus was on literary representations of the African diasporic religions Regla de Ocha and Candomblé in Brazil, Cuba, and the United States; to include Haitian authors referencing Vodou would be irresponsible on my part, as I did not and do not know the religion to the extent that would warrant producing knowledge about it.

I wrote the review of Chancy's book after I had submitted the manuscript of *Oshun's Daughters* for publication, and yet her words stayed with me. The year after the review appeared, in 2015, I began a sabbatical that I dedicated to the writing of *Diasporic Blackness: The Life and Times of Arturo Alfonso Schomburg* (2017). Studying Schomburg's life and works, I once again read about Haiti; indeed, his first published essay was an examination of Haiti's political and economic future. "Is Hayti Decadent?" appeared in print in 1904, as part of a celebration of the independence of the island. Schomburg was enthralled with the history of the first Black republic in the hemisphere and was intent on offering to the world an assessment of the country that went beyond tales of corruption and US occupation. The subject of this first essay was the underdevelopment of its agriculture, which he attributes to the "frequency of internecine wars, repeated insurrections, and street riots which are always harmful and demoralizing to the people as a whole."[2] Eleven years later, in a paper circulated within the American Negro

Academy entitled "The Economic Contribution by the Negro to America," Schomburg reminds his audience: "The name of Haiti will always stimulate us to revere the memory of men who have stamped their names on the scroll of time, for not only did that island strike the first effective blow for the liberation of the Black slave, but, having accomplished this purpose, the Haitians aided in the liberation of all America from the yoke of Europe."[3] Here, then, Schomburg makes explicit the debt that all Americans, that is, all inhabitants of the lands of the Americas, owe the men and women of Haiti, for he identifies this nation as the cradle of independence for all, particularly for those of African descent.

Schomburg would make even more clear his admiration for Haiti when, in 1932, the Division of Negro History, Literature, and Art, at his urging, sponsored a dinner in honor of Dantès Bellegarde, then serving as the Haitian ambassador to the United States. Bellegarde later offered one of four talks as part of the series "The Negro in the New World."[4] One of the first exhibits at the West 135th Street Branch after Schomburg's death featured Haitian books, photographs, and prints; it was promoted in the *New York Amsterdam News* as evidence of Schomburg's legacy.[5] Schomburg's love of and passion for Haiti, its culture, and its people was characteristic of a man who embraced and celebrated Black communities throughout the Western hemisphere; Bellegarde was later quoted as having stated that Schomburg knew more about Haiti, its history, and literature than any living man.[6] He understood the concerted resistance to Haiti, particularly within Spanish-speaking circles, as emblematic of the anti-Blackness he had experienced throughout his life, beginning in his childhood. For him, there was no contradiction between love and admiration for the people of this nation and for the Spanish-speaking world, as all of the cultures of these regions were shaped by the contributions of peoples of African descent.

Perhaps more illustrations of his passion for this country can be found in an accounting of his collection: two weeks prior to his death in 1938, the Historical Records Survey, a project funded under the Work Projects Administration, had finished assessing the holdings of what would shortly thereafter be renamed as the Schomburg Collection. As curator Lawrence Reddick points out in an introductory essay accompanying the publication of these findings in 1942, while texts related to African Americans comprised the majority of the holdings, "every section of the globe where Black folk have lived in considerable numbers is represented. Thus, writings from Africa, the West Indies, Brazil and other regions in South America are included. The Haitian Collection is, perhaps, the best in this country."[7] For Schomburg, then, Haiti, was instrumental in understanding the Caribbean in particular and the Americas as a whole; our understanding of Afro-Latinidad is made more profound when taking into consideration the hemisphere holistically, as Schomburg himself demonstrated during his lifetime.

The combination, then, of having scholarship on Haiti shared at a conference I had organized, of having read Chancy's text, and of having studied and written on Schomburg himself inspired first a digital consideration of Haiti's relationship to the Hispanophone Caribbean literary imagination, published in *sx salon* in June 2016 and organized by this author, followed by the present collection of essays.[8]

Racialized Visions is a contribution to the ongoing work reconsidering Haiti in relation to the Hispanic Caribbean from the perspective of the humanities. As referenced in the introduction, the life and imagination of nineteenth-century free Black José Antonio Aponte has proven to be incredibly generative; in May 2015, New York University hosted the two-day conference "José Antonio Aponte and His World: Writing, Painting, and Making Freedom in the African Diaspora." The gathering gave rise to *Digital Aponte*, a website that is a detailed reexamination of his life and work; led by Linda Rodriguez, Ada Ferrer, Kris Minhae Choe, and Eric Anderson, we are encouraged to understand this man as paradigmatic of Black populations in the surrounding Caribbean islands inspired by the Haitian revolts for independence. In December 2017, *Visionary Aponte: Art and Black Freedom* opened in Miami in the Little Haiti Cultural Center; it is an art exhibit inspired by Aponte's book of paintings that were found in his house upon his arrest and cited as evidence of his imaginings of freedom for Cuba's Black population. Included among the fourteen artists from Cuba, Haiti, the Dominican Republic, Honduras, France, and the United States are Juan Roberto Diago, Édouard Duval-Carrié, Clara Morera, and Vickie Pierre. All of them reconceive Aponte's collection of images, thereby offering their own visions of Black freedom. The exhibit moved to New York University's King Juan Carlos I of Spain Center in February 2018, where it remained until June, and again to Duke University's Power Plant Gallery in September 2018.[9]

Concurrent with the *Visionary Aponte* show in New York was *Bordering the Imaginary: Art from the Dominican Republic, Haiti, and Their Diasporas* by BRIC, Brooklyn Information and Culture, in downtown Brooklyn. Curated by Abigail Lapin Dardashti, the show put in conversation Dominican and Haitian artists as they reconsidered their common cultural exchanges between the two nations ("Revolutions and Unifications: The Contemporary

Resonance of 18th- and 19th-Century History"), deliberated on the border as a dynamic space ("Borders, Fragmentations, and Intertwinings"), and confronted the legacy of racism ("Bodies Transformed"). The exhibit opened with an accompanying conference at the City University of New York's Graduate Center, "Art and Literature in Contemporary Dominican Republic, Haiti, and Their Diasporas." It later closed with a conversation between author Ibi Zoboi, scholar Edward Paulino, activist Albert Saint Jean, and community organizer Suhaly Carolina-Bautista, each of whom had published reflections on their understandings of the relationships between these two countries on the site *Remezcla*.

This digital platform, one created by and geared toward specifically Latinx millennials, has been important in its coverage of Haiti as part of Latin America. In February of 2017, it promoted *Life between Borders: Black Migrants in Mexico*, a sixteen-minute documentary directed by Ebony Bailey, a self-described Blaxican and California native.[10] Bailey's film sheds light on Mexico's Black population, including a Haitian community that lives in Tijuana, Mexico, at the border between that country and the United States. Composed of migrants who had left Hispaniola in the aftermath of the earthquake to find work in South America, these men, women, and children had traveled from countries such as Chile and Brazil through Central America with hopes of applying for asylum in the United States, only to find themselves in political limbo when the Obama administration rescinded humanitarian visas in September of 2016.

Supporting this population and examining the border is the subject of the class "Mexico-United States Border: Diaspora, Exiles, and Refugees," cotaught at Pomona College in California in the spring of 2018 by scholar April Mayes and her colleague Miguel Tinker Salas. Mayes, a specialist in Dominican history and author of *The Mulatto Republic: Class, Race, and Dominican National Identity* (2014), is a founding member of the collective Transnational Hispaniola, a group of scholars dedicated to rethinking the histories of these nations in order to emphasize their commonalities rather than antagonisms.[11] In an effort to "make history relevant to the present, to put [their] skills to use for the cause of social justice, and to build relationships with new community organizations," she and Tinker Salas took the class to San Diego and Tijuana, interviewed Haitian migrants, and created a website linking their work with their community partners, BAJI (Black Alliance for Just Immigration) and Haitian Bridge Alliance.[12]

The reimaginings of relations between the Dominican Republic and Haiti have been occurring for some time; led by scholars such as Frank

Moya Pons and Silvio Torres-Saillant and writers such as Junot Díaz and Edwidge Danticat from at least the 1990s, they began in earnest again after La Sentencia in 2013. Activists and educators alike critical of the Dominican High Court's decision to denationalize Dominicans of Haitian descent continue to lobby for a reconsideration of that ruling. Amarilys Estrella has written the first book-length study on the work of Reconoci.do, an activist group of Dominicans of Haitian descent denationalized by the Dominican Constitutional Tribunal's ruling 168-13 with her 2019 dissertation, "Recognizing Blackness: Grassroots Human Rights Activism Against Racism in the Dominican Republic." Based in New York and founded a month after the court's decision, the group We Are All Dominican continues to hold discussions, vigils, and panels in an effort to confront anti-Haitianism directly and to support the hundreds of thousands who have effectively lost Dominican citizenship in the wake of that judgment.[13] Another activist effort is Dominicans Love Haitians Movement, founded in 2009 and led by Clarivel Ruiz who, through poetry readings, performance, and storytelling, brings together artists to directly confront renderings of Dominican national identity that actively erase Haitian history. Ruiz is intent not only on challenging anti-Haitianist sentiment specifically but anti-Black responses more broadly; an example of this is her Black Doll project, an effort to send one thousand Black dolls to children in the Dominican Republic, Haiti, Cuba, and Puerto Rico.[14] Finally, there is Incultured Company, an organization of young Black Latinx youth leading conversations around difficult historical themes in order to facilitate increased dialogue and reconciliation. Since 2018, the focus of these gatherings have been on Haiti and the Dominican Republic, with events such as "Decolonizing Hispaniola," "Intro to Haitian Vodou and Dominican Vudú," and "1865: Is the Dominican Republic the Second Black Republic?"[15]

On multiple fronts, then—both within the ivory tower and without, in popular media—there is a growing awareness of the need to interrogate outdated renderings of a Eurocentric Hispanic Caribbean and replace those narratives with accurate ones that restore the contributions of Black men, women, and children to our histories. An academic gathering such as the Exploring las Afrodominicanidades symposium, held in March of 2017 at New York University and organized by Saudi García, a graduate student in anthropology at the time, would have been unthinkable decades prior to the event. Ayanna Legros created conversation with the publication of her essay "As a Haitian-American Woman, I Know I'm Afro-Latina but It's Time for You to Acknowledge It Too" in the women's channel, Fierce, of another digital outlet, *Mitú*.¹⁶ As to be expected given their shared histories and geographic proximity, and as made evident in this collection, Haiti in relation to the Dominican Republic receives a great deal of attention when recentering Haiti, and Blackness more broadly, in Caribbean studies. Next is Haiti and its historical relationship with Cuba; the Haiti–Puerto Rico relationship receives very little scholarly attention.

Interestingly enough, this extends even to the archive itself: in a recent digital article for *sx archipelagos*, Marlene L. Daut writes of the underutilized Alfred Nemours Collection of Haitian History located at the University of Puerto Rico. A Haitian military officer, Nemours (1883–1947) collected primary sources—books, manuscripts, pamphlets, letters, prints, and so on—related to the waning years of the colony of Saint-Domingue and the first years of the Haitian nation, and so the collection spans documents covering roughly fifteen years, 1791–1806.¹⁷ While scholars of Haiti know about this resource, many of us who are scholars of the Hispanic Caribbean, particularly of Puerto Rico, have no idea of its existence.¹⁸ One wonders about its maintenance, particularly in light of the economic difficulties of Puerto Rico in the last decade, which include significant budget cuts to the University of Puerto Rico system that were implemented prior to the destruction wrought by Hurricane Maria in September of 2017 and subsequent US bureaucratic incompetence that resulted in more than four thousand deaths on the island. The underutilization of this archive also opens a conversation regarding the kinds of scholarly inquiries in which we are engaged; it suggests little interest at best and an apparent inability to link the histories of Haiti and Puerto Rico. It is for this reason that I included my essay on Dantès Bellegarde's 1936 lectures at the University of Puerto Rico: as the one responsible for organizing this collection of essays, it is my duty to at least attempt to attain some sense of parity in terms of the distribution of subject matter in the volume. As the author of a study about a friend of Bellegarde's who happened to be one of the early twentieth century's greatest proponents of recognizing Haiti's importance in the creation of Latin America, it would have been a grievous oversight to not include it here. In this way, this collection continues the instruction of Schomburg from his most famous essay, that we must "dig up our past."¹⁹

In addition to its significance to me as a personal project, *Racialized Visions* is one of the first studies to be published under the banner of the Afro-Latinx Futures series at State University of New York Press; this is one of several series to emerge from university presses within the last decade. Within the academy in the United States, the turn to Afro-Latinidad has been long in the making; the study of peoples of African descent in the Americas has a long history here, particularly by academics of African descent. This work, however, has traditionally focused on areas in which English is spoken: namely, the United States itself, the Anglophone Caribbean, and, across the Atlantic, West African countries such as Nigeria and Ghana. For its part, Latin American studies tends to be dominated by work on Argentina and Mexico and, within those national contexts, to focus on European heritage (Argentina) or European and indigenous heritage (Mexico). Scholarly work on peoples of African descent began in earnest in Latin American and Caribbean studies during the civil rights movement in the 1960s. Still, Afro-Latinidad remains an area of vibrant scholarly potential waiting to be realized. Not only does study of Latin American and the Caribbean often get divided along national and linguistic lines, with scholars focusing on either predominantly Hispanophone or Francophone countries, but the lack of conversation between these scholars and the privileging of one linguistic community over another has tended to shape—and to misshape—our full understanding of these regions. The culture and history of Haiti, for example, are not taught or studied within a Hispanophone context, ultimately at the expense of our capacity to appreciate Haiti's intranational diversity or hemispheric significance. *Racialized Visions* represents a step toward a more formal integration of the study of the Latin Caribbean, as Myriam Chancy refers to the region in the foreword; it brings together in one volume distinct perspectives on the cultural production of these adjacent nations, thereby serving, hopefully, as a harbinger of how we, students and scholars alike, will approach future research.

Notes

1. Valdés, "Liberatory Potential."
2. Schomburg, "Hayti" 55.
3. Schomburg, "Economic Contribution" 58.
4. Schomburg Committee of the Trustees of the New York Public Library Collection, Manuscripts, Archives and Rare Book Division, Schomburg Center for Research in Black Culture, The New York Public Library.
5. "Colorful Haitian Exhibit Now on Display at the West 135th Street Library Branch."
6. In an appreciation of Schomburg published weeks after his death in the *Chicago Defender*, Lucius C. Harper writes: "The Haitian consul in New York [presumably Bellegarde] said Schomburg knew more about Haiti's history and its

literature than any living man, and when he desired to clear up some points about his native land, he always consulted him" (16).

7. Reddick xiv.

8. Valdés, "Haiti."

9. Rodriguez and Ferrer write about the conspiracy, the creation of the digital site, and the art exhibition in "Collaborating with Aponte: Digital Humanities, Art, and the Archive" on the digital platform of *sx archipelagos* (2019).

10. Vargas n.p.

11. She is also the coeditor, along with Kiran Jayaram, of *Transnational Hispaniola: New Directions in Haitian and Dominican Studies* (2018).

12. Private correspondence between Vanessa K. Valdés and April Mayes, 8 May 2018.

13. We Are All Dominican, wearealldominicannyc.wordpress.com/.

14. Dominicans Love Haitians, dominicanslovehaitians.com/home/.

15. Incultured Company, www.inculturedco.org/.

16. Legros.

17. Daut.

18. In commemoration of the bicentennial of the Haitian Revolution, Humberto García Muñiz, Aura Díaz López, Axel Santana, and Doralis Pérez-Soto published their 2004 essay "La Colección Alfred Nemours de Historia Haitiana, una fuente olvidada, en el bicentenario de la independencia de Haití," in which they state clearly in their title that this is a forgotten resource. It can be found at https://www.redalyc.org/articulo.oa?id=39232206. I thank one of the anonymous readers of this manuscript who called my attention to this unimaginably rich repository of materials from eighteenth- and nineteenth-century Haiti.

23. Schomburg, "Negro Digs Up His Past."

Works Cited

"Art and Literature in Contemporary Dominican Republic, Haiti, and Their Diasporas." 15 March 2018, www.centerforthehumanities.org/programming/art-and-literature-in-contemporary-dominican-republic-haiti-and-their-diasporas. Accessed 18 Mar. 2018.

Bordering the Imaginary: Art from the Dominican Republic, Haiti, and Their Diasporas. 15 March–29 April 2018, BRIC, New York, www.bricartsmedia.org/art-exhibitions/bordering-imaginary-art-dominican-republic-haiti-and-their-diasporas. Accessed 18 Mar. 2018.

Carolina-Bautista, Suhaly. "The Case for Adopting the Term 'HaitianDominican.'" remezcla.com/features/culture/haitiandominican-not-haitian-dominican/. Accessed 18 Mar. 2018.

"Colorful Haitian Exhibit Now on Display at the West 135th Street Library Branch." *New York Amsterdam News.* 27 Aug. 1938, p. 7.

Daut, Marlene. "Haiti @ the Digital Crossroads: Archiving Black Sovereignty." *Slavery in the Machine,* edited by Jessica Marie Johnson. Special issue of *sx archipelagos* 3, 2019, n.p., smallaxe.net/sxarchipelagos/issue03/daut.html. Accessed 10 Aug. 2019.

Digital Aponte. aponte.hosting.nyu.edu/. Accessed 1 July 2017.

Dominicans Love Haitians. dominicanslovehaitians.com/home/. Accessed 10 Aug. 2019.

García Muñiz, Humberto, Aura Díaz López, Axel Santana, and Doralis Pérez-Soto. "La Colección Alfred Nemours de Historia Haitiana, una fuente olvidada, en el bicentenario de la independencia de Haití." *Caribbean Studies,* vol. 32, no. 2, 2004, pp. 181–241.

Harper, Lucius C. "Dustin' Off the News: One of the Most Interesting Men I've Ever Known." *Chicago Defender,* 25 June 1938, p. 16.

Incultured Company. www.inculturedco.org/. Accessed 10 Aug. 2019.

"José Antonio Aponte and His World: Writing, Painting, and Making Freedom in the African Diaspora." 8–9 May 2015, aponteconference.wordpress.com/. Accessed 1 July 2017.

Legros, Ayanna. "As a Haitian-American Woman, I Know I'm Afro-Latina but It's Time for You to Acknowledge It Too." *Mitú,* 5 June 2018, fierce.wearemitu.com/identities/why-i-haitian-woman-identify-as-afro-latina-and-my-sisters-should-too/. Accessed 5 June 2018.

Mayes, April J., and Kiran C. Jayaram, editors. *Transnational Hispaniola: New Directions in Haitian and Dominican Studies.* UP of Florida, 2018.

Paulino, Edward. "The Dominican-Haitian Border Has Always Been a Revolutionary Space." remezcla.com/features/culture/the-dominican-haitian-border-has-always-been-a-revolutionary-space/. Accessed 18 Mar. 2018.

Reddick, Lawrence D. "Introduction." *Calendar of the Manuscripts in the Schomburg Collection of Negro Literature.* New York: Work Projects Administration, 1942. pp. xiii–xviii.

Rodriguez, Linda M., and Ada Ferrer. "Collaborating with Aponte: Digital Humanities, Art, and the Archive." *sx archipelagos,* vol. 3, July 2019, smallaxe.net/sxarchipelagos/issue03/ferrer-rodriguez.html. Accessed 10 Aug. 2019.

Saint Jean, Albert. "Kiskeya Is a Term That Belongs to Both Dominicans and Haitians." remezcla.com/features/culture/kiskeya-for-short/. Accessed 18 Mar. 2018.

Schomburg, Arthur A. "The Economic Contribution by the Negro to America." *Papers of the American Negro Academy Read at the Nineteenth Annual Meeting December 28–29, 1915.* American Negro Academy, 1916, pp. 49–62.

———. "Is Hayti Decadent?" 1904. *Arthur A. Schomburg: A Puerto Rican's Quest for His Black Heritage.* Centro de Estudios Avanzados de Puerto Rico y el Caribe, 1989, pp. 51–58.

———. "The Negro Digs Up His Past." *Harlem: Mecca of the Negro*, special issue of *Survey Graphic*, vol. 6, no. 6, 1925, pp. 670–72.

Schomburg Committee of the Trustees of the New York Public Library Collection, Manuscripts, Archives and Rare Book Division, Schomburg Center for Research in Black Culture, The New York Public Library.

Trouillot, Michel-Rolph. *Silencing the Past: Power and the Production of History*. 1995. Beacon: 2015.

Valdés, Vanessa K. "Haiti in the Hispanophone Caribbean Literary Imaginary."*sx salon*, vol. 22, June 2016, http://smallaxe.net/sxsalon/discussions/haiti-hispanophone-caribbean-literary-imaginary Accessed 1 Sept. 2016.

———. "The Liberatory Potential of Caribbean Women." *Anthurium*, vol. 11, no. 2, 2014, http://doi.org/10.33596/anth.277. Accessed 10 Dec. 2014.

Vargas, Andrew S. "You Should Stream This Uplifting Doc about the Black Immigrant Experience in Mexico." remezcla.com/film/you-should-stream-life-between-borders-black-migrants-mexico/. Accessed 14 Feb. 2017.

Visionary Aponte: Art and Black Freedom. aponte.hosting.nyu.edu/visionary-aponte/. Accessed 1 Feb. 2018.

We Are All Dominican. wearealldominicannyc.wordpress.com/. Accessed 18 Mar. 2018.

Zoboi, Ibi. "Haiti and the Dominican Republic Share a Common Hero: Anacaona," remezcla.com/features/culture/haiti-and-the-dominican-republic-share-a-common-hero-anacaona/. Accessed 18 Mar. 2018.

Timeline

Pertinent Events in the Greater Antilles Cuba, Haiti, the Dominican Republic, and Puerto Rico

28 October 1492	Christopher Columbus lands on Cuba, which he names Isla Juana.
5 November 1492	Christopher Columbus lands on Ayiti, which he names La Española.
November 1493	Christopher Columbus lands on Borikén, which he names San Juan Bautista, today known as Puerto Rico.
1500	Spanish settlement of Santo Domingo begins.
1503	Rebellion by enslaved Africans in Santo Domingo
1508	Spanish settlement of Puerto Rico begins.
1511	Spanish settlement in Cuba begins.
1522	Uprising by the enslaved in Santo Domingo.
1527	Uprising by the enslaved in Puerto Rico.
1697	Treaty of Ryswick divides the island of La Española so that the French control the western side of the territory, known as Saint-Domingue, and Spain the eastern territory of Santo Domingo.
1773	San Mateo de Cangrejos, a maroon settlement near San Juan, is officially recognized; 101 years later it will be the birthplace of Arturo Alfonso Schomburg. Today it is better known as Santurce.

1791–1804	Series of insurrections and battles that have come to be singularly known as the Haitian Revolution.
1 January 1804	Haiti proclaims independence.
9 April 1812	The public execution of José Antonio Aponte in Havana.
1 December 1821	The establishment of the Republic of Spanish Haiti by José Núñez de Cáceres.
9 February 1822	Arrival of Haitian president Jean-Pierre Boyer to Santo Domingo, signaling the establishment of the western Republic of Haiti and the unification of the island. Slavery is abolished, all male citizens are declared equal in the eyes of the law, and discrimination based on color is prohibited.
February 1844	The retreat of Haitian troops from Santo Domingo, as it is renamed the Dominican Republic. In Cuba, a widespread plot of uprisings to be led by the enslaved was discovered; known as la Conspiración de la Escalera (the Conspiracy of the Ladder), in which the ladder referenced the implement to which thousands of free and enslaved Afro-Cubans were tied and whipped. The year is known in Cuban history as el Año del Cuero—the Year of the Lash.
1861	Spain recolonizes Santo Domingo.
1862	The United States officially recognizes Haiti as an independent nation.
1863–1865	War of Restoration in Santo Domingo; Dominican independence is restored.
1868	El Grito de Lares, the first uprising for independence from Spain in Puerto Rico, occurs and is quickly suppressed. El Grito de Yara in Cuba sparks the Ten Years' War (i.e., the first war of independence from Spain).
1873	Abolition of slavery in Puerto Rico.
1880–1881	The Guerra Chica or Little War in Cuba (i.e., second war of independence from Spain).

1886	Abolition of slavery in Cuba.
1895–1898	The third Cuban War of Independence; it is recorded in US history books as having lasted one year, 1898, and is traditionally named the Spanish-American War; historians of Cuba have renamed it the Spanish-Cuban-American War. The United States' defeat of Spain effectively ends the Spanish Empire in the Caribbean and the Pacific, as it loses Cuba and Puerto Rico, along with the Philippines and Guam. Still, it maintained its colonies on the African continent: Spanish West Africa and Equatorial Guinea.
25 November 1897	Spain signs a Carta de Autonomía, allowing for the organization of autonomous governments in Puerto Rico and Cuba.
25 July 1898	The United States Navy lands in Guánica, Puerto Rico.
11 April 1899	Treaty of Paris goes into effect: Spain cedes Puerto Rico, the Philippines, and Guam to the United States; Cuba becomes a protectorate of the United States.
1901	The Insular Cases, a series of cases brought before the US Supreme Court, establish that Puerto Rico is an unincorporated territory.
20 May 1902	Cuba gains independence from the United States, becoming the Republic of Cuba; with the inclusion of the Platt Amendment in the Cuban Constitution, the United States secures a military base in Guantánamo.
1912	The War of 1912—the Cuban government massacres more than three thousand Afro-Cubans, many of whom were veterans of the third war for independence and who had been members of the Partido Independiente de Color.
1915–1934	US Marines occupy Haiti.
1916–1924	US Marines occupy the Dominican Republic.
2 March 1917	The Jones-Shafroth Act grants US citizenship to inhabitants of Puerto Rico.

16 August 1930	Rafael Leónidas Trujillo assumes power in the Dominican Republic.
11 May 1930	Pedro Albizu Campos is elected president of the Puerto Rican Nationalist Party.
1 January 1934	On the 130th anniversary of Haitian independence, the United States formally retreats from Haiti.
24 October 1935	Río Piedras Massacre—police kill suspected members of the Puerto Rican Nationalist Party on the flagship campus of the University of Puerto Rico.
23 February 1936	Two members of the Puerto Rican Nationalist Party kill the police chief of Puerto Rico, an appointee of the United States.
21 March 1937	Ponce Massacre—on Palm Sunday, Puerto Rican police open fire on a peaceful protest held by the Nationalist Party. More than two hundred marchers are wounded, nineteen killed.
2–8 October 1937	El Corte—Dominican troops massacre more than fifteen thousand Haitians and Dominicans of Haitian descent in the northern borderlands.
10 June 1948	The Ley de la Mordaza (Gag Law) is signed into law barring any demonstration of Puerto Rican independence, including the display of the Puerto Rican flag; it remains in effect until 1957, when it is declared unconstitutional.
2 January 1949	Luis Muñoz Marín, the first Puerto Rican elected governor, takes office; prior governors had been appointed by the United States.
30 October 1950	Gritos de Jayuya y Utuado—widespread revolts take place throughout the island, including attacks on the governor's mansion, led by the Puerto Rican Nationalist Party.
25 July 1952	The political status of Puerto Rico is officially declared to be as an Estado Libre Asociado (Free Associated State).

26 July 1953	Fidel Castro leads failed attacks on the Moncada Barracks in Santiago de Cuba, Cuba.
2 December 1956– 31 December 1958	The Cuban Revolution; Castro marches into Havana on New Year's Eve.
22 September 1957	François "Papa Doc" Duvalier assumes power as president of Haiti.
1961	Bay of Pigs invasion.
30 May 1961	Assassination of Trujillo.
27 February– 25 September 1963	Presidency of Juan Bosch.
24 April– 3 September 1965	Dominican Civil War; US military intervention of the Dominican Republic.
1 July 1966– 16 August 1978	Presidency of Joaquín Balaguer.
21 April 1971	Duvalier dies; his son, Jean-Claude "Baby Doc" Duvalier assumes power.
7 February 1986	Duvalier resigns and leaves Haiti for France.
16 August 1986– 16 August 1996	Presidency of Joaquín Balaguer.
7 February– 20 September 1991	Jean-Bertrand Aristide wins the presidency of Haiti.
29 September 1991	A military coup deposes Aristide.
1994–1996	Aristide regains the presidency.
2001–2004	Aristide is deposed by a second military coup-d'état.
19 February 2008	Fidel Castro steps down as president of Cuba; he is succeeded by his brother Raúl.
10 January 2010	A catastrophic earthquake strikes Haiti.
23 September 2013	La Sentencia, Ruling 168-13 by the Constitutional Tribunal, the Supreme Court of the Dominican Republic, that declared that children born between 1929 and 2007

	are not citizens if their parents were undocumented at the time of their birth. The result is that more than two hundred thousand Dominicans of Haitian descent are declared stateless.
30 June 2016	PROMESA bill signed into law, establishing a Fiscal Control board that oversees the governance of Puerto Rico.
7 February 2017	Jovenel Moïse assumes the presidency of Haiti.
20 September 2017	Hurricane Maria strikes Puerto Rico and St. Croix of the US Virgin Islands.
19 April 2018	Raúl Castro stepped down as president of Cuba; he is succeeded by Miguel Díaz-Canel.
7 July 2018	New taxes on diesel, kerosene, and gasoline lead to protests in Haiti that last intermittently until November 2018.
7 February 2019	Protests begin again in Haiti, as demands for the resignation of president Moïse due to corruption increase; they continue for the majority of the year.
25 July 2019	Ricardo Rosselló, son of former governor Pedro Rosselló, resigns as governor of Puerto Rico after weeks of protests, as the citizenry mobilizes against the corruption of the governing class.

Contributors

Cécile Accilien is Professor and Chair in the Interdisciplinary Studies Department at Kennesaw State University in Kennesaw, Georgia. Her areas of study are Francophone African and Caribbean literatures, and culture and film and media studies; her primary research areas are Caribbean popular cultures; film and media studies; women, gender, and sexuality studies. She is the author of *Rethinking Marriage in Francophone African and Caribbean Literatures* (2008). She has also coedited and contributed to two collections of essays, *Revolutionary Freedoms: A History of Survival, Strength and Imagination in Haiti* (2006) and *Just Below South: Intercultural Performance in the Caribbean and the U.S. South* (2007). She cowrote with Jowel Laguerre *English-Haitian Creole Phrasebook* (2010) and *Francophone Cultures through Film* (2013) with Nabil Boudraa. She has published articles in the *Journal of Haitian Studies, Women, Gender, and Families of Color, Revue française, Southern Quarterly,* and *Diaspora in Caribbean Art*. She is finishing a coedited volume *Teaching Haiti from Transdisciplinary Studies* (forthcoming, 2021) and a monograph temporarily titled *Haitian Hollywood: Representing Haiti and the Haitian Diaspora in Popular Cinema* (forthcoming from SUNY Press). In 2019, she became the chair of the editorial board of the journal *Women, Gender, and Families of Color*. She is also on the advisory board of the Haitian Studies Association.

Ángela Castro is a visiting assistant professor at Colorado College. She earned her master's and PhD in Hispanic literatures and cultures at the University of Minnesota. She published "Power-in-Passivity: A Study of the Body and the Hegelian Consciousness in Jamaica Kincaid's *Lucy*" in the *Journal of Commonwealth and Postcolonial Studies*. Her research focuses on predominant representations of the twentieth-century Afro-Caribbean female body through comparative analysis. She uses the concept of the palimpsest as a means of reconfiguring the Afro-Caribbean female body as a site of empowerment born within the struggles of postcolonial and neocolonial history.

Myriam J. A. Chancy is a Guggenheim Fellow and the Hartley Burr Alexander Chair in the Humanities at Scripps College. Her academic publications include: *Autochthonomies: Transnationalism, Testimony, and Transmission in the African Diaspora* (2020), *From Sugar to Revolution: Women's Visions from Haiti, Cuba, and the Dominican Republic* (2012), *Framing Silence: Revolutionary Novels by Haitian Women* (1997), and *Searching for Safe Spaces: Afro-Caribbean Women Writers in Exile* (1997; Choice OAB Award, 1998). Her novels include: *The Loneliness of Angels* (2010; 2011 Guyana Prize in Literature Caribbean Award, Best Fiction 2010), and *Spirit of Haiti* (2003; shortlisted, Best First Book Category, Canada/Caribbean region, Commonwealth Prize 2004). She is a recent editorial advisory board member of *PMLA* (2010–2012) and of the Fetzer Institute (2011–2013). Her novel, *12*, on the aftermath of the Haiti earthquake, is forthcoming (2021).

Claudy Delné obtained his bachelor's degree and then his master's degree in education from the University of Montreal, his juris doctor degree from the University of Moncton, and his PhD from the City University of New York (CUNY-Graduate Center). His area of specialization is in colonial and postcolonial discourse of the nineteenth and twentieth centuries and his research interests in Francophone Caribbean literature with a particular focus on narratology, representation, race, and otherness. In addition to teaching high school, since 2003 he has taught as an adjunct professor at various colleges, most recently at Sarah Lawrence College in Yonkers, New York, as a guest professor from 2015 to 2018. His first book is entitled *L'enseignement de l'histoire nationale en Haiti: état des lieux et perspectives* (2000) and his most recent, *La Révolution haitienne dans l'imaginaire occidental: occultation, banalisation, trivialisation* (2017).

Mohwanah Fetus, PhD, is a creative writer and researcher. Her research and writing focus on the geographies and temporalities of Black women's pleasure, trauma, and memory in African American and Caribbean American literatures. During her graduate career at Northwestern University, she has cochaired a public humanities symposium entitled "Beyond Coasts: Haiti in the Midwest," a two-day conference that explored Haitian diasporas, cultures, and politics in the Midwest. As a creative writer, she produces romance novels, science fiction/fantasy novels, and nonfiction essays. You can find her work in publications like *Queenies, Fades, and Blunts* and *Elixher.com*.

Carrie Gibson is the author of *El Norte: The Epic and Forgotten Story of Hispanic North America* (2019) and *Empire's Crossroads: A History of the Caribbean from Columbus to the Present Day* (2014). She received her PhD from Cambridge University in 2010, and her thesis examined the reaction to the Haitian Revolution in the Hispanic Caribbean. Prior to this she worked as a journalist in the United Kingdom, mainly for the *Guardian* and *Observer* newspapers. More on her work can be found at carriegibson.co.uk.

Philip Kaisary is Associate Professor in the Departments of Law and Legal Studies, English Language and Literature, and the Institute for Comparative Studies in Literature, Art and Culture (ICSLAC) at Carleton University. He is the author of *The Haitian Revolution in the Literary Imagination: Radical Horizons, Conservative Constraints* (2014) as well as essays in publications including *Atlantic Studies, MELUS: Multi-Ethnic Literature of the United States, PALARA: Publication of the Afro-Latin/American Research Association, Slavery and Abolition*, and *Law and Humanities*.

Natalie Marie Léger is Assistant Professor of English at Temple University. She received her PhD in English literature from Cornell University, completed an Andrew W. Mellon Postdoctoral Fellowship at Tufts University in 2011, and was 2016–2017 Ford Postdoctoral Fellow. Her research specialized in anti-Blackness and anti-colonial thought, decolonial philosophy, and settler colonial politics in Caribbean literature and hemispheric American fiction. She coedited the Spanish language collection *Toussaint Louverture: Repensar un icono* with Mariana Past in 2015 and is completing a manuscript titled *Haiti and the Unseen: The Persistence of the Radical Decolonial Imaginary*.

Mariana Past is Associate Professor of Spanish and chair of Latin American, Latinx, and Caribbean Studies at Dickinson College. She cotranslated (with Benjamin Hebblethwaite) Michel-Rolph Trouillot's (1977) *Ti difè boulè sou istoua Ayiti* (*Stirring the Pot of Haitian History*) from Haitian Creole to English. Past has published poetry and prose translations in *Sirena: poesía, arte y crítica, Metamorphoses, Transition,* and *World Literature Today*, as well as critical essays about representations of the Haitian Revolution and Haitian-Dominican relations in *Revista del Caribe, Revista de la Casa de las Américas, Global South, Journal of Haitian Studies, PALARA, Cultural Dynamics,*

Atlantic Studies, and *sx salon*. She coedited (with Natalie Léger) *Toussaint Louverture: Repensar un icono* (*Rethinking an Icon: Toussaint Louverture and Caribbean Cultural Production*), published in 2015.

Erika V. Serrato is Assistant Professor and Lineberger Fellow in the Department of Romance Studies at the University of North Carolina at Chapel Hill. She received her PhD in French from Emory University. Her research focuses on intellectual and aesthetic exchanges between voices, texts, and figures from the Francophone, Hispanic, and Anglophone Caribbean. Her main questions concern what Édouard Glissant calls "l'Autre Amérique," indigeneity, language, aesthetics, "l'entour," and intersectional subjectivities. She has published in *Women in French*, *sx salon*, and has a forthcoming chapter on Taína cacica Anacaona's representation in the works of Edwidge Danticat. She is currently working on a book manuscript regarding indigeneity in the Francophone Caribbean.

Vanessa K. Valdés is Director of the Black Studies Program and Professor of Spanish and Portuguese at the City College of New York, CUNY. Her research centers on the cultural production of Black peoples in the Americas. She is the editor of *The Future Is Now: A New Look at African Diaspora Studies* (2012) and *Let Spirit Speak! Cultural Journeys through the African Diaspora* (2012). She is the author of *Oshun's Daughters: The Search for Womanhood in the Americas* (2014) and *Diasporic Blackness: The Life and Times of Arturo Alfonso Schomburg* (2017). She is series editor of the Afro-Latinx Futures series at State University of New York Press.

Ramón Antonio Victoriano-Martínez (Arturo) is Assistant Professor of Spanish (Caribbean Literatures and Cultures) in the Department of French, Hispanic, and Italian Studies at the University of British Columbia (Vancouver). He was born in the Dominican Republic (1969), where he studied law at the Universidad Católica Santo Domingo (class of 1994). He is the translator into Spanish of *The Struggle for Democratic Politics in the Dominican Republic* (Jonathan Hartlyn, Ramón A. Victoriano-Martínez), published by the Global Foundation for Democracy and Development in 2008 with the title *La lucha por la democracia política en la República Dominicana*. He earned his PhD from the University of Toronto in the area of Hispanic and Latin American Literatures in 2010. His book *Rayanos y Dominicanyorks: La dominicanidad del siglo XXI* (2014) analyzes Dominican identity, departing from the figure of the "rayano" (the one from the border) and leaning on a critical reading of the following texts: *El Masacre se pasa a pie* (Freddy Prestol Castillo), *The Farming of Bones* (Edwidge Danticat), *Dominicanish* (Josefina Báez), and *The Brief Wondrous Life of Oscar Wao* (Junot Díaz).

Index

1822, 12, 13, 19n5, 31, 79, 191, 230, 260
1844, 9, 13, 19n5, 31, 74, 161, 173n7, 191, 202n3, 230, 260
1937 Massacre, 14, 32, 33, 39, 43, 44, 45, 48, 50, 68n15, 73–74, 77, 79, 83, 167, 177–179, 184–185, 189n1, 221, 229, 231, 237, 238, 262

Africa, 13, 51, 73, 77, 84n9, 98, 128, 135–137, 139, 140, 147, 151, 152, 154, 155n27–28, 156n33, 212, 214, 223n11, 228, 239, 247, 255, 261
Africans, 2, 4, 5, 11, 12, 13, 19, 20, 62, 74, 93, 98, 101, 108n11, 114, 116, 123, 124, 128, 137, 145, 150, 161, 168, 171, 173n2, 174, 212, 213, 216, 217, 223n11, 230, 242, 248, 250
Albizu Campos, Pedro, 55, 56–59, 65–67, 67n1, 67n3, 68n4, 68n6–8, 69n22–24, 262
Alexis, Jacques Stephen, 14, 16, 28, 35–39, 43–45, 47–48
Andrews, George Reid, 13, 18n1
anti-Blackness, 2, 3, 10, 11, 45, 76, 81, 91, 93, 94, 98, 161, 160, 211, 212, 214, 216–219, 222, 223n11, 250, 253

anti-Haitianism, xv, 3, 4, 10, 11, 13, 17, 21, 31, 45, 47, 50n7, 74, 76, 81, 91–94, 106, 111, 161, 189n3, 196, 201, 211, 214, 215–219, 222, 223n11, 229, 253
antillanismo, 160, 163, 168, 173n8
Aponte, José Antonio, 8, 21n15, 103, 105, 110n27, 251, 256n9, 260
Aranjuez, Treaty of, 41, 49n3
Aristide, Jean-Bertrand, 20n13, 90, 193, 263
Augelli, John P., 30, 38, 49n2, 50n6

Balaguer, Joaquín, 36, 74, 81–83, 200, 201, 203n19, 263
Bellegarde, Dantès, 16, 55, 59–67, 68n10–14, 69n18, 69n21, 250, 254, 255n6
Bellegarde-Smith, Patrick, 59–60, 66, 68n10
Benjamin, Walter, 188–189
Betances, Ramón Emeterio, 10, 57, 66, 162
blanqueamiento (whitening), xv, 2, 13, 18n1, 36, 45
Bois Kaïyman, 95, 100, 109n24, 129
Bolívar, Simón, 7, 12, 20n11, 21n22, 23, 80, 170
border, xv, 12, 15, 16, 27–50, 51n9, 51n12, 68n15, 73–74, 77, 84n11,

271

border *(continued)*
  164, 167, 180, 185–189, 191–202, 214, 219, 223n6, 224n13, 227–242, 252, 262, 268
Bosch, Juan, 173n7, 196, 263
Boukan Ginen, 89–91, 107n1, 107n10
Boyer, Jean-Pierre, 8, 12, 41, 95, 109n25, 260
Bragadir, Nathalie, 28, 29, 32, 33, 48n1, 49

Candelario, Ginetta, 84n3, 206n37
Carpentier, Alejo, 16, 22n25, 91–93, 95–107, 109n20–22, 110n26, 127, 129, 162
Castro, Fidel, 108n11, 114, 131n13, 144, 155n21, 263, 264
Césaire, Aimé, 91, 116, 131n9–10, 162
Chancy, Myriam J. A., 1, 2, 4, 5, 15, 164, 177, 227, 234, 248, 249, 251, 255
Christophe, Henri, 8, 20n12, 44, 51n11, 95, 95, 97, 102, 103, 171, 172, 174n11
cimarrones, 7, 16, 92, 106–107, 143. *See also* maroons
Citadel Laferrière, 40, 51n11, 96–97, 102
Cook, Mercer, 59, 68n10
Creole Choir of Cuba, 90–91
Cuban Revolution, 17, 91, 92, 94, 102, 106, 108, 114, 130, 136, 139, 141, 152, 153n2, 154n11, 165, 167, 263
CUNY Dominican Studies Institute, 11, 21n20

Dalleo, Raphael, 21n25, 68n14
Danticat, Edwidge, 14, 17, 28, 38, 39, 43–48, 73, 83, 177–180, 182–188, 189n2, 191, 229, 234, 236–238, 253

Dash, J. Michael, 68n14, 167, 173n6
Daut, Marlene L., 15, 254, 256n17
Derby, Lauren, 30–31, 32, 80, 81, 243n3
Dessalines, Jean-Jacques, 8, 11, 41, 44, 78, 81, 84n15, 95, 103, 109n25, 110n28, 120, 171, 174n11
Díaz, Junot, 191, 192, 194, 198–199, 209–222, 229, 253
Digital Aponte, 21n15, 251, 256n9
Don Quixote, 147–148, 155n27–29
Du Bois, W. E. B., 59, 60, 68n11, 130
Duvalier, François (Papa Doc), 144, 165, 205n29, 231, 241, 263

earthquake, 2010 (Haiti), xv, 1, 161, 162, 172, 194, 247, 252, 263
Eller, Anne, 11, 12, 19n5, 20n13, 75, 84n1, 84n5–6, 206n36
Escalera, Conspiración de la, 8, 9, 21n17, 260

Fanon, Frantz, 113, 116, 124, 131n9
Farming of Bones, The, 14, 17, 28, 43–47, 73, 177–189, 189n2, 234, 236–237
Ferrer, Ada, 9–10, 20n10, 21n15, 99, 109n23, 130n3, 251, 256n9
Finch, Aisha K., 9, 21n17
Firmin, Anténor, 168
Fischer, Sibylle, xiv, 5, 10, 11, 14, 20n11, 21n15, 75, 131n12, 131n14, 167, 173n6, 192
Franco Pichardo, Franklin, 21n23, 192, 243n4
freedom, xvi, 3, 5, 7, 19n5, 20n10, 28, 32, 34, 35, 66, 67, 89–107, 110n31, 113–130, 147, 154n11, 173n8, 186, 188, 239, 251
Fumagalli, Maria C., 15, 46, 51n9

Gaceta del Caribe, 137, 153n9

García-Peña, Lorgia, 30, 32, 48, 49n3, 81, 189n1
Garvey, Amy Jacques, 22n25
Garvey, Marcus, 22n25, 141, 142, 154n15, 155n26
Geffrard, Fabre, 8, 20n13
Geggus, David, 6, 7, 34–35, 49n4, 84n4, 170
General Sun, My Brother, 28, 35–39, 47
Geographies of Home, 234, 236–237
Gibson, Carrie, 6, 20n10
Giral, Sergio, 115, 131n7
Glissant, Édouard, 142, 145, 162, 170, 174n9, 237–238
González Echevarría, Roberto, 93, 110n26
Gran Colombia, 7, 12, 20n11, 80
Grito de Lares, 10, 260
Grupo Vocal Desandann. *See* Creole Choir of Cuba
Guerra Chica (Little War), 9–10, 260
Guillén, Nicolás, 135, 137, 153n9, 162, 171, 172
Gutiérrez Alea, Tomás, 113–130

Haitian Revolution, xvi, 3–7, 9, 12, 13, 14, 17, 19n5, 29, 31, 34–35, 50, 55, 62, 76, 81, 84n4, 91, 92, 94–107, 108n12, 108n17, 110n27–31, 113–116, 118, 120, 122–124, 127–129, 130n3, 131n5, 131n11–15, 154n11, 160, 162, 164–165, 167, 170–172, 192, 202n2, 230, 251, 256n18, 260
Helg, Aline, 6, 20n11
Henri Citadel. *See* Citadel Laferrière
Hernández, Rita Indiana, 192, 196
hooks, bell, 227–228, 233, 241, 242, 242n1–2
Hostos, Eugenio María de, 10, 57, 66, 162, 168

Hudson, Peter James, 20n13, 63, 68n14, 69n22, 129
Hume, Yanique, 94, 108n14, 110n26, 110n32

Indemnities, 8, 20n13
Independent Party of Color. *See* Partido Independiente de Color
Indigenisme, 13, 84n3, 75, 137

James, C. L. R., 21n25, 84, 114, 130, 131n4, 131n13
Jean-Louis, Felix, 68n11, 68n14
Johnson, Sara, 15, 19n6, 20n14, 160, 162
Jolibois, Joseph, fils, 57, 67n3, 68n15

Kaisary, Philip, 15, 16, 17, 102, 131n5
Kingdom of this World, The (El reino de este mundo), 91–107, 110n28, 127, 129
Kreyòl, 205n30, 209

Lacan, Jacques, 178–180
Lahens, Yanick, xv, 1–2
Latin Caribbean, xiii–xiv
Lora Hugi, Quisqueya, 79, 84n13, 85n17–18
Louverture, Toussaint, 8, 11, 41, 44, 78, 95, 103, 110n28, 114, 120, 127, 131n13, 141, 142, 154n15, 155n26
Lucumí, Regla de (also Regla de Ocha), 155n30, 168, 213, 249
Luperón, Gregorio, 162, 168

McKittrick, Katherine, 224n14, 224n16
Manzano, Juan Francisco, 8, 21n18
maroons, 6, 7, 16, 29–31, 90, 95, 105, 129, 143–146, 151, 155, 156, 259. *See also* cimarrones

Marcallé Abreu, Roberto, 191–202
Martí, José, 10, 163, 197
Martínez, Samuel, 47, 76, 83, 85n28, 195, 201
marvelous real. See *real maravilloso, lo*
Massacre River, 28, 39–43, 47, 51n10
Matibag, Eugenio, 12, 13, 191
Mayes, April, 13, 49, 80, 84n3, 161–163, 168, 173n8, 252, 256n11–12
mestizaje, 214–219, 222, 223n8
Middle Passage, 137, 139, 141, 145, 147, 155n32, 174n9
Mieses, Juan Carlos, 191–193
Moten, Fred, 218, 224n15
Moya Pons, Frank, 19n9, 21n23, 28, 30–32, 34, 75, 252–253

Nationalist Party, Puerto Rican, 16, 55, 56–58, 64–66, 69, 262
Nessler, Graham T., 19n5, 84n6
Núñez de Cáceres, José, 12, 21n22, 80, 260
Nwankwo, Ifeoma Kiddoe, 14, 20n14, 21n18

occupation of Dominican Republic, 13, 15, 50, 80, 230, 261
occupation of Haiti, 13, 15–16, 50, 21n25, 55, 59–64, 68n14–15, 69n17, 80, 186, 224n13, 230, 249, 261

Palés Matos, Luis, 151, 162, 164
Pan-Antilleanism. See *antillanismo*
parsley. See *perejil*
Partido Independiente de Color, 108n17, 261
Partido Nacionalista de Puerto Rico. See Nationalist Party, Puerto Rican
Paulino, Edward, 11, 13, 28, 189n5, 252

Peña Batlle, Manuel A., 74, 192, 196, 201
Peña Gómez, José Francisco, 82–83
perejil (parsley), 42–43, 177–179, 184, 221, 223n5, 236
Petión, Alexandre, 7, 95, 171, 174n11
Philoctète, René, 28, 39–43, 47–48, 162
Plácido (Gabriel Concepción Valdés), 8, 21n18
plantation economy, 50n5, 114, 150
Platt Amendment, 108n13, 109n18, 261
Prestol Castillo, Freddy, 14, 164
Price-Mars, Jean, 14, 77–82, 84n13, 201, 243n5

*rayano*consciousness, 48, 51n12
real maravilloso, lo, 16, 96–97, 109n19
rebellions, regional, 9, 21n16
Renda, Mary A., 21n25, 68n14, 69n16
Reyes-Santos, Alaí, 160, 162–163, 168
Ricourt, Milagros, 12, 232
Río Piedras Massacre, 16, 57, 59, 68n6, 262
Rodriguez, Linda M., 21n15, 251, 256n9
Roosevelt, Franklin D., 58, 62, 64
Roumain, Jacques, 12, 17, 68n15, 135–153, 154n17, 155n26, 156n33, 171, 174n11
Ryswick, Treaty of (1697), 49n3, 230, 259

Sagás, Ernesto, 50n7, 75, 77, 84n13, 85n28
Saint-Domingue, 27, 29, 49n4
San Miguel, Pedro L., 14, 75, 76, 84n13, 85n21, 201, 243n4
Santiago de Cuba, 98–107, 110n26, 136, 142, 153n1, 167, 263

Santo Domingo, 27, 29, 50n5
Schomburg, Arturo, 21n18, 249–251, 255n2–3, 255n6, 256n23, 259
Schomburg Center, 19n8, 250–251, 255n4–5
Sentencia, La (2013), 18, 46, 83, 166, 173n4, 178, 184–185, 202, 209, 229, 235, 263–264
Silié, Rubén, 33–34
slavery (and anti-), xv, 2, 4–9, 11, 12, 17, 18, 21n15, 29, 34, 45, 48, 91, 92, 95, 99–101, 103, 104–106, 114–120, 124, 126–127, 129, 130, 131n7, 139, 140, 145, 146, 147, 151, 160, 161, 173n7, 211, 217–219, 221, 223n4, 230, 233, 235, 240, 259–261
Smith, Matthew J., 61, 68n15, 153n5–7
Suárez, Lucía M., 14, 191, 213, 232, 237, 240

Théodat, Jean-Marie, 27, 29
Torres-Saillant, Silvio, 11, 21n20, 76, 161, 216, 223n11, 253
Trouillot, Michel-Rolph, xiv, 3–4, 14, 56, 65, 75, 83, 110n29, 131n12, 131n14, 162 228–229, 243n4, 247, 267
Trujillo, Rafael, 13, 16, 30–45, 51n7, 73–77, 80–83, 84n11, 85n18, 161, 165, 167, 177–178, 182, 183, 188, 189n3, 192, 196–197, 201, 203n19, 205n35, 211–222, 223n5, 223n11, 230, 231, 241, 243n3, 262, 263
Turits, Richard L., 30, 33, 167, 191

Ulysse, Gina, 18, 247
unfreedom, 90, 92, 107n5
University of Puerto Rico, 16, 55, 56, 57, 59, 61, 66, 67, 163, 254, 262

Valdés, Vanessa K., 21n18, 21n19, 255n1, 256n8
Valerio-Holguín, Fernando, 169, 203n6, 231, 239
Vodou/Vodun, 21n25, 95, 96, 98, 100, 101, 106, 107, 115, 127, 129, 145, 200, 205n28–29, 213, 214, 223n7, 223n10, 241, 247, 249, 253

Žižek, Slavoj, 178–180, 185, 186, 190n7

www.ingramcontent.com/pod-product-compliance
Lightning Source LLC
Chambersburg PA
CBHW022107150426
43195CB00008B/297